Eighth Edition

TECHNIQUES OF CRIME SCENE INVESTIGATION

Also by Barry Fisher

with David Fisher and Jason Kolowski
Forensics Demystified (2007)

----

with William Tillstone and Catherine Woytowicz
Introduction to Criminalistics: The Foundation of Forensic Science (2009)

Eighth Edition

TECHNIQUES OF
CRIME SCENE
INVESTIGATION

Barry A. J. Fisher   David R. Fisher

CRC Press
Taylor & Francis Group
Boca Raton   London   New York

CRC Press is an imprint of the
Taylor & Francis Group, an **informa** business

Cover photo by Deputy Dale Falicon (Retired), Los Angeles County Sheriff's Department.

Cover design by Ms. Shayna Murry, Graphic Designer.

The views of the authors of this book are their own and are not necessarily those of the City of New York, the County of Los Angeles, the National Disaster Medical System, or the US Department of Health and Human Services. Commercial products mentioned in this book should not be considered as endorsements of such products by the authors.

CRC Press
Taylor & Francis Group
6000 Broken Sound Parkway NW, Suite 300
Boca Raton, FL 33487-2742

© 2012 by Taylor & Francis Group, LLC
CRC Press is an imprint of Taylor & Francis Group, an Informa business

No claim to original U.S. Government works

Printed in the United States of America on acid-free paper
Version Date: 20120411

International Standard Book Number: 978-1-4398-1005-7 (Hardback)

Library of Congress Cataloging-in-Publication Data

Fisher, Barry A. J.
    Techniques of crime scene investigation / Barry J. Fisher, David Fisher. -- 8th ed.
      p. cm.
    Includes bibliographical references and index.
    ISBN 978-1-4398-1005-7 (hardcover : alk. paper)
    1. Crime scene searches. 2. Criminal investigation. I. Fisher, David. II. Title.

HV8073.F49 2012
363.25'2--dc23

2012009447

Visit the Taylor & Francis Web site at
http://www.taylorandfrancis.com

and the CRC Press Web site at
http://www.crcpress.com

for
Susan and Deena

Contents

8   Blood, Forensic Biology, and DNA   193

Foreword

The efforts of law enforcement to stay one step ahead of those who actively choose to violate the law are part of an ongoing and evolutionary process. When there are those who are creating new ways to commit the "perfect crime," the law enforcement community must respond and scour the evidence left behind, no matter how obscure or limited it is, to find the person(s) responsible for those crimes and bring them to justice. This process frequently involves the dedicated men and women of local, state, and federal forensic laboratories. They cannot settle for the status quo but must continue to push forward in scientific endeavors to support the judicial system in its search for truth and justice.

The education of those fine forensic science professionals is also an ongoing endeavor that can take years of study and training to reach the required level of competency, which is then followed by a lifetime of continuing education to remain proficient. This text is a resource for those who have chosen their specialty within the field but still want to keep up on the advances and capabilities of the other disciplines in the forensic sciences.

With the repercussions of the congressionally directed report by the National Academy of Sciences, *Strengthening Forensic Science in the United States: A Path Forward,* still echoing across the land, a new spotlight has been brought on those who provide forensic services for public agencies. Ensuring that the appropriate scientific techniques and principles are used to bring out the truth in criminal investigations will continue to be the task for all levels of forensic practitioners throughout the nation. Validating the science underlying those techniques will also be the responsibility of this generation's forensic scientists. With that in mind, this text that has been a standard for years will continue to be used as a resource for those who wish to study and master the noble field of forensic science.

The Los Angeles County Sheriff's Department was honored to have Barry A. J. Fisher as the director of our Scientific Services Bureau for more than two decades. Leaders like him have helped build it into one of the largest and most respected municipal crime laboratories in the world. I am honored to once again write a foreword for this volume, the eighth edition of *Techniques of Crime Scene Investigation* and look forward to its contribution as a trusted resource for the criminal justice community.

Leroy D. Baca
Sheriff, Los Angeles County

Preface

In the late 1970s, I was invited to revise the classic criminal justice textbook, *Techniques of Crime Scene Investigation*, which was first published in 1949 in Swedish under the title *HANDBOK I BROTTSPLATSUNDERSÖKING* and subsequently in English in 1964. The original authors were Arne Svensson and Otto Wendel, two police investigators from Sweden. In 1981, I revised the text in the third edition and since then have served as the principal author. In this eighth edition, I have the pleasure to introduce a new collaborator, David R. Fisher, a supervising criminalist with the New York City Office of Chief Medical Examiner, Department of Forensic Biology. The reader might notice that we share the same last name; David is my elder son. It certainly makes a father feel proud to have his son follow in his career path.

You may ask why we wrote this new edition; after all, crime scene investigation is a fairly static field with few changes. True enough. However, recently there has been an increased focus on the forensic sciences due in large part to the report put out by the National Academy of Sciences, *Strengthening Forensic Science in the United States: A Path Forward*. New practitioners and students of crime scene investigations must be made aware of the increased scrutiny that they will face in the judicial system. Judges are taking a more involved role than ever before as far as the types of evidence and testimony that they allow into their courtrooms. No longer will substandard forensic science or crime scene investigations be acceptable.

Having said this, criminal investigations remain as complex as ever and require professionals from many disciplines to work cooperatively toward one common goal: the delivery of justice in a fair and impartial manner. The effective use of science and technology is critical to crime solving, reducing the number of wrongful convictions and exonerations. Police investigators, prosecutors, and defense attorneys must be able to use these resources to their fullest potential.

Science and technology applied to the solution of criminal acts solve crimes and potentially save lives. Scientific crime scene investigation aids police investigators in identifying suspects and victims of crimes, clearing innocent persons of suspicion and ultimately bringing the wrongdoers to justice. When the justice system is able to remove a criminal from society, innocent persons do not become new victims of criminal acts.

This book is about the proper and effective use of science and technology in support of justice. The eighth edition of *Techniques of Crime Scene Investigation* is written for students of crime scene investigation, police investigators, crime scene technicians, forensic scientists, and attorneys. The material presented in this text is basic, covering the proper ways to examine crime scenes and collect a wide variety of physical evidence that may be encountered at crime scenes. It is not possible to cover every imaginable situation, but this book is a guide that attempts to promote best practices. The areas are discussed in general terms to give the reader some idea of the information that can be developed from physical evidence if it is collected properly. Few of the procedures mentioned in the book are inviolable, meaning that readers should not presume that practices referenced in the text can never be modified. On the contrary, crime scene investigation requires a degree of common sense and innovation. It is not possible to conjure up every imaginable situation a crime scene investigator may encounter in a case.

The authors of this edition do not claim to know thoroughly every discipline presented. Neither will studying the contents of this text make you an expert in all types of crime scene investigations or forensic science. Instead, we hope that it gives students, police investigators, and others engaged in or interested in the subject some insight into the field and helps interested readers to pursue further studies.

Some of the new topics in this edition include the following:

- Discussion on professional ethics
- Challenges facing forensic science laboratories and suggestions for addressing them
- Expert witness testimony
- CSI in HAZMAT environments
- Low copy number DNA/Touch DNA
- CODIS databases/familial searching
- Forensic science and terrorist acts
- National Academy of Sciences report on Forensic Science
- Digital evidence

The use of forensic science in criminal investigations depends on a number of factors. Police investigators must be knowledgeable about the capabilities of the forensic science support services available to them and appreciate how to use them effectively. Forensic practitioners must be familiar with police investigative procedures, the scientific theory that supports their own activities, and the legal aspects needed to convey the information from the crime scene to the ladies and gentlemen of the jury. Prosecutors, as well as defense attorneys, must understand the scientific and technological issues of the case and be able to work with the expert to admit expert testimony into court. Police agencies that run forensic science labs must fund them at an appropriate level to ensure quality, reliability, and timely service to the criminal justice system. All of these efforts require the cooperation and willingness of different professionals within the criminal justice system to work well together. Those of us who apply science and technology to the solution of crimes have a duty to do our best for the criminal justice system we serve in the interest of justice.

Acknowledgments

In preparing the eighth edition of *Techniques of Crime Scene Investigations,* we contacted many colleagues for interesting cases. Although we were unable to use all the material submitted to us, we do wish to thank them for their time and generosity. If we managed to miss anyone, we apologize for the oversight.

The names are listed in no particular order:

SC Leung, Former Head of Forensic Science Division of the Government Laboratory, Hong Kong, China; Roger Kahn, PhD, Forensic Biology Director, Harris County Medical Examiner's Office, Houston, TX; Andrew Singer, Product Manager, Bode Technology, Lorton, VA; Michael Lyford, Sergeant, Washoe County Sheriff's Office, Forensic Science Division, Reno, NV; Christophe Champod, PhD, Professor, School of Criminal Sciences, Institute of Forensic Science, University of Lausanne, Switzerland; Staff Inspector Richard P. Nuzzo, Division Headquarters, New York State Police, Albany, NY; Mike Havstad, Supervising Photographer, Scientific Services Bureau, Los Angeles County Sheriff's Department; Frederic A. Tulleners, Director, Forensic Science Graduate Program, University of California, Davis, Davis, CA; Steve Nash, Manager of Business Development and Customer Relations, Cogent Systems, Petaluma, CA; Joseph Almog, PhD, Professor, The Hebrew University, Casali Institute of Applied Chemistry, Jerusalem, Israel; Antonio A. Cantu, PhD, Forensic Scientist (retired), U.S. Secret Service, Washington, DC; Anna Barbaro, PhD, Chief of Forensic Genetics Dept., Office of Medical and Forensic Investigations, Messina, Italy; Angela L. Williamson, PhD, Director of Forensic Casework and Assistant Vice President, Bode Technology, Lorton, VA; Senior Criminalists Manuel Munoz, David Vidal, Deputy Dale Falicon (retired), Scientific Services Bureau, Los Angeles County Sheriff's Department; Lisa Jackson, Forensic Supervisor, Santa Monica Police Department, Santa Monica, CA; Melissa Simons, Forensic Scientist, Oregon State Police, Central Point, OR; Jeffrey C. Kercheval, Supervising Forensic Scientist, Western Maryland Regional Crime Laboratory, Hagerstown Police Department, Hagertown, MD; Suzanne L. Noffsinger, Trace Evidence, Miami Valley Regional Crime Laboratory, Dayton, OH; Diana Faugno, Forensic Registered Nurse Consultant, San Diego, CA; Jay Jarvis, Alliance Forensics Laboratory, Inc., Ft. Worth, TX; General Jacques Hebrard and Yves Schuliar, MD, PhD, IRCGN (Institute of Criminal Research of the National Gendarmerie), France; William J. Bodziak, Bodziak Forensics, Palm Coast, FL; Tony Grissim, Public Safety & Forensic Account Manager, Leica Geosystems Inc.; Ray A. Wickenheiser, Laboratory Director, Montgomery County Crime Laboratory, Rockville, MD; Peter Diaczuk, John Jay College of Criminal Justice; Wendy van Hilst, Senior Forensic Investigator, Forensische Opsporing Amsterdam-Amstelland, Amsterdam, the Netherlands; Dan Cheswick, Suffolk County Crime Laboratory, Suffolk County, NY; Lucian C. Haag, Forensic Science Services, Inc., Carefree, AZ; and C.M. Bowers, DDS, JD, Ventura, California; Jeff Buszka and Norm Marin, Special Investigations Unit, NYC Office of Chief Medical Examiner; Doug Schiff, 3rd Tech; and Abacus Diagnostics.

Recognition also goes to Lydia deCastro, Latief Dickerson, Dan Rothenberg, and Peter Diaczuk, who reviewed portions of the manuscript and offered valuable suggestions on ways to improve it. Any mistakes, however, are solely our own.

We also wish to thank our editors Becky Masterman and Jill Jurgensen who were patient with us in making this edition a reality. We appreciate your kindness. Dennis Troutman, our project manager, and Kyle Meyer, our project editor, were instrumental in getting this book through the production process.

Alexis Anderson helped in preparing an updated bibliography and list of websites and Daniel Winderich developed end of chapter questions to be used as study materials and Powerpoint slides for use by instructors. We greatly value their efforts.

And finally to our wives, Susan and Deena, for their encouragement and support throughout this project.

Barry A. J. Fisher
Los Angeles, California
bajfisher@earthlink.net

David R. Fisher
New York, New York
davidfisher100@gmail.com

About the Authors

Barry Fisher served as the crime laboratory director for the Los Angeles County Sheriff's Department, a position he held from 1987 until his retirement in 2009. He began his career in criminalistics with the Sheriff's crime lab in 1969 and worked in a wide variety of assignments.

Fisher is a member of many professional organizations. He is a Distinguished Fellow and past president of the American Academy of Forensic Sciences and was awarded the Academy's highest award, the Gradwohl Medallion. He served as president of the International Association of Forensic Sciences, president of the American Society of Crime Laboratory Directors, and is a past chairman of the American Society of Crime Laboratory Directors—Laboratory Accreditation Board.

Fisher is a member of several editorial boards: *Journal of Forensic Sciences, Journal of Forensic Identification, Forensic Science Policy and Management,* and the *McGraw-Hill Encyclopedia of Science and Technology.* He is a coauthor of two other books, *Forensics Demystified* and *Introduction to Criminalistics: The Foundation of Forensic Science* and has lectured throughout the United States, Canada, England, Australia, Singapore, France, Israel, Japan, China, Turkey, and Portugal on forensic science laboratory practices, quality assurance, and related topics. In 2000, he led a forensic science delegation to lecture to forensic scientists in the People's Republic of China.

Since retiring, Fisher has consulted for the United Nations Office on Drugs and Crime, the United States Department of Justice, International Criminal Investigative Training Program (ICITAP), and Analytic Services Inc., a not-for-profit institute that provides studies and analyses to aid decision makers in national security, homeland security, and public safety.

Fisher, a native New Yorker, received his Bachelor of Science degree in chemistry from the City College of New York. He holds a Master of Science in chemistry from Purdue University and an MBA from California State University, Northridge.

David Fisher currently works as a criminalist supervisor in the Department of Forensic Biology at the Office of Chief Medical Examiner in New York City. He has worked on hundreds of homicide, sexual assault, and property crime cases and has testified in court and in the grand jury as a DNA expert on numerous occasions. He is a coauthor of *Forensics Demystified,* an introductory text about forensic science published by McGraw-Hill. Fisher is certified by the American Board of Criminalistics and is a Fellow in the American Academy of Forensic Sciences. He also maintains membership in the International Association for Identification, the Northeastern Association of Forensic Scientists and is an associate member in the International Association of Bloodstain Pattern Analysts.

Fisher also has much experience in mass fatality incidents. After the events of 9/11, he helped with the identification of victims from the World Trade Center attack. (His agency continues to identify human remains from Ground Zero.) As an intermittent federal employee with the U.S. Department of Health and Human Services Disaster Mortuary

Operational Response Team (DMORT), he was deployed to the Gulf region in 2005 to aid in the identification of victims from Hurricane Katrina.

Fisher received his BS degree in biochemistry and cell biology from the University of California, San Diego and attended graduate school in forensic science at John Jay College of Criminal Justice at the City University of New York.

"You shall investigate and search and ask diligently…"

(Deuteronomy 13:15)

"If the law has made you a witness, remain a man of science;
you have no victim to avenge, or guilty or innocent person to convict or save.
You must bear testimony within the limits of science."

Dr. P.C.H. Brouardel
Nineteenth Century French Medicolegalist

Prologue

Crime scene investigation and forensic science operate within a legal framework. Thus, it is not surprising that a number of cases or legal rulings define some of the aspects of forensic science and crime scene investigation. The goal of any criminal investigation is not only to figure out what happened and who did it, but also to bring the wrongdoer to justice. As the final stop in a criminal investigation is in the courts, regulations, rules, legal precedents, and case law must be taken into consideration throughout the investigation. The following is a review of some of the case law and rules of evidence that deal with forensic science.

> ***Frye v. United States*, 293 F. 1013 (D.C. Cir. 1923).** *Frye* is one of the earliest cases in the United States to address the notion of admissibility of expert testimony. Expert testimony is used to help jurors understand complex issues generally beyond a layperson's knowledge. The Frye case dealt with the polygraph and whether its results were admissible. The court made the following statement in its opinion that sums up its ruling: "Just when a scientific principle or discovery crosses the line between the experimental and demonstrable stages is difficult to define. Somewhere in this twilight zone the evidential force of the principle must be recognized, and while courts will go a long way in admitting expert testimony deduced from a well-recognized scientific principle or discovery, the thing from which the deduction is made must be sufficiently established to have gained general acceptance in the particular field in which it belongs." Polygraph evidence was not held to be admissible in this case. The Frye Rule essentially lays out the notion of general acceptance within the *relevant scientific community*.
>
> *Frye* is still the standard in a number of states and has been modified in Federal cases by the Federal Rules of Evidence, specifically Rule 702.
> - *Daubert v. Merrell Dow Pharmaceuticals*, 509 U.S.579 (1993). The Daubert case modified the way courts view expert testimony. The trial judge serves in the capacity of gatekeeper and decides what expert evidence may be admissible. *Daubert* also expands the requirements for admissibility beyond general acceptance and adds the notion of reliability. (The Daubert standard, however, is not used in all states.)
> - *Federal Rules of Evidence, Rule 702* codifies *Daubert* and other later cases into the federal rules. "If scientific, technical, or other specialized knowledge will assist the trier of fact to understand the evidence or to determine a fact in issue, a witness qualified as an expert by knowledge, skills, experience, training, or education, may testify thereto in the form of an opinion or otherwise, if (1) the testimony is based upon sufficient facts or data, (2) the testimony is the product of reliable principles and methods, and (3) the witness has applied the principles and methods reliably to the facts of the case." Different states use

one or more of the above standards to govern the admissibility of expert scientific testimony. Some have adopted the federal rules, while others continue to follow *Frye*, and still others have adopted a hybrid version. These legal issues are of interest to lawyers and judges who must deal with them in evidentiary hearings.

- *Melendez-Diaz v. Massachusetts*, 129 S.Ct. 2527 (2009) is a relatively new decision by the U.S. Supreme Court. The Sixth Amendment of the U.S. Constitution gives the defendant the right to confront his/her accuser. The question considered in *Melendez-Diaz* was whether lab reports constitute testimony and thus require the analyst who wrote the report to testify in court about his findings. The court concluded that the expert who wrote the lab report, not an affidavit, must testify as the witness for the State against the defendant to give the defendant the ability to examine the witness concerning the work he did in the case.

- Following the Melendez-Diaz case was the 2011 Supreme Court case, *Bullcoming v. New Mexico*, 131 S. Ct. 2705 (2011). The question presented in *Bullcoming* was whether the confrontation clause (Sixth Amendment) permitted the prosecution to introduce a forensic laboratory report containing a testimonial certification—made for the purpose of proving a particular fact—through the in-court testimony of another scientist who did not sign the certification or perform or observe the test reported in the certification. The Supreme Court held that surrogate testimony of that order does not meet the constitutional requirement. The accused's right is to be confronted with the analyst who made the certification, unless that analyst is unavailable at trial, and the accused has an opportunity, pretrial, to cross-examine that particular scientist. This case will have significant ramifications, particularly in cases in which the original expert and the evidence are no longer available for reexamination. Consider an old serial murder case that occurred many years prior. The pathologist who performed the autopsy might no longer be available and the deceased's remains are buried. The question yet to be determined is how evidence in such a case might be presented.

- As of this writing, the U.S. Supreme Court has also heard oral arguments in *Williams v. Illinois*, (10-8505). Although the court has not yet ruled in this case, the issue at hand is whether a defendant's rights under the confrontation clause are violated when an expert witness testifies about the results of testing conducted by another analyst who has not appeared in court to be cross examined. It remains to be seen how the ramifications of this case will affect forensic science operations throughout the country.

Brady v. Maryland, 373 U.S. 83 (1963). *Brady* requires the prosecution to provide material evidence to the defense that may exculpate the defendant. *Brady* material readily adapts itself to forensic evidence and may become an issue in criminal proceedings.

What Is Required under Brady?* Prosecutors are required to disclose to the defense evidence favorable to a defendant that is either exculpatory or impeaching

---

* Adapted from the Los Angeles County District Attorney, Special Directive 02-08, http://da.co.la.ca.us/ sd02-08.htm.

and is material to either guilt or punishment. Evidence is "favorable" to the defendant if it either helps the defendant or hurts the prosecution. In *Strickler v. Greene* (1999) 527 U.S. 203, 280-281, the U.S. Supreme Court stated:

> In *Brady* this Court held "that the suppression by the prosecution of evidence favorable to an accused upon request violates due process where the evidence is material either to guilt or to punishment, irrespective of the good faith or bad faith of the prosecution." *Brady v. Maryland*, supra, 373 U.S. at 87. We have since held that the duty to disclose such evidence is applicable even though there has been no request by the accused, [*United States v. Agurs (1976)* 427 U.S. 97, 107], and that the duty encompasses impeachment evidence as well as exculpatory evidence, [*United States v. Bagley, (1985)* 473 U.S. 667, 676]. Such evidence is material "if there is a reasonable probability that had the evidence been disclosed to the defense, the result of the proceeding would have been different." Id at 682; see also [*Kyles v. Whitley (1995)* 514 U.S. 419, 433–434].

Prosecutors must determine what *Brady* evidence there may be *before* trial. The definition of "material evidence" is generally provided in the context of an appeal from a conviction. Evidence is material if there is a reasonable probability that the result of the proceeding would have been different had the evidence been disclosed. A reasonable probability of a different outcome is shown where suppression undermines confidence in the outcome. Such evidence must have a specific, plausible connection to the case and must demonstrate more than minor inaccuracies. Exculpatory evidence is evidence favorable to the defendant and material to the issue of guilt or punishment. Impeachment evidence is also included under *Brady*. For example, the California Evidence Code section 780 states in part that

> Except as otherwise provided by statute, the court or jury may consider in determining the credibility of a witness any matter that has any tendency to prove or disprove the truthfulness of his testimony at the hearing including, but not limited to, any of the following:
>   His character for honesty or veracity or their opposites.
>   The existence or nonexistence of a bias, interest, or other motive.
>   A statement made by him that is inconsistent with any part of his testimony at the hearing.

 Further examples of possible impeachment evidence of a material witness include the following:

1. False reports by a prosecution witness
2. Pending criminal charges
3. Parole or probation status of the witness
4. Evidence contradicting a prosecution witness' statements or reports
5. Evidence undermining a prosecution witness' expertise (e.g., inaccurate statements)
6. A finding of misconduct by a Board of Rights or Civil Service Commission that reflects on the witness' truthfulness, bias, or moral turpitude
7. Evidence that a witness has a reputation for untruthfulness

8. Evidence that a witness has a racial, religious, or personal bias against the defendant individually or as a member of a group
9. Promises, offers, or inducements to the witnesses, including a grant of immunity

Strengthening Forensic Science in the United States: A Path Forward

In February 2009, the National Academy of Sciences issued a report, *Strengthening Forensic Science in the United States: A Path Forward.*[*] The NAS Committee made 13 recommendations that are summarized as follows:

1. Create an independent federal forensic agency.
2. Establish standard terminology.
3. Support scientific research on forensic practices.
4. Ensure independence of forensic labs.
5. Research to minimize bias.
6. Set standards for forensic practice.
7. Require accreditation and certification.
8. Require quality assurance and quality control.
9. Establish a national code of ethics for all forensic science disciplines.
10. Students should be encouraged to pursue graduate studies to improve and develop applicable research methodologies in forensic science. Continuing legal education programs for law students, practitioners, and judges should also be established and supported.
11. The coroner system should be eliminated, and funds should be provided to establish a medical examiner system.
12. The Government should launch a new effort to achieve nationwide interoperability for fingerprint data.
13. Congress should provide funding to bring the Centers for Disease Control, FBI, forensic scientists and crime scene investigators together to develop roles as first responders in counterterrorism preparedness.

National Academy of Science reports have no force of law but are advisory. As of this writing, the White House and Congress are considering implementation of some of the recommendations made in the report but nothing is certain at the moment. The report has been cited in some court cases, most notably in *Melendez-Diaz v. Massachusetts*; however, it is not possible to say what the ultimate outcome of the NAS report will be. Furthermore, it is unclear how much influence the federal government can exert on the states, other than through the power of the purse in the form of grants. This is another example of an unfolding situation that will have to be followed closely.

Forensic science is more than just applied science. There is much more to crime scene investigation than simply proper police investigative techniques. Appearance and perception as well as the ability to communicate effectively to a jury are equally important. It is not only important to be sharp; you have to look sharp as well. To put it another way,

---

[*] Readers may find this report interesting as it covers many issues concerning modern forensic science and crime scene investigation. http://www.ncjrs.gov/pdffiles1/nij/grants/228091.pdf

appearances and perception are every bit as important as knowledge, skills, and ability, at least in the eyes of the jury and the public.

It would be naive for anyone planning a career in police work, forensic identification, or forensic science to underestimate the importance of the role of the expert witness in the courtroom. An investigator with the cleverness of Sherlock Holmes or a forensic scientist with the wisdom and understanding of Albert Einstein would be ineffective in a criminal investigation if he or she were unable to convince a jury made up of laypeople. Verbal communication skills are every bit as important as technical expertise in being a successful expert witness.

Professional ethics are also crucial. In a small number of instances, ethical failings among practitioners make restating some fundamental principles necessary. Criminal justice practitioners must know how to behave and what actions are right and honorable. For whatever reasons, notions of ethics, duty, and honor are ideals that have been forgotten by some. A brief discussion on the subject is in order because forensic practitioners and crime scene investigators occasionally forget their public duty. In addition, those new to the profession must be told what their role in the criminal justice system is in clear, unmistakable terms.

A colleague once explained ethical conduct by using a simple statement: "It takes a career to build one's reputation, and only a moment to ruin it!" In a forensic context, several examples of dishonorable conduct come to mind. These situations, unfortunately, refer to actual incidents:

- Planting evidence at a crime scene to point to a defendant
- Collecting evidence without a warrant by claiming exigent circumstances
- Falsifying laboratory examinations to enhance the prosecution's case
- Ignoring evidence at a crime scene that might exonerate a suspect or be a mitigating factor
- Reporting on forensic tests not actually done out of a misguided belief that the tests are unnecessary, or "dry labbing"
- Fabricating scientific opinions based on invalid interpretations of tests or evidence to assist the prosecution
- Examining physical evidence when not qualified to do so
- Extending expertise beyond one's knowledge
- Falsifying positive and/or negative controls
- Stealing narcotic evidence from drug cases
- Using unproven methodologies
- Misstating credentials
- Overstating an expert opinion by using "terms of art" unfamiliar to juries
- Failing to report a colleague, superior, or subordinate who engages in any of the previously listed activities to the proper authorities
- Charging for one's testimony based on the outcome of the trial

This list of wrongdoings can be categorized in several ways. Some failings are actually criminal in nature; they are felonies that could result in prison terms for the perpetrator. Others represent negligent conduct and could result in civil litigation against the expert, a superior, or the agency. Yet another class of failings constitutes professional misconduct that could result in censure, suspension, expulsion from professional organizations, or termination from employment. Occasionally, situations arise that contain an element of ambiguity. How might one determine the best course of action? Although the answer may not be clear in every case, one method is to ask the following questions:

- Would I be proud to tell my children or my parents what I did?
- How would my actions look on the front page of the morning newspaper?

If it remains uncertain whether actions are inappropriate or improper, seek the advice of a trusted professional colleague. Every forensic discipline has members who serve as pillars of the profession; seek out those individuals and ask for guidance.

Those of us who work for public agencies and who investigate criminal acts carry a difficult burden. The consequences of our conduct are considerable. Defendants convicted of capital crimes may face the death penalty or long years of incarceration, in part from the physical evidence we collect and about which we provide expert testimony. It is troubling to think that those responsible for committing a criminal act may be set free because of actions committed or omitted by a forensic investigator. Indeed, few professions carry this amount of responsibility or hold such public trust as do forensic scientists and crime scene investigators.

Training and continuing education are important for all practitioners within the criminal justice system: uniformed officers, detectives, crime scene investigators, forensic scientists, prosecutors, defense attorneys, and judges. Continuing education and attendance at professional association seminars and workshops are essential to professional competency and professional development. To demonstrate this point, one should ask themself, "Would I consider going to a physician, dentist, accountant, lawyer, or other professional who does not periodically attend continuing education classes to keep up his or her professional competency?" Funds for professional development should be considered a priority in all law enforcement organizations that conduct forensic science testing. It cannot be overstated enough that we all need to stay abreast of current developments in our field. Practitioners should also be willing to give back to the profession by teaching, giving papers or talks at conferences, or organizing a workshop.

Written standard operating procedures must be developed and reevaluated periodically. All law enforcement personnel involved in the investigation must follow their agency's policies and physical evidence procedures. Agencies must "say what they do and do what they say." The reasons for this are evident. Defense attorneys will attempt to show that the written policies and procedures were not followed or, if policies and procedures do not exist, that the practices used were not generally acceptable or personnel lacked appropriate training. The results are the same; even if forensic tests point to the defendant, improper or inadequate evidence collection and preservation techniques will render the evidence inadmissible or its value will be diminished.

A better-informed defense bar will also raise questions about the quality of forensic science laboratories and their forensic practitioners. One way to evaluate a laboratory's quality is to inquire if it is accredited. In the United States and several foreign countries, the American Society of Crime Laboratory Directors—Laboratory Accreditation Board (or ASCLD/LAB*) provides that accreditation. Other programs such as Forensic Quality Services also provide ISO 17025† accreditation programs. In fact, with the number of

* http://www.ascld-lab.org/
† ISO 17025 is the main standard used by testing and calibration laboratories.

public forensic laboratories that have already become accredited, it is only a matter of time before accreditation will be a de facto requirement for evidence admissibility. No one is likely to undergo surgery in a nonaccredited hospital; similarly, courts, prosecuting and defense attorneys, the police, and the public should demand that their laboratories meet basic forensic science laboratory accreditation standards.

Just as a forensic science user should expect a laboratory to be accredited, a similar question may be asked of the forensic science practitioner: Is he or she board certified? There are a number of professional certifying bodies. In the criminalistics arena, it is the American Board of Criminalistics. The International Association for Identification (IAI) offers an exemplary certification program in fingerprint identification, crime scene investigation, reconstruction, and other disciplines. There are also other forensic science and medical certifying bodies in areas such as questioned documents, toxicology, dentistry, pathology, anthropology, and psychiatry that help to identify competent practitioners.

Certification of forensic scientists (1) measures quality, (2) enhances credibility, (3) introduces a degree of peer standardization, and (4) enhances consumer confidence. However, not all certifying programs are to be trusted. Persons considering a board certifying program are encouraged to evaluate them critically. A program that does little more than require the payment of a fee should raise questions.

Just as accreditation and certification are important, so is ongoing proficiency testing for forensic practitioners. There are a variety of proficiency testing modalities that demonstrate mastery of technical procedures. Proficiency testing can be blind, declared, reanalysis, interlaboratory, or "round robin." Proficiency test results are public records and can be subpoenaed to demonstrate how well laboratories and practitioners perform in such tests.

Forensic science funding needs are often ignored until some big problem is brought to light. Often inadequate funding goes along with inadequate oversight from the local criminal justice establishment. Quality and timely work have a price tag and inadequate funding has consequences. Parent organizations must remember to fund staff and support operations in addition to line units. Failure to provide adequate funding to ensure quality work and timely lab service is unconscionable. The damage done when failures in the forensic science delivery system occur can be appalling. Several states in the U.S. have established oversight committees (i.e., the New York State Forensic Science Commission) comprised of forensic science professionals, judges, defense attorneys, prosecutors and lay leaders of the community. These commissions oversee forensic labs operating in their state. The citizens of a democracy have a right to expect that justice be administered fairly, impartially, and in an expedient manner.

Crime scene investigation and forensic science are complex processes that are essential components of the criminal justice system and public safety. It is the duty of all stakeholders to keep them strong and vibrant.

Introduction

1

The application of science and technology plays a critical role in the investigation and adjudication of crimes in our criminal justice system. But before science can be brought to bear on evidence, it must be recognized and collected in an appropriate manner at crime scenes.

Webster's Dictionary defines evidence as something legally submitted to a competent trier of fact as a means of ascertaining the truth of any alleged matter under investigation. Police investigators deal with evidence on a daily basis. Their ability to recognize, collect, and use evidence in criminal investigations determines to a large degree their success as investigators as well as the outcome of the case.

Evidence can be divided into two broad types: (1) testimonial evidence and (2) real, or physical, evidence. Testimonial evidence is evidence given in the form of statements made under oath, usually in response to questioning. Physical evidence is any type of evidence with an objective existence, that is, anything with size, shape, and dimension.

Physical evidence can take any form. It can be as large as a house or as small as a fiber. It can be as fleeting as an odor or as obvious as the destructive results at the scene of an explosion. In fact, the variety of physical evidence that may be encountered in an investigation is infinite. Physical evidence may also be considered either direct evidence (evidence that supports a conclusion of fact without inference) or circumstantial evidence (evidence that requires inference to connect it to a conclusion of fact).

What is the value of physical evidence and why should police investigators concern themselves with an understanding of the uses and ways to collect physical evidence?

Physical evidence can prove a crime has been committed or establish key elements of a crime.

Case

Proof of rape requires showing nonconsensual sexual intercourse. In an alleged rape case, the victim's torn clothing, bruises, and vaginal tearing may be sufficient to prove nonconsensual intercourse. (Figure 1.1 is an example of one of the first uses of photography at the scene of a rape-homicide.)

Case

Arson investigators dispatched to the scene of a suspicious fire collected some burned carpeting. Later analysis proved that gasoline was present in the carpet, proving that the fire was intentionally set and, therefore, arson.

Physical evidence can place the suspect in contact with the victim or with the crime scene.

Figure 1.1 This is a photograph of a 1907 rape-homicide case taken by the founder of the Institute of Scientific Police at the University of Lausanne, Switzerland–Rodolphe Archibald Reiss. The French criminologist Alphonse Bertillon is usually credited with turning the haphazard practice of forensic photography into a systematic science in the late nineteenth century. But it was his younger colleague Reiss who developed and disseminated those methods and who founded the world-renowned institute in Lausanne. Reiss helped to establish scientific police services in Russia and Brazil, and in 1914, he became the Serbian government's official investigator into the atrocities committed by the German and Austrian armies in World War I. A contemporary wrote that he would have made an excellent model for Sherlock Holmes: tall and youthful well into his fifties, he had eyes that shone with intelligence and a passion for deciphering signs and traces. (Courtesy of Prof. Christophe Champod, Institute of Scientific Police at the University of Lausanne, Switzerland.)

Case

A suspect was apprehended shortly after an alleged murder in the victim's home. A bloody fingerprint at the crime scene after a search of the Automated Fingerprint Identification System (AFIS) ended up matching the suspect. DNA typing showed that the victim was the source of the blood. The suspect was at a loss to explain how his fingerprint made it inside the victim's house (Figure 1.2).

Physical evidence can establish the identity of persons associated with the crime.

Case

Every safe burglar knows not to leave fingerprints at the crime scene, so it was not surprising to find in the trash at the scene surgical gloves that were used on the safe. The identity of the burglar was established by developing fingerprints inside the rubber gloves (Figure 1.3).

Case

DNA typing proved that a lone defendant was responsible for a series of auto theft cases in a major metropolitan area after finding his DNA on multiple cars' steering wheels.

Figure 1.2 A latent fingerprint in blood.

Figure 1.3 Gloves left behind at a crime scene were cut open to develop the fingerprints inside.

Physical evidence can exonerate the innocent.

Case

An 8- and 9-year-old brother and sister accused an elderly neighbor of child molestation. They claimed that the man gave each of them pills that made them feel drowsy and then he molested them. The investigator had a physician examine the children, and blood and urine specimens were collected for a toxicology screen. The analyses of the blood and urine specimens were negative. When presented with this information, the children confessed that they had fabricated the entire story because they disliked their neighbor.

Physical evidence can corroborate the victim's testimony.

Case

A motorist picked up a female hitchhiker. She claimed that he pulled a knife and attempted to rape her. During the struggle, the woman's thumb was cut before she managed to escape. She related her story to the police and the suspect was eventually arrested. During the interrogation, the suspect steadfastly proclaimed his innocence. The investigator noted a small quantity of dried blood on the suspect's left jacket lapel. He claimed the blood came from a shaving mishap. The investigator submitted the jacket along with blood samples from the suspect and the victim to the crime laboratory. The results indicated that the blood on the jacket came from the victim. The physical evidence was instrumental in obtaining a conviction for attempted rape.

A suspect confronted with physical evidence may make admissions or even confess.

Case

Dog fighting still occurs from time to time. Blood found on a suspect's shirt was species-tested and determined to be canine, that is, from a dog. The suspect, who first claimed the blood was his own, made a full admission when confronted by the evidence.

Physical evidence may be more reliable than eyewitnesses to crimes.

Psychological experiments have shown that observations made by test subjects in simulated violent crimes are sometimes inaccurate after the event. Volunteers in a psychological test were witnesses to staged assaults. At the conclusion of the mock crimes, they were asked to detail their observations in writing. The study showed that the mind fills in gaps to physical features. If a portion of a physical characteristic was not seen or did not make sense, the subjects made up descriptions that seemed reasonable. This behavior occurred subconsciously; subjects were not aware that it was taking place. They simply reported what they believed they had seen. This in turn has sometimes, unfortunately, led to wrongful convictions due to mistaken identity.*

Juries in criminal cases expect physical evidence.

Two unrelated factors have biased the public's notion of the role of physical evidence in criminal cases. The "CSI effect" has made jurors expect, even demand, physical evidence in a trial. This is due to the countless shows that glamorize forensics on TV such as *CSI, CSI:NY, CSI:Miami, Court TV, Bones, Law and Order: Special Victims Unit, NCIS, Dexter,* and many others. Second, science and technology are perceived by most of the public to be unbiased and not subject to manipulation. If scientific testing is used to evaluate and characterize physical evidence, the public is more inclined to believe that the police investigation was properly conducted.

---

* The Innocence Project (www.innocenceproject.org) has worked towards the exonerations of many wrongfully convicted individuals from mistaken eyewitness testimony through the use of post-conviction DNA typing.

Negative evidence—the absence of physical evidence—may provide useful information and even stop defense arguments at the time of trial.

Case

In an insurance fraud case, the victim claimed his home was burglarized. No evidence of forced entry could be found and eventually the fraud was discovered.

Classification and Individualization of Physical Evidence

Some investigators may think that every item of physical evidence can be directly associated to a specific person, place, or thing and believe that it is possible to link that evidence to a unique source. This is generally not the case. Although some types of physical evidence may come from one and only one source, most physical evidence may only be associated with a class or group. Only a few kinds of physical evidence can be individualized. A broken piece of plastic physically fitted to reconstruct an item is an example of individualization. Other types of evidence including biological stains, fingerprints, tool marks, and fired bullets are examples of evidence that may be associated with a unique source (Figure 1.4).

The majority of physical evidence found at crime scenes can only be classified. Classification means that an item of evidence shares a common source. These items can be placed into groups with all other items having the same properties or class characteristics.

Figure 1.4 The victim in this case was raped and strangled in her home in a suburb of Beijing. The perpetrator tried to disguise the crime scene by tying a lamp cord from a desk lamp around the victim's neck and making the death appear to be a suicide. A latent fingerprint was discovered on the base of the lamp using superglue. The case was solved when the latent print was matched with that of a neighborhood youth who had claimed never to have been in the victim's apartment. (Courtesy of the Institute of Forensic Science, Beijing, China.)

Note: The ability to associate an item of evidence to a sole, unique source is currently being hotly debated. Proponents argue that experts are able to offer unequivocal conclusions, for example, a latent fingerprint with sufficient ridge detail was left by one person to the exclusion of all others. Opponents to this proposition point out that there is insufficient statistical data at this point in time to make such a claim. It is likely that the courts will settle this question at some point. Statements that evidence came from one source to the exclusion of all others may result in sharp questioning on the part of the opposing lawyer in a case. Currently, more research into the application of statistical pattern recognition to physical evidence in forensic science is underway.

Examples include fabric from a mass produced item of clothing or automobile paint from a specific make and model.

The difference between individualization (Figure 1.5) and classification can be understood by using a hypothetical case. Consider the following example: a blue-colored cotton fiber is found at the scene of a burglary. A suspect wearing a torn blue cotton shirt is apprehended. All the tests conducted at the crime laboratory on the evidence fiber and exemplar fibers from the shirt show that they cannot be differentiated. Can it be concluded that the blue cotton fiber found at the scene definitely came from the torn blue cotton shirt worn by the suspect? No! The best that can be stated from this information is that the fiber *could have* come from the shirt in question or any other one manufactured with similar blue cotton fibers. The item has been classified as a blue cotton fiber and can be placed into a class of all other similar blue cotton fibers.

A follow-up question for the expert testifying about the identification of the fibers might be to inquire about the significance of finding this evidence. Can anything be stated about the fact that the evidence was found? Stating this another way, suppose that blue cotton fibers are routinely found on random people. How might this factor impact a jury versus fibers that are rarely found?

Contrast the fiber evidence with a pieced together broken plastic reflector lens. One can easily conclude the broken pieces originally came from one and only one source because of the pieces' unique shape and jigsaw puzzle fit (Figure 1.6).

Historically, when sufficient markings are present on *pattern evidence* (e.g., fingerprints, firearms evidence, footwear evidence, tire impressions, and tool marks), practitioners would offer a conclusive opinion that the known and questioned item came from a common source to a reasonable degree of scientific certainty. Thus, a latent fingerprint could be compared to a known inked fingerprint and the examiner would report that the questioned print and the known came from a unique source to the exclusion of all others. This source attribution conclusion is now being questioned by some in the criminal justice community. Critics of this conclusion argue that such a definitive conclusion as to the source is not possible because there is insufficient data to back up this claim. Specifically, the contention is that there have not been enough studies to determine the statistical likelihood of various marks to quantify the observation. The examiners' conclusion is subjective, they argue, and is based on their training, experience, and inductive logic, not on statistical data. Research is currently underway to develop the empirical data needed to give weight to source attribution conclusions for pattern evidence.

(a)

(b)   (c)

Figure 1.5 This case is an example of a physical match or jigsaw match. A comb (a) with three missing teeth was found in the suspect's possession. Two plastic teeth (b) found at the crime scene were fitted exactly to the comb (c). The evidence placed the victim at a burglary. (Courtesy of the Los Angeles County Sheriff's Department.)

It appears that the interpretation of forensic DNA evidence has become the "gold standard" and has changed a long-held view on source attribution: connecting an item to a unique source requires statistical weight. DNA testing uses the statistical occurrence of discrete pieces of genetic material or alleles. These alleles have different frequency values developed from population databases. Alleles at different locations, or loci, are statistically independent from other locations. This allows for the calculation of the likelihood of finding all of them together in a given sample by multiplying the individual frequencies together. Thus with DNA evidence, we may report that a given DNA profile has a random match probability of greater than one in a trillion or is extremely rare. The question then

Figure 1.6 Physical matches are an example of individualization. In this hit and run, the top portion of this car part was found at the crime scene and was able to be matched to the broken part on the suspect's car. (Courtesy of the Los Angeles County Sheriff's Department.)

becomes what is the best way to give objective statistical weight to an examiner's conclusion for other types of pattern evidence?

In the case of fingerprints or firearms evidence, such a simple calculation is more difficult. We do not know the likelihood of each mark occurring or whether the marks are independent of one another. Intuitively, the examiner concludes that finding so large a number of seemingly random events must make the comparison unique to a single source. More research that is currently underway in the application of statistical pattern recognition to pattern evidence will allow the examiner to give a numerical value with his conclusion. By attaching a statistical number to a conclusion, juries will be in a better position to decide how much weight to give the expert's testimony.

Most physical evidence by its nature, however, cannot definitively connect a suspect to a crime as pattern evidence essentially can. This should not diminish the usefulness of that evidence. Physical evidence that is identified can corroborate testimony, place a subject at a scene, and be useful in a variety of ways as an interrogation tool. It also provides valuable information for juries to assist them in their deliberations (Figure 1.7).

Collection and Preservation of Physical Evidence

The major theme of this text concerns the proper handling of physical evidence. Two of the main areas that must be considered in any discussion of the proper techniques of collection and preservation of physical evidence are the legal and scientific issues concerning the collection and preservation of physical evidence.

Figure 1.7 The order of clothing fragments caught in the hollow-point round fired by a deputy sheriff helped to reconstruct the sequence of events in an officer-involved shooting. An innocent bystander and an armed robber were killed by the shot and it was up to the laboratory to determine who was struck first. The order of the fragments of clothing proved that the bullet first hit the robber and then the bystander. (Courtesy of the Los Angeles County Sheriff's Department.)

Although laws regarding physical evidence vary somewhat from state to state, they have many similarities. Before any evidence is seized, the need for a search warrant or court order should always be considered. Case law is constantly changing, so investigators should keep abreast of the latest developments. Depending on circumstances, court orders may be required for searching the crime scene and collecting evidence, such as blood samples, hair specimens, medical tests, and teeth impressions, from a suspect. The prosecutor's office should be consulted if there is any doubt. Naturally, in exigent circumstances, failing to obtain a warrant may be excused. Thus, if police believe that a suspect is likely to destroy critical evidence if the police wait for a warrant to be executed, courts are likely to allow the evidence, even when seized without a warrant, to be admitted.

Failure to secure a search warrant may result in legal sanctions by the court. In some cases, the physical evidence seized at a crime scene may be inadmissible in court for lack of a warrant. In fact, a legal doctrine called *fruit of the poison tree* provides that any subsequent information derived from illegally seized physical evidence is inadmissible in court and cannot be used.

The concept of a "chain of custody" or "chain of evidence" is important to understand. The court will require proof that evidence collected during an investigation and the evidence ultimately submitted to the court are one and the same. To prove that the integrity of the physical evidence has been maintained, a chain of custody must be demonstrated. This *chain* shows who had contact with the evidence, at what time, under what circumstances, and what changes, if any, were made to the evidence. It can also be used to help locate evidence years down the road in case additional testing is required (i.e., post-conviction testing).

Typically, evidence is placed in a container with a label or is tagged. Identifying information pertaining to the case is written on the container or tag as well as in reports and logs to establish the chain. Police department policy may dictate which information is required, but usually the following types of information are needed to establish the chain of custody:

- Name or initials of the individual collecting the evidence and each person subsequently having custody of it
- Dates the item was collected and transferred
- Agency, case number, and type of crime
- Voucher or property clerk number
- Victim's or suspect's name
- Storage location
- Brief description of the item

This information serves to prove the chain of custody to the court and assists in admitting the items into evidence.

Storage of physical evidence has legal implications. Evidence must be held in a secured area after it is gathered and before transportation to court. Evidence reasonably assumed to have been tampered with by unauthorized persons because it was kept in an unsecured area may be inadmissible in court. Evidence should be maintained in a specific secured area, with limited access by only authorized persons.

Several scientific issues concerning the proper collection and preservation of evidence require discussion.

Sufficient material should be collected. Evaluating the amount of specimen to gather is largely a matter of experience. As a general rule, however, as much material as is reasonably possible to collect should be taken. Generally, it is impractical and sometimes impossible to return to a crime scene at a later time to collect more material if more physical evidence should be needed. As a general rule, more is better than less, as it is easier to explain why you did collect something, as opposed to why you did not collect something. However, as a crime scene investigator or detective who collects physical evidence at the crime scene gains experience and understands the requirements of the crime laboratory that he submits evidence to, the amount of material will become less over time. Evidence storage facilities do not have an infinite amount of space available to store any and all evidence, so some degree of reasonableness must be exercised.

Many forensic science laboratory examinations compare known specimens with questioned specimens. Known samples or exemplars are needed for these comparative laboratory analyses. For example, if a bloodstained shirt is submitted to a crime laboratory, the DNA typing results must be compared with something to provide useful information, although a search against the DNA database may result in a "cold hit" from an unknown assailant. Blood samples or *buccal* (cheek) swabs from the victim and suspect are needed. In addition, elimination samples from consensual partners in cases of sexual assault and people who may have had legitimate access to a crime scene must also be submitted to the crime laboratory as well. Similarly, if an automobile paint specimen is submitted for laboratory analysis, a known sample of paint from the questioned vehicle must be submitted for comparison. These are examples of known or reference samples. They are also referred to as exemplars.

Case

A unique reference sample was needed after a robbery of a Baskin–Robbins® ice cream store. A suspect was apprehended a few blocks away with what appeared to be ice cream stains on his shirt. The crime laboratory requested a known reference sample of chocolate ice cream from the store to compare to the stains on the suspect's shirt.

Blank samples may also be important. Consider an arson investigation. An issue can be raised that heat from a fire may cause wood or carpeting to give off products that might be confused with combustible material. Unburned samples of wood or carpet can be collected for testing to clarify this contention. Blank samples, or substrate controls, are used to verify that the uncontaminated samples do not interfere with the analysis. Many DNA labs, however, no longer test substrate controls because they do not act as adequate negative controls.*

Physical evidence should be handled as little as possible. Too much handling may obliterate fingerprints; dislodge minute trace evidence such as hair, fibers, and debris; break apart brittle evidence; or contaminate evidence. Forceps, latex gloves, masks, special containers, and a clean work area are required for the handling of physical evidence.

Crime scene investigators should have an assortment of envelopes, containers, evidence tape, and assorted packaging material on hand to properly collect and preserve physical evidence. Plastic bags are generally to be avoided (Figure 1.8). This is usually the

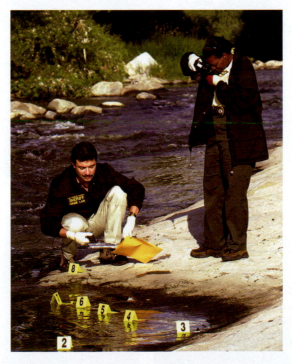

Figure 1.8 Crime scene investigators have to work in various locations and have to have on hand many different types of containers and packaging materials to collect various types of evidence and to mark areas to show the location where physical evidence was collected at the scene. (Courtesy of the Los Angeles County Sheriff's Department, Crime Laboratory.)

* Gill, P. 1997. The utility of "substrate controls" in relation to "contamination." *Forensic Science International*. 85:105

case when preserving biological evidence such as bloody articles because plastic bags accelerate deterioration and mold growth. However, if it is necessary to transport blood-soaked articles that cannot be air-dried at the crime scene directly to the laboratory for processing, plastic containers may be used for such purposes and for short periods of time.

Airtight containers are used for volatile evidence such as gasoline-soaked debris. Clean glass jars with lined screw-cap lids or clean metal paint cans with wide mouth openings make excellent containers for arson evidence. Burned debris that is to be checked for combustible materials should never be packaged in plastic bags or plastic jars because volatile evidence will pass through most plastic containers.

It is good practice to double-wrap very small objects such as hair, fibers, or glass fragments. These items should first be folded up in a sheet of paper, such as a pharmacist's fold, and then placed in an envelope. Careful packaging of minute items of evidence will ensure that they are not lost (Figure 1.9).

It is also important to safely package evidence. Evidence should be labeled with any potential hazards such as biohazard stickers before submitting these items to the laboratory (Figure 1.10). Sharp objects such as knives, blades, or needles should not be placed in a paper bag. These items should be packaged in strong cardboard boxes and secured

(a)

(b)   (c)

Figure 1.9 In this case, clothing was found along with skeletal remains (a). Close-up photography shows cut marks to the fabric of a bra (b) and a close up of a cut fiber from the bra (c). Trace evidence such as this must be handed carefully so as not to lose it. (Courtesy of the Los Angeles County Sheriff's Department, Crime Laboratory.)

Figure 1.10 Sharp items such as knives should be secured in a cardboard box or puncture proof container with zip-ties when submitting to the laboratory. (Courtesy of www.spexforensics .com.)

with zip-ties to prevent the analyst from accidently cutting themselves. Firearms should be packaged unloaded and rendered safe. Boxes especially made for these types of evidence can be purchased from commercial crime scene equipment suppliers.

Contamination is a concern for proper preservation of evidence. Items of evidence should be packaged separately in individual containers. Each piece of evidence should be completely segregated from other evidence, especially known samples from questioned items.

Case

A burglary suspect was apprehended near a residential tract; he had broken into a house through the rear door. The arresting officer observed splinters, paint, and other building material on the suspect's jacket. Samples from around the point of entry were collected for comparison and submitted with the jacket to the crime laboratory. However, all the evidence was packaged together in one paper bag. When it arrived at the crime laboratory, it was not possible to tell whether the debris on the jacket was from the crime scene or from the known samples collected by the investigator and placed into the bag with the suspect's clothing.

Microscopic or trace evidence presents unique collection problems (Figure 1.11). A number of techniques are available to collect this type of evidence. Vacuum cleaners

Figure 1.11 Hair samples are one of the small and easily lost types of physical evidence requiring special care when collecting, packaging, marking, and storing for subsequent examination at the crime laboratory. (Courtesy of the Los Angeles County Sheriff's Department, Crime Laboratory.)

specially equipped with traps can be used to collect trace evidence such as hairs, fibers, glass fragments, and debris. Evidence collection vacuums are available commercially, or normal household vacuum cleaners can be modified to collect trace evidence. However, the technique indiscriminately collects relevant trace evidence as well as large amounts of debris with no relationship to the crime.

Alternative methods for collecting trace evidence consists of shaking, sweeping, or picking trace evidence off of clothing or other large surfaces and allowing the trace materials to fall on a clean sheet of paper. Others prefer to use specialized clear plastic tape. A 4-inch length of tape, or tape-lift, may be pressed onto suspected areas and then placed, sticky side down, on a microscope slide for examination and further treatment.

Each of these techniques has advantages and disadvantages. Before one technique is chosen over another, it is highly recommended that the crime laboratory used by the police agency be consulted because the laboratory may prefer one practice to another.

Specially trained personnel—forensic scientists, criminalists, forensic technicians, or identification technicians—examine physical evidence collected at crime scenes. These specialists prepare reports and testify in court as expert witnesses. Because scientific principles relating to physical evidence are often beyond the knowledge of laypeople, courts permit persons with specialized training and skills to testify in court to explain and interpret scientific evidence to juries, as well as offer their opinion based on the evidence. Expert witnesses can be used when the subject of the testimony is beyond the experience and knowledge of ordinary laypeople and when the expert has sufficient skills, knowledge, or experience in his or her field to help the judge or jury determine the truth.

Those entrusted with the investigation of criminal activity carry a weighty burden. Although the ultimate solution of the crime is a primary goal, one cannot forget that all activity surrounding the investigation will be scrutinized at some later time. Actions taken during the investigative phase, for example, interviews, collecting and preserving physical evidence, documenting the crime scene, etc., must be done in the proper legal fashion so that evidence can be admitted when the case goes to trial. Mistakes are often unforgiving; there are scores of examples where unintentional errors have tainted the evidence, or worse, caused the evidence to be declared inadmissible by the courts. The best advice is to consider all the ramifications before taking action.

Important Considerations in Crime Scene Investigations

In addition to the "how-to" elements of crime scene investigation, several other issues need to be discussed. These represent a philosophical approach to the subject and should be considered an integral part of forensic science and forensic identification.

Forensic scientists, crime scene specialists, and investigators are the individuals whose jobs apply science and technology to the solution of criminal acts. They shoulder an important role in the criminal justice system. Their skill and knowledge in the criminal investigation may establish the innocence or guilt of a defendant. Professional ethics and integrity are essential to their effort.

Many forensic specialists work for law enforcement agencies that are responsible for the criminal investigation and/or the prosecution of cases. While some may argue that employment by police agencies offers the potential for bias, in fact, it is the integrity of the professional and the organization that is the deciding factor.

All forensic practitioners owe a duty to the truth. They may never be biased for or against a suspect in an investigation. The forensic practitioner's sole obligation is to serve the aims of justice. It makes no difference whether a defendant is ultimately found guilty of the crime or not. What is important is that the forensic practitioner conducted the investigation in a thorough, competent, and unbiased manner.

Forensic practitioners have an obligation not to overstate or understate scientific findings. As experts in the criminal justice system, they are placed in positions of authority and responsibility. Because of their education, training, experience, and skills, their opinions on technical matters often carry considerable weight and importance.

For forensic science practitioners to perform their function within the legal system properly, they must exercise independence and integrity. Stated simply, forensic scientists cannot be prejudiced for or against an investigation in which they are involved. Their job is to champion their own expert opinions based on accepted, properly performed scientific inquiry. Forensic scientists who understand their role in the criminal justice arena help to protect individual rights and freedoms while ensuring that justice is delivered.

Like practitioners, managers of forensic science laboratories must be concerned about professional ethics. The American Society of Crime Laboratory Directors* (ASCLD) has a code of professional practices, *Guidelines for Forensic Laboratory Management Practices* (Adopted 1987, Revised 1994). They are included here as a definition of good laboratory management practices.

Guidelines for Forensic Laboratory Management Practices

Introduction

The ASCLD is a professional organization of managers and supervisors employed in forensic laboratories. We are the holders of a public trust because a portion of the vital affairs of other people has been placed in our hands by virtue of the role of our laboratories in the criminal justice system. The typical users of forensic laboratory services are not in a position to judge

* http://www.ascld.org/

the quality of our work product or management for themselves. They must rely on the expertise of individual professional practitioners and the standard of practice maintained by the profession as a whole.

The purpose of this document is to provide guidelines for the conduct of managers and supervisors of forensic laboratories so as to safeguard the integrity and objectives of the profession. These are not immutable laws nor are they all-inclusive. Instead, they represent general standards, which each manager and supervisor should strive to meet.

Laboratory managers must exercise individual judgment in complying with the general guidelines in this document. The guiding principle should be that the end does not justify the means; the means must always be in keeping with the law and with good scientific practice.

Responsibility to the Employer

Employers rarely have the ability to judge the quality and productivity of their forensic laboratory. Therefore, the employer relies on the forensic manager to develop and maintain an efficient, high quality forensic laboratory.

Managerial Competence

Laboratory managers should display competence in the direction of such activities as long range planning, management of change, group decision making, and sound fiscal practices. The role(s) and responsibilities of laboratory members must be clearly defined.

Integrity

Laboratory managers must be honest and truthful with their peers, supervisors, and subordinates. They must also be trustworthy and honest when representing their laboratories to outside organizations.

Quality

Laboratory managers are responsible for implementing quality assurance procedures that effectively monitor and verify the quality of the work product of their laboratories.

Efficiency

Laboratory managers should ensure that laboratory services are provided in a manner that maximizes organizational efficiency and ensures an economical expenditure of resources and personnel.

Productivity

Laboratory managers should establish reasonable goals for the production of casework in a timely fashion. Highest priority should be given to cases that have a potentially productive outcome and that could, if successfully concluded, have an effective impact on the enforcement or adjudication process.

Meeting Organizational Expectations

Laboratory managers must implement and enforce the policies and rules of their employers and should establish internal procedures designed to meet the needs of their organizations.

Health and Safety

Laboratory managers are responsible for planning and maintaining systems that reasonably assure safety in the laboratory. Such systems should include mechanisms for input by members of the laboratory, maintenance of records of injuries, and routine safety inspections.

Security

Laboratory managers are responsible for planning and maintaining the security of the laboratory. Security measures should include control of access both during and after normal business hours.

Management Information Systems

Laboratory managers are responsible for developing management information systems. These systems should provide information that assists managers and the parent organization in decision making processes.

Responsibility to the Employee

Laboratory managers understand that the quality of the work generated by a laboratory is directly related to the performance of the staff. To that end, the laboratory manager has important responsibilities to obtain the best performance from the laboratory's employees.

Qualifications

Laboratory managers must hire employees of sufficient academic qualifications or experience to provide them with the fundamental scientific principles for work in a forensic laboratory. The laboratory manager must be assured that employees are honest, forthright, and ethical in their personal and professional life.

Training

Laboratory managers are obligated to provide training in the principles of forensic science. Training must include handling and preserving the integrity of physical evidence. Before casework is done, specific training within that functional area shall be provided. Laboratory managers must be assured that the employee fully understands the principles, applications, and limitations of methods, procedures, and equipment they use before beginning case work.

Maintaining Employee's Competency

Laboratory managers must monitor the skills of employees on a continuing basis through the use of proficiency testing, report review, and evaluation of testimony.

Staff Development

Laboratory managers should foster the development of the staff for greater job responsibility by supporting internal and external training, providing sufficient library resources to permit employees to keep abreast of changing and emerging trends in forensic science, and encouraging them to do so.

Environment

Laboratory managers are obligated to provide a safe and functional work environment with adequate space to support all the work activities of the employee. Facilities must be adequate so that evidence under the laboratory's control is protected from contamination, tampering, or theft.

Communication

Laboratory managers should take steps to ensure that the employees understand and support the objectives and values of the laboratory. Pathways of communication should exist within the organization so that the ideas of the employees are considered when policies and procedures of the laboratory are developed or revised. Communication should include staff meetings as well as written and oral dialogue.

Supervision

Laboratory managers must provide staff with adequate supervisory review to ensure the quality of the work product. Supervisors must be held accountable for the performance of their staff and the enforcement of clear and enforceable organizational and ethical standards. Employees should be held to realistic performance goals, which take into account reasonable workload standards. Supervisors should ensure that employees are not unduly pressured to perform substandard work through case load pressure or unnecessary outside influence. The laboratory should have in place a performance evaluation process.

Fiscal

Laboratory managers should strive to provide adequate budgetary support. Laboratory managers should provide employees with appropriate, safe, well maintained, and calibrated equipment to permit them to perform their job functions at maximum efficiency.

Responsibility to the Public

Laboratory managers hold a unique role in the balance of scientific principles, requirements of the criminal justice system, and the effects on the lives of individuals. The decisions and judgments that are made in the laboratory must fairly represent all interests with which they have been entrusted. Users of forensic laboratory services must rely on the reputation of the laboratory, the abilities of its analysts, and the standards of the profession.

Conflict of Interest

Laboratory managers and employees of forensic laboratories must avoid any activity, interest, or association that interferes or appears to interfere with their independent exercise of professional judgment.

Response to Public Needs

Forensic laboratories should be responsive to public input and consider the impact of actions and case priorities on the public.

Professional Staffing

Forensic laboratories must hire and retain qualified personnel who have the integrity necessary to the practice of forensic science. Verification of academic, work experience, and professional association credentials is essential.

Recommendations and References

Professional recommendations of laboratories and/or analysts should be given only when there is knowledge and an endorsement of the quality of the work and the competence of the laboratory/analyst. Referrals of clients to other professional colleagues carry a lesser degree of endorsement and are appropriate when a laboratory is unable to perform the work requested.

Legal Compliance

Laboratory managers shall establish operational procedures to meet constitutional and statutory requirements as well as principles of sound scientific practice.

Fiscal Responsibility

Public laboratories should be managed to minimize waste and promote cost effectiveness. Strict inventory controls and equipment maintenance schedules should be followed.

Accountability

Laboratory managers must be accountable for decisions and actions. These decisions and actions should be supported by appropriate documentation and be open to legitimate scrutiny.

Disclosure and Discovery

Laboratory records must be open for reasonable access when legitimate requests are made by officers of the court. When release of information is authorized by management, all employees must avoid misrepresentations and/or obstructions.

Work Quality

A quality assurance program must be established. Laboratory managers and supervisors must accept responsibility for evidence integrity and security; validated, reliable methods; casework documentation and reporting; case review; testimony monitoring; and proficiency testing.

Responsibility to the Profession

Laboratory managers face the challenge of promoting professionalism through the objective assessment of individual ability and overall work quality in forensic sciences. Another challenge is dissemination of information in a profession where change is the norm.

Accreditation

The ASCLD–Laboratory Accreditation Board* (ASCLD/LAB) provides managers with objective standards by which the quality of work produced in forensic laboratories can be judged. Participation in such a program is important to demonstrate to the public and to users of laboratory services the laboratory's concern for and commitment to quality.

Peer Certification

Laboratory managers should support peer certification programs that promote professionalism and provide objective standards that help judge the quality of an employee's work. Meaningful information on strengths and weaknesses of an individual, based on an impartial examination and other factors considered to be important by peers, will add to an employee's abilities and confidence. This results in a more complete professional.

Peer Organizations

Laboratory managers should participate in professional organizations. They should encourage employee participation in professional societies and technical working groups, which promote the timely exchange of information among peers. These societies prove their worth to forensic science, benefiting both the employee and the employer, through basic training as well as continuing education opportunities. Personal contacts with other agencies and laboratories with similar interests are also beneficial for professional growth.

Research

When resources permit, laboratory managers should support research in forensic laboratories. Research and thorough, systematic study of special problems are needed to help advance the frontiers of applied science. Interaction and cooperation with college and university faculty and students can be extremely beneficial to forensic science. These researchers also gain satisfaction knowing their work can tremendously impact the effectiveness of a forensic laboratory.

* http://www.ascld-lab.org/

Ethics

Professional ethics provide the basis for the examination of evidence and the reporting of analytical results by blending the scientific principles and the statutory requirements into guidelines for professional behavior. Laboratory managers must strive to ensure that forensic science is conducted in accordance with sound scientific principles and within the framework of the statutory requirements to which forensic professionals are responsible.

Another key set of principals developed by the ASCLD/LAB sets forth principals for forensic scientists and laboratory managers to follow.

ASCLD/LAB Guiding Principles of Professional Responsibility for Crime Laboratories and Forensic Scientists

Preamble

These Guiding Principles are written specifically for forensic scientists and laboratory management. The concepts presented here have been drawn from other professional codes and suggestions made by leaders in the forensic community. The Guiding Principles have been vetted and adopted by the ASCLD/LAB Board of Directors and staff with the hope that laboratory management will use them in training sessions, performance evaluations, disciplinary decisions, and as guides in other management decisions. It is also important that all laboratory personnel, including forensic scientists and other laboratory employees who assist forensic scientists in their work, are equally aware of these Guiding Principles and support forensic scientists and managers by incorporating the principles into their daily work.

These Guiding Principles provide a framework for describing ethical and professional responsibilities in the forensic laboratory community. While not all inclusive, they describe key areas and provide some specific rules to supplement existing codes of ethics adopted by professional organizations and individual laboratories. The Guiding Principles are designed to promote integrity among practitioners and to increase public confidence in the quality of laboratory services, whether or not the laboratory is accredited by any accrediting body.

ASCLD/LAB has adopted the ASCLD Guidelines for Forensic Laboratory Management Practices, many of which have been incorporated into the ASCLD/LAB accreditation standards. Those practices provide for management support of the guiding principles set forth below and are intended to create a culture of ethical behavior and professional responsibility within the laboratory. The ASCLD practices should be implemented and followed to give practical meaning to the Guiding Principles of Professional Responsibility for Crime Laboratories and Forensic Scientists.

Professionalism

The ethical and professionally responsible forensic scientist and laboratory manager…

1. Are independent, impartial, detached, and objective, approaching all examinations with due diligence and an open mind.
2. Conduct full and fair examinations. Conclusions are based on the evidence and reference material relevant to the evidence, not on extraneous information, political pressure, or other outside influences.
3. Are aware of their limitations and only render conclusions that are within their area of expertise and about matters that they have given formal consideration.
4. Honestly communicate with all parties (the investigator, prosecutor, defense, and other expert witnesses) about all information relating to their analyses, when communications are permitted by law and agency practice.

5. Report to the appropriate legal or administrative authorities unethical, illegal, or scientifically questionable conduct of other laboratory employees or managers. Laboratory management will take appropriate action if there is potential for, or there has been, a miscarriage of justice due to circumstances that have come to light, incompetent practice, or malpractice.

6. Report conflicts between their ethical/professional responsibilities and applicable agency policy, law, regulation, or other legal authority and attempt to resolve them.

7. Do not accept or participate in any case on a contingency fee basis or in which they have any other personal or financial conflict of interest or an appearance of such a conflict.

Competency and Proficiency

The ethical and professionally responsible forensic scientist and laboratory manager…

1. Are committed to career-long learning in the forensic disciplines that they practice and stay abreast of new equipment and techniques while guarding against the misuse of methods that have not been validated. Conclusions and opinions are based on generally accepted tests and procedures.

2. Are properly trained and determined to be competent through testing before undertaking the examination of the evidence.

3. Honestly, fairly, and objectively administer and complete regularly scheduled

a. relevant proficiency tests

b. comprehensive technical reviews of examiners' work

c. verification of conclusions

4. Give utmost care to the treatment of any samples or items of potential evidentiary value to avoid tampering, adulteration, loss, or unnecessary consumption.

5. Use appropriate controls and standards when conducting examinations and analyses.

Clear Communications

The ethical and professionally responsible forensic scientist and laboratory manager…

1. Accurately represent their education, training, experience, and area of expertise.

2. Present accurate and complete data in reports, testimony, publications, and oral presentations.

3. Make and retain full, contemporaneous, clear, and accurate records of all examinations and tests conducted, and conclusions drawn, in sufficient detail to allow meaningful review and assessment of the conclusions by an independent person competent in the field. Reports are prepared in which facts, opinions, and interpretations are clearly distinguishable and which clearly describe limitations on the methods, interpretations, and opinions presented.

4. Do not alter reports or other records or withhold information from reports for strategic or tactical litigation advantage.

5. Support sound scientific techniques and practices and do not use their positions to pressure an examiner or technician to arrive at conclusions or results that are not supported by data.

6. Testify to results obtained and conclusions reached only when they have confidence that the opinions are based on good scientific principles and methods. Opinions are to be stated so as to be clear in their meaning. Wording should not be such that

inferences may be drawn which are not valid or that slant the opinion to a particular direction.

7. Attempt to qualify their responses while testifying when asked a question with the requirement that a simple "yes" or "no" answer be given, if answering "yes" or "no" would be misleading to the judge or the jury.

The term "forensic scientist" is used throughout this document. These Guiding Principles are meant to apply to all laboratory personnel, including technical support personnel and others who assist forensic scientists in their work.

Courtroom Testimony Tips

Everything that occurs at the crime scene, the investigation of the crime itself including work conducted at the crime laboratory all comes together at the trial. The following are some helpful guidelines to assist when you are called to testify in court.

Forensic practitioners are often called to court to testify as expert witnesses. Testifying in court is a challenge, particularly for an inexperienced practitioner. Training and experience eventually make it easier. The following are some hints for effective expert witness testimony:

Before Going to Court

- Keep thorough notes, records, photos, diagrams, etc.
- Carefully prepare your reports and consider appropriate language, completeness, and opinions.
- Prepare your prosecutor through a pretrial conference.
- Review the case before you arrive in court.
- Never allow a prosecutor or defense attorney to push you beyond your area of expertise or opinion. Ask yourself, can my testimony withstand the evaluation of a competent opposing expert?

Giving Expert Testimony

- Dress the part of an expert. Wear conservative clothing. Remove any piercings on the face other than earrings. Avoid wearing lapel pins or jewelry that designates membership in a club or group. Your appearance carries a tremendous amount of weight in how well juries are willing to believe what you say.
- When answering questions, respond to the jury, not the lawyer. Talk to the jury and make eye contact. Look at the individual jurors. (In a bench trial without a jury, make eye contact with the judge.)
- Sit up straight. Do not slouch or look too comfortable. Do not swivel in your chair.
- Turn off all cell phones.
- Pause before giving your answer. Give the opposing counsel a chance to object. Also, consider what you are going to say.
- Try to avoid "ums" and "ahs" when speaking.
- Present a professional demeanor. Not only is what you say is important, but also how you say it and how you look saying it.

- Be aware of your physical presence—how you sit and your body language. Do not fumble with exhibits or props; watch out for change in pockets.
- Do not fidget or sway when standing.
- Watch your demeanor. Do not appear too confident (it may be construed as arrogance).
- Avoid animosity. Appear sincere, objective, polite, and fair. Concede, if you do not know the answer.
- Listen to your speech, volume, and pace. Be deliberate, but not slow.
- Present your opinions with *emphasis.* Educate using nontechnical language. Use analogies. Make your testimony interesting!
- Concentrate: listen to every word of counsel. Do not jump the gun with your replies.
- Pause to clarify concepts.
- *Remember*: A court reporter is recording everything you say. Be specific when giving your testimony. Consider bringing a spelling sheet for the court reporter of any technical words you might use in your testimony.
- Respond directly to the question.

Cross-Examination

- The witness dictates the pace. You do not need to answer any question yes or no. Explain your rationale.
- Be careful with questions such as "Is it possible that …?" or "Is it fair to say?"
- It is acceptable to say, "I don't believe I am qualified to answer that question."
- Listen to all aspects of the hypothetical question. If you are unsure what the question is, ask for clarification.
- If you are not given a chance to explain your answer, ask if you can respond to clarify your statement.
- Remember your demeanor and attitude. You are not supposed to take sides.
- The louder and more belligerent the lawyer becomes, the more composed and polite you should become. Do not lose your temper.
- If you are asked a particularly lengthy, confusing question, simply say, "I don't understand your question. Could you rephrase it?"

Other Points

- Speak in a manner that laypeople can understand. Avoid jargon, especially "scientific-ese."
- Go over prior testimony, reports, and exhibits before the trial. Try to have a pre-trial conference with the prosecutor.
- Remember the "KISS" principle and keep it simple!
- Be objective. You are not an advocate. It should not matter to you whether the case results in a guilty or not guilty verdict. Your salary will stay the same. *Your job is to be an advocate for **your** opinion.*
- Use visual aids, analogies, illustrations from everyday life, the overhead projector, and/or PowerPoint presentations.

- Pay attention to the judge. Wait for the judge to rule on an objection before answering. Objection sustained means you cannot answer the previous question. Objection overruled means that you can answer.
- Do not box yourself into a corner. Beware of questions like, "Have you ever made a mistake" and "Isn't it possible?"
- Do not try to avoid a difficult question. Juries are suspicious of evasive answers.
- Be aware of the cross-examination trick of taking an excerpt from a publication out of context or an excerpt from a *nonexistent article*. You can always ask the lawyer to show you the article to refresh your memory or even to read.
- Be able to say, "I don't know" or "I was wrong."
- Take the lead to meet with and talk with counsel.
- Mentor new, inexperienced prosecutors. If he or she is new or inexperienced in a given area, be patient and offer your assistance as an expert. Try to remember how you felt the first few times you appeared in court.

Teamwork

The final element in crime scene investigation is teamwork. The investigation of criminal acts involves scores of people who often work for different agencies. This system was purposefully designed so that no one person or entity can operate independently. As such, turf issues will always arise, and it is important to remember to "stay in one's lane" as best as possible. In addition, as we move to larger and more complex criminal justice systems, we are more likely to be dealing with people who are faceless voices at the other end of the telephone.

For any complex system to work, teamwork is essential. Each element of the criminal investigation—uniformed officer, detective, crime scene specialist, forensic scientist, coroner, forensic pathologist, photographer, prosecutor, defense attorney, plus all the other vital players in the "system"—must work cooperatively with the other elements to make the entire process work.

No one element or person is more important than any other person or element. Each person has a vital role to play and each portion of the case must be accomplished in a responsible, professional, and timely manner to make every component function properly. Everyone working on a case should feel that he or she is essential to the successful completion of an investigation. Each must feel empowered to do what needs to be done, if only for the sake of justice. Prima donnas have no place in this process!

This chapter has introduced some of the major concepts concerning physical evidence, including its definition and value, the difference between classification and individualization, a brief discussion of the collection and preservation of physical evidence, ethical conduct, and teamwork. Subsequent chapters will explore these topics in greater detail as they relate to specific types of evidence and investigations.

Professional Development

Crime scene investigation, forensic identification, and forensic science require continuing education and networking with other professionals. It is unthinkable, for example, that a physician, dentist, accountant, or lawyer would not maintain ongoing study through professional conferences and continuing education. This is equally true in the forensic science professions.

Law enforcement agencies employ most crime scene investigators and forensic science professionals. Many police agencies fund continuing education in their annual budgets. This economic commitment is essential to the ongoing professionalism of practitioners and is used for professional association dues, professional conferences, workshops, and other continuing education.

Finally, a note on professional organizations for those engaged in crime scene investigation work. The International Association for Identification* (IAI) is one of the oldest professional associations of its kind. For those following a career in crime scene work, the IAI is an excellent organization to help maintain competency in this field. The IAI publishes the *Journal of Forensic Identification* and holds an annual seminar that brings colleagues together to attend workshops and technical presentations and to exchange information. The IAI is worthy of consideration for membership for any serious practitioner. In addition, the IAI offers crime scene certification at four different levels: Certified Crime Scene Investigator, Certified Crime Scene Analyst, Certified Crime Scene Reconstructionist, and Certified Senior Crime Scene Analyst. Each certification requires a vigorous testing process with a minimum passing score of 75%. Certification can also be obtained in the following disciplines: bloodstain pattern analysis, footwear, forensic art, forensic photography, forensic video, latent print, and tenprint.

Chapter Questions

1. Define the term "evidence."

2. Give some examples of testimonial and real evidence.

3. Which of the following pieces of evidence would be more probative in associating the defendant to the victim in a murder trial?
   a) A fiber found on the defendant's jacket when he was arrested that is similar to those from the carpet at the crime scene
   b) A bloodstain found on the defendant's jacket that subsequently matches the victim's DNA profile
   c) A hair found on the defendant's jacket that is similar to those of the victim's dog
   d) Eyewitness testimony of a neighbor who saw someone matching the defendant's build at the scene

* http://www.theiai.org/

4. List the identifying information that should be listed on the container when collecting evidence at a crime scene.

5. (True/False) When collecting evidence, the general rule is that more is better than less.
   a) True
   b) False

6. Which of the following would be considered a known sample?
   a) Hair from the crime scene
   b) Bloodstains
   c) Unburned carpet from an arson scene
   d) Buccal swabs from the suspect

7. You arrive at the scene of a homicide and see a blood-soaked shirt on the floor. Once it is properly documented, which of the following containers should you place it in for transportation to the crime lab?
   a) A sealed paint can
   b) A paper bag
   c) A sealed plastic bag
   d) The trunk of a police car

8. The forensic practitioner's sole obligation is to serve the aims of _____.
   a) Justice
   b) Their agency
   c) The legal system
   d) The prosecutor

9. Which organization has a professional code of ethics that is applicable to forensic science laboratory managers?

10. List some testifying tips that can be used when undergoing cross examination.

First Officer at the Crime Scene

2

"Wherever he steps, whatever he touches, whatever he leaves, even unconsciously, will serve as silent evidence against him. Not only his fingerprints or his footprints, but his hair, the fibers from his clothes, the glass he breaks, the tool mark he leaves, the paint he scratches, the blood or semen he deposits or collects—all these and more bear mute witness against him. This is evidence that does not forget. It is not confused by the excitement of the moment. It is not absent because human witnesses are. It is factual evidence. Physical evidence cannot be wrong; it cannot perjure itself; it cannot be wholly absent. Only its interpretation can err. Only human failure to find it, study and understand it, can diminish its value."

Prof. Paul L. Kirk, 1953

The Case of the Lady in Cement

In late 1987, the skeletal remains of a middle-aged woman, unceremoniously labeled "Jane Doe No. 9," were found buried in the foundation of a residence in an area of Los Angeles. Examination indicated that she had died of multiple stab wounds. The upper portion of her body was encased in cement, a factor that led to her identification through a variety of unusual scientific measures. The wet cement that had flowed over her body had settled in a vivid outline of her skull. This allowed the composite artist of the Los Angeles Police Department, Scientific Investigation Division, to cast a death mask of the victim (Figure 2.1). The mask and artist's rendering presented a startling likeness to the victim, who was ultimately identified.

When the drawing appeared on television, a citizen produced a photograph of a woman resembling the drawing. This led to the possible name of the victim. A fingerprint card was found on file because she had been fingerprinted for a routine job application.

Her arms, crossed over her body, left telltale finger holes in the cement where her hands had rested. Portions of the cement were surprisingly smooth textured, leading to speculation that the preservation of fingerprint evidence might be possible (Figure 2.2).

Meanwhile, the concrete-walled grave in which the victim was found also contained items of clothing and other artifacts. The Comparative Analysis Unit was able to pin down a meaningful estimate of an entombment date to provide detectives with a time frame in which to target their investigation. They determined that the most likely item found with the body for dating was a partly deteriorated cigarette package. The name of the manufacturer, Liggett & Myers (L&M), was discernible. A partial reconstruction of the deteriorated package was necessary to determine additional package characteristics, such as the style, color, location, and content of the imprinted information, tax seal dimensions, and package components. Detailed photographs were taken to record the pertinent information.

(a)

(b)

Figure 2.1 Wet cement had flowed over the victim's body creating an outline of her skull (a), which allowed the artist of the Los Angeles Police Department to cast a death mask (b) of the victim. The mask and artist's rendering (c) presented a likeness of the victim.

(c)

Figure 2.1 *(Continued)*

Figure 2.2 The silicone casts contained sufficient detail on the fingers and palm to enable a positive identification of the victim. The casts also clearly showed additional cuts and stab wounds on her hands and finger, a result of defending herself at the time she was attacked by her killer.

Figure 2.3 The concrete-walled grave also contained items of clothing and other artifacts. One artifact was a partly deteriorated cigarette package showing the name of the manufacturer, Liggett & Myers (L&M). L&M had test marketed a menthol long cigarette soft pack in March, 1974, in their western region, which included California. The product was withdrawn in March, 1975. (Courtesy of the Los Angeles Police Department.)

As part of a test market in March, 1974, in the Liggett & Myers western region (California, Arizona, New Mexico, Colorado, Nevada, Idaho, Montana, Wyoming, North and South Dakota, Washington, Oregon, and Utah), the company had introduced a soft pack of L&M "longs." The product was withdrawn in March, 1975, and the L&M packaging was changed. Furthermore, the tax-stamp dimensions, affixed to a package by the local wholesaler, were consistent with the type used in California (Figure 2.3).

This narrow time frame of one year, bracketed by March, 1974, and March, 1975, when the cigarette package was marketed and probably purchased, helped detectives target a suspect who had access to the house during that time span. Although other items of evidence were available and dramatically important in this particular case, the cigarette package clearly demonstrated the hidden potential of physical evidence. Murder charges were filed against the suspect.

First Officer at the Scene

Crime scenes are dynamic, rapidly changing environments. The first officer to arrive on the scene must be concerned with countless details. One of his/her major tasks is to protect the crime scene. To a great extent, the success of the investigation and, perhaps, any chance for a successful resolution of the case hinges on actions and steps taken by the first officer to arrive at the crime scene.

Think of the crime scene as a snapshot of what occurred in the final moments of a crime. The scene is the place from which much of the physical evidence associated with the crime is obtained. It provides investigators with a starting point for the inquiry to determine the identities of the suspect and victim and to piece together the circumstances of what happened during the crime. Physical evidence found at the scene can be the key to the solution of the crime. The first officer's most important task at the scene is to prevent the destruction or diminished value of potential evidence that may lead to the apprehension of the criminal and the ultimate resolution of the crime.

The responsibility of the first uniformed officers at the scene can never be minimized. What these officers do or don't do, whether innocent or intentional, may have serious ramifications to the course of the investigation. (Figure 2.4 was a significant case which ultimately had a major impact on the criminal justice system. The first officers on the scene probably did not realize the impact of the case.) Some police agencies have very specific policies for uniformed personnel concerning their duties and responsibilities at the crime scene. First responders should be familiar with their duties and responsibilities and execute these tasks to the best of their ability. Superior officers and training officers should monitor the performance of both new and experienced uniformed personnel. Police agencies should understand the importance of ongoing training and continuing education, not only for investigative and technical personnel but also for first responder personnel as well.

The duties of the first officer to arrive at the crime scene are the same, no matter what his/her rank, and remain the same regardless of the seriousness of the crime. The first responder at the scene must assume that the criminal left clues or physical evidence behind. The first responder's actions or inactions must not be allowed to destroy or change anything at the scene. Information developed from evidence left at the scene may help to reconstruct the crime or prove the identity of the suspect. Furthermore, the first officer must not inadvertently add material that may mislead investigators.

Figure 2.4 The infamous St. Valentine's Day Massacre occurred on February 14, 1929, in Chicago. Two rival gangs were fighting over the illicit liquor market created after prohibition made selling alcohol illegal. One of the gangs dressed as police officers entered a warehouse and gunned down their competition. This is an actual copy of a crime scene photograph, courtesy of the Chicago Police Department. The case played a major role in the future of forensic science in the United States and marked the beginnings of forensic firearms identification.

Common sense strongly suggests that a crime scene will yield useful information. It is not possible for anyone to enter a place without changing it in some way, either by bringing something to it or by removing something from it. The notion of an individual coming in contact with a scene and changing it in some way is known as the *Locard exchange principle*, named after the French forensic scientist, Edmond Locard (1877–1966). A popular restatement for this principle may be summarized as: *Every contact leaves a trace.* Although changes to a crime scene may be extraordinarily small, the course of an investigation may well hinge on their detection. Therefore, the first officer's action or inaction may affect the future of the investigation.

The value of detailed, meticulous note taking throughout all phases of the case cannot be overemphasized. All officers have many jobs to perform during the beginning phases of an investigation. Police handle many investigations, and it is not inconceivable that one case blurs into another—a very human reaction. Thorough, detailed contemporaneous note taking, that is, recording significant as well as mundane observations at the time they are noticed, is the most effective way to minimize loss of information.

Naturally, a general rule of protecting the crime scene cannot be applied in every case. The resources of a police agency as well as the nature of the crime must be taken into account. Petty thefts and similar misdemeanors will not receive the same in-depth investigation as a case involving murder, rape, or assault. Some police agencies may arbitrarily set a lower limit to the property value lost in a burglary as a way to determine the scope of their investigation. Some police agencies, for example, employ smaller *Evidence Collection Teams* for smaller crimes and full *Crime Scene Units* for larger, more violent crimes.

In certain serious crimes, it may not be possible to preserve the crime scene because of its location. A busy street or highway with heavy traffic is an example of a situation in which it may not be possible to protect a crime scene properly for a sufficient period of time. In situations like this, the deciding factor in safeguarding the crime scene concerns the likelihood that the criminal has left clues that can be recovered versus the negative factors of holding up traffic flow. Each case must be decided on its own merits.

At first glance, the actions to be taken by the first officer on the scene may seem simple and not well beyond the scope of routine police duties. Some further examination of these duties will show that this is not the case.

First of all, first responders should not approach the scene in haste. All movements should be calm and deliberate. Officers should expect the worst and take the position that it is better to be overly cautious and remember the popular wisdom: *if something can go wrong, it will!* Approaching the assignment with an open mind helps an officer avoid carelessness and false moves that may prove to be disastrous. Note too that in today's terrorist atmosphere, it is not impossible that seemingly innocent items may harbor explosive devices. While officers should not become overly paranoid of such possibilities (after all, such events happen in a very small number of cases), they must keep this and other possibilities of danger in mind as they begin their investigation at a crime scene.

Mistakes made during the interrogation and other aspects of the preliminary investigation can perhaps be corrected, but errors committed in the protection and examination of the crime scene may never be set right. The eventual success of the investigation may be dependent on the preventative and preliminary measures taken by the first officer to arrive at the crime scene. Unfortunately, there are too many examples of how an omission or a mistake on the part of the first responder proved fatal to the investigation and resulted in an unsolved crime. It is often the small things that cause these problems. For example, using a toilet at the scene and flushing it may wipe away an important fingerprint, or using a glass on a kitchen counter or smoking at a scene are simple, unintended cases that have resulted in important evidence being contaminated or destroyed. A simple watchword is: be AWARE! (Figures 2.5, 2.6 and 2.7 are examples of important fingerprint evidence that might have been destroyed but for the careful attention to detail of the first officer and subsequent personnel at the scene.)

In a difficult situation, the officer may be faced with a dilemma that requires quick analysis of the circumstances and the taking of appropriate steps. However, if the basic rule of always anticipating the worst and taking extensive rather than minimal precautions is followed, the most serious errors can usually be avoided.

Because conditions and situations can vary greatly from one crime scene to another, it is not possible to set hard and fast rules to govern all situations. However, certain guidelines can be established. These are mainly applicable to homicide cases and other serious crimes because it is in just these cases that the officer is faced with the most difficult tasks and the actions taken have the most far-reaching consequences. These rules are applicable to less serious crimes as well.

Figure 2.5 A suspect discharged a weapon in a Fairbanks, Alaska, nightclub and subsequently fled, discarding the gun in the snow. A previously convicted felon was interviewed about the crime but denied any knowledge or ownership of a weapon. A latent print was developed using cyanoacrylate ester and photographed using direct reflective lighting. The felon's prints were compared with a latent print on the trigger and identified. He was charged with "Felon in Possession of a Firearm." (Courtesy of the State of Alaska, Scientific Crime Detection Laboratory, Latent Print Section.)

Figure 2.6 This latent print was developed with cyanoacrylate fuming. The .30 caliber bullet was recovered from inside a loaded rifle magazine; the crime involved the shooting death of an elderly white male. The photographic technique employed "shadow" photography and inner negative reversal of the ridge color. The reader is referred to the article on shadow photography in the *Journal of Forensic Identification* 38(5) Sept./Oct., 1989. (Courtesy of the State of Alaska, Scientific Crime Detection Laboratory, Latent Print Section.)

Figure 2.7 The suspect stated that he had never been in the murder victim's house in Ninilchik, Alaska. Trash from the victim's wastebaskets was examined for latent prints. A print was developed on the ring tab of a beer can using cyanoacrylate ester fuming. The latent print was compared to and identified with the suspect in the case. (Courtesy of the State of Alaska, Scientific Crime Detection Laboratory, Latent Print Section.)

Crime Scene "Dos" and "Don'ts"

Do	Don't
Limit access to the crime scene by using tape and a major incident log.	Permit unnecessary personnel to enter the crime scene.
Attempt to identify possible routes used by the suspect.	Use routes possibly used by the suspect.
Note original conditions at the crime scene.	Assume others will note original conditions, etc.
Record changes in conditions especially in regard to your activities (or paramedics').	Fail to document any changes or contamination at the scene.
Protect evidence from adverse environmental conditions.	Allow evidence to be compromised by nature.
Conduct all administrative duties outside the tape (coffee drinking, smoking).	Eat or use any facilities or the phone within the crime scene.
Record the location of evidence before moving it.	Remove items and package without documentation.
Package trace evidence (paint, glass, etc.) into large envelopes.	Package trace evidence in a bundle.
Keep an open mind as to what might be evidence.	Ignore items that appear out of place or are difficult to explain.
Be aware that you are a potential source of evidence and contamination.	Touch anything unnecessarily.
Take photographs of items at 90° with and without L-scales.	Photograph items without scales.
Call expert personnel to crime scenes for detailed or difficult collection or documentation.	Assume that the expert can always answer the questions from nonexpert collection or documentation.
Take photographs of all aspects of crime scenes, perspective shots, 90° photos of items and bloodstains, and close-ups.	Limit your photographs to overalls and item locations.

This list was originally developed by Ronald Linhart and Elizabeth Devine, Los Angeles County Sheriff's Crime Laboratory.

Recording the Time

Precise notations of the time are very important in an investigation. They are most important for checking a suspect's story and can often be quite important in other circumstances as well. Therefore, the first officer at the scene should write down arrival times and other times that may turn out to be important. Notation should be made of the time that the crime was committed, the time that the officer was first called, the time of arrival at the scene, and so on. Such notations lend precision and credibility to the officer's statement if testifying in court should become necessary. Keeping track of the time spent at the scene also maintains a chronological record of the way things were done during the crime scene investigation. These notes will prove invaluable when specific details about the investigation are needed as the case proceeds.

When a Suspect Is Found at the Scene

The first thing an officer should do when entering a scene is to render the scene safe, as the suspect may still be in the location. The officer should always remember that their own safety is of paramount importance! The first officer to arrive at a crime scene may need to arrest or detain a suspect. In such cases, the most important duties should be done first. The police officer must use common sense in taking whatever measures are necessary to protect the scene. If it is not possible to hold the suspect at the scene or in the police vehicle, and if a backup officer is unavailable, a possible alternative is to find a reliable person to protect the scene until other officers arrive. The first officer must instruct such persons on how to guard the premises because the task is likely to be unusual for them.

The first officer should also be aware that the longer the suspect remains at the crime scene, the greater the possibility becomes for changing or contaminating the crime scene. The suspect could, for example, remove evidence, leave new evidence, or even gain information from the opportunity of observing the scene in detail. Thus, the suspect should be searched and removed from the location as quickly as possible.

Entering the Scene Proper

After making sure the scene is safe, the officer should attempt to form an estimate of the situation—what happened here—as quickly as possible. This assessment is the basis for any subsequent actions. When entering the scene proper, or the focal point of events, the officer must proceed with extreme caution and concentrate his/her attention on possible evidence that may be found on doors, doorknobs, light switches, floors, and other areas.

An effort must be made to observe details, particularly those that are fleeting, and to take written notes as soon as possible on such points as

- Doors—Open, closed, or locked? On which side was the key?
- Windows—Open or closed? Were they locked?
- Lights—On or off? Which lights were on?
- Shades, shutters, or blinds—Open or closed?
- Odors—Cigarette smoke, gas, gun powder, perfume, decomposition, etc.?
- Signs of activity—Meal preparation, dishes in the sink, house clean or dirty, etc.?
- Date and time indicators—Mail, newspapers, dates on milk cartons, stopped clocks, spoiled foods, items that should have been hot or cold but were at room temperature.
- Messages on answering machine, voicemail/texts on cellphone?

Nothing at the crime scene should be moved initially unless absolutely necessary. The crime scene should remain as close as possible to its original condition for the detectives or investigating officers to see when they arrive. If it becomes necessary to remove any object because others may disturb it, the officer should consider the possibility that the item may have fingerprints present and act accordingly. Before any object is moved, its location should be noted. The exact position of an object at a scene may become important later in the case. Its position should be noted in the report, outlined in chalk, sketched, photographed, or videotaped.

Under no circumstances should anyone be allowed to wander about the crime scene simply to satisfy his curiosity and pick up and handle objects. Regrettably, there have been too many instances where first officers arrived at the scene and toured it, leaving fingerprints and DNA on a variety of surfaces. Such carelessness cannot be tolerated. Such activities are all the more problematic when senior officers or department brass show up out of curiosity to see what is going on.

Those at the crime scene should never use the toilet, turn on water, eat, drink, smoke, or use towels. The criminal may have used any of these objects—a towel could have been used to wipe a bloodstained weapon. Evidence may have been caught in the sink trap. The rule is simple: the first officer at the crime scene should not touch anything unless absolutely necessary or unless he is charged with the responsibility of processing the scene for physical evidence. Any first officer to arrive at a scene would consider it embarrassing if their fingerprints or DNA were found and identified at the crime scene due to their sloppiness at handing the scene.

First officers should realize that the lead investigator might call on them later to account for their movements at the crime scene. This may be necessary in order for the investigating officer to get a better idea of the original condition of the crime scene proper or to explain seemingly out-of-place items at the scene.

On occasion, the victim or a relative may attempt to clean up the scene—perhaps to put everything in proper order when the police arrive or to try to conceal something. Occasionally, cleaning serves a psychological need to put everything back in its proper place. If a cleanup is in progress when the officer arrives, it should be stopped. If the cleanup has been completed or the officer suspects that is the case, a detailed inquiry should be made to determine the original condition of the scene. It may be possible to recover material or undamaged items that were thrown out or discarded.

Protecting the Integrity of the Scene

As soon as possible after arriving, the officer should take steps to protect the scene from anyone not directly involved with the investigation, including other officers, supervisors and command personnel, the press, curiosity seekers, and family members. This is no easy task and sometimes requires some ingenuity because, initially, personnel may be insufficient to protect the crime scene.

Simply locking a door or stringing rope or commercially available crime scene tape around the perimeter can secure the crime scene. If these measures do not suffice, first responders may resort to using vehicles, boards, or furniture gathered from another area away from the scene to help keep curiosity seekers out. Even with devices such as police barricades, yellow crime scene tape, and ropes, officers may still need to take an active role in keeping unauthorized people away.

The extent of any protective measures must be decided on a case-by-case basis. As a general rule, if the scene is indoors, the barricade should include the central scene and, where possible, the probable entry and exit paths used by the criminal. In this regard, it is important to focus attention on potential evidence on the ground outside a window, in rooms through which the criminal had to pass, in stairways, or in entrances.

If the location is outdoors, an ample area should be roped off to include the paths taken by the criminal to and from the crime scene proper. Sometimes, critical evidence may by found on or near a route leading to or away from the scene. It is important to search paths carefully. In some cases, prior to the arrival of the police, onlookers trample the crime scene.

In open areas, barricades can be set up only if an officer is stationed outside the perimeter to man them. The protection of the scene in open areas merely requires that the officer not walk around aimlessly inside or immediately outside the roped-off area. Limiting movements permits later accountability for the officer's own tracks.

The first officer should remain at the scene whenever possible and should send others to call headquarters or detective personnel. Leaving the supervision of the crime scene to persons other than police officers should only be done in exceptional circumstances. Protective measures at the scene should be taken as early as possible to prevent valuable, often vital evidence from being destroyed. It is also important that barricades be sufficiently extensive from the beginning of the investigation. Sometimes, a sufficient area around the crime scene is not protected early enough in the investigation.

When large outdoor areas are to be protected, officers may take the initiative by enlisting the aid of police cadets, police reserves, or others who can be trusted to assume responsibility for protecting the scene.

Injured Person on the Scene

Saving lives is the first priority and takes precedence over all other considerations. If an injured person is on the scene, first aid should be administered immediately even if it means valuable evidence may be lost or destroyed. If first aid to the injured is not immediately essential, the officer should note the victim's position on a simple sketch, by marking the floor, or by forming a mental picture of the position. The officer should note how the victim is lying or sitting, the position of the hands, arms, and legs, the condition of clothes, and so on. It is also important to notice if the victim's hands have anything in them such as hairs, fibers, etc.

When paramedics or emergency medical personnel arrive, the officer should—without interfering in their work—instruct them how to enter the scene without disturbing it unnecessarily. Observing the movements of medical personnel and noting whether any objects were moved is a necessary task. (Also, disposal of medical equipment like gloves, gauze, etc. should be done outside of the crime scene.)

If civilian emergency medical personnel transport the injured person, a police officer should accompany the victim. An alert investigator may hear an important word or accusation or what might be equivalent to a dying declaration that might be the key to the entire case. In one case, a dying woman uttered the name of her assailant. This vital information fell on the untrained, inattentive ears of the civilian emergency medical personnel, and no amount of interviewing could sharpen their recall.

The officer should arrange for proper removal and custody of the victim's clothing. Occasionally, when the hospital or mortuary is contacted to obtain the victim's garments, the clothing has been incinerated or wadded into a hopeless mess after being cut from the body. Representatives of police agencies should make periodic visits to local hospitals to instruct medical personnel in the proper handling of evidence. The medical profession's lack of interest in and knowledge about evidence is disheartening, considering the broad range of their training and the media attention to criminal investigations.

Dead Person on the Scene

If the first officer on the scene is able to establish certain signs of death, such as clear rigor mortis,* odor, lividity,† beginning decomposition, and so forth, the body is not to be touched or removed until a detailed examination can be made. Once the first officer at the crime scene has established that the victim is dead and has made a cursory inspection of the crime scene, superiors must be notified regarding the nature of the case. The officer's cell phone should be used for this purpose rather than a police radio because it is not uncommon for the press and other news sources to monitor police radio frequencies. The phone at the scene should not be used.

Summoning the Coroner/Medical Examiner

Whether the medical examiner or coroner should be contacted at this point of the investigation is often a matter of local custom. Some agencies, by agreement with the coroner or medical examiner's office, first wait for the investigating officers to arrive and begin their investigation. Notification of a death may be made at this time, with an estimate of the time the coroner should arrive. This can save the medical examiner's staff time by not having to wait needlessly at the scene until the police have completed their portion of the investigation. Policies should be arranged with the medical examiner's or coroner's office on such callout matters.

The medical examiner or coroner's office in most cases has legal jurisdiction over the body at the crime scene. Therefore, the body may not be moved or searched without the consent of the medical examiner or coroner.

On rare occasions, the first officer must take immediate steps to remove the body from the scene. In these situations, the officer must ensure that the deceased is placed on the stretcher in the same position in which the body was discovered, provided that circumstances permit. Limbs rigidly fixed in a certain position should not be straightened. If the victim is found face down, the body should remain in that position because lividity may change position and appearance, and trickles of blood may change direction.

If the rigidity or rigor mortis must be broken in order to transport the body, the officer must make note of it, preferably with sketches or photographs showing the original position. Before the body is moved, its position must be marked on the floor, sketched, and photographed. It is important that the position of the head, arms, hands, knees, and feet is shown on the sketch. The officer should also note the condition of the clothes and bloody tracks that may be present. This can be extremely important in answering the question of whether the body had previously been moved. Blood may run while the body is being removed. A question may later arise about the source of this secondary flow of blood.

---

* Rigor mortis is a recognizable sign of death that is caused by a chemical change in the muscles after death. The limbs of the corpse become stiff and difficult to move or manipulate. It begins after about 3 hours of death, reaches maximum stiffness after 12 hours, and gradually dissipates after about 72 hours.
† Postmortem lividity or livor mortis is another sign of death. It is caused by the settling of the blood in the lower portion of the body, causing a purplish red discoloration of the skin due to the action of gravity. The discoloration does not occur in the areas of the body that are in contact with the ground or another object. The presence of livor mortis can be used by forensic investigators to determine whether or not a body has been moved (for instance, if the body is found lying face down but the pooling is present on the deceased's back, investigators can determine that the body was originally positioned face up).

Suspicious Death

A woman was found dead on the floor in her bedroom. The first officer at the scene made a superficial examination of the scene. Some of the deceased's relatives stated that the woman had been very ill. Concluding that she had died of natural causes, the officer had the body removed from the scene without examining it further. After the deceased was moved, it became apparent that she had died of strangulation. A scarf had been tightly wound around the neck three times and knotted at the throat. A trickle of blood had run over one cheek from the mouth in an upward direction in relation to the position of the head at the time of the brief examination. The investigation of the case was complicated and impossible to decide because of the officer's premature decision to allow the body to be removed. It never could be established whether the blood flowed during or before transportation.

In cases of strangulation or hanging where unmistakable signs of death are observed, the first officer at the scene should do nothing to the body. If there is a danger that the rope might break, the officer may attempt to support the corpse, but it should not be cut down. If obvious signs of life are present, the officer must try to save the person.

Knots in ropes should not be untied, if possible. The knot may be typical of a certain occupation or skill level. The noose may be cut and the loose ends labeled appropriately. An alternative to labeling is to tie the ends back together with string or thread. If these materials are not available, the noose or rope should be placed so that the officer can later recall which ends belong together. In emergencies, the knot may be loosened somewhat and the noose pulled over the victim's head. It is also important to remember which end of the rope was anchored to a fixed object or pulled over a branch or beam. The direction of distorted surface fibers on the rope may indicate whether the victim was pulled up because it is always possible that a hanging was staged to cover-up a murder.

Firearms and Ammunition on the Scene

The general rule is that any firearms or ammunition should be left untouched until investigating personnel arrive. However, recovery of weapons and ammunition may become necessary. If they may be inadvertently moved or lost during the removal of an injured person, or if conditions are such that the first officer cannot effectively protect the scene alone and bystanders might disturb the evidence, then the evidence may be removed.

When weapons are recovered, the officer should concentrate on the possibility that valuable evidence may be found on cartridge cases as well as on weapons. If there is a reason to believe that fingerprints are present in oil or grease on a weapon found at an outdoor crime scene in cold weather, the weapon should not be moved to a heated room; the heat may destroy the evidence.

When picking up pistols and revolvers, a pencil or a stick should never be inserted into the barrel in order to lift the weapon as seen on TV. Dust, blood, particles of tissue, and other debris in the barrel may become dislodged. To move a handgun, grasp the checkered surface of the grips with two gloved fingers to lift the weapon. If the grips have a lanyard ring attachment, the gun can be lifted by the ring. Before the weapon is recovered, its position should be marked on a sketch or by outlining its position on the floor. This marking is important. There might also be a mark in the floor under the weapon, indicating that the gun fell from the hand of a suicide. The position of bullets and cartridge cases may reveal the direction of the shot and possibly the location of the assailant. The positions of hammer and safeties should be noted. Care should be taken so as not to disturb potential touch DNA evidence.

Suspicious Death

A man with a bullet wound in his head was found in his apartment. A police officer and emergency medical personnel transported the dying man to a hospital where he was pronounced dead on arrival. The officer accompanied the injured person to the hospital, which complicated the investigation because the first officer was not available to communicate any information to detectives, who immediately began an investigation of the apartment.

A bullet and a cartridge case were found in the room where the victim had apparently been shot, but no weapon was located. An automatic pistol was found on a shelf in the hallway. It appeared to have been recently fired. A suspicion of murder arose because the injured man could not have placed the gun there. Thus began a thorough and time-consuming examination of the apartment. After the first officer who had gone to the hospital was questioned, the case was determined to be a suicide. The first officer had found the gun by the victim and, without thinking of the consequences, examined it and placed it on the shelf before leaving the apartment. If the investigators had known the facts from the first witness—the first officer—much time and effort could have been saved. Certainly, the detectives acted properly by assuming the worst; however, the first officer at the scene failed to brief the investigators adequately.

If a weapon is found, it should be in the same condition in which it was recovered when delivered to a firearms examiner for examination. When the firearm is packaged for submission as evidence, a detailed description of what was done to it should be prepared and sent to the crime laboratory. The only acceptable changes to the weapon would be to unload it. An investigator with firearms experience should render the weapon safe while wearing gloves before sending it to the crime lab.

What to Do Until Investigating Personnel Arrive

While waiting for investigators to arrive, the first officer on the scene should attend to the following:

- **Write down the names of witnesses and other persons who entered the scene.** This is important for the subsequent sorting of fingerprints and DNA and other clues found at the scene.
- **Note who was at the scene when the officer arrived.** This information can become particularly important if the crime has just occurred.
- **Establish the basic facts.** A factual account of what happened is of great assistance to the detectives when they arrive because it helps them to decide on the next move. However, the officer should never undertake lengthy and detailed interrogations that may damage later questioning or give rise to misleading suggestions in the statements of witnesses. Furthermore, the officer cannot properly guard the scene if occupied with interrogations.

- **Keep the suspect and witnesses separated wherever possible.** Allowing the suspect and witnesses to talk may interfere with later questioning. Family members may be left in the care of neighbors when necessary, taking care that no alcoholic drinks or sedatives are administered. Remember that the dramatically grieving relative may be the prime suspect.
- **Instruct witnesses not to discuss the events.** This can prevent distortion by suggestion. If possible, the principal witnesses should be separated. In relating events to one another, witnesses may distort each other's impressions to a point at which they believe that they saw things that they really did not see or that never happened.
- **Do not discuss the crime with witnesses or bystanders.** This is also intended to prevent suggestion and distortion. Furthermore, circulating details of the crime may hinder the investigation.
- **Listen attentively, but unobtrusively.** An alert officer can often pick up information of vital importance to the investigation simply by being a good listener.
- **Protect evidence that is in danger of being destroyed.** During inclement weather such as rain or snow, divert water and cover tracks with boxes, cardboard, tents, etc. If the crowd of onlookers becomes large, it may become necessary to expand the protective measures at a given location to prevent trampling of the evidence.

When the investigating officers arrive, the first officer should report all that has been learned and observed and the actions taken. This is very important to the evaluation and planning of the crime scene investigation. It is particularly important that reports be given of the extent to which the scene has been altered and whether objects have been disturbed or moved.

Continued Protection of the Scene

In protecting the scene after the investigators have arrived, the officers detailed to protect it should act only on orders from the detective in charge. During the technical examination of the scene, it is the crime scene investigator who is in charge of the officers on security duty as well as of the scene proper.

No one should be allowed access to the crime scene without the investigator's permission, not even other investigators or superior officers. Command officers would render a fine service to their investigators if they would preserve the integrity of the crime scene with a passion and set an example for other officers by keeping out of the scene. Unfortunately, there are numerous instances of police officers on sightseeing tours through crime scenes. Sometimes they destroy more evidence than any group of laypeople could possibly accomplish. At one crime scene, it was reported that the presence of one more police official would have threatened the collapse of the building. Even experienced investigators are guilty of allowing these tours, especially in murder cases and other serious crimes.

News reporters sometimes arrive at the scene before investigators. People in the neighborhood usually call them or they may have heard a call on the police radio. The first officers on the scene should not, under any circumstances, give information about the case to reporters. To inform the press is the responsibility of the police chief, sheriff, or public relations officers designated by them. Officers should not favor one reporter or news agency by giving out information that may not be available to the competitors through prescribed channels. In dealing with reporters, officers should be neither curt nor nonchalant, but they should be firm, even when reporters are persistent. The officer should remember that reporters often give invaluable assistance in the investigation of major crimes. Press passes should be disregarded during the protection of a crime scene.

Case

In one of California's most celebrated serial murder cases, an individual dubbed the "Night Stalker" by the press terrorized the Los Angeles area in the mid-1980s. Before his reign of terror ended, at least 13 people were viciously murdered and numerous others were assaulted. His murder spree ranged from San Francisco to Orange County. A regional task force was led by detectives from the Los Angeles County Sheriff's Department, Homicide Bureau. Evidence of a satanic link—upside-down pentagrams (Figure 2.8a and b)—and an AC/DC cap were noted at early crime scenes and attributed to the assailant. After his capture and during his trial, upside-down pentagrams were found on the dashboard of his car and in his holding cell.

The crime scene attributed to the Night Stalker started to show a grisly pattern: restraints (i.e., cords, belts, handcuffs, and thumbcuffs) were found at many scenes as well as various tools that were used to bludgeon his victims. A characteristic shoe impression was linked to several crime scenes. The unusual shoe pattern was preserved through the use of photography, plaster casting, and tape lifts (Figure 2.8c and d).

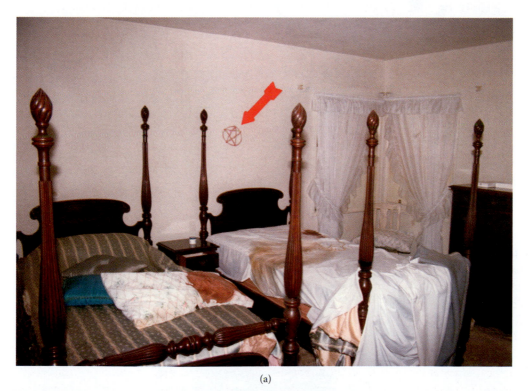

(a)

Figure 2.8 (a,b) Photos from earlier murders attributed to the "Night Stalker" serial killer show evidence of a satanic link. (c,d) A characteristic shoe print was found at several of the crime scenes, but the shoes were never recovered. (e,f) Fingerprinting linked items found in a bus depot locker to Richard Ramirez. (g,h) Live ammunition from the bus locker matched expended cartridges found at four of the crime scenes and Ramirez was later convicted.

(b)

(c)

Figure 2.8 (*Continued*)

(d)

(e)

Figure 2.8 (*Continued*)

(f)

(g)

Figure 2.8 *(Continued)*

The shoe impressions were compared and found to have similar class characteristics to the Avia Aerobic, size 11½. After consultation with the owners of the Avia Company, it was determined that only one pair of size 11½ shoes was distributed in the Los Angeles area, of 97 pairs in the entire state. After a public official mentioned the existence of the shoe prints at a press conference, those prints stopped showing up at subsequent crime scenes and the shoes were never recovered.

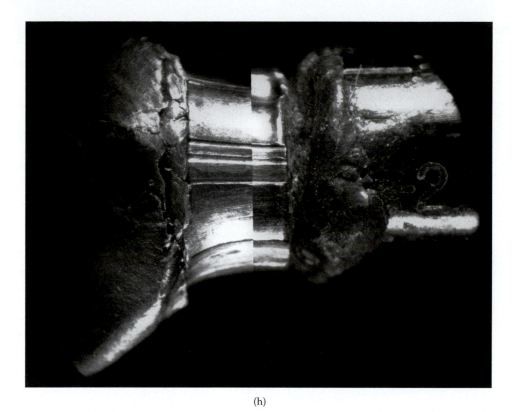

(h)

Figure 2.8 (*Continued*)

The Firearms and Latent Print sections of the Los Angeles County Sheriff's Department, Scientific Services Bureau, played an important part in the perpetrator's conviction. Rifling marks from bullets recovered at different scenes were compared. It was established that they were fired from the same handgun. This substantiated the initial hypothesis that the same individual committed the crimes. On the day of his arrest, items belonging to Ramirez were seized from a local bus depot locker (Figure 2.8e). Among these items were a yellow flashlight and live rounds of ammunition. A latent fingerprint (Figure 2.8f) on the flashlight was identified as belonging to Ramirez, thereby linking him to the recovered property. More important, the live rounds exhibited a magazine signature identical to markings on expended cartridges found at four of the Night Stalker crime scenes (Figure 2.8g and h).

Based on a latent fingerprint from a vehicle the Night Stalker had used in an assault in Orange County, California, he was identified as Richard Ramirez. A mug shot photograph was released to the press the following morning. That same morning, as newspapers were being distributed, Ramirez was on a bus returning to Los Angeles from Arizona. Within hours he was spotted and captured by citizens in East Los Angeles. Once in custody, he was positively identified as Richard Ramirez, alias the Night Stalker. Four years elapsed before Richard Ramirez was found guilty of all counts brought against him, which included 13 murders and 30 other felonies. He was sentenced to death.

Chapter Questions

1. Which of the following is a major task that the first responder must be concerned with?
   a) Calling for backup
   b) Contacting their supervisor to apprise them of the situation
   c) Protecting the crime scene
   d) Arresting the suspect
2. Which of the following principles is associated with processing crime scenes and is often summarized as "every contact leaves a trace"?
   a) Locard's exchange principle
   b) Trace evidence principle
   c) Bertillion's principle
   d) Lacassagne's principle
3. Describe why it is important for the first responder to record the times associated with a crime scene investigation.

4. When entering a crime scene, the first responder should proceed with extreme caution and concentrate their attention to possible evidence at which locations?

5. List some of the points that should be covered when taking notes on the condition of the crime scene.

6. When is it appropriate for the first responding officer to move a piece of evidence?
   a) When the evidence is a gun
   b) When he is charged with the responsibility of processing the scene for physical evidence
   c) Only when the scene is secured
   d) If the crime is serious such as a homicide

7. You are called to the scene of a sexual assault that took place at a park. Describe how you would secure the scene.

8. The position of _____ and _____ may reveal the direction of the shot and possibly the location of the assailant.
   a) Bullets, cartridge cases
   b) Bullets, fingerprints
   c) Cartridge cases, fibers
   d) Bullets, firearms
9. Describe the proper procedure when dealing with multiple witnesses at the scene of a crime.

10. List five crime scene "dos" and five crime scene "don'ts."

The Crime Scene Investigator

3

Introduction and Objectives

Case[*]

On August 20, 1996, a 12-year-old victim was walking home along a wooded bike trail behind her school in Charles County, Maryland (Figures 3.1 and 3.2).

She noticed a male walking in the general vicinity, waved to him, and continued on her way. Moments later, the victim was grabbed by her neck and carried through the woods. While being dragged through the woods, her face was struck by a tree. The suspect then proceeded to pull down the victim's shorts and underpants and then vaginally assaulted her. During the assault, the suspect pulled the victim's shirt up to cover her face. The suspect then sodomized the victim. The suspect threatened to kill the victim if she was not quiet and told her that the attack was her fault. The victim managed to remove the shirt from her face and noted that the suspect was wielding a knife. However, she was unable to get a good look at the suspect's face.

Following the assault, the suspect placed a piece of cloth in the victim's mouth, then tore pieces of the victim's shirt apart and used those sections of cloth to bind the victim's arms and legs. The suspect told the victim to remain where she was for 30 minutes while he fled the scene. After approximately 10 minutes had passed, the victim managed to untie her legs and ran to a nearby residence for help with her hands still bound (Figures 3.3, 3.4, and 3.5).

James Clinton Cole was identified as a likely suspect shortly after the rape occurred. He had been convicted of raping his own daughter when she was approximately 7 years old, and had served 8 years in prison. He also admitted to abducting a teenage girl at knifepoint in the early 1980s; this story was later verified by that victim. After being released from prison, his wife had accepted him back into the family. On August 22, 1996, James Cole raped his own daughter for the second time and was subsequently convicted and sentenced to life in prison plus 15 years. He blamed the rape on money trouble and an addiction to crack cocaine. When confronted about the crime that occurred on August 20, 1996, he admitted being in the woods near the time of the rape and stated that he most likely left DNA behind near the crime scene since he had been smoking crack cocaine in the same area. However, he stated that he would not admit to raping the 12-year-old victim.

---

[*] The James Clinton Cole case study is a 1996 cold case that was resolved by touch DNA and was submitted by Dr. Angela Williamson, Bode Technology. The following investigators also worked aspects of the case: Amy Jeanguenat, Bode Technology, Shelly Progovitz, Charles County Sheriff's Office, Ernest J. Jones, Charles County Sheriff's Office, and Joseph Goldsmith, Charles County Sheriff's Office, Charles Co. MD.

Figure 3.1 A Google Maps® overview of the crime scene area. (Courtesy of Bode Technology.)

Figure 3.2 The area where the victim was walking at the time of the assault. (Courtesy of Bode Technology and the Charles County, MD Sheriff's Office.)

The victim's clothing and Sexual Assault Kit (SAK) were collected and tested for DNA. From 1996 to 2008, the evidence was subjected to forensic testing on four separate occasions:

1. In December 1996, the victim's clothing and SAK swabs were tested for the presence of blood, saliva, foreign hairs, and semen. Very low numbers of spermatozoa were identified on the SAK swabs and only one sperm cell was identified on the shorts. No other probative results were obtained.

Figure 3.3 The ligature used to tie the victim. (Courtesy of Bode Technology and the Charles County, MD Sheriff's Office.)

Figure 3.4 The outdoor area where the assault took place. (Courtesy of Bode Technology and the Charles County, MD Sheriff's Office.)

2. In January 1997, HLA-DQA1 testing was performed on a stained area from the neckband of the victim's shirt (used as a bind during the assault) and compared to reference standards from the victim and James Clinton Cole. The DNA from the stain matched the victim and excluded James Clinton Cole.

Figure 3.5 The area at a neighbor's house where the victim was able to remove the ties used to restrain her and some of her clothing. (Courtesy of Bode Technology and the Charles County, MD Sheriff's Office.)

    With no other leads, the case went cold and no further DNA testing was conducted for 10 years.

3. In May 2007, Bode Technology rescreened the victim's shorts for the presence of semen and screened the SAK swabs and slides for the presence of male DNA. No semen was detected on the shorts. No male DNA was detected in the SAK swabs or samples from the slides.

4. In January 2008, Bode Technology applied touch DNA* testing to items with which the suspect would have had the most contact during the assault. Bode tested the waistband/fly area of the victim's shorts, the damaged areas/pieces of the shirt, and the cloth used to gag the victim for the presence of touch DNA. None of these items yielded enough genetic information for comparison purposes.

    However, the neckband of the victim's shirt that was used to bind the victim still contained a knot. The area an assailant would have touched to create the knot was sampled. This touch DNA sample resulted in a profile consisting of two individuals and was suitable for comparison. Both the victim and James Clinton Cole could not be excluded from this sample.

---

* Touch DNA refers to DNA evidence made up of very small quantities of DNA such as what might be left behind if an item were touched or handled and skin cells were left behind. It is similar to traditional DNA testing, but uses more sensitive methods.

James Clinton Cole was charged with the rape of the 12-year-old victim in late 2008. He was found guilty of first-degree rape and first-degree sexual assault and sentenced to two consecutive life sentences on July 13, 2009.

Police agencies use uniformed or patrol divisions as well as detectives to process crime scenes. The patrol officer, who is usually the first police officer to respond to the crime scene, and the detective, who may arrive later, are responsible for the investigation and processing of the crime scene. This division of labor by function is useful because it allows for a certain degree of specialization and hence the likelihood of better performance in the respective responsibilities. Although patrol or detective personnel may be used for crime scene processing in serious crimes, many police agencies delegate the task to detectives and/or to specialists such as crime scene investigators, fingerprint specialists, or forensic scientists. Modern police agencies typically use specialists to search the crime scene and collect and preserve physical evidence. Patrol or uniformed officers may process crime scenes in less serious crimes. Uniformed officers may respond to residential burglary scenes to investigate the crime, take a report, photograph the crime scene, dust for latent fingerprints, and collect evidence, without calling a detective or using specialized personnel such as crime scene evidence technicians. However, in major criminal investigations—such as homicides, rapes, assaults, arsons, and robberies—personnel with more extensive training and experience are most likely to be used in processing crime scenes.

Although different law enforcement personnel may process the crime scene, the rules are the same in all cases. Crime scenes contain potent information that, if sought in a systematic, legal, and scientific way, can help the investigator determine what happened, who was responsible, and who was involved. Law enforcement personnel involved in criminal investigations must be able to derive the maximum possible information from the crime scene.

The objectives of a crime scene investigation are to

- Reconstruct the incident
- Ascertain the sequence of events
- Determine the mode of operation
- Uncover a motive
- Discover what property was stolen
- Find out all that the criminal may have done
- Determine the perpetrator of the crime
- Recover physical evidence of the crime
- Identify the victim in some cases

In some cases, the investigation yields results that point directly to the criminal and provide solid evidence against the offender. Generally, this happens when the perpetrator's DNA or fingerprints are found at the scene and the profile or prints are already on file. The use of the Combined DNA Index System (CODIS) and Automated Fingerprint Identification Systems (AFIS) has greatly improved the chances of identifying the criminal, and many cold cases have been solved through CODIS & AFIS technology, often in relatively short periods of time.

The work of crime scene investigators* is often thankless. Frequently the public and police officers think of them as modern-day incarnations of Sherlock Holmes or more likely, one of several popular characters on television portraying crime scene investigators. Some expect that real-life crime scene investigators are capable of magically establishing complete information on the identity of the criminal and solving the crime quickly, as an investigator on television is able to do within the hour allotted to the usual TV show. When a crime scene investigator does not succeed in doing just that, he may be considered ineffective. This attitude is, of course, absurd. It is the duty of detectives to pursue and apprehend the criminal; the duty of the crime scene investigator is to gather all evidence available at the scene. For the investigative process to function best, the detective and the crime scene investigator need to work cooperatively. Each must consider the other as part of the team.

The notion of teamwork in criminal investigations is a key factor to the solution of the case. Each person in the process plays a vital role. Any one individual can do something that might have disastrous consequences to a case or make a significant contribution. No one, including the uniformed police officer, the detective, the forensic specialist, the medical examiner, or the prosecutor, can fulfill his duty without the cooperation and assistance of all the other people on the team.

Crime scene investigators understand that criminals leave trace evidence behind and take away minute material from the scene and/or victim. The crime scene investigator's job is to find these traces and preserve them. Such evidence may be used to reconstruct the crime or to prove or disprove that the suspect committed a criminal act. The value of any item of evidence to a criminal investigation—such as an apparently unimportant object or fact—may turn out to be extremely important later in the investigation. No item, however small, should be overlooked.

The crime scene investigator's job at the scene is similar to that of the first police officer to arrive on the scene. Each must proceed calmly and deliberately. The crime scene investigator should not approach the task with preconceived ideas or draw premature conclusions. Investigators should scrutinize the scene with their eyes open for details. Experience teaches the investigator to expect the worst† and to be more thorough than needed. A good rule to remember is: it is better to have processed the scene more thoroughly than needed than to have overlooked something seemingly insignificant that later turns out to be a critical item of evidence in the investigation. A complete investigation may produce information that substantiates a confession or refutes a defense contention raised at the trial. Mistakes made during the investigation often may never be rectified. Also keep in mind that it is always easier to explain to a jury why you did do something than why you did not do something.

Naturally, making the statement, "investigations should be conducted as thoroughly and carefully as possible," belies the fact that investigators are only human. Even experienced, dedicated professionals make mistakes. Remember that conducting thorough

---

* As used in this chapter and elsewhere in this book, the term "crime scene investigator" refers to a specialist whose principal job is to identify, collect, and retrieve physical evidence from the crime scene or to a detective or investigator who has the collateral duty of collecting and preserving physical evidence.
† Those new to crime scene investigations will do well to consider the wise sayings found in the folk wisdom of Murphy's law: (1) If something can go wrong it will and (2) If there is a worst time for something to happen, it will, at that time!

investigations is a goal for which to strive. Even with the best of intentions, mistakes and oversights may occur.

The O.J. Simpson case is a classic example of how the actions of investigators can be misconstrued. During the trial, the defense team raised questions about the crime scene practices of the police and even cited a prior edition of this textbook to suggest that the police acted improperly in processing the scene. An important lesson from this case is that appearance and perceptions, as well as the ability to communicate effectively to a jury, are equally important. Appearances and perceptions are every bit as important as knowledge, skills, and ability, at least in the eyes of the jury and the public. If the defense can make it appear that evidence was handled in an improper manner, that is, create reasonable doubt, the jury may agree.

There are few absolute rules in crime scene investigations. An important concept to note is that most rules outlined in this text and others are guidelines, based on common sense, that are applied to crime scene investigation. There are always cases in which guidelines cannot be followed. An example is packaging wet, bloody evidence in plastic trash bags. Wet, biological evidence packaged in plastic bags deteriorates more quickly than air-dried evidence and should not be used. However, when faced with a crime scene with blood-soaked clothing or bedding, separate packaging in a clean plastic trash bag for immediate transportation to a crime laboratory is an appropriate way to handle such items if the evidence cannot be dried at the scene. Situations demand that investigators be flexible and creative when necessary.

Because investigators are human beings, it is impossible for them to conduct investigations without making mistakes. It is necessary to try to make as few errors as possible and to learn from past faults. Unfortunately, critics will always have a compelling urge to be "Monday-morning quarterbacks" and advise any who will listen about how something should have been done. An investigator would be wealthy if he could have a dollar for each time he said, "If only I had thought to collect that item of evidence" or "I should have done this a different way" or "Why didn't I think of that at the time? It seems so obvious now." The adage that "hindsight is always 20–20" is a fact of life. Through experience, the same mistakes should not be made again. It is a good practice to ask if anything more should be done before quitting and releasing a crime scene.

A further lesson to be learned from the O. J. Simpson case is that the focus of forensic science has shifted from the laboratory to the crime scene. Defense attorneys are quick to learn that if they can show that the initial handling of the physical evidence at the crime scene was faulty that will call subsequent lab work into question. The evidence may be kept out of the trial or at least tarnished in the eyes of the jury.

Crime scene investigators should not allow superiors or others at the scene to influence their deliberations on the case before or during the actual crime scene examination. They should also try to minimize bias as much as possible.* The investigation should not be rushed. Others must wait. The investigator is personally responsible for his mistakes and has the right to determine personal and personnel actions at the scene.

An experienced crime scene investigator asked to describe how he/she proceeds at a scene may find this difficult to explain. Each crime scene is different, and it may not be possible to lay down absolute rules for conducting an investigation; however, a generalized

---

* Dr. Itiel Dror has done extensive research on the results of bias in forensic identifications. Readers are encouraged to read more about his work at www.cognitiveconsultantsinternational.com.

outline on how to process a scene can be made to fit a vast number of conditions. No matter how experienced an investigator is, there are always new situations to be faced and completely unfamiliar problems to master. The best advice to give in an extraordinary situation is to be calm, adaptable, and flexible.

The essential qualities of a good crime scene investigator are intuition and an eye on what needs to be done in every individual case, along with a thorough knowledge of the methods of locating and preserving physical evidence. It is also worthwhile for the crime scene investigator (CSI) to understand the capabilities and procedures of the forensic laboratory in their jurisdiction. Before any actual work at the scene begins, an investigator should try to stand back at an appropriate vantage point on the periphery of the scene and formulate a systematic plan, considering the following:

- How the search should be conducted
- What needs to be photographed at the scene
- Where the possible sources of physical evidence are located

Following this initial assessment, the crime scene investigation can begin.

The start of the crime scene investigation begins with documenting the scene. This process includes the following:

- Photography and/or videotaping (overall views)
- The investigation of the crime scene proper (when needed, combined with photography and videotaping detailed views)
- Sketching* (detailed sketches may be required during the investigation) (Figure 3.6)
- Note taking (to be done throughout the investigation—constant interruptions for notes are the rule)

Note taking at a crime scene is essential. Well-written, contemporaneous notes are invaluable later in the investigation and especially at the time of trial. It can be extremely frustrating for an officer assigned an old open case if the case notes of the original investigator's initial observations are inadequate or even shoddy. There are no substitutes for good note taking at all phases of the investigation.

The order in which work is done at a scene is not sacrosanct. The rule is to be flexible and to use common sense. Sometimes, an investigator must examine a detailed part of a scene or make a sketch of an object that had to be moved immediately on arrival at the scene (Figure 3.7). Consequently, the order of the various phases of processing a crime scene must be decided on a case-by-case basis.

Investigators should adopt an air of curiosity about everything concerning the crime scene, even the smallest items. The perpetrator may have forgotten or dropped something. A seemingly innocuous item may become the decisive piece of evidence later in the investigation. All investigators should develop a healthy skepticism. Things often are not as they seem. Be critical and never accept conditions or appearances without first questioning them. Simulated crimes or crimes masquerading as accidents to cover-up criminal activities do take place.

---

* Crime scene sketches can later be the basis of computer-aided drawing.

Figure 3.6 Computer-aided drawings (sometimes referred to as CAD) have gained wide use for crime scene documentation. They provide the investigator and juries a visual way to better understand the crime scene. (Courtesy of the Los Angeles County Sheriff's Department.)

Figure 3.7 The ScanStation C10 from Leica Geosystems deployed at a postblast investigation scene. (Courtesy of John DeHaan and Leica Geosystems.)

Actual Examination of the Scene

Investigators should think through and recreate the actions of the criminal. If the reconstruction does not make sense or if there are inconsistencies, consider starting over to reevaluate the sequence of events. One way to proceed is to eliminate scenarios while reasoning that "It couldn't have been done this way, how might it have happened?" Continue the process until one or two possibilities remain.

A useful suggestion is to carry a few pieces of chalk or crayons in the crime scene equipment kit. If it becomes necessary to move an object, the location of the object can be marked with chalk, pencil, or crayon.

Examining an outdoor crime scene at night is to be avoided, unless there is a compelling reason. Outdoor crime scene searches in daylight are more effectively examined, yield more information, and are easier to conduct. If an outdoor search must be conducted at night using artificial lighting, the scene should be kept intact as long as possible for a final search in daylight. No matter how powerful the lighting equipment, daylight is better. Experience teaches that some evidence, invariably missed in artificial light searches, is more readily detectable in daylight.

A crime scene investigation should not start if it is obvious that specialized personnel need to be called in to take over the job. The crime scene specialist's task is complicated enough and does not need to be made more difficult by the necessity of finishing what someone else began. The specialist should be permitted to take charge of the intact crime scene after being fully briefed by the detective in charge of the investigation. This guarantees the best possible results.

"Two heads are better than one"—using two crime scene investigators to search for and collect physical evidence is the most effective staffing level for most major crime scene investigations. A single crime scene investigator can do an effective job of searching for and collecting physical evidence, but two are better. Two investigators are more thorough. Notwithstanding this recommendation, in some instances just one investigator will suffice. Emergency circumstances and small, limited crime scenes are such examples. The crime scene investigator may call on an officer who has experience in photography to photograph the scene. Similarly, the investigator may use uniformed police and detectives as assistants to help with some of the simpler tasks. However, this practice should only be used when temporary assistants can be supervised closely and given detailed instructions.

The two crime scene investigators should be used to working on crime scenes together and should be able to cooperate. They should work as a team rather than on separate tasks. One way to divide the work is for one investigator to do the actual examination while the other keeps notes and assists by making personal observations, making measurements, and helping to examine a particular area. Two persons, working together, are able to observe much more than a single person can. Whatever one of the investigators discovers should immediately be reported to the partner. They also should discuss the different possibilities of how a certain clue might have been left at the scene and how the criminal proceeded. An idea that might not occur to one person may well occur to a second.

In homicide cases and other serious assaults, crime scene specialists should not assume any other investigative duties. Their full attention should be devoted to the case to get the most from their efforts. If crime scene work and the detective functions are combined, one of the activities, typically the crime scene duties, usually suffers. Specialized personnel assigned to crime scene duties must cooperate closely with the detective in charge. This division of labor between duties of specialist personnel and detectives may not always be possible due to a lack of personnel. However, the two types of work should be separated whenever feasible.

On arriving at the scene, the crime scene investigator should first obtain the basic facts from the officers already present. It is important that crime scene investigators be well briefed about the case before starting their examination of the scene. Arrival times and weather conditions should be noted. It is also important to determine which persons had prior access to the scene and whether any changes in the original conditions occurred.

When entering the crime scene, investigators should proceed cautiously, aware of potential clues on floors, doorknobs, light switches, and other areas that may have been touched by the criminal. Even when chances are slight that evidence may be found, investigators should not dismiss the possibility that important evidence is present. Investigators should never walk about the crime scene aimlessly. They should exercise the same caution that is expected from inexperienced personnel. Even if many people have already trampled the crime scene, it is important to watch one's step. Although it might be excusable for untrained officers to destroy evidence by inadvertently handling items or stepping on items of evidence, such actions are unpardonable for experienced crime scene investigators.

Before starting work, investigators should first thoroughly consider the crime scene. Significant circumstances may be overlooked if the scene is not thoroughly evaluated first. The investigator should make a complete and systematic survey of the scene and its immediate surroundings, both indoors and outdoors. The investigator should attempt to reconstruct the actions of the criminal by constantly asking "Why?" and "How?" Why did the criminal do this, how was the building entered, how was this mark made? Distractions should not be allowed to interfere with the investigator's initial reconstruction of the case. Quiet deliberation is essential to plan the course of the investigation intelligently and get the most information out of the scene.

Everything the crime scene investigators learn during the investigation should be written down as it is discovered. Clear, concise, contemporaneous notes should be taken during the entirety of the examination. The location and description of objects should be recorded in the notes before they are moved or examined in detail. In some cases, before moving an item of evidence, it is helpful to make a detailed sketch and take close-up photographs with a scale or ruler in the photograph (Figure 3.8). Examination notes at the crime scene should be made in the order of the work done and should not be edited. Any editing and report writing should be done after the initial stage of the investigative process and, preferably, back at the office. The extent of the notes is somewhat proportionate to the seriousness of the crime; a burglary investigation may not merit as many detailed notes as a murder investigation. In the murder case, the statute of limitations never runs out, so notes must be complete enough to be understandable and helpful even 15 or 20 years later.* All objects and details pertinent to the description of the scene must be noted. The report of the investigation of a major crime can never be too detailed. The

---

* The advent of forensic DNA typing and AFIS technology has had an interesting side effect. Murders committed 15 and 20 years ago are being solved. Computer systems storing DNA results and unidentified fingerprints wait patiently for a "hit." Unidentified criminals, whose DNA is tested and added to states' DNA databases or whose prints are entered into AFIS databases because of an unrelated arrest, have been identified and many unsolved cases cleared, often to the criminal's surprise.

(a)

(b)

Figure 3.8 A quick and easy way to make a sketch at a crime scene is to (a) upload a photo into Adobe Photoshop on a laptop and (b) convert it into a sketch, and print it out. (Courtesy of Cedar Crest College, Allentown, PA.)

completeness of the report is especially important in crimes that are not solved within a reasonable time. Rough notes and sketches made at the scene should never be discarded but should be included with the case file.

Although the press has a legitimate role in reporting criminal activity, the media should not be permitted into the crime scene proper to photograph the actual scene without express permission from the officer in charge. In sensational crimes, news photographers will often try to photograph the crime scene and victims, along with police officers. Police personnel should not pose for such pictures; they usually look ridiculous. These news photographs only serve the doubtful purpose of satisfying the public's desire for sensationalism. One should also be aware that journalists can use telephoto lenses to capture pictures of active crime scenes through windows. Additionally, crime scene notes and diagrams should be protected from view when exiting a crime scene so that news cameras cannot photograph any sensitive information about the crime scene.

Personnel at the crime scene should never divulge specific information or conditions at the crime scene to reporters. In fact, only public information officers or lead detectives should speak to reporters at crime scenes. The general rule is not to give out essential information, which is key to the solution of the crime. Usually, only the criminal gains from these news accounts. In one high-profile serial murder case, at a press conference the mayor of a large U.S. city released critical information about unique shoe prints found at several crime scenes. Needless to say, those shoes were never located when the suspect was apprehended. Suspects in a criminal investigation may claim that they learned about particular facts relating to the case on television or in the newspapers. Such information should be given to the press only if it would assist the investigation, and only the officer in charge or a superior may give permission for its release. In cases in which the press becomes privy to sensitive information, they should be asked to hold off reporting it to the public in the interest of solving the case.

Once the first phase of a death investigation has been completed, the coroner may be called. Investigators should work to cultivate good working relationships with their medical examiner and coroner's representatives. Close cooperation between the police and the coroner is requisite for successful investigations (Figure 3.9).

A crime scene investigation is characterized by three essential conditions for success: organization, thoroughness, and caution. Confusion, incompetence, and imprudence may result in a failed investigation.

Following the initial attempt at reconstructing the crime scene, the crime scene investigator's task is to photograph the central crime scene.* The actual investigation should follow with the central scene, unless an initial survey indicates that physical evidence is present along the route used by the criminal to enter or leave and this evidence cannot be well protected. In such cases, the investigator should first examine and recover these items of evidence before continuing at the central crime scene. The search of the criminal's route should start from the central scene.

In an indoor homicide scene, the central crime scene can be searched beginning with the criminal's suspected point of entry and point of exit, followed by the area adjacent to the body, and finishing with the rest of the room. Crime scene investigators should attempt to work according to an established routine that does not vary greatly from case to case. This helps to reduce the risk of overlooking a seemingly insignificant article of trace evidence or a larger object that the perpetrator may have left behind or accidentally dropped. A good idea is to use a checklist.

Investigators should not start the crime scene investigation with a detailed examination of the body until the basic examination of the scene has been completed. Other aspects of

* The terms "central crime scene" and "crime scene proper" are interchangeable and refer to the area where the crime took place.

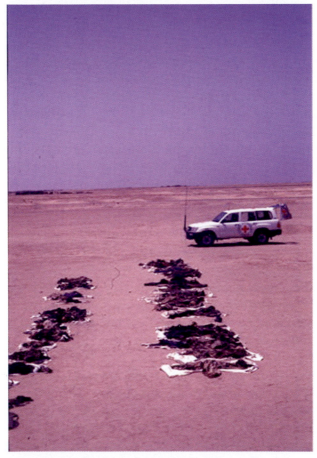

Figure 3.9 Some crime scenes can be more complicated than those that are generally encountered. Situations involving mass deaths from terrorism or political upheavals may well be considered criminal investigations. Moreover, many of the same sorts of practices used in ordinary criminal acts are used in mass fatality incidents that result from natural disasters like hurricanes, tsunamis, earthquakes, and the like. (Courtesy of the International Committee of the Red Cross.)

the crime scene may require attention first. Also, if investigators form a clear picture of the circumstances of the case by first examining the scene, the examination of the body might provide more information. Unknown facts may be discovered that are of value in relation to findings on the body. A preliminary inspection of the body to suggest the mode of death can precede the crime scene search. Noting a gunshot wound suggests that bullets or cartridges may be present. If investigators expect it will take a great deal of time to complete the initial crime scene search, body temperature and other time-of-death indicators should be collected.

Sometimes, it is helpful to leave significant objects in their original positions during the investigation to aid in reconstructing the crime. This practice is useful if the reconstruction of events or the logical steps of the reconstruction do not mesh. If this happens, start over and retrace the steps in the thought process. The body should not be moved in haste if its presence is needed for the reconstruction. In some cases, it may even be appropriate to leave the corpse overnight, but consideration should be given to the availability of the forensic pathologist. If the autopsy can be performed right away, it should take place as soon as possible after the body's position is recorded.

At the very start of the investigation, investigators should designate an area as a "trash pile" in which things may be put that should not be lying about the scene. A certain amount of waste normally accumulates from used swabs, blood-testing materials, gloves, Tyvek suits, etc. The trash collection point should be located as far away as practical from the central crime scene. Spreading a newspaper or using a paper trash bag and marking it accordingly is enough to establish the trash pile. Large evidence collection bags can also be used as trash bags. A work area should also be designated for filling out evidence tags, developing fingerprints on small objects, handling casting material, and so on.

For special methods of detecting, preserving, and evaluating evidence found at the crime scene, the reader is referred to subsequent chapters that deal with methods used at different kinds of crime scenes.

Chapter Questions

1. List the seven key objectives of a crime scene investigation.

2. The notion of _____ in criminal investigations is a key factor to the solution of the case.
   a) Experience
   b) Expertise
   c) Teamwork
   d) Duty

3. Which of the following can be a benefit of doing a complete and thorough investigation?
   a) The guilty are punished.
   b) The case can be closed.
   c) A confession can be substantiated.
   d) A victim can find closure.

4. What important lesson can be learned from the O.J. Simpson trial?
   a) Appearance and perception, as well as the ability to communicate effectively to the jury are equally important.
   b) CSIs must never make mistakes or the trial can be easily lost.
   c) Detectives must never consider economic status of the suspect when undertaking a criminal investigation.
   d) Only the most experienced personnel should be used in high profile cases.

5. (True/False) There are always cases where guidelines cannot be followed.
   a) True
   b) False

6. The recent report issued by the National Academy of Sciences has focused attention on which of the following?
   a) The crime scene work
   b) The work at the crime laboratory
   c) The prosecutor
   d) The supervisors of the crime scene unit

7. The start of the crime scene investigation begins with documenting the scene. List what takes place during this process.

8. Well-written, _____ notes are invaluable later in the investigation and especially at the time of trial.
   a) Handwritten
   b) Typed
   c) Contemporaneous
   d) Historical

9. During a homicide investigation, a preliminary inspection of which of the following can be valuable before conducting a crime scene search?
   a) The body to suggest the mode of death
   b) The inner perimeter
   c) The entry and exit paths
   d) The weapon

10. Where is the most appropriate location for the disposal of trash at a crime scene?
    a) At the command vehicle
    b) Within the scene to save time
    c) In the inner perimeter
    d) As far away as possible from the central scene

Specialized Personnel at the Crime Scene

4

Introduction

Uniformed officers and detectives do not possess the full range of special skills and expertise needed to process all crime scenes. A wide range of specialized support personnel—some employed regularly and others occasionally—can provide these talents when called into a crime scene investigation. Bomb squad technicians, fire marshals, and underwater crime scene divers are some of the specialized personnel who might be needed at a crime scene. Sometimes a particularly serious case may warrant outside assistance, such as hazardous material (HAZMAT) specialists in the case of clandestine drug laboratory cases or federal authorities (e.g., Federal Bureau of Investigation; Bureau of Alcohol, Tobacco, Firearms and Explosives; Drug Enforcement Administration; or Disaster Mortuary Operations Response Team) when investigating mass disasters, terrorist acts, bombings, or major fires.

CSI officers and evidence technicians are police or civilian personnel specially trained to process a crime scene.* These persons are equipped to collect and preserve physical evidence at a crime scene. They arrive at the scene with evidence collection kits and all the tools and equipment needed to conduct the search and collect the evidence thoroughly (Figure 4.1).

There is no single classification of personnel or a sole way in which crime scene personnel are represented in public safety organizations. Some police departments employ identification (ID) officers. The ID officers photograph the crime scene and search for latent

Figure 4.1 Police agencies and the offices of medical examiners/coroners frequently use standard cars, trucks, and vans specially outfitted as crime scene vehicles.

---

* The International Association for Identification offers a well-regarded certification program for crime scene investigators. More information is available at their web site: http://www.theiai.org/

Figure 4.2 A three-dimensional computer graphic that provides complete measurements of a crime scene. (Image courtesy of Deltasphere, Inc., http://deltasphere.com/SceneVision-3D.htm.)

fingerprints; they may not be responsible for collecting other types of physical evidence at the crime scene. ID officers are generally experts in fingerprint collection and sometimes fingerprint comparison. They may be subpoenaed as expert witnesses to establish the identity of the suspect by comparison of latent fingerprints with inked prints.

Some cases may require an accurate architectural rendition of the crime scene. Forensic surveyors, forensic artists, or other specially trained crime scene personnel may be used for this purpose. Relying on accurate measurements, notes, sketches, and photographs, they produce an architectural-like drawing or computer rendition of the crime scene for use at the trial. In some instances, three-dimensional models of the scene may be prepared to better assist the prosecution in presenting the case. Today, it is quite common to use computer programs to make accurate drawings of crime scenes (Figure 4.2).

Photographers are used for specialized photography. Aerial photographs may be needed to illustrate outdoor crime scenes (Figure 4.3). Google Earth images can also provide excellent aerial views of crime scene locations. Special photographic situations such as low levels of light, infrared (Figure 4.4), UV (Figure 4.5), or high speed photography may require their expertise. After a digital photo is taken, Adobe Photoshop can also be used to enhance an image or extract additional information from it.

Forensic photographers and police photographers use digital photography almost exclusively for general police photography and crime scene photography. The increased resolution and decreased cost of digital cameras, and ease of storage of digital pictures have been the driving force to change from film to digital photography.

Digital videotaping is also used by some law enforcement agencies as a means of recording crime scenes. Although affordable video units are available, the level of training required to take quality videos goes beyond the skills of a home hobbyist. Specialists require training to operate and maintain the sophisticated equipment necessary to produce quality crime scene videotapes.

Figure 4.3 An aerial photograph of an arson fire at Universal Studios in Los Angeles, showing the extent of the devastation. (Courtesy of the Los Angeles County Sheriff's Department.)

Issues to consider with digital photography and videography are the long-term stability of the stored images and the ability to recover older formats when checking images in the future. New technology has to be able to view older images. Added issues are the ability to sort through many thousands of images as the library grows and to protect the images from alteration.

The criminalist, or forensic scientist, has special training and education in chemistry and biology that are applied to the recognition, identification, collection, and preservation of physical evidence (Figure 4.6). The criminalist is typically called on to assist in more serious criminal investigations such as homicides, assaults, bombings, and arson. A criminalist's special area of expertise in these cases is trace evidence, biological evidence, and crime scene reconstruction. In addition to assisting at the crime scene, criminalists conduct laboratory tests on the evidence, prepare reports, and testify as expert witnesses about their findings.

State and local jurisdictions use a coroner system or a medical examiner. No standardized system is in place across the United States; however, most would argue that forensic pathologists have the training preferred for performing autopsies in criminal cases. The purpose of the medical examiner or coroner system in death investigation is twofold: to determine the cause and manner of death and to identify the deceased.

The forensic pathologist or a trained medico–legal investigator (MLI) from the medical examiner's office is almost always called to the scene of a homicide as soon as the police investigator has completed the initial examination of the scene. It is the medical examiner's responsibility to identify the deceased, determine the approximate time of death, and take

(a)

(b)

Figure 4.4 Photographic techniques using different lighting techniques can sometimes help to visualize important evidence. Writing discovered on the top inside portion of a drawer (a) was barely visible under normal lighting. (b) Reflected infrared lighting enhanced the writing, making the telephone number visible. (Courtesy of the Los Angeles County Sheriff's Department.)

custody of the remains. Ideally, the forensic pathologist or MLI should be present at the crime scene to conduct an initial examination.

Hospital emergency room personnel may play an important role in gathering evidence in criminal investigations. Doctors and nurses who treat rape or assault victims often are required to collect physical evidence relating to the assault. Hospital emergency

Figure 4.5 Using ultraviolet photography to visualize strangulation marks around the neck of one of the victims in the 1970s Hillside Strangler serial murder case in Los Angeles. (Courtesy of the Los Angeles County Department of Coroner.)

Figure 4.6 Hazardous materials are regularly found at clandestine drug laboratories such as this methamphetamine laboratory. Forensic chemists are often called to these types of scenes to sort through various chemical precursors that are present in order to determine what drugs are being made. (Courtesy of the Los Angeles County Sheriff's Department.)

room personnel may not know which evidence is important or the legal requirements of evidence collection. The first officer to arrive at the scene of a rape, for example, may be required to inform the emergency room physician what evidence needs to be collected.

Forensic nurses are another group of professionals who provide a valuable resource to the police. They have training in nursing and in proper evidence collection as well as in other criminal justice-related skills. Today, many are found in hospital emergency room settings and collect sexual assault evidence as part of their duties. They may also play an important role in other medical settings where evidence is collected for criminal investigations such as elder abuse, child abuse, and spousal abuse and in medical examiner and coroner settings.

The district attorney may sometimes become a member of the CSI team. He or she may be called upon to obtain a search warrant for a location under investigation or a court order to obtain known specimens from a defendant.

In special cases, a forensic dentist, or odontologist, may be called to a scene. Mass disasters such as plane crashes (Figure 4.7) or scenes where charred remains are discovered require the expertise of forensic dentists to assist in identification by means of dental remains. They may also be called upon to collect and preserve bite-mark evidence on a victim or on foodstuff (Figure 4.8).

If the crime scene is a burial site, the assistance of a forensic anthropologist or archeologist may prove valuable. The evaluation of skeletal remains at the scene to determine if they are animal or human is important in some instances. Also, excavating a gravesite requires skill; experts with such experience can be helpful.

Cadaver dogs are specially trained to recognize the scent of decaying remains. They are useful for searching an area where investigators believe a body was buried.

Forensic psychologists are available to assist in evaluating a crime scene. One important group of trained personnel is the FBI's ViCAP* (Violent Criminal Apprehension Program) unit. In cooperation with law enforcement agencies throughout the United States, the FBI has made ViCAP an important resource for crime solving. The agency is at the forefront of psychological profiling techniques and has trained hundreds of detectives across the country to review cases involving solved or unsolved murders or attempted murders. ViCAP is appropriate in cases that involve abduction; seemingly random, motiveless, or sexually oriented crimes; or known or suspected serial crimes. ViCAP may be called in for missing person cases in circumstances in which foul play is suspected.

Forensic engineers may play a role in studying the structural integrity of a building, bridge, or other structure in an accident investigation. Sometimes, an item of building material may require engineering tests to determine if it was tampered with. Forensic engineers can be helpful in electrical fires, explosions, examinations of vehicles involved in traffic accidents, and investigations involving other types of vehicles.

Forensic audio specialists may be required to evaluate sound recordings or to assist in reconstructing events by means of studying sound recordings of an event. Sometimes echoes can be used to pinpoint the location from which a weapon was fired.

Forensic toxicologists may become involved in product tampering cases to determine the nature of the adulterant in the foodstuff or consumer product. Using sophisticated laboratory instruments, they may be able to examine products for unknown poisons or other contaminants.

* http://www.fbi.gov/wanted/vicap

Figure 4.7 An aerial photograph of the scene of a plane crash between a commercial aircraft and a private plane that crashed into a residential neighborhood and the remains of one of the accident victims recovered from the site of the crash. (Courtesy of the Los Angeles County Sheriff's Department.)

Figure 4.8 Forensic dentists are often involved with identification of remains by means of dental x-ray comparisons between the antemortem x-rays and postmortem x-rays. (Courtesy of C. M. Bowers, DDS, JD, Ventura, CA.)

The Society of Forensic Toxicology* defines three distinct elements of forensic toxicology as follows:

- Postmortem forensic toxicology, which determines the absence or presence of drugs and their metabolites, chemicals such as ethanol and other volatile substances, carbon monoxide and other gases, metals, and other toxic chemicals in human fluids and tissues, and evaluates their role as a determinant or contributory factor in the cause and manner of death
- Human-performance forensic toxicology, which determines the absence or presence of ethanol and other drugs and chemicals in blood, breath, or other appropriate specimens, and evaluates their role in modifying human performance or behavior
- Forensic urine drug testing, which determines the absence or presence of drugs and their metabolites in urine to demonstrate prior use or abuse

Firearms examiners are often called to assist in a crime scene to recover spent bullets from walls and doors and to assess the trajectory of fired weapons (Figure 4.9). They can

* http://www.soft-tox.org/

Figure 4.9 Trajectory reconstruction of a shooting incident using rods to depict the likely point of the shooter. (Courtesy of the Los Angeles Police Department.)

determine if a bullet came from a particular firearm. They may also assist in determining whether a shooting could have been an accident or was more likely to have been intentional.

A consistent theme throughout this textbook is that police investigation is a team approach; professionals with multidisciplinary expertise are routinely brought together to solve crimes. It is not possible for a police investigator to have complete knowledge of the law, forensic science, and forensic medicine, as well as other training specialties needed to process a crime scene and investigate a crime completely. Investigators should maintain lists of local experts who can be readily mobilized to assist in cases. Such a directory is a major asset for successful police work.

The need for teamwork cannot be overemphasized. Throughout the case, the detective in charge will be responsible for pulling together a vast array of information from many sources. The detective's leadership skills are key to getting the maximum amount of information from those that may have been associated with the case from the crime scene portion of the case onward. Investigators who take time to work closely with their experts and maintain close working relationships with them will be rewarded for the extra effort.

Health and Safety Issues at Crime Scenes

The threat of radiological, chemical and biological terrorism as well as potential exposure to diseases at crime scenes requires unique expertise, which is sometimes not considered by police professionals. The following material is presented as a precaution. Awareness and proper care could save a life.

Figure 4.10 The Bureau of Alcohol, Tobacco, Firearms and Explosives (ATF) maintains a national response team (as do other agencies like the FBI) to offer assistance to local agencies in major incidents. (Courtesy of US DOJ BATFE.)

Terrorist Crime Scenes*

We live in a violent world where the unthinkable can become a reality. The threat of chemical and biological (as well as radiological and nuclear) terrorism is a reality and police and crime scene personnel may become involved wittingly or unwittingly as first responders. Ultimately, federal agencies, such as the Federal Bureau of Investigation, the Department of Homeland Security, the Department of Defense, Centers for Disease Control, Environmental Protection Agency, and other organizations, will be brought into a situation (Figure 4.10). Local public safety agencies, however, may be the first responders on scene and first to assess the situation.

The complete subject matter concerning terrorist incident response and biological and chemical devices is beyond the scope of this book. That said, many law enforcement agencies are engaged in pre-incident planning and preparation. Some understanding is vital for personal safety in weapons of mass destruction (WMD) situations.†

Crime scenes present potential safety risks to personnel. An understanding and appreciation of the potential risks coupled with appropriate safety precautions will minimize these risks (Figure 4.11). Whenever an investigator has concerns about health symptoms, he or she should seek and obtain professional expert advice. BE AWARE!

---

* Contact your local FBI office if you suspect you are dealing with a terrorism incident.
† *Practical Crime Scene Investigations for Hot Zones* by Fish, Stout, and Wallace offers excellent coverage of this topic. The Centers for Disease Control also has a good resource guide for handling decedents contaminated by radioactive materials, https://www.bt.cdc.gov/radiation/pdf/radiation-decedent-guidelines.pdf.

Figure 4.11 Crime scene investigators should also seek training in the use of HAZMAT equipment so that they can perform their duties under different types of hazardous circumstances. (Courtesy Special Investigations Unit, NYC Office of Chief Medical Examiner.)

Conclusion

Because many of the experts with whom investigators must work do not come from police backgrounds, interpersonal skills are important. Most experts, including those who routinely or only occasionally work for law enforcement, are eager to help. However, police investigators should remember that they are working with people from various backgrounds. Working with them in a spirit of mutual cooperation and respect and in a professional manner will aid in achieving successful outcomes to investigations.

Chapter Questions

1. List some of the federal agencies that could respond to cases such as clandestine laboratories, mass disasters, terrorist acts, bombings, or major fires.

2. These personnel are specially equipped and trained to collect physical evidence at a crime scene.
   a) Forensic pathologists
   b) Forensic anthropologists
   c) Crime scene investigation officers
   d) Medical examiners
3. Which of the following specialized personnel would be the most qualified to properly collect a bloody fingerprint found at the scene of a homicide?
   a) Coroner's investigator
   b) Identification officer
   c) Medical examiner
   d) Forensic pathologist

4. List some of the specialized photographic techniques that may be needed at a crime scene and also any unusual photographic problems that may occur.

5. (True/False) When videotaping a crime scene, the level of training required to take quality videos goes beyond the skills of a home hobbyist.
   a) True
   b) False

6. Which of the following are the typical responsibilities of a medical examiner at a homicide crime scene?
   a) Take custody of the remains, identify the deceased, and determine approximate time of death.
   b) Establish a command post and provide direction to the detectives.
   c) Take custody of the remains, transport the body to the funeral home, and turn over their clothes to family members.
   d) Hold a press conference to discuss the case and suspected cause of death.

7. List the typical cases where a forensic nurse would be used to collect physical evidence.

8. You are called to a scene of an apartment fire with multiple victims. Which of the following specialized personnel would be helpful in identifying the victims?
   a) Forensic nurse
   b) Emergency room physician
   c) Forensic dentist
   d) Cadaver dog handler

9. Explain the differences between postmortem forensic toxicology, human-performance forensic toxicology, and forensic urine drug testing.

10. You are the lead investigator in a homicide case where the suspect claims that he shot the victim in self-defense as he was coming at him with a knife. You have several bullet holes at the scene and want to determine the distance between the shooter and the victim by examining the bullet trajectories. Which of the following persons would be the most helpful?
    a) Firearms examiner
    b) Forensic audio specialist
    c) Coroner's investigator
    d) ID officer

Processing the Crime Scene

5

Plan of Action

Processing a crime scene, including careful examination, note taking, sketching, photography, and collection of physical evidence, requires a plan of action. Crime scenes should be approached in a systematic, methodical way; certain steps must be performed before others. Considerations about legal and scientific matters must be made when searching a crime scene. These details must be included in an action plan or method of approach and practiced when examining the scene of a crime.

The plan of action should be readily available to crime scene investigators. It should be included in a written departmental procedure to define crime scene responsibilities, and it may also detail what tasks are to be done and in what order. It is, of course, impossible to anticipate every detail in a crime scene investigation; however, certain ground rules can be set forth to direct uniformed personnel, detectives, and crime scene investigators to a specific goal.

Note Taking

Of all the duties and responsibilities of an officer conducting the crime scene search, perhaps the most important is note taking. Note taking is important for several reasons. It forces investigators to commit observations to writing and to keep a detailed record of everything observed and accomplished. Frequently, a seemingly insignificant item found in an investigator's notebook turns out to be critical to an investigation.

Some general points about notes and note taking are as follows:

1. Notes should be made as events unfold and in chronological order.
2. Notes should detail step-by-step actions.
3. Notes should be complete and thorough.
4. Notes should be clearly and legibly written. Sloppy notes or those that do not clearly state the investigator's meaning will be subject to misinterpretation.
5. Negative or unexpected conditions (the absence of bloodstains or a light that is found on) should be noted.
6. The note taker should be as specific as possible. If an item of evidence is to be located, a description such as "on the living room floor, 6 inches east of the west wall and 3 feet south of the north wall" should be used. Vague statements such as "near" or "to the left of" should be avoided.
7. Case notes, sketches, tape recordings, or photos should never be discarded or deleted. They should be placed into a case folder and retained for as long as the department's policy indicates.

8. The initial investigating officer should remember that some investigations may go on for years and future detectives will have to rely on the case notes made at the start of the investigation.

The investigating officer or detective is responsible for the entire investigation, including the crime scene. Upon arrival at the scene, the detective should obtain a brief statement from the first officer at the scene, detailing what transpired. The investigating officer should gather much information, and any facts and opinions, from the first officers. The investigating officer's first contact with the scene will be a cursory one. Care should be taken not to disturb anything. Evidence should not be moved or touched. Evidence will be properly documented, measured, sketched, photographed, and fingerprinted later. At the start of the process, the investigator will begin to digest information reported by first officers, witnesses, victims, and suspects, together with the overall appearance of the crime scene. These details are used to get a first impression of the circumstances of the criminal act and to formulate a plan to process the crime scene.

Protecting the crime scene is an ongoing concern. Uniformed officers should remain posted at the scene. The victim's family, the public, and the press should be kept away from the crime scene. Fellow officers, especially command officers, who have no business visiting the crime scene, are a more serious problem. In highly publicized crimes, superior officers often exhibit a desire to see (or perhaps tour might be a better term) the scene. This should be avoided if at all possible. The simplest solution is to have a sign-in log so that anyone who enters or leaves the crime scene is accounted for. An alternative suggestion is to set up a command post with a pot of coffee and donuts to help keep unnecessary persons away. A remote video camera may also be set up inside the command post to allow superiors to have a visual inspection of the crime scene without actually entering it. Another possibility to discourage officers who visit a scene is to give them an assignment and require them to file a written report and sign a log. Sometimes it may be necessary for the investigator in charge of the crime scene to inform the superiors politely that the scene is still active and their presence might compromise findings and interfere with collecting physical evidence.

Tape recorders make it easy to take down information that can be transcribed later; some investigators use pocket digital recorders for note taking. Investigators should remember that impromptu remarks from other officers at the scene might later prove embarrassing. Videotaping creates similar problems.

Notes taken at crime scenes should include the following information:

- Date and time the crime was first reported to the police
- Type of crime
- Location of the crime scene and a description of the area
- Description of the crime or event leading up to the investigation
- Name of the person who requested the crime scene investigation
- Names of all officers, witnesses, investigators, and specialized personnel at the crime scene
- Names of the persons who conducted the crime scene search and who took photographs and fingerprints, made sketches, and collected evidence
- Weather and lighting conditions at the time of the investigation
- Description of the primary crime scene, including the location of the body and accompanying details

- Location of any evidence found during the investigation and the names of those who collected it and the results of a search for fingerprints, DNA, and other trace evidence
- Description of the location, including the surrounding houses, streets, and community
- Description of the interior and exterior of the crime scene, including the type of residence, number of rooms, and windows
- Description of the outside of the scene including the terrain, type of plants, soil, etc.
- The date and time the crime scene investigation was concluded

These details represent only some of the many pieces of information that should be included in the investigator's notes; they do not represent all the possible information. Officers should use this list as a guide. Meticulous note taking is one of the keys to good police work and competent crime scene investigation.

Crime Scene Search

Once the investigator has gathered as much information as possible and made a survey of the location, the actual crime scene search may begin. Processing a crime scene consists of the following:

1. Surveying the crime scene
2. Photographing and sketching the crime scene
3. Mapping and measuring the crime scene
4. Recording and documenting the location of physical evidence at the crime scene
5. Searching for fingerprints, DNA, and other physical evidence

As a simple, general rule of thumb, the most fleeting, fragile evidence should be collected first. Thus, taking photographs and making crime scene sketches take priority because crime scenes change with the passage of time and the investigator's objective is to make a record of the scene that reflects as closely as possible its original condition.

A systematic search of the crime scene should be conducted. Criminal investigation texts recommend a variety of search patterns: the strip or lane search, grid search, spiral search, and quadrant search. Some search patterns lend themselves to outdoor areas, while others are more appropriate to indoor crime scenes. The important idea to remember is that thoroughness is the goal of the search plan.*

Indoor crime scene searches are best done with two persons. One easy way of accomplishing a search in a room is to divide it in half. Each investigator searches one half. After they have done a thorough search, they switch halves (Figure 5.1).

Outdoor searches often cover greater areas than indoor ones and more searchers may need to be called upon. Again, a systematic method should be used. The area can be roped off into grids, each square representing a given search area. A 6 × 6 foot area is a reasonable size for a detailed and comprehensive search. As in the indoor search, each area should be double-checked for thoroughness.

---

* Whatever the search procedure, the "mill around" method is never correct. In this method, using a pen or pencil (for indoor crime scenes) or a stick (for outdoor ones), the officer randomly pokes around, pushing aside objects and picking up items that look interesting. This is never a proper way to conduct a search!

Figure 5.1 A workable pattern for conducting a crime scene search should be formulated and used. Several typical patterns are shown here. The specific case will dictate which search pattern is used.

Do not forget to look up! Generally, investigators concentrate on what is on the ground and at eye level when searching a crime scene. However, evidence may be above their heads, on ceilings, or caught in tree branches.

Before walking onto tile floors, crime scene investigators should consider that shoe prints might be present in dust or dirt. Even if others have already walked on the floor, it is still worth the effort to look for prints. A simple technique to look for prints on the floor is to use a flashlight shined at a low or oblique angle to the floor in a darkened room to look for dust prints. If any are present, they can be photographed with a camera on a tripod using oblique lighting. After photographs are taken, the print can be lifted using an electrostatic dust print lifter or a large rubber-backed lifter. Both items are commercially available from police supply companies (Figure 5.2).

Nighttime outdoor crime scene searches present difficult problems. If possible, any search should be put off until daylight hours. If waiting is not possible, high-intensity lighting and portable generators may provide sufficient light. Fire departments or Emergency Service Units generally have such gear.

Vehicle searches demand the same degree of care. The nature of the crime determines the area of the car to be searched. In hit-and-run cases, the exterior and undercarriage are important; the interior is examined more carefully in a rape or murder case. In most cases, examinations begin with an examination of the exterior portions of the vehicle. In a hit-and-run incident, the examination focuses on areas that struck the victim: bumper, grill, windshield, and undercarriage. Look for the presence of dents, broken headlamps,

(a)

(b)

Figure 5.2 (a) Crime scene investigator lifting a foil film to collect a footprint using static electricity. (b) The lift is shown next to a photograph of the shoe's sole. (Courtesy of the Zurich Cantonal Police Forensic Science Laboratory.)

damaged paint, and fabric impressions. Blood, hair, torn pieces of clothing, or fibers may be present. Broken and missing parts of the vehicle should be thoroughly documented. A hydraulic lift can be used to lift the car to examine the undercarriage for evidence. All evidence should be photographed and sketched. Fingerprints and/or touch DNA may be found on door handles, automatic window switches, door locks, radio/CD player, GPS, gear shifts, steering wheels, mirrors, ignitions, or the area above the driver's-side exterior door panel where some drivers rest their left hands.

The interior of the vehicle should be searched for fingerprints. A systematic approach should be taken, such as dividing the interior into sections: front right, front left and back right, back left. Before entering the vehicle, an examination for trace evidence should be made. If anything of evidentiary value is noted, it should be collected before entering the car. Trace evidence such as hairs and fibers can be collected using forceps or tape lifts. Vacuums can be used; however, vacuums pick up too much debris, which causes considerable extra work for laboratory examiners. Considering the possibility of finding trace evidence will cause the investigator to avoid contaminating the interior of the vehicle with foreign material that may be carried inside by the examiner. Fingerprints and DNA should be searched for and collected after trace evidence is collected.

Crime Scene Photography

The well-worn saying "a picture is worth a thousand words" certainly holds true with crime scene photography. No matter how well an investigator can verbally describe a crime scene, photographs can tell the same story better and more easily. The following is not intended to make the reader an expert in photography, but merely to discuss certain issues that relate to photography in general and crime scene photography in particular.

Before a detailed examination of the crime scene is made or before any items are moved or even touched, the crime scene should be photographed. The photographs should be taken to clearly and accurately depict the scene as it was found, the paths taken by the criminal to the scene, the point of entry, the exit, and the escape route. Detailed photographs should be taken to show items of physical evidence in the condition in which they were found by the investigator before their removal or processing (Figure 5.3).

Types of Cameras

Only a few years ago, crime scenes were exclusively photographed using film cameras. Today that is no longer the case. The quality and cost of digital cameras have made it possible to make the change over from film to digital for the vast majority of people working in this field. For historical purposes and because film cameras are occasionally in use in some places, the following is a short summary of film-based photography used in crime scene investigation.

Larger format cameras, such as a 4 × 5 or 120, used to be the trend years ago because they produced a larger negative that resulted in more clarity when enlarging photographs. If two identical scenes were photographed with a 4 × 5 camera and a 35-mm camera using the same type of film and enlargements were made from each, the photograph taken with

Figure 5.3 Skeletal remains found at a crime scene should always be photographed in the condition that they were found before moving or collecting them. (Courtesy of the NYC Office of Chief Medical Examiner.)

the larger format camera gave greater resolution and very small objects were easier to pick out.

Notwithstanding the benefits of large-format cameras, 35-mm cameras became the norm. The 35-mm single-lens reflex camera offered the greatest versatility. Many police departments chose this camera for routine crime scene photography because of low cost and ease of use.

"Point and shoot" cameras were also useful in a variety of instances. They continue to be inexpensive, take acceptable pictures, and are useful for officers who do not have much training in photography. The cost of these cameras and the even more inexpensive "disposable" cameras makes it possible for every police vehicle to carry a camera for use as needed.

Polaroid cameras can still be useful in certain situations such as for identification photographs. If a photograph of a deceased person is needed to identify him, a Polaroid works well. The quality of the photos is acceptable. However, Polaroid film is expensive and not as readily available as it once was (Figure 5.4).

(a)

(b)

Figure 5.4 Although Polaroid film is not in much use, it still comes into play now and again. A robber had his passport photo taken in a store and later returned and held up the proprietor. When the police came, the victim reported that he recognized the perpetrator as the person who earlier came in for his passport photo. The victim gave the Polaroid negative (a), which had a faint image of the suspect, to the police investigator. The photo lab was able to develop a poor-quality, but recognizable photograph (b). The photo was made into a drawing and subsequently into a wanted poster. (Courtesy of the Los Angeles County Sheriff's Department.)

Digital cameras represent the latest technology and are now universal (cell phones, portable gaming systems, smartphones, and other electronic devices all have them.) Prices have fallen and quality has improved, making digital photography a cost-effective choice. Instead of film, photographic images are stored on digital media storage cards. The cards can be placed into a computer and viewed on the screen and printed out using a specialized printer. Digital photos can also be incorporated into a Microsoft Word® document in the investigator's final report.

Types of Media

For digital cameras, the photographic resolution is measured in pixels. Camera prices increase with increased resolution. For crime scene photography, a digital camera with a resolution in the 14 megapixel range is not uncommon and yields excellent results. Some models even include GPS capability to indicate the approximate location where the photograph was taken. Even low end digital "point and shoot" cameras have good quality resolution and are useful for some situations.

While digital photography provides excellent results, its use has created a new set of challenges for law enforcement users. Cameras are able to store hundreds of photos on a single digital storage card. (Care must be taken when "deleting" digital media storage devices as images can still be recovered with special software.) Procedures must be developed to save the images on the cards in a way that allows them to be admissible as evidence. The volume of digital photographs also creates storage issues. Files need to be backed up routinely and the backups should be kept off-site. There are also issues of image stability. Over time, technology must be available to view and print out a variety of different digital formats, for example, TIF, GIF, JPG, etc., as well as newly emerging ones.

Cameras run the gambit from DSLR (digital single lens reflex) cameras to simple "point and shoot" cameras with built-in flash. Naturally, the DSLR cameras have greater flexibility but cost several times more then simpler cameras. The marketplace continues to change at a rapid rate and a degree of research must be done to determine the features required in a camera and laboratory photo equipment to make the use of the camera optimal. (B & H photo offers an excellent selection and professional assistance in navigating the myriad of cameras and equipment available [http://www.bhphotovideo.com]).

It is also possible to distribute photos over the internet from the crime scene to other locations (i.e., police headquarters, crime lab, district attorney's office, etc.) One must be aware, however, of caveats to digital photography. Security of digital images must be thoroughly maintained. Once a digital photo goes "viral" on the web, it can never be retrieved. It is also important to demonstrate any modification that has been made to original images. Software such as Adobe Photoshop, which can be used to enhance and restore poor photographs, allows for claims that the photo was manipulated. Such claims could be used to render a photograph inadmissible in court. Therefore, it is important to retain original photos and keep a log of any digital enhancements made to the photo.

Number of Photographs

How many photographs should be taken? There is no simple answer, but as a general rule, it is better to overshoot a crime scene (take more photographs than are necessary) than to economize and take too few. Another consideration is that the more photos taken, the more which have to be stored. Time, moreover, may be a concern. Certain types of cases must be processed quickly. In the final analysis, the experience of the crime scene photographer will best answer the question of the number of photos to take.

Photographs serve a number of purposes. They aid in refreshing the memories of witnesses and investigators and show the relationships of items of evidence at the crime scene (Figure 5.5). A very important purpose of crime scene photographs is that they help to convey an image of the crime scene and the circumstances of the crime to the jury.

With these purposes in mind, a number of important photographs should be made in almost every crime scene, including the following:

- *Location.* Photographs of the location of the crime scene should be made. In the case of a residence, for example, the exterior of the dwelling should be shot, including the locations of doors and windows. Photographs of surrounding areas of the house should be included, such as the front and backyards and views in each direction. Aerial photographs are often useful to depict the location of the principal site and other areas of interest in proximity to the crime scene. Pictures from Google Maps can also provide useful perspectives.
- *Witness photographs.* Witness photographs are overall photos of the crime scene. They depict the scene as observed by a witness. In the case of a murder crime scene in a house, such photographs might depict the victim lying on the floor as viewed from a number of locations in the room. These photographs are designed to tell a story, to relate what the location looked like to someone who was not present. To accomplish this task, several overlapping photographs should be made. In addition, long- and intermediate-range photographs should be taken to show perspective and the relative positions of different items found at the crime scene. These are also referred to as establishing shots.

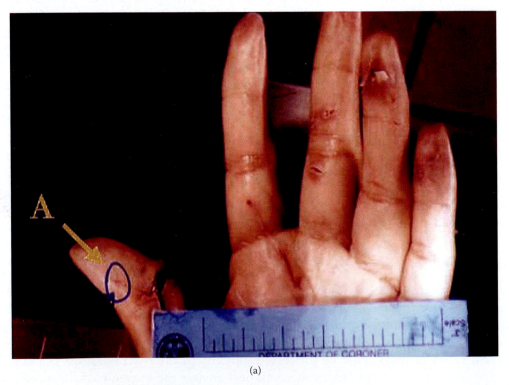

(a)

Figure 5.5 During a violent struggle, the victim's left thumb (a) sustained a defense wound. In the ensuing struggle, the victim's blood was deposited onto the suspect's shirt (b). The suspect claimed that the blood was the result of his attempt to save the victim. Close examination of the lower left side of the shirt shows a transfer stain that looks like the victim attempted to grab the shirt with his bloody left hand (c). (Courtesy of the Los Angeles County Sheriff's Department.)

(b)

(c)

Figure 5.5 (*Continued*)

- *Close-up photographs.* In addition to long- and intermediate-range photos, close-up pictures should also be taken to further clarify the scene. Two photographs should be routinely taken: (1) one showing the item as it actually appears and (2) a photograph of the same item with a ruler or scale included. It is important that the plane of the film be parallel to the plane of the object. The ruler and the parallel film plane ensure the ability later to produce good-quality enlargements or 1:1 photographs of the evidence (Figure 5.6a and b).
- *Evidence photographs.* Photographs of all items of evidence should be made before their removal or changing the location or position of items in any way. Photographs should be made of shoe imprints, fingerprints, bloodstains, weapons, defense wounds, and other such items. Additional photographs should be taken during the crime scene search as new items of evidence are discovered when items at the crime scene are moved.
- *Spectator photographs.* Photographs of onlookers and spectators who have assembled to view the crime scene and police activity should also be captured. Often times the perpetrator remains behind at the crime scene and mixes in with the crowd in order to watch.

When taking photographs, a photo log is recommended. Some police agencies use preprinted forms and others keep track of photographs by some other means. A typical log might include the case number, date, time, photographer's name, type of camera, lens, and a listing of each photograph. The list may include the shutter speed, f-stop, and a very brief description of the location of the evidence. Normally, photographs should be taken at eye level to give the proper perspective of the scene. If the photo is taken from a different perspective, it should be noted in the log. Digital cameras will also mark other photo data in the picture's file when it is saved to the memory card.

The type of lens used also affects the perspective of the scene. A normal lens should be used, such as a 50-mm lens in the 35-mm format. If the crime scene is indoors with cramped quarters, medium-wide-angle lenses may be used; however, the lens change should be noted in the photo log.

When using a flash, in most cases, it should not be mounted on the top of the camera, but should be held off at an angle when shooting. This is to prevent a reflection in the photo from flash bounce. In low-light situations, flash photography is recommended even though high-speed film may handle these situations. Most shooting is done with a handheld camera, but for exposures less than 1/60th of a second, a tripod should be used to ensure sharp photographs.

Photographs should accurately represent the crime scene as seen by the witness or investigator. They should be clear and sharp. Extraneous subjects and items at the scene do not belong in the photographs; crime scene equipment and personnel should not be present in photographs.

Posed photographs that locate where a witness stood when first entering the crime scene may be taken. A photograph should then be taken from that location to show the appearance of the crime scene from that point of observation.

This section is not meant to be an all-encompassing guide to crime scene photography, but rather to present some important points to consider. Several worthwhile classes in general photography that give the beginning crime scene photographer the basics on the subject of photography are offered in colleges and adult education programs. Universities and junior colleges with police science programs may offer classes on crime scene photography.

(a)

(b)

Figure 5.6 (a) Designed by the American Board of Forensic Odontology (ABFO), this scale has become the standard for measurement and photography. The incorporation of three circles is useful in helping to compensate for distortion resulting from oblique camera angles. Graduations are all metric except for the width of the legs, which are 25 cm wide. The 1 cm division lines are traced and extended across the photographic print to grid an image. Measurements within the image are then made relative to these inscribed 1 cm grid lines to compensate for any distortion resulting from no parallelism between the film and the object planes. (b) Scales included in a photo can come in a variety of forms. In a situation where no scale is available, an object of known length should be placed in the photo if the evidence needs to be gathered quickly.

Professional organizations like the International Association for Identification have presentations on crime scene photography from time to time at annual seminars.

Admissibility of Photographs

For a photograph to be admissible in court, the investigator must be able to testify that it accurately depicts the area shown. To be accurate, it must represent the subject matter properly in terms of color, scale, and form. Photographs must be in focus and should show the relationships and distances between objects. Crime scene sketches (discussed later) also assist in depicting the crime scene.

All digital files from the crime scene photographs should be retained. They are important to demonstrate that the picture has not been altered. These are also important if enlargements or enhancements of certain areas of the photo are needed to better depict parts of the crime scene. Computer software (such as Veripic [www.veripic.com]) that can prove that images were not manipulated and can accurately manage photos is available.

Video

Another method of recording the crime scene is video. Lightweight, portable, low-light video cameras are ideally suited for gathering a video rendition of a crime scene. Videography does not do away with the need for still crime-scene photographs, but has the advantage of more graphically depicting the scene.

When videotaping a scene, the investigator should walk the video operator through the location. The video should begin outside an indoor crime scene or with an overall pan of the outdoor location. The detective should narrate the video by recording the audio portion as the video is shot. The narration should include the name of the speaker, time, date, location, case number, and other pertinent identifying information.

If digital recordings are to be used as evidence, they should not be edited or erased. The entire recording must be in its original condition if it is to be admissible as evidence. Some agencies use edited videos solely to refresh the investigator's memory. Courts may or may not admit these recordings for the jury's consideration. As with most generalizations on the legal aspects of crime scenes, it is prudent to check with local authorities to determine what will be acceptable to the prosecution and to the court. It is better to find out in advance rather than to assume the practice is acceptable and then find out that a key piece of evidence is excluded for some legal reason not considered by the investigator.

While the scene is being recorded, other personnel at the location should be silent because their voices can be picked up. Such conversations may prove distracting and sometimes embarrassing if recorded.

As with photographs, close-up video recordings of small items of evidence should contain a scale to show the actual size of the item. Additionally, panning the area and zooming in on the item should show the relative location.

It is also worthwhile to video the crowd of onlookers and spectators that gather around the crime scene. Oftentimes suspects stick around and blend in with the crowd to observe the response of law enforcement to the crime scene. This video can be analyzed later on once a suspect is developed to see if he was in the crowd of onlookers. The video can also be shown to any victims and/or witnesses to see if they recognize the perpetrator in the crowd behind the crime scene tape.

Sketching the Crime Scene

Photographs alone are not sufficient for recording a crime scene adequately. A crime scene sketch should also be routinely made. Sketches and photographs complement each other to depict the crime scene adequately and properly. Sketches clarify the appearance of the crime scene and make it easier to comprehend. It is, therefore, important for investigators to develop the ability to make good crime scene sketches.

A crime scene sketch is not considered an architectural drawing, such as one drawn by an artist or forensic surveyor. It is simply an illustrative diagram or drawing that accurately depicts the appearance of the crime scene. Nevertheless, sketching the crime scene requires some skill on the part of the investigator. Generally, it is easier if two people work on the sketch: one person to draw and the other to take measurements.

Sketches sometimes leave out important information or contain errors. Yet, despite these drawbacks to and problems in making crime scene sketches, they do provide important information and, when done properly, are very helpful. Sketches help investigators recall details of the crime scene. They also aid prosecutors, courts, and juries to better understand the crime scene (Figure 5.7).

Sketches offer a permanent record of the relationship of items at the scene to each other and help to supplement photographs. They depict the overall layout of the location

Figure 5.7 Crime scene sketch. (Courtesy of Jeff Buszka, Special Investigations Unit, NYC Office of Chief Medical Examiner.)

more easily than can be accomplished by photographs. Sketches also allow for selectivity. A sketch may be drawn purposely to leave out extraneous or confusing details that would be recorded in a photograph.

Crime scene sketches can provide a record of conditions that are not readily recorded by other means. Distances can be shown over large areas and topography can be easily illustrated. Paths taken by subjects or vehicles can be demonstrated on drawings more easily than on photographs. Drawings may be used to aid in questioning suspects and witnesses of crimes and to authenticate testimony of witnesses. Sketches combine the best features of photographs and crime scene notes.

Information Included in Crime Scene Sketches

What information should be present on a sketch? Information placed on a sketch is used to make the drawing understandable and admissible into evidence. Like all evidence, it should contain case-identifying information: case number; name of suspect, victim, and investigator; person drawing the diagram; and date and time the sketch was made. It should contain a scale, if required, and distance measurements between items present on the sketch. The location depicted in the drawing and reference points to located items should be included. A legend or key may be helpful to identify and clarify portions of the drawing and the direction of North.

Equipment

Writing materials are, of course, required. Although pens may be used, lead pencils are easier to work with, especially if erasures are made. Colored pencils are also useful to outline important items. Graph paper is best to use, although blank paper will do. Graph paper simplifies scale drawings and provides guidelines for line measurements. Some sort of drawing surface, such as a clipboard, is helpful.

Measuring devices such as rulers and tapes are required. A 50- or 100-foot surveyor's tape is especially useful to measure longer distances. A folding 6-foot carpenter's ruler is also a useful piece of measuring equipment. Inexpensive laser and infrared measuring devices used by realtors and contractors make measuring interiors very easy. Finally, a compass is useful to determine the direction. A total station can also be used to take measurements of outdoor scenes.

Types of Sketches

Different types of indoor and outdoor crime scene locations present different problems in sketching. To best represent the crime scene, it may be necessary to rely upon different types of sketches. The type of sketch chosen by an investigator is not especially important. What is important is that the resulting drawing best depicts the crime scene and most easily illustrates the event to the viewer.

The overview, floor plan, or bird's-eye-view sketch is the simplest and most common one used in diagramming crime scenes. It may be used in nearly all crime scene situations where the items of interest are located in one plane. In addition to its simplicity, it is also the easiest for laypeople, such as jury members, to grasp.

Another type of crime scene sketch is the elevation drawing. This type of sketch is used when the vertical, rather than the horizontal, plane is of interest. Thus, if bloodstains were present on a wall of a house, the elevation drawing of the wall would be used to depict this scene.

The cross-projection, or exploded, view is a combination of the preceding two types. It is similar to the floor plan sketch, except the walls have been folded down into the same plane as the floor.

The perspective drawing is another type of sketch that depicts a three-dimensional drawing of the scene. Although the final drawing will be very clear if done properly, this type of sketch requires considerable artistic skill and, therefore, is generally not recommended.

Locating Objects in the Sketch

Once the drawing has been made and the relative locations of the items have been sketched in, it is necessary to locate them in the sketch. Location is defined as the actual position where the object is located in the crime scene. A position on a plane or flat surface is defined by two measurements. A knife located on the floor of a room requires two measurements from two fixed points to locate its position on the floor accurately. A measurement to show location could be taken from the north wall and the east wall, for example, 3 feet from the north wall and 6 feet, 7 inches from the east wall.

Although perpendicular measurements are the easiest to use, they may be impossible in outdoor crime scenes. In those situations, it is necessary to find fixed points to locate the item in question. This can be done by using telephone poles, fire hydrants, trees, the exterior corner of a building, and so on. Whatever the item of reference used, it must be permanent and identifiable. The number on a telephone pole, a street address, or a roadside marker may be used as a point of reference to locate an object.

GPS, or global positioning system devices, are used in a variety of industries and have become useful for locating the position of evidence in remote outdoor crime scenes. Locations are given using latitude and longitude.

Computer Programs

Commercial computer software and hardware is available to render drawings of crime scenes in two- and three-dimensional views. In addition to the ability to draw crime scenes to scale, computer programs have been used to depict trajectories in shooting scenes and to help reconstruct crime scenes. Some of the programs are able to depict the scene in three dimensions on a video monitor and take a viewer through the scene by means of computer graphics. In the courtroom, these systems have been used to project the video image onto a screen and explain to a jury the sequence of events in a crime scene. Software can be used to depict the crime scene in pictorial form as seen from the perspective of the victim or the suspect. There are a number of relatively inexpensive computer-aided drawing programs available that easily lend themselves to crime scene drawing for jury presentation.

Admissibility of Sketches

As with photographs, the sketch may be entered into evidence only by someone competent to testify about its authenticity. The qualified individual must be able to testify that the sketch is a true and accurate representation of the original scene.

Figure 5.8 Floor plan diagram of crime scene showing results of DNA typing on bloodstains from two different people found throughout different rooms in an apartment. (Courtesy of the Special Investigations Unit, NYC Office of Chief Medical Examiner.)

Crime scene diagrams are extremely useful in court presentations. In major crime cases, the original crime scene sketch is used frequently as the basis for a finished drawing made by an artist or by using a computer program. In some instances where the scene is particularly complex, an architectural model may prove useful to detail the crime scene (Figure 5.8).

Collection of Evidence

Following the initial crime scene search, photography, and sketching of the crime scene, physical evidence may be collected. It is useful to set priorities as to which evidence will be collected first based on the type of case and circumstances surrounding the evidence. While there is no set rule as to in what order evidence should be collected, the most fragile evidence such as fingerprints, touch DNA, and trace evidence should be given attention first (Figure 5.9). Once this has been accomplished, the scene should be searched a second time to make certain that potential evidence was not overlooked.

Evidence that is to be sent to the crime laboratory should be packaged to prevent breakage, spoilage, or contamination that will destroy its value. Evidence containers should be sealed and be strong enough so that they will not break in transit. When evidence consists of several objects, they should be packaged in separate containers or wrapped individually.

(a)

(b)

Figure 5.9 Occasionally, a criminal leaves behind an item that at first glance may not seem important to the case. This flashlight (a) was left at a murder scene; no prints were found on the exterior. Fingerprints, however, were developed on one of the batteries (b) housed in the flashlight that led to the identification and arrest of a suspect in the case. (Courtesy of the Los Angeles County Sheriff's Department.)

Each package should be clearly marked as to its contents and then packed in a shipping container. Bottles and glass containers containing liquid should not be packaged with other evidence because they may break and contaminate the other exhibits. If Styrofoam or other packing material is used for cushioning, any objects that might be altered by contact with such packing material should be separated and wrapped. Commercially available evidence boxes can be purchased from a number of police equipment suppliers, which make packaging evidence very easy.

Even if objects have been individually identified, they should also be marked with the recovering officer's initials and the date collected so that the identity of a given object cannot be questioned. Identification markings may be placed directly on the object or on a tag attached directly to the object. When this is not practical, markings are placed onto the sealed container housing the evidence.

A voucher with a complete inventory of all items submitted and a request for laboratory examination should be included with each shipment. The inventory enables lab personnel to check the contents so that small objects among the many items are not misplaced or overlooked. The request for specific examinations allows the forensic science laboratory to determine what needs to be done.

The written request to the laboratory about the case should be as complete as possible, listing the sequence of events, and the statements of the suspect, the victim, witnesses, etc. This information assists the examiner's evaluation of which laboratory tests are required. The information may also provide answers to questions that come up as a result of the laboratory's findings or provide confirmation of findings that necessarily went beyond those specifically requested. It may be helpful to include copies of pertinent police reports or interrogations. It is also beneficial for the investigator and forensic scientist to speak to each other to determine the best course of examinations to be done on the items of evidence submitted (Figure 5.10).

The following is a brief description of packaging instructions for certain items of evidence:

- Objects with fingerprints or glove prints should be packed so that they do not come in contact with each other or the package sides.
- Tool marks on objects should be protected from contamination and moisture. Marks may be protected from rust by a light film of oil if transfer of trace material is not indicated.
- Clothing containing dry biological stains (blood, semen, or saliva) should be wrapped separately and in such a way that the stains are not broken or rubbed off.
- The victim's clothing must not be packaged or come in contact with the suspect's.
- Strands of hair on garments should not be allowed to come in contact with other garments that may contain hair.
- Firearms should be rigidly fixed inside a container unloaded without further wrapping. Postal regulations should be consulted before mailing firearms.
- Cartridge cases and bullets should be packed separately with soft cushioning material. Federal regulations should be consulted before shipping.
- Live cartridges and explosives should be packed in cushioning material to protect fingerprints and shipped by a parcel carrier clearly labeled.

Figure 5.10 Tests performed on items of evidence should always be clearly documented so that anyone reading a scientist's or examiner's notes later on will know exactly what was done. (Courtesy of the Los Angeles County Sheriff's Department.)

- Stomach contents and organs for toxicological examination should be placed in tightly sealed glass jars and packed in cushioning material. The containers should be of a size proportionate to the amount of fluid so that volatile agents do not evaporate.
- Controlled substances should be tightly cushioned in vials or pillboxes so that they will not break. Absorbent cotton should be used.
- Arson evidence should be placed inside a new metal paint can to prevent evaporation of any volatile compounds and sealed.
- DNA swabs should be dried and placed in an envelope or cardboard swab container and sealed.
- Sharp objects, such as knives or needles, should be secured to a cardboard or plastic container to prevent them from poking through the packaging material.
- Charred paper should be packed in sturdy boxes and supported on all sides with absorbent cotton. The container should preferably not be shipped, but hand-carried to the laboratory. It is also possible to place the charred paper in a large plastic bag that is inflated and sealed tightly.

Proper packaging of evidence cannot be overemphasized. When in doubt, contact the crime laboratory.

Chapter Questions

1. List eight of the general recommended procedures when taking notes at a crime scene.

2. Describe what procedures you would take to prevent fellow officers who are not assigned to the case from entering the crime scene.

3. Which of the following is an important detail to include in your notes when investigating a burglary scene?
   a) The description of the scene and the surrounding location
   b) The name of the victim
   c) Lighting conditions
   d) All of the above

4. Once the initial survey of the scene takes place, the scene is then processed. List the five things that are typically done when processing a scene.

5. You are tasked with searching for footwear prints on the floor at the scene of a breaking and entering. Once located, how would you collect these shoeprints?
   a) Use an electrostatic dust lifter
   b) Make a detailed and scaled drawing of the pattern
   c) Use oblique lighting
   d) None of the above

6. You are processing a vehicle that had been stolen from a homicide victim's home. Which of the following would be the most appropriate course of action?
   a) Fingerprint the interior and then vacuum for trace evidence
   b) Fingerprint the interior and then the exterior and then collect any hairs or fibers
   c) Collect trace evidence from the interior first and then process for fingerprints
   d) Use specialized chemicals to search for fingerprints and then collect trace evidence after the chemicals dry

7. These two things will ensure the ability to produce good quality enlargements or 1:1 photographs of evidence.
   a) A ruler and parallel film plane
   b) A parallel film plane and macro lens
   c) A ruler and macro lens
   d) A ruler and a corresponding establishing shot

8. Describe what information should be included in crime scene sketches.

9. This type of sketch is the most appropriate for depicting only the horizontal plane of the crime scene.
   a) Floor plan
   b) Elevation
   c) Exploded
   d) Perspective

10. Out of the following pieces of evidence, which one should be collected first at a crime scene?
    a) Fingerprints
    b) Gun
    c) Cartridge cases
    d) Clothing

Establishing Identity

6

One of the most important purposes of physical evidence is to establish the identity of the suspect or victim. This identification is possible through a variety of methods discussed in this chapter. Fingerprints are usually thought of first when considering methods of identifying individuals.*† However, techniques such as handwriting examination, forensic anthropology, and forensic odontology are also important and will be discussed. DNA typing is also widely used in establishing identity and will be covered in its own chapter (Chapter 8).

Fingerprints and Palm Prints

Some of the most valuable clues at the crime scene are fingerprints and palm prints (bare footprints are sometimes discovered and may also identify a person, provided there are known exemplars). Prints are conclusive evidence. An expert's report may state three possible findings:

1. The subject made the print.
2. The subject could not have made the print.
3. The print had insufficient detail to be evaluated.

The value of fingerprints is greatly enhanced by the possibility of identifying a criminal through searching a single fingerprint file or an AFIS (Automated Fingerprint Identification System).

In this section, the term "fingerprints" includes all types of prints of friction ridge skin. Prints of the palms or soles of the foot are made under the same conditions as fingerprints and are preserved in the same manner. It is sometimes difficult to decide whether a print has been left by a finger, the palm, or the sole of a foot. For this reason, in ordinary speech, the term fingerprint has come to also include prints of the palms or feet.

How Does Fingerprint Evidence Occur?

When criminals work, they cannot avoid leaving clues in the form of fingerprints unless they wear gloves or some other form of protection. Prints are formed by friction ridges, which deposit grease and perspiration on the object touched, and may be produced when

---

* Forensic science professional organizations play an important role for practitioners who need to stay current in new technologies. The premier association dealing with forensic identification, for example, fingerprints, is the International Association for Identification (IAI). Anyone seriously engaged in the field of forensic identification should consider membership in the IAI as well as state divisions of the IAI.
† SWGFAST, the Scientific Working Group on Friction Ridge Analysis, Study and Technology, http://www.swgfast.org/index.html.

criminals take hold of an object or support themselves with their hands. Prints may be formed when fingers are contaminated with foreign material, such as dirt, blood, or grease, or when the fingers are pressed against a plastic material and produce a negative impression of the pattern of the friction ridges.

Where to Look for Fingerprints

In burglary investigations, the perpetrator's point of entry should be the place at which to start a search for prints. It may be possible at that point to determine if the burglar worked with gloves or uncovered hands. If a door was broken open, prints (including shoe prints) may be located on the lock, the immediate surroundings, or other places on the door where the entry had been forced. With broken windows, particular attention should be given to search for pieces of broken glass, which are useful for standards and may contain prints or blood. The common method to break a window is to knock a small hole in a windowpane. A burglar can then break away pieces of glass with his fingers until he has succeeded in making an opening large enough to be able to reach the window latch. Often, fingerprints or glove prints are found on broken pieces of glass. Broken glass does not always lie just inside the window because burglars sometimes dispose of the broken glass shards to conceal the entry. Fingerprints may be left on the inside of the windowsill, the window frame, and jamb when the burglar climbs through the window and grips these parts of the window frame.

Searches for fingerprints also should be made in areas where the burglar is suspected to have eaten or had a drink.* Prints on glass or china are generally of good quality. If the criminal became drunk at the scene, productive results can be expected from the print search. In some cases, the burglar wore gloves at the start, began drinking alcohol, and gradually became intoxicated. Forgetting caution, the gloves were removed. If the burglar removed liquor bottles from the scene, prints may be found on glasses or china or on bottles that were moved and examined by the thief (Figure 6.1a and b).

Light switches, circuit breakers, and fuses should always be examined, as well as any light bulbs that were loosened or removed. If the criminal wore gloves, special care should be taken at places where the activity was of a type in which gloves would have been a hindrance. For example, opening a case or drawers with difficult locks or searching in the drawers of a bureau may be difficult with gloves. Burglars will remove gloves during the crime and leave fingerprints at the scene. If the thief used the toilet, he might have removed his gloves. Prints should be searched for on the toilet-flush lever, under the toilet seat, on the door lock, and on any paper that may have been used.

Burglars sometimes bring tools or other objects to the scene and leave them behind. Fingerprints may be detected on papers used to wrap tools, on flashlights (do not forget to examine the batteries), and other items such as the inside of latex gloves. All smooth surfaces on which prints could have been left should be examined. Good prints are often found on glass; china; polished, painted, or otherwise smooth surfaces; smooth cardboard cartons, and paper. In some cases, prints have been recovered on rough surfaces, starched

---

* Property crime DNA testing is becoming much more widely used. Investigators should consider the possibility of obtaining DNA samples from foodstuffs and evidence containing saliva (drinking containers and cigarettes) and clothing with possible perspiration and skin cells (hats, headbands, etc.).

(a)

(b)

Figure 6.1 The suspect entered a convenience store in Kodiak, Alaska, where he robbed the clerk, hit her in the head with a gun, and forced her into a back room, where he tied her up with an electrical extension cord and attempted to rape her. The police developed a good suspect, but the clerk was unable to identify him. Inked finger and palm prints were submitted and identification was made from the latent prints developed on the plug (a, b) of the extension cord. (Courtesy of the Alaska Department of Public Safety, Scientific Crime Detection Laboratory, Latent Print Section.)

collars; cuffs, and newspapers. When examining furniture, do not omit places the criminal may have touched when pulling out drawers or moving the furniture. Even if the thief worked with gloved hands, prints may have been left when a heavy piece of furniture was moved because the gloves may have slipped and a part of the wrist or palm left a print (Figure 6.2).

(a)

(b)

(c)

Figure 6.2 Black fingerprint powder is the most common means to visualize latent prints on most nonporous surfaces (a, b). The technique is easy to use and inexpensive, but can be messy. Using a ductless fume hood (c) is an effective way to reduce the amount of fingerprint powder in the workplace. (Courtesy of the Los Angeles County Sheriff's Department.)

A flashlight is a good tool for searching for latent prints. Fingerprints can be observed by holding the flashlight at low angles so that the surface is observed under oblique lighting. However, flashlights may not work on all surfaces. If prints are expected in a particular place and they are not discovered, the area must be examined by special methods described under the heading "Fingerprint Developing Techniques."

Different Types of Fingerprints

Fingerprints can be divided into three main groups: (1) plastic fingerprints, (2) prints of fingers contaminated with some foreign matter or "visible prints," and (3) latent fingerprints.

- *Plastic fingerprints* occur when a finger touches or presses against plastic material and creates a negative impression of its friction ridge pattern (Figure 6.3). These prints are found in thick layers of dust, on substances that melt easily or soften when held in the hand (e.g., chocolate), and on materials such as fresh paint, adhesive tape, plastic explosives, putty that has not hardened, candle wax, sealing wax, fats, flour, soap, thick and sticky oily films, grease, pitch, tar, resin, and clay, to name a few.
- *Prints from fingers contaminated with foreign matter* are common. Dust prints occur when a finger is pressed in a thin layer of dust and some of the dust sticks on the friction ridges. When the finger is then placed on a clean surface, a fingerprint results. In some cases, a dust print may be fully identifiable and may be clear enough to search in a single fingerprint file. Prints can be left when fingers are contaminated with other substances like pigments, ink, soot, flour, face powder, oils, safe insulation, or blood.
- *Latent fingerprints* result from small amounts of grease, sweat, and dirt deposited on a surface. Skin on the hands and soles of the feet have no oil glands. Grease found on fingers comes from other parts of the body that the hands touched. Secretion from friction skin contains 98.5%–99.5% water; the balance is organic

Figure 6.3 This plastic print, in Mikrosil, is a negative impression of the actual print.

and inorganic components. If the hands are cold, practically no liquid is secreted; when they become warm, secretion returns to normal. Latent prints are most often found on objects with polished or smooth surfaces and on paper. However, under some conditions they may also be detected on rough surfaces, and even on smooth fabrics. "Latent prints" include those invisible to the unaided eye plus all others that are visible but only properly examined after development.

Fingerprint Developing Techniques

Many advances in fingerprint technology are occurring continually, specifically in techniques for visualizing prints. Most of these techniques involve chemical reagents that react with materials present in the components that make up the print or contaminants. Collaboration between forensic chemists and forensic identification specialists has made these techniques possible, and continued effort is to be encouraged. Forensic chemists and criminalists should be assigned to identification units within laboratories to work with fingerprint and identification specialists to develop and use chemical-based fingerprint visualization techniques.

Many procedures are available to develop latent fingerprints.* Those listed in the next sections are some of the standard procedures in use; however, new ones are developed regularly. *It is important to understand that practical experience with these procedures is needed to use them effectively.* Certain methods work better than others do for different materials. The sequence of using these procedures is also important because it is possible to use multiple procedures, one following the other, to search for prints. Some procedures have an adverse effect on other types of evidence; for example, certain solvents can cause inks to run on documents or render biological evidence unsuitable for DNA typing. Latent fingerprint examiners are cautioned that they should understand if any of these techniques might adversely interact with other classes of evidence before trying them on casework. Latent print examiners should work closely with forensic scientists to develop procedures for using chemical developing methods with safeguards to avoid destruction of other types of physical evidence. Latent print examiners should consider forming regional user groups to help keep up with rapidly changing technology. Such groups are made up of local practitioners who meet quarterly and share technical experiences with other practitioners. These regional groups are especially helpful in small identification sections with only one or two examiners, who may be unable to attend technical conferences.

Development with Powders

Brushing fingerprint powder over a latent print makes the print visible. The substances that form the print show up, and the print becomes fully visible. The choice of powder depends partly on the kind of surface on which the print is found and partly on how it is to be preserved. If the latent print is of high quality, the choice of powder for development is not especially important. Several types of fingerprint powders are commercially available: black, white, colored, aluminum, copper, fluorescent, and magnetic. The type used is determined by the color of the background and the nature of the surface.

* The Fingerprint Sourcebook by the SWGFAST aims to be the definitive resource on the science of fingerprint identification, http://www.nij.gov/pubs-sum/225320.htm, March 2011.

MSDS or Material Safety Data Sheets for fingerprint powders are available from suppliers and online. Common sense suggests that long-term exposure to fine particulate matter may cause respiratory problems over time. Persons who routinely use fingerprint powders can wear dust masks or specially designed fingerprint hoods to minimize the amount of powder breathed.

Fiberglass, animal hair, and synthetic or natural fiber brushes may be used to develop fingerprints. If the brush is damp or oily, it is useless. The brush is first lightly dipped in the powder and then tapped with the finger so that only a small amount of the powder is left on the brush. The object is then lightly brushed in curved strokes. Powder particles will adhere to all places where there is grease or dirt. If fingerprints are present on the object, they show up more or less clearly.

Powder should not be sprinkled over or tapped onto the object while brushing. Prints from sweaty or dirty fingers or produced by a firm grip may cause the friction ridges to spread out, filling up the spaces between the ridges. Too much powder can destroy these prints. If too much powder is used, it can be "washed" by pressing a fingerprint lifter against the print. The lifter will remove the excess, and the spaces between the ridges may be nearly free of powder. If necessary, the latent print can be reprocessed to get useable results (Figure 6.4a and b).

Some fingerprint examiners use black fingerprint powder as a universal developer on smooth nonporous surfaces. On dark surfaces, such as furniture and firearms, aluminum or copper powders give good results. These powders are useful if the print is to be photographed before being lifted. Remember: aluminum-powdered lifts appear reversed from prints developed with black powder.

Perspiration and grease from fingerprints absorb into porous surfaces such as paper and cardboard and do not usually give results with powdering methods. On porous items,

(a)

Figure 6.4 Latent prints can be developed using a combination of cyanoacrylate, or superglue, and fluorescent powders or dyes that can be visualized under UV light, laser, or alternative light sources. (a) and (b) are latent prints developed on multicolored, glossy-coated papers. (Courtesy of the Zurich Cantonal Police, Forensic Science Department.)

(b)

Figure 6.4 (*Continued*)

Figure 6.5 Magnetic fingerprint powders work well on some items. Only the rays of the magnetic powder come in contact with the surface. (Courtesy of the Los Angeles County Sheriff's Department.)

another method should be used, such as iodine, ninhydrin, or silver nitrate treatment. Another aid to fingerprint development, the Magna-Brush, utilizes magnetic powders and a magnetic applicator. Streamers of magnetized powder are brought in contact with the suspected surface. Powder adheres to the latent print, while the magnet removes the excess. This method has the advantage of not leaving excess powder on the object and the surrounding area. Because of the nature of the process, it can be used effectively only on nonmagnetic surfaces (Figure 6.5). Fluorescent powders are yet another type that may be used in some special cases. Available in powder and aerosol forms, these powders are used to dust paper currency and documents and are sprayed in areas where recurring thefts take place. They are technically not fingerprint powders because they are used prior to the prints being deposited (Figure 6.6a–e).

After the suspect has handled the money or touched the dusted area, the area is examined with UV light. The latent fingerprint is easily visualized by UV light and may be photographed using proper photographic techniques.

Amido Black. This stain turns proteins present in blood blue-black. It does not react with any of the normal components of fingerprints and should be used in conjunction with

(a)

(b)

Figure 6.6 In this series of photographs, (a, b) some of the steps used in super glue fuming in a humidity chamber, followed by (c) using a high-intensity dye-stain, and (d) examining the evidence under high-intensity light, followed by (e) computer enhanced examination of the prints. While these techniques may be time consuming, they can lead to outstanding results. (Courtesy of the Los Angeles County Sheriff's Department.)

(c)

(d)

(e)

Figure 6.6 (*Continued*)

other developing techniques. Other more sensitive stains such as Coomassie blue, a general protein stain used in forensic biology, may be considered. Fingerprint specialists should always consult forensic biologists before using any protein stains on bloody fingerprints because some stains may cause difficulties in DNA testing.

DFO (1,8-diazafluoren-9-one). DFO is a ninhydrin-like analogue. It reacts with proteins to give a highly fluorescent, red-colored product that is more sensitive than ninhydrin. Although some prints developed using DFO will be visible to the naked eye, illumination with high-intensity light improves the sensitivity; however, interference may become a problem from certain colored inks and papers that fluoresce. Longer wavelength light sources, such as mercury vapor lamps at 546 nm, lessen the interference. Ninhydrin may be used in conjunction with DFO; however, DFO must be used first.

Fluorescence examination. Using lasers, alternative light sources, or UV lamps on untreated surfaces may yield prints. Various naturally occurring chemicals and contaminants present in latent prints fluoresce without treatment with laser-sensitive dyes. Although the chance of finding autofluorescent latent prints is limited, the ease of the procedure suggests its use.

Gentian violet or crystal violet. This dye produces a purple color and stains the fatty components of latent prints. It is especially effective when used on the sticky side of adhesive tape. The material is toxic, and appropriate laboratory precautions must be taken. Using a laser increases the sensitivity of the procedure. A yellow-orange light source yields the best results, for example, a copper vapor laser at the 578-nm line. An alternative dye, Basic Fuchsin, yields good results with green excitation and has an absorption maximum at about 500 nm.

Iodine. Iodine is one of the oldest methods of visualizing latent prints on porous and nonporous substrates. The technique is simple to use; however, iodine vapors are toxic and corrosive and the reaction is not permanent. Methods have been introduced for fixing prints developed by iodine fuming, for example, 7,8-benzoflavone, which also increases sensitivity.

Ninhydrin solution. Ninhydrin is another technique for use with porous surfaces, for example, paper, cardboard, wallboard, and raw wood. Ninhydrin reacts with amino acids to form a purple-colored compound called "Ruhemann's purple." The reaction is speeded up by means of humidity and elevated temperatures (Figure 6.7). Treating with zinc chloride

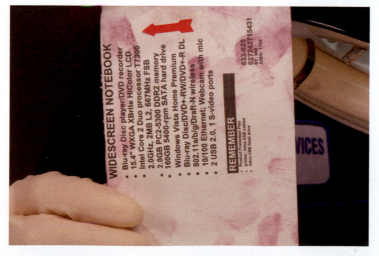

Figure 6.7 The characteristic Ruhemann's purple caused by the reaction of ninhydrin on proteins left on paper products. (Courtesy of the Los Angeles County Sheriff's Department.)

solution and viewing with a laser improve sensitivity of the techniques. Background fluorescence may be overcome by using cadmium nitrate solution cooled to liquid nitrogen temperatures and viewed with a laser. Modifications to the chemical structure of ninhydrin have been synthesized and show usefulness under certain conditions. The importance of these analogues is that they fluoresce at different wavelengths and provide a way to overcome background interference from certain substrates.

Physical developer (PD; also called stabilized physical developer, or SPD). PD is a silver-based solution used as a substitute for the conventional latent print silver nitrate procedure. PD is useful in detecting latent prints on porous surfaces that are wet or have been wet, for example, paper, cardboard, and raw wood. The technique may be used following ninhydrin. PD reacts with components of sweat and appears in shades from gray to almost black. PD-developed prints are preserved by photography.

Silver nitrate. Silver nitrate solution reacts with chlorides in prints, but with the advent of PD it is not in widespread use. It may have some application on raw wood; however, the background staining of the substrate may cause problems in photography.

Small particle reagent (SPR). This is a wet process for developing latent prints on wet surfaces. The reagent is a suspension of molybdenum disulfide particles prepared in a detergent solution. Molybdenum adheres to lipids found in prints as a gray deposit. The process works well on nonporous surfaces, for example, plastic bags, wax paper, glass, and painted surfaces, and may be used effectively on water-soaked firearms. Visible prints may be lifted and/or photographed.

Sudan black. This process is used on nonporous articles, for example, glass, plastics, and metal. Usually less sensitive than SPR, it may be the method of choice if the substrate is oily or greasy. Sudan black reacts with the lipid components of prints and stains them blue-black. It is messy to use and not effective on dark-colored objects.

Superglue or cyanoacrylate fuming. Superglue is used on nonporous surfaces to produce visible prints that are white (Figure 6.8). The visible prints may be dusted with powder, photographed and lifted, or washed with laser-sensitive dyes such as Rhodamine 6G and others, and viewed with lasers or alternative light sources. Superglue fuming is one of the

Figure 6.8 Cyanoacrylate fuming of a credit card.

Figure 6.9 The VMD places a thin film of gold followed by a film of zinc on latent prints left on smooth surfaces such as plastic bags. VMD is a very sensitive technique for fingerprint development on nonporous and semiporous surfaces. (Courtesy of the Los Angeles County Sheriff's Department.)

easier procedures to use; however, in some instances, other latent print visualization techniques may yield superior results.

Vacuum metal deposition (VMD). VMD is an effective technique for most smooth, nonporous surfaces, for example, plastic bags, plastic packaging material, and other smooth surfaces. The major drawback to VMD is that the equipment is expensive and the sample chamber of the vacuum coater is not very large. The procedure evaporates gold or zinc in a vacuum chamber, and a very thin film of the metal is deposited onto the latent print, making it visible (Figure 6.9).

Lasers and Alternative Light Sources

The word laser is an acronym for **L**ight **A**mplification by **S**timulated **E**mission of **R**adiation. The use of lasers and other alternative light sources has been found to be quite effective in locating and visualizing latent prints, as well as other types of physical evidence such as trace evidence and certain types of biological evidence at the crime scene and in the crime lab.

Several types of "alternative light sources" are in current use. No single wave length of light will work best in all forensic applications. Several factors need to be considered in choosing the type of high-intensity light most suitable for use in a forensic laboratory or for field applications. Some of the factors that must be considered are cost, color of light or wavelengths available, light intensity or power output, portability, voltage requirements, safety, available service on an emergency basis, and the ability to use the unit in other forensic applications.

Technology has greatly improved forensic light sources, and a wide variety of units are available; some are very portable and look like handheld flashlights (Figure 6.10a and b).

Naturally, the more sophisticated the unit, the more cost becomes a factor. Some units used in laboratory settings may require special setups and workspace remodeling, for example, darkened work areas to take photographs, laboratory sinks and fume hoods

(a)

(b)

Figure 6.10 (a) A workstation combining an alternative light source, digital camera, and computer hardware and software to achieve good results using chemical processing techniques with latent fingerprints. (Courtesy of the Los Angeles County Sheriff's Department, Scientific Services Bureau.) (b) Cogent Automated Palm and Fingerprint Identification System (CAPFIS) is one of several commercial systems available to law enforcement agencies. CAPFIS is a system that allows for distributed fingerprint and palm print identification/processing systems. (Courtesy of 3M Cogent, Pasadena, CA.)

to handle light-sensitive dyes, power requirements, plumbed in water to cool the unit or additional units to recirculate coolant to the laser, liquid nitrogen for use in certain laser procedures—the list can be formidable and must be considered when budgeting for certain units. Other costs include maintenance and purchase of component parts that must be replaced from time to time.

Safety is a concern with high-intensity light sources. The intensity of the light can cause eye fatigue and eye damage. Persons working with these tools should be required to wear appropriate eye protection to minimize any damage.

Image Processing

New computer technology is being used to enhance latent prints that heretofore were of insufficient quality to be used. Image processing costs have decreased to such a degree that most crime laboratories can afford the hardware and software.

Latent prints are examined by means of a high-resolution digital camera whose output is fed into a computer. Unlike the human eye, the computer is capable of distinguishing among the hundreds of shades of gray that show up as varying degrees of density captured in the image. The computer in turn can process the digital image in several ways. The image can be shown in reverse (equivalent to a photographic reversal or negative) or in color. This is particularly advantageous if the print is on a textured surface that makes it difficult to examine because of the background pattern interfering with the ridge detail of the print.

Various light sources—visible, infrared, UV, high intensity, laser, filtered, and unfiltered—give considerable range to latent print identification. Digitizing images along with readily available computer software gives excellent results.

Automated Fingerprint Identification Systems

AFISs represent the single biggest advance in fingerprint identification technology. They allow for the ability to compare a latent fingerprint discovered at the crime scene to a criminal fingerprint database. The amount of human effort to conduct a manual search for a latent print against several million inked prints is astronomical and prior to AFIS was simply out of the question.

Cold searches or searching a database of several million prints for a single latent found at a crime scene is a daily occurrence. Even more staggering, the search of prints on file in an AFIS database only takes about 10 minutes.

AFIS has revolutionized the way police departments search latent prints for matches. At one time, it was not uncommon for some crime scene investigators to dust low property-value crime scenes to placate crime victims who wanted the police to do something. The effort put into dusting a scene seemed to give victims a feeling that the police were doing something. In only a small percentage of cases would latent prints be matched to those of a criminal. Some police administrators even questioned the value of going through the effort of trying to locate fingerprints in low property-value, residential burglaries and automobile burglaries.

AFIS has completely changed that way of thinking. Simply stated, the more quality latent prints collected at crime scenes and searched against AFIS, the greater is the chance of identifying criminals through an AFIS database.

Several AFIS technologies are in use today. The main drawback at present is that they are not compatible to one another. Prints stored electronically in one state's AFIS database cannot be searched by a system sold by another vendor. The only way around this short-coming is to input the latent, or a copy of the latent, into the other AFIS system. Computer software and hardware to bridge that gap will improve the usefulness of AFIS technology.

The quality of the inked fingerprint cards used to create the AFIS database is critical. Poorly taken fingerprint cards uploaded into the AFIS database eliminates the possibility of making a correct identification when conducting a latent print search. Because a sur-prisingly high number of crimes may be associated to one perpetrator, the quality of the inked fingerprints and the AFIS data entry process become very important.

An alternative to taking inked prints is an electronic technique whose generic name is Livescan. Livescan technology produces high-quality print cards without the need to take inked prints. Each finger is inserted into a reader, and its fingerprint is captured. At the end of the process, a standard print card is produced. The next step of the process is to input the print card into the AFIS database. A shortcoming of the system is that AFIS systems are proprietary and Livescan systems cannot transfer electronic data directly into AFIS.

The FBI has been at the forefront in recognizing the importance of new identification technology. IAFIS, the Integrated Automated Fingerprint Identification System, launched in 1999 is an effort to address the interoperability problems resulting from different AFIS technologies that are incompatible with each other. Of particular note is the effort to inte-grate many forms of identification besides fingerprints, including criminal histories; mug shots; scars and tattoo photos; physical characteristics such as height, weight, hair, and eye color; and aliases.

Preservation Techniques
Preservation by Photography

Fingerprints found at the scene of a crime should be preserved by photography when pos-sible. This procedure has many advantages. Photography leaves the objects intact so that further photos can be taken if the first are unusable. It also makes it easier to show the evi-dence in court because the object on which the latents were discovered can be seen in the picture. The photography of fingerprints and other evidence differs from ordinary picture taking. The photographer must be skilled in photographic techniques and understand how to obtain a reproduction of a fingerprint as accurate and true to the original as possible. Additionally, knowledge of the principles of fingerprint comparison is helpful to appreciate what the person making the print identification requires. The finished photograph should be white on a black background or black on a white background. It should be 1:1, the actual size, and a ruler should be included in the photograph to allow for the printing to be 1:1. The person taking the photograph should advise the person making the fingerprint com-parison whether the print is a direct or mirror image or a positive or negative image.

If the print is visible without fingerprint powder development, it should be photographed as found, in view of the possibility that any measures taken for development might destroy it. This can generally be done by a suitable arrangement of lighting. An attempt can then be made to make the print clearer, for example, by treatment with powders, after which more photographs are taken. Fingerprints should be photographed with a scale in the picture.

Preservation of Plastic Fingerprints

When a fingerprint has been left in material that has hardened or is able to withstand transport and when it is on a small, easily transportable object, it may be sent directly to the crime laboratory. If removing the plastic print poses some special problem, it should be photographed using oblique light to bring out as much detail as possible. An appropriate casting material may then preserve the fingerprint impression.

Frequently, curved surfaces with latent fingerprints present, such as doorknobs, are difficult to photograph or do not lend themselves to the use of cellophane lifting tape. For such surfaces, elastic or rubber material works well. Rubber lifters are commercially available items made of a thin, rubbery material coated with an adhesive. A transparent celluloid material removed prior to use and replaced after use protects the adhesive. The color of the lifter is either black or white for use with different fingerprint powders.

To use this technique, the latent fingerprint is first dusted with an appropriately colored fingerprint powder. The protective covering of the lifter is pulled away, and the sticky surface is pressed against the print and then pulled away. Part of the powder sticks to the lifter and gives the mirror image of the print. After the print is collected, the protective covering is carefully replaced on the lifter.

The lifter comes in different sizes and can be cut for a specific use. It is useful for picking up footprints in the dust as well as fingerprints. The lifting method is simple and easy to master. It requires no knowledge of photography and no photographic equipment. Its use, however, requires greater accuracy in specifying the position of the print. Carelessness in this respect can have disastrous results.

Preservation with Fingerprint-Lifting Tape

The most common method of collecting latent fingerprint evidence today is by special transparent cellophane tape. The material is supplied in rolls and is usually 1 or 2 inches wide. After the surface is dusted with fingerprint powder, the tape is placed over the print. Care must be taken to prevent any air pockets. The tape is smoothed down over the print with the aid of a finger and then drawn off. Particles of fingerprint powder adhere to the sticky surface of the tape and thereby transfer the fingerprint pattern. The tape is finally placed on a card whose color contrasts with the color of the powder used. If insufficient ridge detail is present for any useful comparison, the epithelial cells on the tape can be used for DNA typing.

How Long Does a Fingerprint Remain on an Object?

Plastic prints remain for any length of time provided that the object on which they are left or the substance in which they are formed is stable. In investigations, it sometimes happens that police officers find fingerprints that give the impression of having been made in dust, but on closer examination are found to be dust-filled plastic prints in oil paint made years earlier.

Prints that have resulted from contamination of the fingers with soot, flour, face powder, or safe filling are soon destroyed. Prints of fingers contaminated with blood, pigments, ink, and oil are more resistant and can be kept for a long time under favorable conditions.

Latent prints on glass, china, and other smooth objects can remain for years if they are in a well-protected location. On objects in the open air, a print can be developed several months after it is made. Fingerprints on paper are very stable and will last for years, provided the paper does not become wet and deteriorate.

Effect of Temperature Conditions on the Possibility of Developing Fingerprints

When objects that may contain fingerprints are found outdoors in ice or snow, they must be thawed slowly and placed so that the thawed water does not run over and destroy the prints. A suitable method of treatment is to scrape away as much snow and ice as possible, with the greatest care, before the object is brought to a warm place. Only when the object is dry should the print be developed.

When plastic fingerprints are present in oil or grease, the thawing must be allowed to proceed slowly and under close scrutiny because the print may easily be destroyed by heat. Such prints should be photographed when they appear.

Damp objects should be dried indoors at ordinary room temperature. As a general rule, never examine cold objects, especially metal, until they have been kept for at least some hours at room temperature. In indoor investigations in a cold house, the rooms should first be heated. The heating should be done slowly so that water from thawing does not run off frosted objects or places.

Examination of Developed Fingerprints

The officer who investigates the crime scene should only search for, develop, and preserve the fingerprints. Unless specially qualified by training and experience in the identification of fingerprints, the officer cannot be expected to carry out the continued examination of the developed prints.

A detailed account of fingerprint identification is not included here, partly because it lies outside the scope of crime scene investigation, and partly because it is a vast and specialized subject. Several comprehensive works on this subject are available.

The officer examining the scene should preserve all developed fingerprints. Even small, fragmentary prints that might seem insignificant to a nonspecialist may turn out to be very valuable when examined by an expert. Large fingerprints are not necessarily more valuable than small ones. It happens frequently that the larger print is usable only for comparison with a suspect's fingerprints; it is useless for searching in a single fingerprint file. The smaller print, however, may be usable for both purposes.

Palm Prints

Patterns of friction skin are on the inside of the hand just as they are on the fingers, and they are of equal value as evidence. When part of a palm print is found, the area involved can often be deduced from the position of the print, or from other parts of the hand and possibly fingers having left marks in the form of smears or portions of print. If the position of the hand represented by the fragment can be estimated, a simple sketch of the inside of a hand greatly facilitates the expert's work.

Prints from the Sole of the Foot

Friction ridges on the soles of the feet have the same evidentiary value as fingerprints and are developed and preserved in the same way as other prints. Cases sometimes occur in which burglars lacking gloves for their hands have taken off their socks and put them on their hands to avoid leaving fingerprints. The thought of leaving footprints never entered their minds!

Ear, Lip, and Other Prints

Occasionally, ear and lip prints are found at a crime scene. A suspect might have put his ear to a door or wall to listen to what was taking place on the other side. Lip prints have also been found in lipstick on letters or envelopes placed by suspects. Another method used by criminals is to hold an object between the index and middle fingers like scissors to prevent leaving fingerprints. The sides of the fingers, lips, and ears, however, all have markings that can be used for useful comparisons.

Packing Objects on Which Prints Are Found

The crime scene investigator must decide the best way to transport objects that are to be examined for fingerprints. Wrapping such items directly in paper, cloth, or plastic bags should be avoided because prints may be destroyed. If possible, the object should be wedged firmly in a strong box so that the packing does not touch the surface. Because a rigid suspension can cause breakage or other damage to an object in transit, the box must be wrapped in a sufficient quantity of soft material such as cotton, corrugated paper, crumpled newspaper, etc. If nails are used to fix the object in the box or for the lid, they should not be hammered completely in; the heads should be left free so that they can be pulled out without using much force.

Taking Fingerprints for Elimination

As a rule, persons who have legitimate access to the premises leave the majority of fingerprints found and developed at the crime scene; thus, it is important to eliminate these fingerprints so that the continuing examination may concentrate upon the remaining prints—presumably those of the perpetrator. The investigating officer should, therefore, always take elimination prints of all persons on the premises. These should be submitted to the fingerprint examiner together with the crime scene prints. Because the identification of legitimate fingerprints is as critical as the identification of the criminal's prints, the elimination prints should be as clear as a criminal's prints recorded for filing purposes. Elimination prints should therefore be taken by printer's ink or by specially prepared inkpads. It is not required, however, that they be recorded on standard fingerprint forms as long as they are clearly marked as being for elimination purposes.

A large proportion of latent prints developed at a crime scene are palm prints; therefore, elimination palm prints should also be taken. Inked palm prints require special care in order to be useful for comparison purposes. The palm should be inked with a roller to ensure that all parts of the palm are inked. The prints should be made on a sheet of white paper. Place the inked palm flat on the paper and press on the center of the top of the hand.

Prints of Gloves

The general knowledge of the value of fingerprint evidence has resulted in criminals using gloves as the most usual protective measure. In many cases, when an investigator is looking for fingerprints, glove smears are found and, all too often, little attention is paid to them. The search is concentrated at places where it may be expected that the individual would have preferred to work with bare hands and used a good deal of force so that his gloves would slip and the wrist, or a part of the palm near the wrist, would be exposed, leaving an imprint (Figure 6.11a and b).

(a)   (b)

Figure 6.11 Animal hide is friction ridged and smooth like human skin. It is individual in its minute characteristics and can be conclusively identified. The latent glove print (a) was compared with the test print (b) on the basis of the size, shape, orientation, and interrelationship of "plateau" areas delineated by tension lines in the leather. Three areas have been darkened to serve as a starting point in the comparison. (Courtesy of the Contra Costa County Sheriff's Department, Criminalistics Laboratory, Martinez, CA.)

Prints of gloves, however, may be just as valuable as fingerprints, so it is advisable always to examine and preserve them for closer investigation as long as they are not typical smears formed by the glove-covered hand slipping against a surface. The leather of a glove shows a surface pattern that is often of a very characteristic appearance. It may show furrows in a more or less definite pattern or be perforated in a fairly regular manner. It is much the same with fabric gloves. The surface pattern varies according to the method of manufacture and the yarn or material used. It is the wrinkled or textured surface pattern of leather gloves that can make identification possible.

By contrast, the surface pattern of fabric gloves is regular for each type so, in general, identification cannot be based merely on this. Characteristic and, from the point of view of identification, very valuable formations in the seams may be present, especially at the tips of the fingers. After they have been worn for some time, leather or fabric gloves become shaped to the hands, and typical wrinkle formations often are produced in the leather of the fingers, at the seams, or at places where the gloves do not fit the fingers properly. These wrinkle formations and injuries in the form of tears or holes or, in the case of leather gloves, cracks in the surface of the skin generally show in the print and are most valuable. In rare cases, it is even possible to find fragments of a fingerprint within a glove print. This can occur when the gloves have such large holes that some part of a finger is exposed and leaves a print at the same time as that of the glove.

If prints of gloves and friction ridges appear together, it may be difficult to distinguish the difference without closer examination. At first glance, the print gives the impression of being blurred or composed of two glove prints within each other. On closer examination, however, its regular lines, which lack the detailed pattern of the friction ridges, distinguish the glove print. Glove prints are always formed best on smooth surfaces. Their development requires great care because the prints are not as strong as fingerprints and therefore are easily destroyed if too much powder is used. To ensure not destroying any such prints that may be present at the scene of the crime, the area should not be painted vaguely. A systematic search may be made with the aid of a lamp and then cautious brushing. On the other hand, there is the prospect of finding glove prints at conspicuous and easily accessible places because, in most cases, the criminals abandon all caution and believe that they are fully protected by their gloves and so use their hands freely.

In developing prints, white or black powder may be used. A fingerprint lifter can lift the developed print, but it is better to take possession of the object on which the print is found so that it can be compared directly with prints from the gloves of a suspect. Leather or fabric gloves can produce a print. With the former, the leather contains some fat, while both leather and fabric gloves become contaminated with dirt, skin grease, and the like after being in use for some time. In addition, the warm and moist secretion from the skin of the hands plays an important part, at least with fabric gloves.

Comparison prints from the gloves of a suspect are best made on glass, which is generally most convenient even when the original prints are on furniture. In certain cases, however, it may be necessary to form a print on the same kind of material as that at the scene of the crime. Where possible, such material should be packaged separately when a print and gloves from a suspect are sent for examination. Comparison prints should be made in a manner similar to that used for the original ones. For example, if it is possible to decide how the hand of the suspect gripped the object, this information should be communicated to the expert so that the same grip can be applied for the comparison print. Consideration must also be given to the degree of pressure that may have been used in forming the original print and this should be noted. It is important that neither too much nor too little pressure be used in making the comparison prints because the appearance is greatly affected by pressure.

It is often difficult to make clear prints with a glove, but breathing slightly on the finger of the glove may assist the operation. In certain instances, it may be treated with powder, fat, or the like; however, this technique risks destroying any characteristic details.

Prints of Other Coverings

Instead of gloves, other items such as socks, towels, and handkerchiefs are sometimes used as protection for the hands. It has also happened that individuals have protected the insides of their hands with adhesive tape to prevent the formation of fingerprints. In most cases, when using the above mentioned objects, prints are left only if the material is thin, dirty, or somewhat damp. If, however, it is thick, dry, or relatively clean, it leaves no prints. Prints of such hand coverings rarely have any value from the point of view of identification. Identification is possible only in cases in which the material used has a characteristic surface pattern and shows typical injuries, unusual seams, or characteristic crease formations that are reproduced in the print. In such a case, the investigation is tedious because the extent of the edges of the protective medium is not definitely fixed as it would be in the case of a glove; therefore, it must be searched for before a direct comparison can be undertaken (Figure 6.12).

Although the possibility of identification of hand coverings in such cases is not great, the print should still be given some attention because the method of operation may be typical for a particular individual or gang who has perhaps carried out other crimes in the same or another area.

Figure 6.12 Prints developed from a body by dusting the surface using the Magna-Brush and photography. (Courtesy of the Metropolitan Dade County, Office of Medical Examiner, Miami, FL.)

Latent Fingerprints on Human Skin

Several techniques have been reported for developing latent prints on human skin. These show some value, but success has been limited. One technique is the Kromekote® Lift Technique. The equipment needed includes a fiberglass filament brush, fingerprint powder, and Kromekote cards. Kromekote cards are approximately 5 × 7-inch, high-gloss, 80-lb paper similar in appearance to photographic paper. Kromekote is generally available from local paper suppliers or online. The Kromekote card is used to lift the print from the skin surface by placing the card over the skin in the suspected area and applying pressure for about 3 seconds. The card is carefully removed and then dusted with black fingerprint powder to develop the print transferred onto the card. The fingerprint obtained is the mirror image of a normal print and can be reversed through photography (Figure 6.12).

After the Kromekote technique is used, fingerprint powder can be applied directly to the skin to develop prints. The literature reports that the Magna-Brush gives results superior to a fiberglass filament brush. If a print is developed by this method, it must be photographed and then may be lifted using cellophane lifting tape. Fingerprints on skin surfaces appear to last about 1.5 hours on living victims. Deceased victims should be examined for latent prints on the skin as soon as possible. The technique is still somewhat experimental, but the method's simplicity and ease of use will result in greater use on the part of experienced investigators.

Handwriting Examination

Handwriting is another means of establishing identity. Like fingerprints, it offers the investigator the ability to establish the identity of an individual with some degree of relative certainty. Handwriting characteristics are of two types: style characteristics and personal characteristics.

Style characteristics are the general type to which cursive writing belongs. This general type is learned in school and used by almost everyone. Personal characteristics are changes made in the general style characteristics both intentionally and unconsciously by the writer. Personal characteristics are the ones used to establish the identity of the writer. Handwriting examination can be used to answer two questions: (1) Was a signature or document a forgery? and (2) Were two writings made by the same person? To answer these questions, the document examiner makes a careful examination of the questioned writing and known exemplar writings. Factors such as the relative size of letters, their slope and spacing, the way in which they are formed, and other personal characteristics are used to make a determination.

Written documents occur in every facet of today's society. Daily business transactions include the use of checks, credit card receipts, money orders, purchase receipts, post-it notes, and so forth. Writings may occur on paper as letters and notes, but also may be present on desks, tabletops, walls, floors, doors, and even on dead bodies. Wherever they occur, they should not be overlooked. Once a document is discovered, it must be properly handled and preserved. Failure to do so may result in its inadmissibility as evidence (Figure 6.13).

Excessive handling may damage the document and smudge or obscure important writing characteristics, which may preclude any possibility of identification and eliminate latent fingerprints. The document should be preserved in the same condition in which it is found. Generally, this is best accomplished by placing it into a clear plastic envelope or sheet protector that keeps the document clean, preserves fingerprints, and prevents damage or destruction of minute identifying details. If the document is wet or soaked with blood, it should first be allowed to air-dry at room temperature and be placed in a cardboard box

Figure 6.13 Reconstructing shredded documents in an investigation is very time consuming, but it can be an integral part of the prosecution's evidence. (Courtesy of the State Forensic Science Laboratory, Melbourne, Australia.)

for delivery to the laboratory. Documents should be handled with forceps so as not to leave prints or DNA that may confuse subsequent tests.

Documents should not be altered in any way and should not be folded or creased. If the document is damaged or torn, no attempt should be made to repair it. The investigator should not write on the document to identify it. Documents should not be stapled together or to reports. If the document is stapled, the staple should be removed slowly and carefully so as not to tear the paper. A staple remover should not be used. Do not use a paper punch on a document. Documents should not be left under paper on which the investigator may be writing because indentations may damage the identifying characteristics on the questioned writing. The side of a lead pencil should not be rubbed across the document in order to observe indented writing. Stickers or gummed labels should not be affixed to the document.

The suspect should never handle the document during the course of the investigation. If chemical processing to develop fingerprints on documents is used, the document should first be photographed with a document scale present. After the chemical processing is completed, the paper should not come into contact with other papers because the stain can transfer. Paper should not be handled because additional fingerprints and smudges can easily be deposited onto it. Chemically processed documents should be kept in clear plastic envelopes or sheet protectors.

Documents damaged by fire could contain information valuable to the investigation. Arson has long been used in insurance fraud or to conceal another crime. If possible, burned documents should be left in their container and handled as gently as possible. (Refer to Chapter 7 for a more detailed discussion of preserving burned documents.)

If questioned writings are found on a wall or body in a homicide case, it is advisable to contact a document examiner for possible assistance at the crime scene. If this is not possible, photographs should be taken of the area. Writings on walls, desktops, mirrors, and other surfaces should be photographed with a scale present (Figure 6.14). If possible, the item containing the writing should be removed and submitted to the laboratory. If the writing is confined to a relatively small area, such as a wall, and circumstances justify it, the section should be cut out and taken to the laboratory.

It is necessary to mark documents that later may be entered into evidence during presentation of the court case. The best place to mark a document is usually on the back. This should be done inconspicuously with initials and date and as far away from other writings as possible. In the event this is not possible, the best solution is to use a pen with a different color ink so that the marking cannot be confused with the questioned writing. Red ink should be avoided because it does not survive well when ninhydrin is used to develop latent fingerprints. Extraneous markings and writings should never be placed on the document. If additional information beyond the investigator's initials and the date is necessary, it should be recorded in the officer's notes. It is generally necessary to store documents for varying lengths of time, sometimes several years, pending final disposition of the case. The documents can be stored in protective plastic envelopes or sheet protectors and filed in folders or envelopes large enough to keep them flat. In this way, they will remain in good condition for long periods of time. Photographs can be kept in flat folders or envelopes. Documents processed for fingerprints with ninhydrin or other chemicals must be enclosed in clear plastic envelopes or sheet protectors. Documents should be stored in an area with a relatively cool, dry temperature and away from excessive heat or direct sunlight.

Figure 6.14 Not all handwriting cases involve traditional writings. In this case, a deceased woman was found with Chinese writing in lipstick on her body. The Hong Kong forensic laboratory conducted chemical comparisons on the lipstick as well as writing comparisons in an effort to solve the case. (Courtesy of SC Leung, former head of the government laboratory in Hong Kong, China.)

Once the questioned documents have been discovered and received as evidence and have been properly handled and marked for identification, exemplar writings must be obtained. Exemplar writings are known specimens from the suspect and/or victim. They are extremely important and necessary to connect the suspect or victim to the document. Like the questioned document, exemplars must be properly identified and cared for. They should not be stapled, folded, rolled up, torn, punched, smeared with fingerprints, or otherwise damaged if they are to be acceptable as evidence. The purpose of exemplars is to give the examiner of the document in question a known specimen of the subject's writing, thus providing a source of the writer's individual writing habits and personal style characteristics.

There are two general types of handwriting exemplars: informal and formal. Informal exemplars are also referred to as nonrequest writing. These include the routine, normal course of business writings such as letters, application forms, business records, checks, etc. These documents are sometimes difficult to admit as evidence because their authenticity may be in question; however, they are the best examples of normal or natural handwriting. The subject prepares formal or "request writing" exemplars, usually at the request of the investigator. The format generally used is a handwriting exemplar card designated for that purpose. In addition to an exemplar card, fingerprint cards, booking slips, and, at times, tablet paper may be used to obtain miscellaneous or specific exemplar writing samples. The investigating officer will witness these writings.

The investigator should keep several helpful suggestions in mind when obtaining request exemplars. It is useful to study and become familiar with the questioned document, paying close attention to names, specific words, spellings, and other unusual features of the document. The writing instrument should be in good working order. It is preferable to use a ballpoint pen with blue or black ink. Felt tip pens and pencils should be avoided unless they are the type of writing instrument used in the questioned writing.

The writer should be provided with a comfortable writing area. Generally, exemplars written in the backseat of a police car en route to the station are worthless. The investigator should be present to observe the writing because he or she will be called upon in court to testify to this fact. Only like materials can be compared; that is, cursive writing must be compared with cursive, printing with printing, block letters with block letters, etc. (Figure 6.15a and b).

In addition to the exemplar card, specific writing specimens should be requested, including material contained in the questioned document. The wording of this questioned document should be dictated to the subject; the actual document should not be placed before the writer from which to copy. The writing instrument should be similar to the one used on the questioned document, and the paper should be similar with respect to size,

(a)

(b)

Figure 6.15 In the Ivan "John" Demjanjuk case, the question of identity was proven by forensic document examination. Known as "Ivan the Terrible," Demjanjuk was a prison guard at German concentration camps during World War II. Through a series of legal proceedings in the United States, Israel, and Germany, Demjaniuk, age 91, was ultimately convicted in May, 2011, in Germany, of war crimes and of complicity in the murder of over 28,000 Jews while serving at Sobibor. The court, however, ordered him released pending appeal. He died of natural causes on March 17, 2012. (a, b,) The question of identity was resolved using the following techniques: the chemistry of photographic paper and emulsion; the chemistry of the writing inks; the chemistry of paper and stamp pad ink; the alignment of stamp impressions; and comparisons with ink and paper from known documents of the alleged period from the National Archives, German Archives, and Russian Archives. (Courtesy of Anthony Cantu, PhD, formerly with the U.S. Secret Service Laboratory.)

style, plain, ruled, etc. Several specimens should be obtained as long as the subject is willing to cooperate. If the writer is trying to disguise the writing, it is best to interrupt the periods of writing with conversation and fresh paper from time to time.

This procedure makes it difficult for the subject to maintain a consistent alteration of natural writing habits. In the event of wide variation or difference in the questioned writing and the exemplar, it may be useful to have the writer provide additional exemplars with the other hand.

Because narcotic addicts may show writing that varies from time to time, it may be necessary to obtain writing exemplars at various time intervals, sometimes several days apart. Handwriting reflects the effects of age, illness, injuries, and mental state. It is sometimes necessary for the investigator to obtain additional exemplars of the individual's writing by obtaining informal exemplars.

Identification of Human Remains

The fields of forensic anthropology and forensic odontology (dentistry) have made major contributions over the past decades in the identification of human remains, especially in the area of mass casualty incidents. An in-depth examination is beyond the scope of this book; however, it is worthwhile for the investigator to be aware of some of the information that can be gleaned from semiskeletal remains. Forensic anthropology and odontology techniques are useful in cases in which normal methods of identification, such as facial photographs, fingerprints, physical description, DNA testing, markings on the body, etc., are not available for use. Such cases may involve discovery of buried bodies, badly burned bodies, skeletal remains, major disasters, and so on.

It is possible to determine two types of information from remains. The first is physical characteristics such as sex, ethnicity, approximate age, stature, certain disease states, old injuries, and the like. The second type, which is far more important for forensic purposes, is the actual identification of the individual. To accomplish this identification, adequate records indicating the deceased's physical characteristics must be available as a basis for comparison with the data collected from the examination (Figure 6.16a and b).

Personal identification is one of the most important functions of an investigation. The identity of a living person at a crime scene establishes a strong link between the suspect and the crime. Likewise, the identity, or nonidentity, of a dead person sets the investigation in motion. Because relatives or acquaintances kill the majority of homicide victims, knowing the identity of the victim provides a starting point. From the identity, the character of the victim suggests possible suspects. Although not a responsibility of criminal investigations, the identity of noncriminal decedents enables the deceased person's relatives to collect insurance, settle estates, and provide for the welfare of dependents.

When police are called to a death investigation, relatives or acquaintances of the dead person or documents or possessions found on the body generally help to establish its identity. Caution should always be exercised in making a decision of identity merely because documents concerning a certain person are found on the body—such documents may be stolen, or false, or "planted." Furthermore, the body may be planted to permit someone to disappear. Substitute bodies have been discovered when the dead person's measurements did not agree with those of the alleged victim.

It cannot always be assumed that a relative or acquaintance is competent to identify the body. Instances have occurred in which, owing to the state of the body, even a spouse

(a)   (b)

Figure 6.16 (a) Skeletal remains were discovered in an unused cistern near the Omaha, NE, airport and were positively identified through comparison of antemortem and postmortem dental x-rays. (b) Although nearly 9 years had elapsed between the death and discovery, the bones and teeth revealed evidence of the application of a corrosive substance at or around the time of death. (Courtesy of Douglas H. Ubelaker, PhD, Curator of Anthropology, Smithsonian Institution, Washington, DC, and Norman Sperber, DDS, Chief Forensic Dentist for San Diego and Imperial Counties, San Diego, CA.)

has made a mistake as to identity. It is necessary, therefore, to be careful in establishing a body's identity even though it can be determined with a fair degree of probability. These precautions consist of taking the fingerprints, photographing the body, noting the description (including the dental data), and examining and describing in detail the clothing and objects found on the body. DNA typing may also prove to be of assistance (Figure 6.17).

Sometimes, when the body of an unknown person is found, it is better to postpone a definite conclusion for a few days until the discovery has become generally known through publicity in local papers and/or the national press. Relatives or acquaintances of missing persons who read or hear of the discovery and communicate with the police identify most unknown bodies. The examination by the pathologist at the autopsy of the body will assist greatly in its description, particularly if the body is in an advanced state of decomposition. The pathologist will be able to give such details as apparent age, height, build, weight, and scars (including surgical scars).

However, if all this information, general examination, and publicity fail to establish the identity of the dead person and the body must be buried as that of an unknown individual, it is most important that everything that may be a guide to later identification be preserved for possible future use. DNA and dental data should be recorded.

In the identification of an unknown body, the police officer may need to work with bodies in varying states of decomposition. The most frequent case is that of a body found in water. These cases are considered the most repugnant and difficult. In warm weather, the body will swell up and the skin will become almost black only a few days after death.

Figure 6.17 A gold crucifix found attached to the dentures of an unknown person could provide useful identifying information. (Courtesy of George E. Burgman, DDS, forensic odontologist, Niagara Falls, ON, Canada.)

More rarely, a mummified or petrified body is under inquiry. A dead body may become mummified when it lies in a dry place exposed to sun and air; the tissues do not putrefy but gradually dry up. Under certain conditions, a body can become petrified: the external parts are as if they are calcified due to formation of adipocere (also known as grave wax or mortuary fat) and the body resembles a marble statue. Formation of adipocere occurs chiefly in bodies that lie in a very damp place. It also may be necessary to identify a greatly changed or mutilated body or one of which only the skeleton or certain portions remain.

The deceased may be a murder victim. Therefore, before an attempt at identification, the investigation should be carefully planned. It must be decided how much of a search of pockets and other articles for identifying documents can be permitted without destroying other important evidence. It may be necessary to move the body or other form of remains to a mortuary where a careful examination can be conducted.

Generally, the first procedure is a preliminary investigation of the pockets of the clothes. If any documents or other material that can be a guide to identification are found, careful note should be taken. If this does not lead to any result, the work of identification is continued by taking photographs and fingerprints, preparing an accurate description, and making a detailed investigation and description of clothes and belongings, after which the discovery of the body may be published in a police bulletin for distribution to other agencies and the general press.

A form of identification work that requires exceptionally careful organization is the identification of victims of a catastrophe. The procedure for this type of identification is described later in this chapter.

Taking Fingerprints

Even if an individual is not on record in the fingerprint file, there is a possibility of identifying the body through fingerprints. In many cases, there is reason to assume that a body is that of a certain missing person, but even near relatives are unable to identify it because it has altered so much. Under these conditions, fingerprints are taken in order to compare them with latent prints in the home of the individual or at the place of employment. This type of investigation often gives a positive result.

There is no special difficulty in taking fingerprints from a body after the rigidity has relaxed or when rigidity has only developed to a small extent and the body has not undergone any considerable change. If fingers are rigid, the joints should be bent several times until they are sufficiently flexible. The tips of the fingers are then inked, using a rubber roller and printing ink or commercially available inking materials, and the prints are taken on small pieces of thin card that are pressed against the papillary pattern on the tip of the finger. The finger should not be rolled against the card because the print will inevitably suffer from slipping. With some practice, the card may instead be rolled around the fingertip for satisfactory results.

A number of prints of the same finger are taken so that the best results can be selected. When a sufficient number of prints have been taken from one finger, each piece of card is marked to show to which finger it corresponds. When prints have been taken from all the fingers, the best are selected from each and stuck onto the respective sections of a fingerprint card. It is important to be careful not to get the fingers mixed up when sticking on the prints; if prints of two fingers do happen to get interchanged, then a search in the register will probably be fruitless. It is best to make up two cards, one to be sent to the state or federal file and the other filed with the records. If suitable thin cards cannot be obtained, ordinary glazed writing paper can be used. In such a case, using a piece of wood or sheet metal cut to a form fitting the finger facilitates taking the prints. The pieces of paper are placed on this and fixed or held fast on it when the prints are taken.

Once the rigidity of the body is complete, it is difficult to take fingerprints because the fingers are bent toward the palm of the hand and are so stiff that they cannot be straightened. There is no point in attempting to extend such a finger. In this case, it may be necessary to cut certain tendons in the fingers so that they can be straightened. Certainly, this method is quite effective, but it is not necessary to go to this extreme. It is simpler to bend the hand backward at the wrist to a right or acute angle to the forearm, whereby the fingers will be straightened. It is then possible to hold a finger firmly and lift it up to make the print, with the bend at the wrist becoming slightly reduced. If this method is difficult, then the wrist is bent down again and the required finger is pressed down toward the palm, which makes it accessible from below.

Difficulty is often experienced when the body is considerably decomposed. The changes in the fingers consist either of their drying up and becoming hard or of the tissues becoming loose and filled with liquid and the epidermis becoming fragile and puckered ("dishpan" hands). The first generally occurs when the body has been in a dry place and the second when it has been in water.

When the fingers have shriveled and dried up, fingerprints cannot be taken by the methods just described. Other methods must be employed. The prints may be read directly from the fingers and classified without taking impressions. It is necessary to be very careful and, if possible, perform ridge counting and ridge tracing also on those fingers not required for the classification formulae. A selection is then made of the finger or fingers most suitable for recording with printing ink. When this has been done, a search can be made. Only persons with considerable experience in fingerprint classification can use this method. When reading a pattern directly from a finger, it must be remembered that the print is seen reversed, as in a mirror.

Another method to record fingerprints from deceased persons is by photography. This method is rather tedious and difficult to carry out. If the fingers are stiff and bent, it is necessary to photograph each finger separately.

Frequently, fingertips are so dried out and wrinkled that the friction ridge pattern cannot be read because important parts are concealed in hard folds of the skin. The pattern may be read by removing the fingers from the hand and softening the skin. The pathologist should have an opportunity to view the deceased before this step is taken. The fingers should be cut at the second or middle joint and placed in individual labeled bottles, each bottle noting the hand and finger. Only the pathologist or other competent person should perform this operation. The investigator should be present to verify that the fingers do not get mixed up.

One method for softening dried fingers is to let them soak in a solution of diluted liquid fabric softener for 1 or 2 days, after which they are carefully kneaded until they are sufficiently soft for a print to be taken with the aid of printing ink. If difficulties are still encountered, the fingers must be photographed.

Taking fingerprints from a corpse removed from water is difficult because of changes in the body. In general, changes may be divided into three stages: (1) the epidermis of the fingertips becomes loose and coarsely ridged; (2) the epidermis is loose everywhere and can be removed; and (3) the epidermis is completely missing.

In the first stage, the fingertips must be washed and dried, preferably with cotton or a soft towel. This operation must be done with care and without rubbing so that the skin is not torn off. Fingerprints are then taken in the usual way.

When the skin is wrinkled and granulated, water must first be injected into the upper joint of the finger so that the creases and granulations are smoothed out. For this purpose, a 10-mL hypodermic syringe with a fine needle is used. The needle is inserted approximately at the center of the inside of the middle joint and brought close to the bone in the upper joint, after which water is injected until the skin appears hard and tense. The needle must not be allowed to come too near the skin because the pressure might be sufficient to break the skin, nor should it be put in or too near the outer joint—the return path would be so short that the water would run out again. After the needle has been removed, the print is taken in the usual way. In earlier technical literature, an injection of glycerin, paraffin, or even melted tallow was recommended. However, a properly performed injection with water gives better results and is easier to perform.

In the second stage, when the epidermis has loosened, it is easier to take fingerprints. The loose skin (finger stalls) of the tip is pulled or cut off from the fingertips; the skin from each finger is placed in a labeled test tube filled with water. The finger stalls should not be put in an envelope or other paper wrapping because after a time they will dry up and stick to the paper. When they have been removed this way, the finger stalls may be sent to the fingerprint unit for examination.

For easier handling and photographing, the best procedure is to place the skin from each finger separately between two glass slides. To do this, the fingerprint pattern is cut out of the finger stalls. Because the cutout pieces of skin are then convex, they easily split when flattened between the glass slides. This splitting is unavoidable; therefore, it is necessary to make cuts in the edges so that the splits do not occur in parts of the fingerprint pattern needed for the purpose of classification. When placing them between the glass slides, a small piece of paper or card with the name of the finger is placed near the top of the sample to indicate that the print is being viewed from the correct side. There is not much risk of any such piece of skin being the wrong side because the inside is lighter, smoother, and glossier than the outside. If, however, in a particular case some doubt exists as to which is the inside, taking the piece of skin out and viewing it can determine which side is concave. The glass slides should be taped together. The fingerprint patterns should be photographed by transmitted light; the lines will show up very distinctly.

Prints may also be taken with the aid of printing ink. After careful cleaning and drying, the pattern area is coated with printing ink in the usual way and pressed against a piece of paper. This method is difficult to carry out because the skin is generally so fragile that the print can be destroyed by the slightest carelessness. Occasionally, the finger stalls are so strong that they can be picked up on a finger and the print can be taken as it would be from a living person. However, only in rare cases is the skin on all 10 digits in such good condition that this method can be used.

It often happens that large portions of the epidermis become loose, but small parts remain so firmly attached that the finger stalls cannot be removed whole. Careful scraping of the attached tissues may loosen the tips in a comparatively whole condition. If this is impossible, the part of the underlying tissues to which the finger stalls are attached is cut off, and the whole piece is mounted on a piece of plasticine. The fingerprint can then be taken with printing ink or photographed.

It is far more difficult to take a fingerprint from a dead person when the epidermis of the fingers has fallen away and cannot be found. This occurs generally with bodies that have been in water for a long period of time. Sometimes it is possible to make out the fingerprint pattern in the remaining underskin. Only rarely is it possible to take these fingerprints with printing ink, due to very low ridges in the pattern. The only possible method is to photograph the pattern. In general, however, it can be assumed that the fingerprint pattern will have disappeared entirely because of loosening of the skin.

It is difficult to take a palm print from a dead body, even in a case where the body has undergone little or no change. There is hardly any hope of taking a complete palm print, and it is therefore necessary to take portions of the print on small pieces of paper or card. To simplify the identification of these prints, each piece of paper should have outlined on it a hand on which the part corresponding to the palm print is marked. In taking finger and palm prints from bodies, printing ink is the best medium because the impressions can be mounted directly onto a fingerprint card or other suitable form. These forms can later be filed with other cards. However, an alternate method may be used that employs black fingerprint powder. In some cases, the results of this method may be superior to those with printing ink. The finger or palm is lightly coated with the black powder, using a brush. The impression is obtained by lifting transparent fingerprint tape. The pieces of tape are then mounted directly onto a fingerprint card or on paper cut up into squares for attachment to the card.

In the case of palms, pieces of tape should be laid lengthwise over the whole palm area and removed one at a time. The pieces are then mounted onto a card or paper. This method is somewhat more difficult than the inking method, but it is superior in that a full impression is obtained. A condition for successful lifting is that two persons are available: one to hold the hand and one to manipulate the tape.

Photographing

In photographing an unknown body, full-face and right-profile face photos are always taken. If necessary, further pictures should be taken, including a whole view, left profile—especially with a view to identification from the ears—and detailed photos of scars, injuries, teeth, tattoos (Figure 6.18), clothes, etc. It is good practice to ensure that an unidentified body is not buried before it is photographed; however, it is important to photograph the body before putrefaction sets in and swells or discolors the features. With regard to a body that has undergone some degree of change, although a photograph of the face may be considered quite meaningless, it should still be done. It should also be remembered that the individual may be identified after burial and that the relatives may ask to see the photograph of the face. In taking a full-face picture, the body should be laid on its back with the face turned upward.

When the body is in a mortuary, a wooden rack or other structure that is generally placed under the head should be removed for the photograph. The lower jaw has a tendency to drop, causing the mouth to open, so it is recommended to prop the chin up with a peg or other object that will not be too conspicuous in the photograph. The camera is placed vertically above the face. The color of background material should be chosen so that the outer contour of the head is well defined against it. Often the simplest way is to spread a towel under the head. When profile portraits are taken, the body should be raised so that the camera can be placed at the side of the head. A suitable background is also required for this exposure so that the profile shows up distinctly. The head should not be turned to one side to make it easier to photograph because this might cause considerable alteration in appearance owing to the position of the camera.

In photographing whole-face pictures, the camera is placed high above the body. If this is not possible because of a low roof, then the body can be turned a little to one side, but the procedure must be well thought-out to avoid the possibility of blood running down or other conditions of the body being altered. Under no circumstances should the body be tied or suspended in a leaning position. In photographing scars, injuries, tattoos, and details of clothing, a measuring tape or scale should always be placed on or by the side of the object to provide scale. A ring flash should also be used.

Figure 6.18 Tattoos may help identify victims as well as suspects. A detective was looking through tattoos of gang members when one caught his eye. The tattoo depicted an unsolved murder crime scene he had investigated. It seems the gang member tattooed a depiction of the crime on his chest. (Courtesy of the Los Angeles County Sheriff's Department.)

Photographs are best taken in color. However, in certain instances in which tattoos or other marks present on the body are poorly contrasted, appropriate filters or black and white photography may be helpful.

Even at such an early stage when the changes in the body are limited to rigidity and lividity stains, it may be difficult to distinguish scars, strawberry marks, and birthmarks from livid stains, discolorations of the skin, and wrinkles. The further the deterioration has proceeded, the greater the difficulties. Blue tattooing can be barely perceptible when the skin becomes dark colored and blistered. Under such conditions, the police officer must not rely on personal judgment, but must consult the pathologist. Any special characteristics are described in essentially the same way as for living persons, except in one respect. In the case of a description of a living person with a large number of tattoos, only those that are characteristic or unusual (names, dates, emblems, etc.) are described.* With unknown bodies, however, all tattoos should be described, including the most common types. It is very important that these and other special characteristics be described accurately in a recognized manner with respect to kind, form, size, and position.

UV photography and UV video imaging techniques are useful methods for studying and recording injuries on human skin, such as bite marks and ligature marks, using fluorescent UV photography, reflective long-wavelength UV photography, and short-wavelength UV photography. Taking UV photographs is a cumbersome procedure in that it is difficult to focus UV images because they cannot be seen. One procedure involves using an UV image intensifier. One unit marketed by Hamamatsu has the appearance of an infrared night scope and can be used coupled to a camera or video unit, or by viewing through an eyepiece in the unit. It allows for quick and easy viewing of trauma and even some latent fingerprints on surfaces using UV lighting.

Many people are x-rayed for the purpose of diagnosing medical conditions or for detecting dental cavities. These films are often retained in medical files for many years. Before an unknown body is autopsied or buried, dental and body x-rays should be taken. They not only provide a means of definite identification but might also provide information as to the cause of death.

Marks of Trades or Occupations

Although less common today than in the past, marks and calluses on the hands associated with specific trades may be instructive. When examining victims and suspects, consider the following:

- Clerk, draftsman—hardening of the last joint of the right middle finger at the point where the pen rests when writing or drawing; draftsman—hardening on the part or the ball of the right little finger that lies nearest the wrist
- Baker—hardening on thumb and index fingers of both hands from handling the edges of hot pans and plates
- Engraver, jeweler—wear on nail of right thumb
- Tailor, dressmaker—marks and scars of needle punctures in the tip of left index finger

---

* Gang members often have elaborate tattooing. Such tattooing may suggest specific gang membership.

- Shoemaker, upholsterer—round hollows in front teeth from biting the thread; shoemaker—wear on left thumbnail
- Glazier—hardening between middle and index fingers, arising from handle of diamond being held between these fingers
- Dyer, photographer, chemist—nails dry, brittle, and often discolored
- Butcher—calluses and hardening on inner joints of fingers and on neighboring parts of palm of the hand that holds knives
- Bricklayer, stonemason—hardening of right hand from grip around trowel or hammer; skin of left hand worn very thin from holding bricks or stone
- Carpenter, joiner—hardening in ball of thumb of right hand from grip on plane; unusual number of injuries and scars on left index finger
- Painter—calluses and hardening between right index and middle fingers from grip on handle of brush

If evidence of repetitive operations is observed, it should be noted, sketched, and photographed. It may take imagination, ingenuity, and some practical research in order to connect these calluses to a specific occupation, hobby, or sport.

Making a Description

Making a satisfactory description of a dead body takes time and is often difficult, especially if the body has begun to decompose. In compiling descriptions, it is therefore best to avoid using too definite an expression when describing details for which there is some doubt as to the most suitable choice of words. In case of difficulty, the pathologist should be consulted. The body may conveniently be described in the following order: estimated age, length, build, shape of face, neck, hair, beard, or mustache, forehead, eyes, eyebrows, nose, base of nose, mouth, teeth, chin, ears, hands, feet, and any outstanding characteristics.

If the body has undergone a certain amount of change, it is often nearly impossible to decide the age; even a trained pathologist will often avoid making any definite statement. In many cases, the age can be determined only by postmortem examination.

The length of the body is measured with the body stretched out on its back. The measurement is taken from the heel to the crown of the head. It is often difficult to describe the build. In the case of a swollen body that has been submerged, there may be the temptation to write "well nourished" or "stocky" in the notes, which may be an error. The facial appearance can be described to some degree, but a complete description of the face cannot be specified when a body has undergone considerable change. The color of the hair also may change some time after death. When a body has been in dry earth or in a hot, dry location, the hair may become reddish; however, with a submerged body, hair color may not appreciably change.

In describing the hair, note if it has been well cared for, how it is parted, etc. Hair samples should be taken from bodies that cannot be identified. DNA typing may be possible after compared with hairs found in the home or workplace of a missing person. In describing facial hair, avoid using a term such as "unshaven." That description may be inaccurate as the stubble on the face arises from the hair roots on the face. Hair roots, which lie at an angle to the skin, straighten up after death because of drying and shrinking of the skin—hence the myth that hair and beards grow after death.

It is often difficult to judge the eye color of a dead person because the eyes undergo considerable change after death. Attention should also be given to artificial eyes. The forehead is not likely to change much with respect to form. It is difficult to judge the form and size of the nose because it may swell considerably. On a body that has not undergone any considerable changes, the profile of the nose may be altered considerably due to shrinking of the tissues in the tip of the nose. As a result, a living person's nose that is concave may become straight after death, and a straight nose may become convex. It is usually impossible to decide the size of the mouth because the lips undergo great changes in the very early stages of decomposition.

The size and form of the ears may undergo only minor changes. In cases where the face and body become completely unrecognizable, the ears may look relatively normal.

When examining the hands, note the condition of the fingernails. If applicable, take nail scrapings. Debris under the nails sometimes yields pertinent information. When an unknown body is found without shoes, measure the foot length and width to estimate the approximate shoe size.

The pathologist should take a blood sample from the body. Comparisons with blood found at the crime scene or on the perpetrator may be important. In missing person cases, it may be possible to do reverse paternity typing to demonstrate that the victim was related to someone. A genetic profile may lead to a family connection or to excluding possible identities. Typing of putrefied blood or tissue may be difficult but breakthroughs in forensic biology are improving the chances of identifying missing persons through more sensitive techniques.

Deceased's Clothing

The outer clothing is described first, including accurate indications of the type of material, quality, color, buttons, damage (including, if possible, how the damage is thought to have occurred), stains of dust and dirt, etc. A preliminary examination is made of the pockets and other areas of the clothing, for example, between the clothing and the lining where objects may be found that can be a guide for identification. Garments should be removed one at a time and placed on clean paper and allowed to air-dry at room temperature. If at all possible, the clothing should not be removed by cutting or tearing but should be carefully removed in the usual manner. The person undressing the corpse should be aware that microscopic trace evidence may be present on the clothing, and appropriate care should be exercised so that no useful evidence is lost. If the clothing must be cut from the body, care must be taken to avoid cutting through areas with bullet holes or knife cuts because these areas will be examined in depth later.

After the garment is removed and has been air-dried, it should be packaged and sent to the crime laboratory for examination for debris, trace evidence, and marks of identification such as laundry marks, monograms, manufacturer's markings, and dry cleaning tags.

Shoe size, color, make, and style should be noted. If the size cannot be determined, it is possible to approximate the shoe size by the length of the shoe. Repairs, degree of wear, defects, etc., may also be used as a possible means of identification. Shoes should be submitted to the laboratory for examination for the presence of soil, debris, and other trace evidence that may be helpful in determining identity.

Garments should not be laundered until after the clothing has been carefully examined for trace material and photographed. After these procedures, the garments can be laundered so that clear identification photographs can be made of the clothing and laundry marks can be visible.

Articles of clothing should be repackaged following examination at the laboratory and retained until after adjudication of the case. Under no circumstance should these or any other evidence be destroyed until after all legal proceedings have been completed. This allows the investigator to reexamine the clothing at a later time if new questions arise.

Laundry Marks

In searching for laundry marks on clothing, it should be noted that they may be invisible. Many large laundries now stamp all incoming laundry with a colorless dye imperceptible to the unaided eye, but which fluoresces strongly in UV light. The mark usually comprises the identification mark of the laundry and the number given to the customer. The identification mark sometimes consists of the first letters of the firm's name. The number of the customer is registered with the laundry. The marks are quite durable and remain even after many washings. When the laundry marks the garment, a search is first made for old laundry marks, which are crossed out with invisible ink before the new mark is put on. In this way, a garment may have several laundry marks, which greatly facilitates identification.

It is common practice in the cleaning and laundry industries to identify garments with a paper tag clipped to the article. Unless this tag is attached in an obscure place, the customer usually removes it before wearing the garment.

A good lead for identification can be obtained from monograms, manufacturer's marks, firm's marks, stamp numbers, embroidered initials, and markings made with marking ink. In the case of more valuable garments such as fur coats, overcoats, and suits, it is important to look for marks or alterations often placed on parts turned toward the inside with the idea that the garment may be stolen and that the thief would remove the usual marks. Such identification marks may consist of seams sewn with a different thread, small cuts or pieces cut out of the cloth or lining, threads sewn in, etc.

Watchmaker's Marks

If a watch is found on an unknown dead body, it should be examined for any marks or figures that might aid in the identification. Usually the serial number of a watch is stamped inside the case. Certain watchmakers mark their watches with letters or symbols that indicate their watchmaker's society, together with their membership number. When a sale is made, it may be recommended to the customer to take out insurance on the watch, in which case the purchaser's name and the serial number on the watch are registered by the watchmaker. Some watchmakers mark the date of sale on the inside of the case.

When a watch is taken in for repair, it is customary for the watchmaker to scratch the inside of the case with certain letters or marks and figures that are partly special marks of the individual watchmaker and partly a repair number. The latter is recorded together with the serial number of the watch, name of the owner, and type of repair. The watchmaker's own mark generally consists of one or more initials but may also be a monogram,

Greek letters or other characters, shorthand signs, punctuation marks, private marks, lines, figures, or mathematical signs. Investigators should contact the American Watchmakers–Clockmakers Institute.*

Jewelry

Finger rings usually remain on a body even when it has decomposed to a considerable extent; therefore, they can be a means of identification. Inscriptions may often be found inside engagement, wedding, and other commemorative rings, while signet rings may carry initials, insignia, seals, crests, or other distinctive markings. In a number of countries, graduates of universities wear special rings. Orders, societies, and associations may use rings as marks of membership.

Systems are available for the identification of precious gems. These systems are based upon macroscopic and microscopic imperfections in any gemstone that are not likely to be found in their entire combination in any similar gem.† Also some precious stones, such as diamonds, are microengraved with a serial number. All jewelry should be photographed.

Eyeglasses

Eyeglasses discovered on or near a dead body may provide a means of identification. If the name of the optometrist is on the eyeglass case, it may be possible to determine the victim's name from the doctor's records. Even if the identity of an individual cannot be determined from a prescription, eyeglasses may be useful. Friends or relatives of the victim may be able to identify the eyeglasses as similar to those worn by the victim.

Teeth

Information of special value for identification can be obtained from investigating the teeth of a dead person because they are often characteristic in many respects. This applies not only to the appearance of the dead person who has not altered to any appreciable extent but also to greatly decomposed corpses, badly mutilated victims of airplane accidents, explosions, and catastrophes, and burned bodies. The teeth are very resistant to the normal changes of decomposition as well as to fire and chemicals due to their enamel.

When the teeth are examined, attention is always directed to the changes or injuries in the face of the dead person that may possibly interfere with the subsequent postmortem examination or identification. If a body is altered considerably, the tissues of the face may be missing or may fall apart if the lower jaw is moved out of its position. In such a case, photographing and examining the body should be done first. If for any reason a police officer must examine the teeth of a body before the arrival of the odontologist, he should do so in such a way that no marks of the flow of blood or injuries in the face are aggravated or changed; particularly, the position of any object in the mouth should not be changed.

The first note to make in connection with the teeth is how many are present. A note should be made as to which teeth are missing in the upper and the lower jaws. This may be done by making a sketch of the teeth of each jaw. Special forms and/or computer programs are sometimes used for this purpose and greatly facilitate the work. These sketches

---

* http://www.awci.com/
† The Gemological Institute of America, http://www.gia.edu/, may provide assistance with precious gems.

or forms are marked with the position and size of any visible damage resulting from decay and pieces broken away, cracks, missing fillings, jackets and other crowns, bridge work, implants, root canals, etc. The material used in crowns, fillings, and the like is also noted. Sometimes entire gold crowns melt when teeth are exposed to high temperatures from fire. This is apparent from the amalgam filling running out and around the mouth.

Complete or partial dentures should be kept because the material used in them may possibly be a guide for identification. Dentures may have some identification inscribed on or attached to them. It may be the inmate number, service serial number, doctor's identification, or patient's name. A study of the style of the inscription will give some indication of the probable source.

Furthermore, all characteristics of the teeth should be carefully noted. Teeth can be very light (white) or dark (brown); the teeth of the upper and/or lower jaw may be directed inward or outward, and the teeth may be widely spaced, close together, or wedged in against one another. Exceptionally large spaces may be found between the middle front teeth (central incisors); the central teeth in the upper jaw may be exceptionally powerful (wide); the front teeth in the upper or lower jaw may have noticeably smooth, uneven, or inclined cutting surfaces. Attention should also be given to the bite, that is, the relation between the teeth of the upper and lower jaw when they come together. In a normal bite, the lower edge of the front teeth of the upper jaw fits outside the front teeth of the lower jaw, and the outer chewing surfaces of the upper molars bite somewhat outside the corresponding teeth in the lower jaw. This is called normal occlusion. However, the bite may be such that the front teeth of the upper jaw are quite appreciably outside or inside the front teeth of the lower jaw or that the front and canine teeth in the upper jaw are alternately in front of and behind the corresponding teeth of the lower jaw, resulting in an overbite or underbite.

When examining teeth, the assistance of a dentist should be obtained if possible. This is especially important for root fillings and other work that may be difficult for the untrained individual to detect. A small mirror is valuable help in the examination. If dental work is apparent, identification is possible through the dentist who treated the patient. Dentists keep records of the work on their patients. In an important case, an x-ray examination should be made. Any roots, root fillings, or the like remaining in the jawbones may have a characteristic appearance; an x-ray photograph may agree exactly with one that a dentist has kept.

If teeth are entirely or partially missing from the body, there is reason to suspect that the individual used a full or partial denture. The latter may be found at the house of a missing person or with relatives, and it can then be fitted in the mouth of the dead person, whereby identity or nonidentity can be proved.

In addition to identification of a victim by means of x-rays of teeth compared with dental records, other useful information can be developed through dental examination. These data are useful in identifying the remains of a decomposed or skeletal body.

Age can be determined through dental examination. The ages for eruption of deciduous (baby) teeth and permanent teeth are fairly well established. X-rays of the jaw and examination of the mouth allow the forensic odontologist to make an age determination of the deceased. Habits or occupation may also be deduced through a dental examination. For example, a pipe smoker may have stained and worn surfaces on the teeth, and a tailor may have a groove on the surface of two opposing teeth caused by biting thread. Such characteristics, like those discussed earlier with regard to skin calluses on hands, may prove useful in certain cases.

The arrangement of teeth in the mouth can be useful for identification. Thus, crooked or buckteeth of a deceased may be used as a means of elimination or identification of a particular person. Similarly, disease states, missing teeth, chipped or broken teeth, etc., are helpful for identification.

A tooth found by itself at a crime scene may also yield information. The tooth can be cut open and the pulp can be extracted for DNA typing at the crime lab.

Medical Devices

Permanently installed medical devices, surgical implants, and prosthetics with recorded serial numbers offer another way to identify victims of crimes or natural disasters. There are a considerable number of such medical devices, and a few of the more usual ones include hip and knee replacements and breast implants. The U.S. Food and Drug Administration (FDA) requires manufacturers to establish and maintain a written standard operating procedure related to tracking devices, quality control, and audit procedures (Figure 6.19).

Facial Reconstruction

Occasionally, the police investigator will want to obtain a photograph of the reconstructed face of a mutilated victim. In instances where parts of the face are missing, it is possible to reconstruct the area with various types of mortuary supply materials and cosmetics to a point where a reasonable likeness of the deceased can be made. The procedure requires a fair amount of skill and workmanship but is possible in instances where a reconstruction for identification is needed.

Figure 6.19 In addition to dental x-rays, x-rays of the entire body may be useful. Police investigators obtained medical records of a person reported missing. The records indicated the person had been treated for a fractured forearm. A stainless steel fixation device was placed with screws and remained in place. The autopsy radiographs determined the presence of a similar device in the same forearm of the human remains. The concordance of shape and materials of this device is obvious as seen in both the radiographs. (Courtesy of C. Michael Bowers, DDS, JD, Ventura, CA.)

Determination of Gender

For the determination of gender, the skeletal characteristics are as follows:

Pelvis. Size and form are different for men and women. The preauricular notch and pubic curve are especially significant, and even small fragments can make a determination of gender possible.

Cranium. The walls of the cranium are normally thinner in men than in women. The angle of the root of the nose where it comes out from the forehead (frontal nose angle) is more pronounced in a man. The curve of the eyebrows is generally more rounded in a man than in a woman.

Head of joint of upper arm. This is generally larger in a man than in a woman. Moreover, the size of the head of the joint shrinks only slightly under the action of fire.

Breastbone, thighbone, and shinbones. Both size and form are significant for determination of gender.

Skeleton. The entire female skeleton, with the exception of the pelvis, is in general more lightly constructed than that of a man.

Teeth. In the case of the remains of a child, an important point for the determination of gender is the uninjured crown of the first permanent incisor of the upper jaw. In certain cases, these can show the gender according to whether their width is especially great (boy) or small (girl).

Organs. The uterus or the prostate gland will indicate gender. However, a uterus exposed to decay can become very fragile, so great care should be taken.

Determination of Age

Teeth are especially significant in the determination of age, which is possible even when only one tooth is available; however, it is necessary to allow for a certain percentage of error in this case (according to some authorities, about 15%–20%). If a number of teeth are found, the reliability of the determination is increased. The determination of age from teeth is based on the changes the teeth undergo with aging. These changes are listed below:

1. Wearing down of chewing surfaces (abrasions)
2. Loosening (paradentosis), detected from changes in the attachment of the roots
3. Formation of secondary dentin inside the pulp cavities (can also be formed as reaction to disease of the teeth)
4. Deposition of cement on and around points of the roots
5. Degree of transparency of lowest parts of roots (root transparency)
6. Corrosion of root points (root resorption)
7. Closing of root openings: until the teeth are completely formed, the size of the root openings is in direct relation to the age, so this is of special importance for young individuals

If the body has been completely burned, the crowns of grown-out teeth break up, but the roots often remain whole. If the teeth of a child or young person have not erupted, they do not get broken up. The discovery of teeth that have not erupted or of remains of deciduous teeth thus gives a direct indication of age. When more than one tooth is found, it is important to determine whether the remains come from one or more individuals. DNA can be used for this purpose.

The roof of the cranium gives information that is especially valuable for the determination of the age of an individual; the sutures (ossification lines) are extremely significant. With newborn babies and children up to 3 years of age, the sutures are straight or slightly curved. After this, they begin to become saw-edged in form, growing slowly into the forms typical of the adult. With increasing age, the sutures grow together more and more, finally disappearing entirely; those of a woman, however, join up considerably later than those of a man. The appearance and degree of fusion give an opportunity of estimating an age up to 50 years old.

If the cranium is exposed to great heat, the sutures split up, but if they have grown together completely, the cracks resulting from the heat may take a new path. To some extent, this circumstance makes possible an estimation of age even from small portions of the roof of a cranium. The thickness of the roof of the cranium and also the character of the outside and inside parts of the walls and the intermediate parts give information that may be used as a guide for determination of the age of an individual.

The form of the wedge bone part of the inner ear differs in children and adults. This part is already formed at the fifth month after conception. The epiphyses at the ends of the long bones fuse with the diaphyses at fixed stages in the development of the skeleton. This occurs when the increase in length of the particular limb is complete. Therefore, it is important for the determination of age to note whether this calcification has occurred and to what extent.

Length of Body

The approximate body length of an individual may be determined from the skeleton or a part of it, assuming that some of the longer bones of the limbs (femur, fibula, tibia, humerus, radius, and ulna) are found. The length of some of these is measured, after which the body length is calculated with the aid of formulae and tables developed by anthropologists. The values given by the tables represent the length of the skeleton and should be increased by an inch or so to allow for other tissues and to give an approximately correct value for body height.

Hair Color

Hair is very resistant to change providing it has not been exposed to fire, but it may often be difficult to find at the scene of a discovery when the body has changed greatly. Generally, only the hair of the head—more rarely hair from other parts of the body—can be used as a basis for estimating hair color as required for a description. Great caution should be exercised, however. Surprising changes in the color of hair may have taken place after even a comparatively short time, depending on the character of the soil and other such factors.

DNA as a Means of Identification

DNA testing is a method used to identify both living and deceased persons. DNA testing may not always conclusively identify an individual when there is no reference sample to compare against. However, through kinship testing, it may be possible to determine identity by means of one's parents, children, or other close relatives' DNA.

Blood or other tissue samples from a deceased person can bear results. A deceased person's DNA may be compared against samples collected from personal effects such as hairbrushes, toothbrushes, razors, or articles of clothing, which may hold the person's DNA. Medical specimens, such as biopsies, pap smears, blood tests, etc., may also serve as good exemplars.

The military is also a good source of DNA as all service members have DNA specimens on file to be used to identify battlefield casualties. AFDIL, the Armed Forces DNA Identification Laboratory,[*] maintains such records for such use. DNA typing is discussed in greater detail in the section on forensic biology in Chapter 8.

Identification in Mass Disasters

In occurrences of a catastrophic nature in which a large number of people are killed, such as terrorist incidents, rail and airplane accidents, major fires and explosions, the collapse of a building, accidents at sea, or other natural disasters, the work of identification must be organized as quickly as possible and carried out in such a way that there is no danger of faulty identification of the human remains.

The federal government plays a key role in the recovery and identification of victims of mass casualty. The U.S. Department of Health and Human Services' National Disaster Medical System is a major partner in such efforts. Much of the latest information on these topics is available on the Internet.[†]

The primary responders for a major disaster come from the Disaster Mortuary Operational Response Teams (DMORTs).[‡] DMORT members are required to maintain appropriate certifications and licensure within their discipline. When members are activated, all states recognize licensure and certification and the team members are compensated for their duty time by the federal government as temporary federal employees. During an emergency response, DMORTs work under the guidance of local authorities by providing technical assistance and personnel to recover, identify, and process deceased victims.

It is not only for sentimental considerations that accurate identification is essential. Legal requirements for proof of death must be satisfied. Issues concerning pension rights, the payment of insurance, and estate matters depend on the correct identification of the dead. In addition, consideration of the religious beliefs and psychological health of victims' families are major considerations in mass casualty situations.

If available, it is important to obtain a list showing all persons who may have been killed. In some commercial transportation accidents, this can be obtained from the passenger manifest list. When that information is available, the task of identification is relatively easy as long as the victims are not badly mutilated or burned or the bodies have not undergone any considerable amount of decomposition. When that information is not available, such as in an "open" mass fatality incident like 9/11, the task is extremely more difficult (Figure 6.20).

[*] http://www.afmes.mil/index.cfm?pageid=afdil.overview
[†] http://ndms.dhhs.gov/index.html
[‡] http://www.dmort.org/

Figure 6.20 Identifying human remains from the World Trade Center attack in the aftermath of September 11, 2001. The fragmenting and commingling of the remains made this process extremely difficult. (Courtesy of the NYC Office of Chief Medical Examiner.)

The work of identification should preferably be done by groups, which generally consist of teams made up of a pathologist, dentist, fingerprint examiner, DNA analyst, and law enforcement representative with experience in the identification of dead bodies. The group also needs assistants varying in number for each particular case. The identification group should be present when the first measures of rescue and clearance are started at the scene of the catastrophe, and as bodies are found, they should take charge of them. If the group cannot be organized or does not reach the scene in time, a suitable police officer should be assigned to take the first steps in securing the bodies.

Before beginning, it is worthwhile to establish a command post and chain of command. In certain mass disaster situations, the federal government is in charge of the investigation and local agencies are there as support. In other instances, the reverse may be the case. It will aid the investigation and subsequent identification of victims if these details are worked out ahead of time.

Many public safety agencies today have prepared for mass disaster scenarios, developed procedural manuals, defined responsibilities, and stockpiled supplies for such an event. Those who are faced with a major event for the first time would do well to call for assistance because the task may be enormous and beyond smaller agencies' resources and readiness.

As with any possible crime scene, documentation of the site and the scene must be done. When possible, all items should be photographed. Those present at a major scene should expect a degree of chaos until adequate resources can be assembled. The health, safety, and psychological well-being of personnel who staff a major disaster is an important consideration for those charged with coordination of the investigation and recovery efforts.

The record is made during the course of the work. When the body of a victim is found, it is given a number that is written on a card affixed to the body. Any objects found beside the body are collected in a bag that is also numbered, but should not necessarily be presumed to be personal effects belonging to the deceased. When possible, each victim and object should be provided with a label giving more detailed information, for example, who found it, the time of discovery, and a statement of the nature of the location, preferably in the form of a simple sketch. The objects are entered in the record in succession in a way to which others can easily refer to them, and the position of the object in relation to the body is recorded. Photographing should be done thoroughly. The photographing and sketching must be considered a precaution that may possibly be of use in the work of identification. The numbered places of discovery are also marked on the sketches. If parts of bodies are found, they are given new numbers and placed in bags. As victims are found and the proper measures are taken, the bodies are wrapped in sheets or placed into body bags so that loose objects cannot fall out and get lost. The bodies are then taken to a suitable place where the work of identification is to be done.

When the scene of a catastrophe is so large that the bodies can neither be collected by the identification group alone nor protected by police personnel working under the group, then the victims must first be brought to the identification point by suitable means. There each body or, more likely, portion of a body is given a number and labeled with an accurate statement of the position where it was discovered, time of handing over, and name of the person who found and transported it. If possible, the stretcher bearers who collect the bodies should be given instructions as to their activities so as to avoid any mistakes.

Under all conditions, the scene of the catastrophe should be cordoned off as quickly as possible, and the guards should see that unauthorized persons do not take part in the rescue work. Stretcher-bearer patrols should be under the command of a specially selected supervisor, preferably a police officer. Relatives of deceased persons should not be allowed to take part in this work because they may choose an unidentified body that they think they can recognize, but is possibly a different individual. Relatives of the deceased should be sent to the Family Assistance Center because they can give information that can help in the rescue or identification.

When the scene has been thoroughly searched, all bodies and remains have been found, and all objects assumed to belong to victims have been collected, the work of identification can start. The record made during the first stage should be written up in a clean copy and the photographs arranged in order as quickly as possible so that they will be available for reference together with the sketches.

During the time taken for the rescue and clearing up, and before the actual identification is started, the police authorities should obtain information on the number of persons involved and a listing of their names, occupations, and dates of birth. If it is anticipated that the identification will be difficult, then statements that can assist the identification must supplement the list of names. These are obtained from the relatives of the deceased or from persons who know them sufficiently well. In an especially difficult case, the following information should be obtained:

1. Description, preferably in the form normally used by the police
2. Any illnesses, operations, or bone fractures (possibly x-ray photographs)
3. Fingerprints, if they have previously been taken for any reason
4. Photographs (simple amateur pictures are better than retouched studio portraits)

5. Dental history
6. Description of garments and shoes (if possible, samples of cloth and place of purchase, make, size, markings, repairs, etc.)
7. Description of personal belongings that might be presumed to be the deceased's clothes, together with rings, jewelry, and watch; a statement may also be needed about what would have been near the deceased, for example, a briefcase, handbag, or traveling case
8. Known DNA exemplars

Thus when the work of identification begins, all bodies, portions of bodies, and objects have been numbered in sequence. This numbering is preliminary and should be employed only as an aid to identification.

In the identification, a start is made with the least injured bodies or with those that offer the best possibilities of quick and satisfactory identification. One of the police officers in the identification group keeps the record. In the work of identification, the bodies should lie on a suitable table or bench. All loose objects in or on the clothing or on the body are recorded and then placed in a bag.

If any identifying documents such as a passport, visiting card, driver's license, identification card, or other similar items are found on a body and they agree with statements obtained regarding a person supposed to have been killed, then the identification may be considered complete. However, in some cases identifying documents have been found on a body belonging to another person killed at the same time; when the bodies were thrown against one another, the documents were transferred from the owner to another person. If information regarding the dead person has been obtained, it must be compared with the body to confirm the identification. The first body examined is given the number one, after which numbers are given to the bodies in succession as subsequent measures of identification are taken. The bags containing the belongings are given the same numbers as the bodies to which they belong and clothes are bundled together and given corresponding numbers. Statements regarding injuries and assumed cause of death are made in the usual manner. The pathologist decides whether these statements should be made in a separate report or included in the report of the identification.

As the bodies are identified, they are put to one side. Clothes and belongings are placed next to the bodies. It is safest not to allow a body to be removed before all the others have been identified so that any mistakes can be rectified in time. When the deceased are placed in coffins, the work should be supervised and controlled by at least two members of the identification group. The coffins are marked with number and name.

The work of identification then proceeds to the more difficult cases, and the identification group must rely more on and refer to statements that have been obtained. In due course, it can become easier to work on the principle of elimination. However, this method cannot be employed except in cases where information on the number of victims and their names is absolutely reliable and the statements obtained are detailed and reliable. For the most difficult cases, the group must work according to the methods described in the preceding sections of this chapter. The aid of a computer disaster management system, such as the Unified Victim Identification System (UVIS),* is a must.

* http://en.wikipedia.org/wiki/Unified_Victim_Identification_System

In cases of a large number of victims, the police or other authorities should not allow the body of any victim to be removed before the identification group has been organized and arrives at the scene. Even if, at an early stage, a particular body can be identified with absolute certainty, its removal should not be permitted. The identification group has the responsibility of identifying all the victims. If this group deals only with the difficult cases, it could be under the suspicion that the bodies released earlier might have been wrongly identified, which could eliminate the possibility of certain identification of the last, more difficult cases.

Establishing identity is one of the most important uses of physical evidence. The investigator should make maximum use of experts in various fields, such as finger-prints, handwriting, dentistry, anthropology, DNA, etc., to assist in the identification of a subject.

Chapter Questions

1. (True/False) One of the most important purposes of physical evidence is to establish the identity of the suspect or victim.
   a) True
   b) False

2. Describe how fingerprints are formed at the scene of a crime.

3. You have been asked to search for fingerprints at the scene of a residential burglary. Describe where you would search for any fingerprints left behind by the suspect.

4. List the three main groups of fingerprints that can be found at the scene of a crime.

5. Which of the following chemicals would be the most appropriate when attempting to locate fingerprints on the sticky side of tape?
   a) DFO
   b) SPR
   c) Gentian violet
   d) Ninhydrin

6. Which of the following choices is an alternative to taking inked fingerprints from suspects?
   a) CODIS
   b) Livescan
   c) AFIS
   d) NIBIN
7. Describe the proper procedure for collecting and preserving a plastic fingerprint.

8. You have been asked to collect a knife from the crime scene with a visible fingerprint in blood. Describe how you would package this item up.

9. Can fingerprints be lifted from human skin? If so, describe one of the techniques.

10. Which of the following specialized personnel would be the most appropriate when attempting to identify skeletal remains?
    a) Forensic archaeologist
    b) Criminalist
    c) Forensic anthropologist
    d) Coroner

Trace Evidence[*]

7

Introduction

Trace evidence is a generic term for small, often microscopic material. Such evidence may easily be overlooked in crime scene investigations unless proper care is exercised in the search. The variety of trace evidence is unending. The purpose of this chapter is to examine some of the more common types of trace materials frequently encountered in criminal investigations and to discuss concepts of collection, preservation, identification, and use of these materials.

When an individual comes into contact with a person or location, certain small and seemingly insignificant changes occur. Small items such as fibers, hairs, and assorted microscopic debris may be left by the person or picked up from contact with the environment or another individual. In short, it is not possible to come in contact with an environment without changing it in some small way by adding to it or taking something away from it. This concept of transfer is known as the Locard Exchange principle and is the basis for studying trace evidence.

The importance of transferred trace evidence is that it links suspects to victims or locations. It is physical evidence of contact and, although microscopic, can become a significant part of an investigation.

Case[†]

The body of an 18-year-old female was found on the side of the road near Porvoo (a small town about 50 km northeast of Helsinki, Finland). The deceased was completely naked from the waist down and the upper part of her body was clothed normally. The victim's jeans, stockings, and underwear were bundled on her chest. The technical research team took the clothing of the deceased, fingernail scrapings, head hair and pubic hair combings, and known hair samples.

Fiber evidence was found in the victim's hair. The autopsy determined that the cause of death was strangulation and that the victim had been raped. Semen was found in vaginal and rectal samples collected during the autopsy. The ABO blood group was determined to be "A".[‡] The hope of solving the case centered on the fiber evidence, and a hypothesis was made that the fibers must have had something to do with the crime. Eleven brown, uniform, and multicolored acrylic fibers were found from the combed hair samples. Similar fibers were collected from tape lift samples taken from the victim's clothes. About 200 fibers were found on the clothes. With the help of reference samples, it was deduced that these fibers most probably originated from the seat cover

---

[*] SWGMAT, The Scientific Working Group for Materials Analysis, provides the Guidelines/Best Practices for many types of trace evidence such as fibers, glass, paint, tape, etc. It is an excellent resource for these sorts of evidence. See http://www.swgmat.org/.

[†] Courtesy of the National Bureau of Investigation, Helsinki, Finland.

[‡] This case occurred before the use of DNA typing.

of a car. The police were advised that the laboratory was especially interested in brown automobile seat covers made from pile-type material and that, while searching cars, they should give special attention to red textiles (Figure 7.1).

From the samples combed from the victim's head and pubic hair, two and three viscous fibers were found, respectively, that were unusual in their color and dying. The victim's clothes yielded 28 similar fibers. In the combed samples, an orange-red woolen

(a)

(b)

(c)

Figure 7.1 (a) The roadside near Porvoo where the body was discovered. (b) The body was discovered partially clothed. (c) A close-up of the victim.

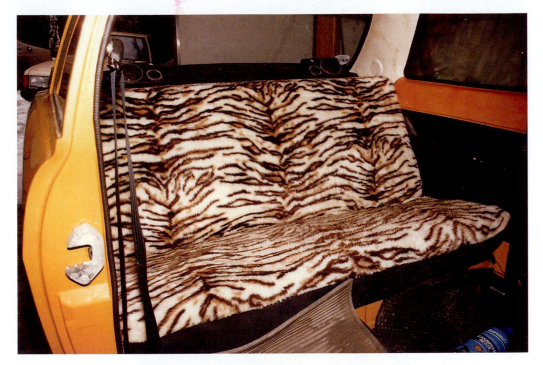

Figure 7.2 The police eventually located the suspect's car because of the leads the laboratory was able to provide concerning the seat cover.

fiber was found that was about 3 cm long; 13 similar fibers were found on the clothes. Because of the number of red-colored fibers found, it was possible to consider primary transfer. It was assumed that the origin of the fibers must have been from a textile other than clothes worn by the suspect because neither of the fiber types belonged to typical cloth textile fibers.

The technical research team examined 12 cars over a 2-month period. They collected seat covers that were a possible match to the fibers, picked hairs and fibers, taped-lifted the seats and searched for the victim's fingerprints. The fiber samples taken from the victim did not match the samples taken from these cars. The victim's clothes were white and light blue and made mainly of cotton; therefore, it was pointless to try to collect these types of fibers (Figure 7.2).

The 13th car to be examined belonged to a person who, 9 years earlier, had been charged with rape but released due to insufficient evidence. The seat cover material in his car matched the acrylic fibers from the hair and the clothes of the victim. Also, the samples taken from the seat covers contained similar red colored viscous and woolen fibers found on the samples taken from the victim. Thirty-nine samples were taken from the interior textiles in the suspect's residence and also from his clothes. The red viscous fibers proved to be the same as the pillowcase cloth fibers found on the sofa in the living room of the suspect's residence. The red woolen fibers were the same as fibers from a blanket found on the sofa (Figure 7.3).

The samples taken from the victim's hair, pubic hair, fingernail scrapings, and clothes were compared to the fiber samples taken from textile material from the furnishings in the suspect's residence and from his clothes. The victim's hair yielded 13 dark blue cotton fiber samples; one of the same types was found in the fingernail

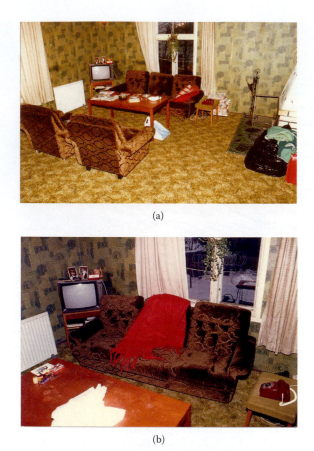

(a)

(b)

Figure 7.3 (a) A search of the suspect's home yielded fibers similar to those found on the victim. (b) Fibers from the fabric on the couch and woolen blanket on the sofa proved to be important evidence in the criminal prosecution.

scrapings. These fibers could not be differentiated from the fibers taken from the suspect's blue trousers. In the clothes of the victim, three thick yellowish-brown V-shaped viscose fibers were found. Their color, quality, thickness, shape, and size were the same as plush fibers found in a velvet sofa cover in the suspect's residence. The sixth fiber similarity was three pink acrylic fibers found in the victim's clothes, which matched samples taken from a sweater in the suspect's residence. All the different types of foreign fibers on the victim were found in the suspect's car seat cover and clothing.

During the investigation, it was concluded that the victim had not been to the suspect's residence. The suspect's untidy habits transferred the fibers from his residence to his car; an exchange known as a secondary transfer. None of these fibers was found at the victim's residence, on her clothes, or at her mother's home. Polarizing light microscopy, fluorescence microscopy, and microspectrophotometry were used in the fiber identification. Fourier transform infrared spectroscopy was used to investigate the brown acrylic fibers. The accused did not confess to the crime but only admitted that he used his car. He was convicted and sentenced to 10 years on the basis of the evidence produced by the fiber identification.

Sources of Trace Evidence

Clothing

Clothing is an excellent source of trace evidence. Microscopic and macroscopic substances may cling to clothing by static electricity or become caught in the fabric. Useful evidence is most likely to be found if the clothes are collected from the suspect or victim as soon after the crime as possible. As time passes, small items of evidence no bigger than a fiber may easily be dislodged from the clothing and lost.

After the suspect is apprehended, his or her clothes should be cursorily inspected for obvious physical evidence connected with the crime. If evidence is observed, its location and description should be noted.

If possible, the subject should be made to undress while standing on clean wrapping paper. The paper will catch any trace evidence that might fall from the clothing. The clothing should then be collected, tagged, or marked for chain of evidence purposes and packaged in paper bags. Plastic bags should be avoided when packaging clothing because the clothes may develop mold or mildew. Care should be taken when placing the garments into paper bags; they should never be shaken because that might loosen or dislodge trace evidence. If the clothes are wet or bloodstained, they should first be allowed to air-dry before packaging.

It is especially important to keep the suspect's clothing away from any sources of trace evidence located at the scene. If known samples from the scene have been collected as exemplars, they should never be packaged with the clothing.

Case

Police were called to the scene of a warehouse burglary. The suspects gained entrance by chopping a hole through the roof. Officers at the scene collected samples of roofing tar, wood, and plaster to be used as exemplars for any trace evidence that might be found on the suspects. The suspects were subsequently arrested a short distance from the scene of the crime. They were taken to the police station and their clothes were examined. Some building materials and tar-like material adhering to their pants in the knee area were noted. The clothes were packaged in paper bags along with known debris specimens collected from the crime scene.

When the evidence arrived at the crime laboratory and was opened, it was discovered that the known material had been thrown into the paper bag along with the clothes. Although building material was found on the pant legs of the suspect's clothing, it was impossible to determine whether the debris came from the crime scene or the exemplars submitted in the paper bag.

Similarly, a subject should not be brought to the crime scene while clothed in the same garments worn during the crime. This will prevent the argument that any trace evidence found on the clothes was from the visit to the scene while in the custody of the police.

Once clothing has been collected and packaged in paper bags, it should be submitted to the crime laboratory for careful examination (Figure 7.4).

Although some police agencies may have equipment to vacuum the garments and send the sweepings to the laboratory, it is preferable to allow the laboratory to conduct the search and collection. In instances when extremely small items of evidence such as a single hair or fiber might be lost, evidence should be carefully packaged in a test tube, pillbox, paper fold,

(a)

(b)

Figure 7.4 When considering trace evidence on clothing, we generally think only in terms of hairs, fiber, and other debris. However, with the advance of more sophisticated forensic biology techniques and procedures, investigators should also consider the possibility of detecting small quantities of epithelial, or skin, cells from clothing and other types of evidence at the crime scene. (a, b) During an aggravated robbery at a jewelry store, one suspect grabbed the complainant's shirt in the shoulder/neck area. A mixture of DNA including the complainant's DNA profile and an unknown male DNA profile was obtained from the right shoulder of the complainant's shirt. The unknown male DNA profile was deduced from the mixture on the shoulder of this shirt and a matched to a convicted offender in the national DNA database. (Courtesy of the Harris County, Texas, Medical Examiner's Office DNA Laboratory.)

post-it note, or other appropriate container. Naturally, the location of this evidence should be noted and the items appropriately marked for identification.

Clothes from murder and assault victims pose other problems for consideration. As on a suspect's clothing, trace evidence may be present on the victim's clothes as well. These garments, however, may have been removed by personnel other than law enforcement who usually are not knowledgeable about proper collection and preservation of evidence. Problems invariably arise when paramedics or hospital personnel remove clothing during life-threatening emergencies. It is not uncommon for clothing to be cut off the victim with the aim of initiating emergency procedures. Often, this results in cutting through bullet holes, tears caused by stabbing, and the like. Frequently, wet bloodstained garments are rolled up and packaged in a large plastic bag and tightly sealed.

In these instances of improper evidence handling by emergency medical personnel, police agencies can do little more than attempt to educate those groups and hope that the potential value of the evidence was not too badly diminished. Crime laboratory personnel should be advised that the victim's clothing was cut off so that they can effectively interpret the information in their attempt to reconstruct the crime.

Clothing on deceased victims requires further considerations. Before the victim is undressed, the body should be carefully examined for trace evidence by the investigator, criminalist, and/or pathologist. An alternate light source is a useful tool in locating trace evidence. The clothing should be carefully removed and placed onto clean wrapping paper. In most instances of violent death, the clothes will be wet from blood. The garments should be air-dried before packaging.

Footwear

Shoes and other footwear are valuable items of evidence. They may have dust, soil, debris, vegetation, or bloodstains on them. In addition to the presence of trace evidence, shoes and other footwear are useful in shoe impression evidence comparison (Figure 7.5). Shoes should be individually packaged to avoid cross contamination. Particular care must be taken when packaging footwear evidence containing clumps of dried soil. Careful examination of the soil might lead to determining the path taken by a suspect. This possibility would be greatly lessened if the soil became dislodged and pulverized in transit to the laboratory.

Evidence from the Body

Useful trace evidence may be discovered by a careful examination of the suspect or victim's body. Injuries caused by a struggle between victim and suspect may be noted. Microscopic particles of gunshot residue are often present on the hands of a shooter following the discharge of a firearm.

Hair is sometimes found on the victim's body in rape cases. Bloodstains on a victim or suspect's body are not uncommon in assault and murder cases. A close examination of the head, ears, fingernail scrapings, and hands may yield traces of debris from a burglary, assault, or other crime in which there was contact between the subject and another person or the crime scene.

Other Objects as Sources of Trace Evidence

Trace evidence may be present on tools and weapons, as well as other objects. When possible, the items should be carefully packaged to protect the material on them. This may be done best by placing the tool in a cardboard box and securing it with zip ties. If the instrument bears larger particles that may be lost, the particles should be carefully removed and placed in appropriately labeled containers.

(a)

(b)

Figure 7.5 (a, b) Unique defects in a shoe can be used as points of comparison in shoe impression evidence. (Courtesy of the Royal Canadian Mounted Police, Forensic Laboratory Services.)

Tools used in burglaries may contain traces of building material, metal shavings, paint, and so forth. These items may be used to establish a connection between the tool and the location. Similarly, a weapon such as a knife may have hairs or fibers present that may prove to be useful evidence (Figure 7.6).

Larger items may be fruitful sources of trace evidence, for example, a vehicle from a hit-and-run accident. Naturally, objects of this size may not be routinely brought to the

(a)

(b)

Figure 7.6 (a) A screwdriver seized from a suspect in a burglary case. (b) Close-up of the blade of the screwdriver showing the presence of a small amount of red paint, which matched the paint at the breaking and entering location. (Courtesy of the Royal Canadian Mounted Police, Forensic Laboratory Services.)

laboratory unless the laboratory has a vehicle garage. However, a careful examination in the field can turn up hairs, fibers, skin, blood, and the like.

Microscopic evidence presents more of a challenge than a problem to modern crime laboratories. Use of low-power and high-power light microscopes and sophisticated instruments, such as scanning electron microscopes and various types of spectrographic tools, make the examination and characterization of minute items of evidence commonplace.

A far greater problem than size is quantity of material. Particles and material collected from vacuum sweepings and careful searches of evidence can yield thousands of microscopic items to be examined. Only patience and the examiner's expertise can ultimately determine the nature and utility of these collected items.

Case

On March 27, 2003, in rural Darke County Ohio, a married couple was shot to death execution-style while asleep in their bed. The only other occupant in the house at the time was their 4-year-old great-grandson who discovered the bodies. The boy attempted to call 911; however, the phone lines had been cut. Knowing that he needed help, he ran nearly a mile to a church where he attended preschool. He told the teacher that his grandparents were "melting." The victims had been shot at point-blank range with a 12-gauge shotgun.

It appeared to investigators that the murderer had intended the crime scene to look like a robbery; however, a deposit bag containing a large amount of cash remained undisturbed in the kitchen and no jewelry or other valuables appeared to be missing. A basement window had been forced open and partial footwear impressions were cast from adjacent soil. Recovered from the head of the bed was a makeshift silencer composed of a quilting material. This material was wrapped in a cone-shaped fashion and exhibited masking tape on one end and black powder on the other.

Over the course of the following week, investigators eliminated a number of suspects and began to focus on the son and stepson of the victims. The suspect's girlfriend informed investigators that the suspect had left for work exceptionally early the day of the murders. An acquaintance of the suspect had also come forward and claimed that the suspect had contacted him shortly before the murders about acquiring a non-registered firearm. Investigators compared the suspect's cell phone records with local ads listing firearms for sale. They located a man who claimed to have sold a 12-gauge shotgun to the suspect just days before the murders. This man still had the firearm box, which included the shotgun serial number. However, investigators did not have a murder weapon for comparison. Subsequent interviews and a search of the suspect's house failed to reveal a shotgun or any probative evidence.

Five days after the murders, an extensive search of nearly 30 miles of roads, bridges, and waterways between the crime scene and the suspect's place of employment was conducted. The search was unsuccessful until, on a hunch, one investigator and a Darke County Sheriff's deputy drove to a bridge over the Stillwater River. In the shallow water right off the side of the bridge, they recovered a 12-gauge shotgun with a piece of masking tape on the barrel. About 1 mile downstream snagged on a tree branch, a large black trash bag was recovered.

The shotgun and trash bag were immediately transported to the Miami Valley Regional Crime Laboratory for examination. Among the items recovered from the bag were two spent shotgun shells, a roll of masking tape, a pair of black athletic shoes, latex gloves, a package of quilting material, and clothing items.

Trace evidence examination of masking tape pieces recovered from the makeshift silencer at the scene, the barrel of the shotgun recovered from the river, and the roll of masking tape recovered from the trash bag revealed numerous fracture matches connecting the first nine feet of tape off a new roll (Figure 7.7a and b). It was conclusive that the tape from the silencer and the shotgun barrel originated from the roll of tape in the trash bag. Also, the quilting material recovered from the bag was the same composition as that used in the makeshift silencer.

The shotgun was processed by the Firearms and Tool Mark Section in an attempt to restore the obliterated serial number. Five of the eight digits in the serial number were successfully raised. These digits matched the corresponding numbers on the box

(a)

(b)

(c)

Figure 7.7 (a, b) Trace evidence examination of masking tape pieces recovered from a makeshift silencer. The shotgun barrel and the roll of masking tape recovered from the trash bag showed numerous fracture matches connecting the first nine feet of tape off a new roll. (c) An initial photograph of the partial latent print on the glove fingertip as observed with RUVIS (Reflected UV Imaging System) before processing.

obtained from the seller. Additionally, the spent shell casings from the bag were found to be of the same brand as those recovered from the victims at autopsy.

The athletic shoes recovered from the trash bag were compared to the partial footwear impressions recovered from the scene and were found to be of the same tread design. It was noted that these shoes were approximately two sizes smaller than those worn by the suspect.

At this point, many of the items from the bag could be linked to the crime scene but nothing could be directly linked to the suspect. That changed upon examination of the latex gloves by a latent print examiner. Remarkably, one of the gloves revealed a partial fingerprint under ultraviolet light. This partial print was intact despite the immersion of the evidence in water for nearly a week. This anomaly was likely due to the deposition of an oily residue on the suspect's hands before donning the glove. Comparison of this partial latent print revealed that it matched a portion of the suspect's right index finger—his trigger finger (Figure 7.7c).

The motive in this case was determined to be financial. The suspect was losing his home to foreclosure and he stood to inherit his father's property if his father and stepmother were deceased. The suspect, age 25, was convicted on all charges and was sentenced to life in prison without parole.

Courtesy of Suzanne Noffsinger
Trace Evidence Examiner
Miami Valley Regional Crime Laboratory
Dayton, Ohio

Collection and Preservation of Trace Evidence

As with all evidence, the investigator or crime scene technician must be concerned with various legal and scientific aspects of collection and preservation of trace materials. Legally, issues of chain of custody and the necessity of a search warrant or court order must always be considered. Generally, case law has dictated what is necessary to fulfill the requirements of a chain of custody, as well as the need for warrants. When in doubt, the investigator should contact the local district attorney's or state attorney general's office for guidance.

Scientific requirements depend upon the nature of the evidence collected and the proximity of the laboratory conducting the examinations. It is obvious that if evidence needs to be mailed or sent by a parcel carrier, extraordinary care must be taken to preserve fragile substances properly.

A question sometimes asked is, "Is it better to remove an item of trace material from a larger item or leave it alone?" The answer is, "It depends." If a hair, fiber, loose paint chip, or other very small and easily lost item of evidence can reasonably be expected to become dislodged or lost from the item to which it is attached, that smaller item should be removed. On the other hand, if in the investigator's opinion the smaller substance will not be lost, then it should not be handled. It is preferable to submit the entire item with trace evidence attached to it to the laboratory for an examination. Of course, in those instances in which the item is too large or inconvenient to transport, the trace material should be carefully removed, packaged, and sent to the laboratory for examination. When possible, photographs depicting trace evidence in its original location should be taken. This is helpful to the laboratory as well as to jurors trying to understand the significance of the evidence.

Small items of evidence should always be double packaged. Double packaging means that the evidence should be first placed into an appropriate container and secured. The first container should then be inserted into a larger container. Both containers should be appropriately marked to indicate the person performing the packaging, the date and time, the case number, and a very brief description of the item. If the inner container should inadvertently open, the outer one will contain the evidence.

As an example of double packaging, consider a hypothetical case. Suppose an investigator has observed a small fiber on the bumper of a car suspected in a hit-and-run accident. Bringing the car to the laboratory or a location where the vehicle could be placed on a lift and raised for a thorough examination of the undercarriage would be the best way to conduct an examination. Assume this is not possible. The detective still wants to collect the fiber for comparison with the victim's clothing. The fiber should be carefully removed and placed in a test tube, small envelope, pillbox, paper bundle (pharmacist's fold), or any other appropriate package. The inner package would be marked with the initials, date, time, case number, and so on and would then be placed into a second or outer package. This outer package would also be appropriately marked.

Control or known samples are required in all cases. The investigator should make every attempt to collect a sufficient quantity of known material to be submitted with the items in question. The known exemplars must never be packaged with the questioned samples. This separation is necessary to avoid cross contamination of unknown by known specimens.

Almost all types of trace evidence can be placed in a class or group, that is, identified. Only in rare cases is trace evidence of the type discussed in this chapter capable of conclusively indicating a specific source or origin. A single fiber cannot be shown to have come from a unique garment, nor a clump of dirt from a specific location. Does this mean that trace evidence is of no value? On the contrary, because of its prevalence, trace evidence may often be the sole means of corroborating testimonial evidence in a case.

Examples of Trace Evidence

Building Materials

Building materials of a wide variety may be encountered in burglary cases. Materials such as stucco, cement, brick, mortar, plaster, sheetrock, plasterboard, window glass, wood, and paint constitute evidence generally considered as building materials. This type of evidence is most likely found on the clothing of burglary suspects, in their cuffs, pockets, and shoes. Another likely location for this type of debris is on tools used to break into a location.

Items suspected of containing building material debris should be carefully packaged and submitted along with appropriate exemplars to the crime laboratory.

The investigator should carefully examine the crime scene to ascertain the nature of the trace evidence. In breaking and entering cases, the point of entry or any other location indicating damage should be examined and exemplars of building material collected. If tool marks are present at the point of entry, samples of building materials should not be collected from the area of the tool mark, but rather adjacent to the mark. Furthermore, if an area is to be cut out, particular care must be taken not to cut through the tool mark.

In cases of building material that show indications of tampering at several locations, it is necessary to collect known specimens of the material in question from each of the damaged areas. This is important because the composition of the building material may vary from site to site. It is very important to package each item of evidence separately, properly marking the package and noting the location where the specimen was collected.

Tools may be useful sources of building material evidence. Bits of paint, plaster, wood, and even glass may become attached to the tool. In addition to the debris they may contain, tools are useful for tool mark comparisons and for physically matching broken pieces of the tool.

If building material is noticed at the end of a tool, the area should be carefully wrapped so as not to dislodge the evidence. If the item is too large to be transported, the trace material can be carefully removed with a clean razor blade onto a clean sheet of paper. The paper is then folded and placed in an envelope. Both paper and envelope should be properly marked.

The interior or the trunk of a suspect's vehicle should be searched for the presence of building materials. Vacuum sweepings may be taken for a later search of debris. Clothing is an especially good place to find building materials. The clothes should be collected from the suspect as promptly as possible to minimize any loss of evidence.

Physical, chemical, and microscopic means can characterize building materials. In most cases, building material evidence can only demonstrate class characteristics and cannot be shown to be unique to a specific source. As with other evidence of this type, it is valuable as circumstantial evidence.

Asbestos

Although asbestos is no longer permitted for use as insulation, it may be present in older buildings and some safes. It can be identified microscopically.

Safe Insulation

Various types of materials are used in fire-resistant safes to prevent the contents from burning. Some common materials used in these safes are diatomaceous earth, vermiculite, and cement, to name a few. These materials may readily become deposited on a safe burglar in the course of opening the safe. Examination of a suspect's clothing, shoes, and tools may yield safe insulation, which can be identified microscopically and chemically. Expertise in recognizing the types of insulation used by various manufacturers may allow the analyst to make an educated guess, useful for an investigative lead.

Paint

Paint evidence is frequently recovered in hit-and-run accidents, burglaries, and forced-entry cases. In some cases, it is possible to show conclusively that the paint came from a specific location if the chips are large enough and the edges can be fitted together in jigsaw puzzle fashion. In most instances, however, only class characteristics can be demonstrated (Figure 7.8).

Paint and other protective coatings such as lacquer, enamel, and varnish can be identified by physical and chemical properties. Physical characteristics such as color, layering, weathering, and texture are useful in characterizing this evidence. Chemical properties such as solubility and composition can indicate the type of paint and identify the pigmentation and fillers used in the manufacturing process.*

---

* ASTM maintains a variety of testing methods used for trace materials. Paint tests are one such example. See, for example, http://www.astm.org/Standards/E1610.htm.

Figure 7.8 A hit-and-run vehicle had apparently struck a parked car. The police, however, suspected that the complainant had struck a steel pole. Paint chips from the vehicle and base of the pole were examined. Not only did the paint from the pole match the transfer to the car, but also a physical match was made of the chip (left) from the pole and the chip (right) from the car. (Courtesy of the Centre of Forensic Sciences, Toronto, Canada.)

Even if a vehicle cannot be identified as to manufacturer, known and questioned specimens can be compared by examining chemical and physical properties. The best that can be stated is that the paint from the control and questioned sources are indistinguishable, that is, they could have come from the vehicle in question or any similarly painted vehicle.

In some instances, vehicles and residences that have been painted and repainted many times may have so many layers of paint that upon examination, the probability is very high that the two specimens share a common source. This, however, will depend on the specific case as well as the expertise of the analyst.

When standard specimens of paint from automobiles or a door or window in a forced-entry case are collected, the specimen should be taken as close to the area of damage as possible to lessen the possibility that an area further away from the location of interest was painted differently. In burglary cases, it is particularly important not to collect a standard or control paint sample from the pry area. The specific area of the jimmy or pry may contain a tool mark that may be compared with a pry bar or other tool found at a later time. (See Chapter 9 for a discussion of tool marks.)

When collecting paint samples in a hit-and-run investigation involving two vehicles, a total of four paint samples should be collected and separately packaged. From vehicle A, collect a sample from the point of impact that contains a paint transfer from vehicle B. Also, collect a standard paint sample that shows no damage but is adjacent to the damaged area. Similarly, two samples should be collected from vehicle B, one from the damaged area and a second from the undamaged area to be used as a standard.

If dislodged paint chips are present in the damaged area of the vehicle, they should be carefully collected and packaged to avoid breaking. They may be able to be fitted with other, larger paint chips collected from the scene of the accident or the second vehicle.

To collect a known paint sample from a vehicle, hold a folded piece of paper and tap the side of the vehicle with a pocketknife or similar device. This will dislodge some paint and allow it to fall into the paper. Care should be taken not to separate the outer layer of paint from the undercoating. Avoid using cellophane tape to collect the paint samples. It is best to place the paint sample into folded paper or a small box with a good seal. Small envelopes are not advised for this type of evidence because the seams of the envelope located in the bottom corners are generally not sealed. Paint chips placed in envelopes usually fall out through the small, unsealed space. Small plastic bags should also be avoided because they have a static electric charge that makes it extremely difficult to remove the chips once the evidence is received at the laboratory. The known paint sample should include the substrate (typically metal or plastic for a vehicle) to ensure all layers of the paint are collected. Multiple known samples may be required if there are multiple areas of damage. Often, different areas of vehicles can be painted differently.

Paint on tools should not be removed. It is preferable to wrap the end of the tool carefully so as not to dislodge the paint and submit the tool to the laboratory with the paint intact.

Rust

Rust stains may sometimes be confused with bloodstains. However, rust can easily be differentiated from blood by a simple chemical field test.

Metals

Filings, shavings, and other metal particles can easily be identified chemically or spectrographically (Figure 7.9). It is possible to make a comparative analysis of a known and questioned metal sample that can show class characteristics. Metal filings located in the jaws of pipe wrenches are fairly common sources of this type of evidence. The wrench is used as a burglary tool by placing it onto a doorknob. Metal filings present in the teeth can be compared to those from the doorknob.

Case

A 13-year-old boy, evidently quite bright, decided to poison his mother slowly with mercury. He collected enough mercury by breaking into a number of homes in the neighborhood with a 17-year-old friend and removing the mercury in their thermostat switches. He may have read that mercury salts are highly toxic and mistook this to mean that elemental mercury and table salt together are highly toxic. Whatever the reason, he placed the mercury in a glass salt shaker along with table salt, shook the contents to break the mercury into fine droplets, and left the shaker to be used by his mother.

Figure 7.9 In the case of an alleged jailbreak attempt, the investigator wanted to know whether the inmate had used a hacksaw blade on his leg chains. When the crime was reenacted, a magnet was able to pick up numerous metal particles from the clothing of the investigator, whose hand was also slightly injured from using the blade. None of this evidence was found on the inmate, calling into question the hypothesis that he had tried to escape on his own. (Courtesy of the Los Angeles County Sheriff's Department.)

The forensic science laboratory was requested to show that the shaker had been used to dispense the mercury. The lid of the shaker was examined using a scanning electron microscope (SEM) with an energy dispersive x-ray detector (EDX). This combination allowed the operator to magnify an image of the object and determine its elemental composition. The lid of the salt shaker was made of plastic coated with nickel and chromium to give it a shiny appearance. The area around the holes in the shaker's lid was examined for traces of mercury and, using the SEM, one fine droplet of elemental mercury, clinging to the nickel plating at one of the holes, was found and identified as mercury by using EDX (Figure 7.10).

Textiles and Fibers

Fragments of cloth may become evidence in a wide variety of cases. Torn fabrics have been examined in murder cases in which the victim was tied and gagged with torn fabric, in burglary cases in which a suspect left a small torn piece of clothing caught at the point of entry, and in hit-and-run cases in which torn clothing was left on the undercarriage of the suspect's vehicle.

Fragments of textile evidence may yield class as well as individual characteristics. A portion of fabric may be physically fitted into another piece of fabric, thereby proving

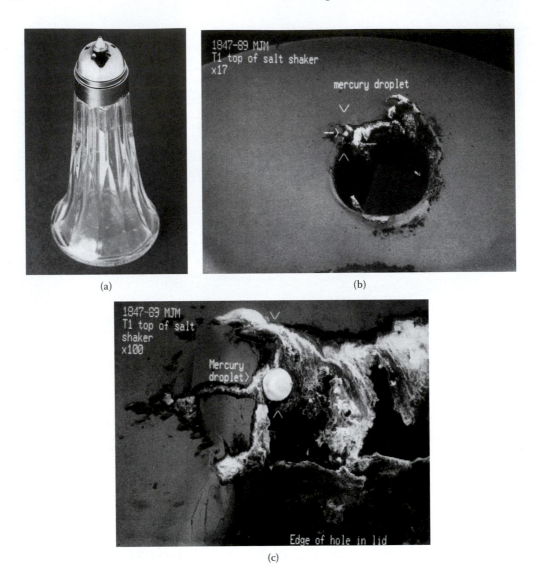

(a)   (b)

(c)

Figure 7.10 (a) A glass salt shaker used by a boy in an attempt to poison his mother. (b) One of the holes of the shaker was photographed using scanning electron microscopy. (c) The magnification clearly shows the droplet of mercury. (Courtesy of the Centre of Forensic Sciences, Toronto, Canada.)

a common source (Figure 7.11). A number of physical, chemical, and microscopic characteristics of textiles can be used for comparison purposes. Properties such as color, type of cloth, dye, direction of yarn twist, and thread count are useful in characterizing the evidence.

When a fragment of fabric is found during the course of a crime scene search, its location should be noted, indicated in a crime scene diagram, and photographed. As with other items of trace evidence, it is preferable not to remove the fabric from the object to which it is attached. If this is not possible, the fabric should be packaged in a clean container, properly labeled with the appropriate chain of custody information.

The location of the evidence at a point of entry or the physical appearance of the fabric may be useful as investigative leads. The detective may be able to theorize the location of a

(a)

(b)

(c)

(d)

Figure 7.11 The bodies of two teenage girls were discovered with multiple gunshot wounds. One of them had been bound with electrical speaker wire and gagged and covered with bedding. The bedding was a sheet with several strips of cloth missing. A search of the suspect's house was conducted and several strips of cloth were found that matched the sheet (a, b) from the scene along with pieces of wire (c, d) that matched as well. (Courtesy of the Detroit Police Department, Crime Laboratory Section, Detroit, Michigan.)

tear on an article of clothing or the type of cloth evidence that needs to be found for comparative purposes.

Investigators may overlook fiber evidence because of its extremely small size compared to fabric evidence. Five types of textile fibers can be encountered as evidence: animal fibers, such as wool; vegetable fibers, such as cotton or hemp; synthetic fibers, such as polyester, nylon, rayon, etc.; mineral fibers, such as glass wool; and blends of synthetic and natural fibers, the most common of which are polyester and cotton. Fiber evidence may be transferred by one person's clothing coming in contact with another's or from articles such as blankets, carpet, upholstery, and so forth. Fibers may be present on clothing, in fingernail scrapings, on hit-and-run vehicles, at points of entry, and on hair covered by knit hats (Figure 7.12 through 7.14).

Removal of fibers from other objects is best done at the crime laboratory. If this is not possible, fiber evidence can be removed by using forceps or cellophane tape or by vacuum sweeping. Of the three procedures, the tape method is probably the best. A length of tape about 4 inches long is taped end-to-end, forming a cylinder with the sticky side of the tape on

Figure 7.12 In a 4-month period between October 1977 and February 1978, the nude bodies of 10 girls and young women between the ages of 12 and 21 were found dumped on hillsides in Los Angeles. All had been raped, tortured, and strangled. One of the victims found lying at the side of a road had a small tuft of fibers on her left wrist. (Courtesy of the Los Angeles Police Department.)

(a)   (b)

Figure 7.13 (a) Fibers were subsequently collected from a chair (b) found in the suspect's home almost 2 years after the murders and compared to the evidence. The suspects, Angelo Buono, a 48-year-old auto upholsterer, and his cousin, a 32-year-old former security guard named Kenneth Bianchi, posed as police officers and "arrested" young women, who were then raped and sodomized and sometimes tortured before being slowly strangled to death. (Courtesy of the Los Angeles Police Department.)

the outside. The hand is inserted into the center of the tape and the sticky side of the tape is pressed on the item of interest. After sampling, the tape is placed sticky side down on a microscope slide or clean transparency sheet for submission to the laboratory. The procedure has its advantage in that it only collects surface material, whereas vacuum sweeping collects huge quantities of debris and forceps may miss many items of trace evidence.

(a)   (b)

Figure 7.14 Fibers from one of the murders linked the victim to the assailants' home. A Monsanto Cadon® fiber (a) made only between 1968 and 1974 and a second rare modified "Y" fiber (b) produced by Rohm and Haas for a short period of time were important evidence in the trial. The defendants were found guilty of nine counts of murder and sentenced to life imprisonment without the possibility of parole. (Courtesy of the Los Angeles Police Department.)

The laboratory can determine the type of fiber and whether it is similar to the control fiber specimen. It is not possible, with fiber evidence, to state with complete certainty that it came from one and only one source because most garments and textiles used today are mass produced. It is usually not possible to determine if a specific sample came from the garment in question or from another garment of similar manufacture.

Buttons

Buttons come in a very wide range of sizes and patterns; only in exceptional cases is it possible to match a button with the buttons of a particular garment. When a button is torn off, generally the thread and sometimes a piece of fabric may be present. If exemplars of the sewing thread and the garment are available for comparison, a more definitive conclusion about the source of the button may be made. If a piece of broken button is discovered, it is possible to match the broken piece physically with another portion of the button. This type of evidence can lead to a conclusive statement about the source of the evidence (Figure 7.15).

Cordage and Rope

Pieces of string or rope are sometimes found at crime scenes. If they were used to tie up a victim, the knots should not be untied; rather, the rope should be cut and tied back together with string. The knots present in the rope may prove to be useful evidence.

Rope and cordage evidence can be compared with exemplars for similarities. Properties that can be examined include the material from which the cordage is manufactured, the number of strands, direction of the twist in the rope, color, diameter, weight per unit of length, etc. All these properties taken together will allow the examiner to determine whether the material is of a similar manufacture.

(a)   (b)

(c)

Figure 7.15 (a) A button found at a burglary scene compared with one found on the suspect's jacket (b). A photomicrograph (c) shows manufacturing marks indicating common class characteristics. (Courtesy of the Orange County Sheriff-Coroner, Santa Ana, California.)

In some cases, rope and cordage evidence may have other trace evidence attached to it. In cases of strangulation, it may be possible to identify epithelial (skin) cells attached to the cordage.

Cigarettes and Tobacco

Cigarettes, cigarette butts, tobacco, and ash are sometimes found at crime scenes and may be overlooked as potentially useful evidence. From the point of view of forensic science, very little work has been done in the identification of tobaccos. This does not lessen, however, the possible use of this type of evidence.

Some laboratories maintain cigarette libraries from which they can often identify the brand from a cigarette butt. In some cases, information about the brand a subject smokes may be useful to the investigation. Similarly, the appearance of ash left at a location may indicate that a suspect smoked a pipe or cigar, which is useful in describing the habits of that individual.

Cigarette butts may be a useful source of other physical evidence. In some cases, latent fingerprints have been developed from cigarette butts by the ninhydrin process. It is also possible to determine the smoker's DNA from the saliva left on the butt. Although latent prints and DNA typing results may be negative, these procedures should be considered.

Empty cigarette packages may also be found along with cigarettes. Besides the brand and the possibility of determining fingerprints, it is sometimes possible to determine the general location of the sale of the cigarettes by the numbers on the package. The ability to determine the area of sale depends on whether the distributor kept records of these numbers (Figure 7.16).

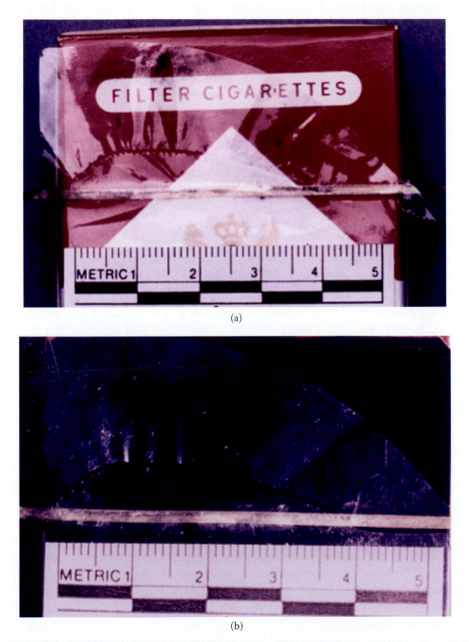

(a)

(b)

Figure 7.16 Sometimes seemingly insignificant items left at the scene are important. (a, b) The cellophane wrapping from a pack of Marlboro cigarettes was shown to have come from a pack of cigarettes found on a suspect. (Courtesy of the Los Angeles County Sheriff's Department.)

Matches

Matches found at a crime scene may be from smokers or from suspects who used them to light their way. Several may commonly be found in burglary cases. The surface of a single match is usually too small to find sufficient detail to identify a latent fingerprint. However, other useful bits of information may be determined from matches.

Matches may be wood or paper. The type of wood, microscopic appearance of the cardboard, color, dimension, and shape are useful in comparing a burned match with some exemplars associated with the suspect. Paper or cardboard matches are by far the most common kind at crime scenes and offer the best chance of directly incriminating a suspect. To show a connection, it is necessary to find the book of unused matches on the suspect or at least at the location with this person's latent prints present. Cardboard matches are made from wastepaper. As such, there is wide variability from book to book. It is possible to show a connection between the cardboard left in the matchbook and that of the match. In some instances, it is possible to fit the match into the book by the appearance of the torn end of the match and the remaining end in the book.

Matches are sometimes used as toothpicks. If the end of the match appears to be chewed, it may be possible to determine the DNA of the chewer from the saliva.

Burned Paper

Burned papers and charred documents are sometimes found in arson investigations or in instances in which an attempt was made to destroy records by fire. Burned documents can be deciphered, provided they are reasonably intact. If the paper has been reduced to ashes it is not possible to determine any writing. For this reason, it is particularly important to exercise extreme care when collecting, preserving, and transporting this type of evidence.

If burned paper is found in a metal file box, it should not be removed from the box; rather, it should be transported in the container in which it was found. If the documents are found in the open, or if the files they are in cannot be taken to the laboratory, the paper should be carefully placed into rigid cardboard boxes. Charred papers can be picked up by gently sliding a flat piece of cardboard under them. Once picked up from the scene, they can gently be placed in boxes.

It is preferable to hand carry boxes to the laboratory because of the fragile nature of this evidence. If this is not possible, the paper must be packaged so that it will not break up in transit. Cotton or any other similar material that will preserve the evidence can be layered in the cardboard boxes.

If the paper is still burning when the investigator arrives at the scene, no attempt should be made to put out the fire, unless the air supply can be shut off without handling the document. Otherwise, the paper should be allowed to burn completely.

If the burned material consists of a book, folded papers, or currency, no attempt should be made to separate the layers of paper. The debris should be kept together and submitted to the laboratory in that state.

Chemical treatment, photography, and examination under ultraviolet and infrared light often make the writing legible in charred documents. However, the documents must arrive intact in order for such examinations to be conducted.

Ash

The composition of ash will vary greatly depending on the source. It can sometimes be identified microscopically, chemically, or by means of spectroscopy. However, the source of the ash may prove difficult to determine. One type of ash common in arson cases is the residue of burned highway flares. This ash contains a significant level of strontium, responsible for the bright red color of the flare.

Soil

Soil evidence may be encountered in a wide variety of criminal investigations. It may be found on shoes, clothing, or the underside of motor vehicles and is useful in tying the suspect or victim to a location. A tire or footwear impression in soil makes it possible to prove that the subject was in fact present. (See Chapter 9 for a discussion of impression evidence.)

Soil is a mixture of decaying and weathered rock and decomposed organic material known as humus. It contains a wide variety of minerals such as quartz, feldspar, and mica as well as partially decomposed leaves, pine needles, pollen grains, and other plant fragments. Thus, it is easy to differentiate soils from various locations by microscopic examination of various components.

Known soil specimens from the crime scene are absolutely required for an analysis of the evidence sample. Samples should be collected from various regions at the specific location in question and several feet away from it, and at other locations, such as the subject's home and work, for elimination purposes.

Known samples can be placed in individual small glass jars. Clean baby food jars are useful for this purpose. (Metal containers should be avoided since metal can be a component of soil, and can add metallic contaminants to the samples.) Two or three tablespoons of topsoil are all that is usually required for known specimens. It is important not to dig deeper than an inch or so when collecting these specimens. The subsoil may have a significantly different composition from the topsoil and lead to confusing results. Again, the containers should be appropriately labeled and the location of each sample noted. When taking soil samples, be aware that footwear impressions may be present.

Soil specimens on shoes and other objects should be carefully handled. In certain instances, in the lab it may be possible to remove successive layers a little at a time and reconstruct the activities of the subject based on the different types of soil present.

Case

A murder victim's home was entered through a bedroom window. Beneath the window was a somewhat muddy planting area. A poorly defined footprint, believed to be the suspect's, was found in the planting area. A suspect was arrested a short time later and the police confiscated his muddy shoes. The suspect maintained that the mud was due to some gardening work he was doing at his home.

Soil specimens were submitted to the laboratory from several locations at the crime scene, the suspect's home, and two other locations where the suspect claimed to have been that day. The examination of the evidence indicated that the soil on one shoe did not come from the suspect's home or either of the two other locations. The soil was consistent with that from the crime scene. The other shoe contained two different soils, one consistent with the suspect's home and the second consistent with the crime scene.

Wood

As evidence, wood may be present as sawdust, splinters, chips, large pieces used as assault weapons, etc. Evidence may be present at the crime scene, on a suspect's clothing, or in a wound. Wood may also have tool marks.

Because of the wide variety of wood types and its use in building, furniture, and hand tools, this type of evidence is most valuable. It is possible to identify, compare, and match sources of wood evidence.

Wood may be divided into two types: hard woods and soft woods. It is possible to determine the type of wood and often the type of tree from pieces the size of sawdust particles. The examination of wood is done microscopically.

If the question is to decide whether two pieces of stem from a tree originally belonged together, the original external contour of the stem is a good guide, if it is in good condition. Cracks in the bark, structures and formations on the surface of the bark, and the position of the sawed surface in relation to the longitudinal axis of the trunk, together with the placing and general appearance of any felling cut have their own significance for the task of identification, which is simply a matter of seeing how the different pieces fit together. By matching them against one another, it is frequently possible to determine the correspondence between two pieces of wood separated from each other in the longitudinal direction of the tree.

The annual rings of a tree are very characteristic. By making a transverse section of an object under investigation, it is often possible to obtain a picture just as characteristic of the tree, within a limited region of the stem. Bruises and decay in the wood are often characteristic in position and extent and may assist in identification.

If an object under investigation is made from wood that has been worked in some way with tools (knife, plane, saw) or has been painted or surface treated in any other way, the possibility of identification is increased. Imperfections in the edge of the knife or plane blade (including planing machines) leave characteristic marks that can possibly be found on both pieces of wood. Unplaned wood, when sawed in the direction of the grain, often shows marks of varying width and depth from the saw used. In the case of frame-sawed lumber, these marks arise during the upward and downward movements of the frame saw. The variations are caused by inequalities in the setting of the teeth and by variations in the pressure on the wood under the saw. The same conditions hold for wood cut with a circular saw; the marks are more or less curved, depending on the diameter of the saw, and differ from the marks of a frame saw, which are straight but may be more or less oblique with reference to the grain of the wood. These saw marks have special significance in the identification of pieces of wood separated from one another in the direction of the grain.

It can be more difficult to determine, solely with the aid of marks from the saw used, whether two cut off pieces originally belonged together. If the cutting was done with a hand saw, identification is sometimes possible because the marks of such a saw are often irregular and show characteristic formations. This is connected with the fact that changes in the position of the saw, in relation to the piece of wood, always occur on the forward and backward strokes of the sawing arm. Also, after a pause in sawing, the saw never takes up exactly the same position again when restarted. In cutting with a machine saw, the marks are generally regular and reproducible and therefore cannot generally be used for identification. A transverse section of wood has a poorer power of reproducing marks from a saw than a longitudinal section, owing to the difference in the structure.

If pieces of wood have been painted or surface treated in any way, shades of color may be useful for identification and the pigment can be chemically and spectrographically examined to confirm the agreement or difference between the constituents. There may be several coats of paint, and agreement or difference in this respect may be noted.

Any knots or cracks in pieces of wood, as well as drill holes, nail holes, or screw holes, are significant when it is necessary to decide whether or not pieces of wood originally were a unit. Based on nail or screw holes or remaining nails or screws, it is sometimes possible to determine whether a certain piece of wood was previously combined with another piece or formed part of a floor or wall.

If pieces of wood are separated from one another by a break running in the direction of the grain, identity can be determined by fitting the pieces to one another. Certain difficulties are associated with a break going across the grain because the broken surfaces are often badly splintered and a number of significant pieces may have fallen away and been lost.

Chips and Splinters of Wood

Considerable quantities of chips or splinters may be found at the scene of a forced entry. They are usually examined to find marks from the tool used to gain entry. Chips of wood can also be valuable in the identification of the tool in another way. Mixed in with chips from the forced doors or windows may be a chip that has broken off the handle of a chisel, hammer, or other tool. A piece from a broken tool handle may be compared later with a tool recovered in the perpetrator's possession. Pieces of wood from the tool may be painted in the same way as the handle of the tool or make a physical match with the tool in jigsaw puzzle fashion.

Sawdust, Wood Meal, or Particles of Finely Powdered Wood

Particles of wood can sometimes be found in the pant cuffs, pockets, hat, or gloves of the suspect or detected on tape lifts of the suspect's clothes. Clues consisting of these particles may also be left behind at the scene if the clothes of the criminal were contaminated with them and the trace material brought to the scene. In some cases, the species of tree can be determined simply by microscopic examination and the occurrence of any foreign bodies on or together with the particles can be confirmed.

Wood anatomy and identification is a narrow specialty not found in many crime labs. University and U.S. Government experts are available for assistance in such cases.*

Plant Material

A wide variety of materials of plant origin may be useful sources of physical evidence. Besides wood, leaves, seeds, bark, twigs, and pollen are sometimes collected as evidence. They may be attached to clothing, found in a vehicle, or present on a weapon (Figure 7.17).

Fragments of plant material generally require a high degree of expertise to identify. Botanists employed at natural history museums or at a local arboretum may be willing to lend their expertise in the identification of such material.

---

* The Center for Wood Anatomy Research, U.S. Department of Agriculture, Forest Products Laboratory located in Madison, Wisconsin, is a good place to start. See http://www.fpl.fs.fed.us/.

(a)   (b)

(c)

Figure 7.17 A small, fresh fragment of *Adenostoma fasciculata* containing growths on its leaves, which were found to be galls of Eriophyid mites (a), was recovered from a suspect's vehicle. This unusual plant specimen was also present at the location where the victim's body had been dumped. This particular plant only exists at certain elevations on east-facing slopes and only near disturbed environments such as a road. Other plant materials, for example, pollens (b, c), are sometimes encountered as trace evidence. (Courtesy of the Los Angeles County Sheriff's Department.)

Pollen is a useful material for determining whether a subject was present in an area where flowering plants are located. Vacuum sweepings of a suspect's clothing may yield microscopic pollen grains whose species can be microscopically identified.*

Glass

Glass may be useful evidence in a wide variety of cases. Hit-and-run cases often have headlamp glass or windshield glass present, burglaries frequently involve window glass, and bottle glass is sometimes found in assault cases. Broken glass may yield information about the direction and speed of a projectile and, in the case of multiple projectiles, the sequence of events.

---

* For more information on forensic botany, see, for example, http://myweb.dal.ca/jvandomm/ forensicbotany/.

Broken Panes of Glass

The police investigator often must decide whether a pane of glass was broken from the outside or the inside or if it was struck by a bullet or by a rock. Pieces from the broken pane or the hole often show marks characteristic of the type of injury and the direction of the force. If correctly interpreted, these indications give useful information (Figures 7.18 and 7.19).

Anyone who examines the edge of a piece of broken glass will note a series of curved lines that form right angles with one side of the pane and curve tangentially with the other side. These fracture lines are a result of force applied to the glass pane and are referred to as rib markings; they can be used to determine from which direction the force came that caused the glass to break.

When an object has been thrown through a glass pane, two types of fractures that form a pattern resembling a spider's web will be seen. These fractures are called radial and concentric fractures. Radial fractures are cracks that start at the center or point from which the object struck the glass and run radially outward or in a somewhat star-shaped pattern from the point at which the break starts. Concentric fractures form concentric circular cracks in the glass around the point of impact.

Determining the direction of force becomes a simple matter of examining rib markings along the edges of radial or concentric fractures. Before drawing any conclusions about the direction of force, the examiner must be certain whether a radial or a concentric fracture is being examined. It is also worthwhile to mark the pane of glass to show the inside and outside clearly.

The determination of the direction of force is accomplished as follows: carefully remove a piece of broken glass, making note of which side faces which, locate an edge that

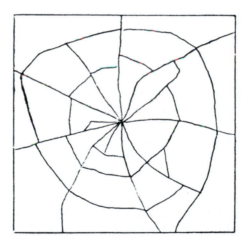

Figure 7.18 Sketch illustrating the radial and concentric fractures in a pane of glass.

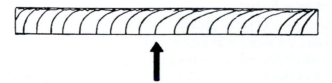

Figure 7.19 Diagram showing the curved lines in the edge of the glass in a concentric fracture. They are almost perpendicular to the side from which force was applied. In radial fractures, the direction is reversed.

(a)   (b)

Figure 7.20 (a, b) The sequence of individual fractures can also be determined. In this example, impact 1 was created prior to impact 2 because the radial fractures from impact 1 "block" the radial fractures from impact 2 from extending. (Courtesy of SIU, NYC OCME.)

corresponds to a radial fracture and examine it edgewise. Observe with which surface of the glass the rib markings make a right angle, because that side of the glass is not the side from which the force came; the force came from the opposite side (Figure 7.20a and b).

The results of concentric fractures are opposite those of radial fractures. In examining the edge of a concentric fracture, the side of the glass forming the right angle with the rib markings is the side from which the force came. Because of this obvious chance of confusion, it is very important to be able to distinguish between radial and concentric fractures. It is also important to have made note of which side of the glass faced which direction.

With small pieces of glass, it is very important not to get the sides mixed up. It is advisable to collect all the pieces of glass and fit them together so that a complete picture is obtained of the broken pane where the force acted. In the case of windowpanes, a useful indication can be obtained from the layer of dirt often present on the outside of the glass.

Definite conclusions should be drawn from the curved lines of the edge surfaces only in the case of fractures that lie nearest to the point of attack. Solely with these closest fractures can one be sure that the fractures resulted from the break in question. Fractures at a greater distance from the point of attack may have been produced, for example, when the object used for breaking the glass was brought back or by projecting and interfering pieces of glass being broken off by hand.

When glass is transported to the laboratory for examination, the pieces should be carefully marked and individually wrapped in paper. The wrapped evidence may then be placed together in a box for easier transportation. Packaging should be done to minimize breakage.

Glass Perforated by a Bullet

If a bullet perforates a pane of glass, the hole is expanded in a crater on the side where the bullet exited the pane. The location at which the cone-shaped crater is narrowest indicates the direction from which the bullet was fired (Figure 7.21).

The appearance of the hole can indicate the velocity of the projectile. High-velocity bullets leave an almost circular hole in a pane of glass without noticeable cracking or with cracks merely starting. Lower velocity ammunition leaves an almost regular polygon with radial cracks running outward.

Figure 7.21 Diagram showing the formation of a bullet hole in a pane of glass; note the crater form of the hole. The arrow shows the direction of the shot.

A shot at very close range more or less completely shatters the glass from the pressure of the muzzle gases; the extent depends on the power of the cartridge and the thickness of the glass. In such cases, it is impossible to obtain a clear idea of the appearance of the shot hole unless the shattered splinters of glass can be pieced together. In most cases, this is not possible because the splinters from the parts nearest the actual hole are too small. In a very favorable case, indications of the metal of the bullet on the edges around the hole may be detected spectrographically. A reliable indication that the glass was shattered by a shot at close range is the presence of gunshot residue particles on the glass.

It is sometimes difficult to determine whether a hole in a pane of glass was caused by a bullet or by a stone that was thrown. A small stone thrown at relatively high speed (such as one flung by the action of a tire of a passing car) can produce a hole very similar to that caused by a bullet. However, the crater-like expansion of a hole caused by a small stone may not show the same uniform fracture in the glass as a bullet hole would. Furthermore, holes caused by small stones generally do not show the same geometrical regularity in the radial and concentric cracks in the glass around the hole as that usually shown by a bullet hole. On the other hand, a large stone can shatter a pane of glass in a manner that nearly resembles the results of a close-range shot. Thus, a careful search for the projectile is necessary to determine the cause of the break.

If a number of breaks are in a pane of glass, it is sometimes possible to determine the order of events producing the holes. Radial cracks produced by the first incident stop by themselves or run to the edges of the glass. On the other hand, cracks from subsequent incidents stop when they meet a crack already present in the glass as a result of earlier fractures. Even when the damage is extensive and large portions of glass have fallen away, the order of the damage can often be established by fitting the pieces together.

Cracked or Burst Panes of Glass

If a pane of glass has been cracked by the action of heat, it shows characteristic long wavy fractures. Pieces that have fallen out are generally found in the same direction as the source of heat. If a limited area of the glass has been exposed to a direct flame, a piece of glass corresponding to that area often breaks off.

Automobile safety glass breaks completely or partially into pieces or small rods of a regular form when subjected to a violent blow or shock. Automobile manufacturers use tempered glass intentionally because it lessens the chance of being cut by flying glass.

A pane of tempered glass shattered by a bullet may still remain hanging in position on the vehicle. In a typical crackle pattern, the crack formation extends over the whole pane, but close around the point of fracture, a large number of small pieces of glass usually come loose and fall away; thus a study of the crater formation in the glass is possible only in rare cases. If pieces that have fallen out are found, however, in favorable cases, they can be pieced together in their places near the point of impact and the appearance of the fracture can be reconstructed.

If a few small pieces believed to be tempered glass are found at the scene of an accident, a simple test can determine whether the glass is in fact tempered. Interference patterns caused by strain in the glass are easily observed by examining the glass with polarized light. A specimen of glass is placed over a light source with a polarizing filter. The glass is viewed with a second polarizing filter and a characteristic pattern is observed, indicating tempered glass.

Glass Splinters

At a scene where the criminal has obtained entry by breaking a window or glazed door, the investigating officer should always remember to collect pieces of glass for comparison purposes. If a suspect is found at a later time, a careful examination of the clothing may show splinters of glass (Figure 7.22). Glass splinters may also be found in the handle of a tool used to force entry into a building.

When such splinters of glass are found on a suspect's clothing or tools from a burglary investigation, they will usually be too small to make a direct physical comparison against the

Figure 7.22 A burglar may be linked to a window he smashed by the tiny fragments of glass that fly backward onto his person and clothing. (Courtesy of the Centre of Forensic Sciences, Toronto, Canada.)

pane of glass from which they possibly came. However, a number of other comparisons can be made to show a common source between the exemplar and questioned glass specimens.

Glass evidence may be examined for a number of physical and chemical properties. Density, refractive index, color, thickness, and chemical composition are some of the common characteristics examined to differentiate glass. Such tests will not result in a definite identification because glass is a mass-produced material with wide use. Nonidentity, however, can be proven and this may be useful information.

When known samples of glass evidence are collected as exemplars, several samples should be taken from different parts of the same pane of glass and packaged separately because there may be variation in glass properties in the same pane. Always note the direction one or both of the sides of the glass face before taking the sample. This is the only way you or the laboratory can definitively determine the direction of the force through the glass.

Objects Left at the Crime Scene

Criminals sometimes leave items behind at the crime scene that they believe have no further use. Items may be lost or forgotten by the suspect. The criminal may have been surprised during the act and forced to leave abruptly without picking up personal effects. Items left behind can be extremely valuable to investigators; they may help connect the suspect to the crime in other ways or prove the suspect's identity if fingerprints or DNA are present.

Paper

Paper such as newspaper, wrapping paper, and paper bags is sometimes left at a crime scene. Besides trace evidence, handwriting, latent fingerprints, and touch DNA may be present. If the paper at the scene is torn or cut, a search of the suspect's home or car may turn up a matching piece of paper that can be fitted together with the evidence. In some cases, watermarks or stains on a piece of paper may be used to show a connection to paper located at another site.

Articles of Clothing

Manufacturer's markings on clothing are occasionally of value. The presence of a foreign label in clothing may indicate the nationality of the wearer; however, because a large number of clothes are imported, any conclusion is open to question. Size and laundry marks may be valuable. Size gives an indication of the physical characteristics of the subject and laundry marks may identify the suspect. Other marks such as initials and even names are sometimes found. One should always search for hair and other trace evidence. If secretions or dried blood is found on an article of clothing left at a crime scene, the subject's DNA type may be determined. Pockets should be searched as a matter of course. In some cases, useful evidence will be found. Torn pieces of clothing are valuable. If a matching piece of clothing can be found in the suspect's home or car, it can easily tie the suspect to the location.

Product Markings

Many commercial products bear manufacturer's marks on the label, package, or container. The markings are used to designate the date, lot number, location of manufacture, and

Figure 7.23 In a highly unusual case, two revolvers each factory stamped had the same serial number. When one of the guns was submitted to the laboratory as part of a criminal investigation, a record check showed that the weapon belonged to an individual residing in northern California. The owner was contacted and advised that his revolver had been recovered. To the investigator's surprise, the owner reported that he had the gun in his possession. The firearms investigator obtained the second gun to photograph this unusual occurrence. The lesson here is never assume anything is as it seems. (Courtesy of the Los Angeles County Sheriff's Department.)

other such details as a control to assist the manufacturer in checking on distribution, sales of the product, and quality control. The markings may also assist the investigator in determining the origin of products found at crime scenes. Because the markings are usually in code form, the manufacturer or distributor must be contacted to determine the meaning of the information (Figure 7.23).

Foodstuffs

Foodstuffs in the form of stains or debris are sometimes found as evidence and may be useful in determining the type of work in which a subject is engaged. For example, if vacuum sweepings are examined and a quantity of wheat starch is found, it could indicate that the suspect had been baking. Through careful examination, it is possible to determine the nature of very small samples of foodstuffs through microscopic and microchemical means.

Cosmetics

Cosmetics such as lipstick, nail polish, and various creams and lotions may sometimes be collected as evidence in cases. If exemplars are available, a laboratory can make a chemical comparison to determine whether the known and questioned specimens share a common

Figure 7.24 Starch, which is sometimes used in cosmetics in place of talc, has a highly characteristic appearance under polarized light microscopy, sometimes referred to as a "Maltese Cross." This photomicrograph is of potato starch. (Courtesy of the Los Angeles County Sheriff's Department.)

source. Cosmetic firms are constantly reformulating their products, and so if the brand of the cosmetic can be determined, it may be possible to determine the approximate time a given specimen was on the market (Figure 7.24).

Hair

Hair evidence is generally associated with crimes involving physical contact such as murder, rape, assault, traffic accidents, and other similar crimes. Hair may be found at the crime scene, on the victim or suspect, or attached to a weapon, tool, vehicle, or article of clothing. Because of its small size, hair may be difficult to find. Care and patience are required to conduct a thorough search for this evidence.

Determining if hairs come from a similar source is a controversial subject. The Innocence Project[*] has uncovered cases in which the interpretation of hair examinations has been in conflict with DNA test results. Examiners suggest that microscopic evaluation of hairs should be further tested using DNA testing (mitochondrial DNA testing if only the hair shaft is present and nuclear DNA testing if a suitable root is present). Hair-testing results are best reported using these two procedures to complement one another.[†,‡] Before DNA testing, microscopic hair examination can be used to exclude a suspect hair as having come from the same source if the questioned and known hairs are of sufficient length.

Reports stating that the known and exemplar hair specimens are "similar and may have come from the same person or a person with similar hair characteristics" only beg the question. A forensic examiner is not able to provide the degree of certainty to a statement of similarity and laypersons may incorrectly conclude that the term "similar hair characteristics" is more specific than it actually is.

[*] See http://www.innocenceproject.org/.
[†] Houck, M. M. and Budowle, B., Correlation of microscopic and mitochondrial DNA hair comparisons. *J Forensic Sci* 47(5), 2002.
[‡] Kolowski, J., A Comparison Study of Hair Examination Methodologies. *J Forensic Sci* 49(6), 2004.

Even though it is not possible to determine the person from whom a strand of hair came, there is probative value in hair examination. Information such as species, location of growth on the body, hair treatment, hair disease, and whether hairs fell out naturally or were forcibly pulled can be determined.

When conducting a hair examination, the criminalist first attempts to determine whether the hair evidence is animal or synthetic in origin. Microscopic examination of a hair quickly determines whether the evidence is animal, synthetic, or simply a plant fiber. Furthermore, it is possible to determine whether the hair is human or animal in origin and, if animal, the species of the animal. Domestic animals such as dogs, cats, cows, and horses are somewhat common. Hairs from wild animals are sometimes collected at crime scenes, for example, at the scene of skeletal remains. It is not possible to determine whether two hair specimens come from a specific animal. Although differentiating between human and animal hair is not difficult, determining the species of animal requires a greater degree of expertise from a hair examiner.

In addition to determining that a specimen of hair is human, it is usually possible to determine whether the hair is from the head or another part of the body. At one time, it was possible to draw a conclusion about the gender of an individual based on the length of a hair strand. Present hairstyles no longer make that deduction valid.

Examination of hair may indicate that it was chemically treated. Hairs that have been bleached, dyed, straightened, or otherwise treated can be compared with specimens from a subject to determine whether the subject's hair has been treated in the same way. Sometimes, hair shows the presence of lice or fleas, which can be useful as a means of comparison. Microscopic examination of the hair root may indicate that the hair was forcibly pulled out as opposed to falling out naturally. Such information may be used to indicate a struggle.

Searching for hair at the crime scene is a tedious process. Subjecting the floor, furniture, and other objects to a very thorough examination is necessary; a flashlight and pair of tweezers are suggested for this purpose. Hair found on an object or in a certain location may be placed in a clean sheet of paper that is folded and placed in a properly labeled envelope. Detailed notes should be made to indicate the date, time, and location of the hair. A sketch or photograph of the area should be made. When a number of hair samples are collected from the same location at the crime scene, sorting the specimens is not recommended. They should be submitted to the crime laboratory for careful and expert examination. If several hairs from different locations are collected, it is important not to package them together. Confusion will arise if the hairs are different and in the same package.

Hair evidence is frequently found on the body of a victim. Pulled-out strands of hair may be found clutched in the hands or under the fingernails of a murder victim. A rape victim sometimes has her assailant's pubic hair present on her body or the bed or location where she was lying.

Pubic hair combings in rape and rape–murder cases are a routine way of collecting hair evidence. It is advisable to collect hair as well as other types of evidence associated with these cases as soon as possible. Trace evidence such as hair is quickly lost unless gathered promptly.

Clothing belonging to the victim of a murder, rape, or assault should be examined for hair evidence. Hairs may become entangled among threads of the fabric. Generally, a very careful examination of the clothing is necessary to locate hairs.

To examine hair evidence collected in an investigation fully, it is necessary to obtain exemplars from the individuals involved. Hair specimens should be gathered from the entire body—head, ancillary, face, chest, arms, pubis, legs, etc. Sufficient numbers of hairs should be taken from each location. Pulling or plucking is the preferred way to collect hair. Head hairs should be collected from several different areas of the head. Specimens should be taken from the front, back, left, right, and top areas. About 25 hairs should be collected from the head. The reason for the large number is because hair varies so much even on the same person. A close inspection of a person's head hair will clearly show several different shades and even colors on a given subject. Thus a large sampling is desirable. It is important to package hairs collected from different parts of the body separately.

Feathers

On rare instances, feathers may be collected as evidence in an investigation. Most crime laboratories have very little or no expertise in analyzing this type of material. Feathers should be collected if discovered and may be identified by experts at museums or academic institutions.*

Electrical Wire

Insulated electrical wire is sometimes collected as evidence. The wire may have been used to tie up a victim of a crime or it is sometimes attached to a car stereo or tape deck stolen from a vehicle. In both cases, it may be possible to show that one end of the wire was once part of another end (Figure 7.25).

Generally, electrical wire that has many strands does not lend itself to tool mark examination. The wires are so fine that sufficient markings are not imparted onto the wire from the tool. If the wire is of a thicker gauge, it may be possible to examine extrusion marks on both ends to determine if each of the pieces has the same class characteristics.

Extrusion marks will also be present on the wire insulation. Because the insulation has a greater surface area, it is easier to work with that portion of the evidence. The extrusion

Figure 7.25 An example of a match of two pieces of wire demonstrating they once were from a common source. (Courtesy of the Los Angeles County Sheriff's Department.)

* For an overview of forensic ornithology see http://www.wilsonsociety.org.

markings along with the cut edge, which sometimes can be made to fit the other piece of wire evidence, can lead to the conclusion that the wires were once from the same continuous piece.

If a positive fit cannot be made, physical characteristics such as the number of strands of wire, the gauge, the appearance of the break, and the color and markings on the insulation may be used at least to show that the wire was of a similar manufacture. Whatever type of examination is made, it is always necessary to have an exemplar to compare with the evidence wire to make a conclusion.

Broken Tools

Broken tools are frequently discovered at burglaries of safes and breaking-and-entering cases. Broken ends from screwdrivers, wrecking bars, and metal punches are important types of physical evidence. Their usefulness lies in the fact that, if the remaining part of the tool is discovered, a positive statement can be made that the piece found at the scene and the tool were once intact (Figure 7.26).

(a)

(b)

Figure 7.26 (a, b) A broken knife blade is shown with pieces recovered from a crime scene. (Courtesy of the Los Angeles County Sheriff's Department.)

Broken knives are another kind of tool found at crime scenes. A piece of knife blade may be discovered at the scene of an assault or murder or be present in the wound of a victim. If the other part of the knife can be recovered, the two parts can be physically fitted together.

In addition to the fit, a microscopic examination of the knife and the broken piece of blade usually shows fine scratches caused by wear and use on the flat surface of the blade. These markings run continuously through the area of the break and can conclusively show that the broken piece and the blade were once a continuous piece.

Tape

Electrical, adhesive, duct, masking, and cellophane tape are sometimes recovered at crime scenes. The tape may have been used to bind a victim or to tape two objects together. If a roll of tape is located in the suspect's belongings, it may be possible to piece together the portion of tape from the scene and that found in the suspect's possession. If the tear at the end of the tape is ragged enough, a conclusive statement about a common source may be made. If the cut on the tape is very sharp, such as that made by scissors, only a statement about class characteristics can be made. Since tape is often torn with the teeth, DNA testing can also be used (Figure 7.27).

Headlamps

Headlamps from automobiles and other motor vehicles are routinely submitted to crime laboratories in traffic accident investigations. A careful examination of the headlamp filament may help determine whether the lamp was on or off at the time of the accident.

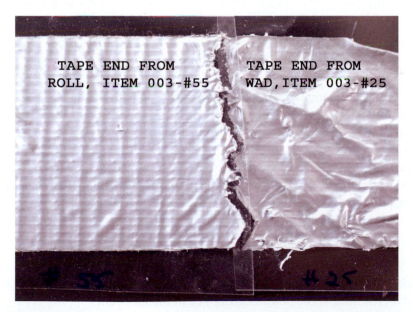

Figure 7.27 Duct tape is commonly used in a variety of crimes. Often, it is possible to demonstrate that the tape found on the victim or at the crime scene and the tape found in possession of the suspect came from the same source by a careful examination of the cut or torn ends. (Courtesy of Frederic A. Tulleners, Director, Forensic Science Graduate Program, University of California, Davis Extension, Davis, California.)

The traffic investigator should be aware of this possibility and collect any pieces of broken headlamp, tail lamp, or other debris present at the scene of the accident.

Chapter Questions

1. Which of the following items would be classified as trace evidence?
   a) Safe insulation
   b) Glass shards
   c) Soil
   d) All of the above
2. Describe how Locard's exchange principle occurs with regard to trace evidence left behind at a crime scene.

3. When dealing with a homicide victim's clothing, which of the following procedures is the best way to capture any trace evidence?
   a) Let the medical examiner collect the clothing at the autopsy.
   b) Examine the clothing for trace evidence before transporting the body for an autopsy and collect any items that you find.
   c) Remove the clothes at the scene and package together to minimize cross-contamination.
   d) Allow the clothes to fully dry on the body before transporting to the autopsy.
4. When is it better to remove an item of trace evidence from a larger object rather than collecting the whole item?

5. The _____ exemplars must never be packaged with the questioned samples.
   a) Known
   b) Unknown
   c) Crime scene
   d) Standard
6. Describe the proper procedure for collecting paint samples from a hit-and-run investigation involving two vehicles.

7. Which of the following techniques would be the best method for collecting fibers found on the floor at the point of entry at a homicide scene?
   a) Using forceps
   b) Tape lifts
   c) Vacuum
   d) All are acceptable

8. (True/False) When trying to determine the direction of force in glass using a concentric edge, the side of the glass forming a right angle with the conchoidal fracture is the side the force came from.
   a) True
   b) False
9. What are some of the characteristics that a criminalist can provide when examining hair?

Blood, Forensic Biology, and DNA

8

It can be said that of all the significant advances made in forensic science during the past couple of decades, forensic biology has made the greatest strides. Deoxyribonucleic acid (DNA) is present at most crime scenes. It can be used to determine the identity of unknown human remains, tie a suspect or victim to a crime scene, establish paternity, and identify the unknown perpetrator to a cold case. Today, forensic DNA typing plays a significant role in criminal investigations and has revolutionized the ability to prosecute criminals and exonerate the innocent.*

A Word of Caution!

Before discussing any testing procedures concerning blood and other biological fluids, some remarks are appropriate about the dangers of blood-borne diseases, for example, hepatitis B, hepatitis C, and HIV. Individuals working around wet or dried blood at crime scenes, autopsies, and in crime laboratories where whole blood or other biological specimens are present are advised to use universal precautions. These include personal protective equipment (PPE) such as Tyvek™ suits, lab coats, gloves, masks, and goggles/face shields. The important thing to remember is that the type of barrier protection should be appropriate for the type of exposure anticipated. Persons who routinely work with blood and blood products should consider receiving hepatitis vaccinations.

Surgical gloves should be worn when working with any biological products: blood, saliva, semen, etc. (Nitrile gloves are available to those with latex allergies.) Cut resistant gloves should also be worn when scraping an item for DNA evidence with a razor blade. Smoking, eating, or drinking in areas that contain these items is not to be permitted. When specific questions arise about proper handling of biological evidence, crime laboratory forensic biology personnel are good resources. Working around biological samples of unknown sources has a potential risk; however, with appropriate care and caution, those risks can be minimized.

Guidelines for handling biological materials should be posted and discussed with personnel who must handle these materials. Periodic briefing, or annual "Right to Know" training, to remind personnel how to handle this type of evidence is important. Appropriate procedures must be taken for disposal of biological evidence as well. Commercial disposal companies that specialize in biohazard disposal should be used to destroy such materials.

---

* Former President George W. Bush's initiative, *Advancing Justice through DNA Technology*, brought much needed funding to help alleviate backlogs, strengthen crime lab capacity, stimulate research, and provide training. As part of the DNA initiative, the Department of Justice launched www.dna.gov as an excellent resource on DNA topics for attorneys, investigators, researchers, and policymakers.

Contamination

Contamination is a big concern when it comes to DNA and biological evidence. Webster's dictionary defines contamination as the "act of making impure or unsuitable by contact or mixture with something unclean or foreign." When collecting evidence or processing a crime scene, it is critical to eliminate, or at least minimize the accidental transfer of DNA as much as possible.

Contamination can occur between items of evidence; it is for this reason that collected items of evidence should be packaged separately. Comingled items that are packaged together run the risk of biological material being transferred from one item to the other. Known and questioned samples also should NEVER be packaged together. One should ensure that any tools or equipment used to collect or process evidence do not become a source of contamination as well. If disposables cannot be used, tools can be wiped down with a 10% bleach solution, followed by 70% ethanol.

Contamination can also occur when an investigator or crime scene technician inadvertently deposits their own DNA on an item of evidence. This can occur by coughing, sneezing, or talking at a crime scene (or in the lab) without a mask. Handling or touching an item without gloves can also leave behind trace amounts of epithelial (skin) cells that could contaminate any DNA profiles that are subsequently developed. Any individual entering a crime scene (including police brass) should submit their own DNA samples to the testing laboratory for quality assurance (QA) measures. Elimination samples such as these are NOT eligible to be uploaded to national DNA databases (i.e., CODIS) but are used by the laboratory solely for in-house comparisons. If elimination samples are not taken from police officers or crime scene personnel at the scene who may have inadvertently contaminated evidence, then any unknown DNA profiles developed could potentially be uploaded to the COmbined DNA Indexing System (CODIS).

Bloodstain Pattern Analysis*

Bloodstain pattern evidence is often present at crimes of violence. Because blood behaves in well-understood mechanisms, the shape, grouping, and distribution of bloodstains can assist the investigator in reconstructing what took place at the crime scene. In addition to determining to whom the blood belongs through DNA, it is often necessary to determine the movement and direction of persons, the sequence of events, the area of origin of a pattern, the number of impacts during an incident, and the object used to create a specific pattern. These determinations can be used to corroborate or contradict the statement(s) made by victim(s), suspect(s), and/or witness(es).

There are three basic classifications of bloodstains: passive, spatter, and altered. Being able to identify the type of bloodstain present and how it was created can aid an investigator in deciding what stains are the most probative to collect for DNA typing. Bloodstain

---

* The International Association of Bloodstain Pattern Analysts is a professional association for those who routinely evaluate this type of evidence. Their website is located at http://www.iabpa.org/. The International Association for Identification offers certification in BPA. See their website at http://theiai.org

patterns often tell a story of what took place at a crime scene; it is up to the investigator to read that story and interpret it.

Two types of bloodstains, for example, are impact spatter (blood that travels through the air from an impact mechanism) and transfer stains (stains resulting from contact with a bloody surface). Determining whether a stain was made by transfer or a spatter producing event will oftentimes be a critical piece of information in a case.

Case 1

Police responded to a 911 call of a husband who said that he came home after a night of playing cards with the guys and discovered his wife on the floor covered in blood and his house ransacked. When questioned by police about the blood on his clothes he said that he got the bloodstains on his shirt and pants when he leaned over his wife's body to administer cardiopulmonary resuscitation (CPR). After examining his clothes, investigators determined that the majority of blood on the suspect's clothes was from a spatter producing event and were not transfer stains. After being presented with this evidence, the suspect confessed to beating his wife with a baseball bat and turning his house upside down to make it look like a break-in.

Directionality of a bloodstain (Figure 8.1) can also be used to help corroborate or disprove a suspect's statement. The pointed or tail end of a bloodstain indicates the direction of travel. The angle of impact can also be determined by using the following formula:

$$\text{Angle of impact}\,(\theta) = \text{arc} \sin \frac{(\text{width of ellipse})}{(\text{length of ellipse})}$$

Figure 8.1 Blood drops that have hit a surface at an angle. The tail end of the bloodstain indicates the direction of travel.

Case 2

DNA typing of bloodstains alone oftentimes does not solve a case. A suspect who claims he was acting in self-defense is not disputing the fact that he caused the victim to bleed. DNA typing showing that blood at the scene and on the suspect's pants came from the victim would not be very helpful in proving or disproving the suspect's claim. Bloodstains, however, showing upward directionality and clustered on a wall close to the floor indicate that it was highly likely that the victim was lying on the floor when the suspect stomped and kicked him, disproving the self-defense claim.

In describing blood marks at a crime scene, some of the terms generally used are bloodstain, swipe, wipe, spatter, drip stain, expired blood, parent stain, satellite stain, insect stain, and several others. The Scientific Working Group on Bloodstain Pattern Analysis (BPA) (www.swgstain.org) has established recommended terminology along with definitions to standardize the terms used in this field. This recommended terminology allows investigators to be on the same page when discussing, writing, reporting, or testifying about these stains.

Case 3

An elderly female was assaulted by her daughter with an oxygen tank and a wine bottle while in the living room of her apartment. The female lived for a period of time but eventually died due to injuries she sustained from the assault.

Figure 8.2 depicts various bloodstain patterns on the entryway floor of the apartment. Eight pressurized oxygen cylinders were also on the entryway floor near the entry door. Impact spatter was noted on seven of the cylinders while one of the cylinders was heavily bloodstained with apparent hair adhering to it. A ring of blood was also seen on the floor beneath this heavily bloodstained cylinder. In addition, impact spatter was seen on the wall behind this cylinder indicating that the cylinder was not in this position when the spatter was deposited. Voids were visible on the wall behind the other seven cylinders indicating that these cylinders were in their current positions

Figure 8.2 Bloodstain patterns were found on the entryway floor of the apartment.

when the assault occurred. A void is a term used to describe an area within a generally continuous bloodstain pattern that lacks bloodstains. Based on the significant amount of blood and apparent hair attached to the one cylinder as well as the presence of impact spatter on the wall behind the cylinder and the ring of blood on the floor beneath the cylinder, the heavily bloodstained cylinder was likely used as a weapon to assault the victim. Figures 8.3 through 8.5 show the locations of the oxygen cylinders, the impact

Figure 8.3 Eight pressurized oxygen cylinders were found near the entry door. (Courtesy of Melissa Simons, Oregon State Police Central Point Forensic Laboratory.)

Figure 8.4 A ring of blood on the floor shows the position of the likely weapon—one of the oxygen canisters. (Courtesy of Melissa Simons, Oregon State Police Central Point Forensic Laboratory.)

Figure 8.5 The wall behind where the cylinders stood shows impact splatter behind the blood-stained cylinder and voids behind the others. (Courtesy of Melissa Simons, Oregon State Police Central Point Forensic Laboratory.)

spatter on the wall behind the heavily bloodstained cylinder and the ring of blood on the floor where this cylinder was positioned, and the lack of impact spatter behind the remaining cylinders. (Case provided by Melissa Simons, Oregon State Police Central Point Forensic Laboratory.)

Bloodstain pattern analysis (BPA) is a field in and of itself and an in-depth discussion of it is beyond the scope of this book.* BPA requires much experience and training to correctly make interpretations about bloodstain patterns. Beginning and advanced blood-stain pattern interpretation courses are available, and it is highly recommended that such courses of study be taken prior to performing crime scene reconstruction on actual cases. Continuing education and experience will allow the investigator to draw the most accurate conclusions. Crime scene reconstruction through the use of bloodstain pattern interpretation is a useful technique but only for those who are properly trained. All too often, unfortunately, investigators overstate their conclusions based on a limited understanding of BPA and crime scene reconstruction.

Presumptive Tests for Blood[†]

Scenes of violent crimes often contain minute quantities of blood that, because of their small size, may not be readily noticed. Presumptive blood tests (sometimes called cata-lytic tests) may be used to search for these small amounts of blood. These chemical tests are also useful at scenes where the suspect cleaned up the crime scene or to differentiate

---

* James, S. et.al., *Principles of Bloodstain Pattern Analysis: Theory and Practice*, CRC Press (2005), does an excellent job in thoroughly covering this topic.
† For an excellent review of presumptive tests, see Cox, M., A study of the sensitivity and specificity of four presumptive tests for blood, *J. Forensic Sci.*, 36(5), 1503–1511, 1991.

between blood and other stains (e.g., rust, chocolate milk, ketchup, lipstick, etc.). It should be remembered, however, that presumptive tests are NOT confirmatory tests for blood.

Historically, several chemicals have been used as presumptive tests to determine the presence of blood: leucomalachite green, phenolphthalein, orthotolidine, and tetramethylbenzidine. All are presumptive or screening tests. Another presumptive test, luminol, is described later.

Presumptive tests are color spot tests that depend on the properties of hemoglobin (the oxygen-carrying molecule found in blood). They are extremely sensitive and can easily detect very small quantities of blood. The test results are easy to perform and lend themselves to use by crime scene technicians. Interpretation of test results is critical because other materials can give false-positive results. A positive result can result from the presence of human or animal blood and a variety of plant materials that contain the chemical peroxidase.

Chemical kits used for presumptive tests are available through law enforcement supply companies or bulk chemicals may be purchased at considerable savings from chemical supply houses.

Of the foregoing tests, phenolphthalein and leucomalachite green are generally considered the most specific, while orthotolidine and tetramethylbenzidine are the most sensitive. Generally, the phenolphthalein test (also known as the Kastle–Mayer test) is a good overall choice. The test may be conducted on filter paper or on cotton-tipped swabs. Performing the test directly on the evidence should be avoided. After collection of the suspect blood, a drop of the Kastle–Mayer reagent is added. Next, a drop of 3% hydrogen peroxide is added. The presence of hemoglobin causes, or catalyzes, an oxidative reaction to occur resulting in a color change from clear to pink (Figure 8.6).

Figure 8.6 The Kastle–Mayer test showing a positive presumptive test for blood. (Courtesy of the Los Angeles County Sheriff's Department.)

Case 4

A suspect physically assaulted the victim and slashed him several times on his body. The suspect fled the scene prior to the arrival of the police and later admitted to washing off the knife that was used in the attack.

The knife was submitted to the lab and examined for the presence of blood. Although the suspect admitted to washing the knife, a small amount of reddish-brown staining was noted around a screw on the handle of the knife as well as on the edge of a clip attached to the opposite side of the handle of the knife. A positive result for a presumptive test for blood was obtained from the staining in each of these areas. The DNA profile obtained from the blood around the screw of the knife handle was a mixture with the major DNA profile matching the victim. In addition, the DNA profile obtained from the blood on the edge of the clip of the knife handle matched the victim. Figures 8.7 and 8.8 indicate the location of the screw on the handle of the knife where the reddish-brown staining was located and the reddish-brown staining around the screw on the handle of the knife taken at 12.5× magnification with a stereobinocular microscope. (Courtesy of Melissa Simons, Oregon State Police Central Point Forensic Laboratory.)

Hemastix® are another good presumptive test for blood and can be purchased at a local pharmacy (they were originally designed to test for the presence of blood in urine).

The luminol test is easily used in the field and very useful for searching large areas for blood, particularly if the area has been cleaned up. A drawback of the test is that the room must be dark because blood reacts with luminol by giving off light, a process called chemiluminescence. The reagent is sprayed with an aerosol sprayer. The glow given off is very faint; therefore, the area must be almost completely dark to visualize the chemiluminescence. The test works best on older stains. In some instances, outlines of shoes and even marks caused by mopping or wiping up an area can be clearly visualized by means of this test. Experience in interpreting this test is required. At times, pinpoint glowing is observed, which is not the result of bloodstains; with a positive test, whole areas are seen glowing. Bleach can also yield false-positive results, so care must be taken in interpreting results. Bluestar® forensic latent bloodstain reagent is also an effective latent blood detection tool that can be used at crime scenes and does not have any deleterious effects on DNA testing. Its advantages over luminol include that it is nontoxic, total darkness is not required, and it has stronger luminescence, longer laster reactions, and higher sensitivity (Figure 8.9).

Figure 8.7 Reddish-brown staining around the screws on the handle of this knife tested positive for blood.

Figure 8.8 Staining around a screw on the handle of the knife shown at 12.5× magnification with a stereobinocular microscope.

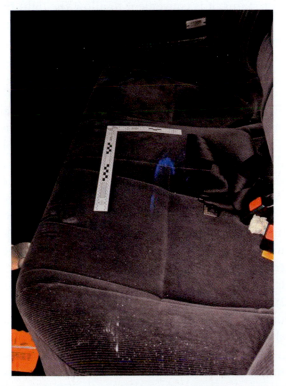

Figure 8.9 The application of Bluestar reagent to latent blood in the backseat of a car shows where a bloody baseball bat was placed after an assault. (Courtesy of Norm Marin and Jeff Buszka, SIU, NYC Office of Chief Medical Examiner.)

Many labs will use a positive presumptive blood test coupled with the presence of DNA to indicate the presence of human blood. The Hexagon OBTI® test (available at many law enforcement supply companies) allows the investigator in the field to confirm the presence of human blood through the detection of human hemoglobin.

Searching for Bloodstains

A dried but relatively fresh bloodstain is generally reddish-brown in color and glossy in contrast to, for example, rust stains. In a very thin layer, the color may be grayish green. The gloss slowly disappears under the action of sunlight and heat, wind, and weather or as the result of an attempt to wash it away. Bloodstains can assume other colors from red to brown or black, or they may appear green, blue, or grayish white. The color and the time required for the change depend on the underlying material: the change is quicker on metal surfaces and slower on textiles. With some types of cloth, the blood soaks into the threads; with others, it lies on the pile. The surface gloss is often less marked on fabric. Bloodstains on wallpaper may show surprising colors because of the blood's taking up color from the paper. Certain other stains, composed of pigment, rust, tobacco, snuff, urine, feces, coffee, and other substances, can easily be confused with bloodstains. In searching for bloodstains, marks should not be classified according to color and character because a stain that appears to deviate from the normal character of a bloodstain may be composed of blood, whereas one that resembles blood may be composed of some other substance.

When searching for stains, it is convenient to allow the light from a flashlight to fall obliquely against the surface under examination. Sometimes, a stain shows up better against a surface when it is illuminated with colored light. Red, green, and ordinary white light have been used successfully. Infrared (IR) light is also useful for locating bloodstains (Figure 8.10).

Occasionally, the assailant will clean up the scene. Furniture is straightened, damage is concealed, and blood is washed off—all for the purpose of concealing the crime, delaying its discovery, and/or destroying evidence. The search of the scene should therefore also be extended to places that are not in direct view. A criminal with bloody fingers may, for example, have opened a drawer, leafed through papers, or grasped a doorknob, a handrail, etc. Washbasins, garbage pails, and similar items should be given close attention. Drain traps should also be examined because blood may be in the trap if the criminal washed his hands there. Towels, draperies, and other fabrics that may have served to wipe off blood should also be examined. If a floor has been washed to remove bloodstains, blood may possibly be found in its cracks, in joints between tiles, under the edges of linoleum, behind floorboards and electric socket plates, and in similar places (Figure 8.11). An item that is devoid of blood that is believed to have the perpetrator's saliva can also be swabbed and/or collected (Figure 8.12).

The search for blood on clothes must be carried out carefully and systematically. Even if blood has been washed off the more conspicuous parts, stains may still be found on the seams, on the lining, inside the sleeves, in pockets, and so forth. Stains that have been diffused by washing may be concentrated in the laboratory. Suspects may also have bloodstains not only on their clothes but also on their body. Clothing can also be scraped for epithelial cells and DNA typed to determine who might have been wearing a particular garment (Figure 8.13).

Figure 8.10 Bloodstains on a black background are almost impossible to see with the naked eye; however, in this IR photo, four bloodstains can clearly be seen on a black cocktail napkin. (Courtesy of Cedar Crest College, Allentown, PA.)

Figure 8.11 Hemascein® is another reagent that is used to reveal latent bloodstains and has a long lasting reaction. (Courtesy of Abacus Diagnostics.)

In the open air, the search for bloodstains is often more difficult. Rain, snow, sun, and wind may have obliterated the marks more or less completely. The blood mark may have changed its color in a very short time because of the character of the ground. If the ground gives an impression of dampness in certain areas, these parts should be given special attention, as should blades of grass, leaves, branches of trees, etc.

Figure 8.12 According to the owner, this beverage container was full when she left in the morning for work. During the commission of a burglary, the thief became thirsty and left the empty container on the counter. (Courtesy of the NYC Office of Chief Medical Examiner.)

Figure 8.13 A sterile razor blade can be used to scrape an article of clothing for skin cells to determine who might have been wearing it. (Courtesy of the NYC Office of Chief Medical Examiner.)

If blood has run through bedclothes on a bed, it is necessary to consider whether it has run through all the bedclothes or has remained in the mattress, for example. This is very important in estimating the total quantity of blood and sometimes in enabling the pathologist to decide on the time that has elapsed since death.

Description and Recording of Bloodstains

In the case of bloodstains, a description should be made of their form, color, size, position, direction of splash, and the like. The best way to preserve the appearance of bloodstains is through photography. Photographs depicting overall, medium-range, and close-up views should be made. A scale should be included for the close-up photographs.

Besides photography, a rough sketch is useful to show the general appearance of the stains as well as their relative position to other areas of the crime scene. The sketch should contain the location and direction of the stains, for example, a drop of blood located 25 in. from the floor and 16 in. east of the doorway on the north kitchen wall indicating a downward direction.

Collection and Preservation of Bloodstains

Wet or damp bloodstains packaged in airtight containers, such as plastic bags, will be useless as evidence in a matter of time. Any type of preservation technique that hastens putrefaction should be avoided. Thus, storing bloodstains that are still damp in airtight containers or in warm environments will accelerate deterioration of the specimen. Conversely, an air-dried sample stored in a paper bag at room temperature will retain its evidentiary usefulness for a significantly longer period of time (Figure 8.14).

Preservation of blood and other biological evidence may require special handling in jurisdictions with case law dealing with preservation of such evidence. Biological evidence, that is, blood, semen, saliva, and so forth, does degrade with time in certain environmental conditions. Drying the specimens slows down this deterioration. Some courts have held that the police have an affirmative duty to preserve evidence for defendants who can prove their innocence. Failure to do this may result, in the entire case being thrown out of court.

Figure 8.14 Samples should be dried before packaging. (Courtesy of the Los Angeles County Sheriff's Department.)

Removal of Bloodstains

Blood may be present in a liquid, damp, or completely dry state. Depending on the circumstance, different procedures may be used. The easiest method of collection of wet blood is to place a cotton swab into the still-liquid pool of blood. Materials such as filter paper and cotton gauze can also be used. A good procedure is to use sterile cotton-tipped applicators, which can be used in the collection of wet and dried bloodstains.

The cotton swab is placed in the liquid blood and allowed to become saturated. The swab can then be left to air-dry and then placed in a coin envelope. The envelopes should be marked to clearly indicate where the specimen came from and who collected it. This is especially important when several blood samples are collected.*

Most blood found at crime scenes is dried. Collection of dried blood specimens may be accomplished in a variety of different methods. It may be collected on a cotton swab moistened with sterile distilled water. After the sample is collected and dried, the swab can be placed into an envelope and marked. For very small stains, it is best to concentrate the blood on one area of the swab, rather than spread it around the entire surface of the swab.

Bloodstained Objects

Generally, it is best to submit the entire bloodstained object or item to the laboratory rather than to remove the blood. The location of the object must be carefully noted and photographed. If blood on the object appears loose and likely to flake off, it should be collected and packaged separately before packaging the item of interest.

Packaging bloodstained items must be done in a way so as not to destroy the evidence. Packaging in airtight containers must be avoided. Bloodstained articles placed in sealed plastic bags or even tightly wrapped in paper will readily putrefy and could render the blood evidence useless.

Items such as damp bloodstained clothing should, if possible, be allowed to air-dry. The drying should be done at room temperature away from direct sunlight. Items should then be packaged separately and loosely in wrapping paper or paper bags.

If wet or damp bloodstained items cannot be air-dried, they should be packaged separately in wrapping paper or paper bags. They should not be tightly rolled or bundled up because this accelerates putrefaction of the stains. Whether wet or dry, newspaper should not be used.†

When items of clothing are collected, a useful habit to develop is to initial the items as soon as the evidence is received. Develop a routine of always marking the item in the same location, such as on the inside collar of a shirt or the back inside waistband of trousers.

Often, it is not feasible to submit an entire large item of bloodstained evidence, for example, a bloodstained carpet or mattress, to the laboratory. There are two ways to collect blood in such instances. The first is to follow the already outlined procedure of using the moistened cotton swab. The second is simply to cut out a portion of the item containing the bloodstain. The cutting is then placed in an appropriate package and marked.

---

* A simple practice is to label the item using your initials followed by a number, for example, BF-1, BF-2, BF-3, etc. Field notes would indicate the location of each item.

† If the items are blood soaked and it is not possible to dry the evidence, it is permissible to use large plastic bags to transport the evidence to the laboratory. However, the evidence should be removed from the plastic as soon as possible to air-dry. Wet, bloodstained evidence should be air-dried first before mailing.

Semen-Stained Objects

One of the most probative pieces of evidence in dealing with a sexual assault case is the presence of semen. It is usually found on bedding, clothing, tissues, towels, condoms, and the like. An alternate light source is often used to locate semen stains due to semen's fluorescent properties under certain wavelengths of light (Figure 8.15a and b). Once a possible semen stain is located, a presumptive test is performed to determine if the stain is

(a)

(b)

Figure 8.15 Using an alternate light source (a) to locate semen stains (b) on clothing from an alleged sexual assault.

presumptively positive for semen. This is done by looking for the presence of an enzyme, acid phosphatase (AP), which is found in large quantities in semen. The presumptive test is a color spot test that changes from clear to reddish-purple (Figure 8.16).

Once an AP positive presumptive test is established, a confirmatory test is required. This is done either by a microscopic visualization of sperm or the detection of prostate specific antigen (PSA), or p30. While PSA is found in low levels of other body tissues in both men and women, high levels of the protein are indicative of the presence of semen (Figure 8.17).

Figure 8.16 A positive presumptive test for the presence of acid phosphatase, an enzyme found in large quantities in semen. (Courtesy of the Los Angeles County Sheriff's Department.)

Figure 8.17 The prostate specific antigen test can demonstrate the presence of semen even in the absence of spermatozoa, such as aspermic men or men that have had a vasectomy. Here the unknown sample is run alongside a positive and negative control. (Courtesy of the Los Angeles County Sheriff's Department.)

Forensic DNA Typing

DNA typing is capable of eliminating suspects as well as incriminating them. However, to give meaning to biological stains collected at a crime scene, DNA samples from victims and suspects must be submitted to the crime laboratory along with the evidence. Elimination samples from consensual partners, people with legitimate access to a crime scene, crime scene investigators, EMS, and other individuals whose DNA might be present at a crime scene should also be submitted to the lab for testing. It is important to collect DNA specimens using the proper collection container. Buccal swabs, or swabs from the inside of the cheek, are an excellent alternative to collecting blood samples of known individuals. Commercial kits are available for this purpose.*

DNA typing is based on our genetic makeup. Anyone who has attended a sporting event or been in a large crowd of people recognizes the obvious: people look different. Differences are manifested by gender, race, stature, hair color, eye color, and shape of facial features, to name just a few of the common features. The fact is that people can easily recognize others through some subjective mental process.

We can also recognize family traits among brothers and sisters, parents and children, and sometimes even more distant familial relationships. How often have people commented that a son looks just like his father or mother or that two siblings look alike? These family characteristics can be seen over and over in family lineage.

An individual's physical appearance and family traits are a manifestation of the biochemical blueprint and building blocks that make people unique. The notion of differences and similarities in individuals has its scientific basis in the study of genetics. Genetics' roots go back to the mid-nineteenth century when Gregor Mendel suggested that genes controlled factors influencing heredity. During the next 150 years, major strides were made in the study of genetics, genes, chromosomes, and DNA.

DNA is the biochemical key to differentiating uniqueness among individuals (with the exception of identical twins).† It has been called the chemical messenger in that it conveys genetic information that is the basis of the way individual living things take shape, grow, and reproduce.

Pictorially, the DNA molecule resembles a twisted ladder or double helix. The steps within the ladder consist of four chemical subunits or bases: guanine (G), adenine (A), thymine (T), and cytosine (C). The bases always pair in predictable ways—A with T and G with C—and form the steps or rungs of the double-stranded DNA helix. The combinations of the A–T and G–C are referred to as base pairs. Over 3 billion base pairs are in human DNA; however, only small portions of these base pairs determine unique traits between persons and are of forensic interest.

DNA is folded into microscopic bundles called chromosomes and exists in all cells that contain nuclei. DNA is not present in red blood cells because these cells have no nuclei; white blood cells contain DNA. DNA is present in blood, seminal fluid, tissues, bone marrow, hair roots, dandruff, saliva, and tooth pulp. Each of these samples has the potential to yield DNA typing results.

---

* See, for example, Bode Technology Group's Buccal DNA Collector at http://www.bodetech.com/collection-products/. Investigators should consult with their forensic science laboratories to determine which known or standard sample collection method is acceptable to the crime lab.
† Fingerprint ridges of identical twins are not the same.

Scientists are able to unravel the DNA code and examine pieces of DNA to look for differences between individuals. In forensic DNA, a polymerase chain reaction (PCR) procedure is used. The methodology is known as short tandem repeats (STR) analysis.

PCR-Based Technology

PCR is a technology that copies short segments of DNA millions of times in a process that resembles the way in which DNA duplicates itself naturally in the body. (Some have described this process as the equivalent of a biological Xerox machine.)

PCR is a powerful technology because it can be applied to any tissue specimen, no matter how small, degraded, or old, and produces billions of copies within a few hours (e.g., a single hair with its root, dried saliva on the back of a letter or postage stamp, small amounts of blood under a victim's fingernails, etc.). After extracting the DNA from the cells, the PCR process consists of initially separating the DNA double helix into two strands by heating the sample. A PCR reaction mixture is then added. It consists of a pair of DNA primers (short segments of DNA that are added to indicate the target segment of DNA to be copied), DNA polymerase (an enzyme that catalyzes the reaction), and the four nucleotide bases (A, C, T, and G). This mixture contains all the ingredients necessary to copy both of the original DNA strands that were separated. The procedure is performed in an instrument called a thermocycler and is typically repeated for 28 cycles, approximately doubling the amount of DNA after each cycle (Figure 8.18).

After the PCR process, the mixture of DNA fragments is separated through a process called capillary electrophoresis (Figure 8.19). A very thin tube, called a capillary, is used to perform DNA separation. A polymer, which is a gel-like compound with tiny passageways, is pumped into the capillary, allowing the mixture of DNA fragments to be separated

Figure 8.18 A thermocycler heats and cools a sample for predefined set amounts of time allowing the PCR process to proceed. Each cycle roughly doubles the amount of DNA. (Courtesy of the Los Angeles County Sheriff's Department.)

(a)

(b)

Figure 8.19 (a) A genetic analyzer instrument contains multiple capillaries that allows for multiple samples to be processed in a single injection. (b) The data produced from capillary electrophoresis results in an electropherogram or DNA profile. The electropherogram can be compared to other knowns and unknowns. (Courtesy of the Los Angeles County Sheriff's Department.)

based on size. A laser then "reads" the DNA samples and software converts this electronic data into an electropherogram.

High Sensitivity DNA Testing/Touch DNA

High-sensitivity DNA testing is used to recover and detect small amounts of DNA (generally this refers to amounts less than 100 pg). It is also referred to as low-template DNA, low copy number (LCN) DNA, or touch DNA. The methods and instruments used are the

Figure 8.20 The NYC OCME uses its own patent pending specialized high-sensitivity swab to maximize the amount of DNA collected from an item. (Courtesy of the NYC Office of Chief Medical Examiner.)

same as traditional DNA typing, except for a few modifications to increase sensitivity (i.e., increased cycle number for PCR and interpretation methods). Examples of items that are candidates for high-sensitivity testing include car swabs, handles of weapons/tools, keys, pens, air bags, objects used for binding, door handles, touched clothing, and degraded/old samples. The New York City Office of Chief Medical Examiner (NYC OCME) Department of Forensic Biology is one of only a few labs in the United States that performs LCN testing on casework. They offer this testing to jurisdictions outside of New York City (Figure 8.20).*

Mitochondrial DNA

Yet another type of DNA typing is called mitochondrial DNA (mtDNA). Mitochondria are found in the cytoplasm of most cells. They play an essential part in generating the energy necessary for cell function. Each mitochondrion contains mtDNA within it. This distinct source of DNA differs from the DNA found in the nucleus of cells (nuclear DNA) in a number of respects:

- mtDNA is a much smaller molecule (it is circular as opposed to helical).
- mtDNA is only inherited maternally.

* See their website on how to submit a case: www.nyc.gov/ocme/highsens.

- mtDNA is present within a cell in multiple copies because there are many mitochondria located in a particular cell and many copies of DNA molecules within each mitochondrion. The actual copy number varies with cell type, depending on the energy requirements of the cell. For example, 20%–25% of a liver cell is composed of mitochondria, whereas 50% of the volume of a cardiac cell comprises mitochondria. Nuclear DNA is only present in two copies per cell (one copy in the case of an egg or a sperm cell).

The most common approach that has been used to analyze mtDNA is based on typing the control region (also called the D-loop region) because it is in this segment of mtDNA that most of the variation (polymorphism) from one person to another is found. The method that is most often used is direct DNA sequencing analysis in which the sample is initially amplified using PCR and the products of this amplification are "read" by DNA sequencing.

mtDNA typing has a number of applications in criminal investigations. It can be used as an investigative tool for the identification of missing persons because it is possible to use the mother, sibling, or any other maternal relative as a reference source since they possess an identical mtDNA type. In the case of nuclear DNA, this is only possible if a person has an identical twin or if multiple nuclear genetic markers are typed from the parents of a missing person. In certain cases, DNA is degraded due to environmental insults, aging, or some other factor limiting the quantity of DNA extracted. The high copy number of mtDNA means a higher likelihood of survival of intact sequences that can be applied to PCR-based technology. Furthermore, the high copy number of mtDNA means a greater chance of success with samples that have little or no nuclear DNA to begin with, for example, hair shafts.

Y-STRs

Y-STRs are found only in males because males possess an X and a Y chromosome, whereas females have two X chromosomes. Since the majority of crimes in which DNA evidence is used involve sexual assaults and since the overwhelming majority of sexual assaults involve male perpetrators, DNA tests that can exclusively examine the male DNA portion are very beneficial. Cases in which Y-STR testing might be used are those that involve very high levels of female DNA mixed with small amount of male DNA or where the number of men involved in a gang rape is unknown. Although Y-STR testing can prove quite valuable in certain types of cases, the results are of a lower power of discrimination than autosomal STRs. This is because the Y chromosome is transferred directly from father to son. A match between an evidence sample and a suspect only means that the suspect *could* have contributed to the sample, as could his father, brother, uncle, son, or other paternal relative.

CODIS

CODIS is the acronym for the *Combined DNA Index System*, an FBI-sponsored initiative similar in concept to an AFIS. CODIS generates investigative leads in cases in which biological evidence is recovered from the crime scene. Matches made among profiles in the forensic database can link crime scenes together. Based upon a match, police from multiple jurisdictions can coordinate their respective investigations and share the leads they developed independently. Matches made between the forensic unknown and convicted offender databases, which contain DNA profiles of individuals convicted of certain crimes, provide investigators with the identity of the DNA source.

Prior to CODIS, forensic scientists could manually compare DNA results to determine if there was a match. The national DNA database has resulted in an increasing number of "cold hits," that is, matches of unknown forensic samples to known convicted offenders. Also common are case-to-case hits.

A key element to utilizing CODIS fully is to make certain that as many offenders as possible are entered into the database. Although most offenders sentenced to state prison have their DNA entered into the felon database, persons sentenced to county jail or placed on probation are not routinely sampled. It is recommended that investigators and forensic scientists be sure that such samples are collected. Some District Attorney's offices have recently included a requirement for any defendant to give a DNA sample in any plea agreement that is reached.

In addition to the forensic and convicted offender databases, CODIS also has four other components:

- Arrestees—contains profiles of arrested persons (if state law permits the collection of arrestee samples)
- Missing persons—contains DNA reference profiles from missing persons
- Biological relatives of missing persons—contains DNA profiles voluntarily contributed from relatives of missing persons
- Unidentified humans (remains)—contains DNA profiles developed from unidentified humans and remains

STR, Y-STR, and mtDNA can be entered into the three missing persons indexes above.

Forensic DNA and Unsolved Cases

The use of DNA typing in crime laboratories has changed the way crime laboratories prioritize their casework, including nonsuspect rape cases. Prior to DNA typing, most laboratories did not perform blood typing on evidence in sexual assault cases in which there was no known suspect. The reasoning was simple: typing results could not be compared with a suspect; because resources are limited, such cases were not typed. The result was that nonsuspect rape cases were not examined.

Forensic DNA capability changed this policy. DNA databanking has the potential to identify unknown suspects based on their DNA type. CODIS makes this all possible. Serial crimes such as rapes and murders have a better likelihood of being solved because DNA typing results can be compared with DNA typing records collected from convicted violent felons. However, two things must happen: the convicted felon's specimen must be collected and typed and the laboratory must routinely examine its nonsuspect sexual assault cases.

Partial Matches and Familial Searching

Occasionally, a partial match between a forensic profile and an offender profile is observed during a routine CODIS database search. A partial match occurs when there is a similarity in profiles between a forensic unknown and a known exemplar. A "partial match" is not an exact match of the two profiles, but when it meets a particular statistical threshold, it is indicative that a close biological relative of the offender may be the source of the forensic unknown. Further DNA testing should be done in such cases (such as Y-STR testing to determine whether the two profiles are of the same paternal relative). A known DNA sample from the biological relative should also be obtained for direct comparison.

Familial searching is an intentional or deliberate search of the database conducted after a routine search for the purpose of potentially identifying close biological relatives of the unknown forensic sample associated with the crime scene profile. This type of search is not done at the national level; however, it is performed currently at the state level in two states, California and Colorado.*†

Scientific Working Group on DNA Analysis Methods

The Scientific Working Group on DNA Analysis Methods (SWGDAM; formerly TWGDAM, the Technical Working Group for DNA Analysis Methods) comprises a group of forensic DNA analysts from local, state, and federal laboratories throughout the United States, who have developed guidelines on QA and quality control (QC). QC pertains to DNA testing standards implemented in a particular laboratory; QA concerns monitoring laboratory operations. One example of QA is proficiency testing, which can be either open or blind. In the former, the analyst is aware that the test is being conducted, whereas in the latter, the sample is submitted for examination under the guise of case samples. Accreditation agencies, which assess sources of error and the corrective measures taken by the laboratory, monitor the results of these tests. The tests are required to be completed twice a year to assess these corrective measures.

DNA Cases

Case 5

Two women were raped in separate attacks. A suspect was arrested and identified by both victims. Meanwhile, two more women were raped under similar circumstances. A second suspect was arrested for those rapes. DNA typing was performed on semen from the victims' vaginal swabs from the second set of rapes and compared to the second suspect. The DNA testing identified him. Because of the similarity of circumstances, the vaginal samples from the first two rapes were also tested and compared to both

---

* http://www.denverda.org/DNA_Documents/Familial_DNA/CBI%20DNA%20Familial%20Search%20
  Policy%20Oct%202009%20-%20Signed.pdf
† http://ag.ca.gov/cms_attachments/press/pdfs/n1548_08-bfs-01.pdf

suspects. The first suspect who had been identified by both victims in court and held to answer was excluded, whereas the second suspect was identified in all four rapes.

Case 6

A comatose teenage female was discovered to be pregnant. A juvenile friend of the victim's brother was the suspect. The fetus was aborted and submitted along with blood from the victim and the suspect for paternity testing. DNA samples from the victim's father and brother were also submitted for elimination. The juvenile suspect was excluded from having fathered the fetus. Unexpectedly, the brother was identified as the father.

Case 7

Three males allegedly gang raped two women. No semen was found in the vaginal samples; however, three used condoms were recovered from a trash can at the scene. Three suspects were arrested and identified by the victims as having participated in the rapes. One of the suspects was adamant that, although he was there, he did not participate in the rape. DNA testing was performed on the semen found inside each of the three condoms. The exterior surfaces of the condoms were tested for the victims' DNA. It was determined that one of the suspects had raped one of the victims and a second suspect had raped both of the victims. Contrary to the victims' statements, the suspect who was adamant about not participating in the rapes did not contribute the semen found in any of the condoms.

Case 8

An adult female was found murdered and left in a position suggesting a sexual assault. Three suspects were generated by the investigation, with no investigative means to determine the true assailant from among them. Fingernail scrapings collected by the coroner's office contained a trace quantity of blood. DNA typing showed the blood was not the victim's. The results were compared to blood samples collected from the three suspects. One was included and the others were eliminated. No other methods available could have yielded a result on such a trace quantity of blood evidence. A charge of murder with special circumstances was filed against the suspect.

Case 9

Police conducting surveillance on an unrelated case discovered decomposing parts of a dismembered human body. The remains included the victim's head. A suspect was identified and blood drops were recovered in a search of his residence. The dismembered remains were too decomposed to provide a reference for genetic typing using conventional methods. Hair was removed from the victim's head and provided sufficient DNA for comparison to the blood drops recovered from the suspect's residence. The blood drops matched the victim and murder charges were filed.

Case 10

In the early 1980s, a young college student was raped and murdered while jogging in a nearby park. A suspect was identified and arrested soon after. He was unable to provide an alibi during the time of the murder. Throughout his trial, the man accused of the brutal rape and murder was adamant that he was innocent of the charges against him. A witness, who originally was not able to identify the defendant, identified him as the murderer at trial that led to the jury's conviction. He continued to maintain his innocence during his prison term and was able to get his state's innocence project to take his case. Recent legislation allowed him to secure postconviction DNA testing on the victim's underwear that was located after a long search of the police department property warehouse. It was never tested for DNA. DNA typing done by a private laboratory excluded him as the semen donor found on the victim's underwear. The profile that was developed "hit" to a CODIS convicted offender already in prison for another rape.

Case 11

An executive in a major southern California business firm received threat letters. A suspect was identified who was an employee of the firm and had an affair with the executive's wife. However, evidence was insufficient for an arrest or a search warrant. Subsequently, the chief of the investigating agency received a mail bomb and a threat letter. The saliva residues on the threat letter envelopes sent to the executive and the Chief of Police were subjected to DNA typing. The results were also compared to saliva residue from love letters sent by the suspect to the executive's wife during their affair. The DNA types matched. This provided sufficient evidence for a search warrant for a sample of the suspect's DNA. The DNA sample also matched the saliva residues on the letters and the suspect was charged with attempted murder. The case was adjudicated by a plea bargain because of the strength of the identification of the suspect using DNA typing.

Molecular Autopsy

DNA can also be used to aid the medical examiner in establishing cause of death. Occasionally, autopsy results produce negative findings as to how someone may have died. The medical examiner can submit a DNA sample from the decedent to a molecular genetics laboratory to screen for certain molecular mutations in genes that may have caused the person's death. This has been referred to as the "molecular autopsy." One example of this is long QT syndrome (a rare genetic inborn heart condition in which delayed repolarization of the heart following a heartbeat increases the risk of episodes of torsade de pointes (TDP), a form of irregular heartbeat, that can lead to sudden death due to ventricular fibrillation).*

* http://en.wikipedia.org/wiki/Long_QT_Syndrome

Missing Persons

The National Missing and Unidentified Persons System* (NamUs) is funded by the Office of Justice Programs, National Institute of Justice and is a clearinghouse for unidentified remains and missing person records. NamUs also includes links to medical examiner and coroner offices, law enforcement agencies, victim assistance groups, and pertinent legislation.

The NamUs system is comprised of two different databases. The first database contains case reports of unidentified remains entered by medical examiners and coroners throughout the United States, Guam, and Puerto Rico. Unidentified persons are people who have died and whose bodies have not been identified. Anyone can search this database using characteristics such as sex, race, distinct body features, and dental information.

The second database contains case reports of missing persons entered by law enforcement and the public; before it appears as a case on NamUs, the information is verified. Relatives of missing persons can submit case information directly to the NamUs.gov website. When a new missing person or unidentified decedent case is entered into NamUs, the system automatically performs cross-matching comparisons between the databases, searching for matches or similarities between cases. NamUs also provides free DNA testing and other forensic services. Close relatives (i.e., parents, children, siblings) of the missing can submit DNA exemplar samples to aid in the identification of unknown human remains through kinship analysis (Figure 8.21).

Figure 8.21 Toothbrushes from missing persons are sometimes used as a DNA exemplar sample. Care must be taken in interpreting results because sometimes multiple people use the same toothbrush! (Courtesy of the NYC Office of Chief Medical Examiner.)

* http://www.namus.gov

Biogeographical Ancestry

DNA Witness* is a DNA test that determines the biogeographical ancestry of a sample. The test determines the relative amounts of European, East Asian, Native American, and Sub-Saharan African ancestry of any given sample. The results can then give information on the general characteristics of a suspect or victim. For example, a person with 95% European ancestry would be expected to have Caucasian features as opposed to Black or Asian features. In addition to racial features, eye color can also be determined from DNA.

The Future

Forensic biology is among the fastest evolving technologies used in crime laboratories today. Within the next several years, we will most likely see faster DNA typing methods, "lab-on-a-chip" technology for typing in the field, and DNA typing for other facial features and characteristics of an unknown individual. The revolution in the biotechnology industry makes it a near certainty that new DNA applications for forensic science will continue to develop for the foreseeable future.

Chapter Questions

1. You are about to enter the scene of a double homicide to begin your investigation and collect evidence. Please list the appropriate personal protective equipment (PPE) you would want to wear while working in the scene.

2. (True/False) When collecting clothing from the same person, you can bag these items together if they are properly labeled.
   a) True
   b) False
3. There are two general categories of bloodstains: _____ and transfer stains.
   a) Cast-off
   b) Volume
   c) Voids
   d) Spatter
4. Which of the following is a presumptive chemical used for screening blood at a crime scene?
   a) PCR
   b) SPR
   c) Acid phosphatase
   d) Leucomalachite green

* http://www.bioforensics.com/conference07/Racial_Identification/DNA_Witness.pdf

5. Describe the most appropriate way to collect a liquid bloodstain at the scene of a crime.

6. Which of the following is the correct pairing of bases within the double helix?
   a) A-T, G-C
   b) A-C, G-T
   c) A-A, G-T
   d) C-A, T-G

7. Briefly describe the process involved when using the polymerase chain reaction (PCR) technology for DNA analysis.

8. You have been assigned a case where human skeletal remains have been found at a city dump. Which of the following DNA techniques would you use to identify the victim?
   a) RFLP
   b) PCR
   c) STR
   d) mtDNA

9. Which of the following is the forensic database for DNA?
   a) NIBIN
   b) AFIS
   c) CODIS
   d) STR

10. This group comprises forensic DNA analysts from local, state, and federal laboratories throughout the U.S. who have developed guidelines for quality assurance and quality control.
    a) SWGSTAIN
    b) SWGANTH
    c) SWGDAM
    d) SWGFAST

Impression Evidence

9

Introduction

Minute imperfections on a large variety of objects such as tools, footwear, tires, and so on produce markings in their normal (and sometimes unusual) usage. These markings are often characteristic of the type of tool or object used. In many instances, very small and sometimes microscopically unique markings are left that can be traced directly to the object or instrument in question.

Such marks caused by a tool are of two general types: compression marks and scraping marks. Compression marks are those left when an instrument is in some way pushed or forced into a material capable of picking up an impression of the tool. Examples include shoe impressions, tire impressions, bite mark impressions, fabric impressions, the mark left by a hammer hitting a piece of wood, the mark of a screwdriver used to jimmy a window, breech mark impressions on shell casings, typewriter marks, etc. Scraping or striated marks are produced by a combination of pressure and sliding contact by the tool and result in microscopic striations imparted to the surface onto which the tool was worked. Examples of scraping marks are those found on fired bullets, left by a cutting tool such as a bolt cutter, from a wrench used on a doorknob, from an ax used to cut wood, from a screwdriver blade dragged over a surface, and teeth marks used to bite through a soft material capable of picking up an impression. In order for compression or scraping marks to be observed, the tool must be made of a harder material than the object on which it is used.

The random nature and microscopic imperfections found on tools are a result of their manufacture and usage. Casting, grinding, and polishing metal instruments, as well as using them, result in small but observable differences from one tool to the next. Such differences have even been demonstrated in consecutively manufactured items.

Comparative examination is the method by which impression-type evidence is studied. The marks left at the crime scene (or castings of the mark) are compared with test markings made by the tool or object in question. Through careful and often tedious examination of the known and questioned evidence, a determination can be made as to whether or not a particular item was responsible for a specific mark.*

Case†

Charlie Richardson was a 30-year-old student completing his final year in medical school and preparing to intern. The victim, Maria Richardson, was the defendant's wife of several

---

* Assertions of uniqueness of pattern evidence examination have been hotly debated in the past few years. Proponents claim that given sufficient random or accidental markings on a tool, experts can proffer conclusive opinions on the source of a tool mark. Others argue that uniqueness may only be described statistically.

† This case was submitted by Norman D. Sperber, DDS, San Diego, California, and Detective Mike Howard, El Cajon Police Department, El Cajon, California.

Figure 9.1 The victim found at the scene of her murder. Note the proximity of the telephone cord to her head. (Courtesy of Norman D. Sperber, DDS, San Diego, California, and El Cajon Police Department, El Cajon, California.)

(a)   (b)

Figure 9.2 (a) The wall telephone and cord used to strangle Maria; (b) a close-up of the ligature marks on the victim's neck; (c) marks presumably made from the telephone cord on the victim's chin. (Courtesy of Norman D. Sperber, DDS, San Diego, California, and El Cajon Police Department, El Cajon, California.)

(c)

Figure 9.2 (*Continued*)

Figure 9.3 The abrasion on Charlie Richardson's right pinky finger, which the defendant explained was due to a burn received while he was cooking. He was unable to explain another less visible one on his left pinky finger. (Courtesy of Norman D. Sperber, DDS, San Diego, California, and El Cajon Police Department, El Cajon, California.)

Figure 9.4 Dr. Norman Sperber making castings of the defendant's left and right little fingers.

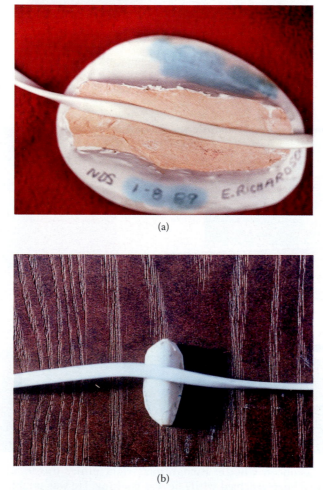

(a)

(b)

Figure 9.5 (a) The telephone cord fitted into a casting of the ligature mark on the victim's neck; (b) the telephone cord fitted onto a casting of one of the defendant's pinkies.

Figure 9.6 (a, b) Two illustrations of how the markings on the defendant's pinkies and on the victim's chin might have occurred; (c) a close-up illustration of how the markings on the defendant's little finger occurred. (Courtesy of Norman D. Sperber, DDS, San Diego, California, and El Cajon Police Department, El Cajon, California.)

years. The defendant and Maria had a marital relationship that appeared normal to those who knew them. One morning, the defendant drove Maria to her workplace, a laboratory located in El Cajon, California. While they were alone at the laboratory, an argument ensued and Charlie strangled Maria with a ligature. After killing Maria, he scattered and misplaced laboratory specimens and the contents of Maria's purse to make it appear that a burglar had committed the murder. Charlie then drove from the laboratory to the University of California, San Diego medical school library to study for an upcoming exam.

Later in the morning, one of Maria's coworkers found her dead in the laboratory. The police arrived and began an investigation. Meanwhile, the defendant purchased items at several locations in the San Diego area, including roses for his wife. At noon, he returned to the laboratory under the pretense of having lunch with Maria. He wondered why he was not allowed to see his wife and why detectives were around the laboratory. Charlie was told of Maria's death and was then asked for background information about her. Charlie related his actions of the morning, explained how he left his wife at work and then went to the library to study. He told investigators that he planned to meet Maria for lunch and produced time-stamped receipts from various locations (Figure 9.1).

The victim had ligature marks around her neck and chin. Several items that could have been used as the ligature were collected, including a long telephone cord attached to a wall phone. During the investigation, a small crescent-shaped abrasion was noted on the edge of Charlie's right pinky finger. Charlie, now a suspect, was read his Miranda rights. He explained the abrasion as a burn received while he was cooking; however, he was unable to explain a very small, less visible matching abrasion along the edge of his left pinky finger. Charlie Richardson was arrested for the murder of his wife Maria. Dr. Norman D. "Skip" Sperber, a forensic odontologist called into the investigation, made castings and took photographs of the suspect's fingers and of the ligature marks on the victim's neck. The castings and photographs were compared with the wall telephone cord from the scene. In this case, the cord became critical evidence. A search of the suspect's home yielded evidence of disharmony in the marriage; investigators also found writings by Maria in which she said she was afraid of Charlie (Figures 9.2 through 9.6).

Although the defense tried to suppress the evidence in pretrial motions, it was admitted in a jury trial. After considering all factors in the case, including the evidence presented by Dr. Sperber, the defense offered to plead to a charge of involuntary manslaughter on condition that Charlie take the stand and tell the jury what had actually happened. The defendant took the witness stand and told how he strangled Maria with the telephone cord during the course of a heated argument.

Footprints

Footprints* are a common type of impression evidence found at or near crime scenes. In favorable situations, such evidence may demonstrate that the suspect was at the scene of the crime. A detailed examination of footprints is tedious and time-consuming work and may be overlooked by the investigator. Although this discussion concerns footwear impressions, the investigator should not overlook soil evidence that might later be discovered on the suspect's shoes.

---

* The reader is referred to an excellent book on the subject, *Footwear Impression Evidence*, 2nd edition, by William J. Bodziak, CRC Press, Boca Raton, Florida, 1999.

When a cast is made of a footprint in soft ground, one would expect to obtain a faithful reproduction of the heel and sole of the shoe that made the print. As a rule, however, the result of casting is actually quite different—the cast has an arched form. The back of the heel and the point of the toe are considerably lower than the other parts of the cast because, in normal walking, the back of the heel is placed on the ground first. After that, each part of the heel and sole is pressed down on the ground in succession until the foot is lifted, with a final strong pressure of the point of the toe against the earth. The pressure that regulates the depth of the impression is the greatest at the back of the heel and at the point of the toe. When running, the footprints are less distinct, partly owing to slipping of the foot and partly to sand and earth thrown into the print. The form of the print depends on the individual's style of running; many people run on their toes, others set both heel and toe hard in the ground, and others set the whole foot down in the earth at once. In deciding whether an individual walked or ran, the length of the step is the only certain guide.

Value of Footprints

Individual footprints are generally preserved only if they contain details of value for identification. The most valuable details are signs of wear, characteristic fittings or marks of fittings that have come off, injuries, marks of nails and pegs, especially when these are irregularly placed, and repair marks. If they are particularly characteristic or occur in sufficient numbers, such details may form decisive evidence. In the interest of thoroughness, footprints should be preserved even if they do not show any details. Although the size and shape of the shoe or a pattern in the heel or sole is of lesser evidential value, a representative print should nonetheless be preserved for its value as an investigative lead.

If footprints are found in snow that has a frozen crust, it is a waste of time to attempt to take a cast of them. When the foot breaks through the hard surface of the snow, the surface snow goes with it and forms a hard bottom to the mark. The coarse grains of ice in the surface layer do not reproduce any details of the shoe—not even such large defects as a hole through the sole—and it is not possible to obtain any useful information of the size by measuring the footprint because the hard snow is broken and pressed down at points considerably outside the outer contour of the shoe.

A footwear print may be a foot impression or a footprint (dust print). Foot impressions occur when the foot treads in some moldable material such as earth, sand, clay, snow, etc. Footprints are formed on a hard base when the foot or the sole and heel of a shoe are contaminated with some foreign matter such as road dirt, dust, flour, blood, or moisture. Footprints may also be latent when naked or stocking-covered feet on a smooth surface have formed them.

Footwear impression evidence and information from the gait pattern may indicate that the subject was walking or running, had sustained an injury or walked with a limp, was possibly intoxicated, had a tendency to walk toe-in or toe-out, or was carrying a heavy object.*

---

* The field of forensic podiatry (http://www.theasfp.org) deals with pedal evidence and the use of podiatry in forensic cases.

Preservation of Footwear and Tire Impressions

Although the focus here is on footprints, much of what follows concerning preservation and collecting this type of evidence applies equally well to tire impression evidence.

Foot impressions are generally found outdoors; the first precautionary measure is therefore to protect the impression from alteration or destruction, preferably by covering it with a box or cordoning off the area. Impressions in thawing snow are especially troublesome, so a box covered with snow to prevent thawing should protect them. If a foot impression is in such a position that it is possible for it to gradually fill up or be damaged by running water, it must be surrounded by a wall of earth, sand, or snow; alternatively, a hole may be dug close to the impression and the water drained toward the hole. However, these protective measures are only stopgaps and the actual preservation should be undertaken as soon as possible.

Footprints on Floors

Interior locations often have footprints present, especially on surfaces such as tiled floors, glass, desktops, countertops, and chair seats. A simple procedure to locate these indoor prints is to turn off all the interior lights and, by means of a high-intensity flashlight, search the surfaces by shining the light at a low angle. Often these impressions are dust prints and very easily destroyed. Once detected, care must be taken to make certain they are preserved (Figure 9.7).

(a)   (b)

Figure 9.7 (a) An electrostatic dust print lifter and (b) a dust print lifted by this technique. (Courtesy of Montgomery County [Maryland], Department of Police, Forensic Services Section.)

Preservation of Footwear Evidence

Preservation should be done by photographing and casting or, in the case of dust prints, by lifting.

Photographing Footwear Impressions

The most common errors made in crime scene photography involve taking photographs of shoe and tire impressions that result in poor-quality photographs. Reasons for this include the following: not using a tripod to support the camera, not shooting perpendicular to the impression, failing to use a scale or ruler in the photograph, and not using oblique lighting. Overall, taking quality photographs is relatively simple, but it requires practice (Figure 9.8a–e).

The camera should be placed vertically above the impression on a tripod with a scale placed next to the impression. The film plane should be parallel to the impression so as not to cause distortion in the photograph. It is good practice to place two scales in the photograph at right angles to each other. One ruler can be placed adjacent to the long axis of the foot impression and a second perpendicular to the first, in the region adjacent to the heel.

If the bottom of the impression is appreciably deeper than the surface of the ground or snow, the scale should be brought down to the same level. Before photographing, any material that may have fallen into the impression after it was formed should be cleaned away. For this purpose, it is convenient to use tweezers, a piece of paper onto which lumps of earth are rolled, or other such objects that cannot be picked up by the tweezers. If it is not possible to carry out this cleaning without injuring details of the impression, it should be omitted. Materials trampled into the impression, such as leaves or grass, should not be removed because they form part of the impression and no details will be found under them. Careless removal of a trampled blade of grass can destroy large parts of the impression. Any water that may be present should be carefully removed by a hypodermic syringe or small pump. If a foot impression has been made in snow, it may be difficult to get a clear picture of it. Hard snow may be dusted with aluminum powder, which gives a clearer picture. With loose snow, aluminum powder can be dusted into the mark by tapping the brush.

Because the details in foot impressions are three dimensional, the photograph should be made under illumination that will bring out those details to the best advantage. Direct sunlight enhances the details by creating highlights and shadows. When the sky is cloudy and the daylight diffuse and practically without shadow, artificial light must be used; photoflood or flash illumination is suitable. These considerations, of course, also apply to situations in which it is imperative that the pictures be taken at night. The important point to remember about the illumination is that the light must not be held at too low an angle because too much shadow will obscure rather than emphasize detail.

Casting footwear impressions is generally done with dental stone. Other materials include paraffin, sulfur, and silicone rubber,* which are less frequently used.

---

* Casting impressions takes practice. It is recommended that one develop skills by working on nonevidentiary footmarks with the material, whether dental stone or any of the other techniques.

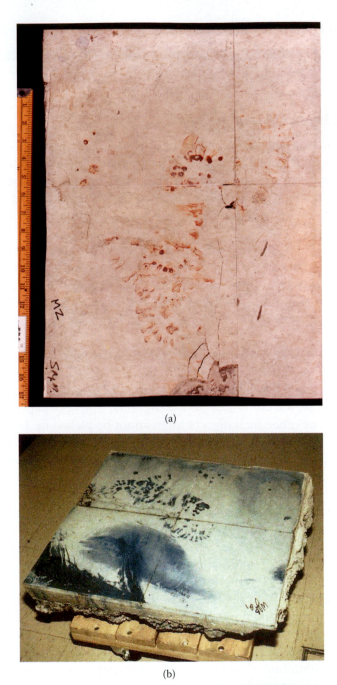

(a)

(b)

Figure 9.8 In 1992, a horrific murder of a young women occurred in Manhattan in the rear of a retail store. The victim was bound and gagged in the rear office and stabbed multiple times with a screwdriver. At the scene, NYPD detectives noted bloody footprints on the cement floor. The piece of floor was cut out and transported to the FBI Laboratory. The suspect's shoes and the prints matched and were a key piece of evidence in the trial. Bloody footprints (a) are visible on a portion of the concrete floor. The actual portion of floor (b) was stained by the examiner to make the prints more visible (c). The soles of the suspect's shoes (d) and a print of the shoes (e) were compared and the examiner concluded the suspect made the prints on the cement floor. He was convicted of first-degree murder and given the maximum sentence. (Courtesy of William J. Bodziak, Bodziak Forensics, Florida and formerly with the FBI Laboratory.)

(c)   (d)

(e)

Figure 9.8 (*Continued*)

Casting with Dental Stone

Dental stone is a type of gypsum or calcium sulfate that can be used to cast shoe and tire impressions. At one time, plaster of Paris was more widely used for this purpose; however, dental stone is superior and readily available from dental supply companies. Dental stone can be used for casting most impressions, even in snow.

Foot impressions in loose, dry sand and earth can be taken without any special preparation. Some literature suggests removing loose twigs and leaves, but this practice can damage the impression and is discouraged. Also, using fixatives such as spray lacquers or talc, practices generally recommended for use with plaster of Paris, are not necessary with dental stone.

Casting Water-Filled Impressions

Dental stone lends itself quite well to casting water-filled impressions. If an impression is very muddy or filled with water, no attempt should be made to remove the water because this may damage the impression.

A retaining wall or frame should be placed around the impression. The retainer should allow for a cast of at least 2 inches in thickness. Dental stone is lightly sprinkled or sifted directly into the water-filled impression to about an inch thickness, followed by normally prepared dental stone that has been prepared with a little less water and is slightly thicker. The cast should be poured to about 2 inches thick and allowed to set in place for an hour.

To cast a footprint, about 2 pounds of dental stone in about 12 ounces of water is used. A clean rubber bowl can be used for mixing. Water should first be added to the bowl followed by sifting in the dental stone. The mixture should be stirred to remove any lumps and air bubbles. The final mix should be the consistency of pancake batter. An alternative method is to use a zippered plastic bag to carry about 2 pounds of dental stone and to mix the material right in the bag. This procedure is reported to be very convenient to use. (Note that when dental stone is mixed with water the solution heats up. This heating causes difficulties when casting impressions in snow. For this reason, a small amount of snow or ice should be added to the mixture to keep the temperature down, and the mixture should be made slightly more viscous than pancake-batter consistency.)

After the material is mixed, it should be gently poured onto an area adjacent to the impression and allowed to flow onto the impression. If it is necessary to pour the material into the impression, a baffle such as a flat stick or spoon can be used to lessen the impact of the material. Great care needs to be taken that the dental stone does not destroy any of the fine material in the impression. Before the cast hardens it should be marked, using a twig, scribe, or other sharp instrument, with information including the date, investigator's name or initials, case number, and location of the impression.

The material will harden sufficiently for removal in about 30 minutes. Clumps of soil and rocks clinging to the cast should not be disturbed and the cast should be allowed to air-dry thoroughly for about 48 hours. If the impression is deep and firmly seated, it should be carefully excavated so that it finally lies on a pillar that may then be cut off.

Casting Impressions in Snow

When casting impressions in snow, the impression is prepared first by spraying a thin layer of Snow Print Wax (available from a number of law enforcement supply companies). The print should be photographed a second time after the application of the Snow Print Wax spray. After the spray has been applied to cover the print completely and then allowed to dry, the dental stone is carefully poured into the impression. The stone is prepared with cold water and snow and should be made slightly thicker than normal. The material should be allowed to set up for at least an hour before removal and should dry for about 48 hours (Figure 9.9).

Sulfur casting is another procedure used by some for snow prints. About 5 pounds of powdered sulfur is needed for a print. The sulfur is melted in a 1-quart aluminum pot and poured into the print, using a channel to direct the flow of the molten sulfur. The trick to using sulfur is not to heat the material too much. Sulfur melts at 115°C but, if heated to 170°C, it changes characteristics and cannot be used. For best results, it should be heated slowly and continuously stirred. The molten sulfur must be poured quickly because it will solidify as soon as it comes into contact with the snow. The cast should remain in place for about an hour; because it will be very fragile, extreme care must be taken when handling it (Figure 9.10).

Figure 9.9 This dental stone tire casting was taken in a case involving the theft of several airplane propellers that was investigated by the Anchorage Airport Police. The tire impression was the first cast that the officer had ever poured in snow and enabled an easy identification because the tire had several bent studs. The technique used in Alaska in snow casting is to spray the impression first with gray automobile primer, which gives good contrast for photography and acts as a shell for the dental stone. The dental stone and water need to be ice cold before mixing. In extreme cold, potassium sulfate is added as an accelerator to the water and has been successfully used to cast impressions in conditions well below zero. (Courtesy of the Alaska Department of Public Safety, Scientific Crime Detection.)

Figure 9.10 A plaster cast from a shoe impression was made in snow and shows good detail of the shoe sole pattern. The cast surface was "colored" with silver spray to enhance the detail for photography. (Courtesy of Zurich Cantonal Police, Forensic Science Department.)

Preservation of Footprints (Dust Prints)

Footprints are always preserved by photographing. After this is done, one of the following methods should be applied:

1. *Recovering the object on which the footprint is made.* Footprints are often found on objects stepped on by the criminal (entering in the dark through a window, for example). If the window is broken, all fragments of glass should be examined. This type of print is usually best detected by low-angle illumination from one side. Rubber heels and soles leave exceptionally good prints on glass. Detailed prints are often also found on paper or cardboard that may be strewn about the room during a safe burglary. All such loose objects bearing prints should be carefully preserved for transport to the laboratory. When the seriousness of the crime warrants it and when the print consists of a dried liquid such as blood or ink, it may be advisable to remove a portion of linoleum or floor tile that bears a clear impression.

2. *Lifting by a special lifter* is preferred whenever dust or a dust-like substance holds the print from the shoe. The lifter is a sheet of black rubber with a slightly sticky surface that is pressed against the print, picking up a faithful replica of the whole print. Oblique light photography under laboratory conditions brings out this dust print to a contrast often better than that observed in the original print. If a sufficiently large fingerprint lifter is available, it may be used instead of the special lifter. Care must be taken not to stretch the rubber lifter because the dust image may become distorted.

3. *Lifting by photographic paper* may be employed when special lifters are not available. Black (exposed, developed, fixed, and washed) or white (fixed and washed) photographic paper is used, as determined by the color of the material in the print. The paper is dampened with water or dilute ammonia, laid emulsion side down over the print, and beaten against the print with a stiff brush or clapped with the

palm. When the whole surface has been thoroughly beaten, the paper is removed and laid out to dry.

4. *Lifting by static electricity* is another technique. Companies selling evidence collection equipment also sell field kits called electrostatic dust print lifters, which pick up dust prints onto Mylar-coated foil by means of static electricity. This procedure has applications in certain situations in which suspects walked on tile floors.

Taking Comparison Footprints from a Suspect

When the original prints are from covered feet, for example, shoes or sneakers, the examiner who makes comparison shoe prints should wear them. When comparison footprints are taken, the soles are coated with water-based ink using a large inkpad. The inked shoes are then carefully stepped onto a sheet of tracing paper or acetate sheet.

In taking prints of bare feet, the feet are blackened by pressing them against a thin layer of printing ink. To get a true picture of the formation of the sole of the foot in different positions, four different prints are taken: normal standing position, standing position with pressure against the outside of the foot and with pressure against the inside, and finally when walking. This also applies to stocking feet.

Yet another method for obtaining known footwear exemplars involves using talcum powder and black carbon paper. A thin coating of talc is spread on a sheet of newspaper placed with talc side up on top of about 10 sheets of newspaper that act as a cushion. The shoe is placed on the foot and walked onto the talc-covered newspaper. The talc-covered shoe is then impressed onto the carbon paper, carbon side up. The carbon paper is similarly cushioned with about 10 sheets of newspaper. The resulting print is photographed 1:1 using Kodalith high-contrast copy film. The developed negative will show a positive reproduction of the impression that can be superimposed over a negative from the crime scene. The same technique can also be done with digital photographs and computer software to superimpose the two images.

Comparison of Footprints

Comparison between footprints found at the scene of a crime and those of a suspect should be made by an expert, but this does not prevent a police investigator from undertaking a preliminary examination (Figure 9.11).

Prints or impressions of shoe-covered feet are seldom the same size as the shoes; even when they are made, slipping and the movement of walking can damage prints. The mark of a naked foot in movement can be as much as 1 inch longer than the mark of the same foot in the standing position. A foot impression in wet earth can become appreciably smaller when the earth dries; in clay, the length can decrease by up to 3/4 of an inch. Thus, in establishing identity, too much significance should not be attached to dimensions. When examining the mark of a shoe-covered foot, the circumference characteristics should be checked. If the marks from the scene of the crime and from the suspect are similar in form, it is less important that they may differ somewhat in size.

Identification is based mainly on characteristic marks on the sole or heel. The examination is best done by direct comparison of the preserved footmark from the scene of the crime with the foot covering of the suspect. These are photographed side by side and characteristic points are marked. With footprints, however, it is generally convenient to take a print of the

Figure 9.11 Comparison of a shoe print found at a scene and that of suspect shoe. (Courtesy of the Los Angeles County Sherriff's Department.)

foot covering of the suspect and compare the prints. When it is a question of prints of bare feet, an examination is made first to see if there are any identifiable friction skin patterns and, if this is the case, the investigation is carried out as for finger and palm prints.

In examining the foot covering of a suspect, dust, dirt, and earth should be kept and, if necessary, compared with similar materials at the scene of the crime. If the perpetrator has left overshoes at the scene, they may be compared with a suspect's shoes. Characteristic marks on the shoes, particularly on the soles, may be reproduced inside the overshoes; for this examination, the overshoes must be cut open. If a shoe is found at the crime scene, it may contain characteristic marks of wear from the owner's foot. Such marks can then be compared with the markings inside shoes and in some cases may be shown to have been worn by the suspect. The shoe and/or laces can also be swabbed for DNA to determine the wearer.

Marks on Clothes and Parts of the Body

If clothing is pressed against a smooth surface, a latent print may be produced. Such a print is developed in the same way as a fingerprint or glove print. Clothing contaminated with a foreign material such as blood can also form a print. When clothing comes in contact with a plastic substance (e.g., clay), an identifiable plastic impression may be formed in it.

Fabric Marks

When a mark from clothing is to be recorded, it must be photographed with the camera placed vertically above or centrally in front of the mark. A scale must be placed at the side of the mark. If the mark is sufficiently large, the scale may be placed in the center of it. In such cases, a number of pictures should be taken and the scale should be moved to either side for each exposure so that details are not concealed.

Marks of clothes are identified with the aid of the structure of the fabric, faults in the fabric, seams, patches and other repairs, damage, and the like (Figure 9.12).

(a)

(b)

Figure 9.12 A suspect picked up a prostitute and, while in her room, produced an Australian Federal Police badge (a), hoping to get some free "service." The prostitute resisted and was assaulted. The badge was a facsimile in a clear plastic wallet. The suspect discarded the badge, which was subsequently located by police; the plastic wallet was found in the possession of the suspect. An examination of the wallet revealed the outlines of a badge (b) of similar size and shape to the one found at the scene. (Courtesy of State Forensic Science Laboratory, Melbourne, Australia.)

Sometimes, a whole section of the body forms impression marks from a body print or impression. In one case, a burglar fell from a water spout onto the damp earth below, making an impression that showed clearly the face with a characteristic nose and both hands, one holding a crowbar and the other a pistol. When a hand has made a print or impression on a plastic medium, one should look for identifiable friction skin patterns. Other marks may also be found such as those of rings, injuries, characteristic skin wrinkles, hand coverings, and so on. The preservation of marks of parts of the body is done in the same way as for footprints.

Tooth Marks

Tooth marks may leave compression or scraping marks and can occur in butter, cheese, fruit, chocolate, and the like. Bite marks may also occur on the skin of victims of rape or sexual murder or on a criminal. Cases have occurred in which the criminal has become involved in a hand-to-hand fight and a tooth has been knocked out or a dental plate broken and parts of the tooth or the dental plate have been found.

Bite marks can, at times, make possible the identification of a suspect. The relative positions of the teeth, their width, and the distance between them, together with ridges on the edges of the teeth and grooves on the back or front, vary for different individuals and may show in the bite mark. Deformations resulting from injuries or illness in the form of portions broken away, characteristic wear of the teeth, fillings, and other dental work, and the loss of certain teeth are noted in the bite. It is good practice to have DNA testing done on bite mark evidence to confirm any identification (Figure 9.13).

(a)

Figure 9.13 In a homicide case involving two suspects, a wad of used chewing gum (a) was discovered at the crime scene. Dental impressions of the victim and suspects were made (b) and compared with the gum. An unusual feature of the gum's impression was a defect corresponding to an opening drilled in the back of one suspect's upper incisor during root canal therapy. In a further comparison, DNA typing revealed a DNA type that was the same as that of the suspect. The case resulted in a guilty plea to second-degree murder. (Courtesy of Norman D. Sperber, DDS, Forensic Odontologist, San Diego, California.)

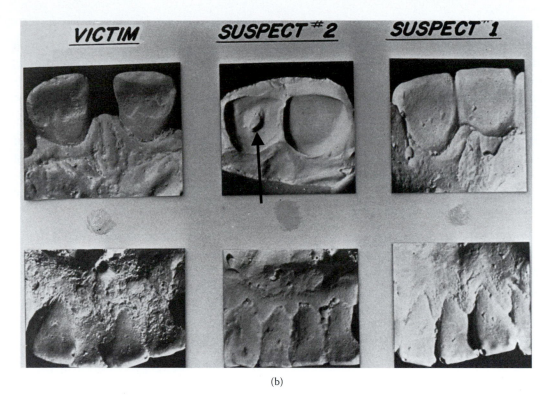

(b)

Figure 9.13 *(Continued)*

Generally, tooth marks come from front teeth in the upper and lower jaws. With children and young people, the edges of the front teeth usually have three ridges (at times more) that are distinguished by shallow incisions, sometimes in the form of furrows, continued on the front and back sides of the teeth. With increasing age, these ridges and furrows generally disappear so that the front teeth are generally smooth by age 30.

Preservation of Bite Marks

Bite marks should be carefully preserved by photographing and casting. They are generally formed in material that cannot be sent away or kept for a long time without the mark changing in appearance due to drying or decomposition of the material. Marks made in fruit can be preserved in 0.5% formalin solution, which prevents changes resulting from drying, decay, and so forth. However, it is not advisable to leave the fruit in solution for shipment by mail to an expert because it may be broken up and mixed with the solution as the result of shaking. An apple showing a bite mark that is to be sent for examination should instead be fixed by soaking in the solution for several hours and then wrapped in tissue paper moistened with formalin solution. The whole package is then packed in a carton or box.

For photography, oblique lighting is used so that details appear most clearly. It should be noted that there is a risk that, for example, butter or soft cheese might melt under the heat from a photographic lamp. All bite marks should be photographed before casting because the casting may go wrong and bite marks are generally altered in such a way that a fresh cast cannot be taken.

Casting Material for Bite Mark Evidence

The casting material must be chosen with regard to the properties of the material in which the bite has been made. If the material contains water-soluble substances, for example, chocolate and certain types of cheese, then the bite mark should be isolated from the casting mass by spraying it with a thin layer of collodion or the like. Suitable casting media for different materials are described next.

Human Skin   Bite marks should first be photographed with a scale; those found on skin should be traced using clear cellulose acetate and a felt-tip marker. The quality of the cast impression will depend on the depth of the bite. Silicone or rubber-based dental impression creams may be used to cast the impression. Because saliva may be present as part of the mark, a swab of the area should be made for DNA typing.

Foods   Bite mark impressions may be left in cheese, butter, sandwich meats, fruit, chocolate, chewing gum, taffy, and other such foods. If the food is water soluble, dental impression cream such as polysulfide rubber-based impression materials may be used. Other materials such as plaster and molten sulfur (provided that the material is not heat sensitive) have applicability. If dental stone is used, the surface should first be lightly sprayed with lacquer or similar material if the item to be cast contains water.

Tool Marks

Marks of tools or of objects that have been used as tools are often found at the scene of a crime, especially in cases of burglary. Marks may have been left in wood, metal, putty, or paint. Among the tools that leave identifiable marks are axes, knives, screwdrivers, chisels, crowbars, pliers, cutters, and drill bits. Some of these tools may be homemade (Figure 9.14).

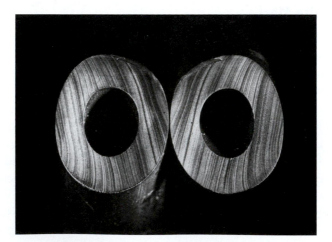

Figure 9.14 A stolen outboard motor was identified by comparison of the tool marks made when the rubber gas lines between the portable tank and motor were cut. (Courtesy of the Centre of Forensic Science, Toronto, Canada.)

These marks are essentially of two types: those in which only the general form and size of the tool are apparent and those in which injuries, irregularities, and other peculiar characteristics are reproduced in the form of striations or indentations. Marks of the first type may not make a definite identification of the tool possible, but do serve as a guide when it is necessary to decide whether the tool of a suspect could have produced the marks. Tool marks that show striations, indentations, or similar details resulting from damage or other irregularities in the tool are the most valuable as evidence (Figures 9.15 and 9.16).

Figure 9.15 The residential community of Castleton, New York, was shocked by the brutal stabbing and bludgeoning of Carolyn J. Finkle, a 42-year-old resident of Rensselaer County. Her two teenage daughters were extremely distraught and claimed they had found their mother slain with multiple stab wounds. Detectives mounted an intensive investigation. Plastic garbage bags used to wrap the murder weapon found in a dumpster matched bags found in the victim's house. The photograph shows backlighting of the plastic bags, revealing sequential striations caused by the manufacturing process. The daughters subsequently confessed to the crime. (Courtesy of the New York State Police Crime Laboratory.)

Figure 9.16 Consecutive manufacture comparison marks of plastic trash bags in a murder case proved to be important evidence. The photograph depicts a single layer of two plastic bags placed edge to edge. Characteristic "die line" and homogeneous mixing in the original plastic sheet are continuous between individual bags. These bags were used to link a box of trash bags from a residence and bags from the alleged crime vehicle to two bags found at the murder scene. (Courtesy of the Oklahoma State Bureau of Investigation.)

Preservation of Tool Marks

Whenever possible, tool marks should be kept in their original condition. This may be done by recovering the whole object or part of the object on which the marks appear. Sometimes, it can be arranged that the marks remain untouched at the scene of the crime but can be recovered later if this is required. This is permissible, however, only when the marks are in such a position that they are completely protected, for example, a small mark on the inside of a door or window frame. If a mark in metal is not immediately recovered, it should be covered with a thin film of oil to prevent oxidation. In recovering the mark, it is important that it be protected against dirt, moisture, and scratching during transport. Tissue or other soft paper should be placed over the tool mark in packaging.

Casting Tool Marks

Casting or other methods of taking impressions of a tool mark should be used only as a last resort. No matter how good a cast is, it can never be equal to the original. This applies especially to marks made in soft materials such as wood, putty, and paint; many of the casting media most suited for these materials are unable to reproduce all the finer details important for identification. Experiments have shown that an impression or a cast cannot reproduce scratches in paint caused by extremely small irregularities in the edge of a tool. Consequently, a microscopic comparison of the cast with a mark made from the suspected tool may not lead to any positive results. If, however, the original mark is compared with one made directly by the tool, then a positive identification is possible.

In the casting of marks, however, very satisfactory results may be obtained with dental impression materials or silicone rubber, and the completed cast will show fine detail.

Difficulties and some expense may be involved in taking possession of the original tool mark. Therefore, it should be subjected to a close examination with the aid of a magnifier to make sure that it shows typical details from the tool before any further steps are taken. In each particular case, consideration must also be given to the type of crime, value of the object, whether a tool from a suspect is available or the probability that such a tool may be found, etc.

Whether the actual mark is recovered or a cast is made, the tool mark should be photographed whenever practical. The picture should show clearly the location of the mark in relation to the rest of the object. Close-up photographs are generally taken in cases in which the mark may be destroyed in the casting process or during removal. The photographs must be made with the film plane parallel to the mark and should include a scale. Oblique lighting is used to enhance details in the mark. Close-up photographs should be in actual size, if possible, or in the case of smaller marks, enlarged. It is generally not possible to identify the tool used from photographs.

Trace Evidence on Tools

In connection with all tool marks and suspected tools, it should be remembered that the tool might also have deposited traces in the form of paint, oil, or other contamination. In turn, clues in the form of wood fragments and paint from the object may be found on the tool. These traces are sometimes just as valuable as the tool mark. Samples should therefore always be taken from the area of the tool mark whenever the actual mark is not recovered. Valuable tool marks are also sometimes found on splinters of wood, loosened flakes of paint, and chunks of safe insulation.

During the examination of the crime scene, the possibility should always be kept in mind that any tool mark found might be compared with marks from previous crimes. It happens frequently that identity is established among tool marks from different burglaries long before the criminal is apprehended or the actual tool is found.

The investigating officer should always endeavor to imagine being in a similar position to the criminal when the tool marks were made to consider how the criminal held the tool, stood, or was supported when breaking in or prying open. A burglary may be faked with the object of concealing embezzlement or of defrauding an insurance company; therefore, the investigator should always examine the opposite part of a mark (e.g., in a doorframe). The fake burglar often overlooks the fact that this other part of the mark must be present.

Moreover, it is essential for the expert who is to carry out the comparative examination of the tool and the tool marks to understand how the criminal held the tool when making the marks. In most cases, if the examination is to have any prospect of leading to the identification of the tool, the expert must make a comparison mark in exactly the same way as the criminal has done. This applies especially to those tool marks that show scratches resulting from damage or other irregularities in the tool. The distance between the scratches varies according to whether a knife, for example, is held at right angles to its direction of movement or is held askew; the appearance of the scratches depends on the angle taken by the knife in relation to the plane of the cut. It is best if the position of a "fixed" mark and the conditions at the place are shown to the expert in a sketch or a comprehensive photograph. A statement that the suspect is right- or left-handed should be added.

It is essential that the comparison mark be made in the same material as the mark at the scene of the crime (with the same paint or surface treatment, of the same degree of moisture, etc.) because the clarity of definition of the microscopic scratches varies with different materials. Thus, a quantity of material for use in producing comparison marks should be sent with the tool and tool mark—it may be necessary to make 10 or more such marks with the suspected tool.

The police officer should not attempt to fit the tool into the mark or make a comparison mark with a suspected tool (Figure 9.17a and b). In most cases, the officer does not have access to an instrument suitable for closer examination of the character of a tool mark, which may be necessary to decide how the comparison mark is to be made. Also, traces of paint or foreign metal on the tool, only observable with a microscope or powerful magnifying glass, may be lost or the tool may be damaged.

Casts or impressions of tool marks should be packed in such a way that they cannot be altered or destroyed during transport. Positive casts should never be made because this may cause fine details to become obscured. If the negative cast of the mark might be destroyed in transmission, it is best to make two and keep one in reserve.

Regarding boring marks, only wood bits and certain spiral bits generally leave identifiable marks. The bottom of the boring, if there is one, and boring chips are important. With other types of bits, identification is possible only in the most favorable cases and then as a rule only when the bottom of the boring is present.

At times, the police officer comes up against the problem of deciding, for example, from which side of a window frame (outside or inside) a hole has been bored. In most cases, this can be seen from the more or less loose wood fibers around the entrance and

(a)

(b)

Figure 9.17 In this case, (a) an unknown tool was used to cause blunt force trauma to the victim's head. (b) A piece of rebar was later found to be consistent with the unique impression patterns in the decedent's skull. (Courtesy of the Special Investigations Unit, NYC OCME.)

exit holes of the bit, but with some bits it may actually be difficult to decide the direction of boring. Reliable information is obtained by cutting through the surrounding wood in the longitudinal direction of the hole—by first sawing through the wood around the hole from each side up to about 1/2 inch from the hole and then breaking the wood apart. It will then be found that the wood fibers are directed upward from the hole in one edge of each half and downward in the other edges. The wood fibers around the boring are displaced in the direction of rotation of the drill, so upon cutting the boring into two parts in this manner, they reveal clearly the direction of boring. The degree of orientation of the wood fibers varies for different types of bits and it is possible to obtain an idea of the type of bit used by carrying out test borings with different bits.

Saw marks usually do not offer any possibility of identifying the saw used. In a few cases, some idea may be obtained by noting the degree of set and possibly also the number of teeth per inch of the saw used, but this can be done only if sawing was stopped before the wood was sawn through. In some cases it is possible to find, in the base of the saw cut, impressions of the teeth of the saw made when the saw was at rest for an instant before it was withdrawn. It is also possible to obtain from the base of the saw cut a measure of the width of cut and therefore of the approximate amount of set.

Hacksaw marks offer little possibility of identification. However, with blades with different numbers of teeth per inch, if the blade did not go through the piece of metal, it may be possible to examine the bottom of the cut and observe the impression of the teeth to obtain an idea of the number of teeth per inch. This may also be observed at the sides of the actual cut where the saw jumped and left shallow marks of the teeth in the surface of the metal, especially when first started.

Preserving a Tool

Once the tool has been found, care should be taken to preserve its evidentiary value. It should be carefully marked or tagged. If markings are made on the tool, they should not be placed in the area of the working surface. Similarly, minute items of trace evidence should be carefully preserved. The tool should be carefully packaged for transportation to the laboratory. It is important to remember that the handles of tools can be swabbed for touch DNA as well.

Tool marks made by cutting tools generally present little difficulty when the object cut is large enough to collect sufficient characteristics, such as the shackle of a padlock. Smaller items such as wire cable and multi-strand wire show identifiable markings only in exceptional cases.

If the wire has plastic insulation as a covering, a physical match may be made by an examination of the extrusion markings on the cable as well as the microscopic jagged cut on the ends of the insulation. Generally, striations on the fine wire will be insufficient.

Manufacturing marks such as casting, extruding, grinding, and so on are important when attempting to match items together physically. These markings and random breaks that occur when tools or other materials break or tear are important means of identification.

Impression or casting media must be chosen for each particular case, taking into consideration the type of material in which the mark is formed and its orientation, that is, on the horizontal or vertical. Some impression materials such as plaster and plasticine have a tendency to shrink or expand after setting; they should not be used for casting. Dental impression creams have been found useful as casting materials. They generally come packaged in individual tubes, with one the catalyst and the other the setting agent, and are simply mixed and easy to apply. Other materials such as moulage, polysulfide rubber-based material, and silicone rubber are also useful (Figure 9.18).

A retaining wall should be built around the impression. Modeling clay or putty may be used for this purpose. The casting material should be thoroughly mixed according to the manufacturer's instructions and applied to the impression by means of a spatula. A tag with string attached may be used for identification purposes. The string may be inserted just below the surface of the casting material.

(a)

(b)

Figure 9.18 Using a honeydew melon (a) to simulate a skull, tests with different hammers (b) suggested one that left a similar shape and dimensions in the victim's skull. (Courtesy of Norman D. Sperber, DDS, San Diego, California.)

Fragments of Tools

At crime scenes where doors, windows, or locked drawers show signs of forcible entry, the investigating officer must remember to examine the floor immediately adjacent to the point of entry carefully before examining the actual tool marks. It is not uncommon for burglary tools to break during forced entry; therefore, large or small fragments of the tool may be found at the scene and prove to be very valuable as evidence. Broken pieces of a tool might also be found inside a lock on which picking or prying has been attempted.

In many cases it is possible to establish that such broken fragments originally were parts of tools found in the possession of a suspect. The physical matching of two or more pieces that originally were one piece—a so-called fracture match—is a most convincing and easily demonstrable type of proof against an offender.

The converse situation should also be kept in mind. A broken tool left by the burglar at the crime scene can be matched with fragments of that tool that may be found in the suspect's clothing, home, or place of business. Pieces may also have been left at the scene of another burglary.

The search for such tool fragments is best done with a flashlight, the beam of which is directed over the search area at a very low angle. When the light strikes a metallic fragment, it will give off bright reflections that make the particles easy to find. Any suspected fragment should be recovered and placed in a vial, envelope, or pillbox that can be labeled as to the time and place of recovery.

A magnet or metal detector can also be used in searching for tool fragments. If a deliberate effort to look for such pieces of broken tools is not made, there is the risk of trampling them into the ground, embedding them in the officer's shoes, or kicking them aside while engaging in other routines of crime scene search.

Impression evidence is often encountered at crime scenes. Submitting that evidence to the laboratory along with the suspected tool frequently results in an identification.

Chapter Questions

1. (True/False) Small and sometimes microscopically unique markings can be directly traced to the object or instrument in question.
   a) True
   b) False

2. Describe the differences between compression marks and scraping marks.

3. Which of the following could be an individual characteristic that might be found on a footwear impression at a crime scene?
   a) Size
   b) Width
   c) Marks of nails and pegs
   d) Brand of the footwear

4. Describe the proper procedure for photographing a footwear impression at the scene of a burglary.

5. How many pounds of dental stone would be needed for a typical footwear impression?
   a) 2
   b) 4
   c) 6
   d) 10

6. Which of the following procedures must be done when casting a tire impression in snow?
   a) Mix the dental stone quickly so that it does not freeze
   b) Use a baffle to pour in the mixture
   c) Spray the impression first with Snow Print Wax
   d) Use an electrostatic lifter before pouring in the mixture

7. Describe the proper method when using sulfur casting on a footwear impression in snow.

8. You are called to the scene of a burglary and notice a footwear print in cooking oil on top of the kitchen cabinet near a broken window. Which of the following techniques would be the best way to collect this print?
   a) Dental stone casting
   b) Rubber lifter
   c) Sulfur casting
   d) Photographing the print at an oblique angle

9. List the two methods for collecting comparison footprints from a suspect.

10. When analyzing a questioned document that was typed, a document examiner may be able to provide which of the following information?
    a) Where the typewriter was purchased
    b) What nationality the writer is
    c) What year the document was typed
    d) The make of the typewriter

Firearms Examination 10

Crimes involving the use of firearms represent a significant area of police investigation. Firearms evidence may be present in crimes such as murder, attempted murder, suicide, assault, and rape. A number of questions may be answered by means of the proper utilization of firearms evidence: What kind of weapon was used? Was the weapon in proper working order? How far away was the weapon fired? In what direction was the weapon fired? Did a specific weapon fire a bullet? Did a particular person fire the weapon?

Because of the importance of reconstructing the circumstances of the crime and corroborating accounts of the crime by witnesses, suspects, and victims, firearms evidence is particularly important. This chapter deals with the major areas of firearms examination as they relate to crimes of violence.

The field of firearms identification is sometimes improperly referred to as forensic ballistics or simply ballistics. This is an improper use of terminology. "Ballistics" generally refers to the trajectory taken by a projectile and assumes an understanding of physics. Firearms identification, on the other hand, refers to the study of firearms and includes the operation of firearms, cartridges, gunshot residue (GSR) analysis, bullet and cartridge case comparisons, powder pattern determination, and the like. Many date the beginnings of modern forensic firearms identification to the Saint Valentine's Day massacre on February 14, 1929, in Chicago. With the aid of a newly developed comparison microscope, Col. Calvin Goddard was able to identify the two Thompson submachine guns used in the infamous crime (Figure 10.1).

Characteristics of Firearms

Today, there are literally thousands of types of firearms. They can be classified broadly into two groups: long arms such as rifles and shotguns, and handguns such as revolvers and pistols or automatic and semiautomatic pistols (bipod, tripod, and other exotic weapons are also sometimes encountered). Of interest to law enforcement, handguns represent the firearm most used in crimes; shoulder arms are used less frequently. Obsolete weapons such as muskets, unusual firearms such as those disguised to appear as something other than a handgun, and homemade weapons such as "zip guns" are used with even less frequency (Figure 10.2).

Firearms may also be characterized by whether they have smoothbore or rifled barrels, the former used in shotguns and the latter in most other firearms. Rifling found in gun barrels is spiral grooves cut into the barrel that impart a rotation motion to the bullet as it leaves the barrel, resulting in more stable flight. Muskets are another type of smoothbore (and sometimes partially rifled) firearm.

Firearms may be single shot, revolver, automatic, and semiautomatic. The single shot firearm is loaded manually, fired once, and unloaded manually. The revolver differs from the single shot pistol, in that it has a rotating cylinder holding from 4 to 24 cartridges. Each time a cartridge is fired, the cylinder revolves by means of cocking the hammer or pulling

Figure 10.1 A modern comparison microscope used to compare two bullets allegedly fired from the same gun. (Courtesy of the Los Angeles County Sheriff's Department.)

Figure 10.2 An operational firearm made to appear like an ordinary object, in this case a cellphone. (Courtesy of http://www.geeky-gadgets.com/wp-content/uploads/2008/11/cellphone-gun1.jpg.)

the trigger, which places the cartridge into position to be fired. The automatic firearm generally found in military weapons is a repeating type. Cartridges are fired in succession as long as the trigger is pressed and until the ammunition supply is exhausted. The semiautomatic pistol (often improperly referred to as an "automatic") functions similarly to the automatic, but fires only one shot each time the trigger is pulled.

In single shot- and revolver-type firearms, the cartridge casing generally remains in the weapon after firing, although single shot weapons have been made that eject cases automatically. With automatic and semiautomatic firearms, the cartridge case is ejected from the weapon automatically.

Shotguns differ in two major ways from other firearms: shotgun barrels are usually not rifled but are smoothbore and fire a different type of ammunition consisting of many lead pellets, rifled slugs, sabots, or shot (Figure 10.3). (There are also some who load shotshells with various other materials like rock salt, flechettes, lead balls, piano wire, or less lethal materials: beanbags, rubber bullets, etc.) Shotguns are of the single- and double-barreled break action for reloading, pump action, semiautomatic, or bolt action types.

The caliber designation of a firearm, a somewhat complicated topic, is a measure of the bore of the barrel and is measured in 1/100 or 1/1000 of an inch or in millimeters. The caliber designation is only an approximation of the bore diameter and is measured from land to opposing land (Figures 10.4 and 10.5). Shotgun bores are measured in gauges; the smaller the number is, the larger the diameter. Thus, a 12-gauge shotgun has a larger

Figure 10.3 The inside of a shotgun shell showing the gunpowder and shot. This type of cartridge is used for trap shooting. (Courtesy of Lucian C. Haag, Forensic Science Services, Inc., Carefree, AZ.)

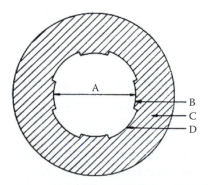

Figure 10.4 The caliber of a rifled weapon is generally determined from the diameter of a bore, measured between two opposite lands. However, there are some exceptions to this rule. (A) Caliber, (B) land, (C) barrel, and (D) groove.

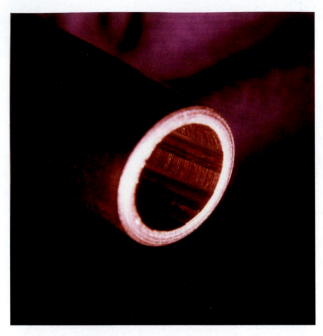

Figure 10.5 The rifling of the barrel of a gun. Note the lands and grooves. (Courtesy of Lucian C. Haag, Forensic Science Services, Inc., Carefree, AZ.)

diameter bore than a 20-gauge shotgun. The term gauge was originally the number of lead balls of that size weighing 1 pound. This system does not hold for the .410 "gauge," which is in actuality a caliber.

Ammunition

Small arms cartridges or rounds are of two general types: rim fire and center fire. Rim fire ammunition is almost exclusively .22-caliber (plus the recently introduced .17-caliber), while larger calibers are center fire.

Some older firearms, other than .22-caliber, did use rim fire ammunition. The terms rim and center refer to the position of the primer located in the base of the cartridge. In a rim fire round, the primer is in the rim in an area around the circumference of the base while center fire rounds have the primer in the center. The primer is a small shock-sensitive explosive charge in the base of the cartridge used to set off the propellant powder when struck by the firing pin.

The bullet is the projectile fired from the weapon. Bullets are generally a lead alloy and jacketed with a harder metal such as copper or brass or nonjacketed. The purpose of the jacket is to keep the bullet intact and from breaking up when it strikes a target, to prevent damage while in the weapon, and to control expansion.

Gunpowder or smokeless powder consists of tiny cylinders, balls, flakes, or discs of nitrocellulose or nitrocellulose and nitroglycerine in so-called double-based powder. When confined and ignited, the powder rapidly burns, giving off a large quantity of gas. The expanding gas is the means by which the bullet is propelled through the barrel and out of the weapon. Black powder is also used in certain ammunition (Figure 10.6).

Figure 10.6 A photomicrograph example of gunpowder, in this case "Hercules Bullseye propellant." (Courtesy of Lucian C. Haag, Forensic Science Services, Inc., Carefree, AZ.)

Firearms Evidence

When a weapon is fired, the firing pin strikes the base of the cartridge detonating the primer, which in turn ignites the gunpowder. Expansion of gases forces the casing against the breech, which resists the rearward movement, and propels the bullet down the barrel. The bullet picks up the tiny imperfections of the rifling as it passes through. The scratches or striations are caused by the imperfections in the lands and grooves placed in the barrel at the time of manufacture and caused through use of the weapon. Characteristic markings from the mechanical action of loading, chambering, and firing the round, as well as from extracting and ejecting the casing, will be present on the bullet, cartridge casing, and cartridge base. If compared against rounds fired from the same weapon, these marks will show similarities that the firearms identification expert can use to determine if the rounds were fired from the same gun (Figure 10.7).

Beyond determining that two rounds were fired from the same weapon, a great deal of other information can be developed from evidence associated with firearms. The presence of cartridge cases may indicate an automatic, semiautomatic, bolt-action or slide-action firearm, or a single-shot firearm when more than one round was fired. The relative location of the casings to the shooter may sometimes suggest the type of weapon fired or that a revolver was emptied at the scene.

Bullets and even fragments of bullets may be used to determine the type of weapon used from the size and weight of the projectile and an examination of the striations on the outside surface. For example, the number, direction of twist, and measurements of land and groove markings can be useful in determining the type, make, model, and caliber of firearm. Examination of the area that the bullet struck will yield information about the path and distance from which the weapon was fired. This is also possible with shot fired from a shotgun.

Tests on the shooter's hands can be made to determine if a weapon was recently fired. Finally, if the firearm is recovered, it can be tested to determine if it is in proper working order and if it could have been accidentally discharged. The owner of the firearm can possibly be determined by serial number examination.

Figure 10.7 Two bullets viewed under a comparison microscope show characteristic markings imparted by the barrel onto the bullet's surface. The firearms examiner uses these striations to determine whether two bullets were fired from the same gun. (Courtesy of the Los Angeles County Sheriff's Department.)

Gunshot Residue (GSR) Analysis

When the firing pin strikes the base of a cartridge, the shock causes the primer to detonate, in turn causing the ignition of the main gunpowder charge. The chemical reaction thus started causes a rapid expansion of gases, which propels the bullet out of the barrel of the gun. The by-products of the reaction are burned and unburned powder and the components of the primer mixture (Figure 10.8).

Primers use shock-sensitive compounds containing such materials as lead, barium, and antimony. Barium, antimony, and/or lead on a shooter's hands indicate that a gun was recently fired. Recently, some ammunition manufacturers have begun to market nonlead-based primers and bullets to limit the lead exposure of shooting enthusiasts.

Upon discharging a weapon, microscopic particles of GSR are deposited on the hands of the shooter as an aerosol.* These particles adhere to the hands but are removed by washing, wringing, or placing hands in the pockets. Handcuffing a suspect behind the back will dislodge these particles. Studies show that GSR material will remain on a shooter's hands for up to 6 hours. The particles are in the highest concentration immediately after shooting

---

* GSR particles can also be detected on clothing and even the area surrounding an automobile window in the case of a drive-by shooting. However, sample collection results in considerable extraneous debris.

Figure 10.8 When a firearm is discharged, gases from the detonation of the primer and burning gunpowder escape from the barrel. These gases along with burned and unburned particles of gunpowder and primer can be used to test whether a person recently fired a weapon or was in close proximity to a weapon being fired. (Courtesy of Lucian C. Haag, Forensic Science Services, Inc., Carefree, AZ.)

and are gradually lost over time. Because of this time factor, GSR evidence must be collected as quickly as possible.

Atomic absorption (AA) spectrophotometry, Scanning Electron Microscopy/Energy Dispersive Xray (SEM/EDX) analysis, and inductively coupled plasma (ICP) spectroscopy are the most widely used methods of testing for GSR. The procedure used by a laboratory determines the way in which the evidence is to be collected.

GSR evidence is collected in one of two ways: with cotton-tipped applicators and dilute nitric acid solution for AA and ICP analysis or with aluminum stubs with double-sided cellophane tape for SEM. The chemical components of the primer present on the shooter's hands are the substances tested for in the GSR procedure. In general, barium, lead, and antimony are characteristic of most ammunition. Certain .22-caliber ammunition, for example, that made by manufacturers other than the Federal Cartridge Company, contains only lead.

GSR evidence collection kits are available commercially and through local crime laboratories. In all cases, the person collecting the evidence should wear plastic gloves to prevent possible contamination of the evidence. Information concerning the subject's occupation and hobbies should be noted. This is important for interpretation of test results.

Obtaining GSR results is straightforward, but its interpretation is another matter. Negative GSR results (no GSR detected) do not conclusively mean that a subject did not fire a handgun. Similarly, positive GSR results do not prove someone fired a gun because a person could have handled a gun or been in close proximity to a gun that was fired.

A shooting suspect's hands should be protected until the test is given. Handcuffing behind the back is likely to remove GSR. Hands may be bagged loosely with paper bags but not in plastic bags, which cause perspiration and hence a cleansing effect. In the case of a deceased subject, the 6-hour time limit is flexible but the hands should be protected until such time as the evidence can be collected.

Because of the ambiguity in conclusions about whether an individual fired a weapon using GSR, a number of forensic laboratories have opted to discontinue this service. Instead, some laboratories opt to swab the gun, including the trigger, trigger guard, backstrap, slide, grip, and/or unspent ammunition for touch DNA typing instead.

Collecting Firearms Evidence

The crime scene in which a firearm was involved should be processed in much the same way as that discussed earlier in the text. In addition, a number of other considerations must be taken into account in these types of cases. (It goes without saying that in life or death situations when a gun needs to be quickly rendered safe, some of the following may not apply. In these situations, the destruction of evidence should be minimized to the extent possible.)

When sketching and measuring the crime scene, it is particularly important to carefully note and measure the location of all cartridge casings, bullet holes, bullets and bullet fragments, and shotgun shot patterns that are found. This information is vital to the reconstruction of the crime and can be used to verify statements by witnesses and suspects. Special care must be taken when walking through the location so that casings or bullets are not stepped on or inadvertently kicked.

If a weapon is found at the scene, it should not be moved until its location is noted through measurement, sketches, and photographs. The investigator should remember that fingerprints and/or DNA might be present, so when the weapon is moved, it must be handled in a way that will not destroy them. The floor below the weapon should be examined for a depression or other marks that would indicate that it was dropped from some height or fell from the shooter's hands. Traces of wood, fibers, paint, building material, blood, and hair should be looked for on the weapon and carefully preserved if found.

If the dead person is holding the weapon, it is important to note the exact grip and position of the weapon in the hand. The murderer may have placed it there. In such a case, the way in which a weapon is held in relation to the injuries on the body is decisive as to whether the dead person could have produced the injuries. In the case of an automatic pistol, the recoil of the slide may have caused a surface graze in the region of the thumb or the web of the hand, and the presence of such an injury is suggestive that the dead person had fired a shot with a semiautomatic pistol. A closer examination of the hand of the dead person may show marks of powder, especially if a revolver had been used. From these marks, the investigator may deduce that both hands were in the vicinity of the muzzle blast or the gap of the revolver. One hand may have been used as a guide while the other pressed the trigger or both hands may have been held up in defense.

In the case of long-barreled guns, rifles, and shotguns, special attention should be given to the possibility of the dead person having fired a suicide shot with the weapon. Special arrangements such as string, belts, sticks, and the like may have been used, and these in turn may have left marks in the form of fibers, dirt, soot, or the like on the trigger or trigger guard. One shoe may have been removed in order that the trigger was depressed with a toe.

The position of cartridges, cartridge cases, and bullets is just as important as that of weapons. From their position it may be possible to deduce the position of firing, direction of the shot, and in certain cases the path of the bullet. If a bullet has penetrated a tree, piece of furniture, or wall, the shot track gives information regarding the direction of the shot and often also the path of the bullet. There is a much better opportunity of determining the exact course of a bullet when it has passed through a fixed object such as a windowpane and then struck a wall. With the aid of the path of the bullet and of shot wounds on the dead person, it is possible to determine the deceased's position when shot. In calculating the distance of the shot, the depth to which a bullet has penetrated, for example, a wall, may be significant. The penetrating power is dependent on the distance of the shot, but allowance must also be made for the loss of energy in passing through an object, such as a body (Figure 10.9a and b). A more accurate determination of distance can be made with the aid of gunshot injuries on the clothes and body of the dead person.

The position of a bullet found at the scene of a crime should be recorded in the same way as for weapons; bullets should be collected separately and packed so that there can be no confusion. If two or more weapons have been used, the bullets should not get mixed up so that, at a later date, the place where each one was found can be fixed exactly. Great care should also be taken in collecting and packing bullets so that the microscopic marks from the barrel of the weapon are not injured or destroyed. For this reason, a bullet that has penetrated or lodged in a wall should not be probed for and dug out by means of a knife, ice pick, or chisel. Instead, a portion of the wall surrounding the bullet should be carefully removed in one piece and the bullet recovered by breaking away the supporting material. Because it may become important to ascertain other objects that came in contact with the projectile, gloves should always be worn when handling bullets or bullet fragments. Trace evidence should not be removed nor the bullet washed until a microscopic study is performed. Care should be exercised that the investigator's marking of the bullet does not destroy this trace evidence. The firearms examiner should also consult with the forensic biologist when DNA typing is needed to determine the best order for the bullet to be examined.

The same considerations with respect to fixing the position and taking possession of weapons and bullets apply to cartridges and cartridge cases found at the scene of a crime. The position of a cartridge that has misfired or of a cartridge case that has been ejected from an automatic pistol may give an indication of the type of automatic pistol used and form a valuable supplement to the determination of the make of pistol from marks left by the weapon on the bullet and casing. Many automatic pistols differ with respect to the ejection of the casings; some throw them out to the left, some to the right, and some straight up. The casing is thrown out with a force that varies for different types of pistols, but is generally considerable, so that it may rebound against furniture, walls, wall coverings, and so on and change direction. The position may give some indication of the type of weapon; however, there is often variation from weapon to weapon. If a cartridge case has not bounced off any object and has moreover fallen onto an underlayer that prevents it from rolling (carpet, lawn, etc.), then its position gives a direct indication of the type of weapon and place or direction of firing. If three of these factors (position of cartridge case, type of automatic pistol, place of firing, direction of shooting) are known, then the fourth can be determined. Outdoors, however, it is necessary to take into account the direction and strength of the wind; in all cases the inclination of the ground must be considered.

(a)

(b)

Figure 10.9 (a) One of the photos of the shooting reconstruction of the Sean Bell case where three men were shot fifty times by undercover NYPD officers in Queens, NY. (b) An overall diagram of the bullet trajectories illustrating that no bullets were fired from inside the car. (Courtesy of the Special Investigations Unit, NYC Office of Chief Medical Examiner.)

The position of wads, which often remain relatively undamaged, from shotgun shells and muzzle-loading weapons, also gives information regarding the direction of shooting. These can generally be found about 5–8 yards or more from the place of firing in the approximate direction of fire, but it is necessary to take into consideration the direction and strength of the wind. The overshot card placed in front of the charge of shot shows, if found, a manufacturing mark and also the size of shot given by a number or letters.

As mentioned previously, weapons and also cartridge cases, bullets, shot, and wads may carry marks from the victim or the criminal who may aid in solving the crime. It should always be remembered that DNA, latent fingerprints, and fingerprints in blood, grease, or the like may be found on weapons and must be protected.

A weapon that has been used in a case of murder, suicide, or assault may contain clues from the victim in the form of blood, hair, fragments of textiles, cloth fibers, and so on. Such clues may appear to be of little value, but if it is necessary to prove that the weapon was actually used in a particular case, these clues are then of the greatest value. Loose hairs, dried blood, fibers, and the like should be placed in a test tube and the weapon taken and packed in such a way that DNA, fingerprints, or other clues are not destroyed. A cardboard container that suspends the weapon with the minimum of bearing surfaces is preferred. Wrapping an object in cotton, gauze, or tissue will more than likely dislodge trace evidence. If epithelial cells, fingerprints, and/or bloodstains are present on a weapon, they might be destroyed if the whole of the weapon is dusted with fingerprint powder. It is therefore appropriate for the latent print examiner to confer with the forensic biologist to determine whether DNA or latent print evidence has the better chance of success. There is no hard and fast rule as to which type of evidence should be collected first; however, examiners should keep in mind that collection of one type of evidence could potentially prevent or inhibit the collection of a subsequent type of evidence.

Contamination in the form of oil, cement, paint, or similar material may also be significant in determining the way in which a criminal acquired a weapon or may give an indication of where a weapon was kept previously. It may possibly have been taken from the criminal's place of work or in an earlier burglary in which the criminal was less careful and left fingerprints or DNA that can be used as incriminating evidence.

If the weapon has been concealed at the scene of the crime or in the vicinity or taken away by the criminal, it is important to know the type of weapon for which one is searching. The only means of determining that is from a study of the injuries on the victim or by removal of the bullet at autopsy. In practice, it is often difficult to draw the correct conclusions from the appearance of the wounds because they are affected by the elasticity of the skin, underlying bones and muscles, angle of application, and other such factors. In these types of cases, however, the pathologist can give valuable assistance.

Handling of Firearms

In lifting firearms, great care must be taken not to destroy evidence. The best way to lift a pistol or revolver is to hold it with two gloved fingers on the checkered part of the butt or possibly by the ring on the butt. Shotguns may conveniently be held around the checkered part of the neck of the butt; if necessary, the weapon can be lifted by a steady grip with the fingers on the trigger guard. It is undesirable to lift a weapon by placing a stick or similar object in the trigger guard, even with a light weapon such as a revolver or pistol, because the weapon may be cocked and a shot might be fired if the trigger happens to be touched. It should be taken as a general rule never to lift a weapon found at the scene of a crime before first making sure that no one is in the direction in which the muzzle is pointing; of course one should not risk being hit if the weapon fires while being lifted. The weapon may actually be cocked so that even the slightest movement could cause a shot to be fired.

The procedure for picking up a gun by putting a pencil or stick in the barrel is absolutely wrong. This may destroy valuable clues in the barrel that might possibly have been of use in elucidating the case. In a contact shot (i.e., when the muzzle is in contact with a body) or close proximity shot, which is common with suicide, it often happens that blood, grease, and textile fibers are forced into the barrel of the gun left by the vacuum from the gas pressure and/or the splash of tissue and blood in all directions. This phenomenon is known as backspatter.

A layer of dust, spider webs, or loose rust particles found in the bore may indicate that no shot has been fired from a weapon for some time. The absence of a powder deposit or the presence of grease in the bore may also indicate that the weapon has not been used, while an examination of the powder layer in the bore may show that the fired cartridge was loaded with black powder or with smokeless powder. It is difficult to decide from the appearance of the powder deposit how much time has elapsed since the last shot was fired from a weapon. Therefore, if the bore of a weapon is to be examined for any such clues, introducing any object into it will interfere with its examination or make it impossible. For the same reason, cotton or the like must not be put in the muzzle during transport of the weapon or when it is sent to an expert. To protect any deposit in the bore, a twist of paper, rubber cap, or muzzle protector can be placed over the muzzle. The layer of dust in the bore is always thickest near the muzzle and decreases in thickness progressively toward the breech, assuming that it has resulted from a long period of storage. The confirmation of such a distribution of the deposit nearest the muzzle is therefore of great importance. Under no circumstances should an investigating officer put the weapon into his own pocket for safekeeping. After only brief contact with pocket dust, the gun will appear to have been unfired for some time.

Case of Homicide

The victim in this case was shot and killed by the suspect and the incident reportedly stemmed from a property dispute between neighboring families. Four firearms were submitted to the laboratory to be test-fired and/or examined for blood. One of the firearms submitted was a Mossberg model 500A 12-gauge shotgun. The interior of the muzzle end of the barrel of this shotgun contained apparent dust, cobwebs, and debris, indicating that the shotgun had not been fired recently and that it could not have been discharged during the reported altercation that took place.

After the weapon has been picked up, any loose objects or particles such as hair, fibers, dried blood, brain substance, and the like that might fall off in transport are removed and kept. With a near shot against a hair-covered part of the body, sometimes strands of hair or tissue can be found held fast between the slide and barrel of an automatic pistol. Also, any traces on the weapon in the form of fibers of wood, paint, cement, or the like, which might indicate that the weapon had fallen on the floor, should be collected while at the scene of the crime.

When a weapon is taken into possession, it should be subjected to a preliminary examination. Fingerprint impressions in grease or blood can easily be seen. If fingerprints, bloodstains, fibers, and so on are found on the weapon, they all must be preserved. It is important for the firearms examiner to also be mindful of subsequent DNA examinations and the potential for their own DNA to contaminate the evidence. Therefore, the firearms examination must be conducted with gloves and a mask covering the mouth and nose at a minimum. If latent fingerprints are to be developed by powder, care must be taken to keep the powder from entering the barrel. Likewise, when a revolver is processed by powder dusting, the front of the cylinder must be protected so that the mouth of each chamber can be examined for flaring.

Everything found in the first examination of the weapon should be written down accurately; any objects, particles, or swabs collected should be placed in a test tube or envelope labeled accurately with the exact place of finding. For the sake of identification, any manufacturer's or type markings should also be indicated, as well as the caliber marking and serial number. The investigator's initials should be inscribed on some major part of the weapon such as the barrel or frame, or the weapon may be tagged. It is most important to write down the condition of the weapon when found, if the safety is on or not, which can be seen from the position of the safety catch, and whether the weapon is cocked and loaded. With some semiautomatic pistols, the latter cannot be observed by a superficial glance, but where it is shown by, for example, an indicating pin, it should be noted. In the most common types of weapon, this condition can easily be confirmed from the position of the rear part of the bolt. It should also be noted whether the bolt (breech block or slide) is closed, partly open, or fully open. A cartridge case jammed in the ejection port should be noted, together with a statement of the exact position of the cartridge, whether the base or neck of the case is turned outward, etc., and also whether the magazine is firm or loose (not pushed right home).

After the exterior of the weapon has been processed for fingerprints and swabbed for DNA, the gun may be unloaded and rendered safe. With a semiautomatic pistol, the magazine is loosened, after which the slide is moved to remove any cartridge in the chamber. In doing this, it should be remembered that fingerprints might be found in grease on the cartridge in the chamber and on the sides of the magazine, which should therefore be examined first before any further handling. The weapon should not be considered unloaded until an inspection is made by looking into the chamber through the ejection port of the gun and physically checking to confirm that the chamber is empty. A broken extractor, jammed cartridge, or other factor may cause a cartridge to remain in the chamber. It is a poor practice to assume that a weapon is unloaded simply because a cartridge was not ejected. The cartridge is placed in an envelope or container with a label attached; a label can also be tied on by a thread around the groove of the cartridge. Any cartridges in the magazine should not be "stripped" if the weapon is to be sent to an expert for examination. Cartridges may carry DNA, fingerprints, and also marks from the guiding surfaces of the magazine, and it may be of significance to confirm them (e.g., whether the cartridges have been charged into the magazine several times). Furthermore, the order of the cartridges in a magazine may be important in certain cases and should always be noted.

In the case of a revolver, nothing should be done with the cartridges in the cylinder if the weapon is to be examined further. The exact position of the cylinder at the moment when the weapon is found is significant from many points of view and should be noted, for example, the position of the fired cartridge in relation to the hammer. The position of the cylinder can be marked if desired with a pencil or chalk mark, provided that this does not destroy other clues. The cylinder should not be "rolled" because then irrelevant marks from the recoil plate or firing pin could be formed on the bases of the fired cases and the cartridges.

In the case of weapons of single shot or repeating types, nothing should be done with the bolt unless the weapon is cocked or has the empty case in the chamber. If, however, the hammer is cocked, an unfired cartridge may be in the chamber and should be removed to prevent any accident. The cartridge is taken out and labeled as described earlier. Semi- or fully automatic weapons generally have a cartridge in the chamber unless the bolt is in the rearward position, so the slide should be moved while making sure that no fresh cartridge is introduced into the chamber. To prevent this, a detachable magazine is removed from the weapon; in the case of a fixed magazine, the uppermost cartridges are held back with a piece of wood or some other object that will not injure the cartridges or deposit any fresh marks on them.

All the precautions taken with a firearm must be put down accurately in the report. Later, possibly, the investigating police officer may be required to describe these precautions in connection with legal proceedings. What may appear to be of subordinate importance during the investigation of the crime may later be especially significant. In connection with all firearms, when a weapon is to be sent to an expert for examination, the only clues that need to be preserved are those that might be destroyed in transit; the only measures taken are those that cannot be omitted without risk of accident or that are essential in assisting the search for the criminal. Many traces on the weapon or significant facts in connection with the mechanism can be of such a character that special instruments or specially trained personnel are necessary to deal with them properly. Perhaps marks of colored lacquer from the sealing around the primer are on the breech face or recoil plate; a chemical examination may be required to confirm whether this could have come from a specific fired cartridge. Even in the bore, lacquer pigments from the sealing between the bullet and case or metallic particles from the jacket of the bullet may be found. In grease and dirt on the breech face, an impression of the markings may also be on the base of the cartridge case; special arrangements will be required for photographing this impression.

As mentioned earlier, from the point of view of identification, any marks indicating maker, type, and caliber should be recorded, together with the serial number. With many weapons, in particular certain pistols and revolvers, such markings are often lacking. The butt plates, however, are usually marked with the maker's or seller's initials, which can be a good guide.

Many weapons also carry proof marks. A number of European countries strictly regulate the manufacture of firearms and require a special mark to be stamped on the weapon's barrel to indicate that it has been tested and found safe. Proof marks are also found on some American-made weapons sold in foreign countries. In cases of inexpensive firearms, the proof mark may be the only clue to the manufacturer of the weapon.

Occasionally, firearms are recovered from which serial numbers have been ground off for the purpose of concealing the ownership of the weapon. When numbers are stamped into the frame of the weapon, changes in the metal structure deep below the surface result. If the process that removed the stamp was not sufficiently deep, the serial numbers or markings can be restored. Depending on the nature of the metal, a number of techniques are possible: magnetic particle testing, chemical etching, electrochemical etching, and heating (Figure 10.10).

Figure 10.10 Serial number restoration. (Courtesy of the Los Angeles County Sheriff's Department.)

Cartridge Cases

If no cartridge cases are found at the scene of a shooting, it may be suspected that a revolver, single shot pistol, automatic pistol with cartridge case collector, rifle, or shotgun was used. Theoretically, one might expect that criminals would attempt to guard themselves by picking up the cartridge cases thrown out by an auto-loading weapon, but in practice, it is hardly ever done because it would waste time and the criminal would run more risk of being discovered, especially if the shooting was heard by persons in the vicinity.

In taking possession of cartridge cases, one should not forget the possibility that significant clues may be found on them in the form of loose particles or fingerprints. These may be picked up by means of a clean swab stick or the like, introduced into the case, and then placed into an envelope marked with the place of finding. The internal diameter of a cartridge case corresponds at the neck with the diameter of the bullet. From the size, form, and appearance of a cartridge case, it is possible to obtain an indication of the type of weapon used.

Revolver cartridge cases are almost always fully cylindrical, with a rim but no extractor groove (a groove for the extractor running around the case with the rim) (Figure 10.11a). They may be made for rim fire (smooth base) or center fire (with primer cap). Many manufacturers make revolvers to take automatic pistol cartridges (Figure 10.11b). Thus, both Colt and Smith & Wesson make revolvers of .45-caliber so that automatic pistol cartridges of .45-caliber can be used in them. Similarly, automatic pistol cartridges of 7.65 mm can be fired in .32-caliber revolvers and automatic pistol cartridges of 6.35 mm can be fired in .25-caliber revolvers. Automatic pistol cartridges (with the exception of .45-rimless cartridges, 9-mm Parabellum cartridges, and bottleneck cartridges) have a rim that, although

(a)

(b)

Figure 10.11 (a) The difference between a revolver cartridge case (left) and a semiautomatic cartridge case (right) is the extractor groove. (b) "Moon clips" allow for chambering of semiauto ammunition in a revolver. (Courtesy of Peter Diaczuk, John Jay College of Criminal Justice.)

not much larger than the cylindrical surface of the cartridge, is quite sufficient to hold the cartridge fast in the chamber of a revolver cylinder when the internal diameter of the latter corresponds with the diameter of the cartridge. In many revolvers provided with one common extractor for all the cartridges, the rim also functions quite satisfactorily when pistol cartridges are used.

Revolver cartridges of .320-caliber can also be fired in certain semiautomatic pistols of 7.65-mm caliber. In some cases, such pistols have also repeated normally and even ejected revolver cartridge cases, but the ejected cases are often ruptured and sometimes jam the pistol.

Smaller caliber projectiles can be fired in larger bore weapons with serious effect. An example of this is the ability of a .38-Special revolver to fire .32–20 cartridges. Desperate persons in need of ammunition wrap cartridges in paper to accommodate a larger chamber, reduce the diameter by filing and even perform the dangerous act of driving a cartridge into a chamber by means of a hammer. Only an expert can determine with reasonable certainty the type of gun that might have been used in a shooting by an examination of the fired bullets or cartridges. An investigator must be careful not to pass up a weapon because it does not seem to correspond to the ammunition at hand.

Caliber and manufacturer's marks generally are found on the base of the cartridge case and sometimes also the year of manufacture. Sometimes, the maker's marks are in code consisting of letters and figures or of only letters or figures.

Fired cartridge cases are especially valuable for identification because they show marks from the weapon that in most cases make it possible to decide with certainty whether they were fired from a particular weapon or not. It is therefore of special importance in an outdoor shooting that all possible efforts be made to determine the location of the shooting so that any cartridge cases left behind can be found. The most valuable marks on cartridge cases are those made by the firing pin on the primer and by the breech face on the primer and base of the case, but the marks produced by the extractor, ejector, and the edge of the breech may also be important (Figure 10.12). Flaws or damage in the chamber may also show on the metal case and make identification of the weapon possible. If, when the criminal is found, he or she has already thrown away the weapon where it cannot be recovered (e.g., in water), it is important to attempt to find out whether the criminal or some other person (e.g., the previous or legal owner) ever fired a test shot, and if so, where. It is possible that the cartridge case and the bullet may be found there. With cartridge cases, it is not particularly important whether the test shot was fired a long time before. The part of the weapon that leaves marks on the case may not have altered even though there was a long interval of time between the test shot and the crime. It is different in the case of bullets because sometimes the bore of a weapon may undergo such changes in a comparatively short time that comparison of a bullet with a test shot fired previously is useless. The nature of the place where the weapon has been kept and the number of shots that have been fired with it are important factors.

From the marks made by the extractor, ejector, and edge of the breech of a semiautomatic pistol on a cartridge case, it is also possible to determine the make of semiautomatic pistol from which the case was fired. Semiautomatic pistols of different types and makes are often constructed differently with respect to the position of the extractor and ejector; this in turn affects the formation of the breech. The combination of these factors forms what is known as a system, that is, the characteristics mentioned allow classification of the type of construction of the pistol. If both cartridge case and bullet are available for determination

Figure 10.12 Ejector marks on a cartridge casing. (Courtesy of Lucian C. Haag, Forensic Science Services, Inc., Carefree, AZ.)

of the make, the possibilities are increased because the number of land impressions on the bullet, their width, and the angle of twist can also be characteristic of a type of weapon and, in any case, form a valuable contribution to the investigation.

Under no conditions should a cartridge case that is to be examined be tried in the chamber of a weapon; any marks made by the weapon on the case may be destroyed and other marks may be formed. It happens sometimes that at the scene of a crime in which a firearm has been used, a cartridge is found that has misfired and been thrown out by movement of the slide or bolt, or that has jammed between the breech-lock and the edge of the breech and been removed by hand. Even such an unfired cartridge may carry valuable marks that can make possible an identification or determination of the make of the weapon used.

Bullets

Bullets that penetrate hard objects are often severely mutilated, sometimes to a degree that the weapon from which they were fired cannot be identified. Therefore, every effort must be made to preserve what little remains of the rifling impression when a bullet is lodged in a wall, tree, or bone.

In the latter case, the method of removal, if at all, will depend on whether the shooting victim is dead. If the victim is dead, the principles for bone, tree, or wall are alike. No projectile should be pried from its position. Instead, the supporting material and the bullet should be cut out as one piece. Then the surrounding bone, plaster, or wood can be broken away carefully, leaving the projectile in the best possible condition, considering all circumstances. If the investigator wishes, the bullet as embedded in supporting material may be sent to the laboratory. Bullets removed by probing show ample evidence of the destructive effect of improper technique. Before removal, some careful testing will indicate the direction of the bullet's track.

Marking Bullets

After removal, the bullet should be initialed on the base. No mark should be placed on the rifling impression or on areas of ricochet. If in doubt as to the proper area to mark, the investigator should place the bullet in an envelope, a plastic vial, or a small box, then seal and mark the container.

Bullets may be of different sizes and shapes and made in different ways. The most common types are entirely of lead, semi-jacketed, or fully jacketed; but there are also bullets with a hole in the point (hollow point), with the point covered with softer metal, lead bullets with a copper cone pressed into the point, and the like (Figure 10.13).

With fully jacketed (solid nose) bullets, the jacket encloses entirely the point of the bullet but is open at the rear end of it, exposing the lead core. With a semi-jacketed (soft nose) bullet, on the other hand, the jacket encloses the whole of the rear end of the bullet while the core is free at the point to a larger or smaller extent. The semi-jacketed bullet breaks up when it meets a bone or other hard part of the body, but if it passes merely through soft parts, it may remain relatively undamaged or it may expand. If it strikes the branch of a tree in its flight, it may actually be split or deformed before reaching its objective (Figure 10.14). On the other hand, a fully jacketed bullet often remains undamaged or only slightly deformed on striking, for example, a body. Less scrupulous shooters sometimes file the point of a fully jacketed bullet to produce the same effect as that of a

Figure 10.13 An example of a hollow point cartridge.

(a)   (b)

Figure 10.14 A fully jacketed bullet (a) is usually not deformed to any extent on striking an object, but a semi-jacketed bullet breaks up (b). (Courtesy of the Los Angeles County Sheriff's Department.)

semi-jacketed one. This result is obtained if the bullet leaves the barrel whole; however, because the jacket is open at both ends, there is a risk of the lead core only being driven out and the jacket remaining behind in the barrel. If this is not noticed, then when the next shot is fired, the weapon will burst or a bulge will be produced in the barrel.

Lead bullets may be of different degrees of hardness. Bullets of soft lead are often greatly deformed and sometimes break up when they strike a body, while those of hard lead may retain their regular shape to the same extent as a fully jacketed bullet.

Ammunition intended for automatic pistols usually has fully jacketed bullets, while revolver ammunition usually has lead bullets. There are, however, also automatic pistol cartridges with lead or semi-jacketed bullets and revolver cartridges with fully jacketed bullets. An intermediate position is taken by the previously mentioned cartridges of .22-caliber with lead bullets, which can be fired in certain automatic pistols, single shot pistols, revolvers, and rifles. Also, as mentioned previously, revolver cartridges of .320-caliber, which are provided with lead bullets, can be fired in pistols of 7.65-mm caliber.

The type of jacket, if any, and the contour, weight, and composition of the bullet, and the number, size, and design of cannelures may give an indication of the maker of the cartridge. In American cartridges, for example, lead bullets are sometimes copper plated. On a fired bullet, the bore of the weapon will have left marks from the lands and sometimes also from the bottom of the grooves. A microscopic examination of these land and groove marks sometimes shows characteristic details that make possible an identification of the weapon. Furthermore, the number, width, and direction of twist of the lands and grooves make possible a determination of the make or makes of weapons from which the bullet may have been fired. The angle or rate of twist can be determined, but this is difficult and inaccurate when the projectile is mutilated (Figure 10.15).

The number and width of the land and groove impressions, together with the direction and angle of the twist, vary for different manufacturers and types of weapons. Under no conditions should a bullet be tested in the bore of a weapon by pushing it into the muzzle, if the bullet and weapon are to be subjected to further investigation with the goal of identification. The microscopic marks on the bullet might be completely destroyed in this way.

Figure 10.15 The direction and number of lands and grooves on this bullet reveal class characteristics as to the type of gun that could have fired this bullet. (Courtesy of Los Angeles County Sheriff's Department.)

If it is necessary to search for a weapon in connection with a bullet that has been found, the police officer can obtain a useful guide from a study of the land impressions on the bullet. The number of marks, their width, and the direction of the twist can be compared with a suspected weapon (Figure 10.16). If it is such a long time after the actual shooting that any deposit of dust or powder in the barrel would no longer be significant or if the barrel has evidently been cleaned or oiled, then a suitable piece of plasticine (and more recently, silicone casting material), molded to a point, can be introduced into the muzzle of the weapon to obtain an impression of the lands and grooves so that their number and width can be compared with the marks on the bullet. Otherwise, this information must be obtained from inspection of the muzzle of the weapon, possibly with the aid of a flashlight.

Generally, the number of "suspect" guns in any investigation is not large. Therefore, it is better to let the laboratory sort these weapons by firing test shots. A number of factors affect the width of land impressions, so that an exact comparison between a cast of the barrel and the bullet cannot be made. Anything within a reasonable range of tolerance should be submitted for laboratory tests.

If there is reason to suspect that a bullet that has been found has ricocheted and it is important to confirm this, it must be remembered that small grains of sand or other foreign matter may have stuck in flaws in the bullet, which should therefore be treated with care so that such particles do not fall off. Damage resulting from a ricochet can often be identified microscopically (Figure 10.17).

If a muzzle-loading weapon has been used, it is possible that the bullet may show marks from the ramrod, so these should be looked for. Homemade bullets can possibly

Figure 10.16 A firearms reference collection can be used to help narrow down the type of gun that was used based on class characteristics found on test-fired bullets. (Courtesy of the Los Angeles County Sheriff's Department.)

Figure 10.17 Ricocheted .357 Magnum bullet. (Courtesy of Lucian C. Haag, Forensic Science Services, Inc., Carefree, AZ.)

be identified with the mold used. In the case of muzzle-loaders, it is also necessary to search at the scene of the crime for any paper wads or the like that might have been used in loading the gun. These often remain uninjured and the paper can perhaps be identified as torn from a newspaper or from a piece of paper in the possession of a suspect. Although the rifled slugs and single balls of lead sometimes used in shotguns may give an opportunity for identification of the weapon, they can give information only as to the caliber. Homemade balls can possibly be identified with the molds in which they were made.

Small Shot

At close range the charge of shot, which has not yet dispersed, makes a large wound in a body, but at longer range the shot spreads out, more or less depending on the degree of choke of the gun, barrel length and size, and amount of shot. The amount of spread gives an opportunity to estimate the distance of the shot. If scaled photographs of the wound or shot pattern are available, comparison shots can be fired using the suspect weapon and ammunition of the same make and vintage. These are usually fired at heavy poster board or blotting paper. Without scaled photographs or comparison tests, only very broad estimates are possible because the patterns produced by various combinations of guns and ammunition vary over a considerable range (Figure 10.18).

Table 10.1 gives an example of the influence of the degree of choke on shot patterns. These figures will not apply to all shotguns and all ammunition. At a distance of 5–8 yards or more from the place of firing, in the approximate direction of fire, one can sometimes find wads. The size of shot is sometimes given by a number and sometimes shown by

Figure 10.18 The distance of the gunshot can be estimated by the degree of stippling and how spread out it is. This wound pattern is from buckshot to the chest. (Courtesy of Lucian C. Haag, Forensic Science Services, Inc., Carefree, AZ.)

Table 10.1 Diameter in Inches of the Spread at Various Ranges of a Shotgun Charge

Boring of gun	Range (yards)						
	10	15	20	25	30	35	40
True cylinder	19	26	32	38	44	51	57
Improved cylinder	15	20	26	32	38	44	51
Half choke	12	16	20	26	32	38	46
Full choke	9	12	16	21	26	32	40

letters. There is no internationally uniform method of designation of shot; the procedure varies in different countries.

By measuring the diameter of any shot found, it is thus possible to find the size of shot that would be marked on the cartridge. In this connection, it should be noted that there might be certain minor variations in size of shot in one and the same cartridge. It is therefore important to collect as many pellets as possible so that the determination is more reliable. Often the shot is deformed to such an extent that it is impossible to measure its diameter with the desired accuracy. In this case, it is convenient to weigh as large a number of shot as possible, calculate the mean weight, then weigh the same number of shot from cartridges with the different sizes of shot that may be in question and calculate their mean weight for comparison.

If a weapon is sent to an expert to determine whether a bullet or a cartridge case has been fired from it, a sufficient number of cartridges (five to six or more) of the same type as that used in the actual incident should be sent with it. This is particularly necessary if powder or shot patterns are to be fired. All ammunition in the weapon and any partial boxes of unfired ammunition associated with the victim or suspect should be submitted with the weapon. Sufficient differences may exist between ammunition found in the gun and other ammunition available to the expert so that comparison tests are difficult, doubtful, or impossible.

If a number of tests must be fired for comparison and transmission to various laboratories, inquiries should be made as to the nature and make of test ammunition desired in each investigation. For best results, these test specimens should be obtained by a laboratory and not by the field investigator.

Test Firing

Test firings of a weapon must be done so that the bullet can be recovered undamaged. For all jacketed bullets and most types of lead bullets, a cotton wad box or water trap is used to stop the bullet. With a cotton wad box, as a consequence of its rotation, the bullet twists itself up in the waste, which finally forms a ball around the bullet, and the velocity progressively decreases until the bullet is finally held in the cotton waste. Occasionally, long staple surgical cotton is placed in front of the cotton waste. This forms a ball around the bullet, further protecting the surface. Because of the mild damage to the bullet's surface due to the abrasive action of the cotton, water is frequently used as a collecting medium. For the collection of projectiles fired from handguns, 5–6 feet of water is ample. Generally, it is undesirable for the police officer to carry out test shots with the weapon personally because the microscopic imperfections in the bore of the weapon may be destroyed in the process. It is particularly important that the expert have an opportunity to examine the weapon before any tests are fired (Figure 10.19).

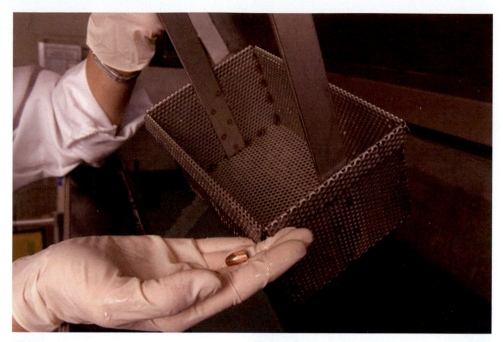

Figure 10.19 Recovering a test shot from a water tank. (Courtesy of the Los Angeles County Sheriff's Department.)

Powder Pattern Examination

When a weapon is fired at close range (up to several feet), burned and sometimes unburned particles of gunpowder are discharged onto the target. This effect is referred to as powder pattern deposit. The appearance of the powder pattern is sometimes helpful in establishing the distance from the fired weapon to the target. If the weapon was fired perpendicular to the target, the resulting powder pattern distribution will be located in an approximately circular area around the bullet entry hole.

The diameter of the circle and the distribution of particles can be used to establish the distance. Type of firearm, barrel length, and type of ammunition are all factors that affect the size and density of the powder pattern. If the muzzle of the weapon is in contact with the skin or within approximately 1/2 inch, the powder pattern is generally absent. This is due to the lack of space available for expansion of the powder, so that at close range it will penetrate the body through the entrance wound.

To make a distance determination, it is important to use the same firearm and ammunition used in the crime. A series of test firings are made into paper or cardboard at different distances and the test patterns are compared with the evidence. In most instances, it is also useful to make the tests on material the same as or similar to the evidence (Figure 10.20).

In certain instances, the powder pattern is not easily visible. Bloodstained or dark-colored clothing causes these difficulties in visualization. Infrared photography is helpful in bloodstained clothing cases. Chemical tests for nitrates present in the gunpowder, such as the Walker test or Griess test or, for lead and barium in the primer, the sodium rhodizonate test, are useful in developing the powder pattern (Figure 10.21).

Figure 10.20 The two test firings on the left (distance of 3″) show a tighter distribution of particles than the two test firings on the right (distance of 6″). (Courtesy of Lucian C. Haag, Forensic Science Services, Inc., Carefree, AZ.)

Figure 10.21 The sodium rhodizonate test can be used to test for lead in this bullet wipe. (Courtesy of Peter Diaczuk, John Jay College of Criminal Justice.)

National Integrated Ballistic Information Network*

In the past, comparing firearms evidence from one investigation to that of another was almost impossible unless there was some connection between the cases. Typically, the investigator determined or thought it possible that the same gun was used in two cases and asked the firearms examiner to compare the two recovered bullets or cartridge casings.

National Integrated Ballistic Information Network (NIBIN) is a networked computer database maintained by the ATF of fired cartridge casing and bullet images used by crime laboratories (Figure 10.22). The system was developed to link firearms evidence and to solve open cases by allowing firearms examiners to compare evidence with fired bullets, cartridge casings, shotgun shells, and firearms recovered in other jurisdictions. By means of a microscope attached to the system, images of bullets and cartridge casings are electronically scanned and stored for later retrieval and comparison with other case images. The system has the ability to compare the new images rapidly with images in regional and national databases. The firearms examiner visually compares the images to determine if there is a hit.

The value of these systems is their ability to associate firearms evidence between unrelated crimes. Test firing all confiscated firearms that come into the custody of the police becomes even more important because of the possibility of developing more information about cases that have appeared to be unrelated. Moreover, it is also important to recover all projectiles and cartridge casings at ALL crime scenes and submit them for imaging.

Figure 10.22 A National Integrated Ballistic Information Network workstation. (Courtesy of the Los Angeles County Sheriff's Department.)

* www.nibin.gov

Firearms evidence occurs in many crimes, such as assault, murder, and the like, and is particularly important because of the large amount of useful information it can provide. Because this type of evidence is encountered so frequently, investigators must be familiar with the proper methods of handling it and its value to the case.*

Chapter Questions

1. (True/False) The field of firearms identification is referred to as forensic ballistics.
    a) True
    b) False
2. Which of the following are the two groups of firearms?
    a) Long arms and handguns
    b) Rifles and shotguns
    c) Revolvers and semiautomatic
    d) Single shot and multiple shot
3. _____ is/are found in gun barrels and impart(s) a twisting motion on the bullet as it leaves the barrel.
    a) Ridges
    b) Minutia
    c) Rifling
    d) Imperfections
4. Describe how shotguns differ from other firearms.

5. Beyond determining that two rounds were fired from the same gun, what other information can be developed from firearms-related evidence?

6. Typically, how long will GSR remain on the shooter's hands?
    a) 1 hour
    b) 3 hours
    c) 6 hours
    d) 24 hours
7. (True/False) When a firearm is found at a scene, it must be rendered safe immediately and then documented.
    a) True
    b) False

---

* Those interested in more training and education in firearms examination can attend the 16-week National Firearms Examiner Academy at the ATF's National Laboratory Center in Ammendale, MD. See www.atf.gov for more information.

8. Which of the following can be used to determine the approximate position of the shooter?
   a) Cartridge cases
   b) Bullets
   c) Cartridges
   d) All of the above

9. In a contact shot to a victim, there is often blood found within the barrel of the handgun. This is called:
   a) Backspatter
   b) Forward spatter
   c) Low velocity spatter
   d) Spatter pressure

10. Which of the following marks found on cartridge cases can be used to identify the make of the firearm?
    a) Striations
    b) Lands
    c) Grooves
    d) Extractor

Arson and Explosives

11

Introduction

Arson investigation can be complex. The consequences can be considerable as the following case study shows:

Cameron Todd Willingham Case

On December 23, 1991, a fire destroyed the Corsicana, TX, home of Cameron Todd Willingham that he shared with his wife and three daughters, killing the three girls. Willingham, who was asleep when the fire started, survived. His wife was at the Salvation Army buying Christmas presents for the girls. At Willingham's 1992 trial, prosecutors claimed he intentionally set the fire to his home in order to kill his own children. Willingham said he was asleep in the home when the fire started and always maintained his innocence. He was convicted based on the testimony of forensic experts who said they had determined that the fire was intentionally set and a jailhouse informant who said Willingham had confessed to him. On October 29, 1992, he was sentenced to death. Thirteen years later, in the days leading up to Willingham's execution, his attorneys sent the governor and the Board of Pardon and Parole a report from Gerald Hurst, a nationally recognized arson expert, saying that Willingham's conviction was based on erroneous forensic analysis. Documents obtained by the Innocence Project show that state officials received that report but apparently did not act on it. Willingham was executed by lethal injection in Huntsville, TX on February 17, 2004.

Months after Willingham was executed, the Chicago Tribune published an investigative report that raised questions about the forensic analysis. The Innocence Project assembled five of the nation's leading independent arson experts to review the evidence in the case, and this prestigious group issued a 48-page report finding that none of the scientific analysis used to convict Willingham was valid. In 2006, the Innocence Project formally submitted the case to the Texas Forensic Science Commission, asking the empowered state entity to launch a full investigation. Along with the Willingham case, the Innocence Project submitted information about another arson case in Texas where identical evidence was used to send another man to death row. In that case, Ernest Willis was exonerated and freed from prison because the forensic evidence was not valid. In 2008, the Texas Forensic Science Commission (TFSC) agreed to investigate the case. In 2009, an arson expert hired by the commission issued a report finding that experts who testified at Willingham's trial should have known it was wrong at the time. Days before the expert was set to testify, however, Gov. Rick Perry replaced key members of the panel, delaying the investigation for months. An investigative report in the September 7, 2009, issue of *The New Yorker* magazine deconstructs every facet of the state's case against Willingham. The 16,000-word article by David Grann[*] shows that

---

[*] http://www.newyorker.com/reporting/2009/09/07/090907fa_fact_grann?currentPage=all

all of the evidence used against Willingham was invalid, including the forensic analysis, the informant's testimony, other witness testimony, and additional circumstantial evidence. On October 14, Texas Judge Charlie Baird held a hearing in the Willingham case to determine whether to hold a court of inquiry. And on October 15, the TFSC discussed the case in depth at its regular meeting. On April 15, 2011, the TFSC issued its final report in the Willingham/ Willis cases with an addendum issued on October 28, 2011. (This report is courtesy of the Innocence Project. For more details, visit their website at http://www.innocenceproject.org/ Content/Cameron_Todd_Willingham_Wrongfully_Convicted_and_Executed_in_Texas. php#summary.)

Fires and explosions account for a large number of property crimes but also may be the cause of serious bodily injury and death investigations. In addition to the requisite expertise needed in many other areas of crime scene investigations, fire scene and bomb scene investigators[*] require added skills to properly investigate these types of crimes. This chapter covers some of the basic information, but those faced with these types of crime scenes would do well to call in practitioners with particular training in these cases. Personnel working in larger municipalities, state agencies, and the federal government possess such expertise. Prudence suggests that these individuals should be brought into the investigation at an early stage, if needed.

Arson is defined as the willful and malicious burning of another's property or the burning of one's own property for some illegal purpose such as defrauding an insurer. As a crime, arson ranks only behind traffic-related incidents in the highest losses of life and property. In dollars, property losses due to arson can be placed in the billions of dollars annually (Figure 11.1).

Arson investigation[†‡] requires a considerable amount of care, attention to detail, and skill on the part of the investigator. Arson scenes present a host of problems that are uncommon to most other crime scene investigations. In most criminal investigations, once the crime has been committed and the police notified, the scene may be secured in relatively the same condition in which it was found. This is anything but the case in fire investigation. By the time the arson investigator arrives on the scene, numerous individuals including firefighters, supervisory personnel, onlookers, and possibly the owner of the property will have visited the crime scene. The preservation of the crime scene is frequently the last thing to be considered by firefighters when "knocking down" a blaze.

The issue of criminal intent is another major difference in arson investigations compared with other investigations. With most other crimes, the investigator frequently knows on arrival or shortly thereafter that a crime has been committed. With arson cases, determining whether a fire was set accidentally or intentionally may require significantly more investigation.

---

[*] Professional organizations focusing on fire investigation and bomb scene investigation are the IAAI, the International Association of Arson Investigators, http://firearson.com/ and the IABTI, the International Association of Bomb Technicians and Investigators, https://www.iabti.org/.

[†] The U.S. Department of Justice, National Institute of Justice, publishes *Fire and Arson Scene Evidence: A Guide for Public Safety Personnel*, available on the web at https://www.ncjrs.gov/pdf-files1/nij/181584 .pdf. The National Fire Protection Association is another important association. Its website is located at http://www.nfpa.org/. The National Association of Fire Investigators has a website at http://www.nafi.org/.

[‡] The Technical Working Group for Fire and Explosives, TWGFLX, http://ncfs.org/twgfex/ is a useful information resource in this area.

(a)

(b)

Figure 11.1 (a) Arsons represent serious crimes against both property and lives. (Courtesy of Contra Costa County, CA, Fire District.) (b) The scene of an arson fire at Universal Studios in Los Angeles showing the clock tower from the movie *Back to the Future*. (Courtesy of the Los Angeles County Sheriff's Department.)

Arson and explosion crime scenes are unique in the amount of destruction and devastation present. An item that normally is identifiable as important evidence in an investigation can be totally or partially destroyed by the fire or by firefighters. In spite of the difficulties inherent in arson investigation, a careful and thorough search of the fire scene can produce much useful information.

A number of motives are frequently associated with arson. Probably the most common motives are concealment of other crimes and defrauding an insurance company. A fire investigator frequently finds that the fire was set to cover up another crime such as murder, burglary, embezzlement, or fraud. The attempt in these cases is to destroy records and evidence of the crime that could make identifying the suspect or the victim of a murder impossible. In insurance fraud cases, the suspect may have suffered a business reversal or be heavily in debt. The fire is set to appear accidental with the intent of filing a false insurance claim. Other motives such as malicious mischief caused by juveniles, revenge, extortion, sabotage, terrorist acts, and pyromania all represent potential reasons for setting fires.

The arson investigator should focus the investigation to answer several questions (Figure 11.2):

1. *Where did the fire originate?* Information can be obtained by questioning firefighters about the location of hot spots, in which direction the fire was moving, how fast, etc. The most information will be gained by going through the scene and noting what areas suffered the most fire damage and exposure to heat. The origin of the fire is evidenced by the depth of char on burned items, degree of destruction, spalling, metal or glass bent or melted by exposure to heat for a longer time than other areas, and burning or heat fading of paint. Be alert to multiple sources or the entire structure as the origin.
2. *How was the fire started?* The investigator should look for faulty electrical wiring, the presence of igniters, matches, ignitable material, kindling, and other means of starting the fire. Ignitable fluids will run into cracks and under objects on the floor and cause burning in locations that would not normally burn. They will also char deeper in areas where they were located, sometimes burning through the floor.
3. *Was the cause of the fire an accident or was it intentionally set?* This is the key issue in determining whether the fire was arson. Evidence such as breaking into and entering the building, presence of ignitable fluids, and multiple points of origin may indicate a maliciously set fire.

Physical Evidence

The presence of ignitable fluids is the most commonly sought physical evidence in arson investigation. Even in cases in which fire damage was particularly extensive or the scene was completely wetted down, there is still a good probability of detecting ignitable fluids when evidence is collected properly. The search for ignitable fluids should be concentrated at the point where the fire started. If charred rags or carpeting are noted, these should be collected and sent to the laboratory. Wood flooring, furniture, and carpet padding into which gasoline or kerosene may have been absorbed should also be collected as well as empty containers or broken glass jars found at the scene (Figure 11.3).

(a)

(b)

Figure 11.2 The following are examples of the aftermath of fires. Determining whether a fire was an accident or purposely set is not always a straightforward task. (a) A burned-out electrical timer device located at a fire scene can give the approximate time at which the power went out as a result of the fire; (b) a melted aluminum awning indicates the approximate temperature of the fire. Aluminum melts at 660.2°C. (Courtesy of the Los Angeles County Sheriff's Department.)

Figure 11.3 Arson dogs trained to detect the odor of ignitable fluids have been used with success in some cases. (Courtesy of U.S. Department of Justice, ATF.)

Ignitable fluids are highly volatile and evaporate easily. For this reason, appropriate packaging must be used to preserve these items for laboratory analysis. Packaging evidence in paper or plastic bags or containers will not preserve it. Such packages allow volatile liquids to dissipate completely. The best manner of packaging these items is in clean metal paint cans (Figure 11.4). Items should be placed into the cans, which should then be tightly sealed with metal lids. An alternative method of preserving evidence is to use glass jars with metal

Figure 11.4 Ordinary clean metal paint cans make for easy collection and preservation of arson evidence.

screw-cap lids. Metal and glass containers retain small amounts of liquids and vapors that can be analyzed by the crime laboratory. The quantity of material needed for chemical analysis of an ignitable substance is extremely small. Laboratory instruments are capable of readily identifying ignitable liquids in quantities of less than a fraction of a drop. In fact, if an odor of an ignitable liquid can be detected, there is a good chance that a forensic lab can identify the source (Figure 11.5).

Laboratory analysis can differentiate among the many types of accelerants used in arson cases. The common types are gasoline, kerosene, charcoal lighter fluid, paint thinner, and turpentine. In some cases, the dyes contained in gasoline can be used as a means of comparison with known samples. Highly sophisticated scientific instrumentation at some laboratories may be able to differentiate brands of gasoline; however, most crime labs do not conduct such examinations, and if only a residue of sample is available, it is not possible to do such testing (Figure 11.6).

A careful search of all entrances and windows should be made to determine whether the building had been forcefully entered. If tool marks are observed, the area should be cut out or an impression made and submitted to the laboratory. Also, samples of building materials such as glass, paint, plaster, stucco, wallboard, cement, etc., that may have been deposited on the suspect's clothing should be collected for purposes of control or known samples. All evidence must be properly marked for identification and packaged properly. In some instances, an apparent forced entry might have been used to cover up arson, so such things as the side from which a window was broken, screen cut, etc., should

Figure 11.5 In this arson the defendant lit a fire after raping and torturing a young college student in her apartment. The victim escaped by using the fire to melt away the cables that bound her wrists and ankles. (Courtesy Norm Marin and Jeff Buszka, Special Investigations Unit, NYC OCME.)

Figure 11.6 Sophisticated laboratory instruments are used to detect the presence of ignitable chemicals such as gasoline and kerosene. This is an example of a gas chromatograph–mass spectrophotometer or GC/MS. It is able to detect very small amounts of chemicals responsible for arsons. (Courtesy of the Los Angeles County Sheriff's Department.)

be checked (Figure 11.7a–d). The investigation should include the search for igniting materials. Burned matches and matchbooks should also be collected. Burned matches, in some cases, can be physically fitted into a matchbook found on a suspect, and matchbooks can be chemically processed for fingerprints. Occasionally, pieces of a timing device used to delay the ignition of a fire may be discovered.

Other types of igniters such as candles, black powder, smokeless powder, sodium and water, electrical devices, and similar items should be noted and collected. It is important that the manner in which the fire started be established. This can help determine the M.O. (modus operandi, a term often used in police work to describe the method or mode used by a perpetrator) of the arsonist (Figure 11.8a–c).

If the scene of the arson is a business establishment, the investigator may notice that file cabinets have been pulled open and papers strewn about. Burned papers should be carefully collected and placed into cardboard boxes, handling them as little as possible. Burned paper may be examined at the laboratory and useful information can be determined. For example, it may be very beneficial to know what files were burned or are missing.

If the fire was started outdoors, the area of the origin of the fire should be examined. Soil from that area should be collected and tested for the presence of ignitable materials. To accomplish this, a clean, gallon paint can should be filled with soil, sealed, and submitted to the laboratory along with a control sample.

Any items left at the scene by the arsonist should be preserved. Traces such as pieces of clothing, hair, blood, tools, broken tools, etc., may prove to be important as a means of establishing identity of the suspect (Figure 11.9a–c).

When a suspect is apprehended, a careful search of his property should be made to determine whether anything can be tied to the crime or the crime scene. Any accelerants such as gasoline or kerosene should be packaged and submitted to the laboratory for comparison with solvents detected at the scene of the arson. Similarly, objects such as tools, matches, matchbooks, incendiary devices, and the like should be collected.

(a)

(b)

Figure 11.7 These photographs depict (a) chipping or splintering, commonly known as spalling, on a brick wall caused by a hot spot at the scene and (b) deformed pipe and (c) melted safety glass as a result of exposure to heat for a period of time. (d) Typical appearance of burned lumber, referred to as "alligatoring," indicating the surface texture of the burned wood. (Courtesy of the Los Angeles County Sheriff's Department.)

(c)

(d)

Figure 11.7 (*Continued*)

(a)

(b)

Figure 11.8 These are examples of improvised incendiary devices. (a) This incendiary device, a light bulb with a small hole drilled into the base, filled with medium petroleum distillate, and sealed with a putty-like material, was found in a light socket connected to a timer in a house under construction. The device probably would not have worked because too much liquid was in the bulb, which covered the filament. (b) A portion of a "Molotov cocktail" with a shot shell. (Courtesy of Illinois State Police, Bureau of Forensic Sciences.) (c) An improvised incendiary device consisting of a cigarette and matches can produce sufficient heat to cause the contents of the bag to burn. (Courtesy of the Los Angeles County Sheriff's Department.)

(c)

Figure 11.8 (*Continued*)

(a)

Figure 11.9 (a) A melted electrical timer device and (b) a close-up showing a portion of a label believed to have been used in an arson case. (c) The example of the intact timer was used in the reconstruction of the device. (Courtesy of the Los Angeles County Sheriff's Department.)

(b)

(c)

Figure 11.9 (*Continued*)

The suspect's clothing and shoes should be collected, packaged, and sent to the laboratory for examination for the presence of these materials.

The suspect's vehicle should be inspected for the presence of material removed from or transported to the scene of the arson. Any search of the suspect's vehicle or residence may require a search warrant. The local prosecutor should be contacted if there is any question.

In cases in which a dead body is discovered in the investigation, a determination of the cause of death is necessary to ascertain whether the victim died as a result of the fire or the fire was set in order to conceal a homicide. The pathologist will be able to determine at the time of the autopsy whether the person died of smoke inhalation or was dead prior to the fire.

Explosives

Explosives are useful tools by which people have accomplished some remarkable engineering feats. However, like many other things, explosives are used for criminal ends as well. Murder, burglary, extortion, terrorist activities, and similar activities involving explosives require the attention of the investigator. Bomb scene investigation is frequently treated as a specialty within some police agencies and is often associated with arson investigation. Although certain aspects of crime scene investigation of bombings differ from a common crime scene, the basics remain the same (Figure 11.10).

In broad terms, an explosive is a material capable of rapid conversion from either a solid or a liquid to a gas with resultant heat, pressure, and loud noise. Many chemicals, alone or in combination, possess the necessary properties for an explosive. Except for chemical compounds classed as explosives, the rest usually come to the investigator's attention only

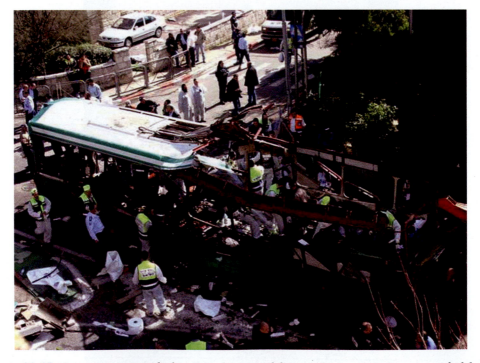

Figure 11.10 A terrorist suicide bomber detonated his explosive vest on a crowded bus in Jerusalem. Crime Scene Investigators work to identify the victims and determine the origin of the explosion. (Photo by Nili Bassan.)

Figure 11.11 Examples of boosters, blasting caps, and dynamite. (Courtesy of the Los Angeles County Sheriff's Department.)

as the result of some accident. In such cases, consultation with a forensic chemist or criminalist will provide a satisfactory explanation for the explosion.

Explosives can be classed into two broad groups: low explosives and high explosives. High explosives consist of primary and secondary explosives; low explosives burn rather than explode. Damage by low explosives is caused by the force exerted by the rapid expansion of gases formed by burning. These types of explosives must be confined to explode. High explosives, in general, are detonated by shock and have much higher detonation velocities; they need not be confined to explode (Figure 11.11).

Low Explosives

Black powder is the most common type of low explosive. It is a mixture of potassium or sodium nitrate, sulfur, and charcoal. There has been wide variation in the formulation of this mixture over the years. Black powder is sensitive to heat, impact, friction, and sparks. When placed into a confined area, such as a pipe bomb, black powder can be a destructive explosive. Detonation can easily be accomplished by means of a safety fuse. If an unexploded pipe bomb is encountered, it is very important to exercise extreme care in opening the device because it can be set off by friction (Figure 11.12). One of the most common uses of black powder is in the manufacture of safety fuses.

Safety fuses are used to initiate explosives nonelectrically; they are generally composed of black powder with a protective covering of cotton yarn or jute followed by an asphalt layer for water resistance. The asphalt covering is then covered with an insulating material such as a polyethylene plastic covering or a wax-impregnated yarn jacket. The color of the fuse is generally white, black, or orange.

Figure 11.12 Debris from a pipe bomb packed with a low-order explosive. (Courtesy of the Los Angeles County Sheriff's Department.)

Safety fuses should normally burn at a definite rate of speed but may burn faster or slower depending on several factors such as age, handling, altitude, and humidity. Usually, they burn at about 30 to 40 seconds per foot; however, the actual rate should be determined by testing a given length.

Smokeless powder is another low explosive encountered in bomb investigations. It is mainly used for small arms ammunition but is frequently used in pipe bombs. Two types of smokeless powder are marketed: single and double base. Single-base smokeless powder consists of nitrocellulose, while double-base is composed of nitrocellulose and nitroglycerine. Although smokeless powder is not as sensitive to friction as black powder, it should be handled with the same amount of care.

High Explosives

Primary explosives detonate when subjected to heat or shock. They are typically used as initiators of high explosives, to detonate main charges, and in blasting caps and firearm primers. For this type of explosive, the major interest in bomb investigation is in blasting caps. Blasting caps are of two types: electric and nonelectric. They are small explosive devices, about 1/4 inch in diameter and from 1 to 3 inches in length. The case may be made of aluminum, copper, or bronze (Figure 11.13a–c). The electric blasting caps have colored wires extending from them.

Secondary explosives detonate by shock from a suitable primary explosive. Their detonation velocities range from 3300 feet per second in the case of ammonium nitrate to 29,900 feet per second in the case of HMX. Typically, high explosives are used to shatter or destroy objects.

Commercial
safety fuse

Military
time fuse (M700)

Black powder
core

0.2 in.

Fiber wrap

Waterproofing

Outer cover

Fiber wrap

0.2 in.

Black powder
core

Dark green plastic
cover with yellow bands

(a)

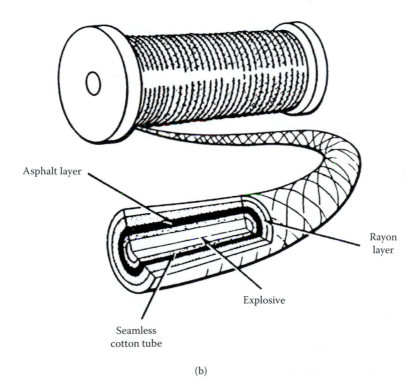

Asphalt layer

Rayon
layer

Explosive

Seamless
cotton tube

(b)

Figure 11.13 (a) Safety fuses. (b) Detonating cord. (c) Examples of use of detonating cord to prime explosive charges. (Courtesy of the U.S. Department of Justice.)

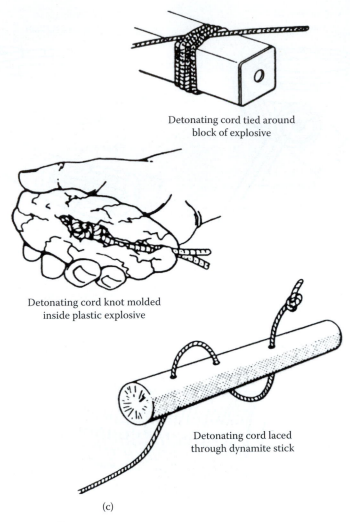

Detonating cord tied around
block of explosive

Detonating cord knot molded
inside plastic explosive

Detonating cord laced
through dynamite stick

(c)

Figure 11.13 (*Continued*)

Detonating cord is a cord-like explosive, similar in appearance to a safety fuse. It contains a central core of RDX or PETN covered with cotton or another textile, followed by a waterproof material or plastic covering.* The cord detonates at velocities from 18,000 to 23,000 feet per second. It is very insensitive to shock and heat and presents no special problems in handling. Detonating cord is used to set off charges of high explosives much in the same way as a safety fuse is used to set off multiple pyrotechnic devices. The detonating cord may be inserted, tied, or knotted inside the high explosive to initiate detonation. Detonating cord is used to set off simultaneous charges and is detonated by means of a blasting cap.

Boosters or primer explosives are used to detonate very insensitive high explosives. The booster consists of a secondary explosive such as RDX, PETN, tetryl, or pentolite and is detonated by means of a blasting cap. Boosters are usually cylindrical in shape with a small opening to permit insertion of a blasting cap.

---

* HMX, RDX and PETN are common names for high order secondary explosives.

A large number of high explosives are used commercially and by the military. Next, some of the more common ones encountered in law enforcement work are detailed; however, the list is not intended to cover all of the many types.

Nitroglycerine was first developed in 1847, but it was not until 1867 that Alfred Nobel developed a method to desensitize this explosive sufficiently so that it could be used commercially. Nobel's invention, dynamite, was a mixture of nitroglycerine and diatomaceous earth. Today, dynamite contains EGDN (ethyleneglycoldinitrate) in addition to other materials used to desensitize the nitroglycerine. Inert materials such as wood pulp or sawdust, cornmeal, sodium nitrate, and many other materials are found in dynamite, which is usually packaged in cylindrical sticks and wrapped in waxed paper. The sticks come in a variety of sizes; the most common is 1 1/8 to 1 1/2 inches in diameter and 8 inches in length. Other sizes may be as large as 12 inches in diameter and 4–36 inches long. There are four basic types of dynamite in use today: straight dynamite, ammonia dynamite, gelatin dynamite, and ammonia–gelatin dynamite.

1. *Straight dynamite*: Manufactured in strengths of 15% to 60% by weight of nitroglycerine. The nitroglycerine is generally absorbed onto a material such as wood pulp or ground meal (such as cornmeal, cornstarch, or the like). Dynamite has a sweet, pungent odor and frequently may cause headaches. Straight dynamite has an oily, slightly moist appearance and resembles a mixture of oil, sawdust, and clay. In older sticks of dynamite, the outer wrapper may often look oil-stained from the nitroglycerine seeping out of the mixture. Police should treat such dynamite with extreme caution because it is in a highly unstable form.
2. *Ammonia dynamite*: Some of the nitroglycerine is replaced with ammonium nitrate. Ammonia dynamite is less sensitive to shock than straight dynamite and has less of a shattering effect but is more suitable for "pushing." The color of ammonia dynamite is light brown, compared with a slight reddish tint in the case of straight dynamite.
3. *Gelatin dynamite*: A water-resistant form of dynamite manufactured by combining nitroglycerine with nitrocellulose. The resulting "gel" forms a thick, viscous liquid useful under wet conditions.
4. *Ammonia–gelatin dynamite*: A combination of the last two formulations. The addition of the ammonium nitrate is a cost-saving factor, and the gelatin allows the explosive to be used in wet conditions.

Ammonium nitrate is a readily available material used as an explosive and, in a less pure form, as a fertilizer. In its pure form, it is a white crystalline material but may be a light tan color in a less pure form. As an explosive, it is relatively insensitive and requires a booster charge to be detonated. Because of its easy availability as a fertilizer, although less pure than explosive grade ammonium nitrate, it is readily available for use in homemade bombs. A modification of ammonium nitrate sometimes used is a mixture of ammonium nitrate and fuel oil, also known as ANFO.

Water gels or slurries are classified as either blasting agents or explosives, depending upon what they contain and whether or not they are cap-sensitive. Water gels typically have an ammonium nitrate base, a sensitizer, a thickener, and 5%–40% water. The sensitizer may be an explosive such as trinitrotoluene (TNT), nitrostarch, or smokeless powder, or it may be a nonexplosive such as sugar, fuel oil, carbon, or a powdered metal. These explosives are rapidly gaining in popularity as substitutes for dynamite. Most slurries require a primer or booster for detonation; however, some manufacturers make cap-sensitive gels.

Blasting Agents

Blasting agents, also known as nitrocarbonitrate (NCN), are insensitive chemicals and chemical mixtures that are detonated by means of a high-explosive primer or booster. In order to be classified as a blasting agent, the material must be unable to be detonated by a No. 8 blasting cap and contain no high explosives such as TNT or nitroglycerine. Blasting agents consist largely of ammonium nitrate. ANFO is considered a blasting agent and consists of 94% ammonium nitrate and 6% fuel oil. The advantage of blasting agents is that safety regulations governing shipping and storage are considerably less severe than those applicable to high explosives.

Binary explosives are two inert, nonexplosive chemicals that, when mixed, form a cap-sensitive high explosive. The materials are either both liquids or a powder and a liquid; in their unmixed states, they are very insensitive to shock or friction. One component is usually ammonium nitrate, while the other is a nonexplosive sensitizer.

Military Explosives

Sheet explosives are flexible, rubber-like sheets approximately 1/4-inch thick that can be cut with a knife. These explosives are used in commercial and military circumstances. The high explosive used is either RDX or PETN. Sheet explosives are known as Flex-X, Datasheet, or M118 Demolition Block (the latter military sheet explosives). The most common type of military explosive is TNT. Military explosives differ somewhat from commercial explosives in that they must be used in combat conditions. Typically, they must be relatively insensitive to heat, shock, friction, and bullet impact, have high destruction power (brisance), be lightweight and convenient to use, be usable under water, etc.

TNT is generally encountered in military explosives in 1/4-, 1/2-, and 1-pound blocks. The blocks have metal ends with a threaded well at one end for a blasting cap. The container is cardboard, and the TNT is a light yellow to brown color although some newer formulations of TNT may be gray due to the addition of graphite.

RDX is used in so-called plastic explosives. Plastic explosives contain plasticizers in addition to RDX and are easy to mold in warm temperatures.

Composition C-3, containing 77% RDX, is a yellow putty-like material that has a distinctive heavy, sweet odor. When molded, it will stain the hands and clothing. The M3 block is enclosed in glazed paper that is perforated around the middle for ease in breaking open and weighs 2 1/4 pounds. The block does not have a cap well.

Composition C-4 is replacing C-3 in military use. C-4 contains 91% RDX, is white to light brown in color, has no odor, and does not stain the hands. The M5A1 block demolition charge contains C-4 in a clear white plastic container with a threaded cap recess at each end. It weighs 2 1/2 pounds. Composition C-4 also comes in the M112 block demolition charge, an improvement of the M5A1 that replaces it as a standard issue. The M112 contains 1 1/4 pounds of composition C-4 with a pressure-sensitive adhesive tape on one surface, protected by a peelable paper cover. The C-4 in some blocks is colored dull gray and packed in a clear Mylar-film bag. In blocks of more recent manufacture, the C-4 is white and packed in an olive drab Mylar bag.

Military dynamite is not really dynamite, but a mixture of 75% RDX, 15% TNT, 5% SAE 10 motor oil, and 5% guar flour. It is packaged in waxed manila paper and marked M1, M2, or M3. Military dynamite is buff-colored granular material that crumbles easily and is slightly oily to the touch. It does not have the characteristic odor usually associated with dynamite because it contains no nitroglycerine.

The explosives discussed to this point are some of the more common ones encountered and represent explosives available through commercial and military sources. The explosives industry, however, is a rapidly changing one, and the reader should understand this when studying the subject. It is suggested that the investigator consult explosive manufacturers, law enforcement agencies that routinely deal with explosive cases, and forensic science laboratories for the latest information on the subject.

Homemade Explosives

If commercial or military explosives are not available, it is not particularly difficult for an individual to improvise from a large number of chemicals that, when mixed together, can produce highly destructive explosive devices. The investigator should recognize at least some of the more common materials that often find their way into homemade explosive devices.

Materials such as starch, flour, sugar, cellulose, etc., can be treated to become effective explosives. Powder from small arms ammunition and from firecrackers, match heads, and ammonium nitrate from fertilizers can be used in explosive devices. To detonate an improvised explosive device, several methods are available (Figure 11.14a and b):

- *Blasting caps.* Caps, especially electrical blasting caps, lend themselves to homemade bombs. Such devices may be set off by a timing mechanism, by movement, by wiring into an automobile ignition system, etc.
- *Percussion primers.* Primers from shotgun, rifle, or pistol ammunition are sometimes used to detonate explosives that are heat sensitive.
- *Flashbulbs.* Flashbulbs may be used to ignite heat-sensitive explosives such as black powder. If the bulb is placed in contact with the explosive, the resulting heat from the flashbulb will ignite materials such as black powder, smokeless powder, incendiary mixtures, etc. As mentioned earlier, because of its relative ease to manufacture, black powder is frequently used in homemade bombs.
- *Match heads.* Match heads are frequently found confined inside pipe bombs. They are sensitive to heat, friction, and shock, and when confined in this type of device, they can produce an effective explosion.
- *Smokeless powder.* Powder from ammunition or for reloading purposes is frequently used as the main charge in pipe bombs.
- *Ammonium nitrate fertilizer.* Ammonium nitrate mixed with fuel oil and an appropriate booster makes an extremely effective homemade explosives device.
- *Potassium or sodium chlorate.* These compounds and sugar are used as incendiary and explosive materials.

In the past few years, two improved explosives, the peroxide-based explosive TATP* (triacetone triperoxide) and urea nitrate,[†] have been used by terrorist organizations.

---

* Used in the London metro bombing in 2005 and by the so-called "shoe bomber," Richard Reid, in 2001.
[†] Urea nitrate was used in the 1993 World Trade Center bombing and has been used in terrorist incidents in the Middle East.

(a)

(b)

Figure 11.14 (a) Debris from a homemade explosives device with a timing mechanism. (b) An example of an unexploded homemade device with a timer. (Courtesy of the Los Angeles County Sheriff's Department.)

Unfortunately, the Internet and terrorist manifestos have become a source of recipes and easy instructions on how to manufacture homemade explosives. Generally, components are readily available and can be obtained at low cost. Investigators should familiarize themselves with these websites and be on the lookout for new types of explosive devices "advertised" on the Web. It would be wise for law enforcement to contact places of business in their jurisdictions that sell materials that could be used in homemade explosives and ask them to report any suspicious purchases.

The list of possible chemicals for improvised explosives is endless. Officers who come upon locations with large numbers of chemicals such as nitrates, chlorates, perchlorates, nitric acid, aluminum powder, magnesium, sodium, sulfur, charcoal, sugar, and sulfuric acid, to name just a few, should be aware that the location may be one where homemade explosives are made.

Bomb Scene Investigation*

Physical evidence in bombing cases is useful in answering many questions. Some of the questions that the investigator will be interested in answering are

What materials were used to make the explosive device?
What was the level of skill or expertise of the suspect?
What was the target of the bomb?
Was the explosion accidental or was there criminal intent?
Where was the bomb made?
Where was the bomb placed?
Where did the suspect obtain the material to construct the device?
Who was the victim or intended victim?
Who made the bomb and who placed it?
How was the bomb detonated?

The nature of the target, whether or not the bomb exploded, the extent of damage, the location of the incident, and weather conditions are some of the factors that influence the action to be taken by the investigator. If a bomb is found that has not exploded, it is necessary to call in a bomb technician to render the device safe. The first priority of the technician is to disarm the bomb safely. If possible, the investigator should photograph the bomb prior to moving it and have the bomb technician note any changes made in the device when dismantling it. If the bomb must be exploded to be disarmed, it should be done in such a way as to avoid total destruction of the device.

The scene should be thoroughly searched for evidence that may have been left by the suspect. Collection of evidence should include a search for a forced entry and accompanying tool marks, fingerprints, footprints, and any other traces that may help link a suspect to the crime scene.

In cases in which the explosive device detonated, the work of the investigator is complicated considerably. The duties of the crime scene investigator are basically the same as outlined in Chapter 3; however, the investigator will have an additional consideration: safety will be a major area of concern. The scene of a bombing is generally very unsafe.

---

* The U.S. Department of Justice, National Institute of Justice, publishes the *Guide to Explosion and Bombing Scene Investigation*, available on the web at http://www.ncjrs.gov/pdffiles1/nij/181869.pdf.

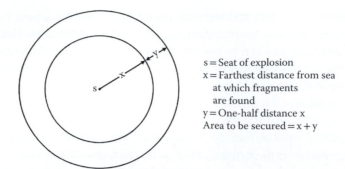

s = Seat of explosion
x = Farthest distance from sea
    at which fragments
    are found
y = One-half distance x
Area to be secured = x + y

Figure 11.15 If the explosion takes place in an open space, the area in which the fragments are found and a surrounding buffer zone should be secured. (Courtesy of the U.S. Department of Justice.)

The structure of the building where the bomb exploded may be seriously weakened and can collapse. Other unexploded secondary devices may still be in the area. Hazards such as broken gas mains and downed electrical lines are potential safety problems. Securing the crime scene is another problem (Figure 11.15). Unlike most crime scenes, bomb scenes frequently attract a large number of people such as police, fire department personnel, medical and ambulance personnel, HAZMAT teams, utility companies' personnel, property owners, the press, and sightseers. One of the first orders of business must be to coordinate the activities of the large number of people likely to be present and to remove individuals who are not needed.

Because of the nature of the crime, bomb scenes frequently contain a certain amount of confusion. It is necessary to restore order and control to the situation quickly to enable the investigator to accomplish the task of processing the scene. The first officers to arrive at the scene of a bombing will be concerned with emergency and safety-related activities such as rescue, evacuation, and assisting fire department personnel if required. Once the emergency phase is complete, efforts should be made to secure the crime scene and begin developing information on the circumstances of the case. Witnesses and victims should be interviewed and as much information as possible about what happened should be gathered.

Because of the number of persons present at the scene and the likelihood of several different investigative agencies being involved in the investigation, a team with representatives from each agency should be established to coordinate and control the investigation. Such a unit can act as a clearinghouse of information so that all information gathered from the investigative process can be integrated and studied.

Investigation of the actual scene of the bombing is a time-consuming task requiring a considerable amount of physical effort and attention to minute pieces of physical evidence. It is also dirty work requiring the investigator to sift through large quantities of debris to locate items of evidence. It is useful to have proper equipment to go through the scene. Coveralls/Tyvek suits, gloves, hard hats, goggles, work shoes, and other such items are useful for the investigator. Hand tools such as shovels, rakes, brooms, a heavy-duty magnet, and cutting tools are useful. Sifting screens of various sizes are needed for going through the debris. Wheelbarrows, trash cans to collect debris, portable lighting, ladders, and the like may be required as well.

An incident commander should be immediately designated to be responsible for processing and directing the bomb scene investigation. The leader also serves as a link between those coordinating the overall investigation and the crime scene investigation. The extent of the crime scene must be identified. The seat of the explosion can be a focal point, and the location furthest from the seat where fragments from the explosion are located will define the outer perimeter of the scene. A buffer area equal to approximately half the distance from the seat to the furthest point should be added. This represents the total area that should be secured and searched.

The bomb scene should be recorded. This may be accomplished in the standard way by means of photography and sketches. If the capabilities exist, the scene may be videotaped. If needed, aerial photographs should be taken. Photographing, measuring, and sketching the crime scene may be done while the scene is searched.

Collecting physical evidence at the scene consists of the search for and recovery of items that may lead to information about the nature and type of explosive and the identity of the suspect (Figure 11.16a and b). A search for the fusing mechanism of the bomb should be made. Items such as timing mechanisms, batteries, pieces of wire, safety fuses, blasting cap debris, and the like may yield information about the way in which the bomb was set to detonate. The scene should be searched for evidence to determine the type of explosive used. The seat of the explosion should be carefully examined for unexploded material and packaging material that may indicate the type of explosive used. If a portion of the container that held the device is found, laboratory tests may indicate the type of explosive. Similarly, the extent of damage to the container, for example, a pipe bomb, can indicate whether the explosive was a low-order or high explosive. In general, large fragments of a pipe bomb indicate a low explosive such as black powder, while small fragments indicate a high explosive.

The package that contained the explosive device may contain evidence to lead the investigator to a suspect. Fingerprints, DNA, names, addresses, and postmarks may be important information in the investigation. The investigator should not forget to search for other evidence besides the bomb debris. Items such as tire tracks, tool marks, and the like are valuable and must not be overlooked.

If a suspect is apprehended shortly after the explosion, the clothing should be collected and submitted to the laboratory for examination for trace evidence and explosive residue. The suspect's hands should be swabbed with cotton applicators moistened with acetone to test them for certain explosives. If the suspect's vehicle is located, it too should be carefully searched for tools, trace evidence, explosive residue, and materials that may have been used in the crime.

All evidence should be photographed where it was found, measured, and located on a crime scene sketch prior to being moved. The investigator should remember also to search high areas such as trees, roofs, ledges of buildings, and other places that may contain pieces of the exploded device.

Because of the large number of persons involved with the bomb scene search and the amount of evidence collected, it is helpful to keep an evidence log to detail each item of evidence collected, including the date, time, and name of the person collecting the material. The use of a log facilitates establishing a chain of evidence and makes inventory of all the evidence somewhat easier.

A word of caution: Terrorists sometimes employ secondary explosive devices. Extreme care should be exercised when searching the crime scene, and consideration should be given to the possibility of other explosive devices!

The crime laboratory plays an important role in bomb scene investigation. Often the nature of the explosive used and information about the type of mechanism used to detonate

(a)

(b)

Figure 11.16 A parcel with an explosive wrapped as a gift was shipped through the U.S. mail. (a) The ribbon used to wrap the package was matched to (b) ribbon found in the suspect's home. (Courtesy of the U.S. Postal Service.)

it cannot be determined in the field. The laboratory will carefully and systematically examine all the items of evidence and attempt to answer some of the questions required by the investigator to assist in the solution of the case.

Bomb and arson scene investigations require much time and patience, and an extreme attention to detail by the crime scene investigating officer. The officer's willingness to carefully and painstakingly go through large amounts of debris and rubble in an attempt to locate pertinent physical evidence may result in a successful conclusion to the case.

Chapter Questions

1. Arson is defined as the _____ and malicious burning of another's property or the burning of one's own property for some illegal purpose.
   a) Illegal
   b) Willful
   c) Reckless
   d) Negligent
2. (True/False) A careful and thorough search at the fire scene does not produce
   much evidence due to the destructive nature of fires.
   a) True
   b) False
3. List the three questions that an arson investigator should focus on when conducting an investigation?

4. You are the investigator assigned to collect evidence from a suspected arson.
   Describe how you would collect evidence containing ignitable fluids.

5. Of the following items, which can be used as an igniter to start a fire?
   a) Matchbook
   b) Black powder
   c) Sodium and water
   d) All of the above
6. This type of explosive is designed to be detonated by shock and has a high detonation velocity.
   a) Low
   b) Medium
   c) High
   d) Black powder
7. List several examples of high explosives.

8. Which of the following items can be used to ignite heat-sensitive explosives such
   as black powder?
   a) RDX
   b) TNT
   c) C-3
   d) Flashbulbs

9. List some of the questions you would be interested in answering while conducting a post-blast investigation.

10. During a post-blast investigation, which of the following is a main concern for the crime scene investigator?
    a) Collecting probative evidence
    b) Bringing the guilty party to justice
    c) Safety of crime scene personnel
    d) Dealing with the media

Illicit Drugs and Toxicology

12

Drugs in bulk form or in blood or urine specimens are often involved as physical evidence in a wide variety of criminal cases. These substances are encountered in cases such as traffic accidents and fatalities, driving under the influence (DUI) of alcohol and/or drugs, public intoxication, possession or sale of controlled substances, and illicit manufacture of controlled substances. The purpose of this chapter is to describe the various types of drugs commonly encountered by police and to examine some of the crime scene investigation issues with regard to this class of evidence. To simplify the topic, a distinction is made between bulk drugs, that is, drugs in their usual solid or liquid form, and toxicological specimens, that is, blood or urine samples that are to be tested to determine whether a drug is present in a person's body.

Psychoactive Drugs*

Drugs that find their way into police investigations† are typically called psychoactive drugs. These drugs affect the user's psychological processes and change his or her mood, thinking, perception, and behavior. Psychoactive drugs may be illicit (e.g., lysergic acid diethylamide [LSD]) or lawful (e.g., barbiturates). They may be controlled (i.e., requiring a prescription) or uncontrolled (not requiring a prescription, e.g., alcohol or certain over-the-counter preparations). Drugs can be divided into several types based upon their effect on the user. The eight major categories discussed in this chapter are central nervous system depressants, central nervous system stimulants, hallucinogens, cannabis, designer drugs, nonprescription drugs, inhalants, and steroids.

Central Nervous System Depressants

Narcotics are an important class of central nervous system depressants. They are used medically for their analgesic (or painkilling) properties and have a high potential for abuse. There are two categories of narcotics: opiate alkaloids and synthetics or semisynthetics. Opiate alkaloids are derived from the opium poppy, *Papaver somniferum* (Figure 12.1). The most frequently encountered opiates are raw opium, morphine, and codeine. Common synthetics and semisynthetic narcotics are Demerol, methadone, heroin, Dilaudid, and Percodan.

The second category of central nervous system depressants is sedative–hypnotics. These are generally prescribed for treatment of insomnia and tension and have a high potential for abuse and addiction. Drugs in this category include barbituric acid derivatives such as

---

* The National Institute on Drug Abuse is an excellent source on the latest information on drugs. Their website is located at http://www.nida.nih.gov/.
† The Drug Enforcement Administration, http://www.justice.gov/dea/, is a source of information on drug related criminal activity.

secobarbital, amobarbital, phenobarbital, and the like and nonbarbiturates such as glutethimide (Doriden), methaqualone (Quaalude), and chloral hydrate. Another drug classified as a sedative–hypnotic is the illicit drug phencyclidine, PCP. Persons taking PCP report feelings of weightlessness, unreality, and hallucination.

The third category of central nervous system depressants comprises tranquilizers and energizers. Tranquilizers are grouped into major and minor tranquilizer groups. Major tranquilizers such as chlorpromazine, prochlorperazine, trifluoperazine, etc., are prescribed for treatment of neurosis, psychosis, and other psychological disorders and

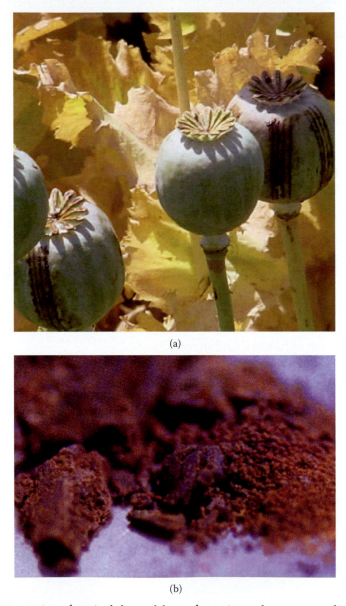
(a)

(b)

Figure 12.1 (a) Heroin is a chemical derived from the resinous latex material extruded from the poppy. (Courtesy of the U.S. Department of Justice (DOJ), Drug Enforcement Administration (DEA).) Heroin, which is synthesized from morphine, has a number of forms: (b) powder (U.S. DOJ DEA) and (c) a tarry material or tar heroin. (Courtesy of the Los Angeles County Sheriff's Department.)

(c)

Figure 12.1 (*Continued*)

are considered addictive. Minor tranquilizers can produce psychological dependence with prolonged use. Drugs in this category include meprobamate (trade name Equanil or Miltown), chlordiazepoxide (Librium), diazepam (Valium), oxazepam (Serax), and chlorazepate dipotassium (Tranxene). These drugs are generally prescribed for treatment of tension and anxiety. Energizers or antidepressants are used for the treatment of moderate to severe depression. Drugs in this group include imipramine (Tofranil) and amitriptyline (Elavil).

Perhaps the most widely used and best-known central nervous system depressant today is ethyl alcohol, or ethanol. Its usual short-term effects are sedation, euphoria, impaired judgment, slowed reaction time, decreased coordination, and decreased emotional control.

Central Nervous System Stimulants

One of the few types of psychoactive drugs that have not become a law enforcement problem is the xanthine alkaloids, which contain such drugs as theophylline, theobromine, and caffeine. Cocaine is another class of central nervous system stimulant (Figure 12.2). It is derived from the leaves of the *Erythroxylon coca* tree native to South America. The drug in its pure state is a white crystalline substance and is not generally used medicinally except as a local anesthetic in certain eye, nose, and throat surgical procedures (Figure 12.3). The third class of stimulants is the amphetamines. Drugs in this group are amphetamine (Benzedrine), dextroamphetamine (Dexedrine), methamphetamine (Desoxyn), mixtures of Dexedrine and amobarbital (Dexamyl), and nonamphetamine stimulants such as Ritalin and Preludin. These drugs are often prescribed

(a)

(b)

(c)

Figure 12.2 Cocaine is seen in two forms: (a) cocaine hydrochloride and (b) crack cocaine. (Courtesy of U.S. DOJ DEA.) "Crack" or "rock" cocaine is the free-base form of cocaine hydrochloride. (c) Parts of the manufacturing process of rock or crack cocaine. The round pieces, called "cookies," are in the shape of the glass beakers used in the final processing. The cookies are broken into "rocks" for sale. (Courtesy of the Los Angeles County Sheriff's Department.)

(a)

Figure 12.3 (a) Kilogram packages of cocaine are often wrapped in fiberglass. This may be an attempt to minimize the odor that drug dogs can detect or to keep the packaging from breaking apart when dropped from aircraft. (b) A large cocaine seizure. (Courtesy of the Los Angeles County Sheriff's Department.)

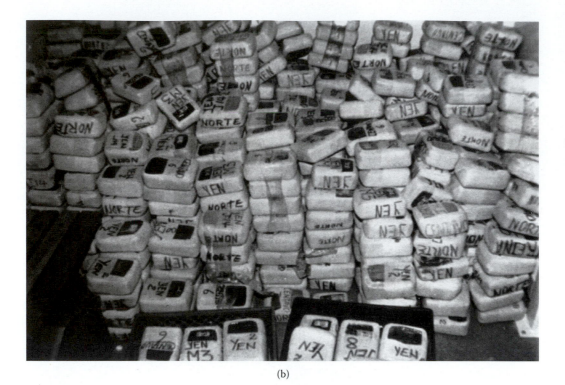

(b)

Figure 12.3 (*Continued*)

for fatigue, narcolepsy, and attention deficit disorder or attention deficit hyperactivity disorder in children, and in combination with barbiturates for (Figure 12.3) treating obesity.

Hallucinogens

Hallucinogens are a group of drugs that currently have no accepted medical use. The drugs produce perceptual alterations, intense and varying emotional changes, ego distortions, and thought disruption (Figure 12.4). Drugs in this group include mescaline, which is derived from the *Lophophora* cactus, psilocybin, which occurs in several species of mushrooms (e.g., *Psilocybe mexicana*), LSD, dimethyltryptamine (DMT), diethyltryptamine (DET), PCP (a central nervous system depressant), and methyldimethoxymethylphenethylamine (STP).

Cannabis

Marijuana is defined legally as derivatives from the plant *Cannabis sativa* (Figure 12.5) and is most often consumed by smoking the dried, crushed tops and leaves or resinous material known as hashish, which contains tetrahydracannibinol (THC). Pharmacologically, marijuana is not classed in any of the preceding drug categories. Its usual short-term effects include relaxation, increased appetite, some alteration of time perception, and impairment of judgment and coordination.

(a)

(b)

(c)

Figure 12.4 Some of the hallucinogenic drugs in this class include (a) LSD, (b) psilocybin, and (c) peyote. (Courtesy of U.S. DOJ DEA.)

Figure 12.5 Marijuana leaf. (Courtesy of U.S. DOJ DEA.)

Designer Drugs

Every few years, new types of drugs become popular. These are the so-called "designer drugs." Designer drugs are a class of synthetic drugs synthesized by chemists working in clandestine drug laboratories. The motive is profit. Clandestine drugs present a serious problem for law enforcement and a danger to those who use them. Illicit chemists do what pharmaceutical researchers do to develop new active drugs. They synthesize drugs with similar structural features to known psychoactive substances. However, with designer drugs, neither quality control nor testing of the substances is undertaken to determine if there are any harmful side effects. Designer drugs include fentanyl analogs, meperidine analogs, and MDMA (3,4-methylenedioxymethamphetamine). MDMA is known on the street by several names, for example, MDM, Adam, Ecstasy, X, and XTC (Figure 12.6).

Synthetic cannabis is a psychoactive herbal and chemical product, which, when consumed, mimics the effects of cannabis. It is best known by the brand names K2 and Spice, both of which have largely become generic trademarks used to refer to any synthetic cannabis product. These drugs are chemically similar to cannabinoids but are not uniformly controlled.

These drugs are often marketed as "herbal incense"; however, some brands market their products as "herbal smoking blends" and are usually smoked by users. Although synthetic cannabis does not produce positive results in drug tests for cannabis, it is possible to detect its metabolites in human urine. The Drug Enforcement Administration has announced it would make five synthetic cannabinoids Schedule I drugs: JWH-018, JWH-073, CP-47497, JWH-200, and cannabicyclohexanol.

Figure 12.6 MDMA. (Courtesy of U.S. DOJ, DEA.)

Steroids

Steroid abuse has long been a factor in professional sports and amateur athletic competition and bodybuilding. Anabolic steroids build muscle mass and thereby enhance performance (Figure 12.7). They are reported to cause liver and adrenal gland damage, infertility and impotency in men, and masculine characteristics in women. Steroids are scheduled, controlled substances. They have become a law enforcement problem as illicit sales of anabolic steroids have been noted. Many of the steroids sold to athletes through illicit channels are not manufactured for use in human beings but rather are veterinary drugs. Frequently, the drugs are manufactured outside the United States; packaging and labeling claiming the drugs to be specific steroids are usually incorrect. The drugs are available in a wide variety of forms and may be injectable solutions, capsules, transdermal patches, or pills.

Nonprescription Drugs

Nonprescription drugs rarely present law enforcement with major difficulties. They are included here as a reminder for officers investigating traffic accidents, fatalities, and cases of driving while under the influence. Over-the-counter drugs, particularly sleep aids, sedatives, and antihistamines, contain materials that make the user drowsy. The investigator who finds a subject who has taken these drugs alone or in combination with alcohol and is exhibiting unusual behavior can reasonably assume that the individual is likely to be under the influence.

Figure 12.7 Labels on pharmaceuticals sometimes describe one drug when in fact the container holds another. In this case, some of the steroids were tested and found to be different steroids from those listed as the contents. (Courtesy of Los Angeles County Sheriff's Department.)

Inhalants

The last group of psychoactive substances is chemicals that are inhaled. Such materials include glue, gasoline, paint, solvents, and the like. Juveniles frequently use these chemicals. The most common method involves placing the material into a plastic bag or onto a piece of cloth such as a sock and sniffing the material to obtain the intended result, intoxication. Another class of inhalants contains amyl nitrite, a vasodilator, used to relieve symptoms associated with angina pectoris.

Crime Scene Search

Searching a crime scene for contraband drugs is somewhat different from other types of cases. In a contraband drug investigation, the officer is looking for evidence that has been hidden on the person, in a dwelling, or in a vehicle. The various rules of evidence including search and seizure and requirements for establishing a chain of evidence hold in these cases as in others, and the investigator must be aware of current laws regulating search activities.

Searching a Suspect

Concerning personal search, the officer must be aware of unusual hiding places in which contraband may be hidden. Clothing and personal property should be carefully examined. Places such as cigarette packages, small cases, film cans, hollowed-out compartments in canes or umbrellas, lining of clothing, luggage, shoes, wallets, cellphones, and similar items may conceal evidence. Suspects have been known to swallow contraband or hide it in a body cavity such as the mouth, nose, rectum, or vagina. Thoroughness and experience will aid the officer in the search.

Searching a Dwelling

When searching a dwelling, the investigation should be done in a thorough, systematic manner. In addition to contraband, investigators should be alert for intelligence information such as telephone and address books, names and telephone numbers on loose pieces of paper, and so on. Sums of money and possibly stolen property should be documented and collected. Additionally, any damage to personal property or to the residence should be carefully noted and, if possible, photographed; the owner should be notified. One officer should be assigned to record the location and the name of the finder of each item of evidence.

To assist in the recording, a crime scene sketch should be made so that each piece of evidence can be charted. The officer should also make certain that each item of evidence is correctly marked for identification and properly preserved. If possible, two investigators should be assigned to a room. The search should begin at one wall, and everything hanging on that wall or resting against it should be carefully examined. Light switches and outlet boxes should be examined to determine whether paint on the screws or around the plate is chipped. The plates should be removed and searched. Molding around doorframes should be examined for signs of stress to determine whether they conceal a hollow area. The tops of doors and doorframes should be examined for indentations. A plug on top of a door or hinges may conceal a hiding place. Walls should be checked to determine whether they were replastered. Wall pictures and the backs of television sets and radios should be examined. Curtain rods, the tops and bottoms of window blinds, and shades should be searched.

After the walls have been searched, furniture should be inspected. Items should be turned upside down and their bottoms examined. Throw pillows and cushions should be unzipped and the contents searched. Rugs should be rolled up. When searching the bathroom, the officer should look for waterproof containers inside flush tanks, and containers under sinks, behind false tiles, or in laundry hampers. Prescription medicine bottles should be examined to determine whether they contain the drug listed on the container and for whom the prescription was intended. When evidence is located, it should be brought to the officer maintaining the evidence log and the search should be continued. It is a good practice to search each room a second time. Occasionally, evidence overlooked the first time will be noticed in the subsequent search.

Searching a Vehicle

Automobiles are often used to hide contraband drugs. Searches involving motor vehicles should be conducted in a systematic and thorough manner. The vehicle can be divided into three areas for the search: the front end, interior, and rear. The front end of the vehicle offers many areas in which to hide contraband. A careful search should include the grill, bumper, radiator, inside surfaces of the fenders, air filter, and body frame. Using a hydraulic lift helps in the examination of the undercarriage of the vehicle. The interior of the vehicle is frequently used in concealing drugs. The seats should be removed from the car and carefully searched. The area behind the dashboard, the door side panels, headliner, and floor are possible areas where drugs may be hidden. Finally, the trunk and rear of the vehicle should be examined. Areas such as the spare tire well, spare tire, rear fender, and bumper area and undercarriage of the vehicle are all potential hiding places.

Clandestine Drug Laboratories

An important source of illicit drugs today is the clandestine laboratory. Illicit drugs such as LSD, PCP, methamphetamine, and other illicit pharmaceuticals are manufactured in illicit laboratories. Police become involved in crime scene investigations involving illicit laboratories through intelligence gathering, complaints from neighbors, fires and explosions, unusually high utility bills, and often from detection of chemical odors while on routine patrol. Whatever the means of detection, the investigator must have an understanding of how such crime scenes are processed. The trained forensic chemist or criminalist should be an integral part of any such investigation. His or her training and experience in dealing with chemicals is extremely important from the standpoint of identifying drugs as finished and intermediate products and also from a safety consideration. In larger police agencies, specialized hazardous chemical response teams have been developed who handle chemical spills and disposal of toxic substances. These teams are especially helpful and should most certainly be included in any clandestine laboratory investigation (Figure 12.8).

The clandestine laboratory scene is a potentially dangerous and hazardous location. Chemicals present are often flammable, explosive, toxic, and corrosive. Proper precautions must be taken to ensure the safety of personnel at the scene. Scenes should be approached with extreme caution. It is not uncommon for chemicals to be unlabeled, and there are even reports of laboratories that were booby-trapped. As soon as the location has been secured, all windows and doors should be opened to ensure adequate ventilation and minimize the risk of fire. Light switches should not be turned on until the area is adequately ventilated; sparks can easily ignite highly flammable chemicals. Under no circumstances should anyone be allowed to smoke. The fire department should be notified and asked to stand by. Certain chemicals are especially dangerous if mixed with others. Chemicals such as lithium aluminum hydride are extremely explosive when combined with water, as is sodium and water. Cyanide salts will liberate hydrogen cyanide gas when in contact with acid. Most chemical solvents, such as ether, benzene, and the like, are highly flammable. Acids and alkaline materials are dangerous and can cause severe burns; others such as piperidine may cause headaches. Prolonged exposure to many volatile organic chemicals may be injurious.

Extreme caution must be exercised in clandestine laboratory investigations! Before any evidence is collected, the laboratory should be photographed. Photographs of individual pieces of equipment, chemicals, laboratory glassware, finished product, and intermediates should be taken. The location should be searched for fingerprints and for laboratory notes, recipes, records, sales receipts from chemical supply companies, and other related items. Samples of chemicals from the final product, chemical precursors or intermediate products, and basic raw materials should be collected for crime laboratory analysis. A complete inventory of all chemicals, equipment, packaging material, and the like should be made.

(a)

(b)

Figure 12.8 Clandestine drug labs used to manufacture methamphetamine, LSD, and other synthetic substances are particularly hazardous to personnel who must go into the field to collect evidence. (a) Sometimes, criminalists must wear personal protective clothing and a breathing apparatus to shut down a chemical reaction and collect samples. Labs can be (b) sophisticated or (c) simple but nonetheless pose a risk. As chemicals are often unlabeled, personnel would do well to consider that they may be dealing with a homemade explosives lab or a drug lab and take suitable precautions. (Courtesy of the Los Angeles County Sheriff's Department.)

(c)

Figure 12.8 *(Continued)*

Such evidence will be very important if no final product is found. Laboratory notes, recipes, chemical precursors, and glassware will be important evidence at trial to prove conspiracy to manufacture controlled substances (Figure 12.9).

A further caution to be considered is that clandestine chemical labs may be homemade explosives laboratories rather than drug manufacturing labs. It is not unreasonable that chemicals are unlabeled; therefore, care should be taken when examination and collecting products.

Collection and Preservation of Evidence

As with all physical evidence, the ultimate aim of collecting drug evidence is its legal admissibility as evidence in court. To assure this end, the investigating officer must be concerned with maintaining the integrity of the evidence from the time of seizure until its presentation to the court. In addition to the usual requirements to maintain a chain of possession of the evidence, some other procedures are important. All drugs should be accurately weighed. The gross weight of the package, including the drug and packaging material, should be determined and recorded. Individual pills, tablets, packets, balloons, etc., should be counted and the number written on the outer package and the report. (In cases involving a large number of units, 100 capsules can be weighed and the total number of units can be estimated by determining the total weight and dividing that weight by the unit weight.) Liquids should be measured in metric units such as liters or milliliters (Figure 12.10).

The packing material seized with the contraband should be kept with the evidence and properly marked for identification. Items should be placed in an appropriate evidence envelope and sealed and marked. Liquids should be placed in a clean, stoppered container or conical tube to minimize evaporation and then sealed and labeled. If the original container can be tightly sealed, it may be used to preserve the liquid.

(a)

(b)

(c)

Figure 12.9 (a) Some of the chemicals used in (b) a methamphetamine lab. (Courtesy of U.S. DOJ DEA.) (c) Meth labs may have elaborate security devices to keep a lookout for law enforcement. (Courtesy of the New York State Police.)

(a)

(b)

Figure 12.10 Other drugs that are also encountered are the so-called "date rape" or drug-facilitated rape controlled substances: (a) gamma-hydroxybutyrate (GHB) and (b) Rohypnol. (Courtesy of U.S. DOJ DEA.)

Field Investigation Drug Officer*

Because of the large amount of drug cases submitted to crime laboratories and the large amount of resources spent on unnecessary drug testing (many cases never make it to trial), the ability to train law enforcement to perform drug testing in possession cases is being considered by several jurisdictions throughout the United States. The Field Investigation Drug Officer (FIDO) program funded by the National Institute of Justice in partnership with the National Forensic Science Training Center offers training to law enforcement to provide immediate investigative information without the need for extensive lab analysis, which often takes months. The program allows trained officers the capability of providing a preliminary identification of the most commonly encountered drugs of abuse (cocaine, heroin, marijuana, and methamphetamine). Field test results can help expedite the adjudication process by being a factor in obtaining an immediate plea agreement and helping reduce the number of backlogged cases and improve the efficient use of resources. Drug evidence can still be submitted to the crime laboratory for complete analysis for those cases that proceed to trial.

* http://www.nfstc.org/programs/field-investigation-drug-officer-fido/

Toxicology[*]

Toxicology is the study of poisons. As used in this section, the term describes the detection of drugs and alcohol in blood and urine samples collected from suspects in certain types of criminal investigations. The presence or absence of drugs or alcohol in a person's body and the issue of whether the subject was under the influence is important in traffic investigations, DUI cases, the legal defense of diminished capacity, and public intoxication cases. The most common substance tested for in most police laboratories is alcohol in blood and urine specimens submitted in so-called "drunk driving" cases.

Cases of DUI of alcohol represent a large percentage of all traffic fatalities and traffic accidents. Implied consent laws require a driver suspected of being under the influence of alcohol to submit to testing—blood or breath—to determine the blood alcohol level. The majority of states in the United States set a blood alcohol level at 0.08% (i.e., 0.08 g of ethyl alcohol per 100 mL of blood) as the level at which a person is presumed to be under the influence of alcohol to an extent that the driver is unable to operate a motor vehicle in a safe and prudent manner. The 0.08% level represents about 3 ounces of 100-proof alcoholic beverage in the body of a 150-pound individual. Blood and breath testing are routine procedures available in all jurisdictions to measure the blood alcohol level (Figure 12.11). Blood that is taken should be collected in a medically approved manner. The syringe used should not have been cleaned with alcohol, and nonalcoholic cleansing agents (e.g., aqueous zephiran) should be used to clean the area of skin from which the blood is to be taken. Approximately 10–20 mL of blood should be collected in a container with an appropriate preservative and anticoagulant. If urine is collected, the subject should first be requested to void the bladder, wait approximately 20 minutes, and then urinate into a container into which an appropriate preservative has been placed. Approximately 25 mL of sample should be collected. The officer should be present in each case to observe the collection procedure and to mark the evidence properly. The specimen should then be submitted to the laboratory for analysis.

Officers will find that some subjects, although exhibiting alcohol-like intoxication symptoms, have no or only a small amount of alcohol in their blood. The reason for this may be that the suspect has taken some other central nervous system depressants with similar physiological effects. When questioning the suspect, the officer should try to determine whether the suspect has taken any other medication; when searching the individual during the booking process, it should be noted whether any solid dose drugs are found. This information is helpful to the forensic toxicologist when running tests on blood and urine specimens. A large number of depressant-type drugs are routinely encountered in traffic-related incidents today. Barbituric acid derivatives, Valium, Quaalude, PCP, cocaine, and marijuana are among the more common substances encountered.

The type and quantity of sample required for analysis may vary from one jurisdiction to another, and the local crime laboratory should be contacted to determine the best sample for a specific drug analysis. In homicide cases in which a suspect is arrested shortly after the killing, it is sometimes a useful practice to obtain blood and urine specimens from the suspect to be screened for the presence of drugs and alcohol. This strategy is

[*] The Society of Forensic Toxicology, http://www.soft-tox.org/, and the International Association of Forensic Toxicologists, http://www.tiaft.org/, are two organizations that can provide further information about forensic toxicology.

Figure 12.11 Chemical instruments such as this headspace gas chromatograph are routinely used in crime labs to measure alcohol in blood from DUI cases. (Courtesy of the Los Angeles County Sheriff's Department.)

particularly useful in those cases in which the suspect may raise the issue of diminished capacity at the time of trial.

Illicit drugs in bulk or in toxicological specimens are encountered in a large number of cases in criminal investigations. Investigators must be familiar with the hazards of various chemicals and the pharmacological effects of psychoactive substances as well as the usual considerations involved in the collection and preservation of physical evidence.

U.S. DEA Drug Schedule Classification*

Schedule I

The drug or other substance has a high potential for abuse.

The drug or other substance has no currently accepted medical use in treatment in the United States.

There is a lack of accepted safety for use of the drug or other substance under medical supervision.

Some Schedule I substances are heroin, LSD, marijuana, and methaqualone.

---

* Source: U.S. Department of Justice, Drug Enforcement Administration.

Schedule II

The drug or other substance has a high potential for abuse.

The drug or other substance has a currently accepted medical use in treatment in the United States or a currently accepted medical use with severe restrictions.

Abuse of the drug or other substance may lead to severe psychological or physical dependence.

This type of drug requires prescription in triplicate.

Schedule II substances include morphine, PCP, cocaine, methadone, and methamphetamine.

Schedule III

The drug or other substance has a potential for abuse less than the drugs or other substances in Schedules I and II.

The drug or other substance has a currently accepted medical use in treatment in the United States.

Abuse of the drug or other substance may lead to moderate or low physical dependence or high psychological dependence.

Anabolic steroids, codeine and hydrocodone with aspirin or Tylenol, and some barbiturates are Schedule III substances.

Schedule IV

The drug or other substance has a low potential for abuse relative to the drugs or other substances in Schedule III.

The drug or other substance has a currently accepted medical use in treatment in the United States.

Abuse of the drug or other substance may lead to limited physical or psychological dependence relative to the drugs or other substances in Schedule III.

Included in Schedule IV are Darvon, Talwin, Equanil, Valium, and Xanax.

Schedule V

The drug or other substance has a low potential for abuse relative to the drugs or other substances in Schedule IV.

The drug or other substance has a currently accepted medical use in treatment in the United States.

Abuse of the drug or other substance may lead to limited physical or psychological dependence relative to the drugs or other substances in Schedule IV.

Over-the-counter cough medicines with codeine are classified in Schedule V.

Chapter Questions

1. Psychoactive drugs are defined as substances that affect the user's _____ process and change his or her mood, thinking, perception, and behavior.
   a) Physical
   b) Psychological
   c) Central nervous system
   d) Coping

2. Which of the following would be an example of a central nervous system depressant?
   a) Ethanol
   b) Caffeine
   c) Cocaine
   d) MDMA

3. List several examples of central nervous system stimulants.

4. Describe the symptoms that a hallucinogen can produce and list several examples of specific drugs within this class.

5. Which of the following are the three classes of designer drugs?
   a) Fentanyl analogs, meperidine analogs, MDMA
   b) MDMA, Adam, XTC
   c) Ecstasy, Adam, Fentanyl analogs
   d) Meperidine analogs, XTC, PCP

6. (True/False) Searching a crime scene for contraband drugs is no different than any other case.
   a) True
   b) False

7. You are searching a person who was just arrested for selling crack to an undercover officer. Which of the following would you focus on during your search?
   a) Cigarette packs
   b) Mouth
   c) Shoes
   d) All of the above

8. During the search of a residence for contraband drugs, the investigators should also be concerned with searching for what?
   a) Legal documents
   b) Intelligence information
   c) Name of the resident's attorney
   d) Documents showing ownership of the residence

9. The majority of states in the United States set a blood alcohol level at _____ as the level at which a person is presumed to be under the influence.
   a) 0.03%
   b) 0.10%
   c) 0.15%
   d) 0.25%
10. Define what is meant by Schedule III drugs and list several examples.

Investigating Sexual Assault   13

Rape

Few crimes rely so heavily upon physical evidence as does the crime of sexual assault. In hardly any other type of case is the testimony of the victim viewed with as much mistrust by juries, courts, and sometimes even prosecutors and police. It is for this very reason that physical evidence is so important to the investigation and prosecution of this crime. Rape investigation is different from many other major crimes. Unlike homicide, robbery, or assault, the first officer at the crime scene plays a much greater part in the collection and preservation of physical evidence. In a murder investigation, the first officer's responsibilities are to secure the crime scene until the investigators arrive. This is not the case in a rape investigation. The first officer is required to make certain that fragile physical evidence that may be lost during the medical examination or by the victim are collected and preserved.

Preliminary Interview

The first officer must be knowledgeable about the types of evidence generally found at the sexual assault crime scene. The officer must also be a skilled interviewer to elicit from the victim the painful details of the assault and from these details determine what evidence may be available.

The first officers at a rape scene may find that training in crisis counseling will help them assist the victim in dealing with their trauma. For example, attitudes that women provoke rape or deserve it because they place themselves in the situation have no place in modern police work. The victim should be treated nonjudgmentally and with sensitivity. Observations about the victim noted in the police report will be important at a later time. The psychological state of the victim may be significant. The officer should realize, however, that people in serious emotional crises might not immediately exhibit states of anguish and grief that might be expected. The victim might appear perfectly calm and in control of themselves when interviewed by the police. This behavior is not uncommon.

The officer should not assume that the victim is untruthful because she is not exhibiting extreme emotion. Statements in police reports, such as "the victim appeared unusually calm, considering her complaint of rape," do nothing but confuse the investigation and raise doubt at the trial. Questions about oral and anal intercourse should be asked. The officer should ascertain whether the victim is sexually experienced and hence able to testify whether penetration and/or ejaculation took place. Another question that should be asked is whether the victim had consensual sex recently. In asking these types of questions, the investigator should be aware that many rape victims do not volunteer particularly sensitive details of the assault.

After a rape, the victim may feel psychologically dirty. She may have an urge to wash, bathe, douche, urinate, throw away her clothing, and clean up the scene of the rape. During the interview, the officer should determine which, if any, of these actions occurred. If any did, an attempt to collect evidence should still be made. A tissue or washcloth used by the victim to clean herself might still have semen present. Underwear, clothing, and/or condoms worn at the time of the crime, even if discarded or cleaned, should be collected for examination. The crime scene should be processed as outlined elsewhere in this book, but several other aspects require attention.

- What was the modus operandi of the suspect?
- Did he practice any unusual acts, such as urination or defecation?
- Did he do or say anything unusual?
- Is there any physical evidence to substantiate these acts?
- Did he bite or lick the victim?
- Was the victim or suspect scratched or bruised?
- Does the victim recall drinking something that may have contained a "date rape" or drug facilitated rape substance?

All of these details, together with any physical evidence, will greatly assist the investigation of the case.

Medical Examination

Following the preliminary interview, the victim should be taken to a hospital emergency room for a thorough examination. (In many cases, the victim goes directly to the emergency room; law enforcement is notified of the alleged sexual assault by hospital personnel.) Because much of the evidence associated with rape is of a fragile nature, time is of the essence. A change of clothes should be obtained so that the clothing worn during the rape may be collected and vouchered as evidence. Many hospital emergency rooms have protocols established to deal with rape victims in which they are ranked in medical priority immediately after life-threatening cases. Hospitals are responsible for the victim's medical and psychological well-being, as well as the collection of physical evidence.

Once at the hospital, the officer should briefly go over the case with the attending physician or registered nurse.* Pertinent information gleaned from the interview should be communicated to the examiner because it may facilitate the examination for physical evidence. The health care provider first takes a medical history from the victim and again goes over the details of the assault. Doctors and nurses should be encouraged to take detailed notes and later couple the notes with medical findings during the examination phase. Details such as the date of the last menstruation, time of last consensual intercourse, presence of bruises not related to the assault, presence of bruises from the assault, and other related factors are pertinent information.

Following the medical history, the examiner should conduct a thorough physical examination. Some hospitals only examine the genital area and miss a great deal of useful evidence (Figure 13.1). If the victim is wearing clothes from the assault, they should be collected and packaged in a paper bag (Figure 13.2). The location of any cuts, bruises, lacerations, or contusions should be noted in the medical report. A helpful practice is the

---

* Many hospitals throughout the United States have Sexual Assault Nurse Examiners (SANE) who are properly trained in conducting this type of examination.

Figure 13.1 Toluidine blue dye highlights fresh injury. It adheres to the nuclei of the white blood cells that have been disrupted. (Photo provided by Diana Faugno MSN, RN, Sexual Assault Nurse Examiner.)

Figure 13.2 The underwear from the victim is examined for the presence of semen. (Courtesy of the New York City Office of Chief Medical Examiner.)

use of an anatomical diagram. The location of cuts, bruises, and the like can be charted on this diagram. Photographs of bruises or wounds should also be taken with an appropriate scale. Wounds on the body that are difficult to see can be enhanced with the help of UV photography. If the hospital does not have this capability, the police officer or CSI may provide a suitable camera. In some instances, the officer may wish to wait a day or so until the bruises become black and blue and better show the location and extent of the assault.

Many hospitals, police departments, and commercial hospital or law enforcement supply firms have sexual assault evidence kits. These kits greatly facilitate the collection and preservation of rape evidence. They also direct the examiner to look for certain evidence commonly found in rape cases (Figure 13.3).

The victim should next be carefully examined for trace evidence adhering to her body. The location of any trace evidence such as debris, grass, soil, vegetation, loose hair, fibers, and so on should be noted and collected. The presence of dried secretions such as semen, blood, and saliva (from bite marks, licking, "hickies," etc.) is especially useful because such

Figure 13.3 Example of the contents of a sexual assault evidence collection kit. (Courtesy of the NYC Office of Chief Medical Examiner.)

Figure 13.4 Crime-lite® by Foster + Freeman is an example of an alternate light source used for detection of bodily fluids and trace evidence. Also shown are the viewing glasses.

evidence may be typed using forensic DNA testing.* Some facilities use a UV lamp or alternate light source to examine for the presence of seminal fluid as semen fluoresces under ultraviolet light (Figure 13.4). Using two slightly moistened cotton swabs, dried secretions can be easily collected and preserved.

Following the examination of the extremities and torso, the genitalia are examined. Pubic hair combings are taken in an attempt to find foreign hairs and fibers or other debris. The hairs, any debris, and comb are all submitted for examination. As with all other evidence, these items should be appropriately documented in the medical report and labeled. A vaginal specimen is collected with cotton-tipped applicators and a portion is smeared onto microscope slides (Figure 13.5). The slides should be air-dried and *not* stained when prepared. The slides should be placed in a slide protector, *not* in alcohol. Some locales also collect specimens from the cervix and vulva as well.

There are also separate sexual assault kits for suspects, acquaintances, and estranged partners. Oftentimes, the collection of evidence from a suspect requires a court order. If a court order can be obtained expeditiously (these kits need to be collected within a shorter period of time than the kit for a victim), penile swabs can be collected to determine if the victim's DNA is present.

If anal or oral contact occurred, appropriate swabs should be collected.† Anal intercourse or sodomy is not limited to female victims. Male sexual assaults occur with some frequency in jail and prison environments as well as elsewhere. Of particular importance in these cases is the physician's examination of the rectum as well as swab evidence taken for the examination of semen. Medical examination indicates if anal penetration has occurred. Beyond the medical examination and search for semen, other evidence is

---

* Independent Forensics offers a rapid stain identification kits, RSID™, for the identification of semen, blood, and saliva (www.ifi-test.com/rsid.htm).
† The Phadebas® Amylase test (www.phadebas.com) detects α-amylase activity that is used as an indicator for the presence of saliva.

Figure 13.5 Microscope examination of a vaginal smear can show the presence of spermatozoa. Sperm cells circled in red seen dyed with "Christmas Tree" stain. (Courtesy of the New York City Office of Chief Medical Examiner.)

sometimes uncovered in such cases. Feces may be found on clothing or other articles. A lubricant such as petroleum jelly may be used and should be looked for. The container for these items can be examined for fingerprints and/or touch DNA. Additionally, any condoms and/or condom wrappers* found at the scene should also be collected. If oral sodomy is suspected, the oral cavity should be rinsed *after* the swab is taken prior to collection of a known buccal (cheek) swab from the victim.

Fingernails may also be examined, and if sufficient debris is present, nail scrapings can be collected for trace evidence examination. The fingernails can also be clipped and submitted for DNA analysis if the victim scratched the perpetrator (Figure 13.6). Toxicology samples should be collected if the victim appears to be under the influence of some substance. Physical evidence collected in rape cases is used for three major purposes:

1. *To establish that sexual contact occurred.* The presence of seminal fluid and spermatozoa in the vaginal cavity is suggestive of vaginal penetration. The presence or absence of this evidence can be explained in any number of ways. The absence of seminal fluid in a case in which it was expected could be caused by the following reasons:
   a. The time period between the rape and medical examination was too long.
   b. The suspect wore a condom.
   c. The suspect penetrated but did not ejaculate in the vagina.
   d. The doctor or nurse examiner did not take an adequate sample.
   e. Seminal fluid and spermatozoa may be present from a consensual intercourse and not from an alleged rape. In this instance, seminal fluid typing is indicated.
   f. Seminal fluid, without spermatozoa, could be present from a male who underwent a vasectomy procedure or is azospermic.

2. *To establish that nonconsensual intercourse occurred.* Physical evidence may substantiate that the victim did not consent to the intercourse. Evidence such as torn

---

* Condom wrappers are often opened with the teeth and can obtain DNA rich saliva.

Figure 13.6 Clipped fingernails from a rape victim can be sent for DNA typing to determine the identity of a scratched suspect.

or soiled clothing, bruises, pulled-out hair, cuts, and other indications assist in proving that a struggle occurred during the time of the intercourse.

3. *To establish identity of the perpetrator.* The suspect's identity may be established by a variety of means: eyewitness testimony, fingerprints, hair, fibers, or bloodstains left behind at the scene. Additionally, it may be possible to determine the assailant's DNA type through semen typing or typing of cellular material at the hair root (especially prevalent with freshly pulled hairs) (Figure 13.7). The suspect may have left an article of clothing at the crime scene or unknowingly picked up some trace material such as fibers from a rug, clothing, or bedding. A cigarette butt, beer can, or piece of paper may yield fingerprint and/or DNA evidence. All are possible from a carefully and thoroughly conducted crime scene investigation.

Figure 13.7 A pulled head hair with root. The abundance of epithelial cells from the scalp makes it ripe for DNA testing. In the absence of a root, a hair shaft can be typed with mitochondrial DNA testing. (Courtesy of the Los Angeles County Sheriff's Department.)

Crime laboratory tests involving comparative analysis such as hair examination require known pubic and scalp specimens. As this can be a painful procedure as the hairs need to be pulled, many victims refuse to submit to collection of these samples. Not submitting pulled hair samples to the lab should be carefully weighed against the pain it causes the victim. Semen and saliva specimens require known DNA samples from the parties involved in the investigation, including consensual partners. Rape investigation presents unusual challenges to the investigator. Issues such as myths about rape, psychological trauma of the victim and, in some cases, the investigator's feelings of discomfort in dealing with the victim must be addressed when investigating this crime of violence.

Date Rape Drugs

If during the course of an investigation, the victim makes a statement such as, "I was at a party, and this guy gave me a drink. Next thing I know, it's morning and I'm in someone's bed. I've no idea what happened in between," consider the possibility that the victim was drugged with Rohypnol or GHB.

Rohypnol, or flunitrazepam, known by various street names (Roachies, La Roche, Rope, Rib, Roche, Rophies, Roofies, and Ruffies), is the brand name of a sleeping pill marketed by Roche Pharmaceuticals in Mexico, South America, Europe, and Asia and first appeared in the United States in the early 1990s. Rohypnol belongs to the family of medications called nitro-benzodiazepines that includes Valium (diazepam) and Librium (chlorodiazepoxide). During the past few years, abuse of Rohypnol has increased; this was initially reported in Florida and Texas, but it is now spreading to other regions. Much of the Rohypnol abused in the United States is obtained by prescription in Mexico and transported across the border. Rohypnol is a fast-acting sedative that can render a victim unconscious within 20 to 30 minutes. Combined with alcohol, it can lead to coma and possibly death. It also produces complete or partial amnesia.

GHB has a number of street names such as "grievous bodily harm," "liquid ecstasy," and "easy lay," plus a host of other names depending on the region of the country. GHB is a depressant affecting the central nervous system and its effects are rapidly felt. Like "Ruffies," it can cause amnesia, unconsciousness, coma, and sometimes (when combined with alcohol) death. GHB generally comes in pure powder form or mixed with water. Body builders sometimes use it. In 1989, the FDA banned the sale of GHB and classified it as a Schedule I drug. A number of states have passed legislation outlawing the possession of GHB by making it a Schedule I drug under state law.

GHB is a liquid that can render a victim unconscious with as little as a teaspoonful mixed into a drink. The onset of symptoms comes within approximately 5 to 20 minutes. The victim experiences a feeling of extreme intoxication and impaired judgment. GHB does not produce the extreme muscle paralysis and memory loss associated with Rohypnol but can cause unconsciousness and strong memory impairment.

The collection of a blood and urine specimen upon admission to the emergency room for analysis is key to the effective investigation of drug-induced sexual assault cases. The cooperation of the emergency room in the collection of specimens greatly helps law enforcement in such cases.

Victims who experience being drugged or are suspicious that they may have been drugged should refrain from voiding their bladders. If voiding is necessary, any clean container is suitable for a urine collection. GHB is eliminated rapidly from the blood (less than 6 hours), but it may be detected in urine. Samples collected from 12 to 24 hours postdose will yield negative results. These samples should be submitted in a drug facilitated sexual assault kit to the toxicology lab.

Investigators should collect any portion of the drink, if it is available, for laboratory examination. Also, if any powdery or crystalline material or pills are found, they too should be sent to the crime laboratory. It should also be mentioned that alcohol by itself is involved in many sexual assaults. Additionally, victims sometimes state that they have been drugged, when in reality they have had way too much to drink.

Finally for any and all evidence that is collected during a sexual assault investigation, a chain of custody needs to be started.

Other Assaults

Sexual Child Molestation and Incest

Child molestation and incest investigations have two related problem areas: difficulty in interviewing the victim and possible problems regarding the child's competency to testify in court. These difficulties, coupled with the family's reluctance to pursue or cooperate in the matter, make these cases a challenge. The key person in a sexual assault case involving children is the physician. The physician's ability to examine the victim and document findings of sexual assault is of major importance in this type of case. Because of the usual inability of the victim to testify, the physical evidence and medical testimony are particularly important. Child psychologists are also playing an increasing role in child abuse and child molestation cases. They help investigators by pointing out specific child behavior patterns generally associated with this type of crime. However, investigators should be aware that a child psychologist might inadvertently cause a young victim to color his or her story so as to tell the psychologist what he or she "wants to hear."

Physical evidence is often minimal in child molestation cases. The child's parents are often unaware of the crime. Telltale signs of child molestation such as nightmares, bedwetting, urinary tract infections, and strange stories eventually lead parents or authorities to a suspicion of the cause. If molestation is suspected, the police are brought into the investigation. If clothing or bedding is available from a recent assault, they should be collected for DNA typing. In cases in which pregnancy results from a case of incest and the pregnancy is terminated, the fetus or products of conception can be used in DNA paternity testing to determine the identity of the father (Figures 13.8 and 13.9). Beyond this, the police will need to rely heavily on medical findings. Child abuse cases also rely upon the findings of the pediatrician. Here, unexplained bruises, x-rays showing broken bones, and so forth will be important in the investigation. In addition to physical abuse, instances of malnutrition and poor hygienic conditions may occur. These types of cases are almost always emotionally charged and are difficult to prosecute and take to trial. To be sure, these crimes certainly do occur; however, investigators must be especially careful in these cases. Innocent people's names can be tarnished irrevocably if a careful investigation is not made. On occasion, children have been known to fabricate allegations of sexual abuse.

Figure 13.8 Some government forensic laboratories will perform criminal paternity testing on the fetal tissue from an aborted pregnancy after obtaining the alleged father's DNA sample. (Courtesy of the Los Angeles County Sheriff's Department.)

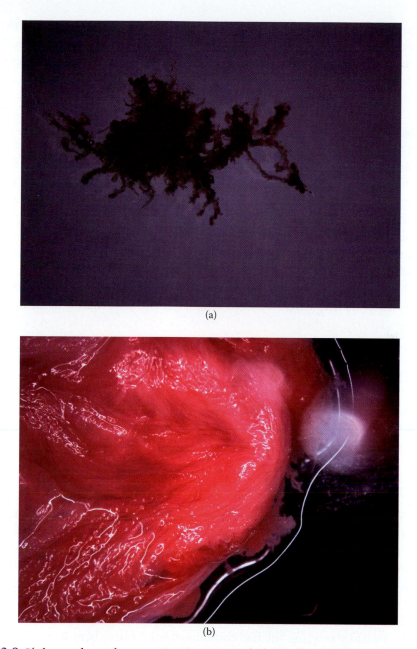

(a)

(b)

Figures 13.9 If the product of conception is not morphologically well defined, the differences between (a) fetal (chorionic villi) and (b) maternal (decidua) parts of the placental tissue can be differentiated under the microscope to be used in DNA paternity testing. (Courtesy of the NYC Office of Chief Medical Examiner.)

Public Lewdness/Forcible Touching

These types of crimes, often misdemeanors, include masturbating in public, or rubbing up against someone on a crowded bus or subway, and ejaculating on them. Swabs of semen or clothing should be submitted to the lab in these types of cases. In cases of groping or forcible touching, items of clothing can be submitted to the lab for high sensitivity DNA typing when a specific region of the clothing was touched by the perpetrator. (The NYC Office of Chief Medical Examiner Forensic Biology Laboratory offers high sensitivity DNA, also referred to as low copy number testing, for jurisdictions outside New York City to recover and detect small amounts of DNA.*)

Conclusion

Recently, the US Attorney General's office announced[†] revisions to the Uniform Crime Report's definition of rape. The reason for the more inclusive definition is to better document the scope and volume of this crime by allowing for a more comprehensive statistical reporting of sexual assault nationwide. The new definition of rape is: "The penetration, no matter how slight, of the vagina or anus with any body part or object, or oral penetration by a sex organ of another person, without the consent of the victim." This updated definition will allow law enforcement to report more complete sexual assault data so that victims of this crime will be more accurately reflected. It is important for this broad range of "special victims" to know that they are supported and that their attackers will be held accountable.

Chapter Questions

1. Explain why the first responding officer is required to play a much greater part in a rape investigation.

2. (True/False) The victim of a rape may appear perfectly calm and in control when being interviewed by the police.
   a) True
   b) False

3. Which of the following statements should not be included in the sexual assault report issued by the first responding officer?
   a) "The victim had several apparent bruises on her left shoulder."
   b) "The victim states that she had consensual sex 3 hours before the rape."
   c) "The victim appears unusually happy considering she was just raped."
   d) "Signs of forced entry were located on a rear window."

4. Of the following examples, which requires immediate attention from the lead investigator?
   a) The victim reports that she called her husband after the rape.
   b) The victim reports that the suspect kissed her on the cheek.
   c) The media is on scene and would like a statement.
   d) The victim has a criminal history.

---

* http://www.nyc.gov/html/ocme/html/hss/hss_home.shtml
† US DOJ Press Release, January 6, 2012, www.fbi.gov.

5. A _____ should be immediately instituted when collecting evidence from the victim at the hospital.
   a) Photo log
   b) Press release
   c) Crime scene log
   d) Chain of custody
6. List the three primary purposes of physical evidence in rape cases.

7. Which of the following is known as a date rape drug?
   a) Rohypnol
   b) Crack
   c) Marijuana
   d) LSD
8. Which of the following can be a problem area when investigating a child molestation case?
   a) The child's ability to testify in court
   b) The collection of probative evidence
   c) Obtaining consent from the parents
   d) Obtaining a search warrant
9. Which of the following is an example of a crime classified as public lewdness?
   a) Rape
   b) Elder abuse
   c) Sexual imposition
   d) Masturbating in public
10. You have been called to respond to a local nursing home for a report of possible elder sexual abuse. List the signs and symptoms you would be looking for.

Burglary Investigation

14

Burglary is one of the most commonly encountered crimes investigated by police. Because the nature of the crime is so varied, it is difficult to set down specific guidelines for its investigation. Many of the techniques and procedures outlined in earlier chapters of the text are pertinent to the burglary investigation. This chapter discusses some of the aspects of crime scene investigation that deal more specifically with the crime of burglary (Figure 14.1).

The first officer to arrive at the burglary scene must be concerned with the suspect's location. In cases in which the burglary is in progress and the officer was called because of the presence of a prowler, silent alarm, or ringing burglar alarm, the first consideration must be to apprehend the suspect. Once the suspect has been located or a determination has been made that the suspect is not at the scene, the location must be secured. Witnesses should next be located and separated for interviewing at a later time.

The crime scene search should commence. The officer conducting the crime scene investigation of a burglary should understand that most experienced burglars attempt to leave only a minimum amount of evidence at the location (Figure 14.2). The officer should also remember that it is impossible for the suspect not to change the crime scene in some small way by leaving traces behind or by picking up small items of evidence when leaving the scene.* The officer, or evidence collection team, must therefore collect evidence left behind by the suspect, for example, fingerprints, DNA, shoe prints, tool marks, etc., and evidence from the suspect that may have been removed from the scene, for example, glass fragments, paint chips, wooden splinters, etc. The investigator should also be aware of the

Figure 14.1 The complainant's home was burglarized. She smelled cigarette smoke upon entering the home and found the cigarette butt in the toilet. A mixture of DNA including a predominant male profile was obtained from the cigarette butt. The profile was submitted into CODIS for an identification. (Courtesy of the Harris County, Texas, Medical Examiner's Office DNA Laboratory.)

---

* This is known as Locard's exchange principle, or "every contact leaves a trace."

(a)

(b)

Figure 14.2 Two apparent burglary scenes. (a) The point of entry turned out to be a homicide case. (Courtesy of the Washoe County Sheriff's Department Crime Laboratory.) (b) The jimmied screen was a point of entry at a "routine" breaking and entry. (Courtesy of the Los Angeles County Sheriff's Department.)

modus operandi, or M.O., of the burglar. Frequently, a suspect may be responsible for a large number of burglaries in an area and similarities in the cases may enable the investigator to concentrate on one rather than a number of suspects. Thus, in some instances it may be useful to examine tool marks left at different crime scenes to determine whether the same tool was used.

Points of Entry

The point of entry is an important location of physical evidence in burglary investigations. The experienced burglar attempts to gain entry by the easiest and safest available entrance.

Entry through Windows

Window entry is usually accomplished by breaking a hole through a pane and removing the broken glass to reach the latch. To minimize the noise from falling glass, the burglar may press a rag against the window; sometimes adhesive tape may be used. In some cases, the burglar may remove the entire windowpane by removing the putty holding the glass in place. It has even happened that the burglar has replaced the glass intact and put in new putty. Where a screen covers a window, a careful examination of the edges for any cuts may show fibers from the sleeve where the suspect's arm was inserted to open or break the window. Glass is one type of evidence often found on the suspect when a window was broken to gain entrance. When the window is broken, it is almost unavoidable that some pieces of the flying glass will adhere to the suspect's clothing. The investigator should collect specimens of the broken window for possible comparison with glass found on the burglar's clothes and also search for any fingerprints present on the windowpane, as well as prints present in the window putty. It is also possible for the suspect to have cut or scraped themselves on the broken glass. Any blood found on glass can be sent for DNA typing.

Similarly, fingerprints should be looked for in the dust that may be present on the window or ledge. Entry may also be gained by forcing in a tool to push back a window latch. In such cases, tool marks should be looked for and samples of wood and paint should be taken for comparison if a tool is later found. A pry bar, screwdriver, or other tool is also sometimes used in forcing a window. In these cases, tool marks and specimens of building debris should be collected. Sometimes, the burglar may try to force several different windows to enter the building. The investigator should therefore examine all windows to determine if any jimmy marks are present and collect appropriate tool mark evidence. Paint chips frequently are dislodged during the course of breaking in and the investigator should always collect samples for later comparison (Figure 14.3). Later, examination of the suspect's clothing and tools may uncover paint that matches paint recovered at the crime scene.

Entry through Doors

A burglar usually opens a door by using a pry bar to attack the door and jamb around the lock until the bolt can be pushed back or is actually freed from the striker plate. A door jamb is sometimes so weak that it may be spread apart far enough to free the bolt. This can

(a)

(b)

Figure 14.3 (a,b) A sliver of wood with multiple layers of paint can be compared to known samples at the point of entry and matched. (Courtesy of the Royal Canadian Mounted Police Forensic Laboratory Services.)

be done by mere pressure from the body or by inserting a jack horizontally across the door-frame. The lock might also be made accessible through a hole that is drilled, sawed, or broken in a door panel. Far too many doors are fitted with glass that is simply broken so that the lock may be reached. Other weak points are mail slots, the frame of which may be removed, and transoms that may have been left open. A common method of entry is to push back spring-loaded bolts by means of a knife (Figure 14.4). The knife is inserted between the door and the jamb and the bolt is gradually worked back. The bolt is kept from springing back by outward pressure on the door. This method is easily detected by the series of scratches that run lengthwise along the bolt. Burglary by this method is prevented by safety catches and dead bolt locks. Snap-lock bolts can also be opened by inserting a knife, spatula, or credit card pressed against the beveled face of the bolt and pushing it back. The instrument can be inserted between the door and the jamb or behind the molding on the jamb.

This method of entry is generally difficult to detect because a piece of plastic can be used without leaving any marks. It is, however, possible that pieces of plastic broke off and may be found in or near the lock. On locks on which the beveled face of the bolt faces inward, the bolt may be pushed back by a suitable tool or a piece of wire that forces the bolt back by a pulling movement. This is usually discovered by scratch marks on the face of the bolt. Special attention should be given to the opening for the bolt in the striker plate for the possibility that it may contain wadded paper or other material. It has happened that a burglar surreptitiously stuffed something in the opening in the door jamb during an earlier visit to the premises. The effect of the wadding is to prevent the bolt from locking so that the burglar may later return and push the bolt back. If there is reason to suspect that the lock has been picked, the lock should be disassembled with great care. The investigator should avoid making new scratch marks inside the lock. If a pick has been used, it may have left marks in the coating of dust and oil usually found inside locks. Broken knife points,

(a)   (b)

Figure 14.4 (a) Exterior doors are another favorite point of entry. (b) Scratches are easily visible on this spring-loaded bolt.

metal fragments from lock picks, and the like may also be found inside the lock. Cases have been recorded in which mechanics who installed the lock made certain alterations to facilitate a later burglary.

Entry can also be gained by cutting the hinge pins off with a bolt cutter. More commonly, however, the pins are simply knocked out with hammer and chisel or screwdriver. With the pins out, the door can be lifted off the hinges. The door may then be replaced and the pins reinserted. This method of entry is readily revealed by the damage to the hinges and the chips of paint or metal on the floor below the hinges. Cylinder (pin-tumbler) locks may be picked by special picks, but usually the whole door is forced or the cylinder is removed. The cylinder may be pulled out by means of a special puller shaped from a pair of large nippers. To avoid detection of the removal, the lock cylinder is sometimes replaced or a similar cylinder put in its place. Sometimes, the retaining screw is removed surreptitiously during an earlier visit to the premises, which facilitates removing the cylinder. Still another means of gaining access through a door is by means of a wrench placed on the doorknob. The twisting motion exerted on the doorknob is sufficient to defeat the locking mechanism of inexpensive locking devices. Examination of the doorknob shows characteristic markings caused by the tool. The doorknob should be removed and submitted to the laboratory for comparison with tool marks made by the wrench and also for comparison of any metal shavings found in the teeth of the tool. In instances in which a padlock was used on a hinged hasp to lock a door, the padlock and cut shackle should be collected and sent to the laboratory. If a pair of bolt cutters or similar cutting device is found, test cuts can be made and compared with tool marks left on the lock shackle (Figure 14.5).

Entry through Basement Windows and Skylights

These windows are forced in the same manner as ordinary windows, but the investigator should pay special attention to the possibility that the burglar's clothes may have become torn and cloth fragments or fibers left behind. The officer should also take samples of the dust and the dirt usually found in such places.

Entry through Roofs

The presence of convenient utility poles, ladders, and other aids, plus the concealment by the edge parapet, makes entry through flat roofs a favorite M.O. Many otherwise well-protected stores have "tissue-paper" roofs. Building material may contaminate the clothing of any burglar using this technique. A careful search will also show signs of ropes for entry and exit. Most stores are equipped with roof ventilators and exhaust fans. Entry through the ventilating system may result in tool marks, DNA, fingerprints, and dust contamination of clothing.

Entry through Walls

Walls are broken by tools or by explosives. A brick wall is easily broken by a hammer and chisel or a sledgehammer. Burglars can be expected to become covered with dust during

(a)

(b)   (c)

Figure 14.5 (a) Burglary tools such as these may be a source of many types of physical evidence such as paint, glass, other building materials, tool marks, etc. Evidence in a burglary case: (b) a cut lock hasp and (c) close-up of the hasp shown pieced together. (Courtesy of the Los Angeles County Sheriff's Department.)

such an operation; samples of mortar and brick should be collected for comparisons. In blasting, a hole is usually chiseled between two bricks and the charge is inserted. Several small charges are normally used to avoid severe detonations and the possibility of the whole wall collapsing. Small hydraulic jacks may be used to force holes into a wall. In this operation, a narrow passageway is usually chosen where the base force can be distributed over a wide area by padding. After the initial hole is made, repeated thrusts are used to enlarge the hole sufficiently to gain an entry. When an empty or infrequently occupied store is adjacent to the target, plaster walls may be cut to a thin supporting layer and the entire section removed at once. Entry into vaults is usually accomplished through the walls, which are easier to force than the door. The walls are often constructed of reinforced concrete that can be broken by repeated blasting or by hammer and chisel and oxyacetylene torch.

Entry through Floors

This method of entry is often preferred in the case of warehouses or other buildings that have a crawl space underneath. The burglar usually drills or saws a hole in the floorboards large enough to crawl through. Entry through walls and floors is also made when the criminal suspects or knows that the premises are protected by burglar alarms on doors and windows.

Because many burglaries occur at night, the investigator should also check any outdoor lights to see whether the bulbs were unscrewed by the burglar to darken the area near the point of entry. These bulbs might contain fingerprints and/or DNA.

Simulated Burglaries

Simulated burglaries are often attempts at insurance fraud. To create a successful imitation of a burglary that will deceive the police, the simulator must strive to carry it out as naturally as possible. Otherwise, there will be gaps in the sequence of events. When windows are entered, the officer should therefore always check whether the windowpanes are in fact broken from the outside, whether footprints are outside the window, whether broken glass has been trampled in these prints, whether the burglar really could have reached the window, whether there are traces of actual entry (sand, dirt, etc.), whether objects inside the window are so placed that the window could be opened to permit entry, and so on. If the outside of the window glass is very dirty, there should be marks from the object used to break it. If the glass is relatively clean, the side on which the force was applied might be revealed by dusting with fingerprint powder. In cases of forced doors, the damage should be examined to see whether it is only on the outside portions. Marks of prying should be present on the door as well as on the door jamb. If the tool marks are located so high up that the burglar must have stood on a box or a ladder, the support should be examined. Whenever a burglary is suspected of being simulated, all tools belonging to the victim should be compared with the tool marks present and, if necessary, recovered for further examination. Holes in floors, walls, and ceilings should be examined to determine the side from which the attack was started. The holes should also be examined to determine any evidence of a person having crawled through. The officer should further make an estimate of how long the burglar spent on the premises. The officer should follow the burglar's actions in searching for valuables—were doors first opened and drawers emptied or did the burglar go directly to the location of the valuables?

Detailed Examination of the Scene

Generally, the detailed examination of the crime scene proper should begin only after the surrounding areas have been searched. Failure to search the surrounding areas initially may result in the inadvertent destruction of evidence by sightseers as well as officers at the location. Approaches leading to and away from the scene should be examined for footprints, tire impressions, drag marks (such as those caused by a heavy object, e.g., a safe), and abandoned items such as tools, clothing, opened cash boxes, and so on. Obstacles leading to the building such as fences and gates should be examined for traces of blood, fabric and fibers, and tool marks. The number of suspects involved should be estimated from footprints when possible. Areas where a suspect had to crawl or climb should be examined for traces of clothing. Samples of building material and soil should be collected for comparative purposes. The location from which the burglar "staked out" the location or where a "lookout" was standing should be examined for footprints, cigarette butts, cigarette package wrappers, matches, food items, and other such evidence. The point of entry should be examined for broken tools, tool marks, broken window glass, fibers, hair, blood, fingerprints, footprints, paint chips, wood, and other building materials (Figures 14.6 and 14.7). Known samples of materials should be collected. Photographs, measurements, and sketches should, as always, be made before any items are moved or collected. The examination of the interior of the burglarized premises must sometimes be carried out while taking into account the wishes of the owner. Business activities cannot be completely stopped. The investigator may allow the owner or manager to specify which area of the premises is available for searching first.

The investigator should carry out the inside crime scene investigation in the normal detailed and systematic way. Attention should be given to evidence such as fingerprints, DNA, footprints, broken tools, tool marks, blood, and any other evidence that will aid in the solution of the case. As the examination of various areas of the location is completed, the proprietor should be notified. If evidence is found that requires time-consuming recovery, the owner and other personnel should be asked to stay out of the area until the examination is complete. A complete inventory of all items missing should be obtained from the owner, as well as a complete description of the items, including brand names, labels, markings, serial numbers, size, shape, color, and value. This facilitates identification of the stolen property in the event the items are recovered.

An apprehended suspect should be thoroughly searched. Cuts and scratches should be noted and photographed. The clothing should be collected for examination for tears and building material that can place the suspect in contact with the crime scene. The suspect's vehicle should be searched for stolen property, burglary tools, and any other items of physical evidence. The investigator should remember that in some instances a search warrant might be necessary before the vehicle may be completely searched.

(a)

(b)

Figure 14.6 (a) An exterior doorknob showing tool marks and (b) a pair of adjustable grips on a doorknob. Investigators should never attempt to match a tool to an object in this fashion.

The investigator should attempt to form a picture of the whole crime scene to estimate whether or not the burglar was familiar with the premises. If the burglar removed valuables from a rather unlikely location without disturbing the rest of the scene or if keys that were hidden were used, the officer might infer that the suspect was familiar with the location. The investigator should try to make a determination about the type of person

Figure 14.7 Many items of evidence may need to be considered in a burglary: tool marks on the bolt and doorknob, paint, wood, building material, glass, etc. Investigators need to be aware of these when searching for physical evidence in such cases.

being sought. Was the burglary the work of a professional burglar? Was the crime simply a case of vandalism involving juveniles? Was anything unusual left at the scene such as feces, which might point to a suspect with a history of sex-related crimes? Answers to these questions, information obtained from interviews, and physical evidence examination will prove useful in the overall investigation.

Safe Burglaries

Safes may be classified into two basic types: fire resistant and burglar resistant. Although providing a minimum resistance to attack by a professional burglar, fire-resistant safes are designed to withstand, resist, and retard the penetration of heat and to protect documents from destruction by fire. Such safes are constructed of metal and insulation consisting of a variety of materials such as vermiculite, cement, diatomaceous earth, sawdust, and the like. Burglar-resistant safes are specifically designed to resist the efforts of safe burglars and are constructed of steel that is resistant to forced entry by tools or torch. Burglar-resistant safes are not burglarproof but are designed to resist attack for a certain period of time.

Safes can be opened by a number of methods such as manipulation, punching, peeling, prying, ripping, chopping, drilling, burning, or by means of explosives. Manipulation is essentially a lost art that involves opening a safe by means of listening to and feeling the combination lock mechanism. Most safes today have manipulation-proof locks; the investigator should therefore assume that the suspect had knowledge of the combination if a safe in which the lock has been opened is found. The punching method involves knocking off the dial and punching the dial spindle into the safe. Newer safes have punch-proof spindles and relocking devices that automatically relock the safe when an attempt at a "punch job" is made. Peeling involves prying or peeling the faceplate from the safe door in such a way as to expose the locking mechanism. This is sometimes accomplished by first pounding the door with a sledgehammer until the door buckles and then inserting a pry bar. Entry by ripping or chopping is achieved by tearing a hole through a part of the safe other than the door such as the top, side, or bottom. Drilling is usually effective, but it is a time-consuming method and therefore only rarely used in safe burglaries. It is commonly done by perforating the doorplate around the keyhole by a series of holes close together. A large portion of the lock mechanism is thereby bared so that the bolts can be manipulated. The front plate of some safes can also be peeled back if some of the screws or rivets in the edge are first removed. The paint covering the rivets is first scraped off so that the rivets are bared. The rivets are then drilled deeply enough for the plate to be separated. After a few rivets have been removed, the front plate is then forced up sufficiently to insert a chisel that is used to break the remaining rivets without drilling.

On some safes, the locking bolts can be reached by drilling through the side of the safe, directly against the face of the bolt. The bolt can then be driven back with a punch. The exact location of the bolts can be determined by the marks in the door frame that occur in daily use when the safe door is shut while the bolts are protruding. In cases of drilling, the burglar can be expected to have used some kind of lubricating oil for the bit. Samples of such oil and samples of metal shavings should be collected because the burglar's body or clothing may contain these materials. Simpler types of safes with combination locks may be opened by means of a thick, square steel plate provided with an opening at the center to be slipped over the dial knob. The corners of the plate are equipped with threaded bolts, the points of which touch the safe door. By tightening the bolts with a wrench, the knob and spindle are torn out. It also happens that safes are opened by a special bridge device screwed to the safe with bolts. The portion of the bridge over the door frame contains a threaded hole. A strong bolt is fitted into this hole and tightened far enough to force the door open.

Another method uses a circular cutter. Such devices are made in several different forms. Some are affixed to one or more holes that have been drilled into the safe, while others are strapped to the safe by long bolts and nuts or steel cable. Common to all types, however, is one or more hardened steel cutters held against the safe under tension and turned by means of a handle. The result is a round hole in the safe wall. These devices are normally not used on the safe door because the locking bars would interfere, but rather on the side or back of the safe. Cutting by oxyacetylene torch is a very effective method against which only specially designed steel chests are completely resistant. A considerable disadvantage of this method lies in the fact that the apparatus required is heavy and difficult to transport. For this reason, the burning method is usually used only where complete welding equipment is available on the premises. Some burglars have used compact equipment that is large enough to do the job but light enough to be carried easily.

Burning is another method used by safe burglars using the so-called burning bar. The bar, a metal pipe, is packed with a mixture of powdered aluminum and iron oxide. The mixture is known as thermite and when ignited gives off a very intense heat that can be directed to the safe. Burning is usually started around the dial hole. A sufficiently large hole is cut in the front plate of the door so that the lock mechanism is accessible. The operator may cut this hole in the form of a tongue that is folded back. Where the cutting is done on the sides or back of the safe, the inside plate must also be cut through. This method often ignites the contents of the safe, whereupon the burglar may use a soda pop bottle as a fire extinguisher. Sometimes, the burglar cuts off the safe door hinges, which reveals an ignorance of the construction of the safe. The manner of opening the safe by burning reveals the skill of the burglar. When the investigator is unable to estimate this skill, a specialist should be consulted. Samples to be collected at the scene are molten particles of metal (beads), slag, molten safe insulation, and the like. Such particles may be found on the clothing of a suspect.

The investigator should also keep in mind the possibility of minor burns in the burglar's clothes from flying particles. When the contents of the safe caught fire, the burglar may have been able to recover paper currency, some of which may be charred. Safe burglaries are often carried out by transporting the safe to an isolated location where it is opened by tools or explosives. In such cases, the burglars are usually less careful in their movements at the place of opening. Valuable footprints or tire tracks may be found at such places. The investigation should be carried out as soon as possible because inclement weather conditions may destroy the most valuable evidence.

Safe Burglary Case

A safe was hauled out during a burglary and transported in a car to a wooded area where it was opened with explosives. During the examination of the outdoor scene, a door handle from an automobile was recovered. The car of a suspect who was later arrested for the burglary was found to have a broken handle. The handle from the scene matched the remains of the handle on the car. It had apparently been broken off while the safe was taken out of the car. The suspect confessed.

Safe Burglaries Using Explosives

It is sometimes very difficult to gather physical evidence that will convict a safe burglar specializing in explosives. As a rule, the burglar is skilled at this method and takes pride in sweeping the crime scene clean of all traces that may be used as incriminating evidence. When examining such burglary scenes, the investigator should therefore proceed very thoroughly and take advantage of the mistakes sometimes made even by this type of burglar.

Experience has shown that these burglars usually make mistakes when disturbed or when fleeing the premises. The burglar may then leave behind or drop objects that have potential value as evidence. One weakness of these specialists is that they usually stick to one method in all their burglaries. The investigator thereby gets an opportunity to tie certain burglaries to a given criminal or to others whom they have trained. This fact may be valuable even when the burglars are not known. Explosives operators usually do not pick locks or make their way into the premises by other light-fingered methods. Their work is carried out with a great deal of noise and this is also characteristic of their method of entry. They generally use great force on doors and windows and may even use a charge on a door that could much more easily have been opened the usual way. On the other hand, they are very careful to protect themselves from surprise. They very rarely work alone and may have several helpers whose only duty is to act as lookouts.

Regarding the placing of the safe for the "blowing," three methods are normally found: it is left in place, it is pulled out from the wall, or it is laid on the floor. The first method is the most common. The second is used by burglars who do not want to have the safe blown against the wall and create vibrations in the building that may be more noticeable than the detonation. It has happened that a safe was thrown so violently against the wall that it broke the wall and started cracks that ran into an apartment above. The third method is seldom used; its advantage is that it facilitates the placing of the charge.

In examining safes that have been moved or laid down, the investigator should be very careful in searching for latent finger and palm prints. Although explosives specialists will be sure to use gloves or other covering, it is still possible that they may leave identifiable fragments of palm prints on a safe that they have moved. The glove may slip during the heavy work, exposing a small piece of the palm, enough to produce a valuable print. In developing prints deposited under such conditions, great care must be exercised because they easily become smeared or even completely filled in because of the great pressure.

The charge is usually placed in the dial spindle hole after the dial is knocked off; it may be dynamite in powder or paste or other explosives. The hazard and the refined technique associated with the use of nitroglycerine usually limit its use to only the elite of the safe burglars. Round door safes have discouraged the use of explosives, however. Wrappers from explosives should be searched for and recovered, even though latent fingerprints are usually not found on waxed wrappers. In a favorable case, the wrapper may still be valuable as evidence. In general, the adhesive material used to affix the detonator that is found on the scene, such as clay, putty, plasticine, or soap, is brought in by the burglar. These substances must be soft and well kneaded to serve the purpose. Because the burglar may have kneaded these materials without wearing gloves before going to the scene, plastic fingerprints and/or DNA may be present. Such evidence should be searched for not only on the surface but also on inside layers of the kneaded material.

Plastic prints or DNA may also be found on strips of tape, but these are usually difficult to detect. The amount of safety fuse—when it is used—may vary in length. Explosives specialists usually cut these lengths before going to the scene and have widely varying ideas of the proper length—a fact that may have some value. Those using the longer fuses usually prefer to light the fuse and then retire to a safe place from which they can observe the effect of the explosion and whether it was noticed. Safe burglars vary as to whether they use a dam or sound-absorbing blanket to contain the explosion. Those who do use a dam probably do so to muffle the detonation and to keep windows from bursting. Because the charge is mostly inside the door, the effect of the explosion is not enhanced by the use of a dam.

When the burglar intends to demolish the door completely, the dam does have some effect, but it is usually an effect that the burglar wants to avoid. The burglar runs the risk that the inside door plate is blown into the safe with such force that new charges must be placed to dislodge it. Many explosives specialists make a habit of not using a dam at all. Instead, they open windows in the room in which the safe is located so that the shock wave will dissipate without breaking windows or attracting unwanted attention. Some burglars soak the dam with water, partly to make it denser and heavier and partly to prevent the possibility of fire. The materials used in dams are brought to or collected at the scene. The damage to the material gives an indication of how many separate charges were used.

Material that has been brought to the scene may sometimes give good leads for the investigation and the search for the criminal. The ideal explosion occurs when the charge is so well balanced that the locking bolts are pulled back and the door flies open. In such cases, the external damage to the safe may be limited to a slight bulge in the front plate around the dial hole. It does happen, however, that the locking bolts remain more or less closed, so new charges must be set off. To avoid this snag, some burglars put weight on the door handle in the direction in which the handle opens. A heavy cord is commonly tied to the handle and a heavy object is attached to the other end. Another method is to tie a heavy metal bar to the handle to act as a lever. At the detonation, the handle is turned by the weight of the heavy object so that the locking bolts are turned back. Locked drawers and compartments inside the safe are either forced open or blown. The investigator should keep in mind the possibility of finding parts of broken tools as well as tool marks at these places.

Fragments of tools should be searched for with a magnet because they are very difficult to find in the powdered insulation that usually pours from the broken safe. The search for fingerprints at scenes of safe blowing is usually complicated by the layer of finely divided safe insulation that settles on everything in the room. This dust should be removed, preferably by careful blowing, before developing with powder. To brush off the dust is wrong because the dust usually consists of gritty particles that will destroy the fingerprints. Visible prints that have been deposited by a dusty finger must be treated very carefully. Whenever an unexploded charge is found in the safe, it should be neutralized with great care. An apprehended suspect's clothes should be thoroughly searched for the presence of safe insulation or paint. Anyone who has been present in a room in which a safe has been blown can hardly avoid getting dust and safe insulation on his or her clothing. The dust may also adhere to the burglar's skin or in the hair, ears, and nostrils and under the fingernails. Such dust may be found on any part of the clothing, but particularly in the pant cuffs and on the shoes, mainly in the seams, in the lace holes, and on the soles.

In addition, paint chips are usually loosened in the explosion and the burglars run the risk of picking them up on their clothing when examining the safe after the detonation. In searching the scene, the investigator should therefore collect samples of the safe insulation and paint on the outside and inside of the safe for use in possible comparisons and also evaluate the possibility of wall paint loosened by the explosion falling on the burglar. The investigator should note the manufacturer of the safe so that the company may later be contacted for information on the composition of insulation and paint. If safe insulation or paint is not found on the suspect's clothes, the investigator should remember that the suspect might have done everything possible to eliminate such traces. The suspect's hands and clothing should also be examined for the presence of trace explosives. If the hands were not immediately washed, traces may be under the fingernails. In the clothing, such traces should primarily be searched for in the pockets—even the gloves may contain traces. If the burglar carried safety fuses in pockets, there may be characteristic stains on the pocket lining.

When a safe is blown, the burglar may be injured by the sharp metal edges. It may also happen that the nose starts bleeding from the shock of the detonation. This is more common when electric detonators are used because the burglar is forced to stay rather close to the safe. If blood is found at the scene, it should be recovered for later examination. The burglar may possibly be so severely injured that immediate aid must be sought. Burglary is such a common crime that frequently a less than thorough investigation is conducted; however, a careful and detailed examination of the crime scene may result in developing evidence useful in an ultimate solution of the case.

Until recently, many crime labs did not have the capacity to test for DNA in samples collected at burglary crime scenes. The reason was that many were faced with major backlogs from violent crimes, for example homicides and rapes, as well as resource constraints. Past cases have shown that when certain types of evidence is left behind at a burglary scene, such as articles of clothing, latex gloves, hats, cigarette butts, partially eaten food, eyeglasses, drink containers, cell phones, PDAs, etc., a considerable number of crimes can be solved by DNA testing. Low copy number (or LCN) DNA can be utilized for touch DNA, where an item does not yield any usable print information. Investigators should consult with the forensic science laboratory in their jurisdictions to determine under what qualifications property crime cases are accepted, and if there are a maximum number of items the laboratory will test. As state and national DNA databases continue to grow, more property crimes will be solved. In addition, if police agencies demand more forensic science services such as DNA in property crimes, forensic labs can make a stronger case for funding in these areas.

Chapter Questions

1. Which of the following things should be done by the officer at a burglary in progress call once the scene has been searched for possible suspects?
    a) Secure the scene
    b) Identify any witnesses
    c) Begin a crime scene search
    d) All of the above
2. Why is it important that the crime scene investigator find the point of entry at a burglary scene?

3. You are called in to process the scene of a residential burglary where a window was pried open. Which of the following pieces of evidence would you want to collect?
    a) Tool marks on the window frame
    b) Paint samples from cans in the basement
    c) Fingerprint standards from the workers who installed the window
    d) Hairs found in the resident's bathroom

4. Describe the various ways that a burglar can force entry through a door.

5. Which one of the following pieces of evidence would be the most useful in identifying the perpetrator of a residential burglary?
   a) Hair on a couch
   b) Blood on broken glass at the point of entry
   c) Mud on the floor inside the point of entry
   d) Glass

6. Describe what a simulated burglary is and list some of the things you should be
looking for when dealing with such a scene.

7. You are conducting a burglary investigation and find a witness who reported seeing a suspicious male sitting in a car across from the scene before the burglary.
Which of the following pieces of evidence would you want to collect when searching that area?
   a) Soil samples from the area
   b) Cigarette butts on the ground
   c) Tire impressions
   d) All of the above

8. Which of the following could indicate that the burglar may have a history of sex-
related crimes?
   a) A hidden key was used to gain entry
   b) Feces on the floor at the scene
   c) Unusual tool marks
   d) The scene was spray painted and things were unnecessarily broken

9. Describe several ways that a safe can be opened by a burglar.

10. You stop a suspect on your way to a call of a burglary where a safe was opened by
explosion. Which of the following pieces of evidence would you look for on the
suspect's clothing?
   a) Hairs
   b) Insulation material
   c) Glass
   d) Dirt

Motor Vehicle Investigation

15

Case

One night a young lady left a nightclub in order to use the pay phone across the street. During her trip back across the four-lane highway, a vehicle that was traveling at a high rate of speed struck her. Found at the scene was a piece of a white body molding kit known to be associated with high-end Corvettes. When the company for this product was contacted, they reported that only two of these white-molding kits had been sold on Long Island in New York.

A witness came forward and stated that he observed a white Corvette at a stoplight take off at a high speed and strike the victim. He believed he might have been racing. After receiving the addresses of the white Corvette owners, the detectives started the investigation with the nearest address. Upon arrival they discovered a white Corvette in the process of being disassembled. After searching dumpsters in the adjacent industrial area, the majority of the pieces were found. The deconstruction of the hood had been achieved through the use of a chain saw, reciprocating saw, and pick axe. When it was reassembled, blood was discovered. Laboratory personnel were in the process of examining the hood for tool marks created by the hinges. Before work was complete, the Corvette owner confessed to the hit-and-run that killed the young lady (Figures 15.1 through 15.4).

The widespread use of motor vehicles in today's society has resulted in automobiles being associated with many different types of police investigations. Motor vehicles may be the instrument of crimes such as hit-and-run cases or traffic fatalities. A vehicle may also be a crime scene, for example, in cases in which a crime was committed in an automobile or in cases of auto theft. This chapter deals with evidence commonly associated with crimes in which a motor vehicle is involved.

Vehicle Theft

A vehicle may be stolen by juveniles for "joyriding," in connection with another crime as a means of fleeing, or for the purpose of stripping the vehicle of parts to be sold for profit. Unfortunately, vehicle theft is a crime of rather high frequency, and some police agencies do not have the personnel resources with which to conduct thorough investigations. This often results in a search for physical evidence that consists of only dusting the vehicle for latent fingerprints. Stolen vehicles may be located in a variety of circumstances. Often uniformed officers while on patrol observe them. The officer may make use of a "hot sheet" listing licenses of stolen vehicles, use a description from a police bulletin or broadcast, or notice some furtive movement on the part of the driver that results in a routine traffic stop and subsequent check for a stolen vehicle.

Figure 15.1 Vehicle part found at scene. (Courtesy of Dan Cheswick, Suffolk County Crime Lab.)

Figure 15.2 Front view of disassembled suspect vehicle. (Courtesy of Dan Cheswick, Suffolk County Crime Lab.)

Once the vehicle has been identified as stolen, the examination for physical evidence begins. A short preliminary investigation will determine whether a full search for physical evidence is needed. In instances in which the driver of the stolen vehicle turns out to be the thief, the need for identity determination by means of physical evidence is removed. It is still necessary to check out the vehicle carefully and inventory the property. It is a good idea to look for evidence of other crimes. In one instance, an automobile was recovered and at the officer's request towed to an impound yard. Some days later, much to the officer's chagrin, a dead body was discovered in the trunk.

It is possible the theft may be only one of other, more serious crimes; with this in mind, the first officer to locate the stolen vehicle should take appropriate precautions. As with other crime scenes, the most fragile evidence should be collected first. This usually means fingerprints. It is recommended that the vehicle be moved to a special location such as a

Figure 15.3 Dumpster where some of the parts were located. (Courtesy of Dan Cheswick, Suffolk County Crime Lab.)

Figure 15.4 Reassembled hood from vehicle. (Courtesy of Dan Cheswick, Suffolk County Crime Lab.)

tow yard or police garage for the purpose of taking prints and looking for other physical evidence. Furthermore, before any extensive search is undertaken, the need for a search warrant should be considered.

When the vehicle is moved, care should be taken not to destroy fingerprints or other evidence. If possible, the vehicle should be towed to the impound yard. Driving it might accidentally destroy certain evidence. Personnel at the tow yard should be reminded not to touch the vehicle until it has been processed for evidence. If the vehicle is wet from dew, it should first be allowed to dry. In cold weather, the vehicle should be placed indoors and allowed to warm up to room temperature prior to taking fingerprints. The examination for fingerprints should be conducted in a systematic manner. Areas most likely to have been handled by the suspect should be carefully fingerprinted. These include the rear-view mirror, steering wheel, shift lever, door handle, glove compartment, and windows. After prints have been lifted, the location, date, time, and other identifying information should be noted on the fingerprint card. Swabs of the vehicle should also be taken for touch DNA in case fingerprints do not produce any useful ridge detail. Signs of forced entry should be noted. Known specimens of broken glass, chipped paint, and similar items should be collected for future comparison.

If the radio, tape deck, CD player, cellular phone, navigation system, or iPod is missing, the electrical wires should be removed for possible comparison against recovered property. The wires should be marked in a way that clearly shows which ends were originally connected to the unit.

Abandoned Vehicles

Any officer who finds or investigates an ownerless vehicle not reported as stolen should not drive it away or subject it to more detailed examination until informed by the driver or owner of the reason why the vehicle was standing at that place. If it is known that a serious crime has been committed, the investigation of the vehicle must be done with the utmost care and thoroughness. The investigation must be planned carefully. The basic search for evidence in and on the vehicle should be carried out in a well-sheltered place, preferably in a garage or other suitable building, because rain or snow or even strong sunlight can destroy certain evidence. The vehicle should therefore be driven or towed from the place at which it was found as soon as possible, but only after certain preliminary investigations have been carried out.

The place where the vehicle is found should be photographed and sketched in the usual way. Photography is done while the vehicle is still on the spot, but sketching can wait until later. In sketches, the distance to the nearest occupied dwelling and to the nearest town or city should be given. If necessary, a sketch plan may be made of the immediate surroundings, and another of neighboring districts, but suitable maps may replace the latter. The recording of the odometer or taxi meter should be noted; it is best to ask an expert whether anything of special significance can be observed. The supply of gasoline is checked. Addresses in the GPS should be checked to determine where the car might have come from and where it was headed. The account information from automatic toll collection devices, such as EZPass in the Northeastern region of the United States, should be checked to establish when and where a vehicle might have been (Figure 15.5). An attempt is also made to determine whether the vehicle stopped at that point for some reason unforeseen by the driver, for example, engine trouble, depleted gasoline supply, inability to drive it further, and so on. The floor in front of the driving seat is examined carefully. Preferably all dust and dirt at this place should be kept. The exterior is examined for the presence of any evidence that might fall off when the vehicle is driven or towed away.

Furthermore, a preliminary examination of the whole vehicle should be made for evidence that is easy to collect or that for any reason might be damaged or destroyed when the vehicle is driven away. The detailed investigation of a vehicle should not be carried out at the place where it is found, but the site chosen should be as near to the place of finding as possible. A long tow can cause a deposit of dust or dirt that may completely destroy any possibilities of finding evidence in the form of fingerprints.

Figure 15.5 Electronic devices such as GPS navigation systems and/or EZPass in cars can provide a wealth of information to investigators.

After removing the vehicle to a sheltered place, a thorough investigation is made of the location where the vehicle was found and the surrounding area. It is possible that the criminal, after committing the crime, unconsciously dropped or threw away objects that show the route taken or supply incriminating evidence. The investigation must be done quickly, especially if snow is anticipated. If larger areas or stretches of road must be searched, it may be advisable to call for a search team; however, they must first be instructed in how to act if they find any evidence. The detailed investigation of the vehicle is done only after it is completely dry.

In general, the floor of the vehicle and seats are examined first; only after this is done are any fingerprints developed and DNA swabs collected. It may be convenient first to examine the outside of the vehicle in order to avoid the risk of anyone unthinkingly destroying evidence or leaving prints. The contents of ashtrays are examined and kept, with various objects noted in the order in which they occur from the top. The contents of the glove compartment and any other storage spaces are examined and noted in a similar way. In and under the seats, objects are often found that the criminal has dropped. Any bloodstains in and on the vehicle are examined for direction of fall, height of fall, direction of movement, etc., after which they are preserved. Marks of swinging a weapon, damage from a gunshot, and the like are preserved. The engine and trunk are examined. In the investigation of a vehicle in which a crime of violence has been committed, it is advisable, after collecting the evidence, to take measurements of the amount of room in the vehicle. A question may arise about the possibility of a criminal swinging an instrument, handling a firearm, and other such acts. Any evidence of the vehicle's being used in any crime should be noted; safe paint and insulation in the trunk, outlines of boxes or tools, even bullet holes should be sought. All VIN numbers should be checked in order to detect alterations in the identity of the vehicle. Any damage to the vehicle may indicate the abandonment and reported "theft" were to hide an accident. The exact condition of damage should be carefully noted and photographed.

Under suspicious circumstances, the temperature of the water in the radiator and the surrounding air temperature should be recorded. From these data, it may be possible to establish the duration of time since abandonment. A careful search of the trunk is indicated in those cases in which it carried a dead body. If the victim was killed in one location, transported in the vehicle, and dropped at another site, only a very small amount of

Figure 15.6 The color of the seat of this car made it difficult to visualize any blood using the naked eye. Luminol was sprayed on the seat in order to determine if the victim was shot in this car. Blood from the victim was found on the seat lever, and the owner of the car was subsequently arrested. In order to capture the chemiluminescence of the luminol in a digital photo (shown in purple), a 30-second exposure was used in a darkened room with a rear curtain flash. (Courtesy of Norm Marin, New York City Office of Chief Medical Examiner.)

evidence may be in the trunk. In some cases, the interior may have been cleaned to remove traces of blood. In such cases, it may be worthwhile to remove the liner to search for blood that has seeped through and was not noticed by the suspect. Removal of the seats should also be considered for a thorough search. Electronic noses can also be used to detect odors of decomposition inside the vehicle. Weapons, tools, and sometimes trace evidence that can link the victim to the vehicle may be uncovered. In cases of homicide, the seat covers or the entire seat should be submitted to the laboratory for testing for the presence of blood (Figure 15.6).

Homicide in a Vehicle

Taxicab drivers are sometimes the victims of robberies, often in combination with assault that may be fatal. For a criminal who is desperate enough, it is a relatively simple matter to order the driver to a desolate area, assault the driver from behind without too great a personal danger, and then rob him. Because it would be dangerous to attack the driver while the cab is moving, the driver is asked to stop under some pretext or other. After the robbery is completed, it is not uncommon for the attacker to hide the victim and then drive the car as far away as possible from the scene.

In cases in which the robbery victim dies, one can expect to find the vehicle and the victim in different locations; sometimes the vehicle is found first. There is a great risk, therefore, that the examination of the vehicle is difficult or impossible because an overzealous officer has the vehicle removed, thinking that it is only a case of "joyriding." For this reason, every officer who finds an abandoned vehicle should suspect the worst and exercise extreme care. After a license check has revealed that the vehicle may have been the scene of a crime, the procedure suggested in the section "Abandoned Vehicles" should be followed, as well as the procedure for the specific type of crime. The search of a vehicle in which a homicide was committed must be conducted with the same degree of care as would be used in conducting the search of an indoor or outdoor crime scene involving a murder. Because of the cramped working area, it is especially important to exercise care so as not to destroy any physical evidence in the vehicle. The procedures discussed elsewhere in the text for processing the crime scene are generally the same for a vehicle.

Cases involving sabotage or acts of terrorism in which the vehicle was blown up by an explosive charge require a thorough investigation to recover as many parts of the device as possible. The debris from the explosion may cover a wide area, and a careful and systematic search is necessary to locate, chart, and recover as many pieces of the damaged vehicle and bomb as possible. Pieces of a timing mechanism, electrical devices, wires, and batteries, as well as explosives residue, may prove to be valuable evidence in the investigation. CAUTION: Investigators should be extremely careful since secondary devices can be used to cause maximum casualties to first responders and investigators!

Hit-and-Run Investigation

Hit-and-run cases include two types: damage to other vehicles or property and death or injury to individuals. In both cases, physical evidence can assist in identifying the hit-and-run vehicle, establishing a connection between the vehicle and the victim or crime scene and reconstructing the scene in general to determine the events surrounding the crime. Cases involving damage to other vehicles are often the result of driving under the influence or in a careless or reckless manner. The usual types of physical evidence found at the scene are paint chips or scrapings, glass, pieces of headlamps or plastic reflectors, and pieces from the grillwork of the vehicle. Most of these items are very small and therefore easily overlooked when searching the crime scene. Also, the impact from the crash may throw certain items some distance from the vehicle, and loose or broken parts still attached to the hit-and-run vehicle may subsequently fall off at considerable distance from the scene. These considerations make a search of a greater area important in these cases (Figure 15.7).

The hit-and-run crime scene often has a factor not present at other scenes: traffic. If the fatality occurred in a busy intersection or on a well-traveled street, the officer may feel pressured to complete the investigation more quickly. Although time may be a consideration, it should not deter the investigator from doing a thorough and complete job of processing the scene. Overall crime scene photos should be taken as well as photographs from different views, including aerial views if possible. Google Maps is a good tool to use for viewing the area surrounding the hit-and-run. Close-up photographs of the victim as well as of items of physical evidence must be taken. If the crime occurred at night, portable lighting should be brought in so that the area is adequately lit. The area should be examined for tire impressions and particularly for skid marks, which can be used to determine the direction and speed of the suspect vehicle and therefore are important in the case.

Trace items of evidence present on the victim's body are also important. Care must be taken when moving the deceased so as not to lose valuable trace evidence. When the deceased is brought to the morgue, clothing should be carefully searched for paint, glass, and other parts from the suspect's vehicle. These items should be packaged, tagged, and submitted to the crime laboratory for examination. If the victim was on a bicycle

Figure 15.7 This close-up of a physical match of broken pieces of a license plate holder proved a vehicle was associated with a hit-and-run accident. (Courtesy of the Los Angeles County Sheriff's Department.)

or motorcycle, it should be carefully examined. Various types of trace evidence, such as paint, may be present that can be used to tie the suspect vehicle to the crime. Lights from the victim's vehicle should be recovered and submitted to the laboratory to determine if they were operational and whether they were on or off. Clumps of soil or dirt found at the scene should be documented and collected. These can be compared with dirt found on the undercarriage of the suspect's vehicle and may demonstrate a connection.

The scene should be examined for specific damage to the unknown vehicle. Broken parts of the vehicle should be collected for possible physical matching. In certain cases, the vehicle's make and sometimes the model can be determined by these parts. This information may be helpful if the investigator contacts automobile repair body shops or parts stores to determine if anyone recently came in to have a vehicle repaired. Occasionally, the force of impact is so great that impressions from the vehicle are made on the victim's body or clothing. Such evidence should be photographed and preserved for later comparison. Airbags, if they have been deployed, should be cut out and sent to the lab for DNA typing. This can help determine who was driving the vehicle and the time of impact.

Paint chips are especially important items of physical evidence. If they are sufficiently large chips, it is possible to fit them physically into the vehicle in jigsaw puzzle fashion. Paint will, at a minimum, be useful to determine the color of the hit-and-run vehicle, and in some instances the make of the vehicle can be determined through laboratory examination. Further, physical and chemical comparisons of paint recovered at the scene can sometimes be made with that from the suspect's vehicle.

As part of the autopsy procedure, specimens of the victim's blood and hair should be collected for later testing. A toxicological sample of blood should be taken to determine whether the victim was under the influence of alcohol or other drugs. Clothing, as mentioned before, should be retained for fabric and fiber exemplars in addition to examining for patterns and other traces present. Once the suspected vehicle is found, it should be taken off the road to a nearby place for examination.

When the vehicle is first found, if any evidence or obviously damaged areas are noted that might be lost in moving the vehicle to a garage, then they should first be collected. If the owner of the vehicle claims that the car had been stolen, fingerprint examination is especially important to help prove or disprove this contention. The exterior of the vehicle should be thoroughly searched, including the undercarriage. The vehicle should be placed on a hydraulic lift to facilitate this examination. Evidence such as hair, blood, skin, and fabric and fiber evidence may be located there. Specimens of grease and dirt should be collected for comparison with debris found on the victim. The front area of the vehicle and the hood should be thoroughly examined. Occasionally, fabric impressions from the impact appear in the dust on the bumper. These should be carefully photographed with a scale, and if possible, the bumper or fender should be removed and submitted to the laboratory. All broken parts and damage to the vehicle are important items of evidence. Damages to the front end such as broken grills, headlights, scratched paint, other scratches, and other damage are to be carefully noted and, if possible, removed and submitted to the laboratory. In some instances, evidence from the motorcycle or bicycle that the vehicle hit may be present; these items should be preserved.

Known specimens from the hit-and-run vehicle should be collected. These especially include paint that should be collected in the area of any damage to the vehicle. If scrapes containing other paint material are noted, these too should be collected to be compared with the victim's vehicle. In some cases, the victim may have been hit and thrown onto the vehicle hood or windshield. Fingerprints belonging to the victim as well as hairs, fibers, and blood should be searched for with this in mind. If the windshield is broken, glass should be collected and a search made for hairs and blood. Headlamps and tail lights should be examined to determine whether they work and, if possible, they should be sent to the laboratory. Examination of the filament can determine if the lights were on or off at the time of impact. Broken headlamp lenses and signal light reflectors should be removed for comparison with evidence collected at the scene. Sometimes it is possible to make a physical match with these items.

Case

During a sailboat race on Lake Ontario, one boat was struck by lightning. The crew radioed to the race organizer that they were dropping out of the race and heading for Rochester, NY; this was the last contact with them. No SOS was sent and no search for the boat was undertaken. Three days later, an American fisherman found two bodies (tied together) floating with a beacon light attached to one of them. The beacon was lit at the time of the discovery. When the beacon later came into possession of Canadian authorities, the bulb was burned out. At the inquest, there was apparently conflicting evidence: the type of light bulb (no. 13) used can only last for approximately 2 hours with a set of new batteries. Thus, if the fisherman found the beacon lit, the boat must have capsized only hours before the bodies were discovered. The examining pathologist from the United States determined the bodies had been dead approximately 70 hours. SEM examination of the filament discovered two breaks, both while the bulb was hot (ON)—an indication that the bulb had a "second life." The conflicting evidence can be explained with the bulb's "two lives" (although it is not proof). In the case of the very fine filament in the lamp, the SEM has a considerable advantage over conventional microscopes in demonstrating the breaks and reestablished contact by providing a clear photograph with good depth of focus and a reflection-free image (Figure 15.8).

If tire impressions were made at the scene, photographs containing a scale should be made of each tire. Inked tire impressions on paper can be made for comparison with tire impressions

Figure 15.8 A scanning electron photomicrograph of a lamp filament showing that there had been a break that reconnected and then a second break. (Courtesy of the Centre of Forensic Science, Toronto, Canada.)

located at the crime scene. If the suspect driver is apprehended soon after the hit-and-run incident, a blood sample should be obtained. The sample should be submitted to the laboratory for testing for alcohol or other drugs to determine if the suspect was under the influence.

Case

Sometimes, what initially appears to be a motor vehicle investigation turns out to be very different, as this case demonstrated:

D. Cotton, a 23-year-old male residing on Vincent Street, Hendon (a suburb of Adelaide), South Australia, died as a result of a motor vehicle accident. He was the sole occupant of a Gemini sedan, which had overshot an intersection in the Adelaide Hills suburb and slammed into a solid stone wall. The Gemini was, in fact, registered to a Mr. Caffrey living on the same street as Cotton. When the police went to question Mr. Caffrey at his home about why Cotton had been driving his car, they found that he had been murdered. Caffrey's body had numerous knife wounds. The crime scene investigation suggested a sole assailant. The Gemini was examined, and a bloodstained knife was found in a plastic bag in the rear compartment. The tip of the knife had been snapped off. Postmortem examination showed stab wounds to the head. The possibility of the knife having left a piece of blade in the skull was confirmed when an x-ray revealed a small metal fragment lodged in the skull behind the left ear. A physical match between the piece of metal and the knife confirmed it as the murder weapon. Combined with the blood evidence (on the knife and a glove worn by Cotton) and the location of bloodied shoe sole impressions at the scene, which were similar in size and pattern to Cotton's shoes, the State Coroner was satisfied that Cotton had been responsible for the death of Caffrey and had stolen his car (Figures 15.9 through 15.12).*

---

* This case was submitted by Sergeant Ted Van Dijk, Police Forensic Science Section, South Australian Police Department, Adelaide, South Australia.

Figure 15.9 An apparent automobile accident led to an unexpected turn of events. (Courtesy of the South Australia Police Department, Adelaide, South Australia.)

(a)   (b)

Figure 15.10 (a) The police found the owner of the vehicle murdered. (b) The autopsy revealed numerous stabbings. (Courtesy of the South Australia Police Department, Adelaide, South Australia.)

(a)   (b)

Figure 15.11 (a) Burglary tools, including a bloody knife, were found in the vehicle. (b) The tip of the knife was broken off. (Courtesy of the South Australia Police Department, Adelaide, South Australia.)

(a)   (b)

(c)   (d)

Figure 15.12 (a) At autopsy, several head wounds were noted. (b) A small metal fragment was found in the skull. (c) A close-up of the fragment. (d) A physical match of the knife blade and the metal fragment leaves little doubt that they were once whole. (Courtesy of the South Australia Police Department, Adelaide, South Australia.)

Marks from Vehicles

Vehicle marks are composed of tracks of wheels or runners. In a specific case, there may also be an indication of a particular type of load, for example, slipping branches in a load of wood or ends of logs in a load of lumber, the smell of fuel oil or lubricating oil, etc. (Figures 15.13 through 15.21).

Wheel Marks

With the aid of wheel marks, direction of movement can be determined. When the ground is damp, the underlayer on which the wheel rolls forward is compressed and the bottom of the mark is formed as a series of steps. The compressed clods of earth in the mark are lifted in the same direction as the wheel is rolling. To assist the memory in this respect, it is easy to remember this rule: for the mark to become level again, the wheel must roll in the opposite direction. A vehicle that travels in a straight line actually leaves only the track of the rear wheels; to observe marks of the front wheels, it is necessary to find some place where the vehicle has turned sharply or reversed.

In examining wheel marks, it is necessary to look for places showing defects or repairs in the tires. With the aid of successive marks of this type, the circumference of the tire can be determined. The track is measured between the center points of the two wheel marks.

Preservation is achieved by photography and casting selected points showing characteristic marks or wear. When photographing, a scale is placed across the track and another along one side of it. Casting is done in the same way as for foot impressions (discussed in Chapter 9). In examining vehicle marks, it should be noted whether wheels that follow

(a)   (b)

Figure 15.13 A Porsche 924 Turbo was stolen and subsequently recovered, but it was missing numerous parts. Automotive parts suspected to have been removed from the stolen Porsche were found in a suspect's possession. Examination indicated that the rear axle link-mounting brackets exhibited sufficient detail for comparison purposes. (a) The right mounting bracket from the vehicle and (b) the right axle link-mounting bracket (reversed) are shown. To enhance the detail of the pattern present on the bracket, UV photography was used. (Courtesy of the Michigan State Police.)

(a)   (b)

(c)   (d)

Figure 15.14 Comparison of (a) wheels from a Porsche with (b) a corresponding mount from the victim's vehicle. Note that the negative has been reversed in (a). Photographs (c) and (d) show comparisons of the markings on each. (Courtesy of the Orange County Sheriff-Coroner, Santa Ana, CA.)

Figure 15.15 (a) Cut hoses in a vehicle theft and (b) a close-up physical match. (Courtesy of the Los Angeles County Sheriff's Department.)

Figure 15.16 (a) A small fragment broken from a vehicle next to the damaged area on a car fender and (b) the piece fitted into the damaged area from a hit-and-run case. (Courtesy of the Israel National Police.)

Figure 15.17 (a) A radio stolen from a vehicle and (b) the faceplate (shown reversed) left at the scene are compared and indicate a common source. (Courtesy of the Michigan State Police.)

one another go in the same track or whether there is any deviation. If dual wheels are found, both tread marks should be recorded simultaneously because the relationship of one tread pattern to the other provides additional characteristics for identification of the vehicle (Figure 15.22).

Skid Marks

The speed of the suspect vehicle at the time of impact is sometimes at issue. If skid marks are present at the scene, a traffic officer with training in skid mark interpretation should be contacted and requested at the scene. A forensic engineer should also be called in certain

(a)   (b)

Figure 15.18 A car that left the road struck a bridge abutment and threw a woman from the vehicle to her death. The officer arriving on the scene found a man unconscious in the backseat. The subject refused to identify the driver of the vehicle. The investigating officer submitted both of the man's shoes, as well as the brake and gas pedals, hoping the laboratory could find a pedal impression on the left side and a puncture mark in the leather. (a) These striations matched the 18 rubber ribs on the brake pedal, and (b) the puncture matched the location and size of the bottom banding wire from the bottom of the pedal, which was bent outward. The subject was subsequently convicted of vehicular homicide. (Courtesy of the Ohio State Highway Patrol.)

Figure 15.19 An investigator submitted a speedometer head to determine the speed of a vehicle at the time of impact. The speedometer dial was examined under UV light, and a "speed mark" was detected in the area of 20 mph. This speed mark is an imprint of the speedometer pointer (needle) on the dial caused by the force of inertia at the time of impact. (Courtesy of the Forensic Laboratory, Office of Attorney General, Pierre, SD.)

(a)   (b)

Figure 15.20 (a) Various imprints and impressions, including round and hexagonal marks found on a victim's coat from a traffic accident. The suspected bus driver denied hitting the victim; however, examination of (b) the bus's underside determined that part of the oil sump could have made the marks. Because several buses had passed the location, they were brought into a garage, and the sumps of each were examined and photographed. A random sample of additional buses was also examined. Because the bolt orientations were shown to be unique, the conclusion was made that the suspect bus caused the imprints. (Courtesy of the Israel National Police.)

Figure 15.21 A careful examination of victim's clothing collected in a hit-and-run investigation clearly showed paint transfer from the red painted car suspected of striking the victim. (Courtesy of the Illinois State Police.)

(a)   (b)

Figure 15.22 (a) A Kirkland tire with unique defects; (b) tire cast with unique marks. (Courtesy of the Los Angeles County Sherriff's Department.)

cases for accident reconstruction. Based upon factors such as the length of the mark and the coefficient of friction of the road surface, an approximation of the speed at which the suspect vehicle traveled may be calculated.

Investigations involving motor vehicles occur in many cases, such as vehicle thefts, abandoned vehicles, homicides, hit-and-run investigations, and so on. Physical evidence consisting of fingerprints, DNA, tool marks, glass, paint, fabric impressions, tire marks, physiological fluids, hairs, fibers, and the like should be carefully searched for, collected, and documented as in all crime scene investigations.

Chapter Questions

1. List the various types of criminal investigations that can be associated with a vehicle.

2. Which of the following motives would explain why a suspect stole a vehicle?
   a) Joyriding
   b) To sell the parts for profit
   c) To flee a crime
   d) All of the above
3. When processing a vehicle, why is it important to collect the most fragile evidence first?

4. Describe the proper procedures for examining an abandoned vehicle.

5. (True/False) The search of a vehicle in which a homicide was committed should be conducted with the same degree of care as would be used when conducting the search of an indoor or outdoor scene involving a murder.
   a) True
   b) False
6. When processing a scene involving the use of a vehicle as an improvised explosive device, which task is most important?
   a) Finding out the exact time the bomb went off
   b) Finding all metal parts of the vehicle
   c) Finding as many parts of the explosive device as possible
   d) Calling the FBI

7. You are the lead crime scene investigator processing the scene of a hit-and-run accident. Which of the following pieces of evidence would you be most concerned about collecting?
   a) Fingerprints on the victim's steering wheel
   b) Mud samples from the tires
   c) Tire standards from the victim's vehicle
   d) Paint transfer on the victim's vehicle
8. Which of the following can be used to determine the direction and speed of a suspect's vehicle in a hit-and-run accident?
   a) SEM analysis of the pieces of rubber from the tire
   b) Skid marks
   c) Glass debris field
   d) Location of vehicle parts
9. Describe what things should be examined when processing a suspect's vehicle in a hit-and-run that killed a pedestrian.

10. How would you properly preserve wheel marks?

Homicide Investigation   16

Of all major crimes, homicide investigation requires the greatest effort on the part of the CSI. The investigator is responsible for collecting a vast amount of evidence and coordinating information from various sources including witnesses, suspect(s), case detectives, forensic pathologists, criminalists, and district attorneys. Death investigation requires a team effort; only through cooperation of persons from many disciplines, coordination of efforts, meticulous attention to detail, and adherence to protocols can a successful conclusion of an investigation be realized. This chapter brings together many of the concepts discussed previously in the text and examines areas unique to the investigation of death.

The finding of a dead body is usually the starting point and initial focus of the death investigation. (Occasionally, a death must be investigated even when a body has not been found, though this is exceedingly more difficult.) The rules for the first officer to arrive at the crime scene are the same as outlined in earlier chapters. The first officer to arrive is required to secure the scene, administer life saving measures and summon EMS if needed, and finally notify homicide investigators if there is any suspicion that the victim has been murdered. Determination of suspicious death at this point is critical. In many cases, the first officer to arrive at the scene has erred and pronounced the death to be from natural causes, only to learn at a later time that the cause of death was the result of an unnoticed bullet wound. The point is that care and attention to detail are critical in these types of cases.

Once the investigation has begun, the investigator should attempt to find and identify all evidence that may be associated with the case. Even items that may seem unimportant and of no value should be considered potential evidence. In murder investigations, there is usually an abundance of evidence even in cases in which the suspect has attempted to clean up after the crime. Even in a so-called perfect murder, there will be much evidence to aid in the crime's solution. In fact, there is no perfect murder—only cases in which a deliberate killing could not be successfully prosecuted beyond a reasonable doubt.

In the majority of cases, it is not difficult to determine that the suspicious death was the result of a murder rather than a suicide or accident. More difficult are those cases that are staged, so at first glance they seem to be an accident or suicide. In those cases, the first officer and investigator must be thoroughly familiar with all aspects of homicide investigation. The initial analysis of the situation and the evaluation of the case require at least as much knowledge as the subsequent investigation of the crime scene.

The officer should keep in mind that if a supposed suicide is judged to be a murder, a serious error has not been committed, even though the investigation may become more extensive than is necessary. If, on the other hand, a murder is judged a suicide, the officer has not only failed in the investigation but may also have made the solution of the crime and the apprehension of the killer more difficult, if not impossible.

Murder, Suicide, or Accident?

When evaluating whether the deceased died from an accident or suicide or if death was caused by another person, it is generally best to suspect the worst—murder. Even if circumstances give the overwhelming appearance of suicide or accident, the investigation should be conducted in as much detail as possible. Murderers have been known to intentionally stage the death to appear to be an accident or suicide. The investigating officer must be aware of this possibility. Only through systematic and accurate investigation can a deception be revealed as that of homicidal intent.

When investigating cases of sudden death, the officer should attempt to evaluate the circumstances revealed at the crime scene as quickly as possible. The following questions should try to be answered as soon as possible: What was the cause of death? Could the deceased have produced the injuries or brought about the circumstances that caused the death? Are there any signs of a struggle? Are there defensive wounds on the victim? Where is the weapon, instrument, or object that caused the injuries or traces of the medium that caused death? Although these are only some of the many questions that will arise in death investigation, they are probably the most important ones for beginning the continued investigation.

Cause of Death

The first question the officer is required to answer is: What was the *cause of death*? It should be noted here that the determination of the cause of death at this time is the *apparent* cause of death and not the *actual* cause of death to be determined by the medical examiner through an autopsy. Determining the cause of death, whether it involves stabbing, shooting, strangulation, or other means, represents a starting point for the investigator and helps him/her to begin putting the facts and circumstances behind the death into focus.

In evaluating the cause of death, it is very useful for the investigating officer and/or medicolegal investigator (MLI) to have a good knowledge of the appearance of different types of injuries and wounds. The investigator is not expected to have the same expertise in this area as that of the forensic pathologist or medical examiner, but he or she must have at least a working knowledge of the subject to take the initial steps of the death investigation. An erroneous estimate of the cause of death may lead the investigation in a wrong direction and may even jeopardize the ultimate solution of the crime. For example, if an inexperienced officer mistakes a gunshot injury for a stab wound, the entire investigation may be sidetracked.

The officer should not confuse experience with expertise, for it is the province of the pathologist to determine the cause of death, no matter how much experience the investigator has. On the other hand, the officer's primary duty should be to keep in mind that success is usually the result of cooperation and teamwork between the medical examiner and the homicide investigator.

The MLI* can also play an important role at the death scene. In some jurisdictions, such as New York City, these professionals are physician assistants who have extensive

---

* The American Board of Medicolegal Death Investigators (http://medschool.slu.edu/abmdi/index.php) certifies individuals who have proven knowledge and skills necessary to perform medicolegal death investigations.

training in medicine and death investigation. They respond to death scenes to assist the medical examiner in their determination of cause and manner of death. The cause of death coupled with other evidence at the death scene helps the medical examiner to determine the manner of death: homicide, suicide, accidental, natural, or undetermined.

Suicide

Could the deceased have produced the injuries or brought about the effect that caused death? A determination of whether death was the result of suicide or murder is extremely important in the initial phase of the investigation. Usually, the decision is based on an evaluation of the injuries that resulted in the death and other factors about the deceased's mental and emotional state before death.

The common modes of death by suicide are drowning, hanging, shooting, poisoning/overdosing, jumping from heights, cutting arteries, stabbing, strangulation, and suicide by cop (the intentional act of provoking a police officer to shoot). These factors must be considered along with the physical and psychological ability of the deceased to accomplish the act.

A detailed examination of the crime scene should be undertaken to determine if the facts are consistent with the theory of suicide. For example, it is reasonable to expect the means of death, such as a weapon or poison, to be close at hand and in proximity to the body. Failure to discover a weapon in the case of a suspected suicide makes that possibility unrealistic.

The nature and position of the injuries are useful considerations in drawing a conclusion. Hesitation marks are quite common in suicide cases involving slashing of the wrists. Similarly, gunpowder tattooing located around a gunshot wound is consistent with the firing of a weapon at close range. Such facts would be consistent with suicide. Defense wounds, however, are not expected to be found on the hands or arms of a suspected suicide (Figure 16.1).

Wound location should be considered. The wound location should be within reach of the deceased, in the case of stabbing or cutting, generally on the wrists, neck, abdomen, or chest. A wound to the back of the head would therefore raise suspicion. Also, wounds are generally grouped in one area, as in the case of hesitation marks on the wrist.

Figure 16.1 Investigators need to be able to distinguish between defense wounds and hesitation marks. This is an example of the latter. (Courtesy of the Los Angeles County Coroner's Department.)

In suicides involving handguns, the victim usually drops the weapon or throws it up to several feet away when the arms are flung outward. In such cases, the floor or ground should be examined for dents or scratches resulting from the impact. Occasionally, the weapon is found in the victim's hand, but this is usually due to the gun or hand having been supported in some way at the moment of discharge.

No blood on the insides of the hands or on the corresponding parts of the gun grip is usually a good indication that the victim fired the shot if the rest of the hand is bloody. The same condition applies to knife handles when the victim causes the slashes. Bloodstains on the palm of the hand and the grip of the gun do not necessarily indicate murder. However, there is reason to be suspicious if the blood marks on the hand and grip do not match. In some cases, a murderer has placed a gun in the victim's hand after rigor mortis has set in.

Someone found dead in a room in which the door is locked from the inside is usually considered to be a case of suicide or natural death. The CSI should not, however, be satisfied with this simple conclusion. Because there are methods by which doors, windows, or other openings can be "locked" from the outside, the investigator should pay particular attention to unusual traces and marks on doors, locks, latches, windows, etc.

Suicide by jumping from buildings or bridges is not uncommon in large cities. The body may land at some considerable distance from the perpendicular. For example, in a jump from an 80-foot vertical cliff, the body was found 42 feet from the base. This circumstance may seem suspicious, but it is explained by the fact that the force of an outward jump continues to act on the falling body.

A determination of suicide should also be based on interviews with the deceased's relatives and friends and on information from a physician or psychologist under whose care the victim may have been. Instances in which the individual had a history of suicide threats or suicidal tendencies are, of course, significant to the investigation. A careful and thorough search for a suicide note at the crime scene, as well as at the victim's residence and workplace, is particularly important. Although such notes are frequently found in plain view, usually near the body, the note may have been written earlier and left in another location. In some instances, several notes have been written and placed around the house or even mailed to friends or relatives. The note should be examined by a document examiner to verify its authenticity. A forensic linguist may also be asked to determine authorship attribution.* The investigator should collect known handwriting exemplars for this purpose and search for the writing instrument and paper used. The document and envelope should also be examined for latent fingerprints and/or DNA. In most jurisdictions, the medical examiner takes custody of the suicide note and not the police department.

Motives for suicide should be considered. A terminal illness may prompt an individual to take his life, and so the investigator should gather information from the deceased's physician, prescriptions, medical records, etc. Poor financial situations may also be a cause, and an investigation of the person's finances and debts should be undertaken. Other motives such as marital or family problems, high stress, and psychological problems must also be investigated. Cases of bullying have also caused young people to take their life in recent years. Investigating a young person's social standing at their school and interviewing teachers and classmates should be done if the suicide victim is a student.

---

* The field of forensic linguistics has recently been growing in prominence. A forensic linguist determines cases of disputed authorship and confessions and uses linguistic knowledge and methods in a forensic context (see www.iafl.org).

In cases of mental disorder, it is not uncommon that killing family members precedes the suicide. These cases must be investigated as thoroughly as other homicides. If the killer in such an instance survives an attempted suicide, it will be necessary to produce evidence about the mental state of the defendant. Psychiatric evaluation of the defendant may be considerably influenced by the findings at the crime scene. Even if the suicide victim does not survive, the investigation must be conducted with care. Inheritance and insurance matters will be influenced by the order in which the victims died.

Cases of suicide in which none of the commonly accepted motivations is apparent—even after some investigation—do occur. The opinions of relatives or friends of the deceased who are reluctant to accept the fact of suicide should not unduly influence the investigator. In many cases, the motivations for suicide are so deeply hidden that they may remain a mystery forever.

Signs of Struggle

If obvious signs of a struggle are found at the scene of a death, the case may be decided from the start as one of death by violence by the action of another person. In a room, the signs of a struggle generally consist of bloodstains, pulled-out hair, overturned or displaced articles of furniture, rumpled rugs, marks of weapons, and injuries caused by the deceased in self-defense.

Signs of a struggle show most clearly when an injured victim retreated or when an attempt was made to avoid the attack. From the visible signs, the course of events can usually be reconstructed accurately. Bloodstains can be considered the best clues for the reconstruction of the course of events in a case of murder. Generally, no bloodstains are produced during the first stage of the attack before bleeding has commenced. If victims do not immediately become unconscious at the first blow, stab, cut, or shot, it can nearly always be assumed that their hands will become covered with blood from touching the injured parts of their body. If victims attempt to escape or resist, their blood-covered hands leave marks that often indicate their position in certain situations. After a struggle in a furnished room, a surprisingly large number of marks of bloodstained hands may be found on the legs of tables and chairs. A frequently occurring bloodstain is the typical one that comes from bloody hair. Bloody hair imprints are often found on the underside of tables and chairs.

Those who examine the scene of a crime should look very carefully for bloody prints on doors (and especially keys, door handles, and knobs), telephones, hung-up clothes, draperies, curtains, and the like. If blood has spattered on a door, it is not sufficient to state on which side; it is necessary to consider the position of the door when the blood was spattered against it and from what direction it came.

Drops of spattered blood can indicate how far the drawer of a piece of furniture was pulled out or whether the door of a closet, kitchen cupboard, or other piece of furniture was open during a struggle. An especially important clue is a footprint in blood. Usually, such a print is blurred and hardly suitable for identification, but it may be possible to decide whether it was made by the victim or the criminal. One should not forget to pull down any window shades to look for marks on them. The parts of the legs of tables and chairs that touch the floor should also be examined. Any voids or areas that show an absence of blood can also be important clues.

Pulled-out hair found in a case of death from violence is a certain indication that a struggle has occurred. When found, it should be collected immediately because it can easily disappear or alter its position, for example, from a draft.

Overturned and displaced furniture gives a good idea of the direction in which a struggle moved or the route by which the victim attempted to escape. Chairs, pedestals, lamps, and other light pieces of furniture fall in the direction in which the struggling persons are moving. If there is reason to suspect that a criminal has righted overturned furniture, the articles should be examined for possible fingerprints or touch DNA. When a print is found on a light piece of furniture, its position should be examined carefully; a firm grip on a chair may give rise to the suspicion that the chair was used as a weapon. When heavy furniture has been displaced, the amount of force required and the way in which this force acted should be determined. Furniture placed irregularly often gives the impression that it has been displaced from its position. Marks of scraping indicate displacement and the floor generally shows clearly whether furniture has stood in the same place previously. Rumpled rugs often provide signs of a struggle, while marks of sliding on the floor sometimes form a useful guide (Figure 16.2).

A murder victim lying in a position of self-defense may kick against a wall, the floor, or furniture and the shoes then leave marks of shoe polish, dirt, and rubber scraping. Such marks should also be looked for on the undersides of furniture.

Marks of weapons may occur, for example, when an ax or other swinging weapon is swung and scrapes the ceiling or slips along a piece of furniture, or when the victim avoids the blow and the weapon hits the wall, floor, or furniture instead. In the case of murder with an ax or similar weapon, a frequently occurring mark is formed on walls or ceilings when the criminal swings the weapon up and back before striking. A bloodstained weapon may also leave cast-off stain patterns on the ceiling or passive blood drops on the floor where blood dripped off the weapon. It could also produce a transfer stain at a place where it was laid down or dropped.

Defense injuries are a fairly certain indication that a fight has taken place. In cases of suicide and accidental death, marks are often found that at first sight appear to be marks

Figure 16.2 Bloodstain pattern after dragging a body through blood at a training exercise. (Courtesy of Cedar Crest College, Allentown, PA.)

Figure 16.3 A shoemark impression in mud was found in the woods far from the road at this outdoor crime scene. A good quality photo using oblique lighting as seen here can help the examiner compare imperfections seen in the impression to the questioned shoe.

of a struggle. Persons weary of life may have taken a number of measures at various places to shorten their life. In a state of confusion, the individual may overturn or move furniture and also leave blood and other marks that at first cause suspicion. A careful investigation of the scene, however, can give a clear picture of the true course of events.

In cases of death by violence outdoors, signs of a struggle are in general not as distinct as those indoors. If a fight preceded the murder, the ground will be trampled. When footmarks made with shoes of different sizes and appearances are found or if the marks have the form that results from feet set down obliquely against the ground, these marks must be considered as evidence of a fight. At the scene of a suicide, especially in a case of hanging, the ground may be trampled, but as a rule the marks have the normal appearance of those of a person walking (Figure 16.3). Other signs of a struggle outdoors may be bloodstains, pulled-out tufts of hair, marks of weapons, and resistance injuries. Broken twigs, trampled leaves, torn-up moss and grass, footprints at places that a person would normally avoid, and other such indications can also be considered signs of a struggle.

Location of Weapon

In cases of violent death, the cause of death must be decided as soon as possible so that a search for the weapon, tool, instrument, or other lethal object can be conducted. The absence of a weapon or instrument at the scene sometimes indicates murder. If the weapon or instrument has been found, then the analysis of the situation must give a preliminary decision as to whether it is a case of murder or suicide. In searching for a weapon, nothing should be moved or altered at the scene of the incident; if evidence may be destroyed in the search, then the search must be postponed. If the weapon is found, it should be photographed and described in the position in which it is found. A pathologist should be consulted when it is necessary to determine which kind of object or weapon could have caused the injuries found on the victim.

Examination of a Dead Body at the Crime Scene

Before examining a dead body, the police officer should consider all the precautions to be taken during the course of the work. A careless move—even one so slight as undoing a button or lifting a flap of a garment—may subsequently prove to be a great mistake. An example is on record of a police officer who, in misdirected zeal, proceeded so far with the examination of a dead body that an attempt was made to determine the track of a bullet and depth it had penetrated into the body by probing the wound with a pencil. Such measures are entirely misguided.

When clothing is found on the body, it must be examined at the same time as the body, but if a pathologist is not present, the examination should include only the visible parts. The clothing's position and state should be described in the report including, among other matters, how clothes are buttoned, attached, creased and wrinkled, marked by injuries and stains, and so on. Any marks, cuts, or tears made by paramedics in life saving measures should also be noted. Discarded gloves, gauze, bandages, and other medical equipment left at the scene by paramedics should not be confused with actual evidence. In cases where necessary, paramedics should be asked to provide fingerprint and/or DNA samples for elimination purposes.

The position of the clothes—for example, how far the pants are pulled up, whether garments are twisted sideways or pulled down, backwards, or even inside-out—may be of great importance. Any displacement from the normal position is measured. Buttons and other fastenings, such as zippers, safety pins and casings, are described. Unbuttoned or torn-off buttons are indicated, as are buttonholes. Shirts should be checked to determine if they button right to left or left to right. Sometimes, men wear women's clothes and vice versa.

Folds in the clothes should be examined, especially on the lower parts of the body. The report should indicate whether the folds go horizontally or vertically and if they have resulted from crumpling of the garment. When a body is dragged along, horizontal creases occur that are dirty on the outside but clean in the folds. When a body is lifted or moved by a grip on the clothing, characteristic formations are produced. If the raised part of a fold is bloodstained but the inner part is free from blood, then the position of a part of the body when violence was exerted can be determined. If a garment is bloodstained and sharply delineated clean areas are on the inside of the bloodstain, then the fold formation can be reconstructed.

Damage to the clothes occurs from tearing, crushing, cutting, or penetration by edged weapons, ax blows, etc. The damage should be measured and the report should contain statements of the type, position, size, and manner of occurrence of the damage. In pertinent cases, the damage to the clothes should be compared during the autopsy with the position of corresponding wounds on the body. In this way, important information can be obtained regarding a particular body position when the injury was inflicted. Mannequins can also be used for this purpose to examine trajectory and other reconstruction scenarios.

Stains may consist of blood, semen, saliva, phlegm, vomit, feces, urine, or other liquid, as well as dust, dirt, or other contamination. They are described with reference to type, location, size, degree of wetness, and, in pertinent cases, direction of flow. If liquid stains go through clothing material, it is necessary to determine from which side the liquid has penetrated.

In describing blood marks on a dead body or crime scene, some of the terms generally used are bloodstain, swipe, wipe, spatter, drip stain, expirated blood, parent stain, satellite stain, insect stain, and several others. The Scientific Working Group on Bloodstain Pattern Analysis has established recommended terminology along with definitions to standardize

(a)

(b)

(c)

Figure 16.4 (a) Expirated blood with characteristic air bubbles. (b) High speed photograph of blood being expelled from the mouth. (Courtesy of Jeff Buszka and Norm Marin, SIU, NYC OCME.) (c) Blood revealed under the linoleum floor at a crime scene. (Photo courtesy of Wendy van Hilst, Forensische Opsporing Amsterdam-Amstelland, Amsterdam, the Netherlands.)

the jargon in this field. This will allow investigators to be on the same page when teaching, discussing, writing, or testifying about these stains.*

Important information can be obtained from blood, saliva, phlegm, vomit, urine, or other liquid stains on a dead body if the direction of flow is observed. Especially, streams of blood can contribute to the reconstruction of events in a case of death by violence. All marks of blood flowing "in the wrong direction" or against gravity are examined and photographed. These suggest that the position of the body was moved.

A special form of bloodstain is expirated blood (Figure 16.4a and b). When a person continues to breathe or cough after blood has entered the air passages, expiration patterns can be found. These sometimes contain air bubbles in them and look similar to other spatter patterns. The presence of air bubbles does not always indicate that the blood has been

* www.swgstain.org

expired, as air bubbles can also result from a transfer stain. Investigators should be very careful in not overstating opinions resulting from bloodstain pattern analysis.

Occasionally, a case of murder occurs in which the criminal wipes or washes the blood away from the victim. Such cleaning is generally easy to detect, especially when the skin is clean around the wound. Washing or wiping the hands generally leaves a thin rim of blood on the nails near the cuticles. When the blood has coagulated, small rolls of blood and dirt are often formed and penetrate cracks and hollows of the skin. If blood has been washed from the head, this fact is often easily detected by the traces of blood that remain in ears, nostrils, and hair. Moisture around the body may also reveal washing with water.

In connection with the occurrence of blood at the scene of a crime, some attempt should always be made to estimate the amount. If blood has flowed out onto an absorbing layer, the depth of penetration should be determined. Floorboards should be lifted, carpet rolled back, etc. (Figure 16.4c).

Murder

Case

A woman was found lying dead outdoors, with her head partly shattered by a number of ax blows, from which it could be assumed that most of the blood had been lost from the body. Under the head of the dead woman, only a small amount of blood, possibly half a pint, was found. From this it appeared that the woman had not been murdered at the place where she was discovered. On further investigation, the majority of lost blood was found at a place about a quarter of a mile from the body. It was determined that the woman had been murdered there at the primary crime scene and that the body had then been transported to the secondary scene where it was found. If the small amount of blood at the place where the body was found had not been noticed, it is possible that that place would have been considered the scene of the crime and investigated as such, while the actual primary scene of the crime would never have been known. Investigation of the latter produced evidence against a local suspect who later confessed to the crime.

In examining a dead body, it is generally possible to take the necessary steps in a certain order, which is a guarantee that nothing will be forgotten or neglected. The various steps in an investigation when a pathologist is present are described next. If the pathologist or MLI does not arrive in time, the investigation is carried out in the same way, but the CSI's moves must be evaluated so that clues that only a medical expert is capable of judging and investigating are protected as much as possible.

The first measure that should be taken without delay is to confirm the appearance of signs of certain death, of which the type and development and the time of their confirmation should be noted in the report. This is sometimes performed by paramedics if they are on scene when they fail to revive the victim.

The body is then photographed. Preferably, all photography should be completed before the position of the body is altered. If for some reason a change has been made after it was discovered, for example, when relatives cover the body or EMS performs life saving measures, the actual position should be photographed first and then the original position is reconstructed and photographed. The camera should be held in readiness for additional pictures during the course of the examination. In addition to digital photos, different types of digital panoramic recording systems should also be used to accurately document, measure, and map the crime scene. One such system is the PanoScan Mark III.* These types of systems can be beneficial to quickly and accurately document the crime scene and create a permanent record that can be gone back to days, months, or years after the incident. The scans also serve as excellent courtroom exhibits for juries to show how the crime scene appeared.

A preliminary investigation of the pockets of the dead person may precede the more detailed investigation only when it is considered absolutely necessary. This is to be avoided if possible, but it may be necessary to confirm quickly whether there are any identification documents, wallet, purse, watch, or other valuable articles in the pockets. This examination must be done carefully so that the original position of the clothes can easily be restored later. It should be noted whether the pockets are turned inside out—this may reveal that they have been previously gone through, possibly by the perpetrator.

A written sketch of the position of the body is then made. The body's position in relation to the nearest article of furniture, object, or fixed point is measured and noted. Then the visible clothing is described. The next step is the detailed examination. Only visible details are examined and described. The original position must not be changed. It is preferable to describe the head, then the trunk, arms, and finally the legs.

The head is described and examined in relation to its position with respect to the body, whether the eyes and mouth are open, color of the skin, injuries, presence of blood, state of the hair, presence of saliva, phlegm, vomit, and foreign bodies (soil, sand, vegetable matter, hair, etc.). The direction of flow of liquids is easily determined on the skin of the face and should therefore be noted.

In examining the trunk, notes should be made of its position, any bending or twisting, the position of visible clothing and condition, folds, injuries to the body and clothes, and the presence of blood, saliva, semen, phlegm, vomit, and foreign bodies (especially hair).

Then the arms and, finally, the legs are examined in the same way as the trunk. The hands should be given special attention. The presence of rings, jewelry, or a wristwatch or marks left by these objects should be noted. Foreign objects are examined, especially fragments of hair or skin under the nails. The hands should be enclosed in clean paper bags tied securely at the wrists. Collection of fingernail scrapings and/or clippings should be taken during autopsy. When examining the legs, the distance between the knees and between the heels should be measured. Special attention should be given to the soles of the feet or shoes with respect to the presence of blood or other material in which the person may have stepped.

After examining the visible parts of the body, the police officer should attempt to visualize the course of events as deduced from observations. The officer's judgment should not be relied on solely; the opinions of others, especially the pathologist or MLI, should also be considered. From a number of opinions it is often possible to get a good reconstruction of the events.

The underside of the body and those portions covered by clothes should not be examined at the scene, unless it is done in the presence and at the request of the pathologist or MLI. Normally, the body will not be turned over or undressed until the time of the autopsy. However, after the body has been photographed and described in all pertinent detail and has been lifted onto a stretcher, the area under the body should be examined. A critical

---

* See http://panoscan.com/DemoVideo.html for a video demonstration of how this system works.

piece of evidence may have been hidden under the body, perhaps in a large pool of blood. Bullets, or fragments of bullets, sometimes penetrate a body completely but are stopped by clothing. The projectile may thus roll out of the clothing of the victim and may even be overlooked, unless great care is exercised in lifting and transporting. The relationship between the location of injuries and bloodstains on the floor should also be established.

The body should be transported in the position in which it was found, if possible. If necessary, the clothing can be fixed in its original position by means of pins. In appropriate cases, the body should be moved on a clean sheet of cotton or plastic, in a body bag, or on an undertaker's impregnated paper sheet. This is partly to protect the body from contamination and partly to prevent minute evidence from being lost.

An officer should accompany the body to the hospital, medical examiner's office/ morgue, or other place where the autopsy is to take place.

Detailed Examination of the Scene of the Crime

After the preliminary investigation has shown that death was caused by the intent or agency of some other person or by suicide or accident, the detailed investigation can begin. How thoroughly this is to be done must be decided for each particular case. In suicide or accidental death, the detailed examination can be limited simply to those matters that appear to be directly related to events. If the death is caused by the intent or action of another person, everything should be investigated, even in cases where the criminal has been arrested immediately after the crime and has confessed. (There have been several cases where confessions have been thrown out or disallowed in court, so one should not rely on them exclusively.) In such cases, the investigation should decide whether the statements of the criminal are consistent. In a first statement, a criminal often makes consciously incorrect statements about personal actions to create extenuating circumstances. Those who investigate the scene of a crime have an opportunity of producing such an accurate reconstruction of the actual course of events that such an attempt by the criminal to evade cannot succeed.

When the examination of the body has been concluded, the body can generally be removed for the autopsy. Photographing the scene of the crime should have been completed before this.

Before the body is taken away, the places at the scene where coroner personnel will need to walk should be examined for evidence that might be destroyed, including the presence of blood. Even if the body is wrapped up well, drops of blood may fall from it as a result of unforeseen circumstances. Such marks can cause much unnecessary work for the investigators later. Those who carry away the body should be warned not to step in any blood.

As a rule, the investigation can then be continued with attention to such details or places where anything of significance might be expected. A methodically planned examination of the scene of the crime as a whole then follows, which will be the basis for the report of the investigation. It is started at a suitable point and everything is inspected in such a way and in such an order that nothing is forgotten. It may be convenient first to examine and describe the entrance, doors, and lock arrangements. Then a description of the room as a whole follows. The length, width, height to ceiling, windows, doors, floor covering, paint on walls and ceiling, color of wallpaper, lighting conditions, and other features should be described. Next, the room is described in detail and investigated in a certain order beginning from the entrance or from the place of death. Everything must be examined and described as a coherent whole. For example, if a writing desk is examined, then a description follows of the nearby parts of the floor and walls and also of the surface of the floor under the piece of furniture. As a rule, it is best for the ceiling to be described and examined last and as a whole. If for some reason a place has been examined in detail and described earlier, then a reference to it is put in the notes to facilitate writing of the final report.

In the investigation everything is noted, even if it appears to have no significance in the case. Such unessential details are sorted out when the report is written, as are similar details that appeared to be important at first but were later found to be immaterial. The notes made at the scene of a crime must not under any circumstances be thrown away but should be placed in the file and kept with the records. Experience shows that such rough notes may be of great importance at some future date if the investigator is required to prove that the examination of certain details was not omitted. It is convenient to develop and preserve fingerprints and palm prints at the same time as the final detailed investigation.

As far as possible, everything should be put back into its original position. When furniture is moved, it should be replaced with the greatest accuracy because the scene must be in its original state in case the suspect or witnesses are returned to the scene for questioning. Before any furniture is moved, a mark should be made around the legs or other suitable parts. Objects placed on furniture can be treated similarly.

A final important step after the sketching of the scene of the crime is measurement. It is desirable to do this earlier, but this may not have been possible because of a risk that those who did the measuring might have destroyed evidence not yet discovered or produced fresh and misleading clues. One method that can be used is to have a preliminary sketch made as early as possible. Gradually, as the investigation proceeds and before each object is moved, measurements are made and recorded on the sketch. This method is somewhat inconvenient, however, because the measuring cannot be done as systematically as is desirable. Under such conditions, even experienced sketchers can easily forget important measurements. Laser scanners and software programs, such as the DeltaSphere-3000 and SceneVision-3D®, are excellent tools that can record measurements quickly and accurately. The scanners rotate 360° capturing thousands of laser data points that can be easily fashioned into a three-dimensional (3D) model (Figure 16.5).

When there has been a shooting at the scene of the crime, it is necessary to look for weapons, cartridges, cartridge cases, and bullets. If a weapon is found, it is photographed at that spot and a chalk line is drawn around it before it is moved. The weapon should always be made safe before sending it to the lab. In cases of presumed suicide, it is necessary to check whether the weapon lies in a place to which it might have dropped or slid. The base on which the weapon lies should always be examined. A dropped or thrown weapon generally leaves a mark, such as a scratch or dent in the furniture or floor, and the absence of such marks should be considered suspicious.

When cartridge cases are found, their position should be noted in the report, on the sketch, and on the envelope into which they are then placed. Bullets and bullet holes are examined. The place from which the shot was fired can be determined quite accurately from the direction of the bullet penetration—a string is stretched along the calculated path of the bullet. The reconstruction is then photographed. Lasers and dowels can also be used (Figure 16.6). A bullet that has buried itself in a wall is cut out, but great care must be used so that the tool used does not touch the bullet. In cases of suicide, the shooter may

Figure 16.5 Three-dimensional models along with measurements of a mock crime scene. (Photo courtesy of DeltaSphere, http://www.deltasphere.com/.)

Figure 16.6 Using sequential image burning to demonstrate the path of a laser in a mock trajectory reconstruction. (Thanks to Brian Gestring for demonstrating this photographic technique.)

fire one or more trial shots before firing the actual suicide shot. Chemical tests can also be performed to see if the suicide victim was actually the one holding the gun.

Case

In a search for a young successful model and her boyfriend, the police arrived at a Jerusalem apartment where they had been living. The door was locked and the telephone went unanswered. The boyfriend's brother forced entry through a porch door and let the police in. They found the dead bodies of the couple. A loaded gun was found next to the girl's right hand. Her index finger was clutching the hammer of the gun (Figure 16.7a).

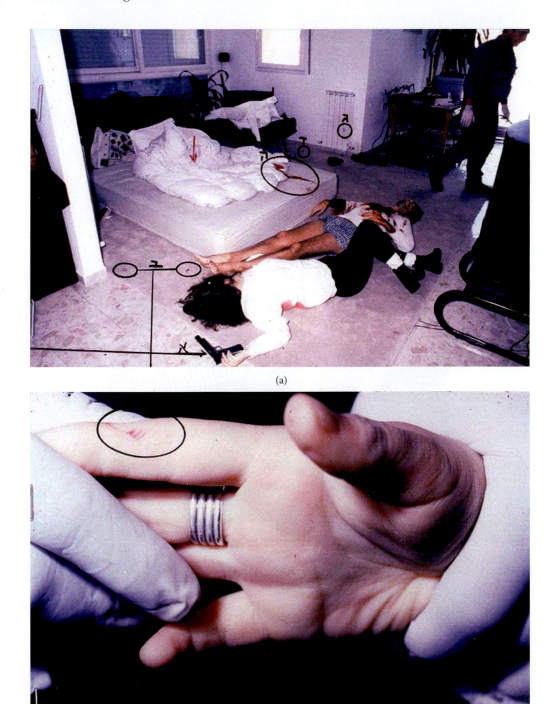

Figure 16.7 (a) The gun lying next to the girl initially led investigators to believe she had shot her boyfriend, then killed herself. (b–d) Further investigation, including testing with Ferrotrace, showed that the woman had never held the gun. (e) Testing of the boyfriend's hand, however, revealed he had held the gun both in the typical shooting position, and in the reverse position indicative of suicide.

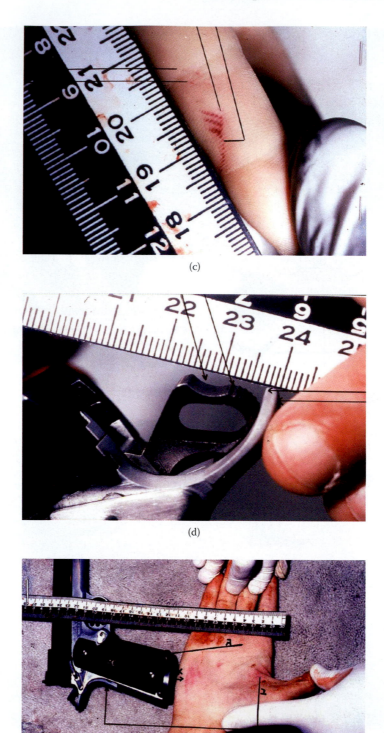

(c)

(d)

(e)

Figure 16.7 (*Continued*)

The man had two bullet holes in his chest, both fired from close range. The girl had one bullet entry wound in the lower section of her left breast and an exit wound on the right side of her back.

In his preliminary assessment, the medical examiner assumed that before committing suicide the woman killed her boyfriend, since he had been shot twice with heavy caliber bullets, and the gun was found next to her. This was also the message released to the media. After the medical team completed their examinations, Ferrotrace (manufactured by Ezra Technology, Jerusalem, Israel and distributed by Arrowhead Forensics) was applied to the hands of the two bodies. (The appearance of a violet-magenta stain on the hand is the result of a chemical reaction between the reagent and iron found on the gun).

The reaction on the woman's index finger was exceptionally strong; its shape matched the upper back of the gun's hammer. There was one puzzling question, however, which had to be answered. The reaction on the finger that touched the gun was very intense, but there was no reaction on the palm of the hand. (Figure 16.7b through d) The absence of a palm reaction raised the suspicion that the woman never really held the gun and that it had been placed near her hand only after her death. The primary suspect in moving the gun became her boyfriend's brother, who had helped the police enter the apartment. Ferrotrace examination of the boyfriend's right hand indicated that he held the gun both in regular position (typical of shooting) and in reverse position (typical of suicide, with the thumb on the trigger, and the index and middle fingers on the safety) (Figure 16.7e). The fact that there were two bullet holes in the man's chest and only one in his girlfriend's did not change the police's conclusion that it was he who shot the girl, then committed suicide. Multiple shots as part of suicide are a known phenomenon when the first shot is not immediately fatal. (*Division of Identification and Forensic Science, Israel National Police.*)

The following is a list of certain details that should be examined where appropriate. Because it consists partly of items of a changeable nature, they should be examined immediately or as soon as possible, especially those easily forgotten or passed over even by an experienced investigator:

- *Stairs, passages, and entries to the scene, together with streets, passages, and yards in the immediate vicinity.* Are there bloodstains or fingerprints on railings (mirrors can be used to help locate these on the underside of railings)? Are objects present that the criminal has dropped or thrown away? Is there illumination? Do trash cans contain evidence? If there is an elevator, the elevator shaft should be examined. Video surveillance footage should also be reviewed to determine possible probative pieces of evidence the suspect might have handled.
- *Outer doors.* Are they bolted and/or locked? Are there marks of breaking in? Does the doorbell work?
- *Windows.* Are they bolted? What is the position of the window catch? Are there marks of breaking in or a possibility of seeing in? What is the position of curtains and blinds? Are there indications of marks outside the windows?
- *Mailbox.* What is the date on mail or papers? Are they in the right order of time?
- *Other papers and mail, newspapers, etc. at the scene of the crime.* Are there date marks? Have letters been opened or do papers give the impression of having been read?

- *Inside doors.* Are they bolted and/or locked? On which side is the key?
- *Hall, entrance.* Are clothing and objects present that do not belong to the place and residents there, especially outer garments, headgear, scarves, gloves, galoshes, umbrellas?
- *Lighting.* Which lamps were on when the crime was discovered? What are the electric meter readings?
- *Television, stereos, MP3 players.* Have they been left on or off?
- *Heating conditions.* Is there a fire or embers in fireplaces or any remaining heat? Do not forget to examine ash and burned residues and the setting on the thermostat.
- *Cooking conditions.* Is the oven or stove on or is there any remaining heat? Was food or drink preparation in progress? In what condition is the food in the refrigerator?
- *Odors.* Gas; gunpowder; strong tobacco fumes; alcohol; perfume; decomposition?
- *Clocks and watches.* Are they running and showing the right time? When did they stop? Is there a time set on the alarm clock? What are the time stamps of e-mails sent or received?
- *Signs of a party.* How many bottles are present? Are there labels on them and what are their contents (not always the same as the label)? Are seals or corks on or in the bottles? How many glasses or cups of different kinds are present? What are their contents, and is there a residue or odor in them? Has liquor been spilled or objects overturned? Have cigarette butts and matchsticks been thrown on the table or floor? How many persons was the table set for and what dishes? Are there any fingerprints? Are the beverage containers suitable for DNA testing?
- *Contents of ashtrays.* Are there remains of smoked tobacco or brand marks on cigarette butts? How were they extinguished? Are there marks of lipstick or burned matches? Remember that DNA and fingerprints may be present on cigarette butts.
- *Drawers and compartments in writing desks, cabinets, or other furniture.* Are they shut and locked? In which drawer is the key? Have drawers been pulled out or taken away or have objects been taken out of them? Are there signs of disorder such as might result from a hurried search? Are cash, bank books, and objects of value exposed in a conspicuous or easily detected place?
- *Wastepaper baskets, trash cans.* Has any object been thrown there by the criminal? Are there torn letters? Did the perpetrator throw out any latex gloves he might have been wearing?
- *Kitchen, bathroom, toilet.* Are towels, rags, and like objects damp or do they show bloodstains? Are there bloodstains on the counter, bath, sink, toilet, or buckets? Are there objects or suspicious liquids in the water trap or toilet? Are there fingerprints on any used paper? Is there evidence that the perpetrator tried to clean up?
- *Damage to ceiling, walls, and furniture.* Investigate how it could have occurred in connection with the crime; marks of plaster or paint soon disappear from the floor due to trampling.
- *Garments taken off.* At what places and in what order, beginning from top, were they taken off? Are they turned right side out or inside out? Are they properly hung up or in disorder? Are there clothes in the washing machine? Hamper?
- *General disorder.* Is this typical of violent happenings or a struggle; can it result from lack of cleaning up over a long period, or incidentally, for example, in carrying out ordinary household operations, etc.

- *Shooting.* The investigating officer should be able to account for the actual number of bullets fired together with a corresponding number of cartridge cases, or give a good explanation of why they are not found or cannot be found in the correct number (consider the possibility of a cartridge case getting caught up in the clothes of the dead person and not being found before the autopsy).
- *Hanging and strangling.* Quickly confirm whether the cord used was taken from the scene or locality. Was it strong enough to support the weight of the deceased?
- *Suicide note.* Is it in the handwriting of the victim? Has the writing instrument been found? Has indented writing come through onto the paper underneath? Is there more than one note? Are there fingerprints or DNA of persons other than the deceased?
- *Hiding places for weapons or objects that the criminal wished to conceal quickly.* Some of the places most often forgotten by the investigating police officer are locations above appliances and high furniture or between these and the wall, behind books in a bookcase, among bedclothes in a bed, behind heating elements, and on high shelves in wardrobe, pantry, and kitchen cupboards. Ordinary items with false bottoms sold in spy shops should also be considered, such as cans, books, and the like.
- *Compost heaps, manure heaps.* These are very convenient for concealing objects without distinct signs of digging.

It is suggested in cases of serious crime that when the investigation has been concluded, the scene of the crime be kept intact until the final report has been written and read through by the superior officer and the prosecutor, recovered evidence has been examined, and the postmortem examination has been completed. It is not uncommon for a second or third visit to the crime scene to be made to collect additional evidence. When material recovered for examination has value as evidence, it should be preserved even after the criminal has been tried. There may be a review of the case, perhaps several years or decades later, and the evidence may then need to be produced.

Outdoor Crime Scenes

The examination of a crime scene located outdoors must be planned quickly and carried out as soon as possible (Figure 16.8). Changes in weather conditions may completely jeopardize the chances of finding evidence that is there. A number of different clues easily detected at first may disappear in a very short time, for example, by precipitation, drying, vegetation, flood conditions, animals, etc. It is even more difficult to examine such a scene at night.

Because bloodstains on grass change color rapidly, they are difficult to detect. A brief shower may completely wash away smaller stains. Other biological evidence, such as hair, seminal fluid, urine, feces, vomit, saliva, nasal secretions, skin fragments, brain substance, and so on, is quickly changed by drying or may be washed away. During the time of year when insects are particularly plentiful, biological evidence may be destroyed by their action. The path of a person through dewy grass may be discernible to the naked eye, but after an hour or so of direct sunlight, the dew is dry and the grass has recovered its original shape. It may subsequently take hours before this track can be followed. Footprints and tire marks should therefore be protected and recorded as soon as possible.

When a shooting has taken place outdoors, the direction of firing must be determined quickly. Fresh twigs and leaves that have fallen to the ground usually mark a bullet's path

Figure 16.8 Identification of decomposed remains requires techniques such as forensic odontology, forensic anthropology, and/or DNA typing. This victim was murdered and dumped in LA County's high desert, where animals consumed the facial tissue and hands. (Courtesy of the Los Angeles County Sheriff's Department.)

through foliage, bushes, or hedges. After a few hours, these traces may have taken on the appearance of the surroundings. Evidence of a bullet striking the ground is usually found in the form of dirt or sand thrown over the surrounding vegetation. A passing shower may wash off these traces and make the location of the impact impossible to find. Cartridge cases may be trampled into the ground. A metal detector might then be the only way to find such evidence.

The crime scene must be effectively roped off and the investigating officer must follow a definite plan of action. Experience has shown that officers who carelessly and aimlessly wander around the area put some of the evidence found at outdoor crime scenes there.

In cases of suspicious death, the officers can anticipate that the person, or persons, who discovered the body did not enter the scene with caution—which is to be expected. One of the first duties of the CSI is therefore to find out where those persons walked. The record of many cases has shown that clues created by these citizens have caused a tremendous amount of unnecessary work that could have been avoided if the person had been properly interviewed.

Case

On a winter day, a neighbor called the police to report the discovery of an apparently deceased female who was located behind his neighbor's residence. He informed the 911 operator that after noticing the body, he had proceeded behind the house to confirm his observation. When the officer arrived at the scene, he met him at the front of his neighbor's residence and stated that he had walked around the right side of the home (as viewed from the front) to view the body and returned by way of the same route. The officer and the caller then proceeded around the right side of the home to view the body together.

When other police officers arrived to the scene, the responding officer had secured the entire scene for protection. He had observed that fresh, undisturbed snow was located to the left and right prior to them walking around the home. The scene was processed with one key piece of evidence in mind; there were only four sets of tracks when there should have been six. The caller had already multiple times locked himself into his story of proceeding around the residence to double-check on the status of the body, therefore arousing suspicion.

During the processing of the scene, crime laboratory personnel discovered additional tracks leading away from the decedent. These tracks did not lead to the front of the house but to the neighbor's backyard through an opening in the fence. Since the caller became the main suspect, he was placed under surveillance. Soon after he was observed dumping several trash bags in a dumpster on a neighboring property. The crime laboratory personnel were called and the bags were retrieved and determined to contain bloody clothing. There was then significant evidence to obtain an arrest warrant for the suspect. (*Provided by Suffolk County Crime Laboratory, New York*)

In making up a plan of action, the officers should decide on a path to be used in going to and from the body. Because this path will be used frequently, it may be marked with stakes. The examination of the body then follows according to the outline given earlier in this chapter. Before too much attention is given to the body, the ground around it should be carefully examined. A second chance will hardly be available after a number of persons have looked at the body and trampled the area. The area surrounding the central scene should then be examined.

The investigators must try to remember their own tracks so that they can distinguish them from others that may be discovered. On snow-covered ground, this is easily accomplished by investigators dragging their feet so that their own tracks become distinctive.

Insofar as possible, examining outdoor crime scenes at night should be avoided. This rule should be followed even when suitable illumination is available. Most clues at outdoor scenes consist of minor changes in the ground cover, such as matted grass, torn moss, broken twigs, indistinct footprints, and the like. Such tracks may be visible from several yards away in daylight but are almost impossible to detect at night even with powerful illumination. If a scene is viewed at night and an estimate made of the topography, it might be found in daylight that the picture is quite different. Because it is difficult to survey the scene and correctly interpret even gross evidence, it follows that it is even more difficult to find evidence as small as bloodstains, fragments of cloth, and fibers. Such evidence may be overlooked or destroyed if a thorough examination is attempted in underlit settings. In these cases, an officer should be placed at the scene to guard the scene overnight until a proper search can be conducted in the morning.

Prevailing weather conditions or expected weather changes play an important role in deciding whether to postpone the examination until daylight. If there is a chance of snow or rain, the examination must be started even if important evidence may be destroyed.

Depending on the type of crime involved, other weather conditions may also have a certain influence. If snow falls before the examination is completed, some evidence may be covered and not retrieved until the snow has melted. In these situations, large tents can be set up over the crime scene during snow or rainfall.

Before the arrival of daylight, certain precautions should be taken. Some flash exposures should be taken of the body. The body should then be covered with a clean sheet over which is laid a tarpaulin to keep out dust, leaves, and other debris. If the body is suspended, the noose may break, and it is advisable to secure the body with a rope tied loosely around the chest. If the body is on the shoreline, it should be lifted far enough onto the beach so that swells will not make changes on the body.

In taking the photographs and the precautionary measures, the officers should not walk around aimlessly. As described earlier, a path should be selected and marked with stakes. The investigator should, of course, make note of changes that may take place on the body, such as signs of death, moisture on the clothing and under the body, and so on.

Discovering a Body Hidden at Another Location

When a homicide victim has been moved from the actual crime scene and hidden at another location, conditions are somewhat different. Although the examination of such places is generally carried out in the same way as at crime scenes, a reliable reconstruction of the crime is usually more difficult. Such locations normally do not yield as much evidence of the perpetrator as the place of attack.

The question often arises as to how long the body has been lying at the place where it was found. The vegetation and other surrounding conditions may give some indications. The path over which the body was transported should be established at the outset. This detail should be attended to immediately, especially when there is risk of precipitation. If the criminal's footprints are not clear enough, the path should be estimated as that most easily traversed if someone were carrying a body. Even when there are no footprints, other signs may be present, such as trampled grass, stains of dripping blood, marks from dragging, broken twigs, etc. If the criminal left the scene by another route, this path should also be examined at that time.

The body should be examined as described earlier in this chapter in the section "Examination of a Dead Body at the Crime Scene." Dust, dirt, and other traces on the skin and clothing that might fall off during transport should be recovered. A preliminary evaluation of such traces may suggest leads for the search for the actual scene. In removing the dead body from the place where it was found, it should be placed in a new body bag, clean plastic sheet, or bed sheet that is then wrapped around the body. Blankets and tarpaulins should not be used because one can never be sure that they are absolutely clean. Because it is difficult to examine and recover trace evidence on the body properly, it should be transported intact to the place of autopsy where the detailed examination can take place.

After the body has been removed, the area underneath it should be examined. The amount of blood and body fluids should be estimated. It should also be determined how deeply into the ground such fluids have penetrated. If the murder weapon is expected to be found in the area, a search for it should be started. If branches, straw, and the like were used to cover the body, they should be examined for the possibility that the criminal may have dropped something while engaged in this activity.

Investigation of a Greatly Altered Body or Skeleton

Often difficulties arise in the identification of a dead body that has undergone such a great amount of alteration that only the skeletal parts remain. Important information can be obtained from a skeleton found whole or dismembered after a very long time or even after burning or other destruction of the body. Clothing or other objects found near the remains can also be used to help identify the deceased (Figure 16.9).

Such bodies or their remains are most frequently discovered outdoors; occasionally, they are found indoors in a cellar, attic, basement, heating furnace, or other places. The remains may be those of a person who was murdered, run over by a vehicle, or committed suicide, was lost and became the victim of exhaustion or exposure, or was suddenly overcome by sickness and death.

Figure 16.9 Skeletal remains found in remote areas offer a special challenge to the investigator. In this case, absent anything more than part of the pelvis, leg bones, and shoes, a forensic anthropologist may only be able to provide the gender, height, and race of the victim. DNA typing can also help identify the remains through the national DNA database—CODIS. Missing person reports and debris scattered in the vicinity of the remains can offer additional information. (Courtesy of the Los Angeles County Sheriff's Department.)

From what has been said, it follows that the nature of the place where the discovery is made can vary considerably. Remains may be found under the ground or under a floor or the like; they may be lying in the open, covered with brushwood, moss, sacks, and so forth, or overgrown by vegetation. If the body was originally in the open outdoors, then the remains (both bones and clothing) are often dispersed over a large area owing to animals having dragged them away. It is not uncommon for remains and objects with some connection with them to be found several hundred yards away from the main site. This also applies to parts of a dismembered or burned body that have been buried or left on the ground because different parts may have been concealed or buried at different places, often far apart (Figure 16.10).

Foreign objects connected with the body or with transport of the body to the site (bags, sacks, cords, etc.), which possibly form the sole proof of a crime and may even indicate how to trace the criminal, may also be found near the remains. A number of cases have occurred in which a correctly performed and accurate investigation of the place of discovery, combined with careful technical and pathological investigation of the remains of the body and other related objects, has led to the identification of the body. In order for the best result to be obtained, the investigating officer needs a good knowledge of the proper method of investigation and preservation of the remains and objects and of the factors that affect distribution of the objects within a larger area.

The detective also needs to know the special methods used for further investigation of the discovery and how these methods can assist in determination of gender, age, and race of the deceased and of the time elapsed since the objects were first placed there. This knowledge is absolutely essential if the detective is to pay the necessary attention to the

Figure 16.10 A body was dumped in a wooded area. By the time it was discovered about 24 hours after the killing, animals had already attacked and eaten a significant amount of it. (Courtesy of the Los Angeles County Sheriff's Department.)

possibly small and apparently insignificant objects that are especially significant in these respects. The precise determination of the characteristics necessary for establishing age, gender, stature, and so forth must be left to the forensic anthropologist. Likewise, the investigator must use the services of entomologists for the life cycles of insects, of botanists for growth rates of roots, grasses, and other plants, of meteorologists for weather conditions that might suggest the time of repose of the body, as well as any other experts whose special knowledge will assist the investigation.

Scene of Discovery

The task of investigating the scene of discovery includes searching for and recovering the remains of the body and all the objects in the area that may be of value for identification. (The methods of identifying human remains are discussed in detail in Chapter 6.) As in all cases in which a body is found under such circumstances that a crime is suspected, the police officer should contact the medical examiner so that right from the start the latter has an opportunity to become familiar with the case. For the purpose of identifying the body, the expertise of a forensic odontologist (dentist) may be needed to compare antemortem dental records to postmortem dental x-rays of the deceased. The forensic biologist can also help to identify the deceased by comparing the DNA type from a known sample (toothbrush, hairbrush, biopsy sample, pap smear, electric shaver, etc.) to the DNA type developed from the remains. The procedure for the investigation is, of course, not always the same.

Outdoors

A discovery outdoors may be one of three different types according to whether the remains are found buried, lying exposed on the ground, or in water.

Remains that have been buried usually come to light during digging, construction, or other similar operations and are generally purely historical finds from old burial sites and the like. (They can also be from much more recent acts used to hide or dispose of a body.) The police officer called to such a scene should first photograph it in the state in which it was found and then expose the body with great care. During this work, preferably done with assistants and in the presence of a forensic anthropologist and/or forensic archeologist, detailed photographs should be taken as necessary to show the position of the body, noteworthy details or conditions, etc.

In exposing the body, special attention should be given to the occurrence of any filling material above it that differs from the surrounding earth, to any objects used as covering near it, and to any foreign material or bodies in the ground or near the body. It has happened that quicklime has been placed on bodies to accelerate the decomposition and make the identification difficult. If anything of this kind is suspected, a sample of the earth should be taken so that it can be examined. Attention should also be given to the properties of the earth (type of soil, dampness, pH, etc.) because this is very important in deciding the length of time the body has been buried.

The color of bones can vary from light grayish-white to dark brownish-black, depending on the age of the find, kind, and properties of the soil, whether the parts are or were enclosed or covered in some way, or the measures that may have been taken with the body before burial, that is, burning. It is often difficult to distinguish between small bones and stones, twigs, or other debris; therefore, the search should be carried out with great care and all remains, even if very small, should be kept and examined by an anthropologist. Certain very small bones and also the teeth are very important for determining the identity of the deceased. If the skeleton is much disintegrated, the earth should be sifted through a small mesh sieve (Figure 16.11a and b).

Of great importance for investigation and identification are all remains of clothing and other objects that may be connected with the find, for example, contents of pockets, buttons, ornaments, rings, coins, etc., and objects that may be connected directly with the crime or transport to the scene of the crime, such as ropes, cords, sacks, bullets,

(a)

(b)

Figure 16.11 (a) After the attack on the World Trade Center in New York City on September 11, 2001, this process of distinguishing between small bones and other debris was never performed before on such a large scale. A special piece of equipment, seen here, was custom-built for the purpose of sifting through large amounts of debris to identify and collect human remains. The work continues as of this writing 10 years later to identify the remains of 9/11 victims at the New York City Office of Chief Medical Examiner. (b) Very small fragmented human remains. (Courtesy of the NYC Office of Chief Medical Examiner.)

duct tape, garbage bags, duffel bags, or objects pushed into the mouth of the victim. Such loose objects are looked for and kept with great care because the risk of breaking into pieces may be great. Objects on or attached to the remains are not moved from their position before the discovery has been fully revealed or unearthed. The position of loose objects in relation to the remains of the body should be accurately marked, sketched, and photographed.

In taking possession of bones and especially of remains of clothing and the like, attention should be given to their association with any vegetation. Roots of trees or shrubs that have grown through them form a valuable aid in determining the length of time the object has been there. A determination of the age of a root of a tree that has grown through clothing gives a minimum value for the time the object has lain in the ground; this can be used as a starting point for further investigations and calculations. As far as possible such roots should be cut off and allowed to remain with the object; otherwise, they must be kept and labeled with the necessary information on their origin.

At the scene of the discovery, attention should also be given to the occurrence of insect larvae and pupae or remains of them on the body. They are placed in a conical tube or other suitable container for examination by an expert forensic entomologist. For example, remains of fly larvae found on a buried body indicate that it was above ground for a certain period of time before being buried; the stage of development of the insect, larva, or pupa can give further valuable information. The amount and type of insect activity can also yield other clues about such things as the time of death.

If only a part of a body is found, then dismemberment may have been carried out before burial. In such a case, a large area of the surroundings must be investigated carefully, with attention directed especially to all changes in the surface of the ground that give the impression of having been produced by human agency. The character of the ground, the possibility of burial at different places, etc., must then be used to guide the search. In some cases, police cadaver dogs can be used to help with the search. Ground penetrating radar is a tool that can be used to search for anomalies in the earth that could reveal evidence of a clandestine grave. Additional staff should be brought in when large areas need to be searched. A sketch should be made of the terrain, giving the place where each object was found, and photographs taken. Using Google Maps® can be helpful in this process. In photographing, each site is marked with a number or letter visible on the photograph and these are also shown on the sketches. The objects found at the different sites are placed in cartons or boxes marked with the number or letter given to the discovery location in the photographs and sketches.

A search for evidence in the vicinity of such a discovery, for example, evidence of the criminal, vehicle tracks, or the like, usually has a low payoff because of the long time that has generally elapsed since the crime was committed. However, marks on stems of trees or the like from vehicles, a bullet, and so on can be found after a comparatively long time, so a routine search should be made if the find is thought not to be too old. It should be remembered that trees and bushes might have grown considerably since the crime, so metal detectors can be helpful in these searches.

The discovery of a dead body found lying exposed on the ground is usually made in a forest, on a mountain slope, or at other remote places.

If dismembered body parts are discovered, the investigation of the scene must be extended to cover a large area. In this case, it is quite normal for the parts of the body to be scattered over a number of places at some distance from one another. The same applies, however, to bodies that have not been dismembered because various animals and birds can drag the parts for a distance of up to several hundred yards from the original site.

Careful attention must be given to those cases that appear to be hiking, mountain climbing, or camping accidents. These may be the result of an attempt to cover up criminal assault or robbery. Lone hikers or naturalists can be easy prey for criminal attacks. Special attention must be paid to the absence of valuables, minor bruises from subduing blows, and evidence of soil or vegetation not found in the immediate vicinity. The investigation of a discovery of this kind is made in exactly the same way as for a body that has been buried. Special attention should be given to the relation of the vegetation to the find because this may be decisive in determining the length of time the body has lain there. Under the remains at the original site, smothered plants may be found or possibly no vegetation at all. Plants may have started to grow over the remains. If the body has lain there for several years, grass, undergrowth, moss, or other vegetation may have completely concealed part of the remains. The remains may have gradually become covered with a layer of soil or leaf mold from falling leaves and dead plants. Roots of trees and bushes may grow through parts of the find and especially remnants of clothing. The vegetative conditions should be described carefully, stating the type of vegetation and supplemented with photographs on which the different remains are marked in the manner described earlier. Any tree or other roots that have grown through the remains are kept for a determination of their age. If there is no risk of the roots falling out of the remains when they are collected, then the roots should be removed with them. A sketch should be made as described previously.

The place of discovery should be cleared and any remains and objects found kept. If necessary, the earth is sifted and may be preserved for further examination or soil analysis. The character of the ground, that is, type of soil, dampness, etc., is described. If there are signs of foreign matter such as lime, samples are taken. When exposing the body, attention should be given to any indications of its having been covered with stones, leaves, brushwood, sand, and the like. When necessary, detailed photographs are taken (Figure 16.12a and b).

If remains of a body are found in water, it is generally much more difficult to investigate the place of discovery accurately, unless it is merely a small pool that can be drained. It must be remembered that currents, ice, floating timber, and other items may have carried parts of the body to places a long way from the place of discovery. Also, the find may be a body part that has been carried to the place of discovery in the same manner, possibly from a considerable distance.

If the discovery has been made in a harbor or river in which there are steamers and motorboats, propellers may have caused some of the injuries on the body. A propeller can cut off a leg or arm in such a way that it appears as if the body has been dismembered intentionally. Injuries to tissues and organs produced in this way often show clean cuts, as from an edged tool. Feeding by aquatic life can also be mistaken for injuries. Besides having crime scene experience, investigators of underwater crime scenes need to be expert divers as well. The Professional Association of Diving Instructors offers courses in underwater crime scenes. The Florida State University also offers a certificate program in underwater crime scene investigation.*

---

* http://www.pc.fsu.edu/Academics/Certificate-Programs/

Indoors

It is very rare for remains of a body found indoors to undergo as extensive degree of change from decay or other causes as in the preceding cases. There have been cases where a body has been buried in a cellar or cut up and burned in the furnace of the heating system or when remains of a dismembered and/or burned body have been placed in a suitcase in an attic or garage. The procedure in such a case is the same as that described above.

If a body has been buried or if remains have been found in a suitcase, sack, or the like, then all objects that have been used to conceal the body or for wrapping are of special interest (Figure 16.13). With such discoveries, the floor, walls, and ceiling of the place should be examined for bloodstains and objects should be looked for that might be supposed to have been used in connection with the crime.

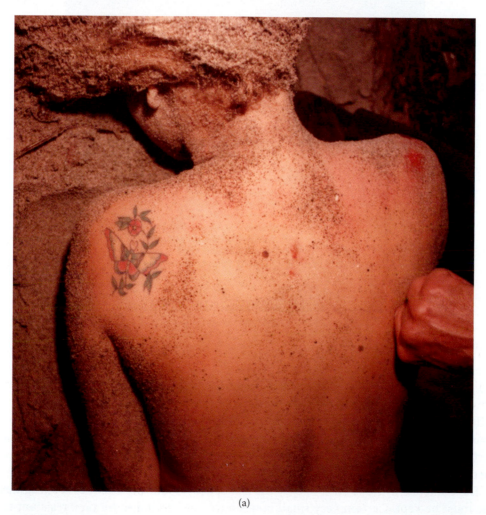

(a)

Figure 16.12 (a) The body of a nude female was found buried in the sand on a beach in Los Angeles County. The unique butterfly tattoo on the left shoulder was used to help identify her. (Courtesy of the Los Angeles County Sheriff's Department.) (b) This adult male was missing for 2 weeks and was eventually recovered on a beach after drowning in the ocean. The condition of the facial tissue from being in the water so long obviously prevented visual identification, so the victim was identified using dental records. (Photo courtesy of C.M. Bowers, DDS, JD, Ventura, California.)

(b)

Figure 16.12 (*Continued*)

For example, if a heating furnace has been used to burn a body, it should be examined very carefully. After a cremation, the volume of the bones of an adult amounts to 2 to 3.5 liters (3.5 to 6 pints). In a freshly burnt state, the bones have a white to yellowish or grayish-white shade, which quickly changes to brown or brownish black in the ground. At a certain state of burning, the bones are soft and may assume peculiar twisted forms that depend to some extent on the underlayer.

The contents of the firebox and of the ash space should be sifted; every fragment of bone must be kept. Certain very small bones have been found to be very resistant to fire and may therefore be valuable for determining the age and gender of the deceased. Teeth are especially valuable. The crowns of teeth generally break up and split under the action of heat, but the roots often remain whole. On the other hand, teeth that have not erupted (e.g., with children) rarely break up and do not change in form or shrink to any appreciable extent; after burning, they have a whitish color and a chalky consistency. It is even possible to recover DNA from the pulp of a whole tooth because of the hard enamel that protects it.

(a)

(b)

Figure 16.13 (a, b) This body was discovered in a suitcase. (Courtesy of the Los Angeles County Sheriff's Department.)

In searching for and taking possession of burnt skeletal remains, great care should be observed owing to their fragile nature. If remains that are especially brittle or liable to fall to pieces are found, they should be packed separately in test tubes, containers, or cartons according to size, with cotton, tissue paper, or the like as underlayer and filling for the container.

Packing and Transporting

Packing the remains of a body with any associated objects to be moved or sent to an expert should be done so as to eliminate any danger of destruction or falling apart of associated objects as the result of shaking or other movement. A skeleton with the long bones still hanging together, with or without remains of soft tissues or organs, should be packed in such a way that it will remain in that state during transport. Styrofoam, rags, tissue paper, or similar materials can be used as filling in the container and for the support of parts so that they do not rest on the bottom. Well-burnt remains should be transported in the custody of a police officer who keeps the package under control at all times and ensures that it is not exposed to shocks or jarring. Suitable packing materials are thin soft paper, soft and flexible cloth, tissue paper, cotton, and the like packed in the container so that the object has a soft support and is also supported in a definite position (Figure 16.14).

Figure 16.14 Charred human remains transported carefully in a body bag to the morgue. (Courtesy of the NYC Office of Chief Medical Examiner.)

Examining Remains of Clothing and Other Objects

The investigation of any remains of clothing and other objects has as its objective the determination of the original appearance of the garments, kind of cloth, color, and so on, and the detection of any manufacturer's or laundry marks. Shoes are examined for maker's marks, size, repairs, and other identifying marks. Any object found in the clothes or at the scene is investigated, keeping in mind that it may be characteristic of a certain trade or in some other way give information about the deceased or conditions in connection with the death (murder weapon, suicide weapon, objects used in transporting the body to the place, objects thrown away or forgotten by the criminal, etc.). In these investigations, special attention should be given to everything that might assist in determining the length of time the remains have been there, for example, alterations resulting from weather conditions, penetration of roots and other parts of plants into clothing, etc.

Everything that arises from this investigation is combined to form, if possible, a description of the deceased and an explanation of the cause of death, time of death, and so on; this information can subsequently be used for identifying the body as some person reported as missing, tracing the criminal, checking the statements of a suspect, and other such objectives.

The examination of any remains of clothing or other objects that may be found and can be connected with the discovery of remains of a body is a matter for the police officer, who can call in the assistance of experts if necessary. The pathologist should always be given the opportunity to be present and should be informed of the results of the examinations because these, like the investigation of the scene of discovery, are closely connected with the pathological investigation. Before the examination is commenced, all objects should be laid out to dry on a table because this facilitates the work considerably.

Clothing

Roots or other parts of plants that have penetrated portions of clothing should be kept and provided with a label showing type of garment and vegetation; afterwards the material is given to a botanist for determination of age. From tree and shrub roots that have penetrated the remains, it is possible to determine the minimum period of time that the object has lain at the site. In the case of *unburied* remains, this estimate must be increased by 1 or 2 years because the material must first "merge" into the soil before it can be penetrated by roots.

The type of cloth, color, type of garment, and the question of whether it is ready-made or tailor-made are determined, possibly with the assistance of an expert. An expert should preferably also be called in to decide the length of time the material has been lying there from any changes in the garments resulting from climatic effects. Manufacturer's and laundry marks are looked for, using an ultraviolet lamp in the latter case. Buttons and the manner in which they are sewn on (by machine or hand) may be significant, as are any repairs in the garments. The remains of clothes are examined also for damage caused by edged tools, firearms, vehicles, and similar objects that may possibly correspond to marks and injuries on the body. The assistance of the pathologist is required for this. The nature of the damage can often be determined with certainty. Damage caused by animals may also occur on clothing, but this can generally be distinguished from other damage. The remains of underclothing and stockings or socks are also examined for color, textile material, manufacturer's marks, other marks, repairs, etc. Depending on the condition of the clothes, clothing can also be scraped near the collar, cuffs, underarm areas, headband, and the like for skin cells to be used in DNA typing.

Boots and Shoes

The original color of boots and shoes may be difficult to determine because of changes to the leather by the action of earth, dampness, etc. The name of the maker, which is sometimes embossed, may be inside or at the back of the heel, or at other points on the inside; stamped marks may sometimes be a guide for identification. The make, size, and types of any rubber soles or heels are also significant. The size of shoes can be determined from the length. Sometimes, a distinct impression of the sole of the foot and the toes can be observed on the inner sole of a shoe and this may be of value for comparison with shoes that may possibly be found in the house of a missing person. Shoe repairs may also help in identification.

Other Objects

Of great importance for identification are all objects found in the pockets of clothing or at the scene of the discovery that may be suspected of having belonged to the deceased. These objects are examined carefully, looking for name, initials, trademarks, and other markings. The description of a missing person may mention such objects or possibly relatives may be able to identify them as belonging to the deceased. It may also be important to determine the application of a particular object, which may be characteristic of a particular trade. A particular collection of objects may be typical of a hiker or a person interested in sports, fishing, photography, or hunting, for example.

Estimating the Time of Death

In cases of murder, suicide, or suspicious death, the determination of the time of death is very important. The most reliable estimate of the time of death comes from a variety of sources: postmortem changes such as body temperature, rigor mortis, lividity, and decomposition and information developed during the investigation such as the last time the victim was seen alive. The correct estimate of the time of death is important when interviewing suspects in a homicide investigation. Such information can serve to eliminate a suspect who was elsewhere at the time of death or establish opportunity, that is, the suspect could have been with the victim at the time of death. The investigator should realize that the estimate of the time of death is only an estimate. In some cases, a more precise determination can be made if the death occurred at or near the time of another event that was known.

Postmortem Signs of Death

After death a number of postmortem changes occur that are useful in determining, within limits, the approximate time of death. The various methods available are useful to make estimates, that is, ranges of times. The precise moment of death can be determined only in rare instances, such as when a bullet stops a clock. The amount of time between the death and discovery of the body also has a bearing on the time-of-death estimate. Generally, the shorter the time interval between death and the discovery of the body, the better is the estimate of the time of death.

Changes in the Eyes

After death, changes become noticeable in the eyes. The cornea becomes dull and a film may appear over the eye. This may appear within several minutes to a few hours depending on whether the eyelid is open or closed, temperature, humidity, and air current. Because of these factors, clouding of the cornea is not considered a reliable indicator of the time of death.

Temperature of the Body

Cooling of the body, or *algor mortis*, is another sign of death. The rate of cooling depends on several factors, including body temperature at the time of death, temperature of the environment, body covering and clothing, and relationship of the surface area to body weight. The body temperature will continue to fall or rise until it reaches ambient temperature, which usually occurs in about 18 to 20 hours.

Core body temperature is generally considered one of the more reliable indicators of the time of death up to approximately 18 hours. The usual way to determine core body temperature is to insert a thermometer into the liver. A comparison between that temperature and ambient temperature is used to determine the approximate time of death.

Rigidity of the Body

Immediately after death, the body becomes flaccid. Biochemical changes in body muscles produce stiffening, known as *rigor mortis*, which usually appears within 2 to 6 hours after death. Rigor mortis is most notable first in the small muscles such as the jaw and fingers and is complete within 6 to 12 hours. The rigidity remains for 2 to 3 days and disappears gradually.

An examination of the body for rigor mortis can help indicate the time of death. If the rigidity is broken, it will generally not reappear unless the body is in the very early stages of rigor mortis. The victim's muscular development will affect the intensity of the rigidity. The very young and very old will likely develop less rigidity than adults with well-developed musculature.

Lividity

After blood circulation stops, blood settles to the lowest portions of the body because of gravity. This is known as *livor mortis* and is noted by the appearance of blue or reddish-violet marks on the skin (in cases of poisoning by carbon monoxide, cyanide or cold, the marks are "cherry red" and with potassium chlorate poisoning, light brown). The first indications of lividity occur in approximately 1 hour, with full development after 3 to 4 hours. Lividity can sometimes be confused with bruising or black-and-blue marks. The pathologist can differentiate between the two during the autopsy.

Under certain conditions, lividity can move or change if the body is moved or the position of the body is changed. Postmortem lividity does not form on parts of the body exposed to pressure, for example, parts that lie against the floor. If the position of the body or the position of articles of clothing pressing on the body is changed within 3 to 4 hours, the original lividity discoloration may partially disappear and a new pattern form. After this time, at least some of the original discoloration will remain. Even 9 to 12 hours after death, and sometimes later, new but successively weaker patterns are produced when the position of the body is changed, although the discoloration that was first formed is usually fixed by this time and does not change. If there was a large blood loss, livid stains will be weak. As a rule, fresh livid stains are not produced by a change in position more than 12 hours after death. Lividity discoloration may provide a limited indication of the time of death but can demonstrate a change of position or movement of the body several hours after death.

Decomposition of the Body

The most certain sign of death, one that cannot be misinterpreted by anyone, is the beginning of putrefaction. Decomposition, or putrefaction, is a combination of two processes: autolysis and bacterial action. Autolysis, the softening and liquefaction of tissue, occurs by means of chemical breakdown of the body. Bacterial action results in the conversion of soft tissues in the body to liquids and gases.

Putrefaction begins immediately upon death and generally first becomes noticeable within 24 hours by a discoloration of the skin in the lower abdomen and groin. The discoloration has been described as greenish-red, blue-green, and even black and is pronounced within 36 hours. Bacterial action produces gases causing the body to swell up, while an unpleasant odor becomes quite noticeable. The swelling is particularly noticeable in the penis, scrotum, breasts, and other areas of loose skin attachment.

Blisters filled with watery fluid and gas appear on the skin, which gradually darkens in color. Material from tissue breakdown (purge) may exude through the mouth, nose, and anus. Within 3 days, the entire body shows signs of decomposition. The environment affects the rate of decomposition of the body. Colder temperatures tend to impede putrefaction while warmer temperatures increase it.

Similarly, if the body is placed in water containing a large amount of bacteria, such as that from sewage effluent, decomposition is accelerated. A body in water generally decomposes more slowly because of colder temperatures and lack of oxygen. Because the body has a greater specific gravity than water, it sinks initially. Prolonged submersion in water causes a wrinkling effect around the skin of the hands and feet. The body orients itself in a head-down position that sometimes results in scraping of the forehead when it comes into contact with the rough sea floor. After a period of 3 to 4 days in warmer water and about a week in cold, the body will surface owing to the formation of gas. Sometimes the skin and tissues burst and the body sinks again to the bottom. The process may repeat itself and the body floats to the surface again (Figure 16.15).

When a body is buried in a shallow grave with loose earth, it is destroyed fairly quickly; in 1 to 3 years all the soft tissue will disappear. The skeleton remains much longer. These time figures will vary greatly according to the type of soil, amount of water, acidity, drainage, and other such factors. In peat bogs, for example, the body will remain relatively well preserved for many years. Bodies buried in clay soil decompose at a slower rate than in other soils. In certain cases, bodies are relatively well preserved through mummification or the formation of adipocere, a wax-like substance caused by hydrolysis of body fat.

Figure 16.15 A body found floating in the Hudson River just to the west of Manhattan. The missing hands and feet are due to injuries from marine animals. (Courtesy of the New York City Office of Chief Medical Examiner.)

In very dry conditions, putrefaction is retarded and mummification may begin. It can become complete in warm, dry air or when a body is buried in dry, porous earth. Formation of adipocere occurs in bodies located in damp environments such as a swamp, wet soil, or even water. Adipocere is characterized by reasonably well-preserved external contours of the body; its formation is noticeable in about 6 to 8 weeks, with complete formation in 18 months to 2 years. When a body lies in a cellar or other damp place, it may become completely covered with mold, leaving black marks on the body. Buried embalmed bodies may also have mold present. (The Anthropological Research Facility, or "Body Farm," at the University of Tennessee conducts research on human decomposition in a variety of settings. More information can be seen on their website at http://web.utk.edu/~fac/.)

Action of Insects and Other Animals on a Dead Body

When a dead body lies above ground, it is generally destroyed quickly by the action of insects and their larvae. Different kinds of insects lay their eggs in the body and these rapidly develop into larvae (maggots) that, when weather conditions are favorable, can appear in such numbers that the dead body positively "teems with life" (Figure 16.16). The body of an adult can be completely destroyed in less than 2 months, with only the skeleton remaining, and that of a child in less than a month. The insects that appear on a body, to feed on it or to lay their eggs in it, always come in a certain definite order, depending on the state of decomposition of the body. This question has attained great importance in medicolegal practice because, by examining the insects found on a body at a particular time, it is possible to obtain a good idea of how long it has lain at a particular place.

Figure 16.16 The lifecycle of maggots found on the body can be used to help estimate the time of death. (Courtesy of the NYC Office of Chief Medical Examiner.)

As a rule, the first insects that attack the body are flies. Even before death actually occurs, the flies may begin to lay their eggs in the body, usually in the mucous membranes—for example, in the eyes, nose, and mouth—but also in wounds and bloody parts of the body. The eggs are white and about 1/16 inch long, and are laid in clumps. On a body lying indoors, they come especially from common houseflies (*Musca domestica*). This may be a significant point in the investigation because if eggs, larvae, or pupae of houseflies are found in a body lying outdoors or buried, it must be concluded that it has previously lain indoors. On bodies lying outdoors, chiefly common bluebottles (*Calliphora erythrocephala*), greenbottles (*Lucilia caesar*), and sheep maggot flies (*Lucilia sericata*) lay their eggs. Flies can also lay their eggs in bodies buried in shallow graves. After only 1 to 2 days, the larvae of the fly come out of the eggs and immediately commence their work of destruction, changing into pupae after 10 to 14 days; after a further 12 to 14 days, the flies come out, to multiply again in their turn after a couple of weeks.

Among the beetles that live or multiply on a body, burying beetles and other kinds of carrion beetles appear on a dead body. Carrion beetles, as their name implies, are an important part of a vast host of scavengers responsible for recycling decaying materials. When a body is buried immediately after death, insects are not able to lay their eggs.

Certain types of boring worms accelerate the decomposition process in the body. Some fly species can live and multiply for long time periods in a buried body.

When larvae, pupae, or insect eggs are found on a body or in clothing, it is possible to estimate the shortest time during which it has been at the scene. This applies also to fully developed insects that, in their natural course, must have gone through all the stages of development in the body. A forensic entomologist should perform these examinations.*

If insects are to be sent for expert examination to an entomologist, they are first killed by placing them in a killing jar that contains a few cotton balls soaked in fresh ethyl acetate. After immobilization, they are then preserved in 75% ethyl alcohol. Insect eggs, larvae, and pupae are killed and preserved by placing in 70% to 80% alcohol.

Animals often attack unburied bodies. Rats attack the projecting parts of bodies, such as nose, ears, and fingers. When they attack the hands, the injuries may produce the impression of being defense injuries. When such injuries are discovered, the pathologist should examine them immediately because they dry comparatively quickly, making it difficult to decide on their origin. Other animals may also produce injuries to a body and sometimes eat it. Gulls, ravens, and crows may eat the loose tissues, for example, in the eye sockets. Bodies in water are exposed to injury from lampreys, crabs, lobsters, water beetles, and mackerel. Eels use the hollows of the body as hiding places, but do not eat it to any extent. Starfish cause injuries by attaching themselves firmly.

Other Indications of Time of Death

In certain cases, the pathologist can draw conclusions from the stomach contents and intestines regarding the time of the last meal, its quantity, and composition. The investigator can assist the pathologist by relaying any information found with regard to the composition of the last meal.

Watches and clocks may be valuable guides in determining the time of death. A clock may stop when it receives a blow during a struggle or is moved from its position by an explosion or shot. When investigating a suspicious death, the police officer should therefore give careful attention to any clock found at the scene, indicate the position of the hands of the clock in the report of the investigation, and see if it has stopped from external action. If clocks or watches are running, it should be noted whether they are showing the right time; the time at which they finally stop should be determined. In the case of alarm clocks, the report should state the time for which the alarm was set and whether the ringing mechanism has run down or the alarm has been shut off. When a more detailed investigation is required, a watchmaker should be consulted.

Watches of older construction generally stop immediately upon contact with water, but a watch provided with a tight-fitting case and glass can run longer before stopping. Watertight watches run for a long time underwater. If a pocket or wristwatch is found on a body, the police officer should not carry out any further examination of it or perform any tests but should consult a watchmaker. Digital watches and clocks do not lend themselves to these techniques.

---

* A useful web page on forensic entomology can be found at http://www.forensicentomology.com/.

In investigating cases of suspicious death, certain conditions can give a good indication for an approximate determination of the time of death. This may be obtained from papers and letters in a mailbox, dated receipts, food materials' state of decomposition, dampness of laundry that has been hung up, dust on furniture, cobwebs, evaporation of liquid in a glass, cup, or other vessel, flowers withering, drying in flowerpots, date on a calendar or diary, food product dating codes, timestamps on sent or received e-mails, cellphone call logs, etc.

When a dead body is found outdoors, the growth of vegetation under and around it can be a good guide in deciding the time when the body began lying there. Flowering plants may be buried and thus may indicate closely the time of burial. The colored matter of plant leaves under the body undergoes certain changes; chlorophyll generally disappears after a week. A good indication can also be obtained from a comparison between the stage of growth of plants under the body and of similar plants in the vicinity. When a body has laid in one place for a considerable time, in favorable cases, the decaying vegetation underneath can indicate the time of year when the body was placed there. If the weather has changed, the amount of moisture under the body, compared with that in the surrounding area, may give some information. When a dead body is found in snow, its position in relation to layers produced by successive snowfalls should be determined accurately.

Some guidance may also be obtained from the extent of decay of clothing. Cotton fabrics decompose after 4 to 5 years; wool after 8 to 10 years; leather and silk only after 20 years or even longer.

Autopsy

The investigator present at the crime scene should also be present at the autopsy. The investigator's attendance is desirable so that the forensic pathologist can be briefed about pertinent finds at the crime scene, as well as other information that will be of value in the examination. Additionally, information uncovered at the autopsy and communicated verbally by the pathologist to the homicide investigator will be helpful in the criminal investigation.

Besides photographs taken at the crime scene, the victim should be photographed at the morgue clothed and unclothed. The pathologist and investigator should be present and carefully examine the victim before undressing the body. Color photographs should be taken of all pertinent details: the overall appearance of the body, close-ups of the face, injuries, ligatures and marks, and the like. A scale should be included in the photographs.

Care should be taken in undressing the body. It should be undressed in the usual way; the clothing should not be cut, if possible. If cutting is required, care should be taken not to cut through bullet holes, knife cuts, tears, or stains. The garments should be packaged separately. If they are wet or blood-soaked, they should be allowed to air-dry at room temperature and away from direct sunlight. The clothes should be hung up to dry with paper draped loosely around the article of clothing to catch any trace material that might fall or be carefully spread out on clean paper. It is important that bloodstained articles be properly preserved to obtain the most from forensic biology testing (see Chapter 8 to review preservation procedures for bloody evidence).

After the clothes have been dried, they may be packaged for submission to the crime laboratory. The investigator and pathologist should be careful to establish a chain of custody of the evidence so it can be admissible in court. Trace evidence present on the victim and the clothing should not be overlooked. Body bags used to carry the body from the scene to the morgue should be carefully inspected for debris and trace material. Any trace evidence found on the body should be removed and properly packaged. Traces noted on the clothing should be removed and packaged only if the evidence might be lost in transit to the laboratory; otherwise the traces should remain and be packaged with the clothing. Investigators at the scene may wish to leave written instructions for the forensic pathologist or assistant responsible for collecting trace evidence from the body when it arrives at the morgue. Of course, it is strongly recommended that homicide investigators make every attempt to be present at the autopsy and to discuss the case with the pathologist.

Following photography, initial examination, and undressing, the body should be fingerprinted. The surface of the body should be searched for bloody fingerprints. The techniques described earlier to obtain latent fingerprints from skin may be attempted on promising areas. An alternate light source can also be used to look for biological fluids on the body. Ultraviolet light can also be used to look for ligature and strangulation marks or other bruises that may not be visible to the naked eye. Fingernail scrapings and hair samples should routinely be taken from all murder victims. A blood specimen should be collected during the actual postmortem examination.

The body should next be washed and rephotographed. Identity photographs of the victim's face should be made at that time. The entire body, including injuries, should again be photographed. Photographs taken during the remainder of the autopsy may be of value in the subsequent investigation and should be encouraged. If the victim died as a result of a shooting, x-rays are necessary to identify and locate the bullet fragments, jacket, etc.

The purpose of the autopsy is to establish the cause and manner of death as well as the circumstances immediately surrounding the time of death. The homicide investigator uses this information together with information gathered from other sources in the solution of the crime. Two factors will have a significant bearing on the outcome of the case: the degree of care and skill in which the postmortem examination is conducted and the level of cooperation between the investigator and forensic pathologist.

Besides the traditional autopsy, new autopsy techniques using computer tomography, magnetic resonance imaging, 3D photogrammetry, and surface scanning has been recently used in the minimally invasive virtual autopsy or "Virtopsy." These techniques can be used in cases where there are religious objections to autopsy, compromised corpses, or to alleviate backlogs.

The remainder of this chapter discusses the various types of injuries by different modes encountered in death investigations.

Injuries from External Mechanical Violence

Injuries from external mechanical violence are made by blunt or sharp instruments and may consist of abrasions, contusions or bruises, crushing wounds, or bone injuries.

Abrasions

Abrasions generally result from violence applied obliquely, which scrapes off the top layer of the skin, but they can occur from violence directed straight against the body and may reproduce the shape of, say, the radiator of a car or the details of a weapon's surface. As a rule there is no bleeding. In a favorable case, it is possible to decide in which direction the body received the violence and, with some degree of certainty, what caused the injury. In general, it is very difficult to determine whether scraping of the epidermis was produced before or after death, although postmortem drying may leave a characteristic yellow parchment-like appearance. Removing or undressing the body must be carried out with care so that no injuries are produced.

Included in abrasions are fingernail marks that are narrow and usually somewhat curved. If the fingers slip, the nails produce scratches or tears.

Contusions or Bruises

Contusions or bruises are injuries to the tissues and organs produced by blunt external violence and result from compression, usually against the parts of the skeleton lying underneath. The most usual type of contusion is an extravasation of blood; when this is close to the skin, it is commonly called a bruise or black-and-blue mark. In extravasation, the blood comes out into the surrounding tissues and remains there, unable to get away to the outside or to the body cavities. A bruise or black-and-blue mark initially shows a swelling and has a reddish color; it then assumes a blackish-blue to bluish-red color, changing gradually to brownish with strong shades of green and yellow. In rare cases, a bruise resulting from a blow with a weapon will have the same form as the striking surface of the weapon. If a bruise is found on a dead body, it may be concluded with certainty that the injury was produced when the victim was alive. At the autopsy, it is usually possible to determine whether a contusion has been produced some time before or in direct connection with the death. Only a pathologist can distinguish the livid patterns from bruises found on a dead body.

Contusions may occur at places other than those where violence was applied. For example, a blow against the back of the head can produce bruises around the eyes. Similarly, with an abnormal accumulation of blood in the blood vessels, as in cases of hanging or other forms of suffocation, bruises can appear in the face. Diffusion of blood may also appear in cases of poisoning and, in some diseases and infections of the blood, injury to the walls of the blood vessels.

Crushing Wounds

Crushing wounds occur most readily, with blunt violence, at those places where the skin is near the bones. They are characterized by irregular form, gaping and swollen edges to the wound, and often considerable bleeding into the surrounding tissues. The wound rarely takes the form of the object producing it, but an impression of the latter may be found. Sometimes a crushing wound is remarkably straight and even at the edges; this occurs when the skin breaks over the uniform edge of a bone or where it splits along a parallel fibered tissue structure. Such a wound may give the impression of having been produced by a sharp weapon. This type of wound can be detected with a degree of certainty, because in deeper lying parts of it, the walls of the wound are uneven and connected by bridges of tissue.

A crushing wound resulting from a blow on the head with a hammer or the head of an ax sometimes has the same form as the round or angular edge that produced it. If a blow of this type is so powerful that the weapon penetrates the cranium, the injury may have the same form.

When blunt violence is used against the body, it is possible for vital organs such as the brain, heart, lungs, liver, spleen, and kidneys to be damaged without any visible external injury. Bite wounds are a special form of crushing wound. The form of a bite wound may reproduce the arrangement of the perpetrator's teeth.

Bone Injuries

Bone injuries may result from blunt external violence, for example, directed against the head. If a bone injury has occurred during life, diffusion of blood is generally found near or around it. Blunt violence against the cranium may produce a fracture. The direction of the crack may make it possible to determine the direction from which the violence came.

Injuries from Sharp External Violence

These may consist of cutting wounds, stab wounds, or chopping wounds.

Cutting Wounds

Cutting wounds have even, sharp edges. When the direction of cutting is across the direction of the fibers of elastic tissue, the wound gapes; when the direction of cut is parallel to the fibers, the edges of the wound generally lie against one another. Often it is difficult to decide whether a cutting wound occurred during life or after death because contusion injuries, which may form a guide in such cases, are not found around the wound. As a rule, a cutting wound is deepest at the place where the cutting object was first applied. The wound leaves hardly any detailed information about the instrument that caused it.

In cases of suicide, the cutting force is generally directed against the throat or insides of the wrists and, sometimes, against other parts of the body. The intent of the suicide is usually to produce bleeding by cutting the arteries. In cases of suicide there may be one or several cuts, generally not of a dangerous type, parallel or running into one another, known as "hesitation cuts." If it is established that such surface cuts were produced before the final fatal cut, it is quite certain that the case is one of suicide; the surface cuts were made because the suicide did not know how much force was required to produce the fatal cut or feared the pain anticipated from the act. The police officer should not, however, draw hasty conclusions from superficial cuts that give the impression of having been made before the fatal cut.

Nothing prevents a murderer who has knowledge of these circumstances from adding superficial cuts after making the fatal one to give the impression of suicide. Only a pathologist is competent to decide in what order the cuts were made. In some cases of suicide, the individual has made a number of trial cuts at places other than the one where the fatal cut was made. Such trial cuts, which as a rule are superficial, may be situated on the temples, arms, or legs. With an active or desperate suicide, the first cut may be a fatal one, but that does not prevent the victim from adding a number of others before losing consciousness.

A suicidal person generally cuts in the direction where the cutting hand is placed. When a right-handed person cuts his or her throat, the position of the cut is generally on the left side of the throat; if the victim is left-handed the position is reversed. In connection with cuts in the throat, it should not be forgotten that a murderer might handle the weapon in exactly the same way as a suicide, if the murderer overcomes the victim from the rear.

In cases of suicide by cutting the throat, incisions made in the free hand can easily be confused with defense injuries. Such wounds may be produced when the suicide stretches the skin of the neck with the free hand so that the weapon can penetrate more easily. Wounds may also be produced from holding the blade to be able to put more force into the cut.

In cases of death from cutting the throat, there is reason to suspect murder when the position of the wound does not correspond with a natural hold on the weapon or the direction of the wound does not correspond with the right- or left-handedness of the victim.

Murder may be suspected if the wound is very deep or if it is irregular. Special attention should be given to the possible occurrence of fingernail marks and scratch injuries that would be produced if the murderer held the head of the victim fast and also to the presence of defense injuries on the hands and arms. If cuts are on the clothing, it may be murder because suicides generally lay bare the part of the body that they intend to cut.

Stab Wounds

Stab wounds are generally produced by a knife, dagger, or scissors, but may also result from other weapons, for example, an ice pick, awl, pointed stick, and similar items. If a stab wound has been produced by a sharp knife or dagger, it is not possible to determine the width of the blade from the size of the surface wound because the wound channel is generally wider than the weapon, especially if it is two-edged. When the weapon is stuck into the body, the edge has a cutting action, so the surface wound is considerably longer than the width of the blade; when the weapon is withdrawn, it usually assumes a different position, so the wound is enlarged still further. The weapon may also be turned when withdrawn, so the surface wound becomes curved or angular. A knife with a thick back produces a wedge-shaped wound.

When stab wounds are produced by a weapon with a blunt point, the outer wound is smaller than the cross-sectional width of the instrument. In such cases, when the weapon is driven into the body, the elastic skin is actually pressed inward and stretched until it breaks. When the weapon is withdrawn, the skin returns to its normal position and the external wound contracts. If the weapon is cone-shaped and rough, the skin around the wound may break in radial cracks.

With a stab wound in the heart, death may not occur immediately. In some cases, people have survived a wound in the heart.

A suicide attempt by stabbing is generally in the region of the heart or, in some cases, in the stomach or other parts of the body. It is often found that a number of stab wounds are concentrated in a small limited region, that is, around the heart. In such a case, the suicide has stabbed the body several times without result, in the same way described earlier in "Cutting Wounds." One fact that indicates suicide is clothes that are unbuttoned or have been taken off. In suicide, the stab is generally directed into the body at right angles.

In cases of murder, the stab wounds are usually not concentrated in one place but scattered, especially when the victim has attempted self-defense. Knife stabs are, as a rule, directed in an oblique direction against the body, with the exception of cases in which the victim was lying down. A number of deep wounds and wounds in the back indicate murder. If the victim tried self-defense, the wound channel may be curved owing to the body being in a certain position when it received the stab. At the autopsy, it may be found that a wound channel does not go right through because the position of the body was such that the muscles were displaced from their normal position when they were penetrated. In such a case, the position of the dead person when he or she was stabbed can be reconstructed.

Case

The body of a dead woman was found by police in a house in Amsterdam, the Netherlands, in 2007. When the police arrived, there were three people in the living room. Two of them pointed out the third and said that he stabbed the woman to death. The man was taken into custody. The job of the CSIs was to determine whether the findings confirmed the alleged accusation.

The whole house was covered with bloodstains, varying from swipes, altered stains, flow patterns, and footprints made with and in blood. In the living room, five knives were found of which two were bloody. After the removal of all the clothing that was placed on the body, the victim was found lying naked on her stomach (Figure 16.17a).

In a closet in the living room, female clothing was found that most probably belonged to the victim. The clothing was examined and in several pieces "perforations" were found. Considering the damage to the clothing, it was very likely that the victim was wearing them during the stabbing. The Dutch Forensic Institute in The Hague examined the clothing for blood of the victim and searched for a comparison between the damaged clothing and the knives.

Large amounts of blood on the mattress and bedding in the first and second bedrooms on the first floor was also found (Figure 16.17b). In the first bedroom, a rope tied to the central heating pipes was found. Similar pieces of rope were found next to the body, and a similar rope on a "roll" was found in the bathroom. It was surmised that the victim was tied to the central heating pipes next to the mattress.

Several bloody sponges, a cleaning mop, and a bucket filled with bloody water were also recovered. Several bloody swipes and efforts taken to clean up the floor were also observed (Figure 16.17c).

Several blood transfers on the seat of the elevator indicated that there had been more than one instance of blood transfer made by a bloody person or bloody object. Looking at the blood pattern on the seat, the guard underneath the seat, and on the footboard of the chair elevator, it is probable that a bloody person was seated on the chair. This hypothesis is supported by the fact that several blood-stained tissues on the chair elevator and also underneath the bare feet of the victim were found (Figure 16.17d).

Further investigation led to a partial visible shoeprint, made with or in blood. This became visible on the floor next to the bed in bedroom number two and in the living room next to the victim. The shoeprint was of a same kind as the shoes the suspect was wearing during his arrest.

The story according to the suspect and witness was that the man and woman had a relationship based on friendship and drugs. They lived together in the house. She asked him to give her some drugs but he did not want to. She kept on asking and he got tired of it. When they were sitting on the sofa he stabbed her in the waist and they got into a fight. Blood fled and (also due to her physical condition) as she was not able to go upstairs, he put her on the stair elevator and moved her to the bedroom. There he tied her with a rope to the central heating pipes. He left her and went downstairs. After a while she managed to get herself loose and went downstairs. There they had another fight which eventually led to her death. She was stabbed several times, her throat was cut, and she bled to death. The suspect did not really know what to do with the situation and covered her with clothing and made an effort to clean up the house.*

---

* Case submitted by Senior Forensic Investigator Wendy Joan van Hilst, Forensische Opsporing Amsterdam-Amstelland, the Netherlands.

(a)

(b)

Figure 16.17 These photos refer to the Case Study on pages 422–423.

(c)

(d)

Figure 16.17 *(Continued)*

Chopping Wounds

Chopping wounds are generally produced by an ax or, more rarely, by a blow with some other edged tool, for example, a heavy knife, sword, broadax, or the like. Usually the wound is similar to a cutting wound, but is easily distinguished from the latter by a ring of contusion injury around the wound and also by the crushing effect produced when the blow meets bony parts. If the edge of the weapon is deformed, tool marks may appear in these bony parts, which can, in favorable cases, lead to the identification of the weapon that was used.

When a blow from an ax or other edged weapon has killed a person, murder can nearly always be assumed. In cases of murder or other violent death from an ax, the wounds are generally in the head and in different directions. In certain cases, they may have the same direction, for example, when a sleeping person, or one who is held, is struck. Usually the criminal first delivers a few blows with the head of the weapon before completing the job with the edge.

Suicide with an ax has occurred, but is rare. Generally the suicide directs the weapon against the forehead and crown of the head. The first blow is relatively light and only produces superficial injuries that are not fatal; then the suicide continues by putting more force in the blows and possibly using the weapon with greater accuracy so that fatal injuries are produced. The wounds have a typical appearance that cannot be mistaken—they are directed from the forehead to the back of the head, approaching one another at the forehead.

Marks or Damage on Clothing

These can be very significant in the reconstruction of events. In cases of blunt violence, an impression of the weapon causing the injury may be found on the clothing, while headgear may show a clear mark of a hammer or other tool. In the case of a blow against the head, the tool used may even chip out a piece or corner of the headgear; this piece will have the same form as the striking surface of the weapon. An impression in the corresponding part of the outer clothing may show that a bruise on the body has resulted from a kick or from trampling. Impressions in clothing may be mixed with dust, dirt, or other contamination from the object producing the injury. Injuries to the clothes may be a good guide for the reconstruction of the course of events in the case of injury from cutting violence. In stabbing cases, the hole in the clothing may have a position different from that of the wound. A victim who has been stabbed may lift his arms in self-defense so that the clothing moves out of its usual position on the body; in such cases the defensive position can be reconstructed. A garment perforated in several places by the same stab indicates creases in the clothes.

Defense Injuries

Self-defense wounds are often found on the hands and arms of the murder victim. If a knife was used, the insides of the hands may be badly gashed from gripping the blade of the knife. Stab and cut wounds may be produced on the arms and hands when a victim attempts to parry an attack. When a crushing weapon is used in a murder, the hands of the victim may be badly injured from putting them on the head to reduce the violence of the blow. Among defense injuries are also included those that occur when the victim attempts self-defense by attacking, for example, knuckles injured from using fists against the criminal or nails broken from scratching.

Firearm Injuries

These must be considered as a special group of injuries because the investigation differs substantially in important respects from the investigation of other injuries. One might think that because a police officer should not touch a wound, it is not necessary to have a detailed knowledge of firearm injuries on a body. They are, however, so frequent and so important that whenever the pathologist cannot arrive in a reasonable time, the police officer should be prepared to make personal observations and to take whatever measures are necessary. Because firearm injuries are frequently covered with blood, it is often impossible for a police officer to distinguish between a gunshot injury and one produced by other external mechanical violence. Under these circumstances it is necessary to wait patiently for the arrival of the pathologist; this holds even when it is important that the type of injury be determined at an early stage. The police officer should never probe in or around a gunshot wound because that may destroy or reduce the chance of the expert being able to determine the type of injury and to reconstruct the course of events.

Bullet Injuries

When a bullet strikes the body, the skin is first pushed in and then perforated while in the stretched state. After the bullet has passed, the skin partially returns to its original position; the entry opening is drawn together and is smaller than the diameter of the bullet. Slower bullet velocities result in smaller entry openings. The bullet passing through the stretched skin forms the so-called abrasion ring around the entrance opening because the bullet slips against the skin that is pressed inward and scrapes the external epithelial layers. The skin in the abrasion ring becomes conspicuous by drying after some hours. In a favorable case, rifling marks on the bullet leave such a distinct mark in the abrasion ring that the number of grooves in the rifling can be counted. The combined section of the abrasion ring and entrance opening corresponds to or slightly exceeds the caliber of the bullet. When a bullet strikes the body squarely, the abrasion ring is round and when it strikes at an angle it is oval.

Along with the abrasion ring, another black-colored ring, the "smudge ring," often entirely covers the abrasion ring. This does not contain any powder residues or contamination from the bore of the firearm, but consists wholly of small particles originating from the surface of the bullet. The smudge ring or "bullet wipe" may be absent in the case of clean-jacketed bullets or when the bullet has passed through clothing.

A bullet passing through the body forms a track that is usually straight, but can also be bent at an angle in an unpredictable manner if the bullet meets or passes through a bone. Thus determining with certainty the direction of the weapon when the shot was fired is not possible from observation of the entrance and exit openings. The pathologist must calculate this direction from the results of the autopsy. The velocity of the bullet has a great influence on the appearance of the track; straight tracks indicate a high velocity, bent and angular ones a low velocity.

In gunshot injuries in soft parts of the body, especially in the brain, the bullet can produce a considerable explosive effect, which is greatest with unjacketed or soft-nosed bullets from high-velocity firearms (Figure 16.18). Such a bullet may split into several parts, each of which forms its own track, and thus several exit wounds may be present. When such a bullet strikes the head, large parts of the cranium can be blown away and the brain scattered around. A soft-nosed bullet that, before hitting the body, is split by striking against a tree branch can produce a number of irregular entrance holes.

A shot through the head is not always fatal. To be immediately fatal, the bullet must produce a bursting effect or injure a vital brain center. A shot through the brain that is not immediately fatal does not always produce unconsciousness. Even when a bullet has perforated the heart, the injured person can sometimes live for several hours, retaining some capacity for movement.

It is often difficult to distinguish the exit wound from the entrance wound, especially at long range with a metal-jacketed bullet, assuming that the bullet passes through the body intact. In a favorable case, the exit wound may have a ragged appearance with flaps directed outward. To determine the direction of the shot with certainty in such a

Figure 16.18 This suicide shows the devastating result of a shotgun blast in the mouth, which resulted in the top of the head being blown away. (Courtesy of the Los Angeles County Sheriff's Department.)

case, an autopsy is necessary. If the bullet has been damaged by its passage through the body or if there has been a bursting effect, then it is generally easy to determine the exit wound. This wound is often considerably larger than the entrance wound and shows a star-shaped, ragged character, with flaps directed outward. Note, however, that in contact shots the entrance wound may be ragged and star-shaped. A bullet that ricochets may strike with its side or obliquely and produce a large and uncharacteristic entrance wound.

Close and Distant Shots

It is very important to be able to estimate the distance from which a shot was fired. In many cases this fact is the only evidence available that can distinguish between suicide, a self-defense killing, manslaughter, or murder.

In practice, a distinction is made among contact, close, and distant shots. A *contact shot* is one in which the muzzle of the weapon is pressed against the body when the shot is fired. In a *close shot*, the distance of the muzzle is less than about 18 inches from the body, while a *distant shot* is one fired at a distance greater than 18 inches.

In the case of a contact shot against an exposed part of the body, soot, metallic particles, and powder residues are driven into the body and can be found there during the autopsy. Blackening, caused by soot and powder, around the entry opening is often absent. A contact shot against a part of the body protected by clothing often produces a powder zone on the skin or in the clothes, while soot, powder residue, and fragments of clothing are driven into the track. With a contact discharge, the entrance wound differs considerably from an entrance wound in a close shot or distant shot. When the shot is fired, the gases of the explosion are driven into the track; however, they are forced out again and produce a bursting effect on the skin and clothes. The entrance wound is often star-shaped with flaps directed outward. It is also possible, in a contact shot, for the muzzle of the weapon to mark the skin, causing an impression that reproduces the shape of the muzzle of the weapon.

A close shot produces a zone of blackening around the entrance wound of the track, on the skin or also on the clothes. Sometimes, the flame from the muzzle has a singeing action around this opening, with hair and textile fibers curled up. The zone of blackening is formed of substances carried along with the explosion gases.

When a cartridge is fired, the bullet is forced through the barrel of the weapon by the explosion gases. Only a small amount of this gas passes in front of the bullet. The combustion of the powder is never complete even with smokeless powder, still less with black powder, and the explosion gases therefore carry with them incompletely burned powder residues, the amount of which decreases as the distance increases. Thus, in a close shot, a considerable amount of incompletely burned powder residue is found on the target. Together with this residue, the gases also carry along impurities from the inside of the barrel consisting of rust (iron), oil, and particles rubbed off the bullet. Metallic residues from the percussion cap and cartridge case also occur in the gases of the explosion. If the shot is fired at right angles to the body, the zone of blackening is practically circular; if it is fired obliquely the zone is oval. The extent of the zone of blackening is often difficult to determine by direct observation, so it is often better to photograph it using infrared-sensitive material, which intensifies the zone so that its extent is more easily determined. The zone of blackening gives valuable information for determining the distance from which a shot has been fired, which may be an important factor in deciding between murder and suicide. It is important that comparative test shots be fired with the *same weapon* and *same type of ammunition* as those used in the actual crime.

Close shots with black powder show marks of burning up to a distance of 4 to 6 inches and a distinct deposit of powder smoke up to 10 to 12 inches. Dispersed grains of powder embedded in the target may be detected even at a distance of 3 feet.

A *distant shot* is one in which none of the characteristics of a close shot can be detected (distance over about 18 inches). *Powder residues* occur on the object fired at in the form of incompletely and completely burned particles. A careful microscopic examination should precede any chemical examination because it is often possible to establish in this way the shape and color of unburned powder particles and to distinguish many kinds of powder.

Black powder, which consists of potassium nitrate, sulfur, and charcoal, is identified by the presence of potassium and nitrate in the entrance wound. Smokeless powder consists chiefly of nitrocellulose or of nitrocellulose with nitroglycerine and is identified by the presence of nitrite, which can be detected by various microchemical reactions. The grains of smokeless powder are generally coated with graphite and occur in many forms, for example, round or angular discs, pellets, and cylinders.

Marks from Primers

At one time a primer generally contained a percussion composition of fulminate of mercury, stibnite (antimony sulfide), and potassium chlorate with a varying amount of powdered glass. Primers now have eliminated the mercury and the rust-forming products from the potassium chlorate. This has resulted in the replacement of the mercury fulminate by lead compounds, such as lead azide and lead styphnate (lead trinitroresorcinate) and in the replacement of the potassium chlorate by barium nitrate. Stibnite is still used, however, to a limited extent.

Thus, in a chemical examination of a gunshot injury, the metals that first come into question are barium, lead, and antimony. For example, by determining the lead content of a bullet wound and comparing it with that obtained from a test discharge against a similar object with the same ammunition from different distances, quite reliable information regarding the distance from which the actual shot was fired can be obtained in favorable cases.

Traces from Bullets

With injuries from plain lead bullets, such as those usually used in ordinary revolver ammunition, there is always a considerable amount of lead in the zone of blackening and in the smudge ring; in the latter it is even possible to detect lead from a distant shot. Lead traces from the surface of the bullet can also be found frequently in the exit hole. In some types of ammunition the bullet is greased; residues from these substances may be carried along with the bullet and found around the entrance opening. Metal-jacketed bullets, which are used chiefly for automatic weapons, consist of an inner lead core with an outer shell of some hard metal or alloy—the so-called jacket; the usual materials are copper, cupronickel, or brass. Traces of all these metals may be found in gunshot injuries.

Traces from Cartridge Cases

It is often possible to detect copper in the track and in perforated clothing up to a range of 6 to 8 inches. This comes from the cartridge case, from which the expansion pressure wears off small particles of metal. Large amounts of copper found in the dirt ring are considered a characteristic indication of a close shot. If, however, a copper-coated bullet has been used, then naturally no conclusion can be drawn regarding the possibility of a close shot because, in this case, even a distant shot shows a distinct amount of copper.

Traces from the Barrel of the Weapon

Iron can be found in and around the entrance wound in a case of shooting with a weapon that has not been used for a long time because the barrel may be rusty. With automatic hand weapons, traces of iron can be detected up to a distance of 8 to 12 inches.

Injuries from Small Shot

With shotguns, the shot column can have a very concentrated effect at distances up to 1 yard. With a distance of up to 4 to 8 inches, the wound is practically circular. The greater the distance is, the more irregular the wound is. At a distance of up to 2 to 3 yards, there is generally a central entrance opening and around it are single small holes from individual scattered shot. At a greater distance the shot spreads out more into small groups; at 10 yards the scattering can amount to 12 to 16 inches.

Damage to Clothes from Shooting

If a shot has passed through clothes, the position of the bullet hole should be compared with the direction of the wound track in the body in the same way as described previously in the section "Marks or Damage on Clothing."

Modes of Death from Shooting

In suicide the weapon is usually directed against the forehead, temple, or heart; a shot fired upward and obliquely into the mouth is quite common. In deciding if a case is suicide, an attempt should first be made to decide to what extent the victim could have fired the shot in the approximate direction given by the track. In the case of pistol or revolver shots against the temple, it is necessary to know whether the deceased was right- or left-handed; however, a person might fire a weapon with the left hand but be otherwise right-handed.

It is an essential condition for the assumption of suicide that the victim be wounded by a close discharge and that the weapon lies in the proper position with respect to the body. If these conditions indicate suicide the question should not be considered settled because nothing prevents some other person from firing the shot under the given conditions and then laying the weapon down in the proper position.

A more certain indication is if injuries produced when firing a shot are found on the hand of the dead person in the form of a mark on the thumb or forefinger or on the web of the thumb. Such marks may result from the recoil of the slide of an automatic pistol. The most certain proof of suicide is found in the form of fragments of tissue and blood spattered from the wound onto the hand of the dead person. Although, in cases of suicide, the hand of the deceased may be blackened by powder, this cannot be taken as proof because the weapon could have been pressed in the hand after the shot was fired. It is also necessary to decide whether the body is in a natural position under the circumstances. A fairly certain sign of suicide is when the person has taken off any hindering clothes or exposed some part of the body before firing. No weapon near the body is a very suspicious circumstance, but hasty conclusions should not be drawn from that fact alone. In some cases a fatally injured person has traveled a long way before finally expiring or has thrown the weapon into a body of water. It has also happened that members of the victim's family have removed the weapon deliberately to create an appearance of murder, sometimes in the hope of escaping what they consider to be the disgrace of a suicide in the family.

It is a certain indication that a person died through the action of some other person when the discharge was beyond arm's reach. "Arm's reach" means the length of the arm plus possible assistance from an extension in the form of a stick or some other convenient means of reaching the trigger of a long-barreled weapon. It is true that it is possible to commit suicide by means of a distant shot, but this requires arrangements of such a type (string-pulls, etc.) that there should be no difficulty in revealing the truth. When the fatal shot was fired from behind, it is safe to assume that it is not suicide. A suicide *could* fire a shot at the back of the head, but such a possibility is very far-fetched. The fact that the deceased has more than one injury cannot always be taken as proof that death was from the action of some other person. Cases occur in which a suicide has fired two or possibly a number of shots, each of which produced a potentially lethal wound, before becoming incapable of continuing the firing.

It is quite common for a person to be shot fatally by accident or through personal fault. During hunting, it is possible to slip or stumble on awkward ground, fall when climbing over a gate or other obstacle, or drop the weapon, whereupon a fatal shot may be fired. In such cases, generally marks at the scene of the accident or marks on the weapon give a clear indication of what has happened. A fatal shot may also be fired accidentally when handling a firearm, for example, when cleaning it. In such cases, the investigating officer should observe the greatest caution and not assume from the start that it was an accident. The victim may very well have committed suicide while giving the incident the appearance of an accident or a murderer may also simulate an accident.

The police officer who carries out the investigation of a fatal shooting must not attempt to carry out any experiments that impinge on the responsibilities of the pathologist or criminalist. However, it may be necessary to undertake precautionary measures in connection with evidence that for some reason may be exposed to destruction. It has been stated before that, in and around a gunshot wound, evidence including traces of incompletely burned powder residues; traces of metals from the primer, cartridge case, and bullet; and grease and dirt from the bullet and the barrel of the weapon may be found. These marks may be of decisive significance in deciding, for example, the distance of the shooting; therefore, they must be protected as much as possible. In cases in which the bullet has gone through the clothes, there is always the risk that evidence may be destroyed by rain or by moving the dead body. The police officer should therefore protect such evidence against destructive action by any suitable means, for example, by covering the actual place or, in suitable cases, by tying or pinning loose layers of clothing in a particular position. If there is any risk that the bullet hole in the clothes may become soaked with blood when the body is moved, the police officer must find some method of preventing it.

The hand that holds the firearm at the instant of firing can become blackened by powder in the area of the web of the thumb and on the thumb and forefinger. The deposit of powder smoke produced in this way can be identified chemically. Wrapping the deceased's hands in clean paper bags should protect them for later examination in the morgue.

Explosion Injuries

Explosion injuries are a variation of gunshot injuries. An explosive charge contains metal parts or is enclosed in a metal container that breaks up, for example, a hand grenade; when it fractures metal objects, stones, or the like in the immediate vicinity, the fragments thrown off have an exceptionally great force that quickly decreases. When such pieces from an explosion hit a nearby body, they can produce very severe damage. A small splinter of only a few millimeters in diameter can perforate the brainpan. When it penetrates the body, it bores a wound channel that can easily be mistaken for a bullet track. The energy in a fragment from an explosion decreases so rapidly that generally it is not able to penetrate the body. At close quarters, air pressure alone can cause fatal injury.

The fatal effect of an explosive charge is limited to the immediate vicinity; at a greater distance, air pressure may cause injury from falling. Another way of committing suicide is to detonate dynamite in the mouth. The effect of such an explosion is generally that the head is torn away, while the skin of the back of the neck, with adhering bone and soft parts, is left on the neck. Suicide by explosion in the mouth can be carried out with nothing more than a blasting cap. In this case, the injuries are to the throat and breathing organs. Generally, no damage is visible in the face; the lips and the skin of the face remain uninjured. Suicide has also been achieved by an explosive charge placed on the chest, in which extensive lacerations are produced.

The police officer should remember that wounds should be photographed, even when they are on a living person. The officer should therefore try to contact the doctor who has treated an injured person to discuss the possibility of photographing. This should not be delayed too long because a wound changes its appearance as it heals or is altered by therapy. Especially in the case of bite wounds and wounds of which the form reveals the character of the weapon or instrument, it is important that photographing should be done before a scab forms or an operation becomes necessary. A scale should always be laid next to the wound.

Death by Suffocation

The actual mode of death may be by hanging, strangulation, by hand, ligature, covering the mouth or nose, blocking the larynx or windpipe, crushing to death, or drowning.

Hanging

A mode of death in which a cord is placed around the neck and tightened by the weight of the body constitutes hanging. The effect of hanging is that the blood circulation to the brain ceases very quickly, which produces immediate unconsciousness; at the same time, the air passages are closed up so that respiration ceases. The action of the heart may actually continue so that death occurs only after some minutes. With violent modes of hanging, injury may be produced to the vertebrae and spinal cord. The noose need not be very tight because only a small part of the weight of the body needs to be taken up for the hanging to be effective; the body does not need to hang free. The effect is the same if the hanging occurs with the body supported in a leaning, kneeling, sitting, or lying position. No one can escape from a tight-drawn noose once hanging in it because vagal inhibition occurs rapidly. This has been shown by a number of cases of persons who wished to try the effect of hanging without any intention of completing it—they found themselves unable to recover from their situation. Thus children have been killed by hanging when, from curiosity, they wanted to test a hangman's noose. Similarly, in some cases, a hanging situation has been arranged to obtain a perverse sexual stimulation. The commonly held view that death by hanging may be preceded by an erotic sensation is, however, certainly incorrect.

In suicide by hanging, quite frequently the rope breaks and the suicide falls down, but subsequently repeats the hanging with another rope and possibly at another place. This may necessitate tedious investigations because the suicide may have contracted bleeding injuries that were caused by the fall or when, after the unsuccessful attempt, he or she wandered around in a daze. In such a case, wounds, marks of blood, and disorder at the scene might be incorrectly interpreted as signs of a struggle.

The rope used is generally slender cord, for example, a clothesline, but other objects may be used, for example, belts, suspenders, towels, scarves, thick shoelaces, etc. After hanging, a typical mark on the neck is usually found: the so-called hanging groove. The broader and softer the noose, the less clearly the hanging groove shows. This is also the case when some part of the clothing comes between the noose and the neck. As a rule, however, the groove is distinct and full of detail, and it is often possible to distinguish marks of twisting, knots, and irregularities, while the width of the cord used can be calculated quite accurately.

The hanging groove generally has a typical appearance. The greatest pressure is exerted opposite the suspension point, that is, if suspended from the back of the neck, the noose, if it is sufficiently thin or narrow, on the front side may have pressed in so deeply that it lies almost concealed by a roll of flesh. The groove then runs upward at an angle around the side of the neck, becomes less marked, and finally fades away as it approaches the back of the neck. The edges of the groove are generally puckered in the direction in which the cord slipped when the noose tightened. When hanging occurs in a lying or inclined position, the groove may be more horizontal, which gives it a certain similarity with a strangulation groove, from which it can easily be distinguished because the hanging groove is less marked and disappears at the back of the neck. In cases of strangling in which the criminal's hands were held between the loop and the neck, the groove also disappears in the direction toward the hands. In general, however, the fingernails or knuckles produce such a great pressure against the neck that contusions appear in the skin. In rare cases, the noose may be applied at an angle on the neck or at the back of the neck, but the effect intended is still obtained because the large arteries of the neck are compressed effectively even when this method of hanging is used. Sometimes the noose may slip upward after the first tightening, whereby two or more hanging grooves are produced. This may give rise to suspicion of a crime, but generally the pathologist finds no difficulty in elucidating the actual circumstances. It can happen that a hanged person's fingers are found between the noose and the neck. This was not due to attempting to loosen the noose, but rather to the fingers not having been removed when the noose tightened.

On the skin of the neck, dead persons may show marks that can easily be confused with hanging grooves. Articles of clothing pressing against the neck can produce such marks. On bodies that have been in water for a long time or that are undergoing decomposition, the hanging groove may have disappeared.

Murder by hanging must be considered an extremely rare occurrence that could be used only against children or persons who are unconscious or unable to defend themselves. In such cases, it is to be expected that the victim will show injuries other than those that occur from hanging. A murderer may attempt to give the appearance of suicide by hanging up the body after the onset of unconsciousness or death. If this is done by hoisting up the body, distinct clues are usually present on the supporting object and on the rope (Figure 16.19). For example, a branch of a tree may show such a clear mark of rubbing on the bark that it is not difficult to elucidate the actual circumstances—especially when the rope has also slipped sideways. On the part of the rope that has lain on and slipped against the support, the fibers are always directed upward against the latter.

Persons who have committed suicide by hanging sometimes show other injuries, which alone could be fatal. In such cases, hanging has been used after an unsuccessful attempt to commit suicide in another way. Such cases are easy to distinguish from those in

Figure 16.19 This hanging by means of a bed sheet at first glance appeared to be a suicide. Upon examining the end of the sheet for touch DNA, the suspect's profile was found and when confronted with this information, he subsequently confessed to the murder. (Courtesy of the New York City Office of Chief Medical Examiner.)

which hanging is the final phase in a murder. Conditions generally give a clear picture of the course of events.

When a body is hanging free but there is no jumping-off point, such as a chair, table, step, stone, or stump in the vicinity, then there is every reason to suspect murder. In such cases, the scene must be examined carefully to determine whether it was possible for anyone to have climbed up to the point of attachment. With trees it is easy to find marks of climbing, such as twigs broken off or leaves, bark, or moss torn away, and similar traces should be found on the clothing of the dead person. An easily removable starting point, for example, a chair, may actually have been removed by mistake before the arrival of the police.

In cases of hanging, livid stains are strongly marked on the feet, legs, and hands, and also immediately above the hanging groove. If such marks should be found on the back of a freely hanging body, for example, there is a question of the hanging having been done some time after death. The same question arises in a case when the arms or legs are bent because it is possible that the body may have been hung up after the onset of rigidity. After the rigidity has relaxed and the limbs have become straight, in some cases the wrinkles remaining in the clothes can indicate that the limbs were previously bent.

The presence of dirt on the clothes, for example, leaves, parts of plants, soil, dust, or other material, that is not present at the scene of the hanging should be noted especially, as should the presence of blood, saliva, or urine flowing in the wrong direction. Such observations may give rise to suspicion of a crime. If the knots and noose are formed in such a way that it is doubtful whether the dead person could have made them, this must be considered a suspicious circumstance.

In suicide by hanging, right-handed persons usually place the knot of the noose on the right-hand side of the neck and left-handed ones on the left; reversal of these positions is suspicious. When investigating a case of hanging, the police officer should always have in mind that the autopsy can rarely decide between murder and suicide. As a rule, the course of events can be determined only from examination of the scene and police investigation.

Strangling

This is usually done by hand or with a cord. In strangulation by hand, death sometimes occurs almost immediately from shock, but usually the squeezing of the neck arteries is incomplete, so death results from interruption of the supply of air to the lungs.

In manual strangulation, typically fingernail marks are on both sides of the throat—from the fingernails on one side and from the thumbnail on the other. If the criminal is right-handed, the mark of the thumbnail is generally on the right side of the throat and on the left side if left-handed. There are often marks of several grips with the hands and abrasion of the skin where the fingers slipped. When death has occurred from shock, marks of nails may be missing. Strangulation is generally preceded by a struggle, so other injuries may be found on the body, usually scratches or bleeding on the face, as well as marks on the clothes.

Strangulation by hand has nearly always resulted from extraneous violence, that is, from another person, although individual cases of suicide by strangulation by hand have occurred, with the suicide using a passive support for the hands so that the grip does not slip when unconsciousness occurs. In strangulation by ligature, death occurs in the same way as with hanging, but the strangulation groove generally has a course and appearance different from that of a hanging groove. Usually, it goes around the neck in a horizontal direction or its back part may be situated somewhat lower down on the neck than the front part on the throat. In some cases it can, like the hanging groove, be directed back and upward. Usually the strangulation groove is located lower on the neck than the hanging groove.

Strangulation with a cord can generally be considered murder and defense injuries are usually found on the victim. Such injuries may be absent if the victim was overcome from behind or if a sleeping, unconscious, or defenseless person has been strangled. In a case in which the cord is left on the throat after the crime, it is generally fixed tightly by means of a number of turns and knots.

Strangulation with a cord is a rare form of suicide. In cases in which suicide can be presumed, the strangling has been carried out with a running noose or by a scarf, rope, or the like, laid around the neck and knotted with a half knot, which is drawn so tightly that the neck arteries are compressed and unconsciousness supervenes. In both cases, one can expect that the hands will hold the noose fast after death or that their position relative to it will give clear evidence of suicide.

In investigating the scene of a hanging or strangling, the procedure to be followed should be the same as described previously for the investigation of murder in general. It is important that the police officer learn something about how the knots and nooses that occur in hanging and strangling are made. The formation of knots and nooses of a certain type often indicates whether or not the person hanged could have made them. When a knot or noose is of a type that could not have been made by the victim, then this must cause suspicion. There is a reason for being suspicious when, in a case of hanging or strangling, skillfully made knots and nooses have been found.

In describing knots and nooses, the usual names may be used, but it is not to be expected that everyone who reads the report will be familiar with them; therefore, their construction should be reproduced by a diagrammatic sketch or sketches and they should also be photographed.

The noose should be examined immediately and the origin of the material used should be determined as quickly as possible. If one or both ends of the cord have been recently cut and the corresponding pieces are not found at the scene, this circumstance must be elucidated. Cut off portions of the material of the noose are often found at the scene and, in such a case, scissors or another edged tool should be found in a likely place.

The ground under or around a hanged person must be investigated as soon as possible so that any evidence will not be destroyed. If the individual was murdered and then hanged to give the appearance of suicide, it is to be expected that distinct evidence will be found because considerable effort is required to hang up a dead body.

It is not uncommon for a person to commit suicide by hanging or strangling but take measures to give it the appearance of murder. These measures may consist of binding the legs and attempts to bind the hands, but this, especially the attempt to bind the hands, is easily detected. The individual may also have used some kind of gag, for example, a handkerchief that is pushed in or bound around the mouth.

Knots in a hanging noose should not be undone or cut except in cases in which the victim's life may still be saved. Where it is possible, cut the rope or cord some distance above the head, loosen the noose, and pull it over the head.

Taking down a dead body must be done carefully so that no new injuries are produced. A convenient way is to raise the body a little so that the cord slackens and then cut the cord. The body is laid down and the noose is allowed to remain on the body. After the noose has been examined and photographed in its original condition, it is up to the pathologist to remove it during the autopsy.

The part remaining on the carrying object should be cut off at such a point that the knots are not altered or damaged, after which the cut off parts are immediately bound together with string. If, for example, a cord is wound in several turns around the carrying object, a diagrammatic sketch of the arrangement is drawn as a reminder, after which the cord is cut and immediately wound around a similar object of the same diameter. When the line is composed of several parts (double or multiple), they are cut one by one and tied together in succession with cord or thread.

If it is suspected that a body has been hung up after death, the fibers in the cord must be protected, most conveniently by placing it stretched out in a long box so that it hangs freely. It can be held fast by loops attached by pins to the sides of the box.

What has been said about removing the hanging noose and strangling cord is the principal rule in cases in which it is expected that the life of the individual can be saved. If, however, the body has been dead for a long time (with certain signs of death present, e.g., putrefaction), the noose or cord is left in an untouched condition. The pathologist will examine it when making the postmortem examination. When, for any reason, the investigating officer must remove the noose or cord from such a body, the knots must not be deranged or loosened. A running noose can be loosened so far that it can be slipped over the head, but before that, the position of the knot on the fixed part should be marked in some way, for example, with chalk or by sticking in a piece of wire or winding a thread around it. If the noose is tight and cannot be passed over the head, it is cut off at a convenient point, generally at one side of the neck, after which the ends are immediately tied together with string. The same method is used for conditions in which the cord cannot be loosened and drawn over the head. In such a case, the position of the knot on the fixed part is marked, after which the cutting is done.

In cases of strangulation, the ligature should be removed in the same way as a noose in the case of hanging. Special care should be taken not to cut through knots that may not be visible from the outside. In general, the ligature should be removed in such a way that the manner of application may be reliably reconstructed. This may require photography and simple sketches to illustrate the various layers and knots.

Because the knots in a cord may be required as evidence, they must be sealed in a suitable manner and the circumference of the constructive loops should be measured and recorded.

Blocking of the Mouth or Nose

This cause of death is rare and commonly occurs with newborn children. The stoppage may result either from a pillow or other soft object being pressed against the face or from a hand pressed against the mouth and nose. Death occurs from suffocation. Suffocation may also result from the mouth and nose being stopped with a handkerchief, piece of cloth, or cotton. When a pillow or other soft material is used there are no typical marks, but saliva or mucus may stick on the cushion and give some information about the course of events. It is possible that the suffocation may be accidental in cases in which a child turns onto his face. When suffocation is done by hand, scratches may be produced on the face. If the investigator suspects that the mouth and nose were stopped with cotton but later removed, an examination should be performed.

Elderly persons are sometimes murdered by blocking the mouth and nose with a soft covering. Murder can also result when a criminal, without intending to kill, has attempted to silence the cries of the victim in a case of rape.

Blocking of the Larynx and Air Passages

Blocking can occur, for example, when food goes down the "wrong way" or vomited stomach contents are unable to get out through the mouth. Infanticide can be committed by a finger pressed down in the throat of an infant causing suffocation. In this case, there will be serious injuries in the mouth and throat.

Squeezing to Death

This can occur, for example, with a panic in a crowd, where the victim is squeezed or trampled or when a person comes under a heavy falling object or is buried by a fall of earth. The external injuries are generally considerable and easily interpreted. Squeezing to death can generally be considered an accident, but the possibility should also be kept in mind that an earth slide was arranged with the intention of murder.

Drowning

This is death due to liquid entering the breathing passages so that access of air to the lungs is prevented. The liquid need not necessarily be water; it may be mud, sludge, or other viscous material. Neither does the whole of the body need to be under the liquid. A person can drown when only the mouth and nose are under the surface. In a more general sense, the word "drowning" is used for every case of death in water, but this is incorrect because a death (e.g., while bathing) may be due to heart failure, cerebral hemorrhage, or shock.

When a drowned person is drawn out of the water, white foam often comes out of the mouth and nostrils, where it forms white spongy puffs that can remain for quite a long time owing to the mucous contained in it.

When the cause of death is simply drowning, murder is comparatively rare and, as a rule, is committed only against children. If injuries are found on a drowned person that might have been produced by some other person, the drowning can generally be considered merely the final phase of a course of events involving murder or manslaughter. It can also happen that a criminal attempts to conceal the discovery of the crime by sinking the victim under water.

In cases of drowning, the question is generally whether it is suicide or accident. If the clothes have been removed or the place is chosen with the idea of avoiding the risk of bumping against a stony bottom, suicide is indicated. The opposite can indicate accident, as can marks of slipping found on stones at the edge of the water and injuries produced when the drowning person attempted a rescue, for example, scraping of the skin of the hands and fingers or broken and torn nails.

The body of a drowned person may be tied in some way or heavy objects attached to it to make it sink and remain on the bottom. In such cases the police officer must proceed very cautiously with the investigation; it can be judged suicide, but suspicion of criminal acts should not be excluded.

A body lying in water is exposed to damage of many kinds. Propellers of boats may produce injuries. A body hit by a propeller can be cut in half. Bodies in water are also often damaged in the breakers offshore, against rocks, or when they bump against a stony and uneven bottom.

Death from Electric Currents

Death from electric currents can occur from the electricity supply or from lightning. Visible injuries may be present at the points of entry and exit of the current—the so-called current marks. If electric sparks or an arc touches the skin, the burn often shows the same form as the object producing it. When the direct injury is slight, characteristically formed fissures and figures indicate the passage of the current. The current marks are often round, sharply delineated, and light in color, or they may consist of edges or surfaces with charred skin. In severe cases, the injury penetrates the underlying tissues of the musculature and bones. The surface of the skin may be impregnated with fine metallic dust, which emanates from the current-carrying object; this can be so great that it appears as a discoloration, sometimes gray or black and sometimes blue or bluish green. The metallic dust can be determined spectrographically. Considerable changes in the skin may also be produced at the point of exit of the current. At the points of entry and exit of the current, the clothing may be torn or charred; sometimes the damage consists of a number of small holes with burned edges.

Death from electric current may be accident, suicide, or murder. In some cases, a trap has been set using house current, with the intention of murder.

Death from lightning is rare. When injuries are present on the body of a person assumed to have been killed in this way, they may consist of current marks on the neck and soles of the feet; the clothes may be badly torn; metal objects in the clothes may be fused together, burned, or thrown away, even in cases where no injury is apparent on the body. So-called lightning figures on the skin are not burning injuries but result from changes in the blood vessels. These arboreal marks generally disappear very quickly after death.

Violent Death in Fires

Only a pathologist can determine the cause of death and injuries on a person who has been burned to death. Death may be due to suffocation by smoke, carbon monoxide poisoning, or injury from falling beams, overturned furniture, falling walls, and so on. Generally, the person is already dead from such causes before the fire begins to attack the body.

Burned bodies usually lie in a distorted position, the so-called pugilistic attitude caused by the contraction of the muscles under the action of heat. The skin and soft tissues crack gradually; the cracks sometimes have quite even edges that can easily be confused with cut and stab wounds. The bones become more or less brittle, so breakages occur. In the inner parts of the skull, the pressure may become so great that the bones of the cranium may shatter. The limbs are destroyed first as heat gradually chars the body. A greatly charred body sometimes has the form of a torso.

For complete combustion, very intense heat for a comparatively long time is required. A newborn baby can be burned away in an ordinary stove in 2 hours, but to consume an adult in the same time, a temperature of 1250°C is needed, after which only certain bones remain.

Murder by burning does occur, but it can generally be assumed that the victim was subjected to other injuries before the fire was started. Disposing of a body by fire after murder is not uncommon. The criminal may in both cases have caused the fire with the objective of destroying evidence. The pathologist can easily decide whether the victim of a fire was alive or dead when the fire started. No signs of inhaled smoke or flakes of soot found in the respiratory organs suggest that the person was dead before the fire. Unburned skin may be found underneath a burned body that escaped burning. Tight fitting clothing may also protect the skin from the fire. In such places, signs of external violence may show clearly. Traces of blood may be found on unburned portions of clothing under the body. Uninjured parts of the skin around the wrists and ankles may indicate that the victim was bound before the start of the fire. A ligature around the neck, destroyed in the fire, may leave a distinct strangling groove.

Death by Freezing

Freezing to death does not as a rule produce any distinguishable injuries or changes in the body. At the autopsy, red spots may possibly be observed on those parts of the body where livid stains occur more rarely, for example, the ears, tip of the nose, fingers, and toes. As a rule, only weak, helpless, insufficiently clothed, or drunken persons freeze to death.

Freezing to death can occur as the result of criminal actions, for example, exposure of newborn or delicate children. A person who has been rendered helpless by an assault can also freeze to death. Persons who have died from freezing are occasionally found more or less undressed. This condition naturally gives rise to suspicions of murder. However, sometimes, at an advanced state of freezing, the victim gets a sensation of heat, which may explain this action.

Death by Poisoning

The determination of death by poisoning is frequently a joint effort on the part of the forensic pathologist and the forensic toxicologist. Only in certain instances will the investigating officer find the presence of physical evidence at the crime scene that indicates the death was caused by the ingestion of some poisonous substance.

Physical evidence located at the crime scene and noted upon gross examination of the deceased may sometimes be indicative of poisoning. Evidence such as drugs, narcotic paraphernalia, markings on the body, or the presence of acids or caustic substances may give an initial basis for forming an opinion about the case.

Corrosion around the mouth and face may be the result of consumption of acids or caustic chemicals such as hydrochloric acid, sulfuric acid, or lye. Odors of ammonia or burned almonds, an odor associated with cyanides, can indicate certain poisons. In cyanide poisoning, lividity is a reddish color.

Certain drugs, such as opium alkaloids and nicotine, cause contraction of the pupils, while others such as atropine (belladonna) produce dilation.

In death from subacute and chronic arsenic poisoning, a large quantity of thin stool resembling rice, often containing blood, may be found. Considerable excretion is also usual in the later stages of poisoning from corrosive sublimate or lead salts.

Strychnine causes convulsions; the corners of the mouth are drawn up and the face is fixed in a grin; the arms and legs are drawn together and the back is severely bent backward from contraction of the muscles.

Different colored materials in the vomit can give clues to the type of poisoning. Brown material resembling coffee grounds indicates poisoning with strong alkalis such as sodium or potassium hydroxide; yellow indicates nitric and chromic acids; blue-green, copper sulfate; black, sulfuric acid; and brown-green, hydrochloric acid. A sharp-smelling vomit indicates poisoning with ammonia or acetic acid.

Murders by using a poison that must be taken internally to be effective are not numerous. Generally, murder by poison is committed only within a family or close group. In such cases, the criminal generally uses some poison that will not arouse suspicion from its color, odor, or taste. Murder or attempted murder by the use of poisonous gas occurs occasionally, for example, carbon monoxide poisoning.

The police officer should know that, in a case of death from poisoning, only the investigation at the scene and examination of witnesses could decide whether a case is murder, suicide, or accident. The autopsy decides only the type and quantity of poison used.

It is not possible to go into a detailed description of different poisons and their actions. The boundary between poisonous and nonpoisonous substances is indefinite. A number of substances normally present in food can cause death by poisoning when they are taken in large amounts. Thus there is a case where the consumption of 13 ounces of table salt caused the death of an adult.

A number of poisons should be mentioned, including those with a powerful action and those responsible for most cases of poisoning:

- *Gaseous and liquid poisons.* Some of the more common of the thousands of these types of poisons are carbon monoxide, hydrogen cyanide, freon, methanol, toluene, benzene, gasoline, and chloroform.
- *Heavy metals and other inorganic poisons.* Compounds and salts of antimony, arsenic, barium, chromium, lead, mercury, and thallium; strong inorganic acids and bases such as hydrochloric acid, nitric acid, sulfuric acid, sodium hydroxide, potassium hydroxide, and ammonia.
- *Ethical, over-the-counter, and illicit drugs.* Ethyl alcohol; barbiturates; heroin; synthetically produced opiates, for example, methadone; phencyclidine; minor tranquilizers such as Valium, Librium, meprobamate, and over-the-counter medication when taken in excess. These drugs may be found in combination with each other and with alcohol.
- *Other vegetable and animal poisons.* Atropine, cocaine, nicotine, scopolamine, strychnine, and snake poisons.
- *Bacterial poisons and food poisoning (botulism).*

The determination of poisoning as the cause of death can be made only by autopsy and chemical analysis. In a number of cases of poisoning, however, certain details in the appearance of the dead person or special circumstances in connection with the death may give some indication. The police officer who investigates the scene of a fatal poisoning can greatly assist the pathologist by recovering any evidence of poisoning.

The most usual indications are, first, residual poison in the form of tablets, powder, or residues in medicine bottles and, second, powder wrappings, boxes, tubes, ampoules, vials, and other containers. All such clues should be recovered and each one packed separately in a tube or envelope. When the dead person is lying in bed, the bedclothes must be examined very carefully because the poison may quite possibly have been in the form of powder and any that was spilled could be difficult to detect.

All medicine bottles and tubes, including empty ones, should be kept, even if the stated contents are considered to be harmless. An apparently empty bottle may contain traces of powder, which can be identified by microchemical methods. The report of the investigation must state where such objects were found. Prescriptions can be useful guides for the pathologist.

Among the most important evidence in poisoning are cups, glasses, and other containers found in the immediate vicinity of the deceased, or in such places and under such conditions that they can be placed in direct relation to the death. If liquids left in a container are found, they should be transferred to an absolutely clean bottle that is then sealed. When a container holds merely sediment or undissolved residues, it should be wrapped in clean paper or, preferably, in a plastic bag. If fingerprints or palm prints are on it, these must be preserved. Spilled liquids can be collected by means of a filter paper, which is then placed in a clean glass jar and well sealed.

When food poisoning is suspected or it is possible that dishes may have conveyed the poison, the dishes used should be collected and packed in a suitable manner. Food dishes and remains of food are packed in a clean, well-sealed glass jar. If such clues are not sent immediately to a public health laboratory, they should be kept in a refrigerator. If there is any suspicion of crime, remains of food should be looked for, including outdoors in garbage cans, compost heaps, the ground, and other such places.

Any hypodermic syringes found should be recovered and kept in such a way that they cannot become contaminated and the contents cannot run out or be pressed out. The needle of the syringe can be conveniently stuck in a cork to prevent its breaking. Fingerprints or palm prints on the syringe must be preserved. When hypodermic syringes are found, ampoules and vials should be looked for in the vicinity.

Vomit, saliva, and mucous on or around the dead person may contain traces of poison and must be kept. Suspected stains on clothing and bedclothes are preserved by spreading each of the articles out on clean wrapping paper and rolling them separately in the paper. Stains of urine and feces can sometimes give the pathologist a guide in making a decision and should therefore be kept.

Cases of poisoning with methyl alcohol occur at times. It can usually be assumed that other persons are involved, so bottles and drinking vessels should be examined for possible fingerprints and palm prints.

Chronic alcohol poisoning can give rise to sudden death, especially after bodily strain. In acute alcoholism, death occurs when the concentration of alcohol in the blood reaches 0.4 to 0.6 g%. However, the alcoholic subject can provoke sudden death through various strokes of misfortune in a number of ways (drowning, falling, traffic accidents, freezing, suffocation from vomit that cannot be ejected, gagging from food in the windpipe). It has often happened that an alcoholic subject, while incapacitated, has died because of falling asleep in a position that made breathing difficult.

If the pathologist is present at an investigation, he or she will decide which evidence should be collected; otherwise, the investigating police officer should keep everything that might be suspected of being poison evidence and should subsequently submit it to the pathologist or toxicologist.

The presence of certain poisons in the human body can sometimes be confirmed a long time after death. Metallic poisons do not disappear with putrefaction. Arsenic can be detected in hair and bony parts hundreds of years after death; lead also remains for a long time in the bone tissues. Scopolomine, atropine, strychnine, and morphine can be detected after several years; carbon monoxide poisoning can be detected up to 6 months after death. Potassium cyanide is decomposed during putrefaction. Hydrocyanic acid and phosphorus remain for only a short time. Hypnotics are decomposed and disappear very quickly—some even in the time that elapses between administration and the occurrence of death. An exception is barbitone (veronal), which can be detected in the body 18 months after death. In cases of exhuming a body of a person suspected to have died through poisoning from metallic poisons (especially arsenic), samples of the soil from the grave should always be taken because the soil may contain the poison.

Carbon Monoxide Poisoning

Carbon monoxide is always produced when the combustion of carbonaceous matter is incomplete. It is a normal constituent of smoke and explosion gases and also occurs in mine gases, natural gas, and the like.

Carbon monoxide is a colorless and very poisonous gas with no odor or taste. The minimum concentration that can be injurious to human beings is 0.01 vol%, while 0.2 vol% is dangerous to life. Continued exposure to such an atmosphere can produce death within 1 hour. If the concentration increases to 0.5 vol% or more, then unconsciousness ensues after a couple of minutes and death follows quickly. With higher concentrations, unconsciousness comes on like a blow. Chronic poisoning by carbon monoxide is quite common, often due to prolonged exposure in shops, garages, traffic tunnels, and streets with high buildings and very heavy motor traffic.

The danger from carbon monoxide is due to the fact that the senses do not give warning in time. With acute carbon monoxide poisoning there is a headache, faintness, and nausea, with flickers before the eyes. This usually is regarded as a temporary indisposition, so the individual in question may make the greatest mistake possible under the circumstances, that of lying down. Gradually, the person becomes sleepy and confused, and the limbs become numb. If the person finally begins to realize the danger, it is usually too late because the body is so weak that the poisoned victim cannot move to safety. In many cases of carbon monoxide poisoning, the victim is found close to a door or window, but was unable to open it or did not think to break the glass.

In cases of carbon monoxide poisoning, it is possible that the death was murder. The investigating officer should therefore not treat the investigation too casually. To decide on suicide or accident immediately is wrong. The case should be considered suspicious from the start and treated accordingly. The analysis of the situation and the result of the investigation must determine whether criminal action should be taken into account. At the autopsy the pathologist can determine only the cause of death.

Carbon monoxide poisoning from exhaust gases of internal combustion motors can occur when the engine of a vehicle is started up and allowed to run for a while in a garage with bad ventilation. Suicide may be committed in this way.

Because of the variety of chemical substances that can be fatal, the determination of the cause of death in suspected poisoning cases is no easy task. Toxicologists play a key role in these types of cases. In some instances, the problem is compounded because the human body is able to metabolize the poison into another related substance, or metabolite. Other problems, such as the small concentration of the poison in the body or the metabolite being naturally present, sometimes make these tests difficult.

Rape–Homicide and Sexual Assault–Related Murders

Rape-homicides are murders committed in connection with rape and can be included with murders involving other sexual acts such as sodomy or anal intercourse. The methods employed in the investigation of such murders are in general the same as those techniques used in the investigation of an "ordinary" murder or suspicious death. The injuries found on the victim are often similar to those encountered in rape investigations, such as bruises on the arms and shoulders caused by forcibly holding down the victim, ligature marks on the wrists if the victim was tied, bruises on the back and buttocks caused by forcing the victim on the ground, and marks on the insides of the thighs and knees, and around the genitalia. Physical evidence such as seminal fluid, hair, blood, skin and blood found under the victim's fingernails, etc., may also be present. Trace evidence found on the victim's clothing might also be noted. The presence of alcohol or drugs should be determined from toxicological analyses.

The investigator should understand that the sexual aspects of these types of murders might manifest themselves in different and sometimes bizarre ways. Thus, sadism and other forms of sexual perversion may lead the inexperienced investigator to assume that a crime other than a sex-related murder is being investigated. Indications such as feces or urine discovered at the scene of a murder may point to a sex-related murder. Sadistic acts such as mutilation of the body and, particularly, the sex organs and breasts, and violent injuries such as biting, strangulation, and multiple stab wounds are especially significant and strongly suggest this type of murder (Figure 16.20).

In investigating the crime scene, one should look for signs of a struggle. Evidence such as marks on the ground, pieces of torn clothing, fragments of textiles, torn-off buttons, blood, semen, and the like should be searched for and collected. Specimens of sand, soil, vegetation, and other materials should be collected for comparison with debris found on the suspect's clothing.

One type of accidental death that could appear to be a sex-related murder is auto-erotic asphyxiation. In this type of accidental death the victim temporarily cuts off their air supply while usually masturbating to heighten their sexual arousal. When the victim is unable to free themself, they end up suffocating to death. Since oftentimes victims are found bound these types of deaths can have the illusion of a sex-related murder.

When a suspect is apprehended, the clothing and body should be examined immediately. Scratch marks on the hands and arms, on the face, bite marks, torn clothing, soiled clothing, hair, and blood may be important evidence.

Figure 16.20 A murder case showing sex-related mutilation. (Courtesy of the Los Angeles County Sheriff's Department.)

A suicidal hanging is frequently associated with sexual homicide; for example, the victim may be dressed in clothing of the opposite sex (typically a man in women's clothing) or have pornographic literature. Other signs, such as loosely binding the hands or legs and binding the genitals, may be noted.

Infanticide and Child Abuse

Homicide investigations of newborn and young children involve circumstances different from adult cases. The type of injuries causing death in infants and children are often non-fatal to adults. Often the abandoned child has no means of identification. In cases resulting in death in the home, the crime scene may show little or no physical evidence to associate the injuries with the victim. Finally, when the young victim of beating or neglect is brought to the emergency room for treatment, the child is almost always unable to communicate the cause of the injuries. These are some of the problems to be addressed in children's murder investigations.

In cases of newborn death, the pathologist is required to determine whether the child was viable, that is, capable of living. The infant is considered to be viable when it has attained a stage of development such that it would remain alive without any special care, for example, in an incubator. Babies with a length of 10 to 16 inches can certainly be born alive, but as a rule are considered not to have reached such a stage of development that they can continue to live.

Infanticide, or killing a newborn child, can be committed in a variety of ways such as intentional neglect, killing with a weapon, suffocation, forcing objects into the nose or mouth, or by drowning.

Intentional neglect occurs when the parents fail to care for the child immediately after birth, in spite of being able to do so. Death may result from exposure, dehydration, or starvation. Heat regulation in the body of a newborn can be a significant factor in exposure-related deaths because the body temperature of a baby can drop rapidly.

Abandonment of the newborn child poses an additional problem. The child may be left without any means of identification. When an infant is left wrapped only in a blanket or even without any clothes, it is frequently impossible to discover evidence to determine the mother. Killing with a weapon may be carried out with blunt objects with the intent to injure the head or by striking the head against some hard object. Stabbing is another means sometimes used in infanticide.

Strangulation is another possible cause of death; manual strangling leaves injuries and sometimes scratch marks on the neck. Suffocation can be caused by placing a pillow on or using a hand to cover the mouth or nose. If the hand is used, scratch marks may be found on the face. It should be noted, however, that suffocation may be accidental and caused by the infant lying face down on soft bedding. Suffocation may also be caused by insertion of objects into the mouth. Items such as cotton inserted into the mouth may be the cause of death.

The so-called battered child syndrome is another area in deaths of children. Frequent beatings and cruel treatment as a means of punishment or discipline sometimes result in deaths of children. Poisoning, starvation, severe beatings, and scalding in very hot water are all means of injury and often death.

Examination by a pediatrician is required in suspected child abuse cases. Often, the child is taken to the doctor or hospital emergency room and the parent may claim that the injury was the result of a fall or other unintentional injury. Careful examination of the injuries may show them to be inconsistent with the "accident" described. Also, x-rays may show several broken and healed bones characteristic of repeated and severe beating.

Trunk Murder, Dismemberment of the Body

Trunk murder is the name commonly used to describe murders in which the criminal, to dispose of the body of the victim, places it in a trunk, chest, large suitcase, box, or similar container, which is then concealed or carried away. Even more commonly, the victim is placed in a sack or covered with a blanket, clothing, or a tarpaulin. This crime is often associated with cutting up the body.

Dismemberment of a dead body may be offensive or defensive. The former is usually conditioned by passion and can be regarded as a form of sadism. A criminal who wants to conceal the body or to make it unrecognizable employs the latter. The method used may give information regarding occupational experience (butcher or person with anatomical knowledge), while the surfaces of the wounds can indicate the implements used (knife, ax, saw). Dust and dirt from the body can, in favorable cases, give information of local conditions where the dismemberment was carried out. The murderer may conceal parts of the body at different places over a considerable area, with the object of making identification of the victim difficult or impossible, or may attempt to destroy the body, for example, in an acid bath or by burning.

Frequently, the place where the body was found is not the same as the scene of the crime. If the murdered person is unknown, success in the search for the scene of the crime depends largely on the possibility of being able to determine the origin of the containers or wrapping around the body or parts of the body. The first step is to determine if labels, stamps, or writing can throw any light on their origin. These examinations involve such delicate procedures that they should be entrusted to an expert from the beginning. The CSI's preliminary examination should therefore not become too extensive.

Dirt or dust present in the wrapping may give direct information regarding what had been in it before. Fingerprints, hair, and other traces of the criminal should be looked for. When looking for fingerprints, no development media should be used until the laboratory expert has completed the examination. Bodies or parts of bodies that are found enclosed in a package are generally wrapped in a large quantity of paper, scraps of clothing, plastic bags, etc.—obviously to prevent blood, other liquid, or odor from betraying the contents. The possibility that the fingerprints of the murderer will be found in blood or blood serum should be considered. Objects used to wrap the body or parts of the body can also be a useful guide in searching for the actual scene of the crime.

Accidental Death

Occasionally, an accidental death raises suspicion. The position of the body, injuries, and appearance of the crime scene can all lead investigators into thinking the accidental death is a homicide. It is always better for an accidental death to be investigated as a homicide than vice versa (Figure 16.21).

Figure 16.21 The unusual position of the body at this scene resulted from the deceased experiencing a heart attack after stepping from her bathtub. (Courtesy of the Western Maryland Regional Crime Lab.)

Serial Murders

Serial murders are distinguished from multiple murders in that the latter are committed at about the same time and the victims are in some way connected with one another, for example, through family ties, socially, or living close by. Serial murders occur over a period of time, sometimes years, and often over large geographic areas. Probably the most celebrated serial murderer in history was the infamous Jack the Ripper who terrorized London in the 1880s. Some infamous modern cases have occurred in New York, Los Angeles, Atlanta, Washington, and Florida. Serial murders are among the most difficult types of homicides to investigate because of their complexity and a component unique to this type of crime: public alarm.

Serial murders follow an almost predictable course. Investigators discover that the M.O. of a case they are working on has similarities to other cases. As the investigation progresses, investigators from various police agencies may become involved in the investigation, as may others, that is, criminalists, pathologists, and so on. Once it becomes clear that the case involves a serial murder, communication with all others in the total investigation is imperative. Principal investigators, forensic scientists, and others who must take an active role in the case should be identified and should coordinate the investigation from this point on. All suspected future cases should be reviewed and, if possible, the crime scenes visited. Because of the delicate balance between the public's right to know and the possibility of public hysteria, all press contacts should be handled from a centralized source and specific details about the case should be withheld from the public so as not to hamper the investigation.

Once the news story breaks, enormous demands will be placed upon those responsible for the investigation. Here "cool heads" must reign. Doubtless, there will be tremendous public pressure to solve the case. Investigators will be deluged with telephone calls, yielding thousands of pieces of information (much of which will be of little value). "Copycat" cases, those with certain similarities to the serial murders, may develop.

Solving cases of the size and scope of a serial murder investigation usually involves little magic; hard work, long hours, and attention to details solve these cases. The ability to sort through mountains of information, recognize behavioral patterns, and, above all, coordinate the efforts of scores of people associated with the various elements of the case makes for a successful investigator.

One final talent for the investigator to master is worth mentioning: leadership. This know-how plays a part in serial murder investigations and may also affect other types of police investigations. The detective is ultimately responsible for running a police investigation. He or she must rely on a host of professionals within the criminal justice system. Interpersonal skills really make a difference. Learning how to ask rather than demand, saying thank you for some extra effort, and establishing good, long-term cooperative working relationships distinguish the great investigator from the adequate one.

Homicide investigation brings together nearly all the skills and principles discussed throughout this text. It requires the coordination and cooperation of many disciplines and the capability of the investigator to assimilate large amounts of information. The skills needed to process the crime scene and the ability to recognize, collect, and preserve physical evidence are crucial. A mastery of the techniques of crime scene investigation is essential to modern law enforcement.

Chapter Questions

1. List some of the initial questions that should be answered as soon as possible during a death investigation?

2. Which of the following individuals have extensive training in medicine and death investigation and respond to death scenes to assist the medical examiner in determining the cause and manner of death?
   a) Forensic examiners
   b) Criminalist
   c) Forensic anthropologist
   d) Medicolegal investigator

3. (True/False) The motivations for suicide can be deeply hidden and remain a mystery forever.
   a) True
   b) False

4. In case of violent death, why is it important to determine the apparent cause of death as soon as possible?

5. This type of bloodstain is created when the victim expels blood through the mouth or nose.
   a) Cast-off
   b) Volume
   c) Expirated
   d) Swipe
6. List some of the details that you should examine when investigating a death scene.

7. Which of the following pieces of equipment would help you to find the location of buried remains?
   a) Alternate light source
   b) Ground penetrating radar
   c) Side scan sonar
   d) Forensic light source
8. Describe the postmortem process of rigor mortis.

9. Which of the following are usually the first insects to attack a dead body?
   a) Flies
   b) Maggots
   c) Larvae
   d) Beetles
10. Describe the differences in appearance between an entrance wound in a contact shot and an entrance wound in a distance shot.

Digital Evidence

17

We live in a digital age. Much of our personal and business information is stored on computers, smart phones, tablet devices, portable USB "thumb" drives, off-line locations such as the "cloud" (virtual web-based information storage locations), on audio and video digital storage devices, and so forth. In fact, the types and nature of storage devices keep growing. It should be no surprise that digital information becomes important in criminal investigations.

In addition, e-mails, even when erased, may provide useful information. Global positioning system (GPS) technology may help locate an individual. Removable storage devices such as DVDs, CDs, thumb drives, and computer backup devices are also useful sources of data.

Caution: It is easy to lose important data when you do not know what you are doing. Therefore, a word to the wise: be certain to know what you are doing *before* you do anything when digital evidence is concerned! Many agencies now have digital evidence or computer forensics units within their agencies. If your agency does not have one, state and federal agencies are available for that purpose. Regional Computer Forensics Laboratories (RCFL) are located across the United States and can offer assistance.*

Like the types of digital devices discovered at crime scenes and criminal investigation in general, the types of crimes that may have pertinent digital evidence are equally considerable. A partial list follows, however, almost any crime may have a digital evidence component:

- Child pornography
- Identity theft
- Gambling
- Fraud
- Terrorism
- Crimes of violence
- Trade secret theft
- Theft or destruction of intellectual property
- Financial crime
- Property crime
- Internet crimes
- Organized crime and drugs
- Public corruption
- White-collar crimes

The FBI defines digital forensics as the application of science and engineering to the recovery of digital evidence in a legally acceptable method. Examiners use digital

---

* Check out the Regional Computer Forensics Laboratory, an initiative started by the FBI. For additional information, visit http://www.rcfl.gov/.

investigation and analysis techniques to determine potential legal evidence by applying their skills on a variety of software programs, different operating systems, varying hard drives sizes, and specific technologies. Examiners are capable of locating deleted, encrypted, or damaged file information that may serve as evidence in a criminal or terrorism investigation.

The scope of digital evidence investigations is far too complex for this textbook; however, we will focus on the most common devices found at crime scenes.

Computer Seizure

With the massive amounts of electronic information being created and stored by individuals and companies, computer crimes are becoming more and more widespread. These computer crimes include a wide variety of crimes: identity theft, child pornography, phishing scams, fraud, embezzling, harassment, bullying, blackmail, and others.

When encountering a computer or any type of computer equipment or data devices (CDs, USB drives, portable hard drives, PDAs, memory cards, smartphones, etc.) at a crime scene, the most important thing to remember is not to be in a hurry. Unless a suspect is destroying something in front of your eyes (which does happen), you can safely assume that the evidence is not going anywhere.

Digital devices like iPods, iPads, cameras, voice recorders, flash drives, and cell phones have become so commonplace that it is easy for CSIs to think that they are not related with a crime. All of these devices can hold both images and documents (Figure 17.1). Officers

Figure 17.1 Besides MP3 music files, an iPod can also have documents and/or images stored on it.

must, therefore, seize all types of electronic equipment because files can be stored on anything that a computer sees as a "drive."

The most common way computer evidence is destroyed is from mishandling seized equipment. Some of the ways this happens are as follows:

- Investigators become impatient and want to look at data by using the normal start-up and access procedures without considering the possibility of computer booby traps set by suspects, which may destroy data.
- The nonexpert uses common software to start up the equipment. The software has properties that destroy the data.
- Equipment (hardware and/or software) is mishandled at the crime scene or en route to the lab by improper evidence packaging or transportation.
- Unauthorized persons get involved in looking at evidence through curiosity or a haphazard request—the "Hey Fred, do you know anything about computers?" syndrome.

You do not need to be an expert to seize a computer, but you should consult an expert. You will need experts to analyze and locate relevant computer data for your case properly and legally. Data and computer equipment must be treated like any other seized evidence. Keep chain of custody procedures in mind.

Steps to Remember

- Call your agency's computer crimes unit or other appropriate experts for advice prior to seizure.
- When approaching computer equipment at a crime scene, clear everyone away from the equipment and do not allow anyone to touch any of the equipment.
- With stand-alone computers (computers without network cables), pull the power cord to turn them off. Do not touch the keyboard or any of the switches! This ensures that no data is written to the hard drive. Depending on the type of alleged crime, a triage tool should sometimes be used to capture data from a live system. Once the power is pulled from the computer, potential probative data can be lost (i.e., whether an encryption application is running).
- If the system involves a network (computers hooked up in a series to each other or to a larger computer), do not unplug them. Call your agency's computer expert before proceeding.
- If possible, take photos of the front and rear of all computers (where cables are attached).
- Before disconnecting any cables, label all connectors and computer connections with numbers or letters. Disconnect as few cables as possible. It may be necessary to disconnect some to avoid unsafe or heavy lifting; but usually one end of a cable can be disconnected, leaving the other end attached to a device.
- Attach an evidence tag to each individual piece of equipment and properly label it with the brand name, type, and model and serial numbers.

- Place all seized data CDs, memory cards, USB thumb drives, portable hard drives, etc., in labeled evidence envelopes (Figure 17.2). Keep magnetic storage media away from magnetic fields. Do not store in a hot area such as the trunk of a car.
- Document where all items were found at the location and who found them.
- Leave an inventory receipt form with persons at the location.
- Transport equipment in an enclosed vehicle. Avoid pickup beds and car trunks. If possible, use boxes and car seats or a van.
- Store equipment in a safe place where it is out of the way and will not be tripped over or stepped on.

(a)

Figure 17.2 (a) CD jewel cases near stereo equipment that appear to be only music CDs oftentimes contain data CDs in an attempt to hide them. (b) Various types of USB flash drives, thumb drives, or dongles.

(b)

Figure 17.2 (*Continued*)

In certain circumstances, it may be necessary to do an on-scene evidence preview to help determine what specific devices to look for. A preview of a suspect's hard drive can show whether an external device like a USB thumb drive or external hard drive was connected and when (Figure 17.3 and 17.4a and b). An investigator should only perform this type of investigation in the field if they have the right training and equipment.

Collecting Video Evidence

The utilization of video surveillance technology is a commonplace occurrence today. CCTV is used in savings and loan institutions, banks, stores, and other places of business for reducing robberies, shoplifting, and other crimes. It is also used for monitoring public areas in casinos, sports arenas, city streets, mass transit, and parking lots. Law enforcement uses include undercover operations, emergency and disaster responses, media releases, and crime scene recording, to mention just a few. Of course, the home video camera plays a significant role not only in television comedy shows, but also in periodically recording unusual and occasionally provocative incidents. The following information is provided as a standard procedure for handling, securing, and protecting video information so that maximum investigative utility may be obtained from it, the odds of conviction enhanced, and investigator's time and effort minimized.

Determine if There Is a Video

One of the first questions asked by investigators responding to the crime scene should be, "Is there a video of the incident? Where are the cameras? Where are the recorders?"

Figure 17.3 This external hard drive was hidden in plain sight on a shelf with toys to make it look inconspicuous. Investigators should remember to search for electronic devices not just near a computer or office.

Stop the Recorder

Often recorders continue after a crime has been committed; therefore, one of the first things to be done at the crime scene is to stop the recorders to avoid accidentally recording over the information captured.

Confiscate the Recording Medium Immediately

When handling video evidence, first stop the recorder. Next, note the time on the recorder and simultaneously note the time on your watch. Do this to the highest accuracy possible, that is, to the second. Often the time on your watch and the time on the recorder will not

(a)   (b)

Figure 17.4 (a, b) A USB thumb drive disguised to look like an ordinary toy figure. Important electronic data can easily be overlooked by an investigator in this situation.

be the same. Therefore, this time discrepancy may be needed and may be important in subsequent analysis. Also note any time differences with any other clocks in the vicinity that may have been noticed by witnesses. Next, note the position counter on the recorder and then write down the information about the recorder. Note the manufacturer, the model, the time-lapse mode, and any other recorder settings.

In addition to locating video equipment at the scene of a crime, look for additional videos that may have a view of a crime (perhaps down the street from the scene) and may contain, for instance, the car driving away. For example, when a crime occurs at a mall, convenience stores or bank ATM videos may record suspects entering or leaving the crime area. In addition, suspects may have been in other nearby locations, for instance, streets used for entry or exit routes. Also, it may be useful to look at recordings made earlier than when the crime occurred because sometimes suspects may have visited the location prior to the crime. If other tapes are located, the collection procedures mentioned previously also apply to them.

If the video is in digital format (more common today), make sure that the video collected is not compressed. Often uncompressed video will be in a format native to the manufacturer of the recording system. Uncompressed video ensures that no data is lost from the recording. It may be necessary to also obtain the software that plays the uncompressed video.

Document the Video System's Physical Relationship to the Crime Scene

Write down the location of the cameras and their views in the report or diagram or photograph this data. Additionally, the size (height, depth, width) of reference objects in the scene should be measured so that they can be utilized to determine physical dimensions of other things such as the height of a suspect.

Protect the video! Make sure that the recording medium (tape, disc, computer, etc.) cannot be recorded over. More modern systems record directly onto a hard drive.

Now that you have a video, what is the best procedure? Although it is often compelling, do not play it; take it somewhere to be copied and play only the copy, thereby saving the original for laboratory analysis. The reason this procedure is recommended is that in case something happens to the recording during analysis and/or enhancement, the original can always be gone back to. If you have gone to the trouble to collect this video as evidence, it should be prudently handled.

From a video surveillance analyst's perspective, the most common errors are the following:

- A tape that has been paused on the critical image for a long period of time for study and is thereby ruined for forensic analysis.
- Only a portion of a recording is analyzed but additional or corroborating information appears in earlier parts of the recording.

Make certain that the original is secured as evidence and stored where it will not be damaged by magnetic fields such as electric motors, solenoids, and magnetic metal detectors. Also, take care that the recording does not overheat, for example, do not leave it in a hot car. Store it in a cool, dry location. Excessive heat and humidity will cause deterioration.

Seek Technical Assistance if Problems Occur

Any of the National Law Enforcement and Corrections Technology Centers may be contacted for advice and assistance if needed. Also, the FBI has the capability to perform video analysis and many of the larger criminalistics laboratories around the nation are available for consultation, guidance, and assistance.

What can be expected from the analysis of video recordings? They can show the crime scene; they often provide a synopsis of a crime and/or a description of a crime scene that would be hard to describe in words or testimony alone. The video is physical evidence similar to a photograph. It may provide images of actions, statements, or other physical evidence that may be part of a crime (handgun, rifle, knife, car) and it provides a format for which associative evidence may be used to establish a connection between a crime scene and an individual—for instance, the car at a crime scene compared with a car of a suspect or shoes observed on a person on the video of a crime compared with shoes of the suspect. Not only might it show a connection between a suspect and a crime, it might also provide an alibi for innocent individuals. In addition, video (even stop-action video) can be used to show action in a fashion from which intent may be inferred. For instance, motion video of a person can reveal vigor of actions (pace), emotions, or other outward indicators of his or

Figure 17.5 An examiner at an FBI digital forensics lab views data extracted from a smart phone. (Courtesy of the Federal Bureau of Investigation.)

her state of mind, not simply identity as a still photograph does. Newer technologies offer enhancements of faces and license plates depicted in video that can provide investigative leads. Video footage of a crime can also aid a criminalist in determining the most probative piece of evidence to collect and/or test. For example, video footage in the elevator of a residential apartment building showed the attacker of a rape victim touching certain areas of the elevator wall. These areas could then be focused in on for fingerprinting and touch DNA collection.

Preparation and planning are the keys to success in any endeavor and certainly this is true in gathering technical evidence from digital equipment (Figure 17.5). Well-prepared technicians knowledgeable in the procedure can make the best use of a powerful tool.

Conclusion

As with other categories of forensic science evidence, a scientific working group made up of digital evidence experts is available: SWGDE, the Scientific Working Group on Digital Evidence.* The SWGDE website has a number of useful links for those interested in learning more about digital evidence.

---

* http://www.swgde.org/.

Chapter Questions

1. List some of the most common ways that computer evidence is destroyed.

2. What are some of the types of crimes associated with digital evidence?

3. Define digital evidence.

Appendix A: Equipment for Crime Scene Investigations

The crime scene investigator needs special equipment to aid in collection and preservation of evidence, photography, and sketching. Equipment should be flexible, portable, and arranged in suitable carrying cases. The following list of supplies and equipment suggests many items generally useful to have on hand at a crime scene investigation. Experience will suggest additional materials that the investigator will find helpful.

Basic Equipment

- Flashlight and spare batteries
- Laptop computer
- Disposable latex/nitrile examination gloves
- Coveralls or disposable clothing
- 50-foot steel surveyor's tape
- 12-foot steel tape measure
- 12-inch ruler
- 6-inch ruler
- Writing paper and report forms
- Graph paper
- Clipboard
- Writing and marking pens, pencils
- Metal scribe
- Chalk and crayons
- Evidence tags
- Evidence sealing tape
- Stapler and staples
- Adhesive and cellophane tape
- Rubber bands
- Scissors
- Scalpel and replacement blades
- Assorted large and small forceps
- Spatulas
- Paper towels
- Hand magnifier
- Disposable pipettes and rubber bulbs
- Cotton-tipped applicators
- Test tubes and corks
- Plastic conical tubes

- Compass
- Magnet
- pH paper
- Antiputrefaction masks
- Odor eliminators (www.morningsicknesssoothers.com)
- Thumbtacks

Evidence Packaging Supplies

- Envelopes of various sizes
- Paper bags
- Plastic bags
- Pillboxes
- Metal paint cans and lids
- Cardboard boxes
- Zip-ties
- Screw-cap glass vials of various sizes
- Paper

Photographic Equipment

- Digital SLR camera
- Lenses—normal, wide angle, and macro
- Filters (polarizing, UV, contrast, etc.)
- Electronic media storage devices
- Flash unit and fresh batteries
- Tripod
- Level
- Rulers and other devices to show scale of items
- Light meter
- Carrying case
- 3D scanner and software
- Lens brush and lens tissue
- Video camera

Fingerprint Equipment

- Fingerprint brushes
- Magna-Brush
- Lift cards
- Magnifier
- Fingerprint powders
- Lifting tape
- Rubber lifters

Hand Tools

- Hammers
- Hand or power saw
- Screwdrivers
- Wrench
- Vise-Grips
- Pliers
- Knife
- Shovels
- Sifters
- Rake
- Bolt cutters
- Power drill
- Electrical extension cords
- Wire cutters
- Hacksaw
- Socket wrench set
- Rope
- Wood chisel
- Ax
- Cotton work gloves
- Pry bar
- Spatula

DNA/Blood Collection Supplies

- K–M reagent, or other presumptive blood test
- 3% Hydrogen peroxide
- Saline
- Distilled water
- Luminol/Bluestar® reagent
- Spray bottle
- Cotton cloth
- Rubber gloves
- Spot plates
- Sterile cotton-tipped applicators/swabs
- 10% Bleach
- 70% Ethanol
- Disposable pipettes and rubber bulbs
- Vacuum blood collection tubes
- Syringes
- Toothpicks

Casting Materials

- Dental stone
- Rubber or plastic mixing bowls
- Wooden spatula
- Metal retaining bands
- Wire or wooden splints for support
- Baffle
- Cardboard boxes to hold finished cast
- Silicone rubber or dental impression material
- Modeling clay for dam
- Ziploc® plastic baggies for mixing

Other Equipment

- Ladder
- Portable vacuum and filters
- Portable generator
- Handheld tape recorder
- Metal detector
- Portable floodlights
- Gunshot residue testing kits

Safety Equipment

- Hard hat
- Hazardous chemical reference material
- Access to breathing devices (i.e., SCBAs) for clandestine drug labs
- Coveralls
- Heavy gloves
- Masks

General Crime Scene Supply

- ACE Fingerprint Equipment Laboratories, Inc.
- Arrowhead Forensic Products
- CrimeTech, Inc.
- Doje's Forensic Supplies
- Evident Crime Scene Products
- Fitzco Forensic Collection Products
- Forensics Source Hippo Evidence Bags LLC
- Identicator-Fingerprint Products
- The Lynn Peavey Company
- Marx Brush-Fingerprint Brushes
- ORC Forensics-Products for forensics and crime scene analysis
- Sirchie Finger Print Laboratories, Inc.
- Spex ForensicsTri-Tech Forensics

Appendix B: Forensic Science–Related Websites

Literally thousands of sites on the Internet offer valuable information on forensic science, crime scene investigation, and related information. These represent only a few.*

General Forensic Information

http://www.forensic-evidence.com
http://www.theiai.org
http://www.aafs.org
http://www.fbi.gov/about-us/lab/forensic-science-communications/index.htm
http://www.forensicnexus.com
http://www.iapsonline.com/forensic
http://www.forensictv.net
http://www.nfstc.org/
http://www.ascld.org/
http://www.criminalistics.com
http://www.forensicnetbase.com/
http://www.forensic.to/forensic.html
http://www.neafs.org
http://www.aafs.org/choosing-career
http://www.forensicpage.com
http://www.forensic-science-society.org.uk/
http://www.crimeandclues.com/
http://www.cacnews.org/
http://www.forensicmag.com/
http://crime-scene-investigator.net/

Bloodstain Pattern Analysis

http://www.iabpa.org
http://www.swgstain.org
http://www.bloody1.com
http://www.physics.carleton.ca/~carter
http://www.gardnerforensic.com
http://www.paulkish.com

* Thanks to Kay Pitluck for providing this information and to Alexis Anderson for reviewing the accuracy of each link.

Bureau of Alcohol, Tobacco, Firearms, and Explosives

http://www.atf.gov

DNA

http://www.dna.gov/
http://www.cstl.nist.gov/strbase/

Drug Enforcement Administration

http://www.usdoj.gov/dea

Drugs

http://www.usdoj.gov/dea/
http://www.drugfreeamerica.org
http://www.drugs.indiana.edu/druginfo/

Evidence Procedures

http://www.iape.org/
http://www.iafsm.com/
http://www.crime-scene-investigator.net/csi-collection.html
http://www.ncsconline.org/wc/CourTopics/ResourceGuide.asp?topic=StoEvi#227
http://www.feinc.net/cs-inv-p.htm
http://www.icsia.org/
http://www.cape-inc.us/

Federal Bureau of Investigation

http://www.fbi.gov
http://www.fbi.gov/hq.htm#lab
http://www.fbi.gov/hq/lab/labhome.htm (FBI's laboratory)
http://foia.fbi.gov/
http://foia.fbi.gov/room.htm (Freedom of Information Act listing of evidence from
    specific cases)

Fire Science

http://www.nist.gov/el/fire_research/index.cfm
http://www.doctorfire.com

http://www.firefindings.com
http://www.interfire.com
http://www.arson-codes.com
http://www.usfa.fema.gov
http://www.fire.nist.gov/bfrlpubs/fire01/art023.html
http://www.nhml.com/resources/1991/3/1/burn-pattern-in-vehicle-fires-forensic-
   analysis

Firearms Identification

http://www.afte.org/
http://www.geocities.com/j_ksinha/index.html
http://library.med.utah.edu/WebPath/TUTORIAL/GUNS/GUNINTRO.html
http://www.firearmstactical.com/index.htm

Forensic Anthropology

http://www.theabfa.org/index.html
http://foil.ucsc.edu/mdc/index.html
http://archlab.uindy.edu/barfaa/index.php
http://www.forensicanthro.com/
http://www.uncwil.edu/people/albertm/

Forensic Dentistry

http://www.abfo.org/

Forensic Entomology

http://www.coleopsoc.org/
http://www.entsoc.org/
http://www.nafea.net/
http://www.forensicentomology.com

Forensic Pathology/Medical Examiners

http://www.thename.org/
http://medschool.slu.edu/abmdi/index.php
http://www.cap.org/apps/cap.portal
http://health.discovery.com/fansites/drg/drg-fansite.html
http://www.ihia.org/

Impressions

http://www.fpsociety.org.uk
http://www.scafo.org/
http://onin.com/fp/
http://www.latent-prints.com/
http://clpex.com/
http://ridgesandfurrows.homestead.com/
http://www.fprints.nwlean.net/index.htm
http://www.forensicITC.com
http://swgtread.org/
http://www.swgfast.org/

Missing Persons

http://www.NamUs.gov/

Profiling

http://www.corpus-delicti.com/profiling.html
http://www.vidocq.org
http://www.johndouglasmindhunter.com/home.htm
http://cognitiveconsultantsinternational.com/index.php?sub=drdror
http://www.crimelibrary.com
http://www.karisable.com/crime.htm
http://www.criminalprofiling.ch/types.html

University Forensic Education

http://www.aafs.org/fepac
http://crime-scene-investigator.net/csi-training.html
http://web.utk.edu/~anthrop/
http://www.jjay.cuny.edu
http://www.gwu.edu/~forensic/
http://www.calstatela.edu
http://www.newhaven.edu/5765/
http://www.olemiss.edu/depts/chemistry/undergraduate/bs_forensic.php
http://chemistry.cos.ucf.edu/undergraduate_degree_forensic.php
http://www.cj.msu.edu/
http://www.grossmont.edu/aoj/forensic.asp

U.S. Department of Justice

http://www.usdoj.gov/

U.S. Fish and Wildlife Laboratories

http://www.lab.fws.gov/ (U.S. Fish & Wildlife Lab)
http://www.fws.gov/

U.S. Marshals Service

http://www.usdoj.gov/marshals/

U.S. Postal Inspection Service

https://postalinspectors.uspis.gov/

Selected Video Demonstations of CSI Techniques

Using Mikrosil to Lift Fingerprints from Irregular Surfaces: http:
//www.youtube.com/watch?v=HkQH0h7BeXo

Developing Latent Fingerprints with Black Powder: http:
//www.youtube.com/watch?v=tqFzVfPRd5s

Developing Latent Fingerprints with Magnetic Powder: http:
//www.youtube.com/watch?v=iomWm3_Qvhk

Casting Footwear Impressions: http:
//www.youtube.com/watch?v=mquyNZaNbPo

Developing Fingerprints with Super Glue: http:
//www.youtube.com/watch?v=R0e8WXkFA64

Photographing Footwear Impressions: http:
//www.youtube.com/watch?v=C29XEOzi8B0

Casting Tool Mark Impressions with Mikrosil: http:
//www.youtube.com/watch?v=ZD-KSGDFX_g

Presumptive Blood Tests: http:
//www.youtube.com/watch?v=pnH2HnB-GrI

Electrostatic Dust Lifter: http:
//www.youtube.com/watch?v=HdAUas4kQw0

Bibliography

The following list suggests further reading relevant to many of the areas covered in the text. Because this book is written primarily for law enforcement personnel, material of a highly technical nature has been intentionally omitted. Thus, certain areas requiring a greater level of scientific knowledge may be limited in this bibliography. The references below serve as a starting point from which the reader wishing additional information may begin, but by no means represents an exhaustive bibliography on forensic science. The Internet is an additional resource for persons interested in the subject and readers are also encouraged to consider membership in the fine professional organizations noted in the text.

Chapter 1

Barnett, P. *Ethics in Forensic Science: Professional Standards for the Practice of Criminalistics*. Boca Raton, FL: CRC Press, 2001.

Bell, S. *Encyclopedia of Forensic Science*. New York: Facts on File, Inc., 2004.

Bergman, R. A. 1988. The impact of technological advancement on forensic science practice. *J. Forensic Sci. Soc.* 21: 169.

Bohan, T. L., and E. J. Heels. 1995. The case against Daubert: The new scientific evidence "standard" and the standards of several states. *J. Forensic Sci.* 40: 1030.

Buckhout, R. 1974. Eyewitness testimony. *Sci. Am.* 231: 2.

Delattre, E. J. *Character and Cops, Ethics in Policing*. Lanham, MD: American Enterprise Institute for Public Policy Research, University Press of America, Inc., 1989.

Doyle, P. 1989. The role of the expert witness. *AFTE J.* 21: 639.

Emergency Response Guidebook. United States Department of Transportation, Research and Special Programs Administration, 2000.

Faigman, D. L. et al. *Modern Scientific Evidence: The Law and Science of Expert Testimony*. St. Paul, MN: West Publishing, 2002.

Fisher, B. et al. *Forensics Demystified*. New York: McGraw-Hill, 2007.

Giannelli, P. C. 1989. Evidentiary and procedural rules governing expert testimony. *J. Forensic Sci.* 34: 730.

Havard, J. D. J. 1992. Expert scientific evidence under the adversarial system. A travesty of justice? *J. Forensic Sci. Soc.* 32: 225.

Hodgkinson, T. 1988. Expert evidence and reasonable doubt. *Law Q. Rev.* 104: 198.

Hollien, H. 1990. The expert witness: Ethics and responsibilities. *J. Forensic Sci.* 35: 1414.

Knight, B. 1989. Ethics and discipline in forensic science. *J. Forensic Sci. Soc.* 29: 53.

Nordby, J. *Dead Reckoning: The Art of Forensic Detection*. Boca Raton, FL: CRC Press LLC, 2000.

Peterson, J. L., and J. E. Murdock. 1989. Forensic science ethics: Developing an integrated system of support and enforcement. *J. Forensic Sci.* 34: 749.

Rosner, R. 1996. Ethical practice in the forensic sciences and justification of ethical codes. *J. Forensic Sci.* 41: 913.

Saks, M. J. 1989. Prevalence and impact of ethical problems in forensic science. *J. Forensic Sci.* 34: 772.

Chapter 3

Buck, S. C. 2003. Searching for graves using geophysical technology: Field tests with ground penetrating radar, magnetometry, and electrical resistivity. *J. Forensic Sci.* 48, no. 1: 5.

Harvey, L. M., and J. W. Harvey. 2003. Reliability of bloodhounds in criminal investigations. *J. Forensic Sci.* 48, no. 4: 811.

Horvath, F., and R. Meesig. 1996. The criminal investigation process and the role of forensic evidence: A review of empirical findings. *J. Forensic Sci.* 41: 963.

Chapter 4

Adrian, D., K. Alibek, and R. D. Thomas. *Chem-Bio Handbook*. Alexandria, VA: Jane's Information Group, 1998.

Bradford, L. W., and A. A. Biasotti. 1973. Teamwork in the forensic sciences: Report of a case. *J. Forensic Sci.* 18: 31.

Chemical and Biological Terrorism. Washington, DC: The National Academies Press, 1999.

Dickinson, D. J. 1976. The aerial use of an infrared camera in a police search for the body of a missing person in New Zealand. *J. Forensic Sci. Soc.* 16: 205.

Emergency Response to Terrorism—Job Aid, Edition 1.0. Washington, DC: U.S. Department of Justice, Office of Justice Programs, 2000.

Gardner, R. Practical Crime Scene Processing and Investigation. Boca Raton, FL: CRC Press, 2005.

Making the Nation Safer—The Role of Science and Technology in Countering Terrorism. Washington, DC: The National Academies Press, 2002.

Richards, G. B. 1977. The application of electronic video techniques to infrared and ultraviolet examinations. *J. Forensic Sci.* 22: 53.

Wood, C. M. et al. *Guidelines for Handling Decedents Contaminated with Radioactive Materials*. Atlanta, GA: Centers for Disease Control, U.S. Dept. of Health and Human Services, 2007.

Chapter 5

Berg, E. 1995. The evolution of the crime scene diagram. *J. Forensic Identification* 45: 25.

Collinson, J. G. 1970. The role of the investigating officer. *J. Forensic Sci. Soc.* 10: 199.

Morse, D., D. Crusoe, and H. G. Smith. 1976. Forensic archaeology. *J. Forensic Sci.* 21: 323.

O'Brien, M. W. 1989. Scale model use in criminal trials. *J. Forensic Identification* 39: 359.

Scott, H. 1970. The role of the photographer. *J. Forensic Sci. Soc.* 10: 205.

Shelef, R., and R. Elkayam. 1997. Collecting and packaging exhibits from the scene of the crime for transfer to the forensic laboratory. *J. Forensic Identification* 47: 276.

Siljander, R. P. *Applied Police and Fire Photography*. Springfield, IL: Charles C Thomas, 1976.

Singla, A. K., and O. P. Jasuja. 1990. Photographing indented impressions under oblique light: A simple modification. *J. Forensic Sci. Soc.* 30: 211.

Warlen, S. 1995. Crime scene photography: The silent witness. *J. Forensic Identification* 45: 261.

West, M. H., J. D. Billings, and J. Frair. 1987. Ultraviolet photography: Bite marks on human skin and suggested techniques for the exposure and development of reflective ultraviolet photography. *J. Forensic Sci.* 32: 1204.

West, M. H. et al. 1989. Ultraviolet photography of wounds on human skin. *J. Forensic Identification* 39: 87.

West, M. H., R. E. Barsley, J. Frair, and F. Hall. 1990. Reflective ultraviolet imaging system (RUVIS) and the detection of trace evidence on human skin. *J. Forensic Identification* 40: 249.

Chapter 6

Abalos, A. 1989. Regenerating finger pads on burnt, putrefied or mummified corpses. *Int. Criminal Police Rev.*, 44: 16.

Allen, M. J. et al. 1988. The dating of a will. *J. Forensic Sci. Soc.* 28: 199.

Allison, H. C. *Personal Identification.* Boston, MA: Holbrook Press, 1973.

Arbouine, M. W., and S. P. Day. 1994. The use of drum defects to link laser-printed documents to individual laser printers. *J. Forensic Sci. Soc.* 34: 99.

Arensburg, B. 1989. Methods for age identification on living individuals of uncertain age. *Can. Soc. Forensic Sci. J.* 22: 147.

Austin-Smith, D., and W. R. Maples. 1994. The reliability of skull/photograph superimposition in individual identification. *J. Forensic Sci.* 39: 446.

Barton, B. C. 1989. The use of an electrostatic detection apparatus to demonstrate the matching of torn paper edges. *J. Forensic Sci. Soc.* 29: 35.

Beck, J. 1995. Sources of error in handwriting evaluation. *J. Forensic Sci.* 40: 78.

Bentsen, R. K., J. K. Brown, A. Dinsmore, K. K. Harvey, and T. G. Kee. 1996. Post-firing visualization of fingerprints on spent cartridge cases. *Sci. Justice* 36: 3.

Berg, E. 1996. Digital enhancement and transmission of latent prints. *J. Forensic Identification* 46: 573.

Bettencourt, D. S. 1991. A compilation of techniques for processing deceased human skin for latent prints. *J. Forensic Identification* 41: 111.

Black, J. 1990. The interaction of visualization fluids and fingerprints. *J. Forensic Identification* 40: 28.

Bobev, K. 1995. Fingerprints and factors affecting their condition. *J. Forensic Identification* 45: 176.

Brandt-Casadevall, C. et al. 1989. Identification based on medical data. *Can. Soc. Forensic Sci. J.* 22: 35.

Breedlove, C. H. 1989. The analysis of ballpoint inks for forensic purposes. *J. Chemical Educ.* 68: 170.

Brill, A. E., and C. Whitcomb, 2006. The Evolution of Computer Forensic Best Practices: An Update on Programs and Publications, *Journal of Digital Forensic Practice* 1: 1.

Brunelle, R. L. 1992. Ink dating—The state of the art. *J. Forensic Sci.* 37: 113.

Brunelle, R. L., C. H. Breedlove, and C. R. Midkill. 1987. Determining the relative age of ballpoint inks using a single-solvent extraction technique. *J. Forensic Sci.* 32: 1511.

Brunelle, R. L., and A. A. Cantu. 1987. A critical evaluation of current ink dating techniques. *J. Forensic Sci.* 32: 1522.

Buquet, A. et al. 1989. The application of statistical methods to the analysis of typewritten documents: regression and covariance. *Int. Criminal Police Rev.* 44: 10.

Burnes, K. R., and W. R. Maples. 1976. Estimation of age from individual adult teeth. *J. Forensic Sci.* 21: 343.

Caldwell, J. P., and N. D. Kim. 2002. Extension of the color suite available for chemical enhancement of fingerprints in blood. *J. Forensic Sci.* 47, no. 2: 332.

Campbell, B. M. 1991. Separation of adhesive tapes. *J. Forensic Identification* 41: 102.

Camps, F. E. *Medical and Scientific Investigations in the Cristie Case.* London: Medical Publications, Ltd., 1953.

Cantu, A. A., and R. S. Prough. 1987. On the relative aging of ink—The solvent extraction technique. *J. Forensic Sci.* 32: 1151.

Choudhry, M. Y., and R. D. Whritenour. 1990. A new approach to unraveling tangled adhesive tape for potential detection of latent fingerprints and recovery of trace evidence. *J. Forensic Sci.* 35: 1373.

Cole, S. A. *Suspect Identities: A History of Fingerprinting and Criminal Identification.* Cambridge, MA: Harvard University Press, 2001.

Conway, J. V. P. *Evidential Documents.* Springfield, IL: Charles C Thomas, 1959.

Cook, S. 1996. The use of embalming fluids in the restoration of mummified fingers. *J. Forensic Identification* 46: 529.

Cowger, J. F. 1979. Moving towards professionalization of latent print examiners. *J. Forensic Sci.* 24: 591.

Cowger, J. F. *Friction Ridge Skin*. Boca Raton, FL: CRC Press, 1983.

Creighton, J. 1997. Visualization of latent impressions after incidental or direct contact with human blood. *J. Forensic Identification* 47: 534.

Crown, D. A. 1989. The differentiation of electrostatic photocopy machines. *J. Forensic Sci.* 34: 142.

Dalrymple, B. E. 1979. Case analysis of fingerprint detection by laser. *J. Forensic Sci.* 24: 586.

Dalrymple, B. E., and T. Menzies. 1994. Computer enhancement of evidence through background noise suppression. *J. Forensic Sci.* 39: 537.

Dalrymple, B. E., J. M. Duff, and E. R. Menzel. 1977. Inherent fingerprint luminescence detection by laser. *J. Forensic Sci.* 22: 106.

Day, S. P. 1985. Evaluation of the application of the argon-ion laser to document examination: a review of casework and experimental data. *J. Forensic Sci. Soc.* 25: 285.

Doherty, P. E. et al. 1990. Deciphering bloody imprints through chemical enhancement. *J. Forensic Sci.* 35: 457.

Drake, W., and L. Lukash. 1978. Reconstruction of mutilated victims for identification. *J. Forensic Sci.* 23: 218.

El-Najjar, M. Y., and K. R. McWilliams. *Forensic Anthropology: The Structure, Morphology and Variation of Bones and Dentition*. Springfield, IL: Charles C Thomas, 1977.

Gamboe, T. E. 1989. Small particle: Developing latent prints on water-soaked firearms and effect on firearms analysis. *J. Forensic Sci.* 34: 312.

Geng, Q. 1998. Recovery of super glue over-fumed fingerprints. *J. Forensic Identification* 48: 17.

Gilmour, C. et al. 1987. The effect of medication on handwriting. *Can. Soc. Forensic Sci.* 20: 119.

Glaister, J., and J. C. Brash. *Medico-Legal Aspects of the Ruxton Case*. Edinburgh: E and S Livingstone, 1937.

Goetz, M. 1996. Cyanoacrylate fuming precautions. *J. Forensic Identification* 46: 409.

Golden, G. S. 1994. Use of alternative light source illumination in bite mark photography. *J. Forensic Sci.* 39: 815.

Gupta, A. K. et al. 1989. Electrostatic detection of secret writings. *Forensic Sci. Int.* 41: 17.

Haglund, W. D. 1987. A technique to enhance fingerprinting of mummified fingers. *J. Forensic Sci.* 33: 1244.

Haglund, W. D., and K. Sperry. 1993. The use of hydrogen peroxide to visualize tattoos obscured by decomposition and mummification. *J. Forensic Sci.* 38: 147.

Hall, R. F. 1979. Latent skin print identification solves homicide. *FBI Law Enforcement Bull.* 48: 9.

Haque, F. et al. 1989. A small particle (iron oxide) suspension for detection of latent fingerprints on smooth surfaces. *Forensic Sci. Int.* 41: 73.

Harada, H. 1988. A rapid identification of black color materials with specific reference to ballpoint ink and indian ink. *J. Forensic Sci. Soc.* 28: 167.

Harris, J. 1992. Developments in the analysis of writing inks on questioned documents. *J. Forensic Sci.* 37: 612.

Harris, J. et al. 1989. Characterization and dating of correction fluids on questioned documents using FTIR. *Can. Soc. Forensic Sci. J.* 22: 349.

Harrison, W. R. *Suspect Documents: Their Scientific Examination*. New York: Frederick A. Praeger, 1958.

Hart, L. J. et al. 1989. Photographically subtracting interfering images from ESDA. *J. Forensic Sci.* 34: 1405.

Hart, L. J. et al. 1989. Typewriting versus writing instrument: A line intersection problem. *J. Forensic Sci.* 34: 1329.

Harvey, W. *Dental Identification and Forensic Odontology*. London: Henry Kimpton Publishers, 1976.

Herod, D. W., and E. R. Menzel. 1982. Laser detection of latent fingerprints: Ninhydrin followed by zinc chloride. *J. Forensic Sci.* 27: 513.

Hewlett, D., and V. Sears. 1997. Replacements for CFC113 in the ninhydrin process: Part 1. *J. Forensic Identification* 47: 287.

Hewlett, D., V. Sears, and S. Suzuki. 1997. Replacements for CFC113 in the ninhydrin process: Part 2. *J. Forensic Identification* 47: 300.

Hicks, A. F. 1995. Computer imaging for questioned document examiners I—The benefits. *J. Forensic Sci.* 40: 145.

Hicks, A. F. 1995. Computer imaging for questioned document examiners II—The potential for abuse. *J. Forensic Sci.* 40: 1052.

Hilton, O. 1979. History of questioned documents examination in the United States. *J. Forensic Sci.* 24: 890.

Hilton, O. *Scientific Examination of Questioned Documents.* New York: Elsevier North-Holland, 1981.

Hilton, O. 1992. Signatures—Review and a new view. *J. Forensic Sci.* 37: 125.

Hongwei, S. et al. 1989. The estimation of tooth age from attrition of the occlusal surface. *Med. Sci. Law* 29: 69.

Hooft, P. J. et al. 1989. Fatality management in mass casualty incidents. *Forensic Sci. Int.* 40: 3.

Horan, G. J. et al. 1988. How long after writing can an ESDA image be developed? *Forensic Sci. Int.* 39: 119.

Jackson, G. R. 1994. A high-resolution electronic imaging system for crime scene use. *Forensic Sci.* 39: 912.

James, J. D., C. A. Pounds, and B. Wilshire. 1991. Obliteration of latent fingerprints. *J. Forensic Sci.* 36: 1376.

Jaret, Y., M. Meriau, and A. Donche. 1997. Transfer of bloody fingerprints. *J. Forensic Identification* 47: 38.

Jones, N. 1990. Arson-for-profit investigations, success or failure? Recovering water damaged business records. *Fire Arson Invest.* 40: 50.

Kahana, T., A. Grande, D. M. Tancredi, J. Penalver, and J. Hiss. 2001. Fingerprinting the deceased: Traditional and new techniques. *J. Forensic Sci.* 46, no. 4: 908.

Kam, M., G. Fielding, and R. Conn. 1997. Writer identification by professional document examiners. *J. Forensic Sci.* 42: 778.

Kam, M., J. Weststein, and R. Conn. 1994. Proficiency of professional document examiners in writer identification. *J. Forensic Sci.* 39: 5.

Katz, J. O. et al. 1988. The present direction of research in forensic odontology. *J. Forensic Sci.* 33: 1319.

Kaymaz, E., and S. Mitra. 1993. A novel approach to Fourier spectral enhancement of laser-luminescent fingerprint images. *J. Forensic Sci.* 38: 530.

Keating, D. M., and J. J. Miller. 1993. A technique for developing and photographing ridge impressions on decomposed water-soaked fingers. *J. Forensic Sci.* 38: 197.

Kempton, J. B. et al. 1992. Comparison of fingernail striation patterns in identical twins. *J. Forensic Sci.* 37: 1534.

Kerley, E. R. In *Forensic Anthropology, Legal Medicine Annual*, ed. C. H. Wecht, 163–98. New York: Appleton-Century-Crofts, 1973.

Killam, E. W. 1989. Is it human? Differentiating between human and animal bones. *Crime Lab. Dig.* 16: 9.

Kopainsky, B. 1989. Document examination: Applications of image processing systems. *Forensic Sci. Rev.* 1: 85.

Krauss, T. C. 1976. Forensic odontology in missing person cases. *J. Forensic Sci.* 21: 959.

Kremer, R. D. et al. 1989. Paper, its material and macro-structural characteristics relevant to analytical and diagnostic test development. *Am. Lab.* 21: 16.

Larson, C. P. 1974. Unusual methods of human identification used in three cases. *J. Forensic Sci.* 19: 402.

Lee, H. C., and R. E. Gaensslen. *Advances in Fingerprint Technology.* 2nd ed. Boca Raton, FL: CRC Press, 2001.

Lee, H. C. et al. 1989. The effect of presumptive test, latent fingerprint and some other reagents and materials on subsequent serological identification, genetic marker and DNA testing in bloodstains. *J. Forensic Identification* 39: 339.

Lennard, C. J. et al. 1988. Sequencing of reagents for the improved visualization of latent fingerprints. *J. Forensic Identification* 38: 197.

Lifschultz, B. D., and E. R. Donoghue. 1993. Deaths caused by lightning. *J. Forensic Sci.* 38: 353.

Lunt, D. A. 1974. Identification and tooth morphology. *J. Forensic Sci. Soc.* 14: 203.

Luntz, L. L., and P. Luntz. 1972. Dental identification of disaster victims by a dental disaster squad. *J. Forensic Sci.* 17: 63.

MacFarlane, T. W., D. G. MacDonald, and D. A. Sutherland. 1974. Statistical problems in dental identification. *J. Forensic Sci. Soc.* 14: 247.

Marchand, P. 1989. A nondestructive method for determining the grain direction of paper. *Can. Soc. Forensic Sci. J.* 22: 69.

Margot, P., and C. Lennard. *Manual of Fingerprint Detection Techniques*. Lausanne: Institute de Police Scientifique et de Criminologie, Universite de Lausanne, 1990.

Marks, M. K., J. L. Bennett, and O. L. Wilson. 1997. Digital video image capture in establishing positive identification. *J. Forensic Sci.* 42: 92.

Masters, N., and J. De Haan. 1996. Vacuum metal deposition and cyanoacrylate detection of older latent prints. *J. Forensic Identification* 46: 32.

McCarthy, M. M. 1990. Evaluation of ardrox as a luminescent stain for cyanoacrylate processed latent impressions. *J. Forensic Identification* 40: 75.

McCarthy, M. M. et al. 1989. Preprocessing with cyanoacrylate ester fuming for fingerprint impressions in blood. *J. Forensic Identification* 39: 23.

Menzel, E. R. 1979. Laser detection of latent fingerprints with phosphorescers. *J. Forensic Sci.* 24: 582.

Menzel, E. R. 1985. Comparison of argon-ion, copper-vapor and frequency-doubled neodymium: yttrium aluminum garnet (ND:YAG) laser for latent fingerprint development. *J. Forensic Sci.* 30: 383.

Menzel, E. R. 1989. Detection of latent fingerprints, laser-excited luminescence. *Anal. Chem.* 61: 557A.

Menzel, E. R. 1989. Pretreatment of latent prints for laser development. *Forensic Sci. Rev.* 1: 43.

Menzel, E. R. et al. 1990. Fluorescent metal-Ruhemann's purple coordination compounds: Application to latent fingerprint detection. *J. Forensic Sci.* 35: 25.

Menzel, E.R., J. A. Burt, T. W. Sinor, W. B. Tubach-Ley, and K. J. Jordon. 1983. Laser detection of latent fingerprints: Treatment of glue-containing cyanoacrylate ester. *J. Forensic Sci.* 28: 307.

Menzel, E. R., and K. E. Fox. 1980. Laser detection of latent fingerprints: Preparation of fluorescent dusting powders and the feasibility of a portable system. *J. Forensic Sci.* 25: 150.

Mittal, S. et al. 1989. The forensic examination of unfamiliar scripts. *Int. Criminal Police Rev.* 44: 11.

Morse, D., J. Duncan, and J. Stoutamire. *Handbook of Forensic Archaeology and Anthropology*. Tallahassee, FL: Rose Printing Co., 1983.

Munson, T. O. 1989. A simple method for sampling photocopy toners for examination, pyrolysis gas chromatography. *Crime Lab. Dig.* 16: 6.

Noble, H. W. 1974. The estimation of age from dentition. *J. Forensic Sci. Soc.* 14: 215.

Olenik, J. H. 1989. Cyanoacrylate fuming: An alternative non-heat method. *J. Forensic Identification* 39: 302.

Osborn, A. S. *Questioned Documents*. 2nd ed. London: Sweet & Maxwell, Ltd., 1929.

Owen, T. 1989. An introduction to forensic examination of audio and videotapes. *J. Forensic Identification* 39: 75.

Parkinson, G. 1996. Certification programs of the International Association for Identification. *J. Forensic Identification* 46: 169.

Penalver, J., T. Kahana, and J. Hiss. 1997. Prosthetic devices in positive identification of human remains. *J. Forensic Identification* 47: 400.

Phillips, C. E. et al. 1990. Physical developer: A practical and productive latent print developer. *J. Forensic Identification* 40: 135.

Pierce, D. S. 1989. Tonally reversed friction ridge prints on plastics. *J. Forensic Identification* 39: 11.

Plamondon, R. et al. 1989. Automatic signature verification and writer identification: The state of the art. *Pattern Recognition* 22: 107.

Reichardt, G. J., J. C. Carr, and E. G. Stone. 1978. A conventional method for lifting latent fingerprints from human skin surfaces. *J. Forensic Sci.* 23: 135.

Richardson, L., and H. Kade. 1972. Readable fingerprints from mummified or putrefied specimens. *J. Forensic Sci.* 17: 325.

Ruprecht, A. 1989. Use of direct positive photographic paper in the preparation of fingerprint exhibits. *J. Forensic Identification* 39: 244.

Ruslander, H. 1997. Super glue fuming of vegetation at crime scenes. *J. Forensic Identification* 47: 42.

Sams, C. 1970. The role of the fingerprint officer. *J. Forensic Sci. Soc.* 10: 219.

Saunders, J. 1993. Macroscopic examination of overlapping latent prints on non-porous items. *J. Forensic Identification* 43: 138.

Sauvarin, A. 1993. Latent fingerprints on a fingernail. *J. Forensic Identification* 43: 35.

Scheuer, J. L., and N. M. Elkington. 1993. Sex determination from metacarpals and the first proximal phalanx. *J. Forensic Sci.* 38: 769.

Sedeyn, M. J. 1988. Handwriting examination: A practical approach. *Forensic Sci. Int.* 36: 169.

Seguss, R. K. 1988. Altered and counterfeit travel documents: A Canadian perspective. *Int. Criminal Police Rev.* 43: 11.

Sekharan, P. C. 1989. Personal identification from skull suture pattern. *Can. Soc. Forensic Sci.* 22: 27.

Sharf, S., R. Gabbay, and S. Brown. 1997. Infrared luminescence of indented writing as evidence of document alteration. *J. Forensic Sci.* 42: 729.

Shelef, R., A. Levy, I. Rhima, S. Tsaroom, and R. Elkayam. 1996. Development of latent fingerprints from unignited incendiary bottles. *J. Forensic Identification* 46: 557.

Shelef, R., A. Levy, I. Rhima, S. Tsaroom, and R. Elkayam. 1996. Recovery of latent fingerprints from soot-covered incendiarized glass surfaces. *J. Forensic Identification* 46: 565.

Shelef, R., I. Rhima, and R. Elkayam. 1996. Development of latent fingerprints from glass surfaces washed in accelerant fluids. *J. Forensic Identification* 46: 561.

Shonberger, M. 1997. A variation of super glue processing of small, immovable, or difficult to move items. *J. Forensic Identification* 47: 47.

Skinner, M. F. 1989. Applied archaeology and physical anthropology in a forensic context: A review of 12 years of forensic anthropology in British Columbia. *Can. Soc. Forensic Sci.* 22: 83.

Skinner, M. F. 1988. Method and theory in deciding identity of skeletonized human remains. *Can. Soc. Forensic Sci. J.* 21: 114.

Sognnaes, R. F. 1977. Progress in forensic dentistry I. *New Engl. J. Med.* 296: 79.

Sognnaes, R. F. 1977. Progress in forensic dentistry II. *New Engl. J. Med.* 296: 149.

Sopher, I. M. 1973. Dental identification of aircraft-accident fatalities. *J. Forensic Sci.* 18: 356.

Stewart, T. D. *Essentials of Forensic Anthropology.* Springfield, IL: Charles C Thomas, 1979.

Stewart, T. D., ed. *Personal Identification in Mass Disasters.* Washington, DC: Smithsonian Institution, National Museum of Natural History, 1970.

Stewart, T. D. 1972. What the bones tell today. *FBI Law Enforcement Bull.* 41: 1.

Taylor, L. R. 1986. The restoration of water-soaked documents: A case study. *J. Forensic Sci.* 31: 113.

Tolliver, D. K. 1990. The electrostatic detection apparatus (ESDA): Is it really nondestructive to documents? *Forensic Sci. Int.* 44: 7.

Trowell, F. 1975. A method for fixing latent fingerprints developed with iodine. *J. Forensic Sci. Soc.* 15: 189.

Tucker, G. 1990. A modified crystal violet application technique for black electrical tape. *J. Forensic Identification* 40: 148.

Twibell, J. D., J. M. Home, K. W. Smallson, and D. G. Higgs. 1984. Transfer of nitroglycerine to hands during contact with commercial explosives. *J. Forensic Sci.* 27: 783.

Twibell, J. D., J. M. Home, K. W. Smallson, D. G. Higgs, and T. S. Hayes. 1984. Assessment of solvents for the recovery of nitroglycerine from hands using cotton swabs. *J. Forensic Sci.* 27: 792.

United States, Federal Bureau of Investigation. *The Science of Fingerprints: Classification and Use.* Washington, DC: FBI, U.S. Dept. of Justice, 1973.

Walton, A. N. 1989. Laser photography using laser beam painted light technique on curved surfaces. *J. Forensic Identification* 39: 177.

Wanxiang, L. et al. 1988. A study of the principle of the electrostatic imaging technique. *J. Forensic Sci. Soc.* 28: 237.

Warren, C. P. 1979. Verifying identification of military remains: A case study. *J. Forensic Sci.* 24: 182.

Weaver, D. E. 1988. Photographic enhancement of latent prints. *J. Forensic Identification* 38: 189.

Weaver, D. et al. 1993. Large scale cyanoacrylate fuming. *J. Forensic Identification* 43: 135.

Weisner, S., and E. Springer. 1997. Improved technique for recovering fingerprints on aluminum foil. *J. Forensic Identification* 47: 138.

Wilkinson, D., and J. Watkin. 1994. A comparison of forensic light sources: Polilight, Luma-Light, and Spectrum 9000. *J. Forensic Identification* 44: 632.

Zugibe, F. T., and J. T. Costello. 1986. A new method for softening mummified fingers. *J. Forensic Sci.* 31: 726.

Chapter 7

Aginsky, V. N. 1993. Some new ideas for dating ballpoint inks—A feasibility study. *J. Forensic Sci.* 38: 1134.

Antoci, P. R., and N. Petraco. 1993. A technique for comparing soil colors in the forensic laboratory. *J. Forensic Sci.* 38: 437.

Blackledge, R. D. 1987. Tapes with adhesive backings: Their characterization in the forensic science laboratory. *Appl. Polym. Anal. Charact.* 413–21.

Bock, J. H., and D. O. Norris. 1997. Forensic botany: An underutilized resource. *J. Forensic Sci.* 42: 364.

Bresee, R. R. 1987. Evaluation of textile fiber evidence: A review. *J. Forensic Sci.* 32: 510.

Brunelle, R. L., and R. W. Reed. *Forensic Examination of Ink and Paper.* Springfield, IL: Charles C Thomas, 1984.

Brunner, H., and B. J. Coman. *The Identification of Mammalian Hair.* Melbourne: Inkata Press Proprietary, Ltd., 1974.

Budworth, G. 1982. Identification of knots. *J. Forensic Sci. Soc.* 22: 327.

Burd, D. Q., and P. L. Kirk. 1941. Clothing fibers as evidence. *J. Criminal Law Criminol.* 32: 333.

Chable, J., C. Roux, and C. Lennard. 1994. Collection of fiber evidence using water-soluble cellophane tape. *J. Forensic Sci.* 39: 1520.

Cole, M. D., and J. W. Thorpe. 1992. The analysis of black shoe polish marks on clothing. *J. Forensic Sci. Soc.* 32: 237.

Crown, D. A. *The Forensic Examination of Paints and Pigments.* Springfield, IL: Charles C Thomas, 1968.

Dixon, K. C. 1983. Positive identification of torn burned matches with emphasis on cross-cut and torn fiber comparisons. *J. Forensic Sci.* 28: 351.

Flinn, L. L. 1992. Collection of fiber evidence using a roller device and adhesive lifts. *J. Forensic Sci.* 37: 106.

Gerhart, F. J. 1992. Identification of photocopiers from fusing roller defects. *J. Forensic Sci.* 37: 130.

Grieve, M. C. 1983. The role of fibers in forensic science examinations. *J. Forensic Sci.* 28: 877.

Hashimoto, T., S. Deki, and Y. Kanaji. 1994. Discrimination of ceramics—Study on the microstructures of ceramics. *Forensic Sci.* 39: 824.

Hicks, J. W. *Microscopy of Hair: A Practical Guide and Manual.* Washington, DC: FBI, U.S. Government Printing Office, 1977.

Junger, E. P. 1996. Assessing the unique characteristics of close-proximity soil samples: Just how useful is soil evidence? *J. Forensic Sci.* 41: 27.

Kirk, P. L. *Crime Investigation.* 2nd ed. Edited by Thornton, J. I. New York: John Wiley & Sons, 1974.

Koons, R. D., C. A. Peters, and R. A. Merrill. 1993. Forensic comparison of household aluminum foils using elemental composition by inductively coupled plasma. *J. Forensic Sci.* 38: 302.

Laska, P. 1996. Forensic search of a landfill. *J. Forensic Identification* 46: 7.

Longhetti, A., and G. Roche. 1958. Microscopic identification of man-made fibers from the criminalistics point of view. *J. Forensic Sci.* 3: 303.

McQuillan, J., and K. Edgar. 1992. A summary of the distribution of glass on clothing. *J. Forensic Sci. Soc.* 32: 333.

Merrill, R. A., E. G. Bartick, and W. D. Mazzella. 1996. Studies of techniques for analysis of photocopy toners by IR. *J. Forensic Sci.* 41: 264.

Murray, R. C., and J. C. F. Tedrow. *Forensic Geology.* New Brunswick, NJ: Rutgers University Press, 1975.

Nickolls, L. C. The identification of stains of nonbiological origin. In *Methods of Forensic Science*, ed. by F. Lundquist, Vol. I, 335–71. New York: Interscience Publishers, John Wiley & Sons, 1962.

Petraco, N. 1986. Trace evidence—The invisible witness. *J. Forensic Sci.* 31: 321.

Petraco, N. 1987. A simple trace evidence trap for the collection of vacuum sweepings. *J. Forensic Sci.* 32: 1422.

Pounds, C. A. 1975. The recovery of fibers from the surface of clothing for forensic examination. *J. Forensic Sci. Soc.* 15: 127.

Robertson, J. et al. 1984. The identification of bird feathers. Scheme for feather examination, *J. Forensic Sci. Soc.* 24: 85.

Roux, C., J. Chable, and P. Margot. 1996. Fiber transfer experiments onto car seats. *Sci. Justice* 36: 153.

Spencer, R. 1994. Significant fiber evidence recovered from the clothing of a homicide victim after exposure to the elements of 29 days. *Forensic Sci.* 39: 854.

Stratmann M. 1987. Identification of textile fibers. *Applied Polymer Analysis and Characterization.* NY: McMillan Publishing Co., 387–411.

Strelis, I., and R. W. Kennedy. *Identification of North American Commercial Pulpwoods and Pulp Fibers.* Toronto, ON: University of Toronto Press, 1967.

Suzanski, T. W. 1988. Dog hair comparison: A preliminary study. *Can. Soc. Forensic Sci.* 21: 19.

Suzanski, T. W. 1989. Dog hair comparison: Purebreds, mixed breeds, multiple questioned hairs. *Can. Soc. Forensic Sci. J.* 22: 299.

Taupin, J. M. 1996. Hair and fiber transfer in an abduction case—Evidence from different levels of trace evidence transfer. *J. Forensic Sci.* 41: 697.

US Dept of Justice, Federal Bureau of Investigation. 1976. Don't miss a hair. *FBI Law Enforcement Bull.* 45: 9.

Vanderkolk, J. 1995. Identifying consecutively made garbage bags through manufactured characteristics. *J. Forensic Identification* 45: 38.

Walsh, K. A. J., J. S. Buckleton., and C. M. Triggs. 1996. A practical example of the interpretation of glass evidence. *Sci. Justice* 36: 213.

Chapter 8

Anderson, A. 1989. DNA fingerprinting on trial. *Nature* 342: 844.

Becker, P. B. et al. 1988. Genomic footprinting. *Genet. Eng.* 10: 1.

Bevel, T., and R. Gardner. *Bloodstain Pattern Analysis.* 2nd ed. Boca Raton, FL: CRC Press, 2002.

Bigbee, P. D. et al. 1989. Inactivation of human immuno deficiency virus (HIV), ionizing radiation in body fluids and serological evidence. *J. Forensic Sci.* 34: 1303.

Boles, T. C., C. C. Snow, and E. Stover. 1995. Forensic DNA testing on skeletal remains from mass graves: A pilot project in Guatemala, *J. Forensic Sci.* 40: 349.

Butler, J. *Forensic DNA Typing.* 2nd ed. New York: Elsevier Academic Press, 2005.

Cawood, A. H. 1989. DNA fingerprinting, *Clin. Chem.* 35: 1832.

Centers for Disease Control. 1996. Case–control study of HIV seroconversion in health care workers after percutaneous exposure to HIV-infected blood—France, United Kingdom, and United States, January 1988–August 1994. *JAMA* 275: 274.

Cherfas, J. 1990. Genes unlimited. *New Sci.* 126: 29.

Cohen, J. E. 1990. DNA fingerprinting for forensic identification: Potential effects on data interpretation of subpopulation heterogeneity and band number variability. *Am. J. Hum. Genet.* 46: 358.

Culliford, B. J. *The Examination and Typing of Bloodstains in the Crime Laboratory.* Washington, DC: U.S. Government Printing Office, 1971.

Evett, I. W. et al. 1989. DNA fingerprinting on trial. *Nature* 340: 435.

Evett, I. W. 1992. Evaluating DNA profiles in a case where the defense is "it was my brother." *J. Forensic Sci. Soc.* 32: 5.

Gaensslen, R. E. 1980. Blood sweat and tears … and saliva and semen—The forensic serologist provides expert identification of body fluids. *Law Enforcement Commun.* 7: 23.

Gaensslen, R. E. *Sourcebook in Forensic Serology, Immunology and Biochemistry.* Washington, DC: U.S. Department of Justice, National Institute of Justice, U.S. Government Printing Office, 1983.

Gardner, R., and T. Bevel. *Practical Crime Scene Analysis and Reconstruction.* Boca Raton, FL: CRC Press, 2009.

Gerberding, J., F. R. Lewis, and W. P. Schecter. 1995. Are universal precautions realistic? *Surg. Clin. N. Am.* 75: 1091.

Gimeno, F. E. 1989. Fill flash photo luminescence to photograph luminol bloodstain patterns. *J. Forensic Identification* 39: 149.

Gindler, J. S., and S. C. Hadler et al. 1995. Recommended childhood immunization schedule: United States 1995. *Morbidity Mortality Wkly. Rep.* 44: 1.

Grispino, R. R. J. 1990. The effect of luminol on the serological analysis of dried human bloodstains. *Crime Lab Dig.* 17: 13.

Grubb, A. 1993. Legal aspects of DNA profiling. *J. Forensic Sci. Soc.* 33: 2228.

Healing, T. A. et al. 1995. Infection hazards of human cadavers. *Commun. Dis. Rep/CDR Rev.* 5: 61.

Heller, E. T., and R. Greer. 1995. Glove safety: Summary of recent findings and recommendations from health care regulators. *South Med. J.* 88: 1093.

Henderson, D. K. 1995. Postexposure prophylaxis for occupational exposures to hepatitis B, hepatitis C, and HIV. *Surg. Clin. N. Am.* 75: 1175.

Hicks, J. W. 1988. DNA profiling: A tool for law enforcement. *FBI Law Enforcement Bull.* 57: 1.

Holland, M. M. et al. 1993. Mitochondrial DNA sequence analysis of human skeletal remains: Identification of remains from the Vietnam war. *J. Forensic Sci.* 38: 542.

James, S. et al. *Principles of Bloodstain Pattern Analysis.* Boca Raton, FL: CRC Press, 2005.

Jeffreys, A. J. 1993. DNA typing: Approaches and applications. *J. Forensic Sci. Soc.* 33: 204.

Karhunen, P. J., H. Brummer, P. Leinikki, and M. Nyberg. 1994. Stability of HIV antibodies in postmortem samples. *J. Forensic Sci.* 39: 129.

Klatt, E. C. et al. 1990. AIDS and infection control in forensic investigation. *Am. J. Forensic Med Pathol* 11: 44.

Lander, E. S. 1989. DNA fingerprinting on trial. *Nature* 339: 501.

Lee, H. E. et al. 1989. The effect of presumptive test, latent fingerprints and some other reagents and materials on subsequent serological identification, genetic marker and DNA testing in bloodstains. *J. Forensic Identification* 39: 339.

Lind, W., and D. Carlson. 1995. Recovery of semen from chewing gum in an oral sexual assault. *J. Forensic Identification* 45: 280.

MacDonell, H. L. *Flight Characteristics and Stain Patterns of Human Blood.* Washington, DC: U.S. Department of Justice, 1971.

MacDonell, H. L. *Bloodstain Pattern Interpretation.* Corning, NY: Laboratory of Forensic Science, 1982.

Montagna, C. P. 1996. The recovery of seminal components and DNA from the vagina of a homicide victim 34 days postmortem. *J. Forensic Sci.* 41: 700.

National Institute of Justice. *Using DNA to Solve Cold Cases.* National Institute of Justice Special Report. Washington, DC: U.S. DOJ, 2002.

Neufeld P. J. et al. 1990. When science takes the witness stand. *Sci. Am.* 262: 46.

Nicas, M. 1996. Refining a risk model for occupational tuberculosis transmission. *Am. Ind. Hygiene Assoc. J.* 57: 16.

Owen, G. W. *A Comparison of Some Presumptive Tests for Blood*. Aldermaston: Home Office Central Research Establishment Report No. 84, 1973.

Petrosillo, N. et al. 1995. Hepatitis B, hepatitis C, and HIV virus infection in health care workers: A multiple regression analysis of risk factors. *J. Hosp. Infect.* 30: 273.

Pitt, M. J. 1994. Safety myths in chemical laboratories. *Chemical Health Safety* 1: 8.

Pizzola, P. A., S. Roth, and P. R. DeForest. 1986. Blood droplet dynamics—I. *J. Forensic Sci.* 31: 36.

Pizzola, P. A., S. Roth, and P. R. DeForest. 1986. Blood droplet dynamics—II. *J. Forensic Sci.* 31: 40.

Plog, B. et al. *Fundamentals of Industrial Hygiene*. 1011. Itasca, IL: National Safety Council, 1996.

President's DNA Initiative. *Identifying Victims Using DNA: A Guide for Families*. Washington, DC: US DOJ, 2005.

Puro, V., N. Petrosillo, and G. Ippolito. 1995. Risk of hepatitis C seroconversion after occupational exposures in health care workers. *Am. J. Infect. Control* 23: 273.

Raymond, M. A., E. R. Smith, and J. Liesegang. 1996. The physical properties of blood—Forensic considerations. *Sci. Justice* 36: 153.

Ross, A. M. et al. 1989. DNA typing and forensic science. *Forensic Sci. Int.* 41: 197.

Saferstein, R., ed. *Forensic Science Handbook*. Englewood Cliffs, NJ: Prentice-Hall, 1982.

Schiro, G. 1997. Collection and preservation of blood evidence from crime scenes. *J. Forensic Identification* 47: 557.

Sepkowitz, K. A. 1996. Occupational acquired infections in health care workers—Part I. *Ann. Intern. Med.* 125: 826.

Stewart, G. D. 1990. Sexual assault evidence collection procedures. *J. Forensic Identification* 40: 69.

Sweet, D. J., and C. H. W. Sweet. 1994. DNA analysis of dental pulp to link incinerated remains of homicide victim to crime scene. *J. Forensic Sci.* 40: 310.

Thornton, J. 1989. DNA profiling: New tool links evidence to suspects with high certainty. *Chemical Eng. News* 67: 18–27, 30.

Tokars, J. et al. 1992. A survey of occupational blood contact and HIV infection among orthopedic surgeons. *JAMA* 268: 489.

Van Buren, J., R. A. Simpson, P. Jacobs, and B. D. Cookson. 1994. Survival of HIV virus in suspension and dried-onto surfaces. *J. Clin. Microbiol.* 32: 571.

Wegel, J. G., Jr., and G. Herrin, Jr. 1994. Deduction of the order of sexual assault by DNA analysis of two condoms. *J. Forensic Sci.* 39: 844.

Zweidinger, R. A., L. T. Lytle, and C. G. Pitt. 1973. Photography of blood-stains visualized by luminol. *J. Forensic Sci.* 18: 296.

Chapter 9

Apolinar, E., and W. F. Rowe. 1980. Examination of human fingernail ridges by means of polarized light. *J. Forensic Sci.* 25: 154.

Beckstead, J. W., R. D. Rawson, and W. G. Giles. 1979. Review of bite mark evidence. *JADA* 99: 69.

Benson, B. W., J. A. Cottone, T. J. Bomberg, and N. D. Sperber. 1987. Bite mark impressions: A review of techniques and materials. *J. Forensic Sci.* 33: 1238.

Bodziak, W. J. 1986. Manufacturing processes for athletic shoe outsoles and their significance in the examination of footwear impression evidence. *J. Forensic Sci.* 31: 153.

Bonte, W. 1975. Tool marks in bones and cartilage. *J. Forensic Sci.* 20: 315.

Cassidy, F. H. 1980. Examination of tool marks from sequentially manufactured tongue-and-groove pliers. *J. Forensic Sci.* 25: 796.

Cassidy, M. J. *Footwear Identification*. Ontario, Canada: Royal Canadian Mounted Police, 1980.

Davis, R. J. 1988. Systematic approach to the enhancement of footwear marks. *Can. Soc. Forensic Sci. J.* 21: 98.

Denton, S. 1981. Extrusion marks in polyethene film. *J. Forensic Sci. Soc.* 21: 259.

Diaz, A. A., A. F. Boehm, and W. F. Rowe. 1990. Comparison of fingernail ridge patterns of monozygotic twins. *J. Forensic Sci.* 35: 97.

Dinkel, E. H., Jr. 1974. The use of bite mark evidence as an investigative aid. *J. Forensic Sci.* 19: 535.

Ellen, D. M., D. J. Foster, and D. J. Morantz. 1980. The use of electrostatic imaging in the detection of indented impressions. *Forensic Sci. Int.* 15: 53.

Facey, O. E., I. D. Hannah, and D. Rosen. 1992. Shoe wear patterns and pressure distribution under feet and shoes, determined by image analysis. *J. Forensic Sci. Soc.* 32: 15.

Fairgrieve, S. I. 1994. SEM analysis of incinerated teeth as an aid to positive investigation. *Forensic Sci.* 39: 557.

Fawcett, A. S. 1970. The role of the footmark examiner. *J. Forensic Sci. Soc.* 10: 227.

FBI Laboratory makes Toolmark Examinations. *FBI Law Enforcement Bull.* (Revised) 1975.

Giles, E., and P. H. Vallandigham. 1991. Height estimation from foot and shoeprint length. *J. Forensic Sci.* 36: 1134.

Glass, R. T., F. B. Jordan, and E. E. Andrews. 1975. Multiple animal bite wounds: A case report. *J. Forensic Sci.* 20: 305.

Gordon, C. C., and J. E. Buikstra. 1992. Linear models for the prediction of stature from foot and boot dimensions. *J. Forensic Sci.* 37: 771.

Hamm, E. D. 1989. The individuality of class characteristics in Converse All-Star footwear. *J. Forensic Identification* 39: 277.

Hebrard, J., and A. Donche. 1994. Fingerprint detection methods on skin: Experimental study on 16 live subjects and 23 cadavers. *J. Forensic Identification* 44: 623.

Hilderbrand, D. 1994. Using manufacturing companies to assist in footwear cases. *J. Forensic Identification* 44: 130.

Hilderbrand, D., and M. Miller. 1995. Casting materials—which one to use! *J. Forensic Identification* 45: 618.

Hodge, E. E. 1988. Guarding against error. *AFTE J.* 20: 290.

Houde, J. 1993. Image enhancement for document examination using the personal computer. *J. Forensic Sci.* 38: 143.

Hueske, E. E. 1991. Photographing and casting footwear/tiretrack impressions. *J. Forensic Identification* 41: 92.

Jungbluth, W. O. 1989. Knuckle print identification. *J. Forensic Identification* 39: 375.

Lennard, C. J. et al. 1989. The analysis of synthetic shoe soles, FTIR microspectrometry and pyrolysis-GC: A case example. *J. Forensic Identification* 39: 239.

Leslie, A. G. 1977. Identification of single element typewriter and type elements, Part I. *J. Can. Soc. Forensic Sci.* 10: 87.

Levinson, J. 1979. Single element typewriters. *Forensic Sci. Int.* 13: 15.

MacDonald, D. G. 1974. Bite mark recognition and interpretation. *J. Forensic Sci. Soc.* 14: 229.

Mankevich, A. 1990. Determination of shoe size in out-of-scale photographs. *J. Forensic Identification* 40: 1.

Nielson, J. P. 1989. Laser enhancement of footwear marks on brown paper. *J. Forensic Identification* 39: 42.

Novoselsky, Y., B. Glattstein, N. Volkov, and A. Zeichner. 1995 Microchemical spot tests in toolmark examination. *J. Forensic Sci.* 40: 865.

Ojena, S. M. 1984. A new improved technique for casting impressions in snow. *J. Forensic Sci.* 29: 322.

Petraco, N. *Color Atlas of Forensic Toolmark Identification*. Boca Raton, FL: CRC Press, 2010.

Pierce, D. S. 1990. Identifiable markings on plastics. *J. Forensic Identification* 40: 51.

Rao, V. J., and R. R. Souviron. 1984. Dusting and lifting the bite print: A new technique. *J. Forensic Sci.* 29: 326.

Sahs, P. 1993. An interesting case involving automotive pedal control/shoe imprinting. *J. Forensic Identification* 43: 20.

Sampson, W. 1996. Latent fingerprint evidence on human skin. *J. Forensic Identification* 46: 188.

Sperber, N. D. 1978. Chewing gum—An unusual clue in a recent homicide investigation. *J. Forensic Sci.* 23: 792.

Springer, E. 1995. Toolmark examinations—A review of its development in the literature. *J. Forensic Sci.* 40: 964.

Stone, I. C. 1988. Fingernail striations: An unusual toolmark. *AFTE J.* 20: 391.

Vale, G. L., R. F. Sognnaes, G. N. Felando, and T. T. Noguchi. 1976. Unusual three-dimensional bite mark evidence in a homicide case. *J. Forensic Sci.* 21: 642.

VanHoven, H. 1985. A correlation between shoeprint measurements and actual sneaker size. *J. Forensic Sci.* 30: 1233.

Von Bremen, A. 1990. The comparison of brake and accelerator pedals with marks on shoe soles. *J. Forensic Sci.* 35: 14.

Von Bremen, U. G., and L. K. R. Blunt. 1983. Physical comparison of plastic garbage bags and sandwich bags. *J. Forensic Sci.* 28: 644.

Wilkinson, D., J. Watkin, and A. Misner. 1996. A comparison of techniques for the visualization of fingerprints on human skin including the application of iodine and α-napthoflavone. *J. Forensic Identification* 46: 432.

Yaron, S. M., R. B. Kennedy, T. Tsach, N. Volkov, Y. Novoselsky, and A. Vinokurov. 2003. Physical match: insole and shoe. *J. Forensic Sci.* 48, no. 4: 808.

Zugibe, F. T., J. Costello, and M. Breithaupt. 1996. Identification of a killer by a definitive sneaker pattern and his beating instruments by their distinctive patterns. *J. Forensic Sci.* 41: 310.

Chapter 10

Andrasko, J. 1992. Characterization of smokeless powder flakes from fired cartridge cases and from discharge patterns on clothing. *J. Forensic Sci.* 37: 103.

Andrasko, J., and A. C. Maehly. 1977. Detection of gunshot residues on hands by scanning electron microscopy. *J. Forensic Sci.* 22: 279.

Andrasko, J., and S. Pettersson. 1991. A simple method for collection of gun shot residues from clothing. *J. Forensic Sci. Soc.* 31: 321.

Association of Firearm and Toolmark Examiners. *Glossary of the Association of Firearm and Toolmark Examiners.* Augusta, GA: Fonville Printing Co., 1980.

Barnes, F. C., and R. A. Helson. 1974. An empirical study of gunpowder residue patterns. *J. Forensic Sci.* 19: 448.

Barnum, C., and D. Klasey. 1997. Factors affecting the recovery of latent prints on firearms. *J. Forensic Identification* 47: 141.

Basu, S. 1982. Formation of gunshot residues. *J. Forensic Sci.* 27: 72.

Basu, S., C. E. Boone, D. J. Denio, and R. A. Miazga. 1997. Fundamental studies of gunshot residue deposition by glue-lift. *J. Forensic Sci.* 42: 571.

Biasotti, A. A. 1964. The principles of evidence evaluation as applied to firearms and toolmark identification. *J. Forensic Sci.* 9: 428.

Brazeau, J., and R. K. Wong. 1997. Analysis of gunshot residues on human tissues and clothing by x-ray microfluorescence. *J. Forensic Sci.* 42: 424.

Burke, T. W., and W. F. Rowe. 1992. Bullet ricochet: A comprehensive review. *J. Forensic Sci.* 37: 1254.

Burnett, B. 1989. The form of gunshot residue is modified by target impact. *J. Forensic Sci.* 34: 808.

Burnett, B. 1991. Detection of bone and bone-plus-bullet particles in backspatter from close-range shots to heads. *J. Forensic Sci.* 36: 1745.

Collins, K. A., and P. E. Lantz. 1994. Interpretation of fatal, multiple, and existing gunshot wounds by trauma specialists. *J. Forensic Sci.* 39: 94.

Dahl, D. et al. 1987. Determination of black and smokeless powder residues in firearms and improvised explosive devices. *Micro-Chem. J.* 35: 40.

Davis, J. E. *An Introduction to Toolmarks, Firearms and the Striagraph*. Springfield, IL: Charles C Thomas, 1958.

DeGaetano, D., and J. A. Siegel. 1990. Survey of gunshot residue analysis in forensic science laboratories. *J. Forensic Sci.* 35: 1087.

Di Maio, V. J. M., C. S. Petty, and I. C. Stone, Jr. 1976. An experimental study of powder tattooing of the skin. *J. Forensic Sci.* 21: 373.

Fackler, M. L. 1986. Ballistic injury. *Ann. Emergency Med.* 15: 1451.

Fackler, M. L. 1989. Wound ballistics: A review of common misconceptions. *AFTE J.* 21: 25.

Garrison, D., Jr. 1995. Reconstructing drive-by shootings from ejected cartridge case location. *J. Forensic Identification* 45: 427.

Goleb, J. A., and C. R. Midkiff, Jr. 1975. Firearms discharge residue sample collection techniques. *J. Forensic Sci.* 20: 701.

Harruff, R. C. 1995. Comparison of contact shotgun wounds of the head produced by different gauge shotguns. *J. Forensic Sci.* 40: 81.

Havekost, D. G., C. A. Peters, and R. D. Koons. 1990. Barium and antimony distributions on the hands of nonshooters. *J. Forensic Sci.* 35: 1096.

Hoffman, C. M., and E. B. Byall. 1974. Peculiarities of certain .22 caliber revolvers (Saturday night specials). *J. Forensic Sci.* 19: 48.

Josserand, M. H., and J. A. Stevenson. *Pistols, Revolvers and Ammunition*. New York: Bonanza Books, 1972.

Kilty, J. W. 1975. Activity after shooting and its effects on the retention of primer residues. *J. Forensic Sci.* 20: 219.

Klatt, E. C. et al. 1989. Wounding characteristics of .38 caliber revolver cartridges. *J. Forensic Sci.* 34: 1387.

Krishnan, S. S. 1977. Detection of gunshot residues on the hands by trace element analysis. *J. Forensic Sci.* 22: 304.

Madea, B. 1988. Determination of the sequence of gunshot wounds of the skull. *J. Forensic Sci. Soc.* 28: 321.

Matricardi, V. R., and J. W. Kilty. 1977. Detection of gunshot residue particles from the hands of a shooter. *J. Forensic Sci.* 22: 725.

McGuire, P. J., and A. Boehm. Analysis of gunshot residue test results in 112 suicides. *J. Forensic Sci.* 35: 62.

Medich, M. G. et al. 1990. Single wound produced by simultaneous discharge of both shells from a double-barrel shotgun. *J. Forensic Sci.* 35: 473.

Meng, H., and B. Caddy. Gunshot residue analysis—A review. *J. Forensic Sci.* 42: 553.

Miller, J. 1993. The value of a firearms open-case file. *J. Forensic Identification* 43: 245.

Missliwetz, J., W. Denk, and I. Wieser. 1991. Shots fired with silencers—A report on four cases and experimental testing. *J. Forensic Sci.* 36: 1387.

Nesbitt, R. S., J. E. Wessel, and P. F. Jones. 1976. Detection of gunshot residue by use of the scanning electron microscope. *J. Forensic Sci.* 21: 595.

Nichols, C. A. et al. 1990. Recovery and evaluation by cytologic techniques of trace material retained on bullets. *Am. J. Forensic Med. Pathol.* 11: 17.

Nichols, R. G. 1997. Firearm and toolmark identification criteria: A review of the literature. *J. Forensic Sci.* 42: 466.

Oliver, W. R. et al. 1994. Three-dimensional reconstruction of a bullet path: Validation by computer radiography. *J. Forensic Sci.* 40: 321.

Petraco, N., and P. R. De Forest. 1990. Trajectory reconstruction I: Trace evidence in flight. *J. Forensic Sci.* 35: 1284.

Rouge, D., N. Telmon, D. Alengrin, G. Marril, P. M. Bras, and L. Arbus. 1994. Fatal injuries caused by guns using shotshell: Case reports and ballistic studies. *Forensic Sci.* 39: 650.

Seamster, A., T. Mead, J. Gislason, K. Jackson, F. Ruddy, and B. D. Pate. 1976. Studies of the spatial distribution of firearms discharge residues. *J. Forensic Sci.* 20: 868.

Simpson, K. 1989. Identification of a firearm in murder without the weapon. *AFTE J.* 21: 62.

Singer, R. L., D. Davis, and M. M. Houck. 1996. A survey of gunshot residue analysis methods. *J. Forensic Sci.* 41: 195.

Smith, O. C., S. A. Symes, H. E. Berryman, and M. M. Le Vaughn. 1993. Characteristic features of entrance wounds from hollow-point bullets. *J. Forensic Sci.* 38: 323.

Stone, I. C., V. J. M. Di Maio, and C. S. Petty. 1978. Gunshot wounds: Visual and analytical procedures. *J. Forensic Sci.* 23: 361.

Stone, I. C., and C. S. Petty. 1991. Interpretation of unusual wounds caused by firearms. *J. Forensic Sci.* 36: 736.

Wolten, G. M., R. S. Nesbitt, A. R. Calloway, G. L. Loper, and P. F. Jones. 1979. Particle analysis for the detection of gunshot residue I: Scanning electron microscopy/energy dispersive x-ray characterization of hand deposits from firing. *J. Forensic Sci.* 24: 409.

Wolten, G. M., R. S. Nesbitt, A. R. Calloway, and G. L. Loper. 1979. Particle analysis for the detection of gunshot residue II: Occupational and environmental particles. *J. Forensic Sci.* 24: 423.

Wolten, G. M., R. S. Nesbitt, and A. R. Calloway. 1979. Particle analysis for the detection of gunshot residue III: The case record. *J. Forensic Sci.* 24: 864.

Zeichner, A. et al. 1986. Improved reagents for firing distance determination. *J. Energetic Mater.* 4: 187.

Zeichner, A., and N. Levin. 1993. Collection efficiency of gunshot residue (GSR) particles from hair and hands using double-side adhesive tape. *J. Forensic Sci.* 38: 571.

Chapter 11

Beveridge, A. D., S. F. Payton, R. J. Audette, A. J. Lambertus, and R. C. Shaddick. 1975. Systematic analysis of explosive residues. *J. Forensic Sci.* 20: 431.

Blackledge, R. D. 1991. Methenamine—An unusual component in an improved incendiary device. *J. Forensic Sci.* 36: 261.

Bomb Investigations. Dover, NJ: National Bomb Data Center, Picatinny Arsenal, 1974.

Boudreau, J. F. et al. *Arson and Arson Investigation Survey and Assessment.* Washington, DC: National Institute of Law Enforcement and Criminal Justice, Law Enforcement Assistance Administration, U.S. Department of Justice, U.S. Government Printing Office, 1977.

Brauer, K. O. *Handbook of Pyrotechnics.* New York: Chemical Publishing Co., 1974.

Brodie, T. G., and A. W. Gleason. *Bombs and Bombings: A Handbook to Detection, Disposal and Investigation for Police and Fire Departments.* Springfield, IL: Charles C Thomas, 1973.

Carroll, J. R. *Physical and Technical Aspects of Fire and Arson Investigation.* Springfield, IL: Charles C Thomas, 1979.

Davis, T. L. *The Chemistry of Powder and Explosives.* New York: John Wiley & Sons, Inc., 1941.

DeHaan, J. D. *Kirk's Fire Investigation.* 5th ed. Englewood Cliffs, NJ: Prentice Hall, 2002.

Dhole, V. R., M. P. Kurhekar, and K. A. Ambade. 1995. Detection of petroleum accelerant residues on partly burnt objects in burning/arson offenses. *Sci. Justice* 35: 217.

Dietz, W. R. 1991. Improved charcoal packaging for accelerant recovery by passive diffusion. *J. Forensic Sci.* 36: 111.

Ellern, H. *Military and Civilian Pyrotechnics.* New York: Chemical Publishing Co., 1968.

Evans, H. K. 1986. An unusual explosive, triacetonetriperoxide (TATP). *J. Forensic Sci.* 31: 1119.

Fire Protection Guide on Hazardous Materials. 8th ed. Quincy, MA: NFPA, 1984.

Fisco, W. 1975. A portable explosives identification kit for field use. *J. Forensic Sci.* 20: 141.

Fitch, R. D., and E. A. Porter. *Accidental or Incendiary.* Springfield, IL: Charles C Thomas, 1968.

Furton, K. G., J. R. Almirall, and J. C. Bruna. 1996. A novel method for the analysis of gasoline from fire debris using headspace solid-phase microextraction. *J. Forensic Sci.* 41: 12.

Garner, D. D. et al. 1986. The ATF approach to postblast explosives detection and identification. *J. Energetic Mater.* 4: 133.

Glattstein, B., E. Landau, and A. Zeichner. 1991. Identification of match head residues in postexplosion debris. *J. Forensic Sci.* 36: 13360.

Henderson, R. W. 1977. Fire investigation from the consultant's point of view. *Fire Arson Invest.* 39: 23.

Hermann, S. L. *Explosives Data Guide.* Scottsdale, AZ: Explosives Research Institute, 1977.

Hoffman, C. M., and E. B. Byall. 1974. Identification of explosive residues in bomb scene investigations. *J. Forensic Sci.* 19: 54.

Introduction to Explosives. FBI Bomb Data Program, FBI/DOJ, 1975.

Jones, B. R. 1988. Putting the fire scene in perspective. *Fire Arson Invest.* 38: 59.

Jones, N. 1990. Arson-for-profit investigations, success or failure? Recovering water-damaged business records. *Fire Arson Invest.* 40: 50.

Kempe, C. R., and W. T. Tannert. 1972. Detection of dynamite residues on the hands of bombing suspects. *J. Forensic Sci.* 17: 323.

Keto, R. O. 1986. Improved method for the analysis of the military explosive composition C-4. *J. Forensic Sci.* 31: 241.

Kolla, P. 1991. Trace analysis of explosives from complex mixtures with sample pretreatment and selective detection. *J. Forensic Sci.* 36: 1342.

Lenz, R. R. *Explosives and Bomb Disposal Guide.* Springfield, IL: Charles C Thomas, 1965.

Loscalzo, P. J., P. R. DeForest, and J. M. Chao. 1980. A study to determine the limit of detectability of gasoline vapor from simulated arson residues. *J. Forensic Sci.* 25: 162.

Meyers, R. *Explosives.* Essen Weinheim, Germany: Verlag Chemie, 1977.

O'Donnell, J. J. 1989. Interferences from backgrounds in accelerant residue analysis. *Fire Arson Invest.* 39: 25.

Perr, I. N. 1979. Comments on arson. *J. Forensic Sci.* 24: 885.

Phillips, S. A. 1988. How wood chars and what it means to the fire investigator. *Fire Arson Invest.* 38: 28.

Pinorini, M. T., C. J. Lennard, P. Margot, I. Dustin, and P. Furrer. 1994. Soot as an indicator in fire investigations: Physical and chemical analysis. *Forensic Sci.* 39: 933.

Posey, E. P. et al. 1988. Outline for fire scene documentation. *Fire Arson Invest.* 38: 55.

Powell, G. L. F., and K. R. Spanswick. 1979. A case of arson? *J. Forensic Sci.* 24: 627.

Price, T. A. 1989. Appliances as a fire cause. *Fire Arson Invest.* 39: 30.

Smith, F. P. 1991. Concrete spalling: Controlled fire tests and review. *J. Forensic Sci. Soc.* 31: 67.

Stoffel, J. F. *Explosives and Homemade Bombs.* Springfield, IL: Charles C Thomas, 1962.

Stone, I. C., J. N. Lomonte, L. A. Fletcher, and W. T. Lowry. 1978. Accelerant detection in fire residues. *J. Forensic Sci.* 23: 78.

Tindall, R., and K. Lothridge. 1995. An evaluation of 42 accelerant detection canine teams. *J. Forensic Sci.* 40: 561.

Townshend, D. G. 1973. Identification of electric blasting caps by manufacture. *J. Forensic Sci.* 18: 405.

Tsaroom, S. 1996. Investigation of a murder case involving arson. *J. Forensic Sci.* 41: 1064.

Twibell, J. D., and S. C. Lomas. 1995. The examination of fire-damaged electrical switches. *Sci. Justice* 35: 113.

Yallop, H. J. *Explosion Investigation.* Harrogate, England: Forensic Science Society Press, 1980.

Chapter 12

American Medical Association. *Alcohol and the Impaired Driver: A Manual on the Medicolegal Aspects of Chemical Tests for Intoxication.* Chicago, IL: American Medical Association, 1970.

Baum, R. M. 1985. New variety of street drugs pose growing problem. *C&EN* 63: 7.

Baumgartner, W. A. et al. 1989. Hair analysis for drugs of abuse. *J. Forensic Sci.* 34: 1433.

Chung, B. et al. 1990. Analysis of anabolic steroids using GC/MS with selected ion monitoring. *J. Anal. Toxicol.* 14: 91.

Cone, E. J. 1988. Marijuana-laced brownies: Behavioral effects, physiologic effects, and urinalysis in humans following ingestion. *J. Anal. Toxicol.* 12: 169.

Cone, E. J. 1990. Testing human hair for drugs of abuse I: Individual dose and time profiles of morphine and codeine in plasma, saliva, urine and beard compared to drug-induced effects on pupils and behavior. *J. Anal. Toxicol.* 14: 1.

Cravey, R. H., and R. C. Baselt. *Introduction to Forensic Toxicology.* Davis, CA: Biomedical Publications, 1981.

Daigle, R. D. 1990. Anabolic steroids. *J. Psychoactive Drugs* 22: 77.

DOT Hazardous Materials Emergency Response Guidebook. Washington, DC: U.S. Government Printing Office, 1981.

Elsohly, M. A. 1989. Morphine and codeine in biological fluids: Approaches to source differentiation. *Forensic Sci. Rev.* 1: 13.

Fasanello, J. A., and R. A. Henderson. 1974. Vacuum searches in narcotics cases. *J. Forensic Sci.* 19: 379.

Garriott, J. C., and N. Latman. 1976. Drug detection in cases of "driving under the influence." *J. Forensic Sci.* 21: 398.

Garriott, J. C., V. J. M. Di Maio, R. E. Zumwalt, and C. S. Petty. 1977. Incidence of drugs and alcohol in fatally injured motor vehicle drivers. *J. Forensic Sci.* 22: 383.

Graham, K. et al. 1989. Determination of gestational cocaine exposure by hair analysis. *JAMA* 262: 3328.

Harkey, M. R. et al. 1989. Hair analysis for drugs of abuse. *Adv. Anal. Toxicol.* 2: 298.

Hudson, J. D. 1989. Analysis of currency for cocaine contamination. *Can. Soc. Forensic Sci. J.* 22: 203.

James, R. D. 1989. Hazards of clandestine drug laboratories. *FBI Law Enforcement Bull.* 58: 16.

Kram, T. C., D. A. Cooper, and A. C. Allen. 1981. Behind the identification of China white. *Anal. Chem.* 53: 1379A.

Le, S. D., R. W. Taylor, D. Vidal, J. J. Lovas, and E. Ting. 1992. Occupational exposure to cocaine involving crime lab personnel. *J. Forensic Sci.* 37: 959.

LeBeau, M. A., and A. Mozyani, eds. *Drug Facilitated Sexual Assault: A Forensic Handbook.* 1st ed. San Diego, CA: Academic Press, 2001.

Lundberg, G. D., J. M. White, and K. I. Hoffman. 1979. Drugs (other than or in addition to ethyl alcohol) and driving behavior: A collaborative study of the California association of toxicologists. *J. Forensic Sci.* 24: 207.

Mason, M. F., and K. M. Dubowski. 1974. Alcohol, traffic and chemical testing in the United States: A résumé and some remaining problems. *Clin. Chem.* 20: 126.

McBay, A. J. et al. 1989. Forensic science identification of drugs of abuse. *J. Forensic Sci.* 34: 1471.

Mule, S. J. et al. 1988. Rendering the "poppy-seed defense" defenseless: Identification of 6-monoacetylmorphine in urine by chromatography/mass spectroscopy. *Clin. Chem.* 34: 1427.

Narcotics Investigator's Manual. Washington, DC: U.S. Department of Justice, Drug Enforcement Administration.

National Fire Protection Association. *Fire Protection Guide on Hazardous Materials.* 7th ed. Boston, MA: NFPA, 1978.

O'Conner, D. L. 1988. Developing a standard operating procedure for crime scene and identification processing of illicit methamphetamine labs. *J. Forensic Identification* 38: 299.

Turk, R. F., A. J. McBay, and P. Hudson. 1974. Drug involvement in automobile driver and pedestrian fatalities. *J. Forensic Sci.* 19: 90.

Willette, R. E., ed. 1974. Drugs and driving NIDA pedestrian fatalities. *J. Forensic Sci.* 19: 90.

Willette, R. E., ed. *Drugs and Driving NIDA Research Monograph 11.* Washington, DC: U.S. Department of Health, Education and Welfare, 1977.

Chapter 13

Brauner, P., and N. Gallili. 1993. A condom—The critical link in a rape. *J. Forensic Sci.* 38: 1233.

Duenhoelter, J. H., I. C. Stone, R. Santos-Ramos, and D. E. Scott. 1978. Detection of seminal fluid constituents after alleged sexual assault. *J. Forensic Sci.* 23: 824.

Enos, W. F., J. C. Beyer, and G. T. Mann. 1972. The medical examination of cases of rape. *J. Forensic Sci.* 17: 50.

Fraysier, H. D. 1987. A rapid screening technique for the detection of spermatozoa. *J. Forensic Sci.* 32: 527.

Hazelwood, R. R. et al. 1989. The serial rapist: His characteristics and victims (part I). *FBI Law Enforcement Bull.* 58: 10.

Hazelwood, R. R. et al. 1989. The serial rapist: His characteristics and victims (conclusion). *FBI Law Enforcement Bull.* 58: 14.

National Institute of Law Enforcement and Criminal Justice. *Forcible Rape: A Manual for Sex Crime Investigators, Police Volume III*. Washington, DC: U.S. Department of Justice, U.S. Government Printing Office, 1978.

Schiff, A. F. 1978. Rape in the United States. *J. Forensic Sci.* 23: 845.

Chapter 14

Building material evidence in burglary cases. *FBI Law Enforcement Bull.* 1973.

Fong, W. 1973. Value of glass as evidence. *J. Forensic Sci.* 18: 398.

Plumtree, W. G. 1975. The examination of disc and pin tumbler locks for toolmarks made by lock picks. *J. Forensic Sci.* 20: 656.

Yallop, H. J. Breaking offenses with explosives—The techniques of the criminal and the scientist. *J. Forensic Sci. Soc.* 14: 99.

Chapter 15

Baker, J. S., and T. Lindquist. *Lamp Examination for On or Off in Traffic Accidents*. Evanston, IL: The Traffic Institute, Northwestern University, 1977.

Basham, D. J. *Traffic Accident Management*. Springfield, IL: Charles C Thomas, 1979.

Clark, W. E. *Traffic Management and Collision Investigation*. Englewood Cliffs, NJ: Prentice-Hall, 1982.

Cousins, D. R. et al. 1989. Data collection of vehicle topcoat colors IV: A trial to assess the effectiveness of color identification. *Forensic Sci. Int.* 43: 183.

Dabdoub, G. et al. 1989. The identification of domestic and foreign automobile manufacturers through body primer characterization. *J. Forensic Sci.* 34: 1395.

Dolan, D. N. 1971. Vehicle lights and their use as evidence. *J. Forensic Sci. Soc.* 11: 69.

Don't overlook evidentiary value of glass fragments. *FBI Law Enforcement Bulletin* 1976.

Drummond, F. C., and P. A. Pizzola. 1990. An unusual case involving the individualization of a clothing impression on a motor vehicle. *J. Forensic Sci.* 35: 746.

Hamm, E. D. 1988. Locating an area on a suspect tire for comparative examination to a questioned track. *J. Forensic Identification* 38: 143.

Lambourn, R. F. 1989. The calculation of motor car speeds from curved tire marks. *J. Forensic Sci. Soc.* 29: 371.

Mackay, G. M. 1970. The role of the accident investigator. *J. Forensic Sci. Soc.* 10: 245.

Monahan, D. L., and H. W. J. Harding. 1990. Damage to clothing—Cuts and tears. *J. Forensic Sci.* 35: 901.

Photography in Traffic Investigation. Kodak Publication M-21. Rochester: Eastman Kodak Co.

Russo, R. E., G. E. Pelkey, P. Grant, R. E. Whipple, and B. D. Andresen. 1994. Laser interrogation of latent vehicle registration number. *J. Forensic Sci.* 39: 1331.

Ryland, S. G., and R. J. Kopec. 1979. The evidential value of automobile paint chips. *J. Forensic Sci.* 24: 140.

Shkrum, M. J., R. N. Green, K. J. Mc Clafferty, and E. S. Nowak. 1994 Skull fractures in fatalities due to motor vehicle collisions. *J. Forensic Sci.* 39: 107.

Zeldes, I. 1980. Speedometer examination: An aid in accident investigation. *FBI Law Enforcement Bull.* 49: 11.

Chapter 16

Adelson, L. *The Pathology of Homicide.* Springfield, IL: Charles C Thomas, 1974.

Anderson, G. S. 1997. The use of insects to determine time of decapitation: A case study from British Columbia. *J. Forensic Sci.* 42: 947.

Blanke, R. V. 1974. Role of toxicology in suicide evaluation. *J. Forensic Sci.* 19: 284.

Burnharn, J. T., J. Preston-Burnharn, and C. R. Fontan. 1976. The state of the art of bone identification by chemical and microscopic methods. *J. Forensic Sci.* 21: 340.

Burton, J. F. 1974. Fallacies in the signs of death. *J. Forensic Sci.* 19: 529.

Byrd, J. H., and J. L. Castner, eds. *Forensic Entomology: The Utility of Arthropods in Legal Investigations.* Boca Raton, FL: CRC Press, 2001.

Chai, D. S. 1989. A study on the standard for forensic anthropologic identification of skull-image superimposition. *J. Forensic Sci.* 34: 1343.

Copeland, A. R. 1989. Multiple homicides. *Am. J. Forensic Med. Pathol.* 10: 206.

Copeland, A. 1989. Suicide among non-whites: The Metro-Dade county experience, 1982–1986. *Am. J. Forensic Med. Pathol.* 10: 10.

Costello, J., and F. T. Zugibe. 1994. Identification of a homicide victim by a Casio data bank watch. *Forensic Sci.* 39: 1117.

Danto, B. L., and T. Streed. 1994. Death investigation after the destruction of evidence. *Forensic Sci.* 39: 863.

Dietz, P. 1985. Classifying sexual homicide crime scenes: Inter-rater reliability. *FBI Law Enforcement Bull.*

Di Maio, V. J. M. *Gunshot Wounds—Practical Aspects of Firearms, Ballistics and Forensic Techniques.* New York: Elsevier Scientific Publishing Co., 1985.

Di Maio, V. J. M., and R. E. Zumwalt. 1977. Rifle wounds from high velocity center-fire hunting ammunition. *J. Forensic Sci.* 22: 132.

Eckert, W. G. 1977. The pathology of self-mutilation and destructive acts: A forensic study and review. *J. Forensic Sci.* 22: 242.

Eisele, J. W., D. T. Reay, and A. Cook. 1981. Sites of suicidal gunshot wounds. *J. Forensic Sci.* 26: 480.

Emson, H. E. 1978. Problems in the identification of burn victims. *J. Can. Soc. Forensic Sci.* 11: 229.

Felthous, A. R., and A. Hempel. 1995. Combined homicide-suicides: A review. *J. Forensic Sci.* 40: 846.

Fossum, R. M., and K. A. Descheneau. 1991. Blunt trauma of the abdomen in children. *J. Forensic Sci.* 36: 47.

Gee, D. J. 1988. A pathologist's view of multiple murder. *Forensic Sci. Int.* 38: 53.

Gilliland, M. G. F., and R. Folberg. 1996. Shaken babies—Some have no impact injuries. *J. Forensic Sci.* 41: 114.

Glassman, D. M., and R. M. Crow. 1996. Standardization model for describing the extent of burn injuries to human remains. *J. Forensic Sci.* 41: 152.

Goff, M. L. 1991. Comparison of insect species associated with decomposing remains recovered inside dwellings and outdoors on the Island of Oahu, Hawaii. *J. Forensic Sci.* 36: 748.

Haglund, W. D., D. T. Reay, and S. L. Tepper. 1990. Identification of decomposed remains by deoxyribonucleic acid (DNA) profiling. *J. Forensic Sci.* 35: 724.

Haglund, W. D. et al. 1990. Recovery of decomposed and skeletal human remains in the Green River murder investigation. *Am. J. Forensic Med. Pathol.* 11: 35.

Henssage, C. 1988. Death time estimation in case work I: The rectal temperature time of death nomogram. *Forensic Sci. Int.* 38: 209.

Henssage, C. et al. 1988. Death time estimation in case work II: Integration of different methods. *Forensic Sci. Int.* 39: 77.

Hirsch, C. S., and L. Adelson. 1976. A suicidal gunshot wound of the back. *J. Forensic Sci.* 21: 659.

Houck, M. M., D. Ubelaker, D. Owsley, E. Craig, W. Grant, R. Fram, T. Woltanski, and K. Sandness. 1996. The role of forensic anthropology in the recovery and analysis of Branch Davidian Compound victims: Assessing the accuracy of age estimations. *J. Forensic Sci.* 41: 796.

Howard, J. D. et al. Processing of skeletal remains: A medical examiner's perspective. *Am. J. Forensic Med. Pathol.* 9: 258.

Keppel, R. D. 1995. Signature murders: A report of several related cases. *J. Forensic Sci.* 40: 670.

Kerley, E. R. 1972. Special observations in skeletal identification. *J. Forensic Sci.* 17: 349.

Kerley, E. R. 1976. Forensic anthropology and crimes involving children. *J. Forensic Sci.* 21: 333.

Kerley, E. R. 1978. The identification of battered-infant skeletons. *J. Forensic Sci.* 23: 163.

Kintz, P., B. Godelar, A. Tracqui, P. Mangin, A. A. Lugnier and A. L. Chaumont. 1990. Fly larvae: A new toxicological method of investigation of forensic medicine. *J. Forensic Sci.* 35: 204.

Klattet, E. C. et al. 1989. Wounding characteristics of .38 caliber revolver cartridges. *J. Forensic Sci.* 34: 1387.

Lord, W. D., M. L. Goff, T. R. Adkins, and N. H. Haskell. 1994. The black soldier fly *Hermetia illucens* (Diptera: Stratiomyidae) as a potential measure of human postmortem interval: Observations and case histories. *J. Forensic Sci.* 39: 215.

Mack, H., Jr. 1995. Identification of victims: The beginning of a homicide investigation. *J. Forensic Identification* 45: 510.

Malik, M. O. A. 1971. Problems in the diagnosis of the cause of death in burned bodies. *J. Forensic Sci. Soc.* 11: 21.

Mann, R. W. et al. 1990. Time since death and decomposition of the human body: Variables and observations in case and experimental field studies. *J. Forensic Sci.* 35: 103.

Masters, N., R. Morgan, and E. Shipp. 1991. DFO, its usage and results. *J. Forensic Identification* 41: 3.

Muramatsu, Y. et al. 1988. Concentrations of some trace elements in hair, liver and kidney from autopsy subjects—Relationship between hair and internal organs. *Sci. Total Environ.* 76: 29.

Murphy, G. E., G. E. Gantner, R. D. Wetzel, S. Katz, and M. F. Ernst. 1974. On the improvement of suicide determination. *J. Forensic Sci.* 19: 276.

Owsley, D. W. 1995. Techniques for locating burials, with emphasis on the probe. *J. Forensic Sci.* 40: 735.

Palmer, C. H., and J. F. Weston. 1976. Several unusual cases of child abuse. *J. Forensic Sci.* 21: 851.

Pfau, R. O., and P. W. Sciulli. 1994. A method for establishing the age of subadults. *J. Forensic Sci.* 39: 165.

Pollanen, M. S., and D. A. Chiasson. 1996. Fracture of the hyoid bone in strangulation: Comparison of fractured and unfractured hyoids in victims of strangulation. *J. Forensic Sci.* 41: 110.

Prahlow, J. A., and P. E. Lantz. 1995. Medical examiner/death investigator training requirements in state medical examiner systems. *J. Forensic Sci.* 40: 55.

Prouty, R. E. 1989. The Zodiac: An unsolved serial murder. *J. Forensic Identification* 39: 165.

Randall, B., and R. Jaqua. 1991. Gunshot entrance wound abrasion ring width as a function of projectile diameter and velocity. *J. Forensic Sci.* 36: 138.

Rentoul, E., and H. Smith, eds. *Glaister's Medical Jurisprudence and Toxicology.* 13th ed. London: Churchill Livingston, 1973.

Ressler, R. K. 1985. Crime scene and profile characteristics of organized and disorganized murderers. *FBI Law Enforcement Bull.* 54.

Rhine, J. S., and B. K. Curran. 1990. Multiple gunshot wounds of the head: An anthropological view. *J. Forensic Sci.* 35: 1236.

Rodriguez, A. *Handbook of Child Abuse and Neglect.* New York: Medical Examination Publishing Co., Inc., 1977.

Rodriquez, W. C., and W. M. Bass. 1983. Insect activity and its relationship to decay rates of human cadavers in East Tennessee. *J. Forensic Sci.* 28: 423.

Rodriquez, W. C., and W. M. Bass. 1985. Decomposition of buried bodies and methods that may aid in their location. *J. Forensic Sci.* 30: 836.

Rumsch, B. J. 1977. Medical examiner report of a Boeing 727-95 aircraft accident. *J. Forensic Sci.* 22: 835.

Simpson, K. 1988. Identification of a firearm in murder without the weapon (a case study). *AFTE* 21: 62.

Skinner, M. F. 1988. Case report in forensic anthropology: Animal and insect factors in decomposition of homicide victim. *Can. Soc. Forensic Sci.* 21: 71.

Snyder, L. *Homicide Investigation.* 3rd ed. Springfield, IL: Charles C Thomas, 1977.

Spitz, W. U., and R. S. Fisher. *Medicolegal Investigation of Death: Guidelines for the Application of Pathology to Crime Investigation.* Springfield, IL: Charles C Thomas, 1973.

Stephens, B. G. 1979. A simple method for preparing human skeletal material for forensic examination. *J. Forensic Sci.* 24: 660.

Sundick, R. I. 1977. Age and sex determination of subadult skeletons. *J. Forensic Sci.* 22: 141.

Thali, M. et al. *The Virtopsy Approach.* Boca Raton, FL: CRC Press, 2008.

Ubelaker, D. H. 1992. Hyoid fracture and strangulation. *J. Forensic Sci.* 37: 1216.

Usher, A. The role of the pathologist at the scene of the crime. *J. Forensic Sci. Soc.* 10: 213.

Vass, A. A., W. M. Bass, J. D. Wolt, J. E. Foss, and J. T. Ammons. 1992. Time since death determinations of human cadavers using soil solution. *J. Forensic Sci.* 37: 1236.

Vieira, D. N. 1988. Homicidal hanging. *Am. J. Forensic Med. Pathol.* 9: 287.

Walker, P. L., D. C. Cook, and P. M. Lambert. 1997. Skeletal evidence for child abuse: A physical anthropological perspective. *J. Forensic Sci.* 42: 196.

Warren, C. P. 1978. Personal identification of human remains: An overview. *J. Forensic Sci.* 23: 388.

Watanabe, T. *Atlas of Legal Medicine.* 2nd ed. Philadelphia, PA: J. B. Lippincott, Co., 1972.

Watson, A. A. 1974. Estimation of age from skeletal remains. *J. Forensic Sci. Soc.* 14: 209.

Wertheim, P. A. 1989. Investigation of ritualistic crime scenes. *J. Forensic Identification* 39: 97.

Wright, R. K., and J. Davis. 1976. Homicidal hanging masquerading as sexual asphyxia. *J. Forensic Sci.* 21: 387.

Chapter 17

Bryant, R. *Investigating Digital Crime.* Malden, MA: Wiley-Blackwell, 2008.

McKenzie Marshall, A. *Digital Forensics.* Malden, MA: Wiley-Blackwell, 2009.

National Institute of Justice. *Electronic Crime Scene Investigation: An On-the-Scene Reference for First Responders.* Washington, DC: US DOJ, 2009.

Nilsson, F. *Intelligent Network Video: Understanding Modern Video Surveillance Systems.* Boca Raton, FL: CRC Press, 2009.

Index